STRATEGIC ADVERTISING CAMPAIGNS

Second Edition

Don E. Schultz
NORTHWESTERN UNIVERSITY

Dennis Martin
BRIGHAM YOUNG UNIVERSITY

William P. Brown
ADCOM, INC.

CRAIN BOOKS

740 RUSH STREET   CHICAGO, IL 60611

Cover photo: Ted Lacey

Copyright © 1984 by Don E. Schultz, Dennis G. Martin, and William P. Brown

Published by Crain Books
Division of Crain Communications, Inc.
740 Rush Street
Chicago, IL 60611

86 85 84 10 9 8 7 6 5 4 3 2 1

ISBN: 0-87251-089-1

Library of Congress Catalog Card No. 83-72177

Printed in the United States of America

Contents

Preface

Second editions should be easier. They aren't. They should be easier because you can always see what was left out, what should be changed, what has worked, and what hasn't. But they are harder to write simply because so many good ideas and suggestions come from students who have studied the first edition or from teachers who have used it in the classroom. The temptation is to try to cram all those ideas into the next edition. It doesn't work. Therefore, this edition is a selection of the good ideas and suggestions we have received, tempered with a good deal of practicality in terms of what is physically possible.

The first thing you'll notice in this edition is the greater emphasis on marketing, planning, and strategy. That's intentional. We're more and more convinced that strategic thinking is what separates the sound advertising campaign from the weak one. And only a glance at the current media seems to verify that belief. The soundly based, strategically oriented campaigns continue while those with only a flash of creativity come and go in a few months.

In this edition, you'll also find some new names. First is Bill Brown, media director, Adcom, Inc., Chicago. Because media is such an integral part of the advertising campaign and because it holds so much excitement for the future, we wanted one of the top people in the field to cover the area. We think you'll agree that Bill has done a great job. The chapter is easy to read, easy to understand, and, most of all, practical and descriptive of the new creative world of media.

Bruce Vanden Bergh, Michigan State University, contributed the chapter on advertising and communications. There are so many new ideas and concepts on how advertising communicates and the effects of advertising on the individual that it is almost impossible to synthesize them all in just a few pages. Bruce has done a great job of relating all of the important ideas in a useful and helpful chapter that ties marketing, advertising, and communciation together. It really sets the stage for the balance of the text.

Many professors, reflecting an increasing sophistication in advertising instruction, requested the inclusion of cases to illustrate the various steps in campaign development. Beth E. Barnes, Miami University of Ohio, developed the cases at the end of each chapter. Beth has managed to condense the basic advertising campaign development decision points and concepts into just two or three pages. That in itself is a unique talent.

Of course, we must thank the students of Michigan State University and Coors Brewing Company for allowing us to reproduce their winning casebook as an example at the end of the text. As you look at their plans book, we think you'll see many of the elements illustrated which we believe are so important in the development of an advertising campaign.

Of course, we didn't develop or create this edition alone. Great guidance came from Kathryn Sederberg and Rich Hagle, formerly of Crain Books, who guided and encouraged us to undertake the second edition. We're also indebted to Jack Graham, now director of Crain Books for his help. Likewise, we're indebted to the many companies, organizations, and individuals who allowed us to either reprint or cite their research and advertising examples so that others could learn. Most of them are cited in the text. For those from whom we borrowed ideas and who are not recognized, you know who you are. Thanks.

Finally, a word of thanks to two people: To BEB for typing the first draft of the manuscript. And, to HFS for ignoring so many times the rattling of a typewriter on an early Saturday morning. You may not be famous authors but you are represented on these pages.

DES

Introduction:
What Advertising Is All About

A Plan Is Vital   In all advertising, regardless of scope, one single thing appears constant: those advertisers who are most successful and who obtain the greatest return on their advertising investment are those who have a well-conceived and well-developed advertising plan. They know *why* they are advertising, to *whom* they are advertising, and *what* results they expect to receive from their efforts. In short, they use advertising as a planned, business-building technique to develop sales and profits, not as a one-shot, scattergun approach to solve short-term problems.

Successful advertisers carefully integrate their advertising into the overall promotional plan for the product or service. And, to guarantee success, they also carefully integrate these promotional efforts into the overall sales and marketing mix of the organization. Without this planning and integration, advertising, just like any other business activity, cannot provide the organization with the necessary return on investment of time and money.

Advertising: A Sales Message for the Product   If there is one fatal flaw in an unsuccessful advertising plan, it is often the mistake advertising people make of viewing advertising as a separate and independent part of the sales and marketing effort. They look at advertising as being somehow "different" or "unique" or "creative" or even an "art form." And that's a major problem today. Too often, it seems, people in advertising lose sight of the fact that they are really only salespersons attempting to sell products and services through the mass media. They seem to forget that the purpose of advertising is simply to deliver a *sales message* on behalf of the product or service to a large number of prospects or customers at a single time. And the only reason that companies use advertising rather than face-to-face selling is that it is much more efficient in terms of time and cost.

Figure I-1.   Sound Advertising: A Commercial for Aunt Jemima

1. (Natural sfx)

2. MAN: Good morning ma'am.

3. This is our Aunt Jemima Buttermilk Complete pancake mix.

4. (Sfx: slam!)

5. Ma'am, our Aunt Jemima Buttermilk Complete...

6. ...has more buttermilk.

7. Makes lighter pancakes.

8. This has more buttermilk than any other mix.

9. Any other. (Sfx: slam!)

10. How do I get to these people? I know.

11. (Sfx: tap, tap) MAN: You can't deny...

12. ...it's a great pancake. (Sfx: slam!)

13. (Natural sfx)

14. WOMAN: What kind of pancake is that?

15. (Anncr VO) Aunt Jemima Buttermilk Complete. You can't deny it's a great pancake.

Source: Courtesy of Quaker Oats Company

The best possible way to deliver a sales message is through personal contact, but in a nation of 220,000,000 people that's neither practical nor possible. It's not even practical or possible for a retailer in a town of 3,000 to meet and present a sales message to all his customers and prospects. Thus, companies use advertising as a surrogate for delivering personal sales messages. They talk to them through the mass media but hope to achieve the results of direct contact. And they hope to achieve the same result: an effective sales message that produces an agreeable response to their message.

A few years ago, Quaker Oats developed a television commercial for their Aunt Jemima Pancake Mix. In just 30 seconds it clearly and succinctly demonstrates what advertising is all about. The Aunt Jemima commercial is a sound advertising lesson. If you keep it in mind when you start to prepare an advertising campaign, it will help you remember what advertising is all about.

The Advertising Campaign

The most common method of planning, executing, and integrating advertising into the overall sales and marketing effort of the organization is through some form of advertising campaign. The campaign approach, in the military sense of the word, means that the advertiser sets a measurable objective or goal for advertising, determines the best method of achieving that goal, develops the tactics necessary to achieve that goal, integrates them with the other selling efforts for the product or service, and then executes the planned activities. And that is what this book is about: setting advertising objectives, developing advertising strategies, and then executing those strategies in the marketplace.

In its simplest form, the advertising campaign consists of:

- Developing the right sales message
- Getting that message to the right audience
- At the right time
- At a reasonable cost

Thus, advertising itself is quite a simple business. It becomes complex, however, when you start to investigate and determine what the right message is, who the right people are, when the right time is, and what constitutes a reasonable cost.

The First Step

If you're going to develop a sound advertising campaign, you first must be sure you're starting at the beginning. And the beginning of an advertising campaign starts with an understanding of the business organization and the various planning activities conducted in an effort to sell products or services to customers and prospects, in other words, marketing. Understanding and using marketing is the first step in the development of an advertising campaign.

1 Marketing, the Marketing Plan, and Advertising

What Is Marketing?

As defined by the American Marketing Association, marketing is "the performance of business activities that direct the flow of goods and services from producer to consumer or user."[1]

This definition, in our opinion, is a bit restrictive. We much prefer the one developed recently by Philip Kotler: "Marketing is human activity directed at satisfying needs and wants through exchange processes."[2] No matter what definition you choose, however, the point of marketing is the development of products or services to satisfy the needs or wants of consumers in the marketplace. That is a definition on which almost everyone will agree.

The Origins of Marketing

The actual process of marketing is very simple. It involves some form of exchange between members of society. It may be an exchange of money, other goods or services, or something else of value, but it always involves some form of transaction between the parties. Thus, there have been marketing activities almost as long as there have been people. One person had something that was needed or wanted by another. Therefore, they marketed to each other. As societies became increasingly complex, however, they moved from individual marketing activities to the collective activities of companies and organizations and to the idea of making a profit on transactions. In addition, the exchange process became increasingly complex as more and more individuals and groups became involved in the development of the parts of products and their distribution. Over time, as

---

1. Committee on Terms, *Marketing Definitions: A Glossary of Marketing Terms* (Chicago: American Marketing Association, 1960).

2. Philip Kotler, *Principles of Marketing* © 1980, p. 10. Reprinted by permission of Prentice-Hall, Inc., Englewood Cliffs, NJ.

more and more organizations moved further and further away from the ultimate consumer and furnished only a part of the final product, the concept of production efficiency sprang up. Companies and organizations that manufactured only parts of products or provided only peripheral services to the marketplace became much more interested in generating their profits from the efficient production of their part of the process than in actually filling the needs and wants of consumers. They became "production oriented" and more involved with producing units or elements than in satisfying consumer wants and needs.

This production-efficiency system continued to grow until the middle part of this century when some farsighted individuals and companies started to practice what they called "the marketing concept." Quite simply, the marketing concept is a return to the basics of the exchange system of centuries ago. It involves first determining what consumers want and/or need and then developing and providing those goods and services in the marketplace at a profit. Thus, marketing, in the broadest sense, has really come full circle to what it was in the beginning.

In spite of the seemingly obvious advantages of the marketing concept, two basic types of companies or organizations, production-oriented and marketing-oriented, still exist in our economy. The production-oriented organization manufactures or develops products or services based on its facilities, capabilities, or interests. It assumes that the market will either absorb or can be sold what it produces based on a price-value relationship. It pays little attention to what the consumer wants or needs or to filling those wants or needs. On the other hand, the marketing-oriented organization first identifies consumer wants and needs and then develops the facilities and products or services to fill those needs. The marketing organization is always oriented to the consumer or user of the final product. While many more production- than marketing-oriented organizations actually exist in our economy, it is from the point of view of the marketing-oriented organization that this text is written.

Marketing in an Organization

In the broadest sense, any individual, firm, or organization that seeks to develop products or services and exchange them in the marketplace develops some form of marketing system; even production-oriented firms have some form of marketing. While these marketing systems vary widely according to the type of organization, they usually have several common elements. These include (a) the *product* or service to be offered for exchange, (b) a *price* at which the product or service is offered, (c) a *place* or distribution system through which the product or service is made available to the ultimate consumers, and (d) some form of *promotion* or communication through which prospective customers are made aware of the product or service being offered. These are often called the "4 P's" of marketing.[3]

The actual task of marketing consists of the mixing and refining of these various elements by the firm to optimize the profitable exchange of its products or services in the marketplace. In basic economic terms, firms in our society take scarce resources in the form of capital, labor, and raw materials, then process or convert them into products or services that they exchange in the marketplace, hopefully at a profit.

Since there are many customers, many firms, and many products, it quickly becomes evident that success is unlikely to occur without some form of planning. This marketing planning process becomes even more vital when a firm's management realizes that its scarce resources are in demand by other organizations in the economy; the marketplace is wide, varied, and constantly shifting; the demand for a product or service is in a constant state of flux; and a multitude of competitors are often offering the same or similar products or services in the marketplace. Without some sort of plan, the organization stands little chance of successfully marketing its products or services. The development of this plan or program usually consists of a series of considerations, evaluations, and decisions by the management of the organization. This usually is called the marketing process because it involves the development of a planned production, pricing, distribution, and promotion program.

The Marketing Process

The so-called marketing process really involves the investigation and evaluation of a number of different areas of the business and marketplace that an organization must consider in order to develop and move products or services most effectively and profitably from their plants to the ultimate consumer. While the depth of study and evaluation of each of these areas will vary widely from company to company, the following are considered primary ingredients in the marketing process and are required decision areas in the development of a sound marketing program:

1. Evaluation of the marketing environment
2. Development of short- and long-term objectives of the organization
3. Strategic planning for the future
4. Marketing opportunity analysis

---

3. The concept of the 4 P's of marketing was originated by E. Jerome McCarthy and most recently discussed in his *Basic Marketing*, 7th Edition (Homewood, IL: Richard D. Irwin, 1981). Others have adapted this concept in various ways over the years.

5. Target market selection
6. Marketing mix strategy
7. Development of a formal marketing plan

Each is reviewed briefly below.

The Marketing Environment

All marketing organizations operate within an environment that dictates what the firm can and cannot do. This environment exists at both the macro and micro levels, i.e., the largest and the smallest. (See Figure 1-1.) At the macro level, the environment consists of all those elements, forces, situations, and restrictions external to the organization itself. These influence the type of products the organization may produce, the prices it may set for those products, the methods by which the products may be distributed, and the manner in which they may be promoted or communicated to prospective consumers. The macro environment generally consists of such elements as:

1. Social environment. These are the characteristics of the people in the society, their values, culture, social class, life style, and goals.

2. Natural environment. The physical situation that exists where the marketer operates, including such factors as natural resources, climate, terrain, pollution, and population density.

Figure 1-1.   The Marketing Environment

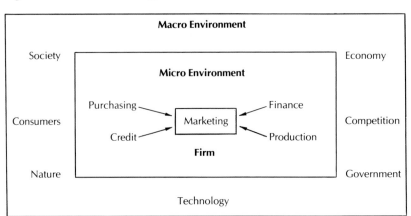

3. Economic environment. The economic system in which the marketing organization operates and how that system influences such things as growth rate, inflation, raw material availability, investment or capital availability, and even interest rates; all those economic factors that impinge on the firm and its marketing activities.

4. Governmental environment. Governments directly affect marketing activities as a result of specific rules and regulations to which the marketer must conform, as well as economic and societal conditions dictated by governmental actions.

5. Technological environment. The increase in knowledge, ability, and application of new inventions or innovations as part of the environment can have either a stimulating or restraining effect on the marketing activities of the firm.

6. Competitive environment. There may be many or few competitors depending on the economy, the type of product or service, the product category, and the like. In addition, there are both direct and indirect competitors for almost all products or services.

7. Consumer environment. The users or purchasers or prospects for the product or service have much to do with the overall marketing environment in which the organization operates.

Most if not all of these macro forces are totally outside the control of the marketing organization. They exist and must be considered and dealt with by the firm as a vital part of any marketing activity. The macro environment for every firm is different. For example, while a company that develops and markets new electronic communications equipment and one that breeds race horses may exist side by side geographically, they have totally different macro environmental considerations when they start to develop their marketing activities. For example, nature has a great effect on race horses and practically none on electronic communications equipment. On the other hand, technology greatly affects communications equipment but has little direct effect on race horses.

The micro environment, or the situation within the firm, also dictates the type and form of marketing actions available for consideration. This micro environment consists of such functions as finance, credit, production, and purchasing. These greatly influence the final marketing activities the firm can use. While the marketer has much more control over micro-environmental situations than over the macro, they still limit or restrain what can and cannot be done in a marketing program.

The environment in which the firm operates is one of the most basic considerations in the development of an overall marketing program. It generally dictates the selection and type of overall goals and objectives that the organization can set for itself and certainly influences marketing objectives and goals. Further, these environmental situations have an effect on the promotional activities the firm can consider, and they impinge specifically on the methods of advertising that can be used.

Short- and Long-Term Objectives

Within the constraints of both the macro and micro environments, most organizations generally define long-term objectives or goals and then supplement these with more short-term objectives. For example, one organization may define its long-term goal as developing and providing consumers with the most effective and efficient personal communications systems possible. Here, the goals are stated quite generally as the business in which the organization sees itself or in which it wishes to participate. These goals also may include such items as the return on investment or capital to be achieved, the length of time the organization is to exist, and so on. These long-range goals may be expanded further to include the geographic area of operation, the share of market to be obtained, some general guidelines on interest in research and development, integration of the manufacturing and marketing functions, projected growth rate, and the like. These are the guidelines by which the company plans to operate.

The short-term goals of the organization tend to be much more specific. Short-range marketing goals would include levels of sales for the next few years, distribution of those sales, introduction of new products, pricing adjustments, and expansion into new areas. From this, it is evident that the broader objectives, or long-range goals, of the organization determine or identify the short-range goals to be achieved.

A firm's long- and short-term goals, as well as its environment, dictate its marketing activities. If, for example, the goal of the organization has been defined as being a supplier of raw materials to the steel manufacturing industry, this goal will have a definite effect on the marketing activities of the organization. If the goal of another firm is defined as being the price leader in the consumer toy market, that goal provides different constraints. Most marketing activities flow out of and are a direct result of the long- and short-term goals of the organization.

Strategic Planning

As a method of developing and implementing both the long-range and short-range goals, many organizations have adopted the idea of strategic planning. While strategic planning can be a very complex process, generally it is a method of evaluating and assessing the market share, growth estimates and potentials, profitability, and cash-generating power of each existing and proposed business unit in the organization. These SBU's (strategic business units) are then evaluated against one another to determine which of them should be supported, maintained, harvested, or terminated to achieve the objectives of the firm.

While strategic planning is the "hot topic" of the 1980s, it is simply a method of advance planning by which the organization hopes to improve its situation in the future. Many methods of strategic planning have been developed. One of the earliest approaches was that developed by the Boston Consulting Group in their work with a number of companies. They suggested that organizations could evaluate their SBU's much like stock brokers might evaluate their portfolios. Thus, one of the principal methods of strategic planning is portfolio analysis as described in Figure 1-2.

Obviously, the strategic planning of an organization has a definite impact on its marketing activities. If, for example, an SBU is identified as being ready to "harvest," little or no marketing funds will likely be invested. However, "rising stars" often are heavily promoted and require considerable marketing support. The advertising support and advertising direction are determined in the same manner. The plans for a particular SBU will have both a short- and long-range effect on the type of advertising campaign developed.

Once the marketing environment, the long- and short-range goals of the organization, and the strategic planning have been identified, actual marketing planning can shift into high gear. Management knows generally what areas of business and the marketplace its marketing activities should be concentrated in. And, this concentration is vital, since most organizations have scarce or limited resources in terms of marketing funds, people, and time.

Market Opportunity Analysis

The next step in the marketing process is a market opportunity analysis, or MOA. An MOA consists of starting with the broadest possible marketing view of the world, the macro environment, and progressively analyzing and refining potential product or service markets in smaller and smaller units to determine their feasibility and the opportunity for the firm to provide a profitable solution to consumer wants or needs. For example, assume that the firm—based on an environmental review, determination of long-range goals, and strategic planning—determines that the production and marketing of beverages best fits present capabilities. Management then must determine if there are marketing opportunities (unmet consumer wants and needs) in the beverage field. The first step would be to investigate the total environment for beverages of all types and descriptions. (See

Figure 1-2.   Strategic Planning

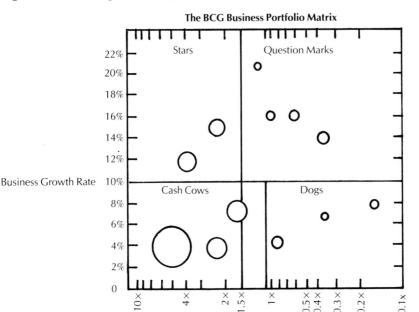

The BCG Business Portfolio Matrix

Source: B. Hedley, "Strategy and the 'Business Portfolio'," *Long-Range Planning* (February 1977): 12. Reprinted by permission.

Strategic planning is the process whereby an organization evaluates the various segments of its overall business and determines potential long-range alternatives and plans. This usually takes several specific steps whereby the firm determines what business it is presently in and where it could logically move to optimize profits and return on investment.

There are many methods of strategic planning. One of the best known is product portfolio analysis. In this method, the organization evaluates various segments of its business or brands as contributors to its overall operation. The Boston Consulting Group uses the business portfolio matrix to make the analysis. It is described briefly below.

For corporate level strategy, the principal visual constructs are business portfolio matrices that help to depict the firm's scope, the major component of corporate strategy. The simplest such matrix is a four-square grid developed by the Boston Consult-

ing Group (BCG). A typical BCG matrix is depicted above. Here, each of the company's businesses is plotted according to the growth rates of the industry in which it competes and its relative competitive position (measured through market share) in that industry, with the size of each circle being proportional to the size of the business involved.

Businesses plotted in the upper left quadrant are called "Stars" by BCG, because they are growing rapidly while being roughly self-sustaining in terms of cash flow. As such, BCG feels they probably represent the best profit and growth opportunities available to a company.

Businesses in the lower left quadrant are called "Cash Cows" by BCG, because, with their combination of low growth and high market share, they should, and usually do, have entrenched, superior market positions with low costs, low growth rates, and the attendant low demands for investment funds that permit them to generate large cash surpluses.

"Cash cows," thus, pay the dividends and interest, provide debt capacity, pay the overhead, and provide the funds to reinvest elsewhere.

Businesses in the lower right quadrant of the matrix are called "Dogs" by BCG, because they usually are not very profitable because of their relatively high cost competitive position. Under periods of high inflation, "Dogs" may not even generate enough cash to maintain their existing position, weak as it is. Thus, BCG feels companies should try to liquidate any such businesses that they have.

Businesses in the upper right quadrant are referred to as "Question Marks" or "Wildcats." They usually have the worst cash flow position of all, since their cash needs are high because of growth and their cash generation is low because of low market share. Consequently, BCG feels that there are only two viable strategies for a "Question Mark" business—to grow it into a "Star" or to divest it.

Once the company's current position is plotted on such a grid, a projection can be made of its future position, assuming no change in its strategy. Viewed together, these two matrices—present and projected—not only help describe the scope and competitive advantage components of the firm's corporate strategy, but they also assist in the identification of some of the major strategic issues that face the firm. Such a grid also isolates some of the basic characteristics of each unit's business strategy.*

The use of the BCG matrix is only one form of strategic analysis and planning. Another of the commonly used methods is the business screening system developed at General Electric several years ago. For more information and detail on strategic business planning, see Charles W. Hofer and Dan Schendel, *Strategy Formulation: Analytical Concepts* (St. Paul: West Publishing Co., 1978); George S. Day, "Diagnosing the Product Portfolio," *Journal of Marketing,* April 1977, pp. 29–38; "GE's New Strategy for Faster Growth," *Business Week,* July 8, 1972, pp. 52–58; and Derek F. Abell and John S. Hammond, *Strategic Market Planning* (Englewood Cliffs, NJ: Prentice-Hall, 1979).

*Charles W. Hofer and Dan Schendel, *Strategy Formulation: Analytical Concepts* (St. Paul: West Publishing, 1978), pp. 30–32.

Figure 1-3.   Market Opportunity Analysis: Market for Beverages

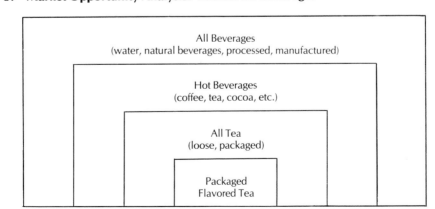

Figure 1-3.) Having looked at all the macro variables such as worldwide or national demographics, climates, societal uses of beverages, cultural biases toward beverages, and beverage use, the firm next would investigate the broad general categories of beverages, such as hot or cold, their social and nonsocial uses, prepared or natural, fluid or reconstituted, and the like. Based on this, management would then decide which general area of the beverage industry the firm could most likely serve.

Assume that the decision is made to enter the hot beverage category. Management then must determine which generic hot beverage category it should compete in, for example, coffee, tea, or cocoa. This decision usually is based on consideration of such factors as sales and growth trends, raw ingredient availability, demographic trends of users, degree of competition, and product margins.

Once the generic category has been determined, the marketing decision is then further refined to determine against what specific brand or positioning segment the company will compete. For example, if management determined that the tea category offers the greatest opportunities in the general beverage area, they whould then have to determine if they should enter the natural or flavored tea market. And, having decided that, they would further have to determine which particular brands they would compete against. This brand competition or positioning decision is usually based on an evaluation of the various consumers using or likely to use the product.

Further assume, for example, that management determined that the flavored tea category is not adequately served by the brands presently available to consumers. Based on that, they could then decide specifically how consumers would be better served with another flavored tea product they might market.

The MOA is most commonly used in the development and introduction of new products, but it is used with existing products as well. Obviously, the market in which the company will compete has a great deal to do with the marketing activities that are to be used. For example, in the flavored tea category, products and pricing situations already exist, and certain channels of distribution have already been established. In addition, competitors are already involved in the flavored tea category, and their present promotional activities as well as their specific advertising campaigns must be considered. The MOA serves to identify the opportunities and problems in developing a marketing program in a specific product category.

Target Market Selection

Having decided in what specific product category the firm will compete, management next must determine which consumer groups are the most likely prospects for the firm and its brand. Commonly, these consumers are defined on the basis of geographic location, demographic and psychographic characteristics, perhaps by their media usage patterns, and certainly by their present buying and use patterns for the product category and brands.

From a marketing standpoint, the most important determinant for the target market selection is to find a group that is either not served or is underserved by products presently on the market. Of course, one of the most important determinations of any target market is that it is sufficiently large or can be expanded to the point that marketing of the brand to the group will provide a financially feasible and profitable use of the organization's scarce resources.

The selection of the target market is often the key element in the overall development of the marketing mix. That is followed by determining which strategy should be used to convince the target market to buy and use the product to be marketed. Once this target market and the basic strategy have been identified, most major sales and promotion decisions can be made. For example, advertising decisions as to what message, what media, what frequency, and the like, can then be developed.

Marketing Mix Strategy

As previously discussed, the marketing organization has four broad elements that can be used to influence consumers' purchases: the product, the price, the availability (distribution or place), and the promotional effort. It is the mix of these elements that usually is the key to marketing success. For example, an incorrectly priced product is not likely to succeed. Similarly, a sound product that is properly priced and well promoted will fail without sufficient or proper distribution. And without promotion, in a complex and increasingly cluttered marketplace, it is questionable whether consumers will seek out or find a single product. Thus, it is the proper mix of these marketing elements that often determines the success of the marketing effort.

Generally, most marketers have two broad strategic alternatives available to them when developing a marketing mix. The primary emphasis can be put on a mix of elements that will influence members of the distribution channel, that is, retailers or distributors. This is often called a "push" strategy since the manufacturer attempts to "push" the product into the marketing channels or distribution system and assumes the distributors and retailers of the product will move it on to the final consumer. This type of strategy is widely used by manufacturers of products where a great deal of personal selling is involved in the final decision by the ultimate consumer or where the distributor or retailer actually seeks out and finds consumers for the product. Marketers of most industrial, business, and agricultural products use some form of push marketing strategy.

The alternative to the push strategy is the "pull"; i.e., the marketer advertises or promotes directly to the ultimate consumer, assuming that the consumer will demand the product of the retailer. Thus, the marketer assumes that his advertising and promotional efforts will be strong enough to generate consumer demand that will "pull" the product through the distribution system or at least that the retailer will believe the promotion will create demand. In most situations where a pull strategy is used, consumers seek out the product in retail stores; personal selling by the retailer doesn't play an important part in the final purchase decision. This type of marketing strategy is widely used by package goods companies that sell their products through self-service food, drug, and discount stores.

Push and pull strategies are actually the extremes of a continuum. In practice most strategies contain elements of both, and the individual marketer determines the exact mix that is most effective for his particular product or service. In line with this, the marketer also determines how and in what way promotion in general and advertising in particular can be used to most effectively and efficiently move the product from the plant, through the distribution channels, and to the ultimate consumer.

After all the decisions previously described have been made—that is, the environmental effects, short- and long-range goals for the company, the determination of how the SBU fits into the strategic planning program, the MOA has been made, the target market selected, and the marketing mix strategy developed—the marketing manager finally is ready to put this material into a formal document called the marketing plan.

The Marketing Plan

The document that defines and describes the overall marketing program developed for a particular organization and includes decisions and plans for various products, the pricing, the distribution systems, and the promotional activities is called the marketing plan.

Marketing plans can take many forms. One example of a marketing plan format, developed by the Association of National Advertisers for their members, is illustrated in Figure 1-4. A more extensive outline covering the background, planning, implementation, and controlling areas may use:

- Company mission, scope, and goals
- Situation analysis
- Current marketing organization
- Marketing objectives

Figure 1-4.   Format for an Annual Marketing Plan

The annual marketing plan comes in many styles and types, with each organization typically adapting a rather basic format to meet its own particular situation and needs. The outline that follows was developed by F. Beaven Ennis for the Association of National Advertisers and is rather typical for a consumer products manufacturing company.

BRAND NAME   19__ Marketing Plan

I. Current Year Performance—How the brand has performed so far this year

II. Recommendations—Brand objective in units and sales and expenditures needed to achieve those sales

III. Profit and Loss Effect of the Recommendation—Summary of marketing effects over three-year period (last year, current year, projected year)

IV. Background
  A. Market
    1. Size—Unit sales, growth rate, and competition
    2. Consumer—Profile of consumers by geographic areas
    3. Pricing—Company and competitive pricing by unit size
    4. Competitive Spending—Media and promotional spending by six-month period
    5. Other—Any other helpful data
  B. Brand
    1. Product—Formulation, unique attributes, sizes/variety, and margins
    2. Manufacturing—Plant capacity, capital investment required, and any production/purchasing problems

    3. Product Research—Major studies relating to brand or its performance
    4. Market Research—All other pertinent research information
    5. Other—Any other helpful data

V. Opportunities and Problems
  A. Opportunities—Where sales are expected to be gained in coming year
  B. Problems—Factors that might jeopardize success of plan

VI. Strategies
  A. Marketing—Brand's basic objective and strategy planned to achieve it
  B. Spending—Investment for the coming year
  C. Copy—Brief review of advertising objectives, strategy, executions, and copy rotation plan
  D. Media—Brief review of media objectives, strategy, and comparison of sales volume to media expenditures
  E. Promotion—Brief review of objectives, strategy, and trade deals by area

VII. Tests/Research—What is planned for coming year and costs

SOURCE: Adapted and used with permission of Association of National Advertisers, Inc. Taken from F. Beaven Ennis, *Effective Marketing Management: Planning and Control Systems for Making Better and Faster Marketing Decisions* (New York: Association of National Advertisers, 1973), pp. 1-32.

- Marketing strategies, policies, and procedures
- Marketing programs
- Schedules and assignments
- Personnel plan
- Budgets
- Pro forma profit and loss and balance sheet
- Controls and continuity

The basic structure and amount of detail of the marketing plan are determined by the management of the organization. For a small retail operation, a simple listing of the target market for the store, the general marketing objectives to be achieved, an outline of the marketing program, and sales forecasts and budgets may suffice. Since the retailer knows the details of his organization and what he hopes to achieve, his marketing plan can be very simple in some sections but expanded into more detail in others. For example, a very complete outline of the promotional calendar may be the key element in a retail plan. Other, more complex organizations may require such information as analysis, factual support, and financial justification for each section. Thus, while all marketing plans include some subjects, they generally are developed to fit the needs of the organization and those who will use them.

Typically, the marketing plan outlined in Figure 1-4 is supported by four basic financial and marketing exhibits. These are:

1. The price and profit structure for the brand
2. The brand's current profit and loss statement
3. The proposed media allocation schedule
4. The proposed promotion spread sheet[4]

The most detailed part of the marketing plan usually is the section that describes the actual activities to be carried out to achieve the goals of the plan. These *marketing tactics* are the specific steps and programs that will be used during the life of the marketing plan and typically include sales, service, promotion, pricing, distribution, and marketing research activities. Since the implementation and coordination of these activities are crucial to the success of the overall marketing plan, they are spelled out in as much detail as is possible and practical.

Of greatest concern to the advertising campaign planner is the overall promotional plan, which is sometimes called the marketing communications section. This section details the specific plans, tactics, and activities that will be used in personal selling, advertising, sales promotion, and publicity to support the sale of the product. Since advertising people are most concerned with these promotional activities, we'll look at them in greater detail in the next section.

The Promotion Plan   The Promotion Mix

The promotion plan of the marketing organization reflects its marketing mix and usually includes the use of (a) personal selling, (b) advertising, (c) sales promotion, and (d) publicity and/or public relations. For each of these

4. Ennis, *Effective Marketing Management,* p. 32.

activities, the idea of communicating a sales message is an integral part of the operation; for example, the salesperson delivers the message through personal contact, the advertising through various media forms, sales promotion most commonly at the point-of-purchase, and public relations and publicity through the delivery of information about the company or organization through news items that will help promote good feelings or understanding of what the company is trying to achieve or how it is serving its various publics.

Depending on the marketing goals to be achieved, both short- and long-term, marketing management will coordinate the various promotional elements. In industrial marketing, for example, advertising, sales promotion, and public relations are used primarily to help pre-sell or generate leads for the personal sales force. Since most industrial sales are made as a direct result of a presentation by a salesperson, the other elements are used to assist or support these personal selling situations. For consumer package goods, however, advertising is commonly the most important element in the promotion mix. The ultimate consumer is told the uses for, the benefits of, the location of, the pricing and other important selling messages about the product through advertising. Usually, little or no personal selling is involved in the sale of these products. In still other instances, sales promotion or publicity may well take the lead in the overall effort to generate sales. In many cases, particularly for widely available products, the most important decision a marketer can make is the correct allocation or mix of the various promotional elements.

Integration of the Promotional Elements

In addition to determining the emphasis of each of the promotional elements in the mix, one of the key jobs of marketing management is to assure the proper integration of these elements into an overall promotional program. While it would seem obvious that all promotional activities should be coordinated to provide a common promotional message to the target market, in actual practice this is not always the case. Part of the difficulty in the proper integration of a promotional plan is that the separate elements are often developed by individual specialists. For example, sales activities are the province of the sales department, advertising is developed and placed by the advertising department and the advertising agency, and sales promotion may be done by a sales promotion manager and perhaps a sales promotion agency. Thus, with a number of different groups responsible for varying parts of the promotional program, one of the most difficult tasks of management is to make sure that all are heading in the same direction.

The Advertising Plan

In the development of an advertising campaign the planner must identify the specific advertising objectives that are to be achieved and then allocate the available funds in the best way to achieve those objectives. For example, a successful advertising campaign combines the proper sales message with the correct media allocation to assure that all messages are presented to the target market. Likewise, it is necessary to allocate the proper advertising media to optimize the results of the dissemination of advertising messages. The formal presentation of this advertising combination and allocation is called the advertising plan.

The advertising plan is an integral part of the overall marketing plan. While it may be developed separately, it usually is a specific subsegment of the marketing plan. (See Chapter 4 for specific details on the development and implementation of the advertising plan.)

An advertising plan consists of the following general topic areas:

- Situation analysis
- Marketing goals
- Advertising recommendations
- Media recommendations
- Sales promotion recommendations (if not included in a separate plan)
- Budget
- Evaluation methods

The development of the advertising plan marks the start of the actual advertising campaign planning procedure. However, we cannot stress too strongly the importance of the analysis, development, and planning of the marketing activities leading up to the development of the advertising plan. Unless the advertising specialist fully understands and incorporates all the necessary marketing material and information previously described into the advertising plan, it is certain to fail. That is why we believe advertising specialists should first be marketing generalists. They must have a full and complete understanding of the marketing process before attempting to develop an advertising campaign. More will be said about this in later chapters.

With this review of the marketing process and the steps leading up to the development of the advertising plan, we now take a brief look at the organization and structure of marketing and advertising organizations.

Marketing and Advertising Organizations

In the development of an advertising campaign, the campaign planner should understand the various structures and functions of businesses, marketing departments, and advertising organizations. Generally, five specific groups or types of organizations are involved in the development or execution of the advertising campaign. They are:

1. Marketing organizations
2. Advertising agencies
3. Media such as newspapers, radio, television, etc.
4. Suppliers such as film studios, typographers, art studios
5. Support organizations such as marketing and advertising research groups, audience data suppliers, etc.

Since we are interested primarily in the development of an advertising campaign, we will deal mainly with the structure of the marketing organizations and advertising agencies. Because the media, suppliers, and support organizations generally sell or furnish services and facilities to the marketer and the agency, we will deal with them only in general terms.

Marketing Organization Structures

Marketing organizations are those companies or firms that develop and/or market products or services to customers. Generally, there are four types of organizational approaches for the marketing operation in a firm: (a) functional, i.e., the grouping of marketing activities into areas of specialization such as sales, advertising, research; (b) market, i.e., the emphasis in the organization is on managing markets rather than functions; (c) product, i.e., specialization and management by product or product line; and (d) product-market, a hybrid system where function, market, and product approaches are combined in some manner. (See Figure 1-5 for illustration of the general makeup of these various organizations.)

Most consumer product marketing organizations in the United States use some form of product management system. Figure 1-6 illustrates a hypothetical marketing organization in the U.S. in the mid-1980s. The figure shows the relationship between marketing and other groups. Of particular interest is the relationship of the brand manager to other service departments.

In today's larger package goods firms, the brand manager is usually entrusted with a particular brand and functions as the responsible agent (or president) of the brand. While a brand manager may delegate much or all of various functions in the marketing and advertising program to others, such as the advertising agency or the package designer, it is the brand manager who is ultimately responsible for the overall success of the brand. The brand manager answers directly to the division brand manager, who in turn reports to the marketing director. Some of the management levels shown in Figure 1-6, e.g., division brand manager, may be eliminated in smaller firms.

Figure 1-5. Typical Marketing Organization Structures

Functional approach

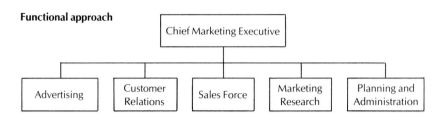

Market approach

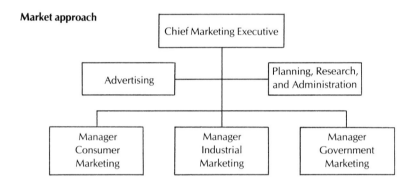

Product approach

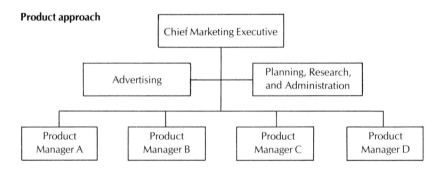

SOURCE: David W. Cravens, Gerald E. Hills, and Robert B. Woodruff, *Marketing Decision Making, Concepts and Strategy,* Revised Edition (Homewood, IL: Richard D. Irwin, Inc., 1980), p. 460.

Figure 1-6.   Hypothetical Marketing Organization in the Mid-Eighties

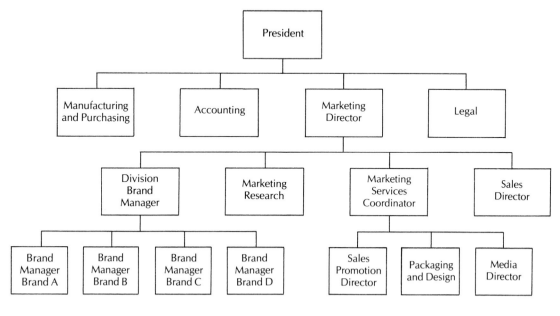

SOURCE: Cravens, Hills, and Woodruff, *Marketing Decision Making*, p. 460.

As illustrated in the lower part of Figure 1-6, brand managers are separated from the service personnel on the right side of the chart. Thus, each brand manager must work through the marketing director to get the support services to accommodate the particular needs of a brand. This is where the brand manager's talents and skills will be put to the test, since he or she must literally compete for the same support resources used by the other brand managers within the organization.

The Advertising Agency

Because the advertising agency is often an important partner in the development and execution of the marketer's advertising campaign, a brief look at the organization of the typical agency should prove helpful.

Typically, the advertising agency operates in a functional manner; that is, there are separate managers for the various functions and activities that the agency conducts. Figure 1-7 illustrates the structure of a typical member of the American Association of Advertising Agencies (AAAA).

The agency illustrated in Figure 1-7 has been organized on a functional basis. One alternative to this form would be a structure based on

Figure 1-7.   Typical AAAA Advertising Agency Structure

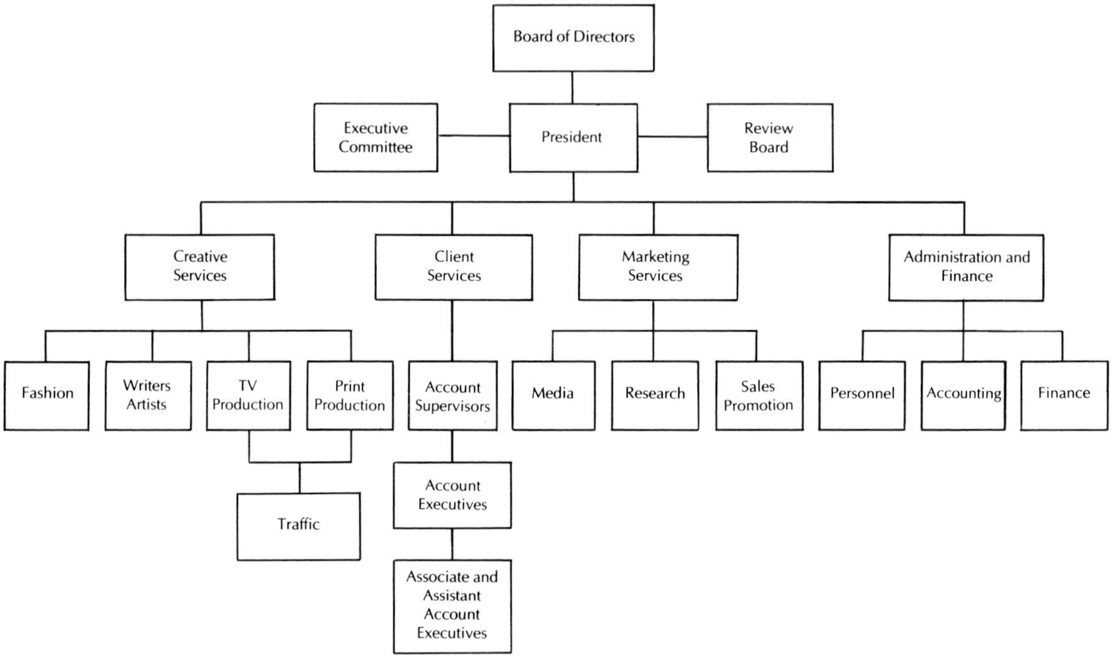

SOURCE: Adapted from material supplied by the American Association of Advertising Agencies. Used with permission.

individual accounts. In that format, client services, creative, media, and sales promotion personnel would be gathered around an individual client or group of clients. The administrative, financial, and market research groups still would be functionally organized.

While the functional structure shown in Figure 1-7 is typical of most advertising agencies, it is perhaps a bit misleading in terms of how specific advertising campaigns are actually developed. For the most part, advertising agencies are structured by account groups, i.e., a group of functional experts assigned to a specific client. This group is usually coordinated by an account supervisor. Reporting to the account supervisor may be several account executives who are responsible for various portions or brands of the general client. The account supervisor and the account executives act as the leaders or coordinators for the various other service functions that the agency may provide to the marketer/client. Figure 1-8 illustrates this typical account group structure. Client services personnel (account supervisors, account executives, associate and assistant account executives) are the coordinating forces that bring all the agency facilities and capabilities together to plan and develop an advertising campaign for the client.

Figure 1-8.   Agency Services to the Client

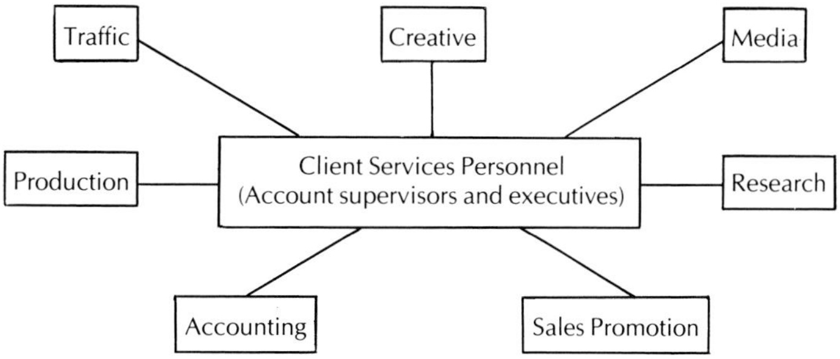

Media, Suppliers, and Support Groups

The development of an advertising campaign, even for a local retailer, is a very complex process, usually requiring a fairly large number of outside specialists in addition to the advertiser and the agency. These individuals or groups furnish the ingredients, materials, or services used by the advertiser and the advertising agency to prepare the advertising campaign. The importance of these specialists varies greatly with the type or complexity of the campaign.

Of particular interest are the media, since they deliver advertising messages to consumers or prospects. In most instances, media are independent of the advertiser or the agency. Thus, the advertiser, often through the agency, simply purchases time, space, or facilities from the media for the campaign.

Organizationally, the media are represented to the advertiser or agency by a group of salespersons. These media representatives, who may be employees of the media or simply represent the media on a commission basis, sell and service the needs of the agency or advertiser by quoting rates for time or space, furnishing information on the media coverage and audience, providing proof of performance, and performing the necessary handling to assure that the advertising appears as ordered. In many cases, the only contact between the advertiser and agency and the media is through these sales or service representatives.

Almost the same pattern exists with suppliers and support groups. (Suppliers include film studios, typography houses, printers, and art studios. Support groups include legal services, talent and residual groups, and accounting firms.) Like the media, these suppliers and support groups are represented to the advertiser and the advertising agency through sales or service personnel. Thus, the immediate contact is with the sales or service representative. Often, in both the media and the service and support groups, the sales representative operates within that organization much like the account executive functions within the advertising agency. He or she marshals all the interior forces of the media, the service, or support group to fill the needs of the advertiser or advertising agency.

Advertising: Investment or Expense?

With this understanding of the basic marketing activities within the various organizations, we come to a final overall area that should be discussed, that is, the financial view of marketing, and particularly advertising, by the firm.

Most financial managers view any expenditure that results in rewards to the organization over a relatively long period as an investment. For example, plants, trucks, warehouse facilities, and the like are considered investments, and their value is depreciated over time. Unfortunately, while marketing activities are typically viewed as being long term (that is, many marketing activities do not result in immediate sales), all firms take marketing as an expense item on their profit and loss sheet. Thus, marketing funds spent this year are taken as an expense item although the results of those activities may not occur until a year or even several years later. This arrangement is quite typical under most accounting systems.

With some marketing expenditures, taking costs as current year expenses is quite reasonable. For example, distribution costs and warehousing, while they are a marketing function, unquestionably are expenses generated in selling the product. Likewise, current year price markdowns or discounts are also costs of selling the product at that particular time. A question arises, however, when we move into such areas as research and development costs for new products and, particularly, when we start to consider advertising expenditures.

The question of whether advertising should be considered an investment or an expense to the firm has long been debated. Marketing people have traditionally tried to view advertising as an investment (or at least to convince financial people to do so). They stress that even though the funds may be spent in one period of time, value often will be received over the longer term. They also argue that in our diffused and complex marketplace, consumers often have little personal contact with the firm except through what they learn about the company and its products through the advertising they see or hear. Thus, consumers may develop their opinions and attitudes about the brands and even the whole company as a direct result of advertising messages they receive. For example, although most people may never purchase or even have occasion to be in the market for an IBM mainframe computer, a definite feeling about the company, its products, and its reputation has been built up through IBM's direct advertising to the consumer. This goodwill for the firm is often cited as a direct result of advertising expenditures. And, goodwill is normally carried on the firm's balance sheet as an asset that has been built up over time.

People in the financial and accounting sections of a company usually have a different view of advertising. Since advertising funds are normally spent in one period of time, say a fiscal year, and since there may be no direct method of measuring the value or effect of advertising, they contend there is no satisfactory way to depreciate the expenditure. The financial view is, therefore, that advertising is a direct expense related to the manufacturing and selling of the product and should be charged to the operation of the firm in the period in which it was expended. Because the federal government, for tax purposes, views advertising as an expense, the debate is somewhat theoretical. However, the question is very important on a practical, operating level when one starts to identify goals and objectives, develop marketing and advertising budgets, and measure program performance.

Summary: How Marketing and Advertising Fit Together

With this brief review of the marketing process, marketing organizations, and the financial view of advertising, it should be clear that advertising is often only a very small part of the overall marketing activities of a company or firm, although it may be a very important part. As was stressed earlier (and this theme will be followed throughout this text), advertising is simply the communication of a sales message for a product or service made through various media forms. As such, it is an integral part of the marketing process, but it is totally dependent for success on the other elements in the marketing mix. No advertising campaign can succeed without a sound product that is properly priced and adequately distributed.

Since advertising is simply the communication of a sales message for or about the product, the next logical step is a brief review of the communication process. That follows in Chapter 2.

Case for Discussion: Bossy Products

As they neared the end of the 1980 fiscal year, management at Bossy Products realized that the company was in a position similar to that of many older companies. Established in 1936, the company produced processed milk products, including powdered milk and canned condensed and evaporated milks. Its products were nationally distributed and had strong retailer support. Bossy sales accounted for 30 percent of the powdered milk and 25 percent of the canned milk market. It was the second and fourth largest seller in these categories, respectively.

Despite its strong showing, Bossy management was actively seeking new alternatives. Sales in both categories had declined over the past decade, as had overall milk consumption. As a result, profits had remained static, and there was little possibility of growth.

Powdered milk was used in approximately 12.5 percent of all U.S. households.[1] The chief buyers were one- or two-person households. Bossy studies suggested that these were people who used milk infrequently and viewed powdered milk as the most convenient form. The milk was used for drinking and baking.

Condensed and evaporated canned milks were purchased by 3.8 percent of U.S. households. The chief users were women aged 35 to 49 in high-income households with no children at home. Unlike most milk products, which showed broad geographic distribution, canned milks were used primarily in the South. Bossy studies revealed that canned milks were used primarily in cooking.

After a major consumer research study conducted in 1978, Bossy had targeted women who baked as a key market for powdered and canned milks. More specifically, the target consumer was defined as:

> A married woman with no children living at home. She works outside the home. During the week, she and her husband either dine out or eat convenience foods. However, she enjoys baking and prepares from scratch breads, pies, and cakes once or twice a month. She does not view liquid milk as a staple and sees Bossy products as a convenient alternative.

---

1. Unless otherwise noted, all demographic information is from 1976/1977 W. R. Simmons & Associates Research, Inc. studies.

Bossy's advertising had been targeted at this woman and was viewed as successful since market share had remained steady.

Realizing that their well-defined market was somewhat limiting, Bossy management was eager to find a way to expand their consumer base. A technological breakthrough in late 1979 provided new possibilities. Bossy researchers had developed a patented process for producing powdered cream, which, like powdered milk, could be reconstituted with water. The researchers also felt that with some modifications, the product could be added directly to coffee or tea as a beverage lightener.

Management explored the potential market for both scenarios. Use of fluid cream had decreased steadily (6,736,000 pounds were sold in 1977; 4,245,000 pounds in 1978).[2] Conversely, prices per pound had increased (92.0¢ in 1977; 102.0¢ in 1978).[3] Based on their knowledge of the powdered milk consumer, management believed that the market for powdered cream would be similar. There was also the probability that other homemakers would buy the product. Unlike milk, cream was not a staple in larger households. Women on a Bossy consumer panel had indicated that they were often reluctant to use recipes calling for cream. They explained that the amount of cream called for was usually so small that much of the package was left over. Because they used cream infrequently, the leftover cream usually had to be thrown out. Bossy could promote their powdered cream as economical and efficient.

Nondairy creamers are used by 14.9 percent of all U.S. households. Bossy felt that a substantial portion of these people would prefer a *dairy* powdered creamer to the nondairy products that were currently available. They cited as evidence the new emphasis on "natural" food products. They also felt that the strength of the Bossy name would help support the natural claim.

In order to more fully evaluate the potential of each alternative, Bossy set preliminary goals for the new products:

- If marketed as a powdered cream for use in baking, the product should have a 10 percent share of the dairy cream market at the end of Year 1.
- If marketed as a beverage creamer, the product should have a 15 percent share of the creamer market at the end of Year 1.
- Distribution would represent at least 65 percent of national all-commodity volume. (Bossy powdered and canned milks had 75 percent ACV distribution.)
- Return on investment would be 30 percent. (This was standard for all Bossy products.)

---

2. United States Department of Agriculture, 1979 Agriculture Statistics.
3. *Ibid.*

Questions

1. Looking at the elements making up the macro environment for a marketing company, evaluate Bossy's actions. Can you see the impact each factor has had on the situation?

2. If plotted on a business portfolio matrix, Bossy's powdered and canned milks would be labeled cash cows, since they have high market share in an industry with low growth. What would the expected matrix position be for the new product under both scenarios—baking aid and beverage creamer?

3. Assume the product will be marketed as a beverage creamer. What recommendations would you make with regard to price and place?

4. How would you market the product? As a baking aid along the lines of powdered milks or as a beverage creamer?

$\mathbb{2}$ Communication and Advertising

Advertising as Communication

The introduction and Chapter 1 have provided an overview of the marketing plan and advertising's role in achieving marketing objectives. The previous sections have also stressed the importance of planning advertising campaigns as opposed to arbitrarily spending money on ill-conceived messages aimed at the wrong target audience or run in the wrong media at the wrong time.

Typical of the wrong approach to the creation and placement of advertising is the small retailer who is lured into buying a package of radio spots to be run at 2 A.M. on a station whose format does not attract his customers. The reason given for buying the spots is usually that they were cheap. Well, cost is only one requirement of good planning. In addition, the message must be right, it must be aimed at the right audience, timing must be right, and finally, the cost must be reasonable.

The costs involved in advertising planning is the subject of another chapter. This chapter is concerned with how advertising can be planned to communicate the right sales message to the right audience. Also, through the study of communication we hope to better understand how our messages are received by and acted upon by our customers.

Ways of Looking at Communication

Since advertising is a special form of communication intended to persuade consumers to respond in a positive way toward a product or service, the study of communication can help us to better understand how our advertising actually works. Through this understanding we will then be in a better position to plan and successfully execute an advertising campaign.

There are three basic types of communication processes that are of value to the advertising planner. These are: individual communication

This chapter was written by Bruce Vanden Bergh, Department of Advertising, Michigan State University.

processes, interpersonal communication processes, and mass communication processes. Each of these areas of communication study provides valuable insight into how advertising works. Let's start with individual communication.

Individual Communication

To successfully communicate our sales message to our customers, a majority of them must decide to select our message from a cluttered media environment and to remember it for future use. At the individual level of communication we are concerned with how people select messages to attend to and how their memories work to retain information and impressions conveyed by advertisements.

Selection of messages occurs at several levels. First, our customers must decide to expose themselves to our messages. This can occur in a very planned way, as in the case where customers actively seek out our ad because they are already interested in our product. Or exposure to our ad might occur because the ad is very unique and breaks through the media clutter to attract customers to it. From the advertiser's perspective, selective exposure necessitates that the sales message be of interest value to consumers, that it be unique or creative enough to seek out consumers, and that it be in those media vehicles where consumers are most likely to find it.

Exposure is not enough. Many people will be exposed to a message yet decide not to attend to it or retain it in their memories. For example, a very unique ad—like those for Federal Express where a fast-talking potential customer symbolizes the need for fast delivery of important packages in this fast-paced computer age—easily achieves wide exposure for Federal Express. However, before this message can be remembered—retained for future reference—a consumer must decide to consciously attend to the ad. Attention is another selective process. If an ad's sales message does not offer a consumer any information worth storing, it will be forgotten, almost immediately. But, if the message does offer something of value, it will be retained in memory.

There are many approaches to the study of memory. For practical purposes, it is important only to know that memory is very limited, and therefore, all of us must be very selective in determining what to remember and not to remember. We simply cannot remember everything we see, read, or hear.

Memory is the cornerstone of the use of creative strategies in advertising. The basic assumption of strategy is that the media environment is cluttered and memory is limited. Since memory is limited, it is important that your advertising give customers something worth remembering. Otherwise, they simply will forget you.

Novelty approaches that tease consumers typically can trick people into exposing themselves to ads. However, once a consumer realizes that there is nothing in the ad for him, he will not waste his precious time and memory on your ad.

Advertising that is creatively unique and offers consumers information or ideas of value to them is the most effective in today's cluttered media environment. Advertising that is just creative for art's sake will likely win awards but not communicate with most consumers. This is the lesson to be learned from how communication works at the individual level.

Interpersonal Communication

Another way to look at communication is to study those factors that lead to successful face-to-face communication. A model of face-to-face communication appears in Figure 2-1.

Face-to-face situations occur most often in personal selling. However, successful copywriters communicate with consumers not by writing to the masses but by imagining that they are talking or writing to one person. In essence, they treat the situation as if it were a face-to-face situation and not a mass communication situation.

The success of face-to-face communication depends on the sender's ability to elicit meanings and feelings in the receiver that both have in

Figure 2-1.   Face-to-Face Communication

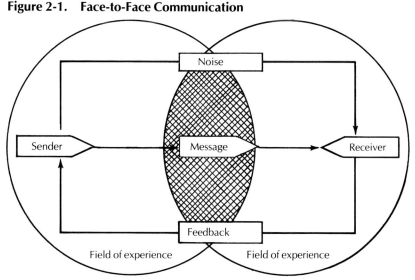

SOURCE: Adapted from Wilbur Schramm and Donald Roberts, eds., *The Process and Effects of Mass Communication* (Urbana: University of Illinois Press, 1971).

common. To be able to do this, both sender and receiver have to have some shared experiences in their backgrounds. These experiences are labeled field of experience in Figure 2-1. The crosshatched area is where these experiences overlap. The key to communication is for the copywriter to be able to identify and tap these shared experiences. This often involves good consumer research to identify these experiences. Additionally, most good creative people have a natural sensitivity or empathy for other people. They are able to see things from the other person's point of view.

Ads that can tap the receiver's field of experience are on their way to communicating successfully. Also, most face-to-face situations have background "noise"—other things that are going on at the same time communication is taking place. For instance, imagine a typical father sitting in his easy chair reading a newspaper. The television is on. His teenage kids are upstairs playing their stereo. The dog is barking, and you can hear a siren in the distance. Now, through all this noise we can vaguely make out a commercial on TV. How successful do you think this commercial will be? The problem is "noise," too much "noise."

Clutter in the media is also a form of noise. Anything that can interfere with the reception of a message is noise. Media planners are largely responsible for placing messages in environments conducive to the reception of the message, and noise is an important consideration. You must try to find the right environment for the message. Riding on buses or subways creates a certain amount of competition for ads. The home environment, often considered one of the best, can also be "noisy." The doctor's office, beach, driving, etc., also present environments that contain different types of noise.

Think of all the competition for the receiver's attention. Add this problem to the limited capacity of our memories, and you get a rather frightening picture of what an ad has to go through to successfully communicate its message.

Up to now we might have given the impression that communication is a one-way process, something a sender does to a receiver. Face-to-face communication has the important characteristic of being a two-way process. When we talk to each other, we provide "feedback" upon which future messages are based. This feedback can be something we say, a facial expression, or the way we are sitting or standing. Mass communication situations generally lack this type of feedback, although this is compensated for through research.

Copywriters also have to compensate for a lack of immediate feedback to their ads by guessing in advance as to a consumer's response. The better a writer is at this, the better he is able to communicate.

Henry Assael has taken the basic structure of the face-to-face communication model and shown how the different advertising institutions

Figure 2-2.   The Advertising Communication Process

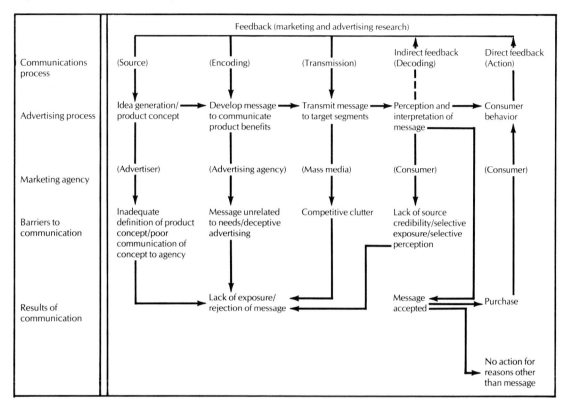

SOURCE: Henry Assael, *Consumer Behavior and Marketing Action* (Boston: Kent Publishing Co., 1981), p. 480.

must work together to effectively communicate with consumers. (See Figure 2-2.)

The communication process components are shown in Assael's model across the top row. Notice the similarities with the face-to-face model. The source component is the same in both models. Assael has also retained the feedback loop. The receiver component has been replaced with the response we hope the consumer will make, and the message has been replaced with the term *transmission*. Transmission includes not only a message but the media through which it will be sent to the audience.

Assael has also included the processes by which messages are developed (encoding) and deciphered (decoding). Encoding involves all those processes writers, artists, and producers go through to translate ideas or product benefits into symbols that consumers will understand and be interested enough in to take action on and, hopefully, buy the product.

Decoding involves all the selective processes discussed previously that consumers use to decide to attend to and remember messages and their components.

Parallel to each element in this basic communication process is an analogous process specific to how advertising works. The source of the message or the advertiser is ultimately responsible for the product concept and the package of benefits that must be communicated to consumers. This is the most important step in the advertising process. The product must be a good one for advertising to be successful. If the product is lacking or not wanted by consumers, then the best advertising available will not be able to sell the product. This barrier to successful communication is shown in the fourth row of the model under the column headed "source."

Next, it is the advertising agency's job to develop messages that will successfully convey the important product benefits to the consumer. If this message incorrectly presents the product benefits or deceives the customer into trying the product, consumers either will not attend to the message or eventually will reject it. Either of these situations will hurt the credibility of the advertiser.

The media provide the channels through which advertising messages can be conveyed simultaneously to large groups of consumers. The environment provided by each vehicle can influence the receptivity of the message. Excessive clutter and noise will impede the communication process. This barrier to communication appears in the fourth row under the column labeled "transmission."

Consumer selection of a message and interpretation for retention in memory are as important as the development of the ad itself. Ultimately, most messages are either rejected or misinterpreted. Consumers will defend against persuasive attempts and misinterpret messages to fit their own biases. If we are lucky enough to get our message through this difficult and complex process and into the consumer's mind as intended, we have a chance of stimulating the consumer to want our product.

All of the major components of the advertising process influence the likelihood of success. They are intertwined in such a way as to make planning essential to successful advertising. Haphazard or arbitrary advertising can only be successful through luck. While planning does not guarantee success, it increases the probability of success substantially.

Assael's model can be seen in action in Federal Express's success in identifying a successful service concept, selecting an agency to convey its message to consumers, transmission of the message, and consumers' positive responses to the whole idea of overnight mail delivery. For Federal Express to be successful, it had to have an idea that could be sold to potential customers and could be executed at a profit.

The overnight delivery concept started with the recognition that as information processing via computers spread and increased in speed, companies and individuals would need a more efficient and quicker delivery system. To do this, a system was designed so that all mail would be delivered to one place and redistributed to its eventual destinations. But the concept was not enough. It had to be communicated to companies and individuals nationwide. An agency was selected that had a style and philosophy consistent with this new maverick of the delivery business. And this agency had to develop advertising that could break through the clutter of television, convey the speedy delivery theme, and convey the personality of the advertiser—all in 30 seconds. The ads developed are now classic. The quick-talking actor has become a celebrity. The ads have won Clio Awards consistently for three years in a row, and Federal Express has kept its dominant name in the intensely competitive overnight delivery business despite the entry of many new companies in recent years.

Mass Communication

The situation that most advertising planners are confronted with is different from the preceding discussion in a number of important ways. First, when we advertise, we generally do not know the people we are trying to communicate with. If we are lucky, we might have some consumer research that describes our best prospects, but we do not know these people the way we know our friends and neighbors. Second, the feedback we get from our communication attempts is very indirect. It normally takes a long time to see if people are reacting positively to our ads. Thus, we cannot react as quickly as we can in face-to-face communication. Clutter is also a problem. Not only messages from competitors, but also everything in the environment is competing for a customer's attention.

In addition to these problems, we still have to deal with the communication problems previously discussed. Consumers' selective processes and memory limitations, noise, and tapping common experiences are problems present in all communication situations from face-to-face to mass communications.

The communication models that best illustrate what we should know about mass communication are called step-flow models. These models simply and clearly describe the way messages such as advertisements flow from the media to the general population and the steps involved in this process. These models are useful to the advertising planner because they give us a picture of how our ads travel through society to their ultimate destination, a target prospect. Additionally, these models focus on the "transmission" of our ads. Step-flow models are concerned with the channels through which our ads must flow and how these channels can influence how our ads are received.

Figure 2-3.   Multistep Flow Model

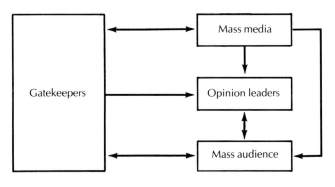

The planning and control of advertising is paramount to its success, and step-flow models can be an important tool for managing the process. Among the step-flow models, the most comprehensive and useful one to the advertising planner is the multistep flow model depicted in Figure 2-3. Control of how a message is received is much easier in face-to-face situations than it is in mass communication situations. The mass communication situation contains intermediaries who influence the ultimate reception of our messages.

When we decide to run a commercial on network television, a number of things can happen to it before it reaches its final destination—the prospective consumer. There are people in our society who, through education and interests, are more active consumers of information than the average population. They tend to see new ads first. They also tend to be very active in talking to others about what they have seen. And they don't merely convey the information in the ads; they interpret the information too. These people have been labeled opinion leaders by mass communication scholars.[1] They are important to advertisers for two reasons. First, they help to disseminate the advertiser's message to people who might not otherwise have been exposed to it. Second, they interpret and sometimes distort the message. Thus, they influence the nature of the content of an ad that is ultimately received by consumers.

Opinion leaders are also important because they generally have more credibility than advertisers and can take advantage of the characteristics of face-to-face communication situations. Their influence is most often

1. Elihu Katz and Paul F. Lazarsfeld, *Personal Influence* (Glencoe, IL: The Free Press, 1955).

exerted through word-of-mouth communication. An advertiser's task is to be able to identify opinion leaders and use them to his advantage. Opinion leaders can act as an extension of a media campaign, but they can also impede a campaign's success. Negative opinion leaders like Ralph Nader can certainly hurt a campaign through his interpretation of the campaign's content. Positive opinion leaders such as doctors, teachers, and fashion leaders can be employed to benefit an advertiser.

Notice the fervor with which personal computer companies are trying to get educational institutions to employ computers in their instruction. Some technologically oriented colleges now require students to own personal computers. In such situations educators are prime opinion leaders in the dissemination of information. Advertisers are frantically trying to reach educators with information they want spread to students and their families. This way the advertisers hope to use the educators' credibility to aid in the communication of their sales messages.

The opinion leader concept can also be employed in the development of ads themselves. The testimonial format is an attempt to use a well-known and credible personality to sell products and services. Bill Cosby, John Houseman, Arthur Godfrey, and many other well-known people have been employed to add their credibility to products and services.

Of course, in many situations advertisers do also communicate directly with the ultimate prospect. Still, there is another type of intermediary who exerts a certain degree of control over the messages we receive. These people are called gatekeepers because they are in positions where they can control the dissemination of information through the media. The gatekeeper concept is more important in the dissemination of news. Editors of newspapers act as gatekeepers of the news we read because they decide what news is printed and what is left out.

In advertising, family members can act as gatekeepers of product information. Different family members typically have different interests and are relied upon for certain types of information. For example, children might be considered more knowledgeable about products they use. Parents will rely on them to bring information concerning these products to the family. Knowing this, advertisers can target both the child, the gatekeeper, and the parent, the person who might ultimately purchase the product.

The flow of information in the multistep flow model is typically from the mass media through gatekeepers and opinion leaders to the mass audience. Yet, we must also remember that gatekeepers and opinion leaders often interact with one another as well as with other people. So, the flow of information is often not as clear as described here.

Some advertisers take advantage of worth-of-mouth communication and the step-flow process simply by creating excitement through their advertising. They intentionally try to get people talking. A recent Seven-Up no-caffeine campaign, is an example of this type of strategy. Also, the introduction of new products necessitates generating excitement to break through media clutter. The lesson to be taken from the step-flow model is the realization that advertising often does not influence consumers directly and opinion leaders can be used effectively to extend and reinforce the effects of a well-planned campaign.

Your Audience: Active or Passive?

An age-old axiom in the advertising business has been: "Know your audience." This truism shows up again and again in communication models and theories. The focus on the individual's selective processes and memory limitations is an attempt to better understand our audience. The emphasis on the importance of shared experiences in the face-to-face model further underlines the importance of the receiver of ads.

Another important distinction to make in trying to better know who it is we are communicating with is, whether our audience members are likely to be "active" or "passive" receivers of our message. To this point, we have been talking about consumers as if they are very "active" participants in advertising campaigns. Among the most active participants are opinion leaders and gatekeepers. They seek out ads and do a lot of the work in the communication process. But these consumers are also very stubborn. They are among the most selective people who will see or hear our ads, and they are not easily persuaded. These people are members of what has been labeled the "obstinate audience."[2]

How do we know if most of our prospective consumers are likely to be difficult to persuade and, more important, how does this influence the success of our ads? To find out if your audience is made up of mostly active consumers you must analyze your product and its importance to your prospects. Highly involving products like shopping or specialty goods tend to attract prospects who are very active participants in the search for information about those products. Shopping and specialty goods tend to be expensive items like major appliances, furniture, automobiles, cameras, sporting goods, and clothing. These items are involving because the importance of making the right choice is very high. If a bad choice is made, the prospect can lose a great deal of money or feel a great deal of social pressure against his selection. To assure a good choice and thus reduce the risk of a poor choice, consumers of these products shop extensively and are difficult to persuade with our ads.

2. R. A. Bauer, "The Obstinate Audience," *American Psychologist* 19 (May 1964): 319–28.

Table 2-1.   Active Versus Passive Learning

Active	Passive
The consumer is . . .	The consumer is . . .
1. A very *selective* processor of product information.	1. Exposed to product information at *random*.
2. A very *active* seeker of product information.	2. A *passive* gatherer of product information.
3. *Involved* with the purchase decision.	3. *Uninvolved* with the purchase decision.
4. A *complex* decision maker.	4. Likely to try the product due to *simple* recognition of the brand name.
The advertising should be . . .	The advertising should be . . .
1. *Informative* and of high interest value to prospective consumers.	1. *Creatively unique* to cut through the clutter.
2. *Rational*.	2. *Memorable*.
3. In *selective* media likely to attract the target prospect.	3. In *general* media, primarily television.

Advertisements for high-involvement products tend to appear in selective print media. The ads give the active consumer reasons for purchasing a particular brand. These ads strive for more than exposure and attention; they often try to get the consumer to retain information about the product or service.

Herbert Krugman of General Electric realized that not all products and ads attract prospects who are highly involved in the selection and purchase process. In fact, many of the packaged goods advertised in the mass media today are greeted by a big yawn from many consumers. Why? Because the products are relatively unimportant compared to the shopping and specialty goods just discussed. These products are your typical "me too" products found on the shelves of your local supermarket. Soap, cereal, soft drinks, dish detergent, and snacks are typical of these products. When confronted by ads for these products on TV, most consumers are "passive."[3] Their selective defenses are down as is their interest in the ads.

Does this mean we cannot get many of these consumers to learn something from our ads? Not at all. In fact, in these situations, passive learning can take place. Passive learning requires interesting advertising to gain the attention of the viewer. A simple 30-second TV spot with an intriguing creative approach like Dr Pepper's "Be a Pepper" campaign is all that may be needed to get consumers to remember the name of the product and try it the next time they buy a soft drink.

Unfortunately, as simple as it might seem, the clutter of ads trying to reach passive consumers places a premium on creativity. These ads are also the most memorable of all advertising from Alka Seltzer's "Spicy Meatball" spot to the current Federal Express campaign. The objective of

3. Herbert E. Krugman, "The Impact of Television Advertising: Learning Without Involvement," *Public Opinion Quarterly* 29 (Fall 1965): 349–56.

advertising in this situation is to get across the name of the product and a simple claim about the product. To do this, your advertising must be very, very memorable. Think of the TV spots you can remember and the ones you talk about at parties. These are usually ads written to make the brand name memorable above everything else the campaign might accomplish.

The basic differences between active and passive learning situations are listed in Table 2-1.

Theories of How Advertising Works

The discussion to this point has been based on a fairly important assumption regarding how advertising works. The assumption is that before a prospective consumer will go out and buy a product, he must know something about it. The consumer must learn something from our advertising and promotional efforts. In high-involvement situations, the active consumer must learn a great deal about competing brands before making a choice. In contrast, the passive consumer only has to learn the name of the product and perhaps a simple message for each purchase alternative. Yet he still must learn something. Learning, therefore, is a key cornerstone of how advertising works.

To be able to use consumer learning processes to our advantage, we must know something about how learning takes place. There are many theories about how we learn things, but the two most important to the advertising planner are the behaviorist approach and the cognitive learning approach. In fact, as we discuss these approaches, refer back to the ideas behind active and passive learning. The behaviorist tradition describes a rather simplistic learning process that has some similarities to passive learning. The cognitive approach is much more closely aligned with active learning. Therefore, both approaches provide interesting insights into how people learn from advertisements.

The Behaviorist Approach

Within the behaviorist approach to learning are two dominant schools of thought. The first is called *classical conditioning* and describes what might happen from repetitious exposure to ads that attempt to convey a brand image. Typically, this type of advertising will attempt to get consumers to associate something unique or pleasant with a product. Through repetition of the association it is hoped that the pleasant or unique imagery will trigger a desire for the product.

An example of the use of classical conditioning principles can be seen in beer advertising. Budweiser beer is presently associating their product with pride in one's work and quality craftsmanship. Through heavy repetition of this theme, Budweiser is attempting to persuade a very specific group of consumers to associate Budweiser with their own pride in their jobs. Budweiser is hoping to trigger a desire for their brand whenever the ''pride-in-job'' emotion is triggered.

The other dominant behaviorist tradition, *instrumental conditioning,* focuses on how reward and punishment can be used to persuade people to learn a correct response. In advertising, the correct response is the purchase of an advertiser's product. The reward that should trigger the response is satisfaction with the product. Advertising is also used to further reinforce this satisfaction by telling consumers why they should be satisfied with their choice.

Instrumental conditioning principles are the cornerstone of the marketing concept. The marketing concept directs a firm to identify and fulfill consumer needs and desires. The fulfillment of these needs should reward the consumer and, in doing so, lead to repeat purchases of a product.

Advertising also offers consumers rewards other than just the product itself. Many rewards in our society are psychological and social. The promises of better looking hair, a better sex life, more comfort, and more excitement are all rewards for purchasing products. If consumers perceive that these promises are fulfilled by a product, then their behavior has been reinforced and should lead to repeat purchase until a better product with a better promise comes along.

Think of advertising for products like cosmetics and shampoo. Physically or tangibly, many of these products are quite similar. At least most consumers cannot tell the difference through simple inspection of the contents. It is the promise of an important benefit (reward) that attracts different groups of consumers to different brands.

Products that do not fulfill advertising's promises act as a punishment for the purchase and will not lead to repurchase. Instrumental conditioning teaches us not to try to trick consumers into trying a product we know cannot live up to the things promised by advertising.

The behaviorist tradition carries with it overtones of a passive consumer who can easily be conditioned into exhibiting a desired response. While most purchase situations are not that simple, we can still see some of the behaviorist principles used in advertising. Repetition, pleasant associations, and reinforcement are all useful devices to employ in many advertising campaigns.

Cognitive Learning

Those who support a cognitive approach to how consumers learn from advertising take a very different view of learning from that of the behaviorists. A cognitive approach assumes that people are more actively involved in learning. This approach sees consumers as goal-oriented people trying to fulfill their needs through the active pursuit of product information and ultimate purchase of the best product available. Consumers are seen as much more rational and complex from this perspective.

Cognitivists focus their attention on a series of intervening variables in the consumer's mind that influence how he will respond to ads and promotional activities. Perception, beliefs, attitudes, motivation, and learning are among the more frequently studied variables.

The Howard-Sheth model of consumer behavior is a good example of the cognitive tradition. Their model consists of four major components that take us away from the simplistic relationships between exposure to advertising and learning supported by the behaviorists. The major components are: (1) input stimuli; (2) intervening factors—perception and learning; (3) exogenous factors; and (4) a hierarchical series of responses—attention, comprehension, attitude, intention, and purchase.[4]

Input stimuli include items such as price and product advertising. Perceptual processes include the consumer's biases, attention, and search for information. Learning, according to Howard and Sheth, is far more complex than a simple conditioned response to an ad or other information. It involves a person's motives, criteria used to select a product, confidence in the choice, comprehension of products, attitude toward products, and satisfaction with a purchase.

Once incoming stimuli are processed, Howard and Sheth theorize that a hierarchical series of responses are possible. This hierarchy assumes that before a purchase can be made, a consumer must pass sequentially through these responses from attention to actual purchase. The hierarchical concept will be discussed further in the next section.

Additionally, factors external to an individual's perceptual and learning processes influence the output of a decision. Culture, social class, personality, time pressure, and financial status can influence a consumer's decision. Culture, social class, and personality will be discussed in the next chapter.

From a learning perspective, the Howard-Sheth model depicts decision making based on learning as a very complex process. In any given situation, every variable in the model can take on a different value. Inputs change from situation to situation as does the way we perceive the inputs. Motives, attitudes, levels of comprehension, confidence, and satisfaction all differ in importance from one purchase situation to another.

The Howard-Sheth model clearly illustrates the complexity of learning. This approach more closely describes an active consumer trying to

---

4. John A. Howard and Jagdish Sheth, *The Theory of Buyer Behavior* (New York: John Wiley and Sons, Inc., 1969).

make a difficult choice from among brands in an important and expensive product category.

The following automobile purchase example describes how a cognitive learning approach might be applied to a purchase decision. Mr. Smith has just seen a spot on TV for a Chevy Blazer. He has a family consisting of his wife and two kids. They presently own a Ford LTD that is four years old. Mr. Smith likes to go fishing and hunting, and the Blazer would be ideal for this sort of activity. But he cannot afford two cars right now so the Blazer would replace the LTD.

Mr. Smith is a factory worker and the recession has hit his firm rather hard. He is not likely to earn any large salary increases for the next two years.

Mr. Smith likes the Blazer because he feels it is large enough to carry his family and he can still use it to go "off-roading." He describes the Blazer as durable yet still comfortable. Mr. Smith also likes the image he associates with the vehicle. It's rough and macho.

Mr. Smith shopped around extensively and looked closely at competitive vehicles like the Ford Bronco and Jeep Cherokee. Due to financial constraints, Mr. Smith decided not to buy the Blazer right now. He is still considering buying another family car.

Notice in this example the inputs and criteria Mr. Smith used to make his decision. Advertising was just a triggering device to get him thinking about the possibility of buying a new car. His financial situation was a key exogenous variable that had a very strong influence on his decision. Mr. Smith's motives and criteria for making a choice were strongly influenced by his sports interests and family considerations. What Mr. Smith learned from this process was that this was not the right time to buy the Blazer.

The complexity of Mr. Smith's situation is in stark contrast to the behaviorist principles employed in less important purchase situations. Advertising is a more influential promotional tool in situations involving simple decisions. In complex decision-making situations, many more variables enter into the learning situation.

The Hierarchical Approach to How Advertising Works

A key advertising planning activity is setting objectives for the advertising campaign. To decide in which areas objectives must be set, it is necessary to understand the relationships between various consumer responses to advertising and the ultimate purchase of a product. Otherwise, objective setting and planning become arbitrary, and we have no way of knowing if achievement of our objectives will contribute to the sale of our product.

A hierarchical scheme for setting and measuring advertising objectives was developed by Lavidge and Steiner and has become the founda-

Table 2-2.   The Hierarchy of Effects

Terminology in the Hierarchy of Effects

Name(s) of theorist(s)	Learning (cognitive)	Feeling (affective)	Acting (conative)
Anonymous	Attention	Interest, Desire	Action
Lavidge & Steiner (1961)	Awareness Knowledge	Liking Preference	Conviction Purchase
Colley (1961)	Awareness Comprehension	Conviction	Action
Rogers (1962)	Awareness	Interest Evaluation	Trial Adoption
Mendelsohn (1962)	Rudimentary response (recall)	Emotional response (affect)	Active response
Wolfe, et al. (1962)	Awareness Acceptance	Preference Interest	Sale
Aspinwall (1964)	Acceptance	Preference	Insistence
A.R.F. (undated)	Exposure, Perception, Communication (knowledge)	Communication (attitude)	Action
M.S.I. (1968)	Awareness Knowledge	Liking Preference	Conviction Purchase
Schwartz (1969)	Exposure, Attention, Retention	Attitude change	Purchase
Howard & Sheth (1969)	Attention Comprehension	Attitude	Intention Purchase
Howard (undated)	Facts-exposed Facts-coded	Attitude	Intention Purchase
Murphy (1971)	Attitude Comprehension	Significance Differentiation	Activation
Taylor & Peterson (1972)	Attention	Interest Desire	Conviction Action
Young (1972)	Attention Communication	Persuasion	
Holbrook (1975)	Attention, Perception, Memory	Attitude	Intention

SOURCE: Charles Ramond, *Advertising Research: The State of the Art* (New York: Association of National Advertisers, Inc., 1976), p. 15.

tion for objective setting in many companies and agencies.[5] Others have also developed hierarchical approaches similar to that of Lavidge and Steiner's. The hierarchical approach to how advertising works assumes that there is a series of steps a consumer must pass through in sequential order from initial awareness of a product to actual purchase. The typical configuration of the hierarchy is indicated at the top of the columns in Table 2-2. This text uses Lavidge and Steiner's approach due to its popularity and usefulness in describing key advertising variables measured in the industry today.

The key components of the hierarchy, regardless of labels given to them, are: learning, attitude formation or feeling, and purchase or the conative component. Table 2-2 includes some of the more popular hierarchies including that developed by Lavidge and Steiner.

The Lavidge and Steiner hierarchy is based on the hierarchy developed by Russell Colley from his book, *Defining Advertising Goals for Measured Advertising Results,* or DAGMAR for short.[6] A comparison of Colley's hierarchical scheme with Lavidge and Steiner's shows some minor differences. The comprehension and knowledge terms under learning are really interchangeable. Colley places conviction under feeling as a strong attitudinal response after comprehension. Lavidge and Steiner include weaker attitudinal responses before conviction. The purchase and action responses are really the same. These two hierarchies are the most popular in the industry today.

Let's use a hypothetical new product introduction to demonstrate how the hierarchy works. A new line of ice cream flavors is about to be introduced called "vegetable flavors." The new flavors range from carrot to broccoli. Distribution has been achieved in all major supermarket chains, and a network television campaign will introduce the new flavors to homes in the top 200 TV markets. Since there is no awareness of this new line presently, an ambitious awareness objective has been set for the first year of the campaign.

The manufacturer of "vegetable flavors" expects some resistance to the idea of combining vegetable flavors with ice cream. Therefore, another goal of the introductory campaign is to teach (i.e., knowledge) consumers about the nutritional value of the ice cream flavors. Due to the current health trend, the manufacturer expects the new health segment to react favorably and like the flavors. To build a preference for "vegetable flavors" an ambitious promotional campaign is planned to support the national

5. Robert J. Lavidge and Gary A. Steiner, "A Model for Predictive Measurements of Advertising Effectiveness," *Journal of Marketing* 24 (October 1961): 59–62.

6. Russell H. Colley, *Defining Advertising Goals for Measured Advertising Results* (New York: Association of National Advertisers, 1961).

advertising. Taste tests and nutritional programs are being planned. The taste tests will occur in all national supermarket chains. The nutritional programs will be offered in booklet form with each purchase of a gallon or more of one of the new flavors.

To bring consumers to the conviction stage, nationally known authors of best selling books on health and exercise like Jane Fonda and Victoria Principal are being used to extol the virtues of the new flavors on talk shows and to civic groups. The combination of all these efforts is expected to pull consumers through the hierarchy to trial and repeat purchase of vegetable-flavored ice cream.

The assumption of the hierarchical approach described is that it is necessary for a campaign to pull a consumer through all the steps before he will purchase the product. Yet there are situations in which a consumer might buy a product after simple exposure to an ad and before developing an attitude about the product. This is exactly what happens for many of the products we buy.

The passive learning situation described previously is exactly the situation Herbert Krugman was referring to. He labeled the hierarchical sequency involved in these situations the low-involvement hierarchy. The low-involvement sequence takes the consumer from passive learning straight to purchase. Only after experience with the product is an attitude formed.[7]

An example of the low-involvement hierarchy in action is when a new advertising campaign breaks for a very unimportant product like a candy bar. The Nestlé Crunch campaign that claims Nestlé Crunch is music to your mouth is a new and interesting campaign for a product you might not have thought about for a long time. The catchy jingle and heart-warming scenes of everyday life draw you into the ads. As a result of this simple yet likable approach, you might buy Nestlé Crunch instead of another brand the next time you want a candy bar. This is how the low-involvement hierarchy works.

The general configuration of this hierarchy is learning followed by purchase followed by attitude formation.

These two hierarchies—learning and low-involvement—account for the majority of the situations confronted by most advertisers. However, advertising and consumer purchase patterns are dynamic. Once someone has purchased a product the sequence of events does not stop. A hierarchy that demonstrates the sequence of events following purchase is the dissonance-attribution hierarchy.

To illustrate this hierarchy, let's return to Mr. Smith's car purchase situation. Now, let's assume he did purchase the Chevy Blazer and not a

---

7. Herbert Krugman, "The Impact of Television Advertising."

Jeep or Ford. What happens next? The dissonance-attribution hierarchy says that Mr. Smith is likely to experience an uneasy feeling about his purchase. This is called dissonance.[8] The uneasy feeling is caused by the realization that the Chevy Blazer is not a perfect purchase. The Blazer has some negative aspects that are now recognized by Mr. Smith. Also, he now realizes that the Jeep Cherokee and Ford Bronco have positive aspects that would make them reasonable purchases. These realizations after the purchase are contradictory to the purchase Mr. Smith made.

Mr. Smith does not like this dissonant feeling so he tries to reduce the pressure by seeking out information that supports his purchase. He now notices all the Chevy Blazers on the road that he never noticed before. He also starts to notice more and more ads for Chevy Blazers. All this information is taken in and reinforces a positive feeling in Mr. Smith for his new Blazer. The dissonance has been reduced.

Advertisers can take advantage of the dissonance-attribution hierarchy by giving consumers reinforcing reasons for their purchases in advertising and promotional materials. By helping consumers reduce dissonance, purchase behavior is reinforced and the likelihood of repurchase greatly enhanced.

Models of How Advertising Works at the Societal Level

The previous section describes how advertising affects individual consumers. Now it is necessary to paint a picture of how advertising affects many people simultaneously.

Two theoretical approaches that deal with how groups of people respond to advertising are diffusion theory and agenda setting. These topics are discussed in some depth in Chapter 3, so they will be treated only briefly here.

Diffusion theory.   Diffusion theory attempts to explain how new ideas and products spread through the population. The basic theory uses the structure of the step-flow models previously discussed but focuses more closely on how word-of-mouth communication helps to disseminate innovations through society.

The major components of diffusion theory are diffusion, adoption, communication, adoption units, innovations, and time. The diffusion model tries to explain how an innovation is tried and adopted by people, groups, organizations, or countries over time. Rogers segmented the population into five groups based on the amount of time it takes for each group

---

8. Leon Festinger, "Cognitive Dissonance," *Scientific American* (October 1962): 93–100.

to adopt an innovation. The earliest group to try a new product are innovators. They are considered risk takers. The second group is labeled early adopters. Next to adopt are early majority members followed by the late majority and laggards. These groups plus the adoption process are diagrammed in Chapter 3.[9]

Of importance to the study of advertising is the role that interpersonal communication plays in disseminating news about products and services. The diffusion model can be observed in operation in the motion picture industry where word-of-mouth communication can make or break a film. Initially, film producers try to create awareness to interest avid film goers in their new pictures. Next, the first group to see a film will tell friends about the film. If the word-of-mouth communication is positive, it will spread quickly, and more and more people will become involved in the communication process as they see the film and talk about it with others. This model is an analogy to the spread of contagious diseases. Advertisers of new products and services hope for an epidemic of positive communication as a result of their advertising.

Advertising's role in this process is to create initial awareness and interest and to give people information content to spread via word-of-mouth communication. This strategy is based on the premise that the best salesperson for your product is a satisfied customer.

The concept of opinion leadership as described previously is central to the diffusion process. Opinion leaders are both active seekers and disseminators of information. Campaigns that target opinion leaders like doctors, teachers, etc. are attempting to use their influence and credibility to spread favorable word-of-mouth communication.

Agenda setting. The major premise of agenda setting theory is that "the mass media don't tell us what to think, but they do tell us what to think about."[10] In essence, the media set our agenda. An agenda setting approach to understanding how advertising works would suggest that advertising focuses our attention on what products, brands, and attributes to think about as opposed to trying to persuade us what to think of them.

The agenda setting approach dovetails nicely with low-involvement learning. It suggests that salience of a brand is important in low-involvement situations where simple recognition might induce product trial. The evoked set concept discussed in the next chapter is a marketing application of the agenda setting idea. An evoked set consists of those brands of a product that are serious alternatives to a consumer. The goal of many

9. Everett M. Rogers, *Diffusion of Innovations* (New York: The Free Press, 1962).

10. Max Sutherland and John Galloway, "Role of Advertising: Persuasion or Agenda Setting?" *Journal of Advertising Research* 21, No. 5 (October 1981): 25.

advertisers is to make sure their brand is in a consumer's evoked set. Products not in the evoked set have little chance of being purchased. The evoked set is the agenda for a product category in a consumer's mind.

**Summary:
How Does
Advertising Work?**

Figure 2-4 summarizes many of the concepts we have discussed to this point. It combines the key elements of individual, face-to-face, and mass communication. As you look at the model, notice the clutter of messages that clamor for the receiver's attention. This clutter represents over a thousand messages a day that many of us are exposed to. To deal with the clutter, the consumer screens out or selects only those messages that interest him. To get through this screen advertisers must appeal to the consumer's needs, tap common experiences, and be unique enough to gain his attention.

The decoding, encoding, and memory processes are also clearly indicated in Figure 2-4. Remember that memory is limited and will influence what information is stored. Also, some information not immediately needed will also be stored for future use.

This model generally describes high-involvement situations concep-

Figure 2-4. How Advertising Communicates

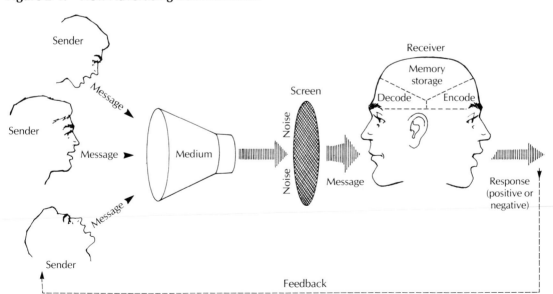

SOURCE: Don E. Schultz and Dennis G. Martin, *Strategic Advertising Campaigns* (Chicago: Crain Books, 1979), p. 6.

tualized by the learning hierarchy. Passive learning situations can be accommodated if we visualize the receiver in a passive model not selecting but merely catching messages that grab his attention.

The active and passive learning situations account for most advertising situations you are likely to encounter. While the models described here might suffer from oversimplification, they are useful to the planner's understanding of how advertising works. And, this understanding will affect the goals he sets for his campaign and the strategies and tactics he selects to achieve these goals.

This chapter has attempted to illustrate the important factors involved in the communication of sales messages to consumers. How consumers respond to these messages is largely influenced by individual consumer characteristics and environmental factors not covered in this chapter. The next chapter will discuss those factors that influence how and why consumers react to our ads as they attempt to make purchase decisions.

Case for Discussion:
Maverick Brewing Company

Background

The Maverick Brewing Company is a small, regional brewer located in eastern Tennessee. Maverick is a family-owned business with a short, 20-year history of brewing and marketing beer in an area of the country not known for its beer drinking. Maverick markets its line under the Ole South and Rebel Flag labels. Until recently, Maverick sold a premium beer under the Ole South label and popularly priced beer under the Rebel Flag label. Last year, a light beer was added to the line and given the name Ole South Light. This addition was made so Maverick could compete locally in the relatively new light beer segment of the beer market.

While Maverick has never attempted to compete head-on against the major national brands, it has enjoyed success as a regional brewer. This success has not gone unnoticed. At least one major brewer is interested in merging with Maverick to gain easy entry into the beer market in the Southeast.

Last year, Maverick sold approximately 3 million barrels of beer in a six-state area from North Carolina to Mississippi (Alabama, Georgia, Mississippi, North Carolina, South Carolina, and Tennessee). Maverick's advertising budget of $500,000 has been spent primarily in local radio and outdoor in the major metropolitan markets in the six-state area. In fact, more than half the budget has been spent during the football season to support regional college and professional teams.

Mr. Ronald Cummings, owner and president of Maverick, described what he thinks are the reasons for Maverick's success in the region in a recent issue of *Southern Advertising News*. Mr. Cummings said:

> What we really try to do is to keep the business simple. We brew three high-quality beers with a formula that gives them a distinctive taste people in the Southeast like. Our market is not New York or the Midwest. We have to appeal to the South's unique taste preferences.
>
> Next, we appeal to local sporting interests and pride through our advertising. If you've never been to an Alabama or Georgia football game, then you don't know what I mean. But it's very important to our customers, and we try to associate our beer with these events.
>
> In our advertising, the beer is always the focus of the ad. It's the reason for the ad's existence. To tie in with pride in local sports, we associate ourselves with local sports heroes who have "made it" in professional sports. Joe Namath is an example. He was a quarterback

at Alabama and with the New York Jets. After he retired, we used him a lot in our ads. People like Joe Namath add a lot of impact to our ads. And on our budget, impact is important.

It's really quite simple. Start with a beer brewed specially for the region and appeal to our customers' pride in their local teams and sports heroes. It's gotten us this far. Why fool with success?

New Competition

Maverick's line of beers has been a success in the past 20 years primarily because other brewers did not see the South as a very lucrative market. However, the Cummings' family saw changes in the region that would lead to the general public's acceptance of social drinking and sale of alcoholic beverages. Now, Anheuser-Busch, Miller, and Coors are making serious promotional efforts in a market Maverick once had to itself. This worries Mr. Cummings because the promotional clout these companies bring into the region is something Maverick has not had to face in the past.

Anheuser-Busch and Miller dominate the national beer market with over a 50 percent combined share of the market. Their dominance is so great that industry experts describe the beer industry as a two-tier industry. The second tier of the industry includes smaller national brewers like Heileman, Coors, and Olympia plus regional brewers like Lone Star, the Pittsburgh Brewing Company, and Maverick.

Even though Anheuser-Busch and Miller dominate the market, second-tier regional brewers have been able to succeed in their local markets by appealing to local pride and tastes. Olympia and Coors are very successful brewers in the West. Lone Star does well in Texas. Iron City Beer and Mustang Malt Liquor do well for the Pittsburgh Brewing Company in western Pennsylvania. The beer industry has a long history of good, regional brewers. In fact, it is not uncommon to find regional brands out-competing the national brands in their regions.

The national brewers who worry Mr. Cummings the most are Anheuser-Busch, Miller, and Coors. Each has different strengths and weaknesses.

The National Competition

Anheuser-Busch's brand list includes Budweiser, Busch, Michelob, Michelob Light, Natural Light, and Budweiser Light. The strength of the list is Budweiser, which continues to be the number-one premium beer in the world.

While Anheuser-Busch has been quite successful with its premium and super-premium brands (Budweiser and Michelob), it has had difficulty competing against Miller's Lite brand in the light beer market. Lite owns a 60 percent share of this market, and Anheuser-Busch's light beer brands command a modest 17 percent share.

Anheuser-Busch continues to dominate the industry's advertising spending. They also have breweries in Virginia and Florida that will provide the production needed to support their serious promotional efforts in the South.

Miller has based its resurgence in the beer industry on three brands— Miller High Life, Lite, and Lowenbrau. Since being taken over by Phillip Morris in the late Seventies, Miller has steadily climbed toward the top of the beer industry behind the success of Lite. Although Miller spends slightly less on advertising than Anheuser-Busch, it only has to spread its budget across three brands of beer. Lowenbrau, Miller's super-premium, has not fared as well as Lite, and the possibility of adding another super-premium to the brand list is being seriously considered.

Coors, like Maverick, is a family-owned brewer that has achieved a reputation for brewing a smooth, light-tasting beer that could only be bought west of the Mississippi. The regional exclusivity of Coors is becoming a thing of the past as the conservative brewer expands slowly east of the Mississippi. Coors markets a light beer, premium, and super-premium all under the Coors' name. Coors does not have the same advertising support as Anheuser-Busch and Miller, but it does have a line of beers specially suited to the Southeast in terms of taste and reputation.

Maverick's Plan

Cummings' first step to fight the increased marketing efforts of Anheuser-Busch, Miller, and Coors will be to add a super-premium to his brand list to compete against those offered by the competition (Michelob and Lowenbrau). Additionally, a deal is being negotiated with another small regional brewer to produce the new super-premium. Although a name has not been chosen, Cummings' preference is to use a variation of one of his two existing brand names. Ole South Golden is the name Cummings prefers, but Rebel Gold is also a possibility.

Cummings plans to compete against the national brands by being aggressive, not defensive. To do this, he plans to invest $2 million in advertising to support the introduction of his new super-premium brand. The problem, to Cummings, is one of gaining a fair share of the consumer's mind for his brands. He feels that he has a definite advantage in the region because he knows the people better than the national brewers. But he does not want to rest on his laurels. In fact, the new super-premium addition is really a rallying point for his new campaign. Maverick needed something "new" to help create some excitement in the marketplace.

Questions

1. Using the step flow model, discuss how Maverick Brewing Company might expand the impact of the new campaign for its new super-premium brand.

2. Analyze Maverick's communication advantages and disadvantages in the Southeast using the individual and face-to-face models of communication.

3. Which hierarchy of communication effects is Mr. Cummings confronted by? Describe how Maverick's new advertising campaign is likely to affect the different steps of the hierarchy.

4. Using the distinction between active and passive audience members, describe what you think Maverick's customers are like. Also, outline a brief plan for what you think the advertising should be like for the new super-premium introduction.

5. Using Assael's model of how advertising works, describe the process Mr. Cummings must go through to successfully gain a strong position for his new brand in the customer's mind.

Marketing, Advertising, and the Consumer

3

The background on how advertising works should help you understand how advertising communicates selling messages to customers or prospects. But to develop an advertising campaign, you also need a basic understanding of consumers—how they act and react to advertising messages and how they go about making their purchasing decisions. Unless you understand the consumer, you really have only a partial view of how advertising works or attempts to work in the market. With a myriad of product categories available to most consumers and with many brands actually substitutable for one another (for example, the flavored tea example in Chapter 1), the primary question in developing a sound advertising campaign becomes, how do consumers make choices in the marketplace? That's called consumer behavior, and it is the subject of this chapter.

Let's start with a definition: "Consumer behavior is the behavior consumers display in searching for, purchasing, using, and evaluating products, services, and ideas which they expect will satisfy their needs."[1] Obviously, to develop the most effective sales message for a product, marketers and advertisers need to know many things about the present or prospective users of the product. They first need to know what consumers and prospects buy, then why they buy what they do, how they buy the product or service, when they buy it, where they buy it, and how often they buy it. In addition, it is usually helpful to know how consumers feel about the product or service they have purchased or how they feel when they use it, if and how and why they might purchase it again in the future, and so on. In short, to devise an effective advertising or sales message, an advertiser needs to know as much as possible about how consumers behave, how they react or don't react, and why they do as they do. This knowledge is the basis of a sound advertising campaign. An overview of the more important

---

1. Leon G. Schiffman and Leslie Lazar Kanuk, *Consumer Behavior*, © 1978, p. 4. Reprinted by permission of Prentice-Hall, Inc., Englewood Cliffs, NJ.

concepts of consumer behavior, particularly as they relate to advertising, will be helpful.

Types of Consumers and Influences on Consumer Purchases

Essentially, in any marketplace in any society, there are two types of buyers: personal and organizational. Personal buyers have the sole or ultimate purchasing decision power, whether they plan to use the product themselves or not. This is usually the case with most consumer products. No doubt, many factors influence people to purchase a particular product category or even a particular brand, but ultimately the choice is up to the individual.

At the opposite extreme, there is the organizational purchaser. For an organizational purchase several people have a direct influence on the product category and the brand purchased. For example, people in a large manufacturing plant are considering the purchase of a new industrial incinerator. While it is true that only one person will likely sign the purchase order, many people will be involved in the decision. The purchasing "influencers" might include the sanitation people in the plant, the plant engineer, and perhaps even the chief executive officer of the company. All may well have a say in what specific brand of incinerator is purchased. These organizational purchasers are usually found in industrial or business-to-business sales fields. It is important, however, for the advertising campaign planner to understand the difference between the two types of buyers because it can make a definite difference in the way the advertising campaign is developed, from the setting of advertising objectives to the design of the message to the advertising media selection. This text will deal primarily with individual consumers as the decision makers, but it is important to recognize the influence of others even on those individual decisions.

While most consumers or prospects for products or services can make the individual decision as to whether to purchase, it is important to remember one fact: even individual purchasers come in two types, those who buy for their own use or consumption and those who purchase products for use by others. In our mobile society and diffuse marketplace, the purchaser of the product is not always the final user. For example, Mom buys peanut butter but consumes none herself. She's buying for the children in the family. In this situation, she may respond to the wishes of the children who will actually eat the peanut butter or she may make the decision on her own. The husband, at the request of his wife, stops at the corner drugstore on his way home from work and purchases her shampoo and conditioner. He may or may not have had an influence on the purchase. The couple make up the shopping list and then allocate the purchases between them, although both may use or consume the products purchased. That is why it is important to keep in mind that the buyer is not always the user, nor the user the buyer. Often, advertising campaigns are developed to encourage the purchaser to influence the user or to encourage the user to influence the purchaser. Perhaps at this point it would be helpful to look briefly at what influences consumers or purchasers in their actual buying decisions.

In our society, few consumer purchasing decisions are made in a traditional, rational, unemotional, economic way. It's quite the opposite, particularly for those products that are used often and consumed. The environment, our emotions, hopes, wishes, and wants often have a greater influence on our purchasing decisions than do sheer economic values. That's why sales of products such as hoola-hoops and pet rocks soar even in economic recessions. While it is difficult to do, the basic task of the advertising planner is to know and understand as nearly as possible what those influences are and what effect they might have on the success or failure of the advertising message being developed. Generally, the influences on consumer purchasing behavior can be separated into internal and external factors.

Internal Influences on Consumer Behavior

Factors that come from the personality or psychological makeup of the individual are considered *internal influences*. These are all those things that make "me" what I am, or what I think I am, or what I would like to be. While often these factors are quite complex, researchers have classified them into needs and wants.

The basic factor that influences nearly all consumer purchases is the arousal of a need or a want within the person. This is the most important factor in marketing and advertising because the entire idea of marketing is built around determining what consumers need or want and then attempting to fill that need or want with a product or service at a profit to the marketing organization. (See the discussion of the marketing concept in Chapter 1.)

While needs and wants are very important, they are quite different when it comes to using them in the development of an advertising campaign. Needs have been defined as "the gap or discrepancy experienced between an actual and a desired state of being. This experience may be biological or social in nature."[2] Needs vary in importance to consumers. It does appear, however, that there is a basic structure for needs among all

---

2. Gerald Zaltman and Melanie Wallendorf, *Consumer Behavior: Basic Findings and Management Implications* (New York: John Wiley & Sons, 1979), p. 318.

Figure 3-1.   Maslow's Hierarchy of Needs

Maslow developed the idea or concept that all human actions are based on a hierarchy of needs (some researchers term them *motives*). He identified the basic needs as physiological, safety, love, esteem, and self-actualization. Maslow's basic concept was that as the lower needs are fulfilled, the next highest order of needs comes into play.

Thus, the most basic needs, the physiological needs of food, drink, shelter, and relief from pain, dominate behavior until they are satisfied. Once that occurs, the factors that most influence behavior are those next up the scale: safety and security. And so on up the scale.

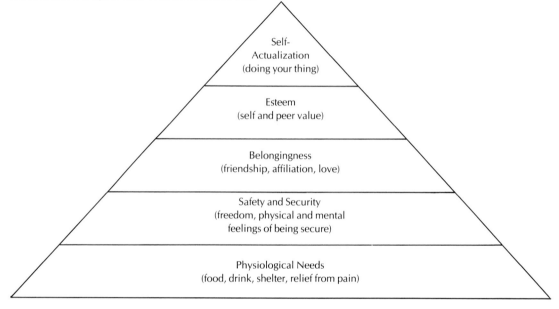

Maslow estimated that the typical adult in our society has satisfied about 85 percent of the physical needs, 70 percent of the safety and security needs, 50 percent of the need to belong and love, 40 percent of the need for esteem, and 10 percent of the self-actualization need. Obviously, every individual has a different method of satisfying his or her particular needs, and each progresses through the hierarchy at a different speed and with different solutions. Maslow's theory is helpful, however, for the advertising planner's understanding of why and how various products or services might fit into the plans, goals, and lives of prospects. One should also remember that as the individual progresses up the hierarchy, there are more and more ways of satisfying

needs. For example, food and drink are easily identified as methods of solving some of the basic needs, but there are many and varied ways in which the needs for esteem fulfillment might be satisfied. The advertising planner must always view the product or service to be advertised in terms of how it might fit into the need patterns of prospective consumers.

While Maslow theorized that all people are born with the basic needs in the hierarchy he proposed, others have argued that many human needs, particularly those at the higher levels, are learned. For example, David McClelland has proposed that many needs are learned through the childhood socialization process. Thus, McClelland and others theorize that each individual has a unique set of motivational needs.*

SOURCE: Abraham H. Maslow, *Toward a Psychology of Being,* 2nd ed. (New York: Van Nostrand, 1968).
*David C. McClelland, *Personality* (New York: Holt, Rinehart and Winston, 1951).

people. One of the most widely known and accepted theories of motivation as a result of needs is the hierarchy developed by Abraham H. Maslow. (See Figure 3-1.)

Generally, most researchers call needs those things that humans require for survival, such as food, clothing, and shelter. These needs are built into all of us. On the other hand, the methods by which we satisfy those needs are often called wants. For example, in most of our northern climates, people need clothing simply to ward off the cold or protect themselves from the elements. However, over time, humans have decided that coats made of animal furs are a better or perhaps more socially acceptable method of keeping warm than are coats woven from cloth. Further, they have decided that mink or sable furs are more acceptable than are those of other animals, such as rabbits or sheep, even though they may provide the same protection. In our society of abundance, marketers primarily try to satisfy the wants rather than the needs of consumers. Coffee may be prepared by boiling the grounds in an iron pot over an open fire. Yet, consumers *want* automatic drip percolators, which, when set in advance, come on at a certain time each morning, perk the coffee, and then turn themselves off and still keep the coffee warm. Consumers may need an iron pot, but they want a Mr. Coffee. Thus, it is consumer wants rather than human needs to which most advertising campaigns appeal.

It is important to keep these two concepts in mind when developing an advertising campaign. Since there are few unfilled consumer needs in our society, it is usually filling the want that products or services try to provide.

External Influences on Consumer Behavior

Our needs and wants, whether we are born with them or acquire them through learning make up our personality. They therefore influence our attitudes toward various products and services. More specifically, we learn or discover through experience or are told by others or by advertising that certain products and even certain brands satisfy various needs better than others. In some instances our attitudes about various products and brands are influenced by what happens to us in society; these are *external influences.*

While we normally bring our needs into a given purchasing situation—that is, we were born with those needs or they have been embedded in our personality at an early age—the same is not true of wants. Wants are largely influenced by factors outside us. These external factors may take many forms, and experts still fail to agree on a detailed listing of all of them. Generally, however, most researchers agree on the basic concept of external influences and that they consist of such things as culture, subcultures,

---

Figure 3-2.   External Influences on Consumer Behavior

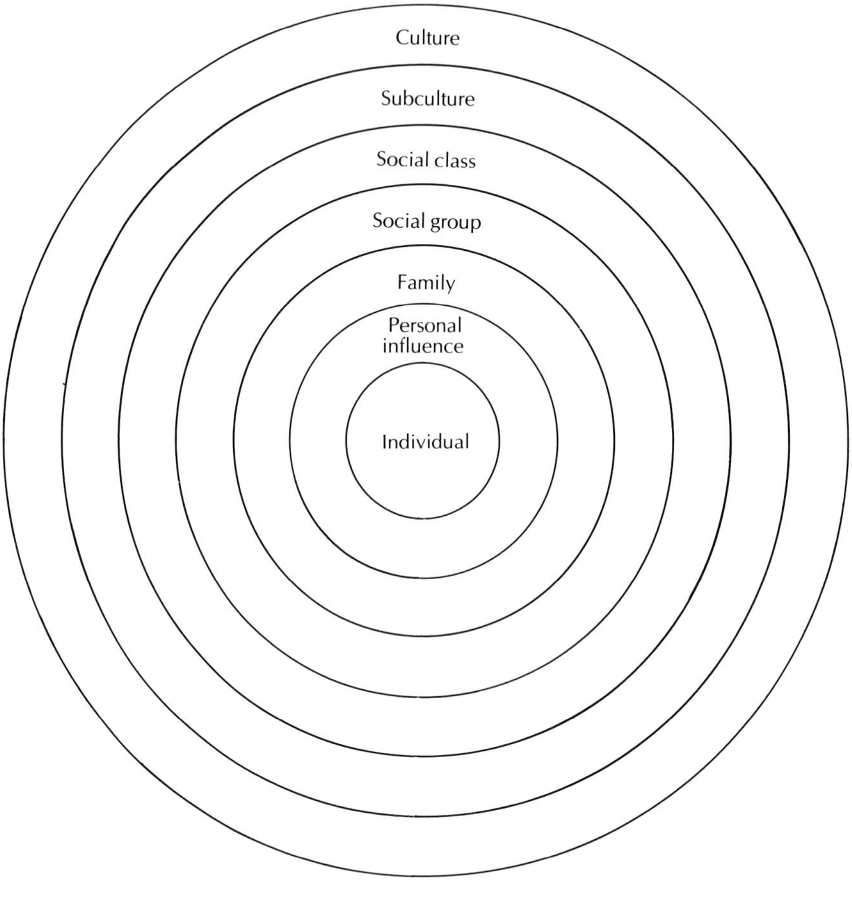

SOURCE: Adapted from David L. Loudon and Albert J. Della Bitta, *Consumer Behavior: Concepts and Applications* (New York: McGraw-Hill, Inc., 1979), p. 122.

---

social classes, social groups, families, and personal influence. (See Figure 3-2.) David Loudon and Albert J. Della Bitta visualize these external influences as a series of concentric circles, with the most general influences on the outside, the farthest away, and the others becoming more and more personal in nature the closer they are located to the individual.

Culture. Culture is a very broad concept, although researchers generally agree that E. B. Taylor's 1891 definition is still appropriate: "that complex whole which includes knowledge, belief, art, law, morals, custom, and any other capabilities and habits acquired by man as a member of society."[3] Culture is the broad, general framework within which many of our ideas and actions are governed.

Cultures are quite different. For example, United States culture is quite different from Egypt or Japan. The U.S. is also different from that of a close geographic neighbor, Mexico.

Cultures are made up of many things. Cleanliness is a major force in our culture. Such is not the case in many other areas of the world. Thus, media in the U.S. are filled with advertising for products such as soap, detergents, shampoos, bleaches, deodorants, and the like, products that are not nearly so important in other countries.

Subcultures. Within most cultures there are several, if not many, subcultures. The most common of these subcultures are usually based on race, religion, or nationality. For example, in the U.S. the most common racial subcultures are blacks, Hispanics, Orientals, and American Indians. Religious subcultures in the U.S. are typified by Protestants, Catholics, and Jews. Nationality subcultures include such groups as Mexican-Americans, Cuban-Americans, Puerto Ricans, and others of a non-U.S. mainland background.

We also find subcultures developing or having developed in the U.S. as a result of age or sex. The senior citizens group is a developing age subculture, while the youth subculture has been important to many marketers in recent years. Subcultures based on sex are quite common. There has been a traditional women's subculture built around home and family. That is now changing and segmenting. As more and more women move into the labor force, new and different types of subcultures from those of fifty years ago are developing.

There also are subcultures based on geographic location. In the U.S., the cultures of urban and rural geographic locations are dramatically different. The same is true for specific geographic areas of the country. For example, the urban cowboy subculture that has developed in Texas has spread its influence across the entire nation.

Finally, in addition to these basic subcultures, some researchers have classified groups that have sprung up around a specific belief or lifestyle as subcultures. For example, over the past several years a definite subculture has sprung up among those persons who use drugs. At this point, it is difficult to determine whether or not the subcultures of this type will survive, although they can be quite a factor in the short term. Advertising campaigns often are significantly influenced by the culture and the various subcultures that exist in the country.

---

3. Edward B. Taylor, *Primitive Culture* (London: Murray, 1891), p. 1.

Table 3-1.   Social Class Placement

	Percentage distribution
Upper-upper class	1.44%
Upper class	
Lower-upper class	1.56
Upper-middle class	10.22
Middle class	
Lower-middle class	28.12
Working class	
Upper-lower class	32.60
Lower class	
Lower-lower class	25.22
Other responses	0.84
	100.00%

SOURCE: W. L. Warner, Marchia Meeker, and Kenneth Eells, *Social Class in America* (Chicago: Science Research Associates, 1949), p. 14.

Social class. Classifying or separating groups of people by social class is probably one of the world's first attempts at stratification. Generally, social class is some type of hierarchy that attempts to delineate the whole society into homogeneous groups based on attitudes, values, lifestyles, and perhaps other variables of the population. Generally, the groupings developed by W. L. Warner are among the best known. Table 3-1 illustrates Warner's stratification and estimate of population distribution several years ago. Most likely, these distributions have changed dramatically during the past decades, but it does indicate the concept, which is still accurate.

Social class is signified in many ways in the U.S., ranging from customs, such as membership in certain clubs and organizations to the physical location of the home. For example, some suburbs are considered more socially prestigious than others. Social class also is signified by possessions, such as automobiles, clothing, and even the colleges or universities attended by members of the group.

One of the most important features of U.S. society is great social mobility. For example, some rock music stars are touted as being part of the upper class although they may have come from very humble beginnings. In addition, the ebbs and flows of financial status greatly influence social class. One of the most important effects social class may have on consumers is lifestyle definition. Often, because of social ranking, consumers may or may not consider themselves to be prospects for some types of products or services.

Social groups. Within a total society, there are various groups within which people interact. These are called social groups or reference groups. These groups are usually determined on the basis of some shared interest or are related through some activity or action. This shared interest can range from rock and roll "groupies" to more traditional organizations, such as civic groups, churches, colleges and universities, and country clubs.

Members of social groups are important to advertisers because their shared interest may provide the key to developing the advertising strategy or message. For example, the "preppie look" favored by some college students has been a boon to manufacturers of khakai trousers, mono-grammed knit shirts, and boating deck shoes. These "badges" of group affiliation are used to signify a person's belonging to or belief in the group. While these badges are often used by members of the group to identify themselves, in many instances they are promoted by advertisers who hope to profit from the association with the group's identity.

Family. The family is the basic external influence on most consumers. It is from the family and individual family members that many personality traits are developed. As a result, there is little question that family influence on future purchasing decisions is great. For example, if the family always used Crest toothpaste and Mom further confirmed the value of Crest to the children as a decay preventive toothpaste, there is a good chance the children will continue to purchase and use Crest toothpaste even after they leave the family situation. Kool-Aid powdered soft drink mix has used this family influence approach in advertising over the past few years. Their line, "You loved it as a child, you trust it as a mother," is designed to build sales and acceptance through family influence.

An important allied concept in the influence of the family on purchase decisions is the idea of a family life cycle. That simply means that a family

---

Figure 3-3. The Family Life Cycle

1. The Bachelor Stage: young, single people
2. Newly Married Couples: young, no children
3. Full Nest I: young married couples with youngest child under 6
4. Full Nest II: young married couples with youngest child 6 or over
5. Full Nest III: older married couples with dependent children
6. Empty Nest I: older married couples with no children living with them and household head in labor force
7. Empty Nest II: older married couples with no children living with them and household head retired
8. Solitary Survivor I: older single people in labor force
9. Solitary Survivor II: older retired single people

SOURCE: William D. Wells and George Gubar, "Life Cycle Concept in Marketing Research," *Journal of Marketing Research* 3 (Nov. 1966): 355–63.

goes through a birth, development, growth, maturity, and then decline cycle just as do the people involved. A typical example of the progression of the family life cycle is that developed by William D. Wells and George Gubar. It is shown in Figure 3-3.

Obviously, the family life cycle is important to marketing and advertising planners alike. In certain situations and in certain life cycles, people will be much better prospects for some products than they will be for others; for example, children's toys to members of Full Nest I. This family life cycle concept can assist the advertising campaign planner not only in selecting the proper persons to whom the advertising message should be directed but would assist in determining what message might be most effective.

Personal influence. The final external influence, and usually the most direct on the consumer, is the result of direct involvement with others. This is the one-on-one influence that may be a result of a friendship, a business relationship, a chance meeting, or any other form of nonfamily human interaction. This is the well-known "word-of-mouth" advertising: one person tries a product or service and tells others about the experience. This is perhaps the strongest external influence on purchasing decisions and is the most difficult for the advertising campaign planner to affect or control.

Opinion Leaders

In most every relationship between groups of people, there are people who have the ability to influence those around them, and sometimes their guidance and opinion is sought out by their peers. In these instances, the advertiser first attempts to locate the opinion leader and favorably influence him or her with the knowledge that this "endorsement" will be passed along to the group. This is the so-called "two-step flow of information." Examples of some of these opinion leaders might be theater or movie critics, gourmet cooks, travel editors, and fashion consultants.

Demand   The purchasing effects of all consumers on products or services are referred to as demand by economists. Advertising campaign planners are most interested in demand and how to increase demand.

As consumer needs and wants develop and as the various internal and external influences activate those needs and wants, demand for products or services develops in society. Consumers are willing to exchange goods, services, and/or labor for products and services they cannot or do not produce themselves. The greater the desire by consumers for those products or services, the stronger the demand. This demand is illustrated by a

Figure 3-4.   Demand Curve

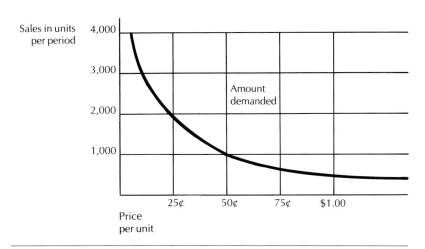

series of curves usually showing the relationship of sales to such factors as availability and price. The best known demand curve illustrates the sales response to price. (See Figure 3-4.) The lower the price, the greater the demand. That simply means that as marketers reduce the price for a product, more and more people usually are inclined to purchase it.

Marketers and advertisers are primarily interested in two measures of demand. First is the measurement of overall demand, the amount of the product or service a certain group of consumers purchased in a certain time period, in a certain geographic area, at a certain price, and under certain economic conditions. Second is demand forecasting, which is the estimate of what a certain group of consumers *might* purchase in a certain time period, in a certain geographic area, at a certain price, under certain economic conditions if a particular marketing program is used. Both measures of demand are very important in the development of an advertising campaign.

For purposes of advertising campaign planning, the market for a product is the demand or estimated demand that may exist for that product by consumers. In advertising campaign planning, three basic market measurements are used: (a) market demand, (b) market forecast, and (c) market potential. While the market forecast shows the estimated demand for the product or service, the potential is the highest possible market demand that might occur under a given set of conditions. Based on the market demand and market forecast, a marketer can calculate potential market share by multiplying the demand by the population. Further market share can be determined by taking sales of the product as a percentage of the total sales in the category. Market shares are an important calculation in terms of advertising planning because they illustrate how well a product is doing in relation to its competition.

For purposes of advertising campaign planning, the total dollar potential market for a product or service is determined by the formula:

$$\text{Number of buyers} \times \text{quantity purchased by average buyer}$$
$$\times \text{ price of an average unit } = \text{ total market potential}$$

Using this simple calculation, a marketer can estimate the value of any given market and determine the desirability of advertising and marketing efforts against that market based on the expected return from the advertising expenditure.

Types of Demand

To properly develop a complete advertising campaign, a planner needs to know two basic forms of demand for the product or service. First, there is the *generic* (total) demand for the entire product category. To develop an advertising campaign for a powdered soft drink mix, for example, a marketer needs to know how much will be consumed in the entire country during the year of the campaign. This is called the generic demand, or demand for the total product category.

Second, while it is important to know the total volume in a category, it is often more important to know what the demand for the brand may be, or could be, for that forms the basis of the development of the advertising campaign. Knowledge of the demand that a marketer believes can be created for a specific brand within a specific category is important when developing the basic advertising strategy and message. For example, should the advertising be designed to develop demand among customers and prospects for the generic product category of powdered soft drink mix, or should it be designed to build demand only for the specific brand among those consumers who already demand powdered soft drink mix? Or, should the advertising concentrate efforts on getting current users of the brand to buy and use more? This knowledge of the basics of demand will often guide the advertising campaign planner in selecting the proper approach to use. Figure 3-5 illustrates this basic concept.

For any product in any category, three basic types of customers or prospects exist. These are (a) non-users of the product category—that is, those who do not currently purchase or use any brand in the product category, although they may be potential users (group N); (b) those who are using competitive products (group C); and (c) the existing customers for our particular brand (group E). These three groups make up all the present and potential customers for the product under any circumstances. (See Figure 3-5.)

Figure 3-5.   Total Market for a Product

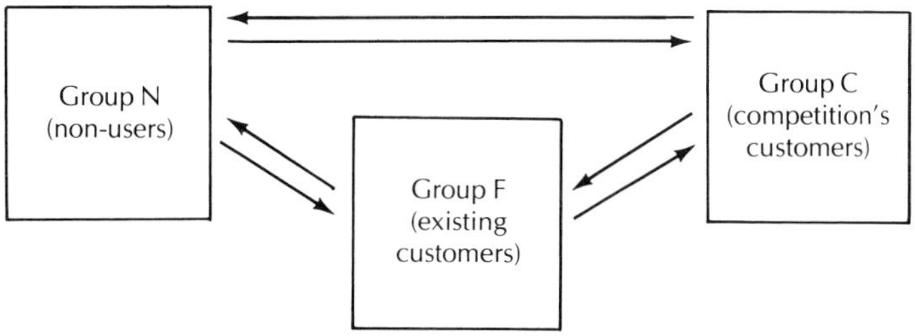

Inherent in this concept, as in the real marketplace for any product or service, is that the market is not static. That is, consumers from one group are constantly moving to another group. For example, non-users of the product category (N) may start using one product and change to a competitor's. Similar changes may occur within the other two groups. Thus, in terms of customers, advertisers are constantly dealing with a passing parade.

In addition, it should be noted that while the categories have been drawn as being discrete for illustrative purposes, in fact, there may be dual users in any of the groups. Some people may buy and use two or more competing products on a regular basis. The same is true of the other groups. There may be those who use competitive brands on occasion but generally are considered to be non-users of the product category because their usage is so insignificant. More about this in later sections on creative strategy.

The Product Life Cycle

Consumer demand for a product or service is not constant over time. Every product or service has a life cycle. This life cycle illustrates how demand for the product is small in the introductory stage, grows rapidly, eventually levels off at maturity, and then declines. Figure 3-6 on the next page describes the product life-cycle concept and how it relates to an advertising campaign.

The concept of the product life cycle is important in the development of an advertising campaign because the stage the product is in often determines the type of advertising strategy that should be used and the advertising message which should be developed.

Estimating Market Demand

The estimated demand for the product or service to be advertised is of great interest to the campaign planner. While the development of this forecast

Figure 3-6.   The Product Life Cycle

The concept of the product life cycle, on which much current marketing management theory is now based, was formalized by the consulting firm of McKinsey & Co., Inc. The description by Donald K. Clifford, Jr. illustrates this concept:

The product life cycle concept derives from the fact that a product's sales volume follows a typical pattern that can readily be charted as a four-phase cycle. Following its birth, the product passes through a low-volume introduction phase. During the subsequent growth period, volume and profit both rise. Volume stabilizes during maturity, though unit profits typically start to fall off. Eventually, in the state of obsolescence, sales volume declines.

The length of the life cycle, the duration of each phase, and the shape of the curve vary widely for different products. But in every instance, obsolescence eventually occurs for one of three reasons.

First, the need may disappear. This is what happened to the orange juice squeezer when frozen juice caught on.

Second, a better, cheaper, or more convenient product may be developed to suit the same need. Oil-based paint lost its position in the home to water-based paint; plastics have replaced wood, metal, and paper in product categories ranging from dry-cleaning bags to aircraft parts.

Third, a competitive product may, through superior marketing strategy, suddenly gain a decisive advantage. This happened to competing products when Arthur Godfrey's personal charm got behind Lipton Tea, and again when Procter & Gamble secured the American Dental Association's endorsement of its decay-prevention claims for Crest toothpaste.

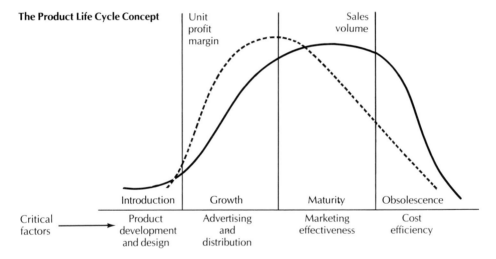

As the chart shows, a product's profit cycle is shaped quite differently from its sales cycle. During introduction, a product may not earn any profit at all because of high initial advertising and promotion costs.

In the growth period, before competition catches up, unit profits typically attain their peak. Then they start declining, though total profits may continue to rise for a time on rising sales volume. In the chemical industry, for example, rapid volume increases often more than offset the effect of price reductions early in the growth phase.

During late growth and early maturity, increasing competition cuts deeply into profit margins and ultimately into total profits. For instance, as a result of drastic price cutting, general-purpose semiconductors, once highly profitable, now return so little profit that many companies have left the business.

Finally, in the period of obsolescence, declining volume eventually pushes costs up to a level that eliminates profits entirely.

SOURCE: Donald K. Clifford, Jr., "Managing the Product Life Cycle" in *Marketing Management and Administrative Action*, 4th ed., Steuart Henderson, Britt and Harker W. Boyd, Jr. (New York: McGraw-Hill, 1978), pp. 237–43.

may not be the province of the planner, a brief look at four basic methods of estimating market demand will be helpful.

Market buildup. This is a very simple approach. One simply determines, through data or estimation, the total number of purchasers for a product or service and adds up what they buy. Often, however, this may be difficult. The number of buyers may not be known, or their volume of purchase may be difficult to determine.

Expert opinion. This is simply a forecast made by asking a panel of knowledgeable people to estimate what they believe the demand for the product will be in the marketplace in a certain time period. A summary of those opinions is then used.

Sales force opinion. Often, companies rely on the estimates of their sales force to determine the estimated market demand. The reasoning is that the sales force is closer to the market and has a better feel for what will actually be purchased in the coming period. This approach is widely used for industrial products or services.

Market research. Various forms of market research, ranging from surveys of buyer intentions to formal test market approaches, are used to estimate demand. Consumer market research is often used because it provides a more direct method of estimating demand by gathering the information directly from those who are likely to be purchasers rather than using surrogate measures such as the opinions of experts or the sales force. Often this information is available in syndicated research studies. (See Chapter 5.)

No matter how the forecast of demand for the product or service is developed, it is a vital ingredient in the preparation of an advertising campaign. If demand for a product is declining, advertising's role in the promotion mix will be much different than if demand for the product is increasing rapidly. While demand forecasting or estimating may be one of the most difficult of all marketing tasks, it is the basis for most of the decisions that influence the development of a successful advertising campaign.

Types of Purchasing Behavior

The determination of consumer demand for a product or service is often based in part on the way in which consumers purchase products. Various products are purchased in different ways by consumers, and not all consumers even purchase the same product, or even brand, in the same way. Often, these purchasing patterns are related to the product life cycle.

Consumers' views of alternative products within a product category (i.e., whether they are new and innovative; established and reliable; or on their way down) will determine how they make a purchasing decision. John A. Howard has identified three basic types of purchasing behavior based on the amount of information, effort, and length of time required by consumers to make their purchasing decision. He labels them as:

1. Extensive Problem Solving (EPS): To make these types of purchasing decisions, consumers normally need a great deal of information on simply whether to buy in the product class at all. With these products, consumers usually make up their minds rather slowly. This often occurs when a consumer is faced with a decision in an unfamiliar product class.

2. Limited Problem Solving (LPS): In these decision situations, consumers have some basis or criteria against which to judge various products—for example, a new product in a known product class. Usually consumers need less information and less time in which to make a decision in LPS than in EPS.

3. Routinized Response Behavior (RRB): In these decision situations, the product category is known, the brands are known, and in many instances the purchasing decision may be based strictly on price or some other marketing variable such as a sales promotion event. In RRB, consumer purchasing behavior has become a habit, and it is done with little thought and may even have become automatic. This type of behavior is exhibited by most consumers purchasing products or services used on a regular basis. It is the basis for the concept of "brand loyalty": consumers simply continue to buy what they have always bought.[4]

All these patterns of purchasing behavior must be considered in the development of an advertising campaign. They are most important in the identification of market segments toward which the advertising campaign may be targeted.

Market Segmentation   As may have become evident, consumer behavior and motivation are extremely complex and not totally understood. In fact, when asked why they purchase various products, consumers often cannot explain how or why they make certain market or product choices. But, while information

4. Adapted from John A. Howard, *Consumer Behavior: Application of Theory* (New York: McGraw-Hill, Inc., 1977), pp. 1–18. See this text for a complete discussion of these concepts.

is limited, marketers must have some method of viewing or grouping consumers to develop an effective advertising approach.

Marketers generally take one of two views toward consumers in the marketplace: (a) market aggregation or (b) market segmentation. Market aggregation assumes that all consumers are somewhat alike and that a given product or service would appeal to many of them. While there is an understanding that not all will buy, it is assumed that a single marketing and advertising program will appeal to enough consumers to make the product successful. The alternative to this is market segmentation. Here, the marketer decides to concentrate efforts on that segment of the total market thought to have the most purchasing potential. Thus, rather than developing a broad-scale marketing and advertising program, a more specific targeted approach is used with all the marketing mix variables, particularly advertising. From this view comes the idea of a "target market" for an advertising campaign. The target market is simply the segment of the market toward which advertising will be directed.

To effectively select a segment, or target market, several factors are required. First, the segment must be identifiable; that is, there must be some basis for determining who belongs and who doesn't belong in the chosen segment. This, of course, implies that the segment can be measured in some way to determine its value in terms of sales or market potential. Next, the segment must be large enough or have the potential to purchase enough so that the advertising and marketing efforts are worthwhile. It is possible, for example, to identify a very tightly organized or available group of consumers, but if there is not enough potential purchasing power or volume usage in the group to justify the advertising or marketing expense, the segment may not be a worthwhile target.

On the other hand, the segment or group must be accessible through marketing and advertising efforts. One of the problems with market segmentation is that media access and usage information are often limited. (See Chapter 12.) Unless advertising messages reach the selected segment, that group is not a practical target from a campaign standpoint. Finally, it is necessary to get some form of specific response from the chosen segment of the market population. If selected segments cannot be expected to respond better or more directly or more strongly to specific advertising messages than the general population will, there is no reason to develop the segmentation program. In such cases the market should be approached on an aggregated basis with a broad-scale advertising campaign.

Methods of Segmenting Markets

Generally, marketers attempt to segment markets on a basis that allows the use of specific advertising media or advertising messages. While it often is

Figure 3-7.   Psychographic Research

One of the important areas of marketing and advertising research is psychographic or lifestyle research. Many purchases are made on the basis of satisfying the customer's inner desire or inner view. In addition, we have become a nation of "exhibitors"; that is, we try to show the type of person we are or hope to be by the type of outward appearance we present, the types of groups with which we associate, the opinions we hold, and the like. Thus, we try to differentiate ourselves by the type of lifestyle we have or seek.

These lifestyle or psychographic approaches are increasingly used by marketers and advertisers as methods of segmenting the population. For example, Joseph T. Plummer has identified several lifestyle dimensions among consumers.* By researching these activities, interests, and opinions, the advertiser often can develop a profile of a group of people who might be an excellent market for a specific product or service.

Activities	Interests	Opinions	Demographics
Work	Family	Themselves	Age
Hobbies	Home	Social issues	Education
Social events	Job	Politics	Income
Vacation	Community	Business	Occupation
Entertainment	Recreation	Economics	Family size
Club membership	Fashion	Education	Dwelling
Community	Food	Products	Geography
Shopping	Media	Future	City size
Sports	Achievements	Culture	Stage in life cycle

Through this type of lifestyle research, advertisers and marketers have attempted to develop and define specific lifestyles that might be used in advertising campaign planning. The research firm of Yankelovich, Skelly, and White has broken the market into 6 segments; Leo Burnett U.S.A. uses 19 lifestyle segments; and Needham, Harper & Steers, Chicago, has defined 10 major lifestyle groups. The latter are, with approximate percentage of the male or female population in each group:

- Ben, the self-made businessman (17%)
- Scott, the successful professional (21%)
- Dale, the devoted family man (17%)
- Fred, the frustrated factory worker (19%)
- Herman, the retiring homebody (26%)
- Cathy, the contented housewife (18%)
- Candice, the chic suburbanite (20%)
- Eleanor, the elegant socialite (17%)
- Mildred, the militant mother (20%)
- Thelma, the old-fashioned traditionalist (25%)†

Obviously, the groups change over time as our social values change. They do, however, illustrate the concept of lifestyle and how important this approach is today to the advertising campaign planner.

One of the newest forms of psychographic analysis being used in the development of marketing and advertising plans is that recently developed by SRI International. Their system, called the Values and Lifestyle System (VALS) is an attempt to categorize consumers according to their lifestyles and values rather than their vital statistics. Through their research, the VALS scientists have identified, isolated, and labeled 3 major groups and 9 subgroups of consumers on the basis of their behavior and emotional makeup:

The Need-Driven.   These are "money-restricted" consumers who are struggling just to buy the basics. They buy more out of need than from choice or whim; but sometimes they splurge, which accounts for large sales of luxury items in lower-income areas. The need-driven represent 17 million people—11 percent of the adult population. This group is divided into two subcategories: *Survivors,* who are old, poor, depressed, and far removed from the cultural mainstream; and *Sustainers,* who are relatively young, angry, crafty, struggling on the edge of poverty, and willing to do anything to get ahead. Many female single heads of households also fall into this category.

Outer-Directed Consumers.   This group, which accounts for more than two-thirds of the adult population, makes up Middle America. These people conduct their lives so that others will think well of them. This group contains three subcategories: *Belongers,* who are traditional, conservative, conventional, nostalgic, sentimental, puritanical, and

(continued on next page)

unexperimental. *Emulators,* who are trying to burst into the system and make it big: they are ambitious, upwardly mobile, status-conscious, macho and competitive, but they are also distrustful and angry, with little faith that they will get a fair shake from the Establishment. *Achievers,* who are the leaders in business, the professions and government. They are characterized by efficiency, fame, status, the good life, comfort, and materialistic values.

Inner-Directed Consumers. These are individuals who generally buy products to meet their own inner needs rather than responding to the opinions of others. This is the only group expected to grow in the next ten years—from about 33 million today to 50 million (or 28 percent of the adult population) by 1990. There are three types of inner-directeds: *I-am-me's,* who are generally young, zippy, exhibitionistic, narcissistic, dramatic, impulsive, fiercely individualistic and inventive. *Experientials,* a more mature variety of the I-am-me's, who want direct experience and vigorous involvement and are concerned with inner growth

and naturalism. *Societally conscious individuals,* who are attracted to simple living and smallness of scale and who tend to support such causes as conservation, environmentalism, and consumerism.

Alone at the top of the VALS hierarchy is the ninth category, the *Integrateds,* who meld the power of outer-directedness with the sensitivity of inner-directedness. These individuals are fully mature in a psychological sense, tolerant, assured, self-actualizing, and often have a world perspective. They account for about 2 percent of the population, and while of little importance to marketers from a numerical standpoint, are heavily represented in corporate and national leadership.‡

Graphically, the groups look something like the hierarchy illustrated in Figure 3-8. From this classification and identification of consumers, VALS researchers believe they can provide advertisers with a clearer picture of the purchasing and media habits of consumers in the marketplace so that the advertising plan can be more finely tuned. Time will tell if they are correct.

*Joseph T. Plummer, "The Concept and Application of Life Style Segmentation," *Journal of Marketing,* 38 (Jan. 1974): 34.

†Peter W. Bernstein, "Psychographics Is Still an Issue on Madison Avenue," *Fortune,* January 16, 1978, pp. 78–84. © 1978 Time, Inc. All rights reserved.

‡Niles Howard, "A New Way to View Consumers," *Dun's Review,* August, 1981, pp. 43–46. Reprinted with the special permission of *Dun's Review,* August 1981. Copyright 1981, Dun & Bradstreet Publications Corporation.

Figure 3-8.   Buying Behavior Exhibited by Groups

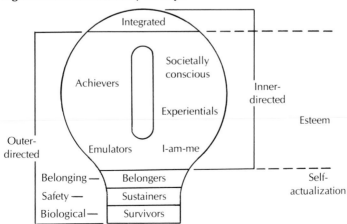

Figure 3-9.   Market Segmentation

Often we segment markets based on volume usage of the particular product or service, employing the terms light, medium, and heavy users. This is particularly helpful to advertising campaign planners because obviously the larger the usage of the product category or brand, the more important that person is to the advertiser. Interestingly, heavy users of a product often consume an inordinately large percentage of the total in a particular product category. Dik

Warren Twedt labeled this group the "heavy half" and, through consumption data, illustrated how important they are in certain product categories.

Numbers above bars are percentages of the population categorized according to non-users, "light half," and "heavy half." Numbers within bars are the amount of total volume consumed by "light half" and "heavy half." For example, in the first bar (Lemon-lime), 42 percent of the population are

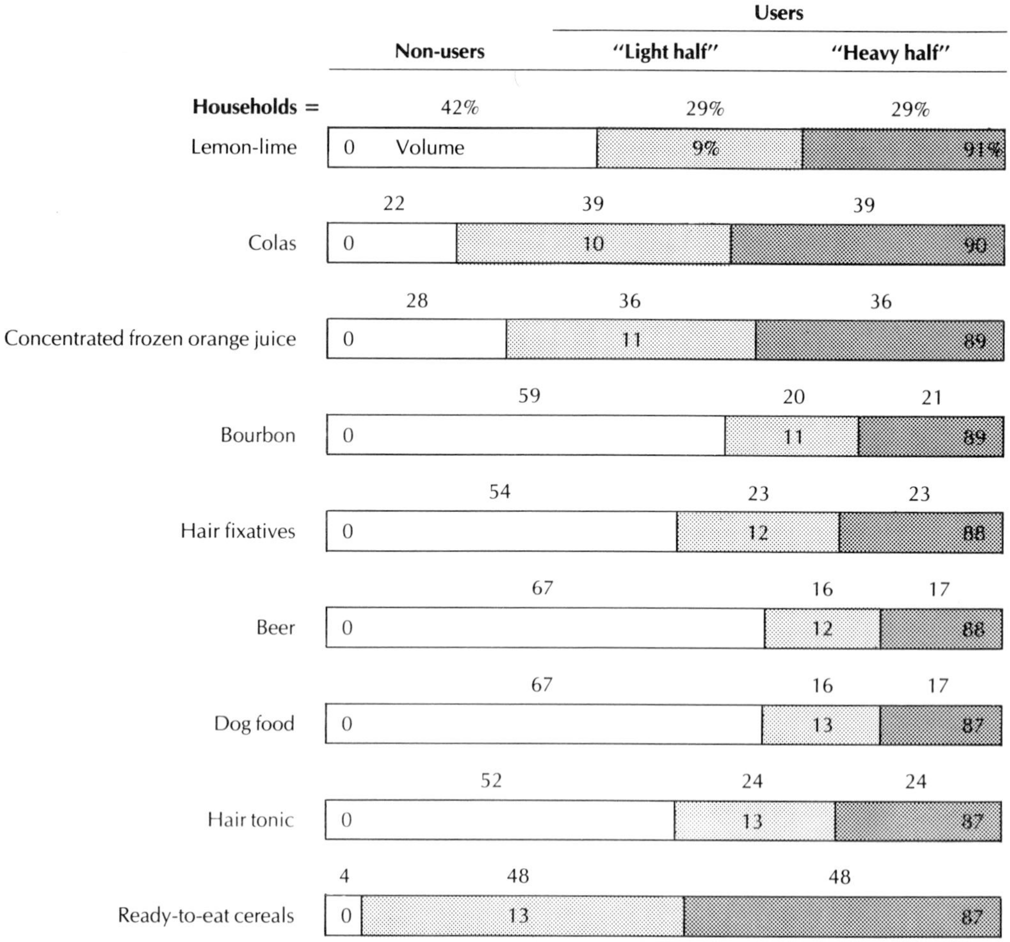

		Users	
	Non-users	"Light half"	"Heavy half"
Households =	42%	29%	29%
Lemon-lime	0 Volume	9%	91%
	22	39	39
Colas	0	10	90
	28	36	36
Concentrated frozen orange juice	0	11	89
		59	20	21
Bourbon	0	11	89
		54	23	23
Hair fixatives	0	12	88
		67	16	17
Beer	0	12	88
		67	16	17
Dog food	0	13	87
		52	24	24
Hair tonic	0	13	87
	4	48	48
Ready-to-eat cereals	0	13	87

non-users, 29 percent are "light half," and 29 percent are "heavy half." Of the 58 percent who make up the user base, 91 percent of the total consumption is by the "heavy half," while only 9 percent is consumed by the "light half."

Through use of this consumption data, advertisers try to group people who are heavy users by other factors such as demographics, psychographics, or media patterns so that they can be reached with advertising messages. For example, heavy users of beer tend to be heavy viewers of sports programming on television, thus the attempt to reach them through that medium.

Of some concern to the advertising planner, however, is the fact that the heavy user of a product tends to be the most difficult to influence. Since many exhibit RRB purchasing behavior, they are often quite difficult to change or to get to consider new brand alternatives.

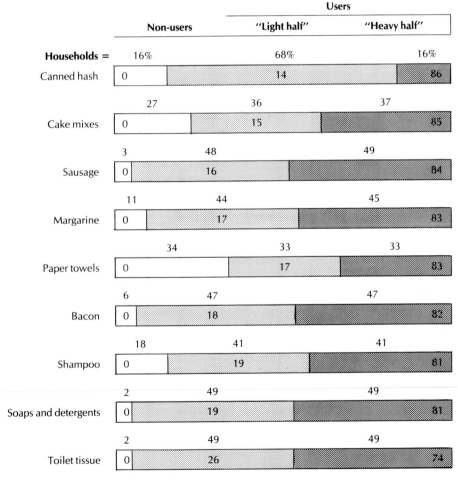

SOURCE: Reprinted from Dik Warren Twedt, "How Important to Marketing Strategy is the 'Heavy User'?" *Journal of Marketing*, 28 (Jan 1964): 72.

possible to identify an extremely important consumer segment, often there is no practical method of reaching that segment through the media. For example, a marketer might identify those people who use or wear only all-cotton socks as the most important segment for the advertising campaign. However, if there isn't any advertising medium that reaches that segment, or any method of contacting the all-cotton sock wearing market segment, the segment becomes useless. As a result, most market segmentation efforts follow rather broad demographic lines (discrete measurable factors about consumers that can be easily determined, such as age, sex, income, marital status, number of children, etc.) and general geographic definitions such as regions, states, and cities. As a general rule, markets are segmented on the following broad lines:

1. Geographics. Nations, regions, states, Standard Metropolitan Statistical Areas, Areas of Dominant Influence, counties, cities, zip codes, and the like.

2. Demographics (as described above). Markets are also segmented on the basis of some socioeconomic characteristics, such as education, occupation, income, and willingness to purchase.

3. Psychographics or lifestyle. An increasingly important method of segmentation involves how people spend their time, how they view themselves, and the things with which they surround themselves. Often these are called activities, interests, and opinions, and they offer another dimension for advertising campaign planners. (See Figure 3-7.)

4. Media usage. Often, markets may be segmented simply by the type of media consumers use or to which they are exposed. For example, daytime television, which includes the well-known soap operas, has brought together groups of people with similar interests and concerns. The same is true for late night television. In addition, many new lifestyle magazines that are dedicated to individual interests, activities, and opinions have sprung up over the past few years. Thus, a marketer may segment prospective customers for products through the media vehicles they use as well as their demographic and psychographic variables.

5. Buying and use. Perhaps one of the most important methods of segmenting people into markets or potential markets is through their purchase or usage of products and services. Here, marketers attempt to identify customers or prospects based on what products they buy, how often they buy, how rapidly they use up the product, when and how they repurchase, and so on. For example, not all consumers use products at the same rate. In fact, there appears to be a very distinct "heavy user" group for most product categories. (See Figure 3-9.)

In addition to identifying heavy users of a product, consumers may also be segmented on the basis of how they use the product. A few years ago, for example, Johnson & Johnson discovered sales of their baby shampoo were increasing in spite of a downward trend in the birth rate. Upon investigation, they learned that younger people, because of longer hair styles, were washing their hair nearly every day. They had started using Johnson & Johnson Baby Shampoo because of its mildness. Thus, consumers themselves had created a new market segment through their use of the product. Now, Johnson & Johnson has developed an advertising campaign designed to reach this segment and others like it. There are many other examples of this consumer-selective market segmentation process.

With this view of market segmentation, we now look at the area where we hope our advertising campaign will have an actual effect—that is, in developing or changing attitudes of consumers toward various products or services.

Attitude and Attitude Change

In Chapter 2 it was stated that the primary purpose of advertising is to help people gain information of interest or benefit about the product or service so that this might result in a change or continuation of attitudes about the product or service. Generally, the influence of advertising on consumer behavior can be depicted as in Figure 3-10. Thus a marketer must first know how consumers behave and how they react to various influences before he can hope to influence their attitudes, which may in turn influence their behavior. As a prelude to behavior change, attitudes must first be influenced.

Generally, the purpose of an advertising campaign is to communicate a sales message for a product or service to a previously selected group of consumers or prospects. In communicating this sales message, an advertiser hopes to trigger some sort of response in the consumer that will have some influence on his or her behavior that will result in the purchase of a product or service. While there are many intervening marketing variables between the advertising message and the actual purchase of a product (for example, the retail price of the product and its availability), the primary

Figure 3-10.   Attitudes and Attitude Change

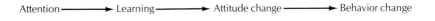

Attention ⟶ Learning ⟶ Attitude change ⟶ Behavior change

effect an advertiser seeks is to influence consumers' attitudes toward or about the product or service. Martin Fishbein and Icek Ajzen have defined an attitude as "a learned predisposition to respond in a consistently favorable or unfavorable manner with respect to a given object."[5]

Most researchers generally believe attitudes are related to an object; they have direction, intensity, and degree; they have some sort of structure, and usually they are learned. All of us have attitudes toward everything around us and everything within us. Usually, attitudes are formed and develop from our needs and wants and the values we place upon objects that will satisfy those needs and wants. Of particular interest in the development of an advertising campaign is how attitudes toward products or brands may be formed. Figure 3-11 illustrates a simplified model of how that is believed to occur.

Almost all theories about attitudes and how attitudes are formed or change are based on the general idea that the human mind strives to maintain a harmony or consistency among currently perceived attitudes. Thus, individuals constantly strive to maintain some sort of consistency among what they currently believe and what is going on around them. They form new attitudes to coincide with what they already believe and events they see or perceive, and they change or modify attitudes to fit with what occurs in the world around them.

Attitudes toward brands and products or services are generally thought to have three basic components: (a) the cognitive component, which is the individual's beliefs and knowledge about the product or service; (b) the affective component, or the emotional reactions toward it; and (c) the behavioral component, or how the person actually reacts toward the brand or product, such as buying it regularly or avoiding it at all costs. To change an attitude, all three of these components must be considered and must be affected in some way.

These attitudes and attitude changes are why advertising often has such a difficult task. Consumers are constantly trying to maintain a mental balance, yet advertising is constantly encouraging them to change in some way. Thus, there is a pull and tug going on between what consumers presently believe about products and services and what advertisers are trying to communicate to them through their advertising messages. The easiest state for the human mind is a constant state, such as one characterized by brand loyalty, or being in an RRB buying situation. However, consumers are constantly being besieged by advertising messages that attempt to create a change in their attitude toward the advertised product, service, or brand.

---

5. Martin Fishbein and Icek Ajzen, *Belief, Attitude, Intention and Behavior: An Introduction to Theory and Research* (Reading, MA: Addison-Wesley, 1975), p. 6. Reprinted with permission.

Figure 3-11.   How User Attitudes are Formed

While there are many models of consumer behavior and many explanations of how attitudes are formed, the one developed by David L. Loudon and Albert J. Della Bitta is a clear, concise explanation as illustrated in the model below.

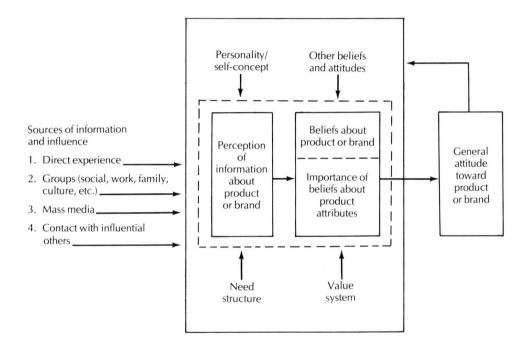

"It shows that several sources provide consumers with information and influence about products, services, retail stores, and other objects. The individual selectively perceives and distorts the information according to his individual needs, values, and personality and according to how well the information 'fits' with currently held beliefs and attitudes. This processed information initiates either development, change, or confirmation in the consumer's beliefs about the product and the importance of each of the product's attributes to him and his current needs. Out of this process is synthesized a general attitude toward a product. Admittedly, this model is an oversimplification. However, it does reflect current understanding of attitudes and presents a concise picture of the psychological and external elements involved in the process of forming attitudes toward products. Also, it should be pointed out that the process is dynamic; it continues to change over time."

SOURCE: Loudon and Della Bitta, *Consumer Behavior* (New York: McGraw-Hill, 1979), p. 392.

Influencing Attitudes

Advertising campaign planners are primarily concerned with either (a) maintaining a favorable attitude toward their brand, product, or service or (b) changing or modifying existing consumer attitudes so they will be more in favor of their brand, product, or service. To do so, advertisers generally concentrate on the cognitive component of the attitude; that is, they hope to influence beliefs or add knowledge to the consumer's information base so that the present attitude will become more favorable. There are five basic methods of changing attitudes toward a product or brand through the use of advertising and advertising appeals.

1. Affect product class linkages with goals and events. If attitudes are related to certain groups or social events, can the advertiser change the attitudes toward the brand by pointing out or linking these certain desirable social groups or events to the brand?

2. Add a salient characteristic. Can something be added to the brand that will be important to the consumer? Can what our product or service is or does be improved through a change or innovation in manufacturing process, ingredient, effect, or the like?

3. Alter the perception of existing product characteristics. Can product disadvantages be turned into advantages? Or can a relatively unimportant product benefit be made the primary decision point in the consumer's selection of a product in that class?

4. Change perceptions of the advertiser's brand. Can consumers' present belief about the brand be changed to something else? Can the product have "more" of something or be "better" or perhaps "improved" to change the consumers' image of the product?

5. Change the perception of competing brands. A common method of attempting to change perceptions of competitors is through comparative advertising. Is it possible to show that the competitor's product is not as good, as useful, or as inexpensive as the brand to offset what consumers now believe?[6]

Almost all advertising campaigns attempt to develop or change consumer attitudes through one or a combination of these five methods. Often this forms the basis for the advertising message and usually is a central part of the actual advertising strategy.

---

6. Adapted partially from Harper W. Boyd, Jr., Michael L. Ray, and Edward C. Strong, "An Attitudinal Framework for Advertising Strategy," *Journal of Marketing,* 36 (April 1972): 27–33.

The Evoked Set

A result of consumer attitudes about products and brands is called the evoked set of brands. Based on the existing attitudes, particularly in the cognitive component, when a consumer feels a need or want for a particular product category, he or she goes through a mental search process. He searches his knowledge, background, and experience to find a solution — that is, a product that might satisfy that particular need. Searching further, the individual "evokes" from his or her own experience and background a specific brand or brands that might fill that need. For example, if a person decided to buy a male friend a new shirt as a birthday gift, first he would recall what types of men's shirts the person liked, considering such factors as type of cloth, pattern, color, and collar styles. Having determined the basic product class, he would then recall brands such as Arrow, Enro, Gant, Manhattan, and Dior—or at least those that come immediately to mind. From that group, he would then do an evaluative summary of each before making the actual purchasing decision. The brands that come immediately to mind constitute the evoked set. The evoked set is those brands one might consider as the solution to a particular problem or situation.

People have evoked sets of brands for all types of products and services, from insurance companies to candy bars to washing machines. Usually, unless the purchase decision is a major one, say in EPS, consumers choose from among brands that exist in their evoked set. For example, when a person stops to purchase a candy bar, the actual brand decision often is made from among brands within the evoked set. Little additional search or decision making is required or involved. The consumer, through the use of the evoked set, attempts to simplify the purchase decision process. It is here in the evoked set, or the formation of the evoked set, that advertising may have its greatest effect. By moving a brand into a consumer's evoked set, an advertiser can assure that the brand will at least be considered for purchase rather than being totally ignored in a particular purchasing situation.

Agenda Setting

Another major method of using advertising to influence consumer purchasing decisions is through the process of agenda setting. Agenda setting is simply the idea that in an unknown situation, or among unknown or infrequently purchased brands or products, consumers may have little or no basis on which to make a buying decision. Thus the advertiser attempts to identify those areas in which her brand is superior to competition and to convince consumers that those areas form the best basis for the decision. The advertiser thus is said to "set the agenda" for the purchase.

An automobile battery is not purchased on a regular basis by most consumers. Other than knowing that the battery is supposed to furnish the electrical power to start and run the automobile engine, most consumers know little about the product class or the brands within the class. The manufacturer of the battery understands this and attempts to influence and inform consumers about the basis on which a battery should be selected. She thus develops an advertising campaign featuring the particular brand attribute in which her product excels.

If Battery Manufacturer A's battery has superior power in cold weather, she would attempt to get consumers to consider cold-weather starting as the primary benefit to seek when making a battery purchasing decision. Manufacturer B, however, might have more cells or plates in his product. He would thus try to "set the agenda" for battery purchase selection as being the number of cells or plates the battery contains. Manufacturer C might stress a warranty or guarantee that is superior to Brands A and B and make that the most important factor. Thus, while all products would essentially serve the same purpose, each manufacturer, through advertising, would attempt to identify the major decision factor or to set the agenda by which consumers should go about deciding on an automobile battery brand. As more and more products reach parity in the marketplace, this agenda-setting approach will likely become more and more important in the development of an advertising campaign.

Diffusion of Innovation and the Adoption Process

While attitude development and change are important concepts, it is also important for the advertising campaign planner to understand the actual purchase behavior of consumers in the marketplace. Often, simply creating or changing an attitude toward a brand or product does not automatically result in a product purchase decision, nor does it guarantee that the brand, once tried, will be repurchased on a regular basis. Researchers have found that most consumers and most social groups go through a set of measurable steps in deciding to try a new product or brand or to change the brand they are presently using. This is called the *adoption process*.

An equally important concept is that not all consumers nor social groups go through these steps at the same time nor at the same speed. Thus, we find that some people adopt new ideas and new concepts more rapidly than others. This is called the *diffusion of innovation*.

Generally, the adoption process consists of several steps that can be predicted and charted. Originally identified by Everett M. Rogers while studying how native tribes adopt a new idea or concept, the steps that Rogers charted are used today to describe the stages of the adoption process:

Step 1—Awareness of the innovation
Step 2—Interest in the innovation
Step 3—Evaluation of the innovation
Step 4—Trial of the innovation
Step 5—Decision as to whether to adopt the innovation
Step 6—Confirmation of the decision to adopt the innovation[7]

While almost all members of society go through Rogers's process in the adoption of an innovation, not all people move through the steps at the same speed nor do all people adopt new innovations at the same time. Rogers and others have found the adoption process, or how the idea diffuses through the population, actually resembles a bell-shaped curve when measured over time. An example of the diffusion process based on time is illustrated in Figure 3-12. The curve illustrates that only a few persons actually adopt the new idea at the very beginning. Only 2.5 percent of the group can really be called innovators. Others in the group are slower to adopt the idea and are a relatively large group; the laggards are the very last to adopt the innovation. In fact, not all members of the group may actually adopt the innovation no matter what the length of time.

The importance of this concept to the advertising campaign planner should be obvious. First, when developing a new advertising campaign, which often consists of relatively new information about the brand in the advertising message, one should remember that not all customers and prospects will become aware of the advertising message at the same time. Usually, this creation of awareness is a consequence of the media selected. In addition, a new advertising message must take the consumer through the various mental steps necessary for the receiver to accept the sales message. (Note the strong resemblance between Rogers's diffusion of innovation and Lavidge and Steiner's hierarchy of effects from Chapter 2.) Further, not all persons accept the sales message at the same rate over time even if they receive equal exposure to the message. Thus, the importance of advertising message repetition through the media plan becomes clear. (See Chapter 12.)

In introducing new products or new advertising ideas, sometimes it may be important for the advertising campaign planner to concentrate efforts on innovators, or those who are most likely to adopt the new idea, new concept, or new advertising message. This further supports the idea of selecting a specific target market for the advertising campaign message. Finally, the advertising planner should keep this concept of diffusion and adoption in mind when developing the advertising strategy and advertising messages in various product categories and for individual brands. If the

---

7. Everett M. Rogers and F. F. Shoemaker, *The Communication of Innovations: A Cross-Cultural Approach* (New York: The Free Press, 1971), p. 23.

Figure 3-12. Adopter Categorization on the Basis of Innovativeness

Innovators	Early adopters	Early majority	Late majority	Laggards
2.5%	13.5%	34%	34%	16%

$\bar{x} - 2sd$ $\bar{x} - sd$ $\bar{x}$ $\bar{x} + sd$

The innovativeness dimension, as measured by the time at which an individual adopts an innovation or innovations, is continuous. However, this variable may be partitioned into five adopter categories by laying off standard deviations from the average time of adoption.

SOURCE: Rogers and Shoemaker, *The Communication of Innovations*, p. 23.

---

product or brand is startlingly new, time will usually be required for the adoption process to occur. If, however, the product or brand is well established and only the advertising message is new, the adoption process and resulting diffusion through the marketplace will take less time. In any event, the diffusion of innovation and the adoption process clearly illustrate why it is sometimes difficult to measure the results of an advertising campaign in a short period of time.

Summary   Understanding your consumer—what he or she wants, doesn't want, what he or she needs or doesn't need—and what motivates a person to purchase one product instead of its competitor is a crucial part of advertising campaign planning. The planner must understand the different types of consumers and the many internal and external influences on them. In terms of campaign planning it is especially important to understand the types of needs, demand, and the product life cycle concept, and how consumers make purchasing decisions.

All of these elements determine the character of market segment which is critical to developing the proper advertising message and choosing the proper media to get that message to the potential buyer.

Case for Discussion: Stearns Food Market

In July of 1982, Amy Louis was sitting at her desk in the back room of Stearns Food Market while sawdust and the sounds of hammers and drills drifted in from the front, where extensive remodeling was well underway. Louis was the manager of the Riverview, Virginia, Stearns store, one of 37 Stearns Food Market Stores in the Washington, D.C., area.

Stearns operated in several East Coast markets and had opened its first stores in Washington in 1961. Stores were located throughout the District of Columbia and suburban Maryland and Virginia. Stearns was the fourth largest grocery retailer in the area, behind two large chains and military base commissaries.

Early in 1981, consumer trends analysts at the headquarters office had proposed a major remodeling change. Based on industry forecasts for the coming decade, these analysts believed that Stearns could get a jump on the competition by instituting design and product-offering changes in advance of widespread consumer demand. Specifically, they cited these trends:

1. Contrary to earlier predictions, specialty store sales had increased by 11.4 percent from 1980 to 1981, as compared to a 10.4 percent sales increase for chain stores.[1]
2. Convenience store sales increased by 18.1 percent in the same period.[2]
3. Husbands are helping with shopping regularly, particularly in the East.[3]
4. Fifty-seven percent of consumers shop in more than one store to take advantage of specials.[4]
5. Nutrition and food safety are becoming increasingly important.[5]
6. Impulse buying is increasing.[6]
7. Because of the large number of working women, one-stop shopping and convenience foods will become even more popular.[7]

The analysts proposed that Stearns respond to these trends through a change in store format that would include:

---

1. "Grocery Industry Report for 1980," *Progressive Grocer,* April 1981, p. 5.
2. "Grocery Industry Report for 1980," p. 5.
3. "Grocery Industry Report for 1980," p. 61.
4. "Grocery Industry Report for 1980," p. 63.
5. "Grocery Retailing in the 80s," *Progressive Grocer,* April 1981, p. 42.
6. "Grocery Retailing in the 80s," p. 42.
7. "Grocery Retailing in the 80s," pp. 104–105.

1. Stores-within-a-store: full-service deli, bakery, butcher shop, gourmet shop, cheese counter, and seafood market, all located at various points within the main store.
2. An expanded produce section.
3. Large wine and beer section.
4. At least 10 checkout lines, including 2 express lanes.
5. "Good through" dating on all dairy items.
6. Full range of regular food store items, including a large frozen food section.

In addition, the analysts urged adopting a "guaranteed low price" policy and regular special price reductions.

Stearns management accepted the analysts' report and decided to select one market as a trial spot for the change. Washington was considered a representative location. Four stores were chosen to undergo the initial remodeling. The Riverview store, where Louis was manager, was one of the first four.

Remodeling had begun in early May and was scheduled for completion in late August. The store had remained open until mid-June, but had been closed once heavy construction began.

Each of the remodeled stores had been given an ample advertising budget to be used in re-introducing Stearns to area shoppers. The managers were responsible for spending these funds in whatever way they felt would be most effective in their particular neighborhood.

Riverview was a middle to upper-middle class Virginia suburb. The Stearns store was located in a small shopping center which also contained a large drug store, several banks, and a number of small clothing, appliance, and craft stores. The shopping center was in a mostly residential area at the intersection of two moderately busy thoroughfares. A very large grocery operated by the no. 1 marketer in the area was located 2½ miles away in a larger mall on a major highway. The no. 2 market's nearest store was 3 miles away, on one of the roads that ran past the Stearns location. This store was in a very small shopping center.

Louis knew that at the time it was closed for remodeling, her store was viewed as second-best by most area shoppers. The majority of business in Riverview went to the no. 1 marketer's large store. Stearns' prices were about equal, but its selection was not as good and the store itself was older and somewhat shabby.

Louis had scheduled a meeting with a local advertising agency to discuss an advertising campaign for the re-opening. She believed that if she could get people into the new store one time, they'd keep coming back. Getting them in could be difficult. Those people who had shopped Stearns regularly would not be a problem, but "store switchers," those who had shopped at both Stearns and the major competitor's would be harder to attract. Since Stearns' temporary closing, many of these people had become regular customers at the no. 1 marketer's store. She would need to attract as many of those shoppers as possible to make the new Stearns a success.

Louis knew that consumer shopping trends had determined the design of the new Stearns. Perhaps consumer behavior techniques could determine her advertising strategy.

Questions

1. Referring to the section on external influences on consumers, Louis' store operates in a culture that prizes cleanliness and quality in foods, a subculture that is suburban, where customer social class is middle to upper middle. How would you expect the three remaining external influences—social or reference groups, the family, and personal influence—to impact on Louis' success in attracting customers to Stearns?

2. Demand and estimated demand were clearly key factors in the decision to remodel Stearns and in Louis' thinking on potential customers. Although everyone shops for food (after all, it's a physiological need), can you think of anyone who could be defined as a non-user for Louis' purposes?

3. How might the product life cycle concept affect Louis' advertising strategy?

4. What market segments might Louis pursue? What benefits would appeal to them?

5. The five methods of changing attitudes are discussed in this chapter. How might these be applicable here?

6. Ultimately, for a grocery store such as Stearns to succeed, especially in a highly competitive market, it must have a large consumer base. Going back to the segments you identified earlier, which would you recommend targeting?

4 The Advertising Plan

While there is no guarantee that great advertising can be produced from a rigid formula, the campaign planner who attempts to develop an advertising proposal without first preparing a carefully written plan is courting disaster. Although a written plan isn't foolproof, it does provide the blueprint that should assure that all the necessary decisions are made in a logical and effective sequence. Further, it assures there are no glaring blunders in the development process.

What Is an Advertising Plan?
Perhaps the best way to define an advertising plan is first to describe what it is not:

A. The advertising plan is not a marketing plan. That means it does not contain marketing objectives such as sales or profits or return on investment. The advertising plan is part of the marketing plan and contains only that information relevant to the advertising or sales promotion program that will be conducted for the brand during the given time period. The marketing information should be in the marketing plan, not the advertising plan.

B. The advertising plan is not a sales document. While it is important to be enthusiastic about the program that has been developed, the purpose of the advertising plan is to provide an outline of what is recommended and what is to be done. As such, the selling arguments should be restricted to the "Conclusion" section or in the formal presentation of the material.

C. The advertising plan is not a ponderous tome. The objective of the plan is not to show how much information has been gathered. The purpose of the plan is to communicate clearly and completely what is proposed for the coming advertising period and why those recommendations are being made. Keep it to that.

What is an advertising plan specifically? It is:

A. The background, history, and past records of the advertising programs that have been conducted for the brand. In addition, it is the recommendation of what is proposed for the coming period in terms of specific advertising, sales promotion, or publicity programs. As such, it contains a record of what has gone before and also provides an outline of what is to come that can be used for reference in future years. Therefore, the plan should contain only those elements that will be helpful in understanding what is proposed, judging the likely success of that program, and preparing future ones.

B. The advertising plan is an opportunity to explain and illustrate the logic and reasoning that has gone into the development of the plan. By explaining the problems and opportunities that the brand or the company face, the planner can illustrate how the proposed program solves problems and capitalizes on opportunities. The plan gives the campaign planner an opportunity to illustrate how all the parts of the plan fit together over time. Since advertising often takes place over a year or longer period, it gives the planner an opportunity to illustrate how the program will build over the course of the campaign.

C. The advertising plan is an action document. Since the development and implementation of an advertising program is usually a very complex scheduling and coordinating activity, the advertising plan lists on paper all the steps that are to be taken. It can also indicate who is to implement the plan. Therefore, the advertising plan serves as a formal document used throughout the period of the campaign.

D. The advertising plan provides management with an outline of the financial commitments being made on behalf of the brand and a general outline of when those funds will be spent. Since many advertising programs for national brands involve millions of dollars, this outline is vital for the financial planning of the company. Further, the advertising plan provides a form of control over the approved expenditures and puts a limit on the funds that will be made available by management.

With this brief look at the advertising plan, the next step is the actual development of the plan—first the entire planning process and then a step-by-step procedure for developing the plan.

Elements of the Advertising Plan

The best way to develop a plan is to first outline the basic steps used in the planning process. Figure 4-1 illustrates one method of advertising campaign planning. As you can see, the development of an advertising plan is actually a series of interrelated steps taken in a logical sequence. None of the steps can be taken until a preceding decision has been made. Similarly, no decision can be made in isolation.

While the model in Figure 4-1 is excellent for visualizing the general decisions that must be made, a more explicit description of the specific items found in an advertising plan follows.

Here are brief descriptions of the major parts of an advertising plan. Following this section is a working model in outline form. The model is suitable either for the management of a consumer products company or as a document prepared by an advertising agency to be presented to a client company. If the audience is different, changes should be made accordingly.

I. The Executive Summary

As the title suggests, this is a brief digest or abstract of the entire plan. The purpose of this summary is simply to provide the highlights of the plan in a form that management can quickly read and understand. Top level executives often simply want a brief thumbnail sketch of what is proposed in advertising since they assume that the planner is expert. Further, if the management has a question about one or more sections of the plan, they can quickly refer to those sections for more detail. Therefore, this should be a one- or two-page summary at most that simply outlines what is proposed and highlights the most important areas, such as spending, advertising, creative strategy, general media schedules, sales promotion, and the like.

II. Situation Analysis

A. Company and product history. It is traditional to include a brief history or sketch of the company in the opening. Generally, a single paragraph will do. The history of the brand may need to be a bit longer, perhaps a half-page or so. It should, however, stick to the key issues that face the brand today and are relevant to the brand's future success. Above all, you should avoid the temptation to stroke management with a verbose, yawn-producing "century-of-progress" report.

Relevant history here may relate to the sales history of the brand and perhaps key competitors. Equally important may be the historical growth of the category if it has not been included in the marketing plan. However, this is not a marketing exercise. It is simply a review of what has happened

Figure 4.1   Components of the Advertising Decision Process

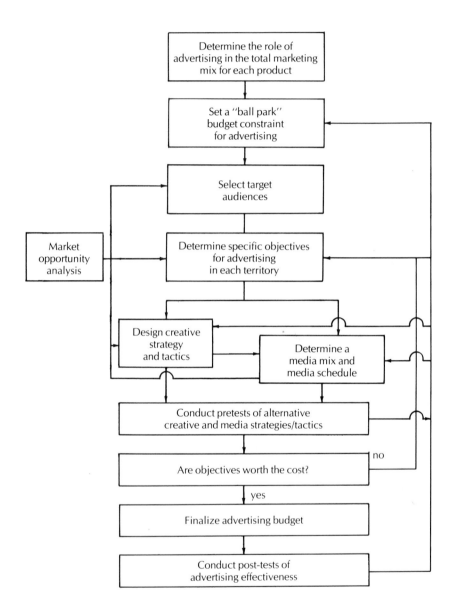

SOURCE: Cravens, Hills, and Woodruff. *Marketing Decision Making: Concepts and Strategy* (Chicago: Richard D. Irwin, 1976).

in the market and to the brand. If possible, this information should be related to the past advertising program for the brand in a way that might indicate why the sales patterns occurred as they did.

Perhaps the most important element to include here is a brief review of the previous advertising plan and its success or failure. For example, if there was a reason the previous year's plan did not meet expectations, here's an opportunity to tell why it didn't work and how the necessary changes have been made for this year. The goal here is to update management on what is happening in the marketplace and set the stage for what the plan proposes.

B. Product evaluation. This is where the plan gets down to serious business. All those elements (discussed in Chapter 1) that might affect sales of the product or service should be compared, including benefits offered, distribution, pricing, and so forth. This information should be in brief outline form and deal only with specifics, not guesses or estimates. It should, however, point out those areas that will impact specifically on the success of the advertising program. For example, if the brand has a distribution problem, that should be pointed out and the expected effect that it will have on the success of the advertising program should be explained. Perhaps as important is the need to point out the assumptions being made about the marketplace and marketing activities during the period of the plan, and which of these will likely affect the program being recommended. For example, if prices are to be raised during the course of the advertising plan, some statement should be made about what effect this might have on advertising response.

This section need not be a total and complete review of the product. It should simply cover those relevant facts which might affect the outcome of the proposed advertising program.

C. Consumer evaluation. This section should give an accurate picture of the target market (TM) to whom the advertising will be directed. It should be as specific as possible, including demographics such as age, sex, income, education, race, occupation, and so on. Most important, how many purchasers there are in the category, how many purchasers the brand has, and the brand's market share should be stated. Those are all-important factors in supporting the recommendations that you are making.

All available psychographic data also should be included. That includes information on the lifestyle of consumers or prospects, how they use the product now, what attitudes they have toward the brand, how they feel about competition—in short, any information that will give a better picture of the target market of proposed advertising messages. This type of material can be vital to management in making a positive decision about the plan. Remember, management doesn't know the prospects and customers as well as you do. So, paint them a picture of whom your advertising will be expected to influence. That can help immeasurably in getting approval for the campaign.

D. Competitive evaluation. Most modern marketing language was borrowed from ancient military strategists. As any commanding officer knows, accurate intelligence on the enemy is crucial if a successful military campaign is to be launched. The same is true in advertising. You must know what your competitors are doing and what they can or might do. That will help guide you into developing a plan that expects and anticipates not only competitive reaction to your plan but also gives you an opportunity to offset any programs you think competition might implement during the period your plan will be in effect.

So, start first with a review of current competitive advertising campaigns. Point out to whom these campaigns are directed, give an indication of the advertising weight being used, and how this campaign might affect the target market. Further, show the timing of previous competitive programs and what strategy this implies they are using. This can be quite helpful in illustrating how and why your creative and media recommendations will be effective. If at all possible, give some indication of the spending level being used by competition. This will help support the budget proposed in the plan and gives management a benchmark against which to measure. In brief, include any competitive advertising information that will show why and how you developed your plan and how you hope to offset competitive activities with the program you are proposing.

III. Marketing Goals

While the advertising plan should deal with advertising and not marketing, it is helpful to include a brief review of the marketing goals that have been set for the brand or company. Often, that review will assist management in seeing how the advertising program is designed to support and assist in reaching those sales and profit objectives.

Typically, marketing goals are stated both short term and long term. Most short-term goals are for the coming year or coming financial period. Long-term goals are for from three to five years. Whether the goals are short or long term, they should be expressed quantitatively, that is, in numbers or figures that can be measured. (See Chapter 1.)

IV. Budget

Generally, the budget should come next. Often the question uppermost in management's mind is, "What will this advertising campaign cost?"

Therefore, the best time to show what you propose to spend is when marketing goals are still fresh in their minds. It is always easier and quicker to review the marketing goals and relate them to the proposed advertising expenditure if they are located close together.

For this section, you may want to include a brief historical note on what traditionally has been spent on the brand and what is proposed. This can take many forms, such as a recap of the past five years' expenditures, a relationship of advertising to sales or distribution or number of units operated or other factors. This will give an indication of the proposed expenditure related to some known factor in the past.

Be sure to include all costs for the campaign here. For example, if evaluation is included as an advertising cost, include that. Don't forget the cost of production of the materials or the research expenditures for pretesting the creative material and so on.

Most advertising budgets can be presented on one page with a back-up page or two of explanation or support for spending amounts. If you do choose to include competitive expenditures, be sure to include the sources of your estimates or information. Or, if you are estimating based on experience, be sure to say so. The more support you can give for your suggestions and recommendations, the better their chances of acceptance.

V. Advertising Recommendations

This section has specifics about what is proposed in the advertising program. If you have thoroughly explained what is happening in the market and what actions competition is taking, your lead-in should show how you have planned an advertising program that will speak to those situations. Therefore, you don't need long explanations of what you propose.

A. Target market. The first step is to profile the group of people to whom the advertising will be directed. This can be a brief summary of the consumer evaluation developed in Section II (Situation Analysis). You should review the numbers, the demographics, the psychographics, and finally, give a rationale of why the particular group of people was selected as the best prospects for sales messages. The clearer you can make this statement, the better your chances for success in achieving your advertising objectives and also in getting approval for the plan.

An important part of this section is the quantification of the TM you have selected. Be as specific as you can in terms of number of people and where they are located geographically. That is vital to support the creative and media recommendations that follow.

B. Advertising communication objectives. This section spells out exactly, in quantifiable, measurable terms, what sales message will be communicated to the target market. In addition, the time period in which these goals will be accomplished should be specified. Generally, advertising goals are stated in terms of what communication is to be accomplished, for example, creating awareness, imparting knowledge about the product benefits, developing preference, and the like. Unless you are in the direct response advertising business, your goals should not include sales or marketing objectives. That's where advertising plans often fall apart. The planner writes into the advertising program activities or actions that advertising alone simply can't accomplish. (See Chapter 1.)

No matter what goals you set for the advertising plan, they must be measurable and specific. For example, here's just one of the advertising goals taken from a recent plan:

> To make 60% of the target market aware of the new coast-to-coast service being offered by Whiz-Bang Airlines in the first four months of the advertising campaign.

Note that the objective is specific. That is, it gives a goal against which actual results can be measured. It specifies the group that will be measured and it sets a time limit for the accomplishing of the goal. Finally, the objective to be measured is specific: it is awareness of "coast-to-coast" service being offered by the airline. That's the way to write effective advertising objectives.

Creative strategy. The advertising strategy tells the message to be communicated in the advertising campaign. It is the companion to the advertising communication objective since it states what is to be communicated. Often, the strategy is stated in the form of a "Promise" to be made to the target market. The creative strategy simply sums up the solution to the advertising problem that has been identified as being faced by the brand or the company. If the first sections of the plan have been properly developed, the creative strategy should be the logical solution to the problem or problems that have been developed in Sections II and III.

Executions. The executions are the form the actual advertising will take. They carry out the strategy that has been developed and put it in a form that allows it to be transmitted to the target audience. Generally, this section contains the actual elements to be used in the campaign, such as storyboards, layouts, radio scripts, and the like. If a central theme for the campaign has been developed, it should be featured here plus any other specific creative recommendations which are being made.

E. Plans. This may or may not be required in your formal document, for it generally includes a brief description of how the creative executions will be accomplished. For example, if new television commercials are to be produced based on results of what happens in a distribution drive in the field, you might want to sketch out a general timetable for the production of those commercials. Or, alternatively, it might include a commitment pattern for production costs if a close rein is being kept on the budget. In short, it is a section that can be used to explain or bring forward specific steps that are contingent on activities within the campaign or as a result of portions thereof.

VI. Media Recommendations

In this section, the planner should outline the complete details of the media program that will be used to get the advertising message to the target market.

A. Key media problem. This starts with the major media problem to be solved, generally in the form of a brief question facing the advertising planner for the campaign. For example, in the advertising objective for Whiz-Bang Airlines above, the goal was to make 60 percent of the target market aware of "coast-to-coast" service from the airline. The problem here might be, how to reach persons who are prospects for transcontinental airline service. Many people fly on airplanes, but not all of them fly on transcontinental routes. Thus, the question facing the campaign planner is how to reach prospects most effectively and efficiently. On the other hand, other media questions might be more important in other situations, such as how to compete in a category in which the brand is being outspent by competition by a substantial amount and so on. This section can often be one or two paragraphs, but it should sum up the problem the media plan is designed to resolve.

B. Media objectives. These are the specific goals established by the campaign planner. They should be stated as quantifiable, measurable goals within certain time limits. In many cases, these goals will be stated in terms of reach and frequency against the target market for the time period outlined.

C. Media strategy. A companion to the media objectives, the media strategy lists the various media that will be employed in accomplishing the media objectives. For example, will television be used? If so, will it be network or spot? If print is the major vehicle, will it be newspaper, magazine, or direct mail? And so on. In short, the planner should use this section to tell how the strategy will be accomplished and give some support and rationale for the choices being recommended.

D. Media plan. With the outline of what is to be accomplished through the media and what media will be used, the next logical section is the actual media plan. This should outline, in as much detail as is needed, the specific scheduling planned for each medium. Depending on the complexity of the overall plan, this may consist of a single flow chart with one or two magazines listed, or it may consist of a number of specific media plans for individual markets or areas of the country. That, of course, depends on the specific brand for which the plan has been developed.

The easiest way to illustrate media plans is through a flow chart. (See Chapter 12.) This gives a graphic illustration of how the media is to be used across the term of the plan and can illustrate how the various media have been scheduled to work together.

Also this section should include a media budget recap sheet. This should show spending for each medium and a total for the campaign. In some instances, you may want to show quarterly or other expenditure patterns, depending, of course, on the needs of the brand.

VII. Sales Promotion Recommendations

Since sales promotion is becoming such an important part of the total spending for many brands and companies, the proposed sales promotion program should be included in the advertising campaign plan. Including the proposed sales promotion program will illustrate how the advertising and promotional efforts have been coordinated to achieve maximum effectiveness. Like the advertising section, you'll want to include the following specific recommendations.

A. Sales promotion objectives. These objectives should be stated in measurable, quantifiable terms. They should indicate exactly what the sales promotion program should accomplish. Actual results may be listed in terms of sales or trial or conversion or similar behavioral activities by the target market. As will be shown in Chapter 13 on sales promotion, this is an area where direct action can be expected. An example of a measurable sales promotion objective might be:

> Using sales promotion, the objective is to increase shelf facings by 25 percent in the top 15 national supermarket chains during the eight months of the program.

B. Sales promotion strategy. This section simply spells out what specific sales promotion techniques will be used to accomplish the goals stated above. Specific tools to be used are generally stated such as sampling, couponing, in-store displays, contests, sweepstakes, and the like. In most instances, specific recommendations will be supported with some information on the strategy being used and the reasoning behind it. If there has been a major change in the marketplace that makes certain sales promotion strategies more practical during this planning period than in the past, you will want to spell that out, too.

C. Sales promotion executions. This section illustrates the specific details for each of the sales promotion strategies listed above. For example, if you are recommending the use of cents-off coupons, you will want to describe the value of the coupons and perhaps how they will be distributed. The same might be true for a contest. You would want to tell what the contest was about, how the winners would be selected, the prize structure, the timing, how the promotion fits in with the advertising, and so on. In short, you should describe each of the sales promotion programs in sufficient detail so that management can quickly and easily see what you have in mind. Be sure to relate the sales promotion plan back to the advertising. In some instances, you may want to refer to the advertising media plan and the other elements so that your reader will have a clear view of how all the elements fit together.

D. Sales promotion plan. Finally, you should include a brief outline of the overall sales promotion program. This can be done in the form of a flow chart or other device that shows when each element takes place and the length of each promotional activity. Overlaying the advertising media plan on the sales promotion schedule is a good way to show how everything is dovetailed together during the campaign period. In addition, this section should include the various costs for each scheduled element, including estimates of various redemption costs or units such as the dollar amount for coupons, number and cost of premiums, expected acceptance and value of trade deals, and the like. This is where you put all the detailed information needed to make your plan action-oriented.

VIII. Evaluation

It is essential to spell out very clearly exactly how the advertising campaign should be evaluated. If various steps need to be taken prior to the start of the campaign, such as a pre-test, that should be listed. A brief description of the recommended methods and their cost and whether or not they are to be considered an advertising or a marketing cost should be included. Generally, evaluation plans are included as an advertising expense.

IX. Conclusions

Depending on the persons to whom the plan is being addressed, you may or may not need to include this section. If the plan is being developed as an internal document, it probably is not necessary since you will have covered most of this "selling material" in the Executive Summary. If, however, the plan is being developed by an advertising agency for submission to a client, a one- or two-page review of why the plan meets the needs of the brand, how it is designed to achieve certain preagreed upon objectives, and the like are in order. In other words, this is the place to put the selling copy to convince a client to approve the plan and for you to "ask for the order." It's really the only chance you have to do some old-fashioned selling of the plan you have developed. A caution though: don't make this section redundant. If you've already given reasons why you're recommending certain things within the body of the plan, don't just repeat them. Use this section, if you use it at all, to summarize the value of this plan compared to any others that might be developed or considered.

Your Advertising Plan—A Working Model

No perfect outline exists to fit every advertising campaign planner's needs. The following outline was developed with three major objectives in mind: simplicity, substance, and clarity. Use this model as a directional guide for your plan. Include things that are not listed but which are important to making your plan clear and complete. Likewise, drop those sections that do not relate to your needs. If it makes a better plan, change the sequence listed here. For example, you may prefer to have the budget section at the end as a summary. If you follow this plan or at least include all the items listed below, you will be sure to have included all the major elements for an advertising campaign plan.

I. Executive Summary

On a single side of a sheet of paper, outline the major issues covered in your plan. Generally, one or perhaps two elements are vital to the success of a proposal. It may be that you want agreement on the proper target market, it might be the creative strategy, or it might even be the media plan. Whatever it is, there usually are one or two issues with which your readers must agree for them to approve the plan. Make sure those points come through loud and clear in the summary. And, be sure you adequately support your views and positions with facts and information. If you can get these major issues down on one page, you're usually well on your way to developing an effective advertising plan.

II. Situation Analysis

Dig up all the facts and information listed below. Then cut away the unimportant information and get down to the real basics of the plan. This section shouldn't run more than 10 to 15 pages.

A simple way to reduce the verbiage in your plan is to use pie charts, graphs, and growth curves. Many times, a small chart can replace hundreds of words of prose.

In terms of content, the following points should be covered or at least considered:

A. Relevant History of the Product or Brand
    1. Background of the product or brand
    2. Past advertising budgets
    3. Past advertising themes
    4. Past media or spending patterns
    5. Patents or technological history
    6. Significant political or legal influence
    7. Current creative theme being used in advertising or promotion
    8. Current problems and opportunities facing the brand
    9. Major events or activities which might affect the brand in the coming plan period
    10. Relevant marketing data from the marketing plan which might be helpful in understanding why the advertising plan is prepared the way it is

Note: Most of the questions asked about the brand's history could also be asked about the major competitive brands. A historical comparison with competition can be made in this section or separately under the Competitive Analysis. Either is acceptable. Use whichever is most efficient and effective in terms of understanding by your readers.

B. Product Evaluation
    1. How does the product compare to competition in terms of features, ingredients, uses, consumer acceptance, etc.?
    2. What has been added or improved in the last few years, deleted or dropped, new uses, new markets, etc.?
    3. Do consumers perceive the product to be new and modern or old-fashioned? Is it a fashion product and affected by changing consumer mores?
    4. How does the product stack up in terms of value? Good? Fair? Poor?

5. Are present users satisfied?
6. Is distribution widespread? Is the product available?
7. How do retailers feel about the product? Do they want to stock and sell it? Is distribution adequate? Etc.
8. What about packaging? Labeling?
9. Is the brand name well known? Accepted?
10. What about service if provided with the product?
11. What problems do consumers have with product if any? Are they correctable?
12. Is there anything in the product or features that is unique or different from competition?

While this is just a partial list, it gives you an idea of what should go in this section. Include any relevant data that will give your reader an understanding of the product and how it fits in the marketplace and why the proposed advertising plan will be effective.

   C. Consumer Evaluation
1. Demographic profile: occupation; marital status; household head; race; education; age; household income; presence of children in household; social class; locality type; geographic region; other geographical or market breakdowns such as high or low CDI areas, county size, and so on.
2. Psychographic profile: any VALS data available? Any psychographic information from Simmons or other lifestyle data bases? Any user data from previous primary research? Any data on lifestyle or how your product fits into the lives of your present customers or prospects? And so on.
3. Analysis of present customer's behavior: information on consumption such as social influences, where used, how used, frequency of use, average amount used, etc.; attitudes about product such as quality, price, packaging, styling, reputation of the brand, etc.; percentage of consumer awareness of present advertising or promotional activities. What problems does the product solve for the consumer? Is the consumer aware of these benefits? How loyal are present customers? Does brand-switching occur? If so, among this brand or others? Who are the best prospects for the brand? Where are they located? Can they be influenced? In short, include any and all relevant information about the present customers and prospects whom you have identified for the product or service.

   D. Competitive Analysis
1. Direct competition
2. Indirect competition

1. Direct competition
2. Indirect competition
3. Advertising strengths and weaknesses of competition
4. Current and past competitive advertising themes
5. Strengths or weaknesses of competitive packaging, branding, etc.
6. Past competitive advertising and sales promotion expenditures
7. Any research on effectiveness of competitive expenditures
8. Trade acceptance of or influence of competitive advertising or sales promotion programs
9. Any apparent weaknesses in competitive programs
10. Any geographic concentration of competitive expenditures
11. Any comments or feelings from the sales force or trade as to unusual strengths of competitive programs.

III. Marketing Goals for the Brand

This can be taken directly from the marketing plan. Be sure to include information on such areas as what marketing objectives have been set in terms of sales, margins, or profits for the period the advertising will cover. You'll also want to include information on expected market share or share improvement, current and proposed market penetration, and where changes should occur.

More specifically, you'll want to refer to the marketing plan to outline the proposed marketing strategy for the coming period. This is important so the reader can see how your advertising plan fits in with the overall marketing strategy. You'll want to include a brief description on how these marketing objectives are being supported by the advertising campaign. That is particularly true if your advertising plan is expected to make a direct and major contribution to the accomplishing of those goals.

IV. Budget. See Chapter 8.

V. Advertising Recommendations

This is the heart of the advertising plan. Below is an outline of the elements you'll want to include.

A. Target Market: The best place to start is to immediately identify the target market to whom the advertising will be directed. This can simply be a summary of the Consumer Evaluation section or it may be more detailed, depending on the needs of your readers. Generally, here's where you outline in general terms the demographics and psychographics of the target market, identify how many of those types of people there are and give some indication of why they are prospects: i.e., are they present users, users of competitive products, or not users in the category? You'll also want to support your recommendation for selecting this particular segment of the population here.

B. Advertising Communications Objectives: This covers the basics of what the advertising is supposed to accomplish. One of the easiest ways to do this is through a formal, structured approach. The form below will help you present this information to management in a clear, easy-to-understand manner.

1. Key fact (usually one or two sentences): A single-minded statement that sorts out all the information about the product, market, competition, etc. The single element which is most relevant to the advertising need or plan.

2. Primary marketing problem (one half page or so): This should grow out of and be directly related to the key fact. It may be a product problem, a marketing problem, or an image problem, but it must be related to an area where advertising can have some influence.

3. Communications objective (one or two sentences): A clear statement of the effect advertising should have on the consumer. What is the message the advertising is to convey to the prospect and how should the prospect react after seeing it?

C. Creative Strategy: Next comes the "what" you'll be saying in your advertising campaign. This probably is the most important element in the entire advertising campaign. Therefore, you'll want to spell this out in some detail. One of the easiest ways to do this is to write a brief description of a representative person in your target market. Giving this explanation of the market as a person, rather than as a faceless mass does much to help management to see customers as people, rather than as simply potential units to sell. To properly describe a representative person in your TM, include at least the following information:

1. Geographics   4. Media patterns
2. Demographics   5. Buying/use patterns
3. Psychographics

Finally, include a brief idea of the competition and the promise and reason-why in your advertising.

a. Principal Competition (two or three sentences maximum): Not a listing of all brands but the segment or area in which the product will compete.

    b. Promise (one or two sentences maximum): Must be phrased as a consumer benefit and made as competitive as possible. It must be strong enough to motivate the prospect. It should not be written in advertising terms, i.e., no jargon or buzz words.

    c. Reason-Why (two or three sentences maximum): All points must support the promise and not wander. Ideally, this is a single fact and not a list of attributes. If no facts are available, an authority must be available to support. This can be done through manner and mood. Above all, these claims must be legal.

    d. Divisional/Corporate Requirements

D. Executions: This section shows how the creative strategy has been fulfilled. Include as much or as little of the actual creative product as you feel necessary to get your ideas across. That may include but not be limited to:

1. Print layouts and copy
2. Radio scripts
3. Television storyboards
4. Theme lines and art
5. Package designs, illustrations, etc.
6. Brochure or catalog layouts
7. Outdoor board designs
8. Advertising specialties

E. Advertising Plan: Outline any details of how the advertising will be done or any special information. For example, if the advertising calls for special travel to photograph locations, specify why you chose this location or area. You might want to suggest a timetable for approval of the creative material to enable it to be prepared in time for the media schedule, or you simply might want to justify in more detail why the approach you have developed should be successful in meeting the advertising objectives. This is the area to cover those important details that need to be discussed and explained if management is to have a complete picture of what you are proposing.

VI. Media Recommendations: In this section you should lay out clearly and completely but very briefly the media program that is proposed. Depending on the complexity of the media plan, you may need to give descriptive material or a simple outline may be sufficient. If you are proposing a media plan that is radically different than that which has traditionally been used for the product or service, you may want to give additional justification for your proposal. In other cases, where you are simply updating plans that have been used before, a quick review of the history of the media program may be sufficient. At a minimum, you will want to include the following information.

A. Key media problem: This is where you should detail the primary problem that your media plan solves in terms of getting the message to the target market. An example might be:

> This media plan is unique to that brand since the marketing activities are being revised from national to regional and local coverage. This plan is designed to maximize media coverage in the 20 markets which have been selected but still give the appearance of a national plan to dealers and the sales force.

This key media problem may be more specific than this example if the situation warrants it but generally, it should set up the basic premise which management will need to approve to get final acceptance of the entire program.

B. Media objectives: This section relates media to the overall marketing and advertising plan—in other words, the specific goal of the media plan in quantifiable terms. At a minimum, you should cover the following areas:
  1. The target audience to be reached, in terms of demographics and psychographics if that is pertinent
  2. Budget available and restrictions on its use
  3. Reach and frequency needed
  4. Effective reach levels needed
  5. Continuity needed
  6. Pattern of monthly and yearly continuity
  7. Special geographic weighting needed
  8. Merchandisability of media if necessary
  9. Flexibility needed
  10. Degree to which media will have to support promotions
  11. Creative strategy implications

In addition, a rationale for each of the decisions should be included here to support the proposal.[1]

C. Media strategy: This section covers the specifics of the media plan. That means you list each of the media you propose and then support why you have made that recommendation. In addition, you must relate each of the strategies back to one or more of the

---

1. Jack Z. Sissors and Jim Surmanek, *Advertising Media Planning,* 2nd ed. (Chicago: Crain Books, 1982), p. 230.

media objectives. In some instances, you may want to explain why other obvious strategies were not used or or why a new plan that doesn't follow historical tradition is needed. At a minimum, strategies should include:

1. Media classes selected (e.g., network television or magazines)
2. Strategy for allocating the budget to geographic areas (roll-out vs. national introduction; spot only or national plus spot heavy-up)
3. Allocation of budget to media classes (dollars and percentages of total)
4. Allocation of budget by months and/or quarters of year; introductory vs. sustaining period strategy
5. Reach and frequency levels desired by months and/or quarters of the year
6. Effective reach and frequency levels per typical month
7. Size of the primary and secondary target markets
8 Weighting of strategic targets
9. Geographical weighting requirements that must be used
10. Cost-per-thousand standards, if required
11. Explanations of why a strategy is different from previous ones
12. Specifications of the size of media units to be used (30- or 60-second commercials; full or fractional pages)
13. Criteria to be used for selecting or scheduling media (need for flighting)
14. Relationship of strategy to that of competitors, with special emphasis on certain key brands that must be dealt with specifically
15. A rationale for each strategy statement[2]

D. Media plan: This section documents and details the specifics of the media proposal. Generally, this information is supported by media flow charts showing exactly when each insertion or broadcast is scheduled, along with costs and other supporting information. Again, at a minimum, the media plan should include the following information:

1. A statement of criteria for determining media values
2. Proof that vehicles selected are the best of all alternatives (using media value criteria) and for the budget (data plus words)
3. Data showing net reach and frequency for targets reached by a combination of all vehicles, including frequency distributions

---

2. Sissors and Surmanek, *Advertising Media Planning,* p. 230.

4. Data showing gross impressions for a combination of all vehicles, especially for target audiences
5. Cost-per-thousand shown for all vehicles selected or considered
6. Cost summary tables showing each vehicle, number of times used per month, cost-per-insertion, and total cost-per-month
7. Yearly cost summary
8. Yearly flow chart (or schedule) showing vehicles, weeks of insertions, reaches, frequencies, and costs per month for the year
9. Any other data that will help buyers implement the plan[3]

VII. Sales Promotion Recommendations
    Since sales promotion now accounts for up to 60 percent of many products' total promotional budget, it may well be that this is a substantial portion of your overall recommendations. In some instances, the sales promotion program is handled as a separate document or it may be included in the general advertising plan for the product or service. Here, we make the assumption that it is a part of the advertising plan.

    A. Sales Promotion Objectives: Start first with a clear, concise, and complete description of what the sales promotion program is designed to achieve. This can vary widely, but the more specific you can make your recommendations, the better. For example, don't use broad, general ideas such as "support the advertising campaign"; that's understood. Be specific: "generate trial of Brand Q among 40 percent of the TM during the first six months of the budgeted period." With clear, measurable sales promotion objectives, management can easily see how your entire plan fits together.
        Some of the common objectives often set for the sales promotion program are:
        1. Generate trial
        2. Hold present customers
        3. Load present customers
        4. Encourage repeat usage of the product
        5. Build more frequent or multiple purchases
        6. Introduce a new or improved product
        7. Introduce new packaging or different size package
        8. Neutralize competitive advertising or sales promotion

3. Sissors and Surmanek, *Advertising Media Planning*, p. 231.

    9. Capitalize on seasonal, geographic, or special events

  10. Encourage customers to trade up to a larger size, a more profitable line, or another product in the line

B. Sales Promotion Strategy: These are the specifics of the sales promotion plan. At a minimum, you should identify the specific sales promotion techniques you propose and justify why they are being recommended. In addition, you may want to outline some of the other strategies that were considered but rejected. One of the basic differentiations in sales promotion should be made between the consumer and the trade. In other words, you should identify what activities are designed to get consumer action and what is recommended to get trade support. Some of the basic sales promotion strategies that might be included are:

    1. Consumer sales promotion strategies
       a. Coupons
       b. Contests and/or sweepstakes
       c. Bonus packs
       d. Stamp and continuity plans
       e. Price-offs
       f. In-packs, on-packs, near-packs, and reusable containers
       g. Free-in-the-mail premiums
       h. Self-liquidating premiums
       i. Refund offers
       j. Sampling
       k. Point-of-purchase materials

    2. Trade sales promotion strategies
       a. Trade deals
       b. Trade coupons

C. Sales Promotion Executions: To illustrate what you are proposing, you will likely want to include examples of the specific sales promotional activities. This can consist of sketches or simply descriptions of the specific nature of the event. Generally, rough sketches of art or illustrations of specific promotion are needed at a minimum here. For example, if you are proposing items such as samples, you'll want to include a sketch of the mailer or distribution package along with any sales material or information which might be included. Some of the more common items often included in this section are:

    1. Coupon advertisements or mailers
    2. Trial or sample packages
    3. Layouts of sweepstakes ads

4. Direct mail folders or forms
5. In-store take one pads or display material
6. Illustrations or sketches of premiums proposed
7. Sketches of bonus pack labels or stickers

By including examples of the specific sales promotion activities you propose, there will be no question in the mind of the reader as to exactly what will be used in the sales promotion program.

D. Sales Promotion Plan: An outline in calendar form usually follows examples of the illustrations of the sales promotion executions. This is done to give management a view of how all the various parts fit together and will interact in the marketplace. If you have not done so previously, you will also want to include a recap of the cost of the sales promotion program, including not only immediate expenditures proposed for sales promotion activities but also a description of the reserves that will be necessary for such things as coupon redemption, premium purchases, fulfillment of promotional programs, and the like.

In this section you will also want to list the response you expect for each of the activities. For example, what percentage of the coupons will be redeemed? How many premiums will be needed? What is the cost of the contest or sweepstakes prizes and judging? What will it cost to return refund coupons to those who participate, and so on.

VIII. Evaluation

A brief statement of how the advertising campaign is to be evaluated should be included. This should cover the proposed methods, for example, a telephone tracking study, or the purchasing of Nielsen data, or the measurement of shelf space in retail stores so that the stated objectives of the campaign can be evaluated. Usually, some specific directions are given as to who will be responsible for this evaluation and how it will be carried out. Since often the advertising campaign planner relies on the research department or even an outside research organization for this portion of the plan, it is vital that direction and control be identified in detail.

Finally, the estimated cost of this evaluation plan should be included. This is particularly true if the evaluation plan is to be included as a part of the total advertising campaign cost.

IX. Conclusions

As previously stated, this page may or may not be included in the advertising plan, depending on whom the audience is and the position of the advertising campaign planner. If it is included, it should be short and to the point. Don't simply repeat previously included material. If it is to be used at all, it should summarize and bring out the major factors that make the plan especially appropriate to the problems and opportunities facing the product or service at this particular time.

Some Tips on Writing an Advertising Plan

While everyone has his or her own writing style, there are some general guidelines for the preparation of an advertising plan. These should be helpful to both professionals and novices.

A. Be Brief. An advertising plan is not a test of your literary ability. It is written to enable you to communicate your ideas in a clear and concise fashion. Therefore, summarize, outline, categorize, cut out all excess words. Edit and trim. Make the plan lean and easy to read and follow.

B. Avoid Redundancy. One of the biggest hazards of an advertising plan is repetition of the same ideas over and over. If you have covered the idea in one section, refer to it. Don't repeat it.

C. No Pronouns. Readers of advertising plans don't really care who had the idea or suggestion. They want only facts. Therefore, leave out the references to ''I'' or ''me'' or ''we'' or ''us.'' If you wrote the plan, the reader knows you did and you don't need to remind him or her of it.

D. Inductive, Not Deductive. Start with the most important points and then support them. Advertising plans are not novels. They shouldn't be written to build up suspense.

E. A Summary at the Beginning. One of the best ways to develop an advertising plan is to put a brief summary at the beginning of each section. That way, the reader can quickly and easily see if that is the section that contains the detailed information he is seeking.

F. Show Sources of Information. A must for any advertising plan is to show the sources of data that are used. It lends much more credence to your proposal if you do so. Further, it illustrates that you obviously have based your recommendations on solid information not just opinion or guesswork.

G. 50 to 60 Pages Maximum. While there are occasions in which you may have to break or bend this rule, generally, no advertising plan should run over 50 to 60 pages. If it is longer than that, there's a good chance you've overwritten. One way to handle the ''number of pages'' problem is to move charts, graphs, and supporting material to an appendix and identify it as such. Thus, if your readers need more information, they have it available, yet you don't clutter the basics of the plan with detail.

In summary, be brief, be complete, but most of all, pack the plan with usable, useful information.

Advertising Information Sources

While most of the material you will need for the development of the advertising plan will be developed in the research section, here are some suggested sources of information that may be helpful to you in finding information about a company, an organization, a product, service, category, or the like.

I. Financial Information Sources
   A. Finding out what books exist on a subject
      1. Library card catalog
      2. *Cumulative Book Index*
      3. *Books in Print*
   B. Finding journal and newspaper articles
      1. *Funk and Scott Index of Corporations and Industries*
      2. Business Periodical Index
      3. *Wall Street Journal*
   C. Financial services
      1. Moody's manuals
         a. Moody's Industrial Manual
         b. Moody's OTC Industrial Manual
         c. Moody's Bank and Finance Manual
         d. Moody's Municipal and Government Manual
         e. Moody's Public Utility Manual
         f. Moody's Transportation Manual
      2. Standard and Poor's Corporation
         a. Standard Corporation Records
         b. New York Stock Exchange listed stock reports
         c. American Stock Exchange stock reports
         d. Over-the-counter and regional exchange stock reports
   D. Company information
      1. Annual reports (often available from stock brokerage firms)
      2. House organs
      3. Prospectuses

II. How to find information about an industry
   A. Guides to sources
      1. Wasserman's Statistics Sources
      2. Encyclopedia of Business Information Sources
   B. Other sources
      1. Standard and Poor's Industry Surveys. Covers 49 industries and their principal companies.
      2. U.S. Census publications
         a. Annual Survey of Manufacturers
         b. Census of Agriculture
         c. Census of Business
         d. Census of Construction Industries
         e. Census of Housing
         f. Census of Manufacturing
         g. Census of Mineral Industries
         h. Census of Population
         i. Census of Transportation
      3. Survey of Current Business
   C. Directories listing corporations
      1. Thomas Register of American Manufacturers—includes alphabetical listing of trademarks
      2. Conover-Mast Purchasing Directory

III. How to find information about a geographical area
   A. U.S. Census publications (in addition to those listed above)
      1. Statistical Abstract of the United States
      2. County and City Data Book
      3. County Business Patterns
   B. State statistical abstracts
   C. State industrial directories
   D. "Survey of Buying Power Issue," *Sales/Marketing Management* magazine (annual)

IV. Special advertising sources
   A. Standard Rate and Data Service
      1. Consumer Magazines
      2. Business Publications
      3. Canadian Advertising
      4. Network Rates and Data
      5. Newspaper Rates and Data
      6. Spot Radio Rates and Data

      7. Spot Television Rates and Data
      8. Transit Advertising Rates and Data
      9. ABC Weekly Newspaper Rates and Data
     10. Print Media
     11. Directorio de Medias
     12. Newspaper Circulation Analysis

  B. Standard Directory of Advertisers

  C. Standard Directory of Advertising Agencies

  D. National Advertising Investments

V. Syndicated marketing studies
Note: Companies listed here will often provide "year-old" data to universities and colleges for cost of postage and handling.

  A. Simmons Market Research Bureau
Audience exposure estimates and product-usage studies correlated with both broadcast and printed media. A major source of consumer research data and marketing studies for all major consumer product categories.

  B. A. C. Nielsen Company
Several kinds of syndicated services are available:
    1. NTI (Nielsen Television Index) is a national television rating service that estimates audience size for all the network TV shows using audimeters installed in approximately 1,200 U.S. TV households.
    2. NSI (Nielsen Station Index) is the Nielsen's service for measuring local TV audiences.
    3. Nielsen Food & Drug Index is a service that measures movement of products in retail stores. From these store audits, companies are able to estimate their brand shares.

  C. LNA-BAR
Leading National Advertiser-Broadcast Advertiser Reports provides a monthly estimate of TV commercial expenditures and gross time billing for all major national brands. Also available are estimates of production costs for programs and talent costs along with station lineups. Network Radio station lineups by program and advertiser is another service syndicated by LNA-BAR.

  D. SAMI (Selling Areas Marketing, Inc.)
This syndicated research company estimates inventory withdrawals by major food and drug chains and stores.

Summary The advertising plan is a very important element in the campaign because it forces the planner to consider all elements that might influence the success of the campaign and explain to others (i.e., top management) how the campaign will work. Key components of the plan are executive summary, situation analysis, marketing goals, budget, advertising recommendations, media recommendations, sales promotion recommendations, evaluation, and conclusions.

Case for Discussion:
Sidley's Soft Drinks

Mort Sidley, president of Sidley's Soft Drinks, decided to hire an outside advertising agency in May of 1983. Sidley's manufactured and distributed six soft drinks regionally. Their market area included retail outlets in North and South Carolina, Georgia, Alabama, Kentucky, and Tennessee. In the past, all promotional efforts had been handled in-house and had consisted mostly of consumer sales promotions and store displays. Sidley's average market share was 10 percent, giving it a good showing behind the national brands. Sidley had decided to allocate more of his budget to advertising and to develop a campaign to be used throughout the region. With the new product introductions from the national brands, he was afraid Sidley's might lose share in the shuffle. Accordingly, he contacted three agencies who had experience in the region and asked them to study the situation and submit a written plan outlining their analysis and solution. Sidley set a June 15 deadline for submission of the plans.

The three plans Sidley received were very different from one another, both in content and format. Plan A contained a detailed analysis of the entire soft drink industry, outlining competitive expenditures and campaigns for the past five years. It also contained an in-depth look at the national brands' new products—formulations, positioning, pricing, trade deals, and consumer promotions. The plan briefly outlined Sidley's activities and product characteristics, noting that the product was comparable to the national brands in quality and that its distribution was quite good in the region it served. Plan A identified price as the primary benefit. (Sidley's was priced an average of 10 percent below national brands.)

The target market was defined as that sought by the national marketers, with special emphasis on young professionals aged 22–34. A psychographic study of these people revealed them to be very quality-conscious, but also concerned about price. Sidley's was a known brand, but they were unaware of its high quality. This segment currently purchased national brands, but were not brand loyal.

Marketing objectives included a 5 percent increase in market share during the first 8 months of the campaign. The plan also recommended expanding distribution into Mississippi within the next 18 months. These objectives would be accomplished through the increased ad budget, which would be used to develop a major regional campaign.

The advertising campaign was centered around the theme "Quench it with Sidley's quality." Advertising would be carried over regional television and in regional magazines and would feature members of the target market drinking Sidley's after a day's activity (tennis, swimming, biking, etc.). The plan explained that, by using television, Sidley's would actively compete with the national brands.

Sales promotion activities would include coupons ("Sidley's quality for less than ever") and premiums such as coolers and beach towels with the Sidley name. These premiums would help increase recognition.

The evaluation plan called for a straightforward analysis of sales increases.

Plan B began by briefly reviewing Sidley's activities and the competitions' spending in the region. Sidley's "home-grown" appeal was identified as the product's unique feature and the bulk of the plan was devoted to a detailed explanation of the advertising campaign that would bring this feature to the general public's attention. The "Drink of Dixie" would be advertised on television, radio, and billboards. With an appeal to all "true Southerners" to support the South's own soft drink, the campaign included such elements as a commercial showing Robert E. Lee and Stonewall Jackson enjoying Sidley's before a victorious battle, billboards where Sidley's grew on magnolia trees, and a jingle to the tune of "Dixie":

> Oh, I'm so glad I have my Sidley's,
> It's the drink that's really Dixie,
> Drink it down, drink it down,
> Drink it down, it's for me.

Plan B defined a target market that was very southern oriented and primarily rural. It recommended that Sidley's set up soft drink machines that would dispense Sidley products in small towns throughout the area. The Dixie appeal would help strengthen Sidley's image against the national brands and was expected to increase market share 5 percent in six months.

Plan C began with a look at Sidley's growth over the past five years, its primary areas of strength (medium-sized communities and suburbs of larger cities), seasonality (like most soft drinks, sales dropped slightly from November to February), and distributor attitudes (well liked). It contrasted these findings with those for the national brands, which were stronger in the big cities. The plan also noted that retailers had no strong attitude toward the national brands, suggesting that they would be willing to support any consumer promotions Sidley's might institute.

Consumers were described as liking Sidley's, and a large proportion of Sidley's buyers were identified as being fiercely brand loyal. The target market for the campaign was described as households of three or more persons living in suburban and nonmetro communities and having yearly incomes of $10,000+. The best prospects among this group were brand-switching national brand buyers.

Marketing goals were for a 7 percent market share increase after the first year, and a 30 percent increase in brand recognition.

The advertising campaign identified Sidley's as "The South's Favorite Son." Ads were to be run in local newspapers and were in the form of turn-of-the-century advertisements. Each ad would feature a tintype-style photo of a local resident with a can of Sidley's. Copy would explain that Sidley's was that person's favorite soft drink. The newspaper ads would be augmented by a radio commercial featuring a "politician" introducing "the South's favorite son—Sidley's." The plan explained that using newspapers would set Sidley's apart from the national brands and give it strong local appeal, particularly in the smaller towns.

Sales promotions would include coupons in the form of ballots ("Pick your favorite son—any of Sidley's six flavors at a savings"). Store displays would also be used.

Evaluation would consist of an analysis of sales increases by community type and a pre-post measure of brand awareness among the target market.

Questions

1. Based on the information given in the case, evaluate each plan. Is the information relevant to the situation? Adequate?

2. Does the analysis seem to justify/lead logically to the solution?

Research: The Foundation for the Advertising Campaign

5

Few successful campaigns can spring full-blown from the mind of the advertising planner. The products, the consumers, and the marketplace are simply too complex for campaign planners to rely totally on intuition and inspiration when developing an advertising campaign. And, the risks are too great as well. In spite of the massive use, and often misuse, of research, it is still one of the most helpful though misunderstood tools available to the advertising campaign planner.

The Reasons for Research

Research is needed and must be used to develop an effective advertising campaign. The first reason has already been alluded to above, that is, the increasing complexity of products, consumers, and the marketplace. A few years ago, when there was less competition, fewer markets, fewer media, fewer distribution systems, and less communication, it was possible for a marketer and an advertising agency to sit down and develop a simple advertising campaign just by writing some rather winning prose about the product, putting it in the form of an ad, and then placing it in the local newspaper. That was possible because the customers and prospects were usually the friends and neighbors of the marketer and agency people. They knew the market, and they knew the people they were trying to communicate with. In addition, the product was often simple and the demand was great. That's not the case today: now, the marketer and agency are often separated from the market not only in terms of space and time but also in terms of culture and social class. And there are many products competing not only in the same category but in the same market as well. In our complex society and increasingly complex marketplace, research is vital.

Second, the penalty of failure in today's marketplace is tremendous. Where once the advertiser risked only a few hundred dollars on a newspaper advertisement, now a single 30-second television commercial, broadcast nationally, can run well into six figures. With that sort of money involved, advertisers and agencies, as a matter of good business practice, must remove as much of the risk from advertising as possible.

Third, if one truly accepts the marketing concept, that is, to fill consumer needs and wants, it is necessary to conduct research simply to learn what those consumer needs and wants are. In order to move from a production-oriented to a marketing-oriented system, research, with its resulting consumer and market information is not only helpful, it's a must.

While the research background is vital to the planner in developing a successful advertising campaign, there is one caution. Research can provide information on where a product or service stands in the marketplace and what products and services consumers want and need. Research might even indicate the direction in which an advertising campaign should move. It can provide the information base on which to make various advertising campaign decisions, but it cannot dictate the actual method of accomplishing those goals. That direction depends on the skill and talent of the advertising campaign planner. Once the planner knows the situation, the direction, and the potential rewards, he or she must set the advertising objectives and then develop the advertising plan and implementation to achieve those goals.

Types of Research

The campaign planner is often faced with a multitude of advertising and marketing needs ranging from identification of present users to competitive themes being used in the marketplace, to methods of evaluating the advertising campaign after it is completed. In addition, there is often a bewildering number of methods and techniques of gathering information used by researchers. And, to complicate matters even more, the planner often faces research results computed or analyzed by rather sophisticated statistical techniques that the person who did the research may consider more important than the actual information being learned.

Since this is not a text on how to conduct research, we assume you, the campaign planner, are more interested in gathering the needed information than in being able to conduct the research in person. The key element for the planner is to understand the various research techniques used, be aware of the availability of information, and have a sufficient understanding of research analysis so that the needed information can be gathered in the least possible time and at the lowest possible cost.

Marketing Research vs. Advertising Research

The campaign planner typically uses two types of research in developing and evaluating an advertising campaign.

1. Marketing research—information on the market, competition, prospects, distribution, and pricing.
2. Advertising research—information directly related to the advertising campaign, normally in connection with the development, pre-testing, placement, and evaluation of the actual advertising campaign or materials.

The planner should keep these two differing kinds of research activities clearly in mind. Although both marketing and advertising research are needed to develop, implement, and evaluate an advertising campaign, there are several differences in what information is gathered, what sources are used, and the availability of the information needed. Market research is covered in this chapter. Advertising research is discussed in Chapter 6.

The Five-Step Advertising Campaign Research Plan

For most advertising campaigns including the development, testing, and evaluation of the plan, research in five specific areas is needed.

Prospect, market, product, and competitive research. Research in these areas involves gathering information to identify the target prospects for the product or service to be advertised; the size of the market; market location; distribution patterns; pricing; any product tests and/or evaluation; identification of competition and competitive products. This research deals with the development of information necessary to market the product or service whether or not advertising or another form of promotion is used. Generally, these are rather broad studies and often come from existing sources or data. These types of information and the various research tools used to obtain it are discussed later in this chapter.

Strategy development research. Research in this area deals with the sales message or type of appeal to be made to the target market. It may or may not include gathering additional target market information. That usually depends on the scope of market identification available from basic research. Generally (after the basic marketing research has been conducted), this is the first step in the development of the advertising campaign. The objective of all strategy development research is to identify the single strongest advertising sales message that can be developed from all alternatives. This is advertising research. It will be discussed in some detail in Chapter 6.

Advertising performance research. The specific goal of this research is to determine how well the advertising performed or is performing in the marketplace. Measurement is usually based on how well the advertising communicates with prospective consumers. Further, attempts to determine consumer reactions to the advertising may be made. Often, this type of research is called advertising pre-testing. It is discussed in detail in Chapter 9.

Media, media usage, and media placement research. Another type of advertising research is conducted to determine media distribution, media availability, usage of the media by the consumer population, and size of media audiences. The goal of this type of research is to optimize the advertising budget in terms of effectiveness and efficiency in reaching the target market with the advertising campaign messages. This will be covered in detail in Chapter 12.

Measurements of the effects of the advertising campaign. This is pure advertising research. It consists of activities and methods designed to evaluate the results of the advertising campaign among the target market. Often, this is the only research plan developed and specified by the advertising campaign planner and included in the outline of the campaign itself. Most other forms of marketing and advertising research previously discussed are used only to plan and implement the campaign. Measurement research, however, is used to evaluate what the campaign did or did not accomplish. Thus, it is quite different from the other types of advertising research. Measurement research will be covered in Chapter 14.

The planner must have a sound grasp of the entire research spectrum to be able to marshall all the information and material needed to successfully advertise a product even on the lowest level. While the areas and techniques may seem complex, the information on the following pages should provide a sound understanding of the various types of research.

Existing Product vs. New Product Research

While it might seem that the research task is already very complex, one additional caution should be made. The need for information to develop a campaign for a new product is often quite different from that required for an existing product or one that has already been marketed in some fashion. Both of them will be explained in the following section.

Developing a Research Plan

No matter what the product or service, where the market is located or the size of the campaign to be prepared, all research information gathering must start with a plan. Without a planned approach to research, costs in time and money mount quickly. In addition, the planner may find himself with too little or too much information on which to base a decision. While there are as many ways to develop a research plan as there are researchers, the outline that follows has worked quite well in providing a research base of information for the development of an advertising campaign. It is management oriented and can be used with any type of product or service and for any type of campaign anticipated.

A. Define the advertising problem.

B. Determine specifically how research can help solve the problem:
1. The data or particular information, i.e., target market, size of market, creative direction, message design, etc. needed to solve the problem.
2. The cost or time impact on the project to obtain or use the research.

C. Project the form in which the material will be presented or used in the campaign plan.

D. Determine what additional information is needed above what is already on hand.

E. List the alternative methods available to obtain the needed information and select the most effective and efficient ones:
1. Secondary research
2. Primary research

F. Estimate the cost of each form of research and weigh the cost against the potential value in the development of the advertising campaign.

G. Develop the final research plan or proposal.

This outline focuses directly on that material needed in the development of the advertising campaign. The campaign planner inevitably finds some information that, while valuable or interesting to know in the development of the plan, is just too costly to collect. The cost-benefit relationship between the need for information and the need for precise information must be weighed against the cost of obtaining that data or obtaining that precision. For example, it is quite unusual for an advertising campaign researcher to use a strict probability sample in a research study. The costs simply outweigh the potential benefits. The advertising planner is constantly making such trade-offs between the ideal and the practical.

As noted above, the first step in a research plan is to define the research problem. And, usually that's the key to a successful research study. If the information to be gathered is clearly stated, the alternatives usually become quite clear. The vague, loosely worded, imprecise problem statement causes most research problems. If the information cannot be defined clearly, consumers or marketers or retailers or any other research source cannot be expected to give clear, precise answers to questions. It's simple. A clear understanding and statement of the information provides a basis for a problem statement.

Three basic elements go into the makeup of a good research problem statement:

1. The information to be gathered must be measurable.
2. It must be relevant to the problem being considered.
3. The various pieces of information or knowledge to be gained must somehow be related.

A good example of a research problem statement follows:

> Sales of the 20 oz. size of Reckless Ralph's Window Cleaner have declined 10 percent in the past six months. Is the decline in sales due to a decline in the total category, the package size, or are sales being lost to another brand? If sales are being lost to another brand, which brand is it and why?

This problem statement clearly and concisely sums up what information is needed and offers some direction toward solution. The research problem is measurable. The questions are relevant to the problem. And the information requested is directly related to the overall problem. With this approach, the researcher can clearly identify the various sources of information needed and develop a sound research plan.

Three basic sources of information are used in the development of an advertising campaign plan: (a) secondary research, (b) primary research, and (c) observation. Generally, secondary research and observation are the basic methods of gathering information for products or services that are presently being marketed and advertised. Primary research is often used in planning the advertising to help in the introduction of a new product or the marketing of an existing product or service in a new area.

Identifying Prospects, Markets, and Competition for Existing Products or Services

Generally, advertising campaign planners work with products that are already on the market. New product development also tends to grow out of experience with existing lines. So, by understanding how and where various types of information for existing products are available, the planner can often develop information bases for almost any type of new product.

Types of Information Needed

Four types of information are needed about presently marketed products:

1. Information on consumers or present users
2. Basic market information
3. Information about the product or service to be advertised
4. Information on competition and competitors

Information on consumers or present users. Obviously, the best advertising prospects for a product or service are those who are already using or persons like them in some way. That is why research begins with present users. Generally, the planner needs to know who users are geographically, demographically, and psychographically; how they buy the product (one at a time or in multiple units); and when they buy it (in a particular season); etc.

Many other characteristics also must be defined. Where do users normally purchase the product and what price do they pay? How do they use the product and are they using it in familiar or unfamiliar ways? To what degree are users satisfied with the brand? Are they generally loyal to the brand or do they switch to other brands? Further, are there groups of heavy users, i.e., people who use more than the normal amount of the product? If so, who are they, where are they, why do they use such a disproportionate amount? Obviously, it is necessary to know how consumers feel about the brand, what information they have, how past advertising has affected them, and so on.

Of course, in developing a research plan, each brand will have different needs and may require different information. Generally, however, the planner wants as clear a profile of present users as possible in order to understand to whom advertising should be directed, where they are located, and what sales messages might best motivate them to continue using or perhaps to increase their usage of the brand.

For example, assume you are in the baby food business as Gerber Products is. From your research, you will want to learn as much as you can about how mothers feel about baby food, what they consider important, what they are concerned about, and so on. Knowing how mothers feel and how they use your products would be particularly helpful in developing advertising to keep present customers purchasing and almost as important in getting new mothers to start and stay with Gerber baby foods. (See Figure 5-1.)

The planner uses the profile of present customers and users to select and segment other population groups who might be likely prospects for the brand. By knowing present users, the planner should be able to expand the present user base by bringing new users to the brand and switching users of competitive brands.

Figure 5-1. Advertising Must Be Based on Information about Current and Potential Users

SOURCE: Courtesy Gerber Products Co.

Market information. In addition to knowing who present users are and who prospects might be, the planner needs to know something about the marketplace in which these consumers operate. The place to start is with the general economic conditions in the country or the area where the advertising campaign will be placed. For example, the planner should know if there is inflation or recession; the level of unemployment; consumer attitudes toward the economy, and so on. That will help define how the product fits in the overall scheme.

From this general view, the planner moves next to the product category in which the brand competes and learns as much as possible about that area. Information of this sort includes the total value of sales in the category, the category sales trends, and usage trends. That tells how the category is faring. Further, the planner needs to know information on such things as pricing and pricing stability, distribution patterns, and type of retailers who carry the product, as well as the general profile of persons who use a product in the category—their demographics, geographics, purchasing patterns and the like, if they are different from present customers. In short, the planner needs as clear a picture as possible of the total market for the particular product category and brand and the marketplace in which the brand is competing. For the specific brand, the planner needs to know the areas of and levels of distribution, types of retailers who stock, existing pricing patterns, forms and methods of discounts given retailers, type of sales force, and the like. This information is used to match the brand against the total market. Often, the standing of the brand in the market among both retailers and consumers dictates how the advertising campaign can be developed.

Information about the product or service to be advertised. The product's construction, contents, length of service, background, and its advantages and disadvantages when compared to competition—it is important to have all such information and to look at the brand from the consumer's view. The manufacturer of a brand may believe certain product ingredients are very important—for example, it has twice the amount of ingredient R compared to competition. If, however, these ingredients can't be translated into consumer benefits, they aren't truly important in terms of advertising potential. For purposes of the advertising campaign, the planner needs to gather as much information about the brand as possible and then compare it against competitive brands. This information should include more than just ingredients or manufacturing differences. Warranties, guarantees, product tests, previous advertising campaigns, and any psychological benefits that may have been built up over time also should be included.

Campbell Soup has obviously done a great deal of research on their products, as illustrated in the advertisement in Figure 5-2. Note how they have used several pieces of research information as a basis for their claim that "Soup is good food."

Information on competition and competitors. Advertising does not exist in a vacuum. It is necessary to know competitive products, their claims, distribution, pricing, customers, product strengths and weaknesses in order to develop the most effective advertising campaign possible. Only by knowing competition can the planner know what advertising may or may not be able to say.

One special note is important here. Competitors for a product or a brand are often more than just specific competitive brands in the category. There may be competition for sales from other categories as well. Thus, it is necessary to identify all general competition. For example, direct competition of a Florida resort might be other Florida resorts. But indirect and, perhaps, more important competition for the tourist dollar might be resorts in Mexico, the Caribbean, California, and other sunny spots. Going a step further, even less direct but perhaps as important competition for a Florida vacation might be the use of that money to purchase a new automobile, a new home, swimming pool, or a college education for the children. Thus, advertisers must look at all forms of competition for the money that would be spent to purchase their product or service and then attempt to relate to the most important ones. In a sense, all products and services in the marketplace are competing with one another for the consumer's limited funds. How the product is viewed and how the consumer can be led to view the product often are the responsibility of the advertising campaign planner.

From the description above, it should be clear that different products and different brands have different research needs. A specific list of information and materials is required in order to develop the most effective advertising plan. In some instances, the information may already be on hand. In others, it may be necessary to locate or generate the information prior to developing the advertising campaign. In the next section, we look at some of the most common sources of consumer, market, product, and competitive information for consumer products and where that information might be found.

Sources of Information

The campaign planner needs two basic kinds of information or material: (a) that which has already been gathered or exists in a form the planner may

Figure 5-2.   Base Your Research on Sound Product Information

YOU ALWAYS HAD A GOOD FEELING ABOUT SOUP. AFTER YOU READ THIS YOU'LL KNOW WHY.

Soup makes you feel good in so many ways. It's the wholesome food that satisfies your appetite and your spirit.

You know that when you've got to go somewhere on a cold windy night, a bowl of steamy Clam Chowder can stoke you up for the trip, and insulate you inside till you get there.

Or, when the midday sun is sweltering you, a bowl of refreshing, chilled Consommé (maybe with a salad and iced tea) tastes great and keeps you going through the day.

But did you know nutritionists are now finding out that nutrition-wise, soup is super. Three different sources support the goodness of soup.

Using data from one of the largest studies ever made on nutrition (conducted by Government health agencies), experts from leading universities identified differences in people's diets.* It was found that soup can be a significant part of a balanced and healthful diet.

And when compared to other foods in a Nutrient Density Rating System** used by nutritionists, many of the most popular soups come through with flying nutrients. In fact, some soups have more nutrients per calorie than other good foods you think are very nutritious. For instance, calorie for calorie, Campbell's Chicken Noodle Soup has more protein and thiamin than peanut butter, or rye bread.

In another way of rating soup, based on U.S. Department of Agriculture data, one 10 ounce serving of Campbell's Old Fashioned Vegetable Soup has more Vitamin A than 2 heads of lettuce, 12 ears of corn, or four tomatoes.

And soup is not only good for your body. It's good for your soul. When you come home from a hard day all frazzled, a heart-warming cup of zesty Minestrone can really unwind you. Because what could be more soothing than soup?

And so digestible. If you've got a little empty spot late at night, a bowl of delicious Mushroom Soup will hit the spot perfectly and let you sleep like a log.

So you can see, there's a good reason for the good feeling you get with soup. One of the many reasons why Soup is Good Food.

Campbell's
SOUP IS GOOD FOOD.

*As published in The American Journal of Clinical Nutrition, April, 1981
**Source: Hansen, R.G., Wyse, B.W., Sorenson, A.W., The Nutritional Quality Index of Foods, AVI Publishing Co., Inc., Westport, Conn. 1979
Note—Mean value sources for nutrient comparison: USDA Handbooks No. 8 and 456 and Campbell Soup Co.

SOURCE: Courtesy Campbell Soup Co.

use; and (b) that which must still be gathered or collected in some way. Existing information is called secondary information. Research based on this information is called secondary research. If the information is not available and requires a research program specifically designed to get it, that kind of research is called primary research. In most cases, secondary research is used in planning much of the advertising campaign for an existing product. Since information for new products is often not available, primary research is required. It will be discussed later.

Company records or company marketing intelligence. The prime source of information for a brand and, unfortunately, one of the most overlooked, normally consists of sales records, product shipments, customer reports, and the like. The amount of information that is gathered and stored by a company and can be useful to the advertising planner is amazing. The secret is to locate it, and the key to obtaining and using existing company information is a clear, concise description of what is needed and what form it is needed in. If the needed information can be adequately described to the accounting or financial people, it can usually be obtained. In addition to existing records, many organizations also have what they may call a marketing intelligence or marketing information system. This may consist of records and data on the product and product sales, competitive situations, customers, prospects, and the like.

Previous company research. In many cases a great deal of information can be taken from previous research studies conducted by the company for various reasons other than advertising. This may consist of consumer data, product tests, distribution information, and pricing tests. In some instances, this information is held in the marketing department and in others it may be found in a research department or even in the sales organization.

Syndicated market and consumer information. When specific research or information is not available for the individual brand, often generalized market and brand standing information may be purchased from organizations that gather and make this type of information available for a price. Some of these suppliers provide information that may be very general and include only such basic market data as the size of the total market, distribution patterns, geographic dispersion and the like. In other cases, the data may be brand specific and designed to provide just the information the planner needs to analyze the total market. In all instances, however, this data is gathered by an outside source, who usually also gathers the same data for other organizations and competitors as well and provides the information for a fee. Some of the major sources of syndicated market and consumer data are described in Figure 5-3.

Figure 5-3.   Major Sources of Syndicated Market and Consumer Data

Sales Marketing Areas, Inc. (SAMI)
This organization provides continuous measurement of sales and distribution of food and related products based on a computerized warehouse withdrawal technique. Measured are dollar volume and share of market data and reports are issued every four weeks. Base is approximately 28,000 individual items at over 400 chain and wholesaler warehouses plus rack jobbers. Information is available from 39 retail markets covering about 77 percent of the national food sales. In addition, SAMI offers an on-line interactive system to facilitate analysis by subscribers. In some selected supermarkets, scanner store sales and consumer purchase data are also gathered.

Market Research Corporation of America (MRCA)
MRCA provides continuous consumer diary reports of weekly purchase information from a national sample of 7,500 households. Each year, MRCA develops a menu census, the most comprehensive study of eating habits available in the country. This census data contains information on each menu served at each meal, including snack items and carry-out foods for each member of the panel. The census also indicates whether the item was used as a basic dish, an ingredient, or an additive; how the item was prepared; who was present at the meal; what was done with the leftovers; and so on.

Nielsen Retail Index
Nielsen provides a continuous national and regional measurement of consumer sales and sales-influential factors in retail outlets for numerous consumer packaged goods. The sales data is obtained every 60 days by auditing inventories and sales of carefully selected sample stores throughout the U.S. The audit data provides purchasers of the service with reports of total sales of the product class; sales of their own brand and that of competitive brands; retailer inventory and stock turn; retail and wholesale prices; retail gross margins; percentage of stores stocking; special manufacturer's deals

and local advertising. The data is gathered and provided for the entire U.S. market and for Nielsen-defined geographic regions by type of store ownership groups and sales volume groups. Nielsen subsidiaries and affiliated companies conduct store audits similar to those in the U.S. in approximately 20 foreign countries.

National Purchase Diary, Inc. (NPD)
NPD is the largest supplier of diary panel data in the U.S. The basic panel consists of some 13,000 families selected to be representative of the entire U.S. population. Regional breakouts are possible in areas representing as little as 5 to 8 percent of the total continental U.S. population from the data base. The company can also provide local market data in 35 separate areas of the country.

The data base is built on monthly diaries submitted by panel members. Participants list their purchases in 50 basic consumer-good product categories. NPD data are reported by selected demographics, regions, product ownership, and media habits. Panel data format permits analysis of sales and share trends by brand, package size, product type, and retail outlet. Special analyses can provide information about heavy vs. light users, users of a product class, dealing strategy, price ranges, and brand loyalty.

Simmons Research Associates
Simmons is a research firm that specializes in communications media and product usage research. The information form is an annual data base called Simmons Market Research Bureau Syndicated Media/Marketing Survey. This report contains audience measures for magazines, newspapers, radio, television, and outdoor media usage and attendance. Marketing data is also collected for 500 product categories, including brands purchased and volume used. Media and purchase data are then cross-tabulated by various demographic and psychographic variables to provide tables of product usage and media-related information.

Trade and association studies. Many trade journals and associations conduct surveys of their readers and collect data about their particular field or industry as part of an ongoing service. Many trade associations develop quite sophisticated data and information for their members, and they may be available if the advertiser company is a member of the group. In many specialized or limited fields or activities, the trade association may be the only source of market and/or marketing information.

The major problems in using data of this sort are locating it and then determining its accuracy. Information other than that collected by the government must have been gathered for a purpose and funded by an organization. Care should be taken in analyzing the data-gathering method, sample size, and age of the information when it is being used for a research base. Most marketing research texts have excellent lists of sources of this information. Additional sources are available at most libraries or through various trade organizations.

Census and/or registration data. One of the most overlooked sources of information about markets and consumers is that developed or gathered by various governmental organizations. Federal, state, and local governments are particularly good sources of data on almost any subject. The federal government publishes information through the Census Bureau on such topics as population, housing, retail trade, wholesale trade, service industries, manufacturers, agriculture, and transportation. In addition, states also publish census data on such factors as population, retail sales, income levels, and employment. Moreover, even cities and counties issue census data on population trends and projections, income, economic and planning studies, traffic counts, and demographic factors. Virtually any large library can provide most types of census data. Because new census material is constantly being published, a thorough study of existing information should be made before additional research is undertaken.

Libraries and universities. Public and private libraries provide an almost endless source of information on all possible topics. Perhaps of most interest to the advertising campaign planner is the fact that most librarians can and will provide sources to the researcher and in many cases will actually locate and provide the information at no cost.

Universities are also a good source of information for the advertising planner. Many advertising and marketing departments conduct ongoing research in various phases of marketing, advertising, and advertising campaign planning. Not only can they often provide leads on how to locate various types of information, but they may even have the information available.

Miscellaneous sources. The supply of data sources for the advertising campaign planner seems almost endless. Individual companies, market research organizations, and others often gather and publish data on various industries and various consumers. The same is true of advertising and marketing consultants, advertising agencies, and the like. A quick check of the telephone book and a few calls can often turn up additional sources or leads as to where information might be found. One of the best sources of information is scanning current marketing or research journals. This will often turn up leads particularly when a bibliography is included. In short, data is usually available. It takes only a bit of investigative interest and creativity to turn up the leads and the material.

Extrapolation of Data

Although it is true that data often exists for presently marketed products or services and that the real task is to determine what is needed and to gather it, that is not always the case. For example, even though the product may have been on the market for a long time, the campaign planner may decide to develop a new strategy or to advertise to another consumer segment or to suggest another use. In those cases, if the use is new and the consumer purchasing group isn't fully established, specific market, usage, or consumer data may not be available. Here is where the advertising campaign planner really gets to use some creativity in research by converting existing data into usable information in another area. This is called data extrapolation, and it is a very common practice in advertising and marketing research and should not be overlooked by the planner. Perhaps an example will illustrate the point.

Assume the planner's brand is in the coffee category. A new technique that has just been developed removes coffee acid without removing the caffeine. The resulting new brand tastes much smoother than other brands on the market. Of course, smooth taste is important to many coffee users, but the planner doesn't have much of a description of users of other brands other than knowing they exist. However, the planner can develop a profile of prospective new users from existing market information by extrapolating some existing data.

The planner starts with people who have demonstrated they dislike black coffee. That would seem to indicate there was something about the coffee taste they didn't like. What do people add to their coffee to change its taste? Some add cream or nondairy creamers, some add sugar. The assumption can be made that people who use nondairy creamers don't like the taste of black coffee. In other words, they may be looking for a smoother tasting coffee. Since people use sugar for many things in addition to changing the taste of coffee, cream or creamer users might provide a better answer as to whom prospects might be. Since nondairy creamers is a large market, the information on who purchases and uses them should be available. Obviously, not all of them might be prospects, but the planner can estimate a logical number who might—that is, the extrapolated market for a smoother tasting coffee.

This is just one way existing market data can be used in developing data and information that can be helpful in the planning of an effective advertising campaign. The extrapolation of data is limited only by the ability and creativity of the person seeking the information. Research, just like advertising strategy and advertising executions, can be a very creative field.

Using Marketing Data to Determine Market Position

After information about the market, the consumer, and the competition has been gathered, the next step is to develop some method of identifying the brand's position in the marketplace. This is particularly important when the brand has varying levels of sales or penetration in markets across the country. Advertising and marketing people use a system of indices to illustrate the standing of the product in various markets: a category-development index (CDI) and a brand-development index (BDI), both of which are computed against the all-commodity volume (ACV) in the particular type of market. The calculation of these indices provides convenient numbers that help identify the best markets or the proportion percentage of distribution for individual products or services. All-commodity volume gives the total amount of sales in a given category. For products sold in food stores, for example, sales of all food stores would comprise the all-commodity volume. Because a small number of food stores often generates a large share of total food store sales, it is possible to achieve a high percentage of distribution of the ACV in a disproportionately small number of stores.

For example, if total sales of canned tuna fish in Tulsa are 2,000 cans per month, that would be the ACV, or total number of cans of tuna sold. Further assume that the sales by each chain by month were as shown in Table 5-1.

The ACV is 2,000 cans of tuna fish sold each month. Yet, these sales are not equally divided among the chains in the market nor among the individual stores. For example, Chain A has only 12 stores, yet sells 850 cans of tuna per month, an average of 70.8 cans per store per month. On the other hand, Chain D has 23 stores and sells 154 cans per month, or an average of 6.7 cans per store per month. Closer examination probably would show that sales by individual store are not equal either. Some stores may sell much tuna, others almost none.

Table 5-1.   Sales by All-Commodity Volume Index

Chain	Number of stores	Number of cans of tuna sold	Percent of ACV
A	12	850	42.5
B	16	420	21.0
C	19	180	9.0
D	23	154	7.7
E	4	103	5.2
All others	116	293	14.6
Total	190	2,000	100.0

A company that markets tuna obviously wants to get as wide a distribution as possible to take advantage of its advertising. By obtaining distribution in Chains A and B, whose 28 stores account for only 14.8 of the 190 stores in the market, a marketer would have distribution in stores doing 63.5 percent of the ACV. This instance is not at all unusual. In some product categories, 60 percent or more ACV distribution can be achieved in less than 30 percent of the retail outlets across the country.

Category- and brand-development indices are calculated in a similar manner. For the CDI, total sales of the category may be indexed against sales for a certain geographic region or type of store. In a product category such as soft drink mixes, for example, the category development index may be quite high in the Midwest, say, 130 (Index = 100), while somewhat lower in the Southwest, e.g., 89. Here, the CDI calculation is based on the percentage of total sales that occur in each geographic region.

The brand-development index is the comparison of brand sales indexed against total product sales calculated on a geographic or other basis. In the above example, Brand A might have a brand-development index of 125 in the Southwest, indicating that sales are very good in that region. This, however, would be offset to a certain extent because the CDI for that area is rather low. The use of these shorthand indices helps to better identify the present sales or potential market for a brand or category. They are widely used by commercial research organizations.

A major factor in any market analysis is the sales trend for the category or brand. Trend lines that show patterns of sales over several years are developed. Five-year trends are usually best because frequently there are wide fluctuations in the marketplace in one- or two-year periods. Trend lines are especially important for products that have shown consistent growth or decline for a number of years. Being able to spot a trend can often be very helpful in planning the campaign.

Identifying Prospects, Markets, and Competition for New Products or Services

As was stated in the previous section, the largest number of advertising campaigns are created for existing products or services. However, the most exciting task for the advertising campaign planner is often developing the plan for a new product or brand to enter a new market. While new product advertising campaigns may be the most exciting, they are also the most difficult and often the riskiest for planner and product because of the lack of information on which to make campaign decisions. With new products, services, or brands, there usually isn't adequate information on which to make the necessary estimates or evaluations. Thus, the campaign planner may be forced to rely on intuition and management judgment. The alternative course is some form of marketing research study. The true problem with new product research isn't that it can't be done, but that the cost and the time for the research are high and that consumers often are unable to verbalize what they might do in new purchasing situations.

As with research for existing products, there are two basic ways to gather information on new products: (a) secondary and (b) primary research.

Secondary Research

The easiest and quickest source of information is through secondary research. The problem, though, is that if the product is totally new, there is usually little published information available. As would be done with existing products, the first step is to check company records and market intelligence information. If the manufacturer or marketer has been planning the new product for some time, a file usually has been built up so there is some previous research information. With any new product, all company sources should be checked before going on to other information.

Other major sources of secondary information are the same as those listed for existing products. Also, research organizations in many major cities often will do library or data searches on a product category for a fee. In addition, major research organizations have data files of previous research studies they have done in categories which might be of value. For example, a company planning to enter the pet food drink category might find that some organizations have gathered data on that product area and might make their findings available for a price.

The alternative to finding existing information is to do extrapolations from other data. As was illustrated in the previous example on the new type of smooth coffee, a planner may be able to extrapolate market information from data that has been gathered for another purpose or might be similar to the category the company plans to enter.

A caution here on both previously gathered and extrapolated data: use this information only as a general guide for planning. The planner should be sure to check the date of the material and the purpose for which it was gathered. The marketplace changes rapidly. It is possible to take the giant leap to error by using out-of-date or inconclusive secondary data.

Primary Research

Primary research is original research carried out to gather specific information about the problem being studied. Usually, primary research is conducted when existing information is not available, the existing information is suspect, or additional specific information is needed.

Primary research may be carried out for either an existing product or a new product. The comments and suggestions that follow apply equally to both.

Four general types of primary research are used in advertising campaign planning. They are: exploratory or qualitative, primarily used to better define the problem, the market, or the consumer; descriptive or quantitative, the most widely used type of research in advertising campaign planning; experimental, widely used in new product research that consists of laboratory tests in which a cause-and-effect relationship is sought; and tracking or performance evaluation, often used to evaluate the effects of an advertising campaign (see Chapter 13).

No matter which type of research is used, data is usually gathered either by observation or by survey research. In observation data gathering, consumers or users are observed as they shop, evaluate products or services, make purchasing decisions, or are otherwise involved with the product or service under study. Survey data gathering entails asking a number of customers or prospects questions about the product or service or having them keep a diary of their purchases, product use, or other measurable activity.

Exploratory or qualitative research. Exploratory research is undertaken when the information needed is to be directional or diagnostic. Such research is usually done with fairly small groups of people, and the sampling is conducted on a quota or availability basis.

Definitive conclusions usually cannot be drawn from exploratory or qualitative research. Instead, an attempt is made to get a general impression of the market, the consumer, or the product. Two types of qualitative research can be quite helpful in the exploratory stages of the campaign. These are intensive data gathering and the use of "projective" techniques.

1. Intensive data gathering. The informal research approach consists of gathering information or data through discussions with interested groups or individuals such as consumers, prospects, and retailers who have knowledge about the product or service. An excellent source of information is often the sales force who are in direct contact with consumers and resellers.

   A more formal approach would be a more systematic method of data gathering such as conducting focus groups or doing individual "depth interviews."

   Group interaction of focus groups usually generates a great deal of insight into the research problem and can lead to more detailed methods of information gathering.

   An alternative intensive data-gathering approach is the "depth interview." Interviews are conducted in the same way as those in a focus group, except they are done on an individual basis. Respondents are asked to discuss the product, the problem, or the situation. By asking carefully structured questions, the interviewer tries to probe the deeper feelings of the respondent rather than simply expose surface opinions, which may be readily offered.

   Both focus groups and depth interviews are best carried out by a trained researcher. Untrained persons may obtain general information through focus-group discussion, but errors may creep in or the group may be inadvertently led to a false conclusion unless the person directing the questioning or analyzing the data has had adequate previous experience with this form of data gathering.

2. Projective techniques. Many forms of projective techniques may be used. All have the same basic approach: the person being interviewed is asked to involve himself or herself in a situation or experience in which he or she "projects" feelings and experiences about the product, brand, or problem set up by the interviewer. The assumption made in these projective techniques is that the person being interviewed, by involving himself or herself in a situation, will disclose underlying feelings, thoughts, and desires about the problem or situation which might not otherwise be revealed in direct questioning.

   Projective research projects can take many forms, from word association to role playing to cartoon completion to Thematic Apperception Tests. Only skilled, experienced researchers are capable of developing successful projective research instruments. If this methodology is contemplated, a commercial research organization should be consulted.

Exploratory or qualitative research should be used by the advertising campaign planner in the first stages of the development of the plan.

Qualitative research is generally inexpensive, since it can be done with small numbers of consumers, with selection based on a quota or availability sample. This type of research is often conducted to determine general trends or to identify areas that need further exploration.

Qualitative research may be sufficient to answer the campaign planner's questions. The information gathered, however, because of the limited sampling methodology, is subject to wide variations in reliability and validity. If exploratory or qualitative primary research is to be used as the basis of the campaign, this should be referenced in the campaign plan.

Quantitative or descriptive research. Quantitative or descriptive research is usually primary research. The results can be projected to various portions of the marketing universe, and the laws of statistical probability can be applied to lend support to or cause rejection of the findings.

Boyd, Westfall, and Stasch differentiate between exploratory (qualitative) and descriptive (quantitative) studies as follows:

> Descriptive studies differ from exploratory studies in the rigor with which they are designed. Exploratory studies are characterized by flexibility, while descriptive studies attempt to obtain a complete and accurate description of a situation. Formal design is required to ensure that the description covers all phases desired. Precise statements of the problem indicates what information is required. The study must then be designed to provide for the collection of this information. Unless the study design provides specified methods for selecting the sources of information (sample design) and for collecting the data from these sources, the information obtained may be inaccurate or inappropriate.
>
> Descriptive data are commonly used as direct bases for marketing decisions. After analyzing the data, the investigators attempt to predict the result of certain actions.[1]

Thus, qualitative or exploratory research is used primarily to give direction to the advertising campaign planner, while quantitative or descriptive research is used in choosing between alternatives or in decision making.

Quantitative or descriptive research is also distinguished by the method in which the data is gathered. The two types are observation and survey. Because the first is not widely used in advertising campaign planning, only a brief overview will be given. More emphasis will be placed on survey research methodology.

---

1. Harper W. Boyd, Jr.; Ralph Westfall; and Stanley F. Stasch, *Marketing Research: Text and Cases*, 4th ed. (Homewood, IL: Richard D. Irwin, 1977), p. 48.

1. Observation. In quantitative research, the activities or habits of persons in the marketplace are observed either personally or through some mechanical means. Because historical data is gathered according to what the given person was observed doing or had done in the past, many researchers believe predictions of what that person might do in the future based on observation are difficult to make.

   Another form of observation is the so-called pantry check made in consumers' homes. Pantries are checked to determine the various brands that have been purchased and the amount of product on hand. By correlating this observed information with the demographic characteristics of the respondents, the present users (or general target market) for the product can be identified.

   Observation is also used by several commercial research organizations such as Nielsen or Audits & Surveys. These groups visit retail outlets and make shelf audits of products. They might, for example, gather data on what products are being stocked, what brands are available, what sizes are available, prices, and out-of-stock. This information is used by the advertiser to determine his or her position in the marketplace.

   Observation can be helpful to the advertising campaign planner, but it is usually quite expensive since a large number of observations is required to develop a conclusive answer.

2. Survey. Survey research is the most common method of primary research data gathering used for advertising campaigns. As the name implies, data is obtained through a survey of present or prospective consumers of the product or service. The usual goal is to obtain information necessary to develop a profile of the target audience or to determine the most effective advertising message to be used.

   Survey research methodologies differ according to the method of data gathering employed. The most common forms are personal interviews, mail surveys, consumer panels, and telephone interviews.

   a. Personal interviews. Personal interviewing may take many forms ranging from traditional door-to-door canvassing to intercepts in shopping malls and laundromats or outside food and drugstores. The key to success in personal interviewing is to find situations in which respondents have the time available to answer questions. The usual data-gathering form is a series of questions, scales, evaluations, or other devices that allow the respondent to express his or her ideas, concerns, or opinions. Interviews in the home may last an hour or more, while interviews with persons interrupted while shopping, such as in a mall intercept, must be confined to five or ten minutes. There is literally no limit to the type of data that can be gathered. In each case, the result depends on the kind of information desired and the situation in which the interview occurs.

The primary advantages of the personal interview are the opportunities to probe, to ask followup questions, and to use examples or samples of the product or advertising material. The major disadvantages are the extremely high cost of personnel and diminishing cooperation, particularly in door-to-door calls.

b. Mail. Much useful information can be gathered through a mail survey. Respondents tend to give more complete answers since the interview is relatively anonymous. Respondents also can indicate answers to questions that might not be readily available in a personal or telephone interview. Since no one is there to give directions, the questionnaire form must be made as easy as possible to follow with primarily closed-end questions. The questionnaire may be any length and may cover almost any subject.

Data gathering by means of the mail questionnaire is relatively inexpensive. The main costs are for the mailing list, the questionnaire form, and postage. A nominal reward is sometimes included in a direct mail questionnaire to encourage response.

Mail questionnaires ordinarily have a fairly low return rate. A 30 to 40 percent response to a mail questionnaire is considered normal. Obtaining a return of 60 to 70 percent is exceptional. All results, however, depend on the product interest, the quality of the questions, and the mailing list.

c. Consumer panels. Pre-formed or existing panels of consumers have long been used for research data gathering. A number of commercial panels offers services that may be purchased. One example is National Family Opinions, Inc. (NFO).

Data gathering from consumer panels has the same disadvantage as do mail surveys in terms of time required. Response rates, however, often reach near 100 percent because the panels are established groups and are rewarded for participation. The representativeness of panels may be questionable because they answer many research questions during the course of a year.

The major advantage of panel data gathering is that the information obtained is more complete and more detailed. The panel is accustomed to furnishing information through questionnaires and tends to be quite cooperative. Based on total research expenditure, cost per response by a panel is usually lower than in most other types of interviews.

d. Telephone interviews. An increasingly important method of data gathering is use of the telephone. With the advent of Wide Area Telephone Service (WATS) lines, interviewing throughout the country can now be done from a central location that provides complete control over the interview. Costs of WATS line interviews are relatively low compared to other forms of data collection, and when time for data gathering is considered, this is probably the lowest cost of all research methods.

Telephone data-gathering usage has increased as samples have been improved. Originally, telephone samples were limited to persons whose names were listed in telephone directories. Newer systems of random digit dialing now make all connected telephones part of the sample frame, and every telephone home is a potential respondent, including the approximately 20 percent or more unlisted numbers.

Telephone interviews are excellent for obtaining a relatively small amount of information from a large number of people. Because contact is by voice, only certain types of questions may be asked. Questions that require visuals or thorough understanding of a complex question are not practical. A telephone interview may last 10 to 15 minutes with many closed-end questions, that is, questions for which a list of answers is supplied or made available. Some questionnaire callers have kept people on the line for a half-hour or more. Surprisingly, telephone respondents may provide information they would not ordinarily give in a personal interview. Apparently, the telephone offers a certain amount of anonymity.

The major advantages of telephone interviews are low cost, a complete sample frame, the ability to call any geographic area (with WATS lines), and very rapid data gathering and reporting. Moreover, the telephone is the only practical method of conducting a coincidental survey, a study which is conducted at the same time the advertising is appearing.

Telephone surveys do have disadvantages, however. Answers usually must be shorter and not as in-depth as those obtained through other methods. There is no opportunity to use props or other materials that might help explain the questions or to display package designs, advertisements, or other items that the subject must see to be able to respond to. Despite these disadvantages, more emphasis will likely be placed on telephone-data gathering, particularly as the costs of personal interviews increase.

Experimental research. Experimentation is a type of laboratory or otherwise controlled research in which a cause-and-effect relationship is sought. Strict controls are employed so that the variable that causes the effect can be identified. Experimentation is used only on a selective basis, since it is very difficult to control all marketing variables.

Several research organizations offer forms of experiments to gather data. One of the best known is Yankelovich, which has developed a testing method for new product introductions.

The most common form of experimental research in advertising occurs in the use of a test market for new products or in new advertising campaigns. Here, two or more individual markets are matched as closely as possible according to such marketing variables as population, category sales, and income. Using these matched markets, an advertising campaign is run in one market (or set of markets) and not in the others. Then the results are observed. An alternative method is to use differing advertising campaigns in a given set or sets of markets and to observe the differences that result. A third method is to use media weight tests. Here, varying levels of media promotion are used in matched test markets. Again, because other variables are held as nearly constant as possible, the influence of the media can be evaluated in terms of such effects as attitude changes and awareness.

Experimentation, particularly in advertising, is an expensive method of obtaining information, since the effects may not be immediate. It is widely used for new products, however, e.g., to test the viability of the product on a small scale or to test various advertising or marketing alternatives prior to a major national introduction.

Sampling for data gathering. The success of any research design depends on the sample selected for data gathering. The major objective is to make sure that respondents to be interviewed are representative of the entire target population. It is important to determine who is to be sampled, the procedure to be used for selection of the sample, and the size of the sample.

1. Who is in the sample? Persons to be interviewed must be representative of the target population. If a planner wants to learn about cat food, owners of cats should be interviewed. In advertising and marketing research, this is done through screening questions such as, "Do you or your family own a cat?" Those who do not have a cat would not be included in the study; they would automatically be screened out of the sample.

    The research sampling frame for an advertising campaign study can be easily defined. It may be as broad as "all women 18 to 49 years of age with children in the home under 12 years of age," or it might be as restrictive as "those persons owning canaries in the state of Idaho." The sampling frame depends on the type of specific data to be gathered and a general idea of the information sought. A common definition used as a sample frame is "present users of a product category or brand."

The key point in any sampling plan is to state clearly and concisely in advance the sample universe. If this is done, no confusion will arise as to whether an individual selected for interviewing is qualified.

2. Sample selection. There are two types of sampling techniques. Probability samples are those in which every known unit in the universe has an equal probability of being selected for the research. For example, if the universe were defined as drugstores in the city of Dallas with sales in excess of $1,000,000 annually, a complete list of potential stores could be developed from various sources such as tax receipts and licenses. Knowing the names and locations of all the drugstores in Dallas which fit the qualifications makes possible the development of a probability sample such that each store has an equal chance of being selected.

Probability samples are used when the number of units to be measured is fairly small; a complete list of the items in the universe exists (such as all drugstores in Dallas); the cost per interview depends on the location of the items; and the need exists for precisely measuring the risk of sample error. Because of these conditions, the use of probability sampling in advertising and marketing research is quite limited unless the universe can be very precisely defined.

A nonprobability sample does not provide every unit in the universe with an equal or known chance of being included in the sample frame. If, in the above example, the restriction might be relaxed from stores doing over $1,000,000 in Dallas to simply those drugstores in North Dallas that are high volume and which are located within easy access of the freeway system, this then would not be a probability sample. It would be a nonprobability sample because not all drugstores would be included in the sample frame. For example, large stores that might qualify in every other respect might not be located near the freeway system or might not be considered high volume by the researcher, and so on.

Nonprobability samples are widely used in marketing and advertising research because, in many categories, no listing of the complete universe is available. Such samples are also used when the costs for a true probability sample are prohibitive because (a) of geographic dispersion, (b) only a general estimate of the data is needed, (c) there is a possibility of obtaining a larger sample with a decrease in the magnitude of error, (d) the nature and size of the bias can be estimated fairly accurately.

Most advertising and marketing research studies are of the nonprobability type—for example, the planner doesn't really know the true universe of users of the product or competitive products. The dispersion of product users is normally great, particularly for those sold on a national basis. Error can be estimated based on sample size, and the amount of bias can also be determined. The primary reason for non-probability sampling in advertising and marketing research is simply the cost of obtaining data. Once again, the advertising campaign planner is faced with the cost-benefit trade-off. Planners are usually willing to trade some validity and reliability to avoid the large costs entailed in developing a true probability sample.

3. Sample size. One of the most difficult tasks in planning or evaluating primary research is determining the sample size required to achieve a given level of confidence. Statistical techniques are available for developing confidence levels of probability samples. The problem becomes more complex with nonprobability studies because the true universe is usually unknown.

   A number of rules of thumb exist for determining sample sizes that are helpful to the advertising campaign planner. While they lack precision, such rules do give general approximations of sample sizes for various types of nonprobability studies. In data gathering such as depth interviews or focus groups, for example, most major ideas or answers concerning a product or service will be verbalized after the first 30 or so persons have been interviewed. This happens because most consumers have the same basic, general ideas about various products and services. Therefore, when about 30 persons have answered, repetition of the major ideas begins to mount rapidly. Similarly, interviews with 100 to 200 users of products or services, given a standard questionnaire in a limited geographic area, will tend to indicate the general attitudes of the population. After 100 interviews, reliability tends to mount as more and more respondents give the same answers to the questions being asked. For a regional study covering several cities or a few states, a sample of 300 to 400 qualified respondents is normally considered to be sufficient. A sample of 1,000 to 1,200 qualified consumers, selected according to a probability sample, will generally reflect the opinions and feelings of the national population on most subjects. While these sample sizes are only estimates, they have been proved to the extent that only in unusual circumstances will major errors occur.

4. Problems. Four major problems are usually encountered with sample respondents: not-at-home, refusals, respondent bias, and interviewer bias.

   Not-at-home and refusals create more problems in a probability sample than in a nonprobability one. For a group to constitute a true probability sample, the actual persons selected in advance must be interviewed. Obviously, this is not always possible. Steps must be taken, therefore, to select a large enough original sample so that substitutions for nonrespondents can be made without destroying the representative makeup of the original sample.

The biases of both the respondent and interviewer are most difficult to control. Respondent bias usually appears when the person is truly anxious to assist the interviewer and the respondent often gives answers that do not reflect his or her true feelings. In some cases, respondents, in an attempt to appear knowledgeable, give answers to questions on which they have no information.

Interviewer bias usually comes about when the interviewer, through either the question itself or the manner in which it is asked, indicates the type of answer that would be most acceptable or is generally regarded as correct. The advertising campaign planner should be aware of the bias problem, particularly if the sample is small, or if the interviewers are not professionally trained, or if the interviewers or respondents have strong feelings about the particular subject under study.

Summary   Research isn't a cure-all. It won't make a bad campaign a good one. But it can provide important information about the size and makeup of the potential market for the product, and it is the key to advertising campaigns as *planned* efforts. This chapter reviewed the basic kinds of information needed and how to use them effectively.

Case for Discussion: "POPCORN!"

In March of 1981, the newly formed market research team at "POPCORN!," a Boston-based subscription television service, was given its first assignment. It was to estimate demand for the company's product in 1986 and, if the resulting prediction warranted it, recommend changes to improve the outlook.

"POPCORN!" began operation in Boston in late 1979. It is one of the many subscription television services (STVs) that have sprung up in the nation's major metropolitan areas (Chicago, Los Angeles, Washington, and Dallas, among others). In most cases, STV developed as a predecessor to cable television. Although many parts of the country are already wired for cable television, the process of awarding local franchises to operators and subsequent hookup is a slow one, especially in large metropolitan areas, where each suburban community may select its own cable service.

STV developed in response to the growing interest in cable television and its multiplicity of programming. Many consumers want an alternative to traditional network television fare *now*. If cable is not available in their area, what are the alternatives? STV services like "POPCORN!" offer programming similar to that of such cable networks as Home Box Office (HBO) and Showtime. This is primarily "movie television," programming consisting mainly of first-run motion pictures, along with occasional sports and musical events.

Most STV services broadcast using a "scrambled" frequency. The frequency can be picked up by any television set within the broadcast area. Subscribers are given a decoder box that is attached to their television. When the decoder is activated, the signal is "unscrambled" and subscribers can watch the STV programs.

"POPCORN!" charges a one-time installation fee of $47 and a monthly subscription fee of $20. It currently has 24,500 subscribers throughout the Boston metropolitan area (1.4 percent of all Boston TV households). Subscribers receive a monthly program guide and are eligible for bonus gifts for referring new subscribers.

Boston is the nation's fifth largest market area, with 2.48 percent of all U.S. TV households.[1] Several suburban communities, including Melrose, Everett, Revere, Chelsea, and Belmont, have already awarded cable franchises. Most of the metropolitan area, however, will not have cable available for two to three more years.

---

1. A. C. Nielsen Co., September 1975.

"POPCORN!" had previously developed a description of the "typical" subscriber family based on the results of response cards filled out by subscribers at the time of installation:

> A young couple (35–45 years old) with one or more children living at home, their income in the upper middle range ($20,000–$50,000). They are heavy television viewers, watching an average of four hours per day.

This description also fits the average cable television viewer.[2]

In a preliminary meeting of the research team held to discuss the new assignment and determine a course of action, Meyer Terry, an analyst, summarized the situation:

> Clearly, our main focus, since we're looking at 1986, will be a city that's wired for cable. I've talked to council members from most of the metro communities and they're all expecting cable by fall of 1985 at the latest. Downtown will be wired by then too. So, what we've got to determine is who'll want us then, if anyone does.

Another team member, Carla Douglas, spoke up:

> I've visited some of the cable companies in the suburbs. Their pricing will be a big factor. Right now, they're offering basic service at $7.50 to $15.00. HBO is another $7.50. So, that's between $15.00 and $22.50 for a movie channel *and* all the basic community, sports, news, and weather channels.

"You know," Dario Thomas, a third team member, said, "we didn't have a lot of subscribers in those cable areas to begin with. I think they were waiting for their area to be wired. Most of those that we did have have since disconnected. That could be a key to our prediction."

Terry asked, "Has anyone seen any figures on how successful cable has been in those communities? Are most people having their homes connected to the system, and are they going for extras like HBO along with the basic programming?"

After some additional discussion, the team decided they needed answers to the following questions in order to make their prediction and recommendations:

1. Do our present subscribers like our service? What complaints do they have?
2. How do our subscribers feel about our price?

---

2. *Advertiser Pocket Guide to Cable Communications* (Chicago: J. Walter Thompson Co., February 1981).

3. In the communities with cable, what kind of penetration does cable have?
4. Are cable viewers buying the extra services?
5. How do cable viewers feel about its pricing?
6. What kind of people are turning down cable? Why?
7. Why have former "POPCORN!" subscribers dropped us? Have they taken something else instead?
8. What do cable viewers like most about cable? Least?

"POPCORN!" management wanted to review the team's findings in mid-April, which gave them four weeks to work. All research was to be handled by the department, and costs were to be kept low. The five-member team was very excited, seeing this project as a chance to demonstrate the strength of research and an opportunity for them to get a better "feel" for the consumer.

Questions

1. List any possible primary and secondary sources for each of the team's questions. In each case, which source would be most effective? Why? Which source would be most efficient if the time limit were two weeks? three months?

2. What competitors (other than cable television) might have an impact on the team's recommendation? What information would be needed regarding these competitors?

3. In cases where you have recommended use of primary sources (no. 1, above), is a probability sample necessary?

4. Based on the questions and the team's discussion, do you foresee any bias problems?

5. In addition to the areas identified in their questions, are there other topics the team might want to explore before making their recommendation?

⑥ Advertising Strategy Research

After the basic information has been gathered on the marketplace, the consumer, the product or service to be advertised, competition or competitors, and other basic marketing information, the next step is to start the physical development of the advertising campaign. That starts with the "what" the advertiser plans to say about the product or service to be advertised. That is then followed by the information needed on media or where to place the advertising, and then the evaluation of the effect of the advertising, and so on. Charles Ramond has suggested that three steps are required in each of the areas of campaign development. (See Table 6-1.)

The market research that has been completed should provide the second decision in Table 6-1: to whom should the advertising be addressed or who is the target audience? Following that, the next step is to determine what to say. That involves, as Ramond calls it, "theme or copy platform research." Planners call it advertising strategy research.

Table 6-1. Steps in Campaign Development

To make this decision	One must choose a	Using techniques variously known as
What to say	Theme, copy platform	Concepts tests, positioning studies
To whom	Target audience	Market segmentation studies
How to say it	Copy, commercial execution	Copy research, commercial tests
How often	Frequency of exposure	Studies of repetition
Where	Media plan	Media research models, audience studies
How much to spend	Budget level	Sales analysis, marketing models

SOURCE: Charles Ramond, *Advertising Research, the State of the Art* (New York: Association of National Advertisers, 1976), pp. 3–4.

Some Definitions   Some definitions are needed at this point.

1. Advertising objectives. A clearly stated, measurable end result of an advertising message or messages. Usually the objective is measured in terms of a change in awareness, preference, conviction, or other communication effect.

2. Advertising strategy. The formulation of an advertising message that communicates the benefit or problem solution characteristics of the product or service to the target market. It is generally developed for use in the mass media.

3. Advertising execution. The physical form in terms of art, illustration, copy, music, etc., in which the advertising strategy is presented to the target market to achieve the advertising objective(s).

These are the major terms used in this text. They will be referred to often.

Advertising Research to Develop the Advertising Strategy   Once the general market for the product, service, or brand is known, the next step is to determine what advertising message; i.e., what advertising strategy will most likely influence the target market to consider the product or service for purchase? That's the "what to say" about the brand, which is the most important advertising decision a campaign planner can make. Unless the message is correct, the media used to carry the message or even the amount of investment made cannot assure success. The development of the advertising strategy is where the planner usually succeeds or fails in the overall development of the effective campaign. Some of the more common research methods used to provide a sound base for the development of an advertising strategy are explored here.

Research among Present Users

As with market research, advertising research activities for strategy development can be divided between those for existing and new products. While some of the techniques are similar, the approaches differ.

Generally, the objective of the research needed to develop an advertising strategy for an existing product is to learn why present users purchase and use the brand or why other users purchase competitive products. The planner needs to determine, as accurately as possible, why various purchasing decisions are made and then match those purchasing decision points against the various brands. This is not an easy task. What consumers purchase is fairly easy to determine. *Why* they do so is much more difficult. Often, even purchasers don't know the true reason why they prefer a certain brand over others. Even more difficult is to learn what would likely encourage them to switch to another brand. This is very true for commonly purchased, low-risk products such as beer, detergents, canned foods, and even bar candy. Consumers simply don't go through a deep mental process in determining which brand in a product category to buy. They have images in their minds of certain brands, they may remember a few catch phrases or even recognize the label among a host of others, but when asked why they purchased Detergent A over Detergent B, they often are hard-put to come up with an answer. In spite of these difficulties, the advertising planner must have some guidance in developing an advertising strategy. And that guidance can only come from consumers. Obviously, Dove has done its research homework with consumers. (See Figure 6-1.) By first talking with users, they are now able to give prospective users sound, valid reasons why they should try Dove.

While there are many ways of gathering information for strategy development, five basic approaches are widely used. These are (1) focus groups, (2) perceptual or brand mapping, (3) usage studies, (4) motivation research, and (5) benefit segmentation. Each is briefly described below. More information on any of these methods can be found in most market or advertising research texts.

Focus groups. As discussed in Chapter 5, focus groups are comprised of individuals who are asked questions about a particular product. The purpose is to determine what is important to them, what is unimportant to them, and how they make a purchase in that product category. Often, the focus group mixes users of one brand with users of competitive products. The attempt here is to learn why purchasers of one product are different from users of competitive products and to determine what they consider to be the key benefits they receive from the brand. Generally, focus groups provide only broad, general ideas or provide general direction that may be pursued through other forms of quantitative research described previously.

Perceptual or brand mapping. In an effort to understand how consumers position various brands in their minds and to learn more about how consumers feel about brands in a category, researchers use an approach that requires participants to evaluate existing brands. It is called perceptual or brand mapping because it requires consumers to identify how they feel about or perceive various products in terms of certain benefits or attributes.

A five- or seven-point rating scale is constructed using bipolar adjectives that might apply to the product or the product category. (In some in-

Figure 6-1.   Matching the Product to the Reasons for Purchase

Figure 6-2.   Rating Scale for Perceptual Mapping

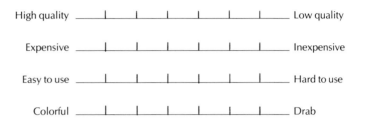

stances, the scale is used to determine which benefits or attributes are most important in the brand decision first and then the comparison is made.) For example, the scale might look like the grid in Figure 6-2. The respondent then marks the position on the scale for the product being studied.

These adjectives may use any attributes that are considered important to either the users or the marketer. Often these terms come from the results of focus group sessions where various product benefits and attributes have been discussed.

The idea of mapping is to determine how the brand relates to competition on these various benefits or features. This is done by constructing a two-dimensional matrix that compares the scores of the brand being investigated against those of a competitor or group of competitors. Figure 6-3 is an example.

In Figure 6-3, Brands J, M, R, and Z are compared in regard to the

Figure 6-3.   Two-Dimensional Matrix for Mapping

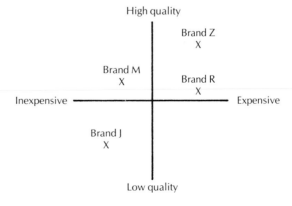

attributes of high or low quality and expensive or inexpensive price. The researcher averages respondents' scores and plots them on a grid. The result is a visual picture of how consumers view the various products or brands. In this example, Brand R is viewed as being expensive but of not very high quality while Brand Z seems to be equated with relatively high price and high quality. This type of mapping approach is quite helpful in spotting weaknesses in one's brand or those of competitors. It is also beneficial in determining what perceptions consumers have or don't have about a brand. It should be noted, the reactions of consumers may or may not be correct. That isn't important. It's how they think or how they believe that is the key element in this research because it is the basis on which they buy.

Usage studies. Often, research is conducted with existing users of the product or service to determine the reasons they purchase the product. In these studies, which may be large or small, the intent is to determine the benefits the consumer seeks or finds in the brand and to use this as a strategy to bring more users to the brand. The basic approach is to ask current users why they buy or the benefits they receive from the brand through some form of discussion or questionnaire.

For example, several years ago a manufacturer of baby shampoo was surprised to see sales of the product increasing while the birth rate was declining. Through usage studies, it was learned that because of changes in hair styles, teenagers had started using the product. Because these teens washed their hair every day or several times per week, they were looking for a product that was mild. The baby shampoo gave them that benefit. The manufacturer picked up the new usage idea and turned it into an advertising campaign. They now promote the product to all age groups but particularly to those people who wash their hair frequently.

Motivation studies. Several years ago, motivation research (MR) was the rage. It has since declined in popularity although it still has a rightful place among techniques used to learn more about products and brands. Motivational research uses a depth interviewing technique to determine why people act as they do. This might include why they use a product or brand or why they avoid it, how they feel about competitive brands, what they look for in a brand to purchase, and so on. The objective of MR is to discover some of the important aspects that might not be uncovered in only surface interviews. Often, MR is used to determine basic beliefs about the category or the brand. These beliefs can then be confirmed in more formal and quantitative research. Generally, MR research is conducted only by skilled researchers who have the ability to do the necessary probing interviews and then to interpret the results.

Benefit segmentation. From the foregoing techniques, it should be obvious that one of the goals of all this research is to determine or identify important segments of the population. Few, if any, advertisers have products or services that interest the entire population. Even if the product were of interest, it would be practically impossible to finance a campaign directed toward the entire population. While segmentation and segmentation research were discussed in Chapter 5, a brief review here will be helpful.

Segmentation studies attempt to group consumers in some fashion so that a specific advertising message might be directed at them. Some rather sophisticated computer programs have been developed that can group or assimilate consumers on a common basis as a result of various types of research. General segmentation studies attempt to group customers or prospects along various lines such as demographics, geographics, psychographics or lifestyle, and the like.

Of perhaps more interest to the advertising campaign planner are benefit segmentation studies. Benefit segmentation attempts to determine the various benefits consumers seek from products, services, or brands and then to quantify consumers based on these benefits. For example, an early study of toothpaste determined there were four basic benefits consumers sought from the toothpaste they bought (1) cavity prevention, (2) tooth whitening, (3) breath freshening, and (4) economy. Thus, in addition to basic geographics and demographics, advertising planners can separate or segment the population on the benefits they seek from toothpaste brands. By knowing these were the four basic benefits sought, advertising strategies could be developed for individual brands of toothpaste. Benefit segmentation is a complex research process in many cases, but it can provide some valuable answers for the planner.

It's likely that Aqua-fresh toothpaste has done some additional research on the various market segments in that category. In the ad in Figure 6-4, they are appealing to people who want protection from cavities, those who want fresh breath, and also those who want whiter teeth. All these benefits are rolled into the one advertisement.

Research among New Users

Typically, focus groups, perceptual mapping, benefit segmentation, and motivational research are all used in determining what consumers might find most important about new products just as with existing products. There is a basic difference, however, in this type of research. Often, the product isn't available or it hasn't even been manufactured. In many cases, only a description of what the product might be is used in the research. When this is the case, the research methodology used is called a concept

Figure 6-4.   Benefit Segmentation

SOURCE: Courtesy Beecham Products.

test. This concept testing attempts to determine consumer interest in a product or brand based simply on a description of what the product or brand might be or might do and then to determine the best method of communicating that benefit.

Generally, concept testing is a two-step procedure. First, the advertising campaign planner must determine which of several potential product benefits is most important to the consumer. For example, if a company plans to introduce a new, fortified, nonsugar-added fruit drink in a pouch container, the first step would be to determine which of these benefits would be of the most interest to the target market. Would it be the added vitamins and minerals? The absence of sugar? Or the unique pouch container? A separate concept statement would be written for each benefit (even though the product was the same in each case). Then these concepts would be tested with prospects. A good concept statement should have three basic attributes according to Eugene Cafarelli:

1. A statement of the problem that the product is meant to solve.
2. A definition of the type of solution that the product provides.
3. The necessary supporting attributes (both physical and communications) that lend credibility to the product's ability to solve the problem.[1]

Once the best concept statement has been selected, the next step is to determine the best way to communicate that benefit. That requires a concept statement of another sort. It's the alternative ways in which the benefit can best be communicated to or understood by consumers. For example, in the fruit drink case above, assume consumers said that the most important benefit of the new product would be the absence of added sugar. The question then is, how best to use this as an advertising strategy. Here the planner constructs various ways the benefit can be communicated and puts this in the form of a strategy statement or advertising promise. When testing an advertising strategy, two points must always be included:

1. The promise or the end benefit the consumer will receive by purchasing or using the product.
2. The reason why or supporting product attributes that make that promise possible. These are the things which provide a rational basis for the promise being made.

---

1. Eugene F. Cafarelli, *Developing New Products and Repositioning Mature Brands* (New York: John Wiley & Sons, 1980), p. 110.

In the no-sugar-added strategy above, this might be phrased directly as no-sugar-added, or it might be phrased obliquely such as naturally sweet so nothing has been added, or it might be stated as lower in calories since no sugar has been added to the product. In any case, no matter how the benefit is stated, it must be clear, concise, and complete so that consumers can understand the idea in a very short period of time.

The use of concept tests is very widespread and, unfortunately, in many cases not very well done. A good concept statement is difficult to write, but it is a necessity with a new product. Additional information on concept testing can be found in most advertising or marketing research texts.

Evaluating Research

Throughout this chapter, a great deal of emphasis has been put on how research should be developed and the various methods that might be used to gather information. While this is important to the campaign planner, often it is just as or more important to be able to judge existing or just completed research. In many instances, the advertising campaign planner will not actually be doing the research. Instead, the research data may already exist or may be furnished either by the agency or the advertiser. In those cases, the ability to judge, evaluate, and extract information from the research studies is vital. If the campaign planner doesn't have an understanding of research, how it is done, sampling, and so on, then that person is in a very precarious position. He or she must rely totally on whoever analyzed the research to be accurate in interpretation and conclusions. A better way would be for the planner to have a basic understanding of how to evaluate research studies so he or she could be sure of the research base.

Criteria for Evaluation of Research

In any type of research, the key question is whether the results provide solid evidence on which advertising decisions can be based. This is especially true for the advertising campaign planner who may be proposing a new or unique approach. The crucial questions are (a) the soundness of the research, (b) the issues of validity and reliability, and (c) whether the information is germane to the recommendations resulting from analysis of the data.

The Advertising Research Foundation has prepared a guide for evaluating advertising research. They recommend looking at:

1. Under what conditions was the study made? Problems. Sources of finances. Names of organizations participating. Period of time covered.

Date of report. Definition of terms. Questionnaire and instructions to interviewers. Collateral data. Complete statement of methodology.

2. Has the questionnaire been well designed? Dangers of bias. Unreasonable demands on memory. Poor choice of answers. Monotonous questions. Lack of space for answers. Was it pretested?

3. Has the interviewing been adequate and reliably done? Familiarity with prescribed interview procedure. Training. Maturity. Were spot checks made to ensure accuracy?

4. Has the best sampling plan been followed? Random sample is preferable. Quota sample is more likely to be satisfactory for collecting qualitative rather than quantitative data.

5. Has the sampling plan been fully executed? Substitutions or other variations may destroy validity of data.

6. Is the sample large enough? If a probability sample is properly designed, reliability of results can be determined mathematically. In other samples, it is much more difficult to determine adequacy of sample size.

7. Was there systematic control of editing, coding, and tabulating?

8. Is the interpretation forthright and logical? If one factor is interpreted as cause, all others must be held constant. All basic data underlying interpretations should be shown. Validity of respondents' memory should not be overemphasized. Small differences should not be emphasized. Analysis should be clear and simple.[2]

Limitations of Research

In addition to the question of whether the actual research conducted is reliable and valid, a more basic question is, "What answers can research provide?" Dorothy Cohen suggests six basic limits to all types of advertising and marketing research:

1. Research, no matter how well conducted or under what circumstances, will not provide precise answers to marketing questions.

2. All research is based on past experience and conducted under certain conditions. If those conditions change—and the marketplace is constantly changing—research results may well change with the conditions. Thus, all research is time-and-situation specific.

2. *Criteria for Marketing and Advertising Research* (New York: Advertising Research Foundation, 1953).

3. Research is a business tool, not an answer to all business questions. Research may increase the probability of success. Alternatively, it may help to reduce losses. Doing research to find the answer to the question of why a brand's sales are falling may not give the answer to how to stop the slide. Research may give an indication, though, of how the slide may be reduced.

4. Research is an out-of-pocket expense. Research costs usually are not recoverable. Most research is an investment in the brand or the business. Either way, the advertising campaign planner must recognize research costs as nonrecoverable and regard such costs as an expense against the brand.

5. Research is time-consuming. There must be sufficient time in the advertising planning process to allow for the necessary development, conducting, and evaluation of research.

6. Usually, there are limited personnel available for the research task. Persons who have the ability to conduct skilled research are in short supply. Therefore, there are limits as to the amount of research which can be conducted, no matter how strong the desire for information.[3]

Summary   In summary, research must be the basis for the development of the advertising campaign. Without sufficient research information that will provide an understanding of the market and the consumer, the advertising campaign planner is easily lost or misdirected. And research must provide the basis for determining what the advertising campaign is designed to achieve. We look at that next when we start to set advertising objectives.

---

3. Dorothy Cohen, *Advertising* (New York: John Wiley & Sons, 1972), p. 234.

Case for Discussion:
Noile Shampoo

In February of 1979, the management team of the personal care division of Sullivan Industries met to discuss Noile shampoo. The product had been in national distribution for two years. Targeted at the consumer with oily hair, Noile's market share was .5 percent of the total shampoo market, 4.9 percent of the oily hair category; 7,601,052 units were sold in 1978.

Noile was formulated with a strong cleaning agent to cut through dirt and oil and oil-free conditioners to protect after cleaning. The advertising campaign described the product as "the serious solution for a serious problem." Early research had identified a segment of consumers who were bothered by extreme oily hair.

Although the initial research had indicated that more women than men were in the "seriously oily" category, 68 percent of Noile's purchasers were men. Most of these men were young (20–35) bachelors. Many were very sports-oriented, participating in tennis, skiing, or jogging regularly. Female purchasers were also young and tended to be active.

Tom Dodge, the product manager, felt that sales might increase if a new advertising strategy was adopted. He believed that the "serious solution" theme had reached the limit of its effectiveness. Therefore, Dodge requested permission to have the research department conduct several usage studies to help identify potential new approaches. He was given the go-ahead.

Sullivan Industries had several established consumer panels. Panel A consisted of 200 female homemakers. Half of these panelists did not work outside the home; half were employed in full or part-time positions. The women were between the ages of 21 and 49 and were regular purchasers of one or more Sullivan products.

Panel B was made up of 200 men aged 21 to 49. Approximately 40 percent were professionals, 40 percent worked as skilled laborers, and 20 percent worked in semiskilled positions. They were also regular Sullivan customers.

Panel C consisted of 200 teenagers, half male, half female. These were students in grades 7–12.

Working with Dodge, the market research department developed a questionnaire to assess usage rates and perceived benefits for Noile. The questionnaire was sent to all members of panels A and B. After six weeks, Dodge received the following report:

Noile Questionnaire

1. How often do you shampoo your hair?

Panel A		Panel B	
Daily	.34%	Daily	.28%
3–4 times a week	.52%	3–4 times a week	.49%
1–2 times a week	.14%	1–2 times a week	.23%

2. Is your hair:

Panel A		Panel B	
Dry	.37%	Dry	.29%
Oily	.41%	Oily	.44%
Normal	.22%	Normal	.27%

Panel A		Panel B	
Longer than shoulder length	.26%	Longer than shoulder length	.0%
Shoulder length	.34%	Shoulder length	.1%
Collar length	.23%	Collar length	.38%
Shorter than collar length	.17%	Shorter than collar length	.61%

3. Have you tried Sullivan's Noile shampoo?

Panel A		Panel B	
Yes	.32%	Yes	.57%
No	.68%	No	.43%

(If yes, go to Question 4. If no, go to Question 8.)

4. How many times have you purchased Noile in the past year?

Panel A		Panel B	
One time	.4%	One time	.0%
2–4 times	.48%	2–4 times	.11%
5–8 times	.37%	5–8 times	.26%
9 times or more	.11%	9 times or more	.63%

5. Do you use Noile every time you shampoo?

Panel A		Panel B	
Yes	.36%	Yes	.83%
No	.64%	No	.17%

6. When using Noile, do you also use a cream rinse or conditioner?

Panel A		Panel B	
Yes	87%	Yes	34%
No	13%	No	66%

7. What do you like most about Noile? (OPEN-ENDED, MOST
   FREQUENT RESPONSES REPORTED)

Panel A		Panel B	
Helps control oil	61%	Cuts through oil and sweat	71%
Doesn't dry hair out	17%	Hair stays clean	53%
Hair stays clean longer	37%	Doesn't dry hair out	24%
Has conditioner	12%	Cleans and conditions	22%

(Skip to Question 9.)

8. Why haven't you tried Noile?

Panel A		Panel B	
Don't have oily hair	54%	Don't have oily hair	55%
Too harsh	38%	Too harsh	21%
Like present shampoo	36%	Like present shampoo	38%
Haven't seen it	8%	Haven't seen it	10%
Too expensive	6%	Too expensive	3%

9. Your age:

Panel A		Panel B	
21–25	15%	21–25	13%
26–30	19%	26–30	23%
31–35	21%	31–35	21%
36–40	22%	36–40	16%
41–45	13%	41–45	14%
46+	10%	46+	13%

10. Are you:

Panel A		Panel B	
Married	48%	Married	40%
Single	28%	Single	33%
Divorced	21%	Divorced	25%
Widowed	3%	Widowed	2%

NOTE: 72 percent (144) response from Panel A members and 77 percent (154) response from Panel B members. These figures are provided for your information and analysis. Cross-indexes are available upon request.

Dodge felt that the questionnaire results provided an excellent basis for developing a new strategy for Noile. After lunch, he would request some cross-indexes and set up a meeting with the ad agency account executive.

Questions

1. Would you have included Panel C in the questioning? Why or why not?

2. A cross-index compares two or more questions. For example, cross-indexing questions 3 and 9 would reveal how many people aged 21–25 have tried Noile. Assume that because of time and computer cost restraints, Dodge can only request two cross-indexes. What do you think would be most helpful?

3. If Dodge were to assess Noile against competitors on a perceptual matrix, what attributes might he select for the axis?

4. Do you feel Noile might be a candidate for benefit segmentation?

5. Were there other usage or psychographic areas you would have included in the questionnaire?

6. What, if any, questions do the questionnaire results raise that you would like answered before developing a new strategy?

7 Determining and Establishing Advertising Objectives

After research has been conducted and completed and all the basic questions, problems, and opportunities relating to the brand have been identified, advertising objectives should be determined and established. The planner needs to define and set down those goals and objectives that the advertising campaign should reach.

These advertising objectives are the most important step in the advertising campaign planning process because they determine how the advertising plan will be developed. All the physical elements of the actual advertising campaign—what the advertising strategy will be, what media will be used, how sales promotion will be integrated into the program, what budget will be established, and so on—will be developed and based on what these established objectives are.

While it might seem that establishing and determining advertising objectives should be a rather straightforward task, it often becomes quite complex due to the needs of the brand or the expectations of the advertiser. Often advertisers aren't really clear about what advertising can do for their brand or what the advertising campaign can or should do. Sometimes advertising doesn't have a clearly defined place in the overall corporate program and is not coordinated with the marketing plan. Sometimes an advertiser doesn't have a clear picture of what effects might be produced with an advertising campaign.

Why Set Advertising Objectives? The first question is "Why set advertising objectives at all?" Generally, it's argued, everyone is in some kind of agreement about what the advertising is supposed to do: i.e., increase sales, create product awareness, generate enthusiasm among dealers and/or the sales force, help get the product message across to the consumer, and the like. Beyond this, there seems to be some sort of tacit or unwritten agreement against setting any specific advertising objectives. In fact, that is the best argument *for* setting specific advertising objectives. There must be agreement among all the parties involved in the advertising campaign development and approval process that there are specific, measurable objectives for the campaign. Without this agreement, the campaign is doomed to failure if it ever gets started at all. In addition to assuring agreement among the planners and managers, advertising objectives are required for four basic reasons.

Measurement

The planner needs some method or some way to determine whether or not the advertising campaign was successful. This means setting some form of objectives or goals against which actual results can be measured. In an advertising campaign, the measure of success can be any number of things from determining gains in awareness that the product exists to directly measuring sales produced by each advertisement. By setting goals or objectives, the planner determines in advance the measures that will be used to evaluate the advertising campaign. That's important. It gets advertising away from the idea that results of a campaign are a matter of opinion or executive judgment. Advertising can and must be measured, but first there must be the measure. That comes from measurable advertising objectives.

Design the Plan

If the objectives of the campaign are simply to generate awareness among the general population of the existence of the brand, then that would call for a vastly different plan than if the advertiser were trying to convince a highly segmented group in eastern Montana to purchase a certain brand of sheep dip. The objectives set for the campaign in most cases dictate the specific actions and activities included in the plan. With clear-cut advertising objectives, the development of an advertising plan is usually a relatively easy task for the campaign planner.

Evaluate the Results of the Campaign

If the planner knows the situation of the brand prior to the campaign, has the measure that will be used to evaluate, and knows how the plan was implemented, he or she can clearly and concisely evaluate the results of the campaign. Without these three things it will be extremely difficult to determine whether or not the advertising accomplished what it was hoped it would. Setting advertising objectives tells exactly how the advertising will be evaluated after the campaign has been completed. That prevents any discussion or question between management and the planner when it comes time to evaluate the results.

Relate Advertising to Other Expenditures

Whether the campaign planner likes it or not, today's management often evaluates an advertising investment just as they would any other major expenditure, that is, on a cost-return basis. Increasingly, managements are asking advertising people to justify the investment to be made and to give some actual measures of success for the money expended. Today, advertising must compete for scarce resources as an investment just as would a new plant, an increased sales force, or any other major expenditure on behalf of the brand. For that, if for no other reason, objectives must be set for the campaign so that returns can be calculated and the advertising investment compared to other opportunities.

Setting Corporate Objectives

While it might seem that the objectives for a brand's advertising campaign are only distantly related to the overall goals or objectives of the corporate organization, in truth, they are quite directly related. The common goal of most all corporations is to generate sales and ultimately profits for their management, employees, and stockholders. This profit goal is usually influenced by five basic factors that impinge on the goals that may be set.

The Corporate Strategic Plan

As was described in Chapter 1, most major organizations follow some form of strategic business plan. Based on that strategic plan, while advertising people may find it hard to believe, not all organizations are interested in growth. Some companies find themselves better served if they harvest existing businesses and maintain a low but stable return on their investment. Obviously, the strategic plan being followed by the organization has a direct impact on the corporation's view of advertising and its importance.

Production or Marketing Orientation

Quite closely related to the strategic plan being followed by the organization is business orientation. There are two basic types of companies: production oriented and marketing oriented.

The difference is quite dramatic. The marketing-oriented organization views the market from the consumer's standpoint and determines how to best meet the consumer's wants. The production-oriented organization, however, takes the opposite approach—that manufacturing and distribution of products are most important. Production-oriented organizations concentrate their efforts on developing more efficient means of producing or distributing a given product. The production-oriented company takes the view that, "If you build a better mousetrap, the world will beat a path to your door." The marketing-oriented company provides the opportunities and even the path to their product for the consumer to take. Even in our supposedly enlightened marketing age, many companies in the United States are still production-oriented. This orientation is quite evident in the industrial sector and is prevalent among many consumer-product companies that manufacture or process commodity-type goods. The goals of the company are strongly influenced by this type of orientation and that, obviously, influences the value of advertising to the organization.

Prime Industry

The prime industry in which the organization is involved has much to do with the corporate goals that may be set. If the industry is research oriented, then the orientation of the company may well be more toward research than marketing. The ethical drug business is a good example of a research-oriented industry. Companies in this field believe research is all-important and marketing only peripherally important. The prime business in which the organization operates has much to do with the overall goals that management may set for the business, and those goals will influence marketing and advertising.

Competition

The strength and activity of competition also influences corporate goals and, ultimately, marketing and advertising goals. If the business arena is highly competitive, the corporate goal may be market share first and profits second. If competition is limited, the goal may be optimization of profits or the obtaining of a sufficient share of available profits with minimum investment. Competitive activity often has a greater effect on corporate goals than management would like to admit.

Management

The approach of management in directing the organization has a direct effect on the goals which may be set for the corporation. If management is aggressive and growth-minded, corporate goals will be different than if management is conservative and is content to simply "tend the store" until someone else takes over. The effect of management on company direction is quite clear: some companies even change their top management in an attempt to set the corporation in a different direction.

The objectives of the company have much to do with what advertising and marketing goals are established. For example, if the company were following a "harvesting" strategy with its various divisions or brands, the use and impact of advertising would be minimal. Similarly, if research were the basic goal of the corporation, then that would have an effect on what advertising might be used and what goals would be set. Obviously, the advertising goals of a marketing-oriented, consumer package-goods operation seeking to maximize sales and generate market share would be totally different from a research-oriented firm. Thus, one of the first things a campaign planner has to evaluate is the corporate goals of the organization and their impact on the advertising campaign.

Flowing directly out of the corporate goals are the marketing goals for the company and the brand. These are specified in the marketing plan.

Marketing Objectives

Once the corporate goals are established, the marketing plan for the company or brand can be written. The marketing plan outlines and details all the marketing activities the company will undertake for a given period. Generally, there is a long-term marketing plan developed for a period of five years or more, which is supplemented by an annual marketing plan. The annual plan details the specific marketing activities that will be used during the coming year.

The five-year plan generally looks in broad strokes at what has happened the previous year, the budget for the coming year, the actual results for the current year on a monthly basis, and then a forecast of three years ahead. The headings in a long-term plan usually look something like those in Figure 7-1.

Figure 7-1.   Long-Term Marketing Plan

Immediate past year (actual)	Present year (budget)	Present year (forecast)	Present year +1 (forecast)	Present year +2 (forecast)	Present year +3 (forecast)
$XXX	$XXX	$XXX	$XXX	$XXX	$XXX

Of more direct interest to the campaign planner is the annual marketing plan. The annual marketing plan consists of all data, both physical and financial, that relates to the production, distribution, pricing, and promotion of the brand. Perhaps one of the best descriptions of what a marketing plan should contain is that by Herbert West:

A marketing plan is a written document which (a) examines the major acts in a marketing situation of a product or service; (b) identifies the problems and opportunities in the situation; (c) proposes long-range strategy to meet these problems and opportunities; (d) recommends tactics of selling and advertising for the coming year to carry out this strategy.[1]

While the advertising planner may or may not be involved in the development of a marketing plan, knowing what is included is very helpful. An outline of a marketing plan developed for the Association of National Advertisers is reproduced in Figure 7-2.

The marketing plan incorporates the various aspects of the advertising plan, including the advertising objectives. Thus, until the marketing plan is developed, it is often quite difficult to develop any specific advertising plan or campaign and therefore to establish any definitive advertising objectives. The advertising objectives must be directly related to the marketing plan, for that is the basic guiding document for the brand.

Understanding Advertising Objectives

The advertising campaign, while it is important, is usually only one of the tools needed to execute the marketing plan. Since there is often confusion between advertising and marketing goals, a brief review of the differences will help in planning.

Differences in Marketing and Advertising Objectives

Sales vs. sales messages. Generally, marketing goals are defined in terms of sales and profits. Advertising goals are usually set in terms of delivering sales messages to the target audience or some communication effect. Marketing goals are measured in concrete terms of dollars and cents. Advertising goals are measured by changes in awareness, attitude, and information shifts among consumers.

Current vs. lagged effects. Marketing objectives are generally evaluated for a single specific time period, such as one year. The program either achieves or fails to achieve the sales or profit objectives that have been established for that time. Future sales are not taken into account. Advertising, however, in many cases has a lagged effect. That is, advertising dollars may be invested in this calendar year, but results may not occur until a later period. Often, specific marketing activities don't have a long-lasting effect, but the effects of advertising may linger for some time.

1. Herbert West, "Why You Need a Master Strategy Blueprint," *Advertising Age*, 18 (January 1959): 59.

Figure 7-2. Format for the Annual Marketing Plan

Brand Name 19__ Marketing Plan

Outline	Description
I. Current Year Performance	1–2 short paragraphs summarizing how the brand performed this year relative to sales, share and budget objectives; the reasons for significant variations from plan; the major events that occurred affecting the market, if any; etc.
II. Recommendation	2–3 sentences stating the brand's objectives in total shipping units and in sales value, the total expenditures to support the brand, and the share objective.
III. P & L Effect of the Recommendation	Summarize in a brief table the basic P & L differences between recent performance and the new fiscal year, showing the ratio of each figure to sales, as follows:

	Last year	Current year	New year
Volume			
(value)	$—	$—	$—
(units)	—	—	—
(% increase/decrease)		— %	— %
Share	— %	— %	— %
Cost of goods	$—(%)	$—(%)	$—(%)
Adv./prom.	$—(%)	$—(%)	$—(%)
Other costs	$—(%)	$—(%)	$—(%)
Pre-tax profit	$—(%)	$—(%)	$—(%)

IV. Background
  1. Market
     - Size — 2–3 short paragraphs on the size of the market in units and/or volume, plus its growth rate. Competitive brands and share position versus the company brand should be shown. If the list of competitive brands is extensive, mention only the major brands.
     - Consumer — 1–2 short paragraphs describing the consumer profile (age, income, etc.) and indicating what the total consumption of this product category is by major geographic areas.
     - Pricing — A brief table, preferably without comment, showing competitive and company retail price structures, by unit size. If appropriate, cost per ounce/unit may also be shown.
     - Competitive spending — A table breaking out the previous year's competitive media and promotional expenditures by six-month periods, e.g., Jan.–June vs. July–Dec., plus competitive volume consumed during these two periods if available. Estimates of promotion costs should include only regional and national promotions, and not tests. This table should be arranged as follows:

	1st 6 months				2nd 6 months			
	Vol.	Med.	Prom.	Total	Vol.	Med.	Prom.	Total
Brand A	—	$—	$—	$—	—	$—	$—	$—
Brand B	—	$—	$—	$—	—	$—	$—	$—

(continued on next page)

Figure 7-2.   (Continued)

Outline	Description
	Following this table, brief comments may be made on any significant changes from the above pattern which may be taking place currently.
● Other	State any other facts or statistics about the market that would be helpful to management in reaching a decision on this proposal.
2. Brand	
● Product	1–2 sentences on the general makeup of the product's formula, points of uniqueness, a table on the sizes/variety it is sold in, and the profit margin by size.
● Manufacturing	A short paragraph on existing plant capacity, next year's capital investment requirements if known, and any production or purchasing problems encountered to date. This is an optional section and is primarily concerned with new products.
● Product research	A brief summary of the major pieces of research relating to the brand and its performance. Emphasis should be placed on actual research scores obtained rather than on editorial comments.
● Market research	This encompasses all other significant research studies performed on the brand, to include items such as the major scores obtained from the latest advertising research, test market shares, name and packaging research, etc., if appropriate.
● Other	State any other facts or statistics about the brand that would be helpful to management in reaching a decision on this proposal.
V. Opportunities and Problems	
1. Opportunities	In support of this recommendation, list the key areas of opportunity from which the brand expects to obtain its growth or sales objectives in the coming year.
2. Problems	Similarly, outline the major factors that might jeopardize the brand's ability to meet its objectives, explaining what steps have been taken to minimize these risks.
VI. Strategies	
1. Marketing	A concise, well-defined paragraph or two on the brand's basic objective and marketing strategy. The length of this section will vary according to individual brand needs, but should be limited to approximately a half page.
2. Spending	This section is optional and is primarily intended for brands with heavy advertising expenditures which may vary significantly according to sales areas or marketing opportunities.
3. Copy	This should consist of three brief statements: the first devoted to the primary copy objective, the second to the strategy to achieve this objective, and the third to the brand's TV/print pool or rotation policy. As a guide, this entire section should be about a half page in length.

Figure 7-2.   (continued)

Outline	Description

4. Media

As with Copy, this section should consist of three elements. The first is a statement of objective and the second the strategy to achieve the objective. Every effort should be made to make these two statements as specific as possible, particularly in terms of coverage, frequency of commercial exposure, wave advertising, etc.

The third element of this section should be a table showing sales volume versus media expenditures by major sales areas, the current year compared to the new year, arranged as follows:

Area	Current year			New year		
	Vol.	Med.	Exp'd/unit	Vol.	Med.	Exp'd/unit
1	—	$—	$—/cs	—	$—	$—/cs
2	—	$—	$—/cs	—	$—	$—/cs
etc.						

Significant changes in expenditures per unit in any sales area, from one year to the next, should be explained briefly beneath this table. Depending upon the number of sales areas used, the entire Media Section should probably not exceed three-fourths of a page. Brands with little or short-term media should eliminate the above table entirely.

5. Promotion

Similarly, the three elements of this section should consist of a promotion objective, a well-defined strategy statement, and a table showing the differences in expenditure and deal-pack volume, by major sales areas, from one year to the next, as follows:

	Area 1	Area 2	Area 3	Etc.
Expend./unit				
Current year	$—	$—	$—	
New year	$—	$—	$—	
% Vol. in trade deals				
Current year	—%	—%	—%	
New year	—%	—%	—%	

As a guide, the Promotion Section should probably be no longer than one page.

VII. Tests/Research

This is a brief statement on what major tests and/or research the brand will conduct in the coming year, e.g., media or promotion tests, product tests, package research, etc. Simply give the nature, purpose, and cost of each activity. The entire section should not exceed a half page.

This concludes the written portion of the Annual Marketing Plan, to which the four recommended financial marketing exhibits should be attached.

SOURCE: F. Beaven Ennis, *Effective Marketing Management* (New York: Association of National Advertisers, 1973), pp. 13–16.

Tangible vs. intangible results Part of the difference between marketing and advertising goals is the final result. Marketing goals are usually stated in concrete terms such as units moved, sales or profits, distribution achieved, shelf facings in stores, or the like. Advertising goals, on the other hand, can often be quite intangible. They may include such things as shifts in attitudes, changes in opinion, entry into and establishment in the evoked set, and the like. Therefore, it can be quite difficult to measure the rather soft objectives of advertising in terms of hard, discrete data.

Types of Advertising Objectives

The three types of advertising objectives that the advertising campaign planner usually sets relate to selling, advertising, and measuring results. Advertising is generally considered to be the communication of a sales message to a customer or prospect. Whether the advertising message is delivered through the media with advertising or personally through direct selling, several factors affect the results obtained. For example, some sales messages are simply more effective than others. A promise for a cure for cancer will get more attention than the introduction of a new dishwashing detergent. Similarly, in some situations customers are ready to buy immediately. In others, long, detailed sales presentations may be necessary and even then not succeed. And, even when the sales message is delivered in person, the customer still may not be ready to buy. They still want to shop around a bit. Finally, in all selling situations, problems that just can't be overcome kill the sale. Factors such as high price, wrong color, or non-availability of size stymie even the best salesperson.

The same thing happens to advertising. In most package-goods self-service selling situations, the advertising planner has very little control over the marketing mix elements other than the advertising itself. While the advertising may be right and the message may be delivered effectively, no sale may result. That may be because of improper pricing, lack of distribution, out-of-stock situations, wrong, colors, and so on. Even though the advertising has done its job in communicating a sales message, no sale may result. Since the planner doesn't have control over these marketing variables and since not all consumers are in the market to buy at a given time, surrogate measures are often used to determine the effects of an advertising campaign.

These surrogate measures are important and involve types of advertising objectives. Most advertisers set advertising objectives in one of three ways.

Sales. Some types of marketers, primarily those involved in direct response, can easily set and measure their advertising objectives in terms of unit or dollar sales. They can do that because advertising is the only form of marketing and selling used in moving the brand from marketer to final consumer. The marketing system goes directly from the manufacturer through the media to the consumer. The consumer either reacts with an order or doesn't. Setting advertising goals in terms of sales is wonderful when it can be done. It just isn't possible in very many consumer product marketing situations.

Behavioral effects. When advertising goals can't be set directly in terms of final sales, some type of behavioral activity by consumers can be used as a measure of the effect of the advertising messages. For example, some advertisers attempt to get advertising respondents to take some sort of specific action short of making a purchase, such as sending for more information, returning a reply card, calling a dealer, or the like. This approach is common in many forms of industrial advertising since the advertiser knows most industrial products are sold only through face-to-face negotiation between a salesperson and a buyer. Many industrial marketers use advertising to generate leads for the sales force. Thus, customers or prospects who ask for more information or send in coupons are referred to the sales force for a followup call.

The advertiser may measure many types of activities or actions suggested through the advertising. This will enable the advertiser to identify who is responding to the advertising and what results are being obtained. In cases where direct sales cannot be measured, a surrogate measure of behavior or interest in the product generated by advertising is often used as a measure of success.

Communication effects. In the case of most consumer package goods or products purchased on a regular basis and through various forms of trade channels, the advertising objectives must be even softer than a measure of behavior. In other words, a measure of the effects the advertising has in terms of either awareness, knowledge, preference, or some other mental effect on the consumer is used. Since this type of measurement makes up the greatest portion of the advertising objectives of consumer product advertisers, it will be discussed in detail on the following pages. Before that, however, we need to look at some of the factors that influence the type of objectives the advertising campaign planner can set.

Factors Influencing the Establishment of Advertising Objectives

Several factors influence what objectives can be set for an advertising campaign. The primary ones follow.

Marketing system. The system through which the product or service is marketed has much to do with the type of advertising objectives that can be set. For example, direct marketers can set sales goals, and consumer product marketers, distributing brands primarily through self-service retail operations, usually measure communication effects only.

Type of message. Not all advertising is designed to generate an immediate sale. For example, an oil company attempting to explain the energy situation to the consuming public really isn't trying to sell additional product. It is advocating a position or explaining its operation. In those cases, no actual sales may result. The result may well be only a change in public attitude or understanding of the problem. Thus, the type of information in the message to be communicated through the advertising campaign usually will be quite different from the information given by a company trying to generate, for example, a point-of-purchase sale.

Long- or short-term effects. The intended effect of the message also has much to do with establishing the advertising objectives. For example, an attempt to build an image of the organization in the minds of the consumers may require quite a long time to achieve, for example, convincing consumers that XYZ Corporation makes high-quality automobiles. A product sales message, however, such as the #70 model of XYZ is a high performance auto, may take a very short time to see results. The campaign planner must consider the length of time required for response when setting advertising objectives.

Intended audience. The audience for the advertising campaign also has an effect on the advertising objectives. For example, it is usually much easier to get existing users of a product to use more of the product or to use it in additional ways than it is to get new users to try the brand. It may be much easier to get established retailers to perform some type of sales function than it is to get consumers to try a new brand.

Product familiarity. A product's relative position in its life cycle makes a definite difference in the advertising objectives that can be set for it. The advertising objectives for a product in the introductory stage will be quite different from those that might be set for a product in the maturity stage.

Competitive activity. The amount of competitive "noise" has an influence on how effective an advertising message can likely be. Obviously a company that is the only advertiser in a product category has a better chance of reaching consumers with its message than if it is only one of ten or more.

Setting Advertising Objectives

While there are three basic ways of setting advertising objectives: sales, behavioral effects, and communication effects, there are several views of how to set and measure advertising objectives and results.

Colley's DAGMAR Approach

Russell Colley wrote *Defining Advertising Goals for Measured Advertising Results (DAGMAR)* for the Association of National Advertisers in 1961. He did much to convince advertisers that communication effects are the logical basis for advertising evaluation. A second result of Colley's efforts was the general idea of establishing advertising objectives and then measuring results of the advertising campaign against those objectives.[2]

Since Colley set the form by which advertising communication effects are used as the basis for advertising objectives and advertising measurement, his suggestions will be examined in some detail.

Specifically, Colley states:

Advertising's job, purely and simply, is to communicate to a defined audience information and a frame of mind that stimulates action. Advertising succeeds or fails depending on how well it communicates the desired information and attitudes to the right people at the right time at the right cost.[3]

Colley develops the outline for his approach to measuring advertising results using the following six principles.

1. An advertising goal is a succinct statement of the communication aspects of the marketing job. (It expresses the particular work advertising is uniquely qualified to perform and does not encompass results that require a combination of several different marketing forces.)

2. The goal is expressed in writing—in finite, measurable terms. (If there is agreement among all of those concerned on what advertising is expected to accomplish, then it is no great chore to reduce it to writing. If there is a lack of agreement as to purpose, the time to find this out is before the advertising is prepared, not afterward.)

3. Goals are agreed upon by those concerned at both creative and approval levels. (Planning is separated from doing. Agreement is

---

2. Russell H. Colley, *Defining Advertising Goals for Measured Advertising Results* (New York: Association of National Advertisers, 1961).

3. Colley, *Defining Advertising Goals*, p. 21.

reached on what needs to be said to whom before time and money are spent on how best to say it.)

4. Goals are based on an intimate knowledge of markets and buying motives. (They express realistic expectancy in the light of carefully evaluated market opportunities. They do not express mere hopes and desires arrived at without factual foundation.)

5. Benchmarks are set up against which accomplishments can be measured. (State of mind—knowledge, attitude, and buying propensity—are appraised before and after the advertising, or among those reached versus those not reached by the advertising.)

6. Methods to be used at a later date in evaluating accomplishments are set up at the time goals are established.[4]

Colley's primary theme throughout the DAGMAR approach is that good advertising objectives are both specific and measurable. In his view, the key to measuring advertising results is first being able to define the advertising goals to be accomplished. This decision is one of the most difficult parts of the task. Colley suggests a "6 M" approach, which he outlines as follows:

Merchandise: What are all the important benefits of the products and services to be sold?

Markets: Who are the people to be reached?

Motives: Why would these people buy or fail to buy?

Messages: What are the key ideas, information, and attitudes to be conveyed? (To move the prospect closer to the ultimate aim of a sale.)

Media: How can the prospects be reached?

Measurements: What method is proposed to measure accomplishment in getting the intended message across to the intended audience?[5]

To be able to measure the effect of the advertising message, the campaign planner must be able to detect a change in the consumer's perceptions, attitudes, or actions. Colley proposes the following hierarchy of stages in the communication process designed to achieve the ultimate goal of advertising, which is persuading the consumer to act. The four stages of "commercial communication" suggested by Colley are:

4. Colley, Defining Advertising Goals, p. 14.
5. Colley, Defining Advertising Goals, p. 23.

Table 7-1.   Effect of Advertising on Consumer Response

Product: Filter cigarette	Before advertising (percent)	After advertising (percent)
Aware of brand name:		
Unaided recall	20	40
Aided recall	40	80
Comprehended messages:		
Message A	6	12
Message B	10	20
Message C	8	16
Favorably disposed to buy	4	8
Demonstrated action	2	4
Image: Industrial chemical division		
Aware of corporate name	85	88
Aware that corporation is a leading		
supplier of industrial chemicals	15	30
Comprehended key messages:		
Message A	6	12
Message B	4	8
Message C	5	10
Favorably disposed to buy	5	10
Action leading to purchase	3	6

SOURCE: Colley, *Defining Advertising Goals*, p. 39.

1. Awareness. The prospect must be made aware of the brand or product.

2. Comprehension. The prospect must comprehend what the product is and what it will do for him.

3. Conviction. The prospect must arrive at a mental disposition or conviction to buy the product.

4. Action. Finally, the prospect must take action.[6]

The primary thrust of Colley's approach is that the response to communication can be measured in many instances with existing research tools and methodologies. Colley offers the example given in Table 7-1 of the effects advertising might have on consumers. He uses two different products and compares the effects before and after advertising communication.

Colley does not specifically deal with how the benchmarks are established or the methodology of measurement. His key point is the identification of specific communication goals from the start of advertising to the close of the campaign.

---

6. Colley, *Defining Advertising Goals*, p. 38.

In summary, Colley's DAGMAR approach is best described as a written measurable communications task involving a starting point, a definite audience, and a fixed period of time.

A Recommended Approach to
Setting Advertising Objectives for Measurable Results

The DAGMAR approach is sound both conceptually and practically, with one exception. The hierarchy of steps from awareness to action is somewhat ill-defined. The DAGMAR approach has much to recommend it, but we believe a different hierarchy of effects model should be used. The Lavidge and Steiner model, as illustrated in Figure 7-3, is more specific than Colley's "four stages of commercial communication" and provides a better method of establishing and measuring results. As the authors describe their model:

> Advertising may be thought of as a force, which must move people up a series of steps:
>
> 1. Near the bottom of the steps stand the potential purchasers who are completely unaware of the existence of the product or service in question.
> 2. Closer to purchasing, but still a long way from the cash register, are those who are merely aware of the product's existence.
> 3. Up a step are prospects who know what the product has to offer.
> 4. Still closer to purchasing are those who have favorable attitudes toward the product—those who like the product.
> 5. Those whose favorable attitudes have developed to the point of preference over all other possibilities are up still another step.
> 6. Even closer to purchasing are consumers who couple preference with a desire to buy and the conviction that the purchase would be wise.
> 7. Finally, of course, is the step which translates this attitude into an actual purchase.[7]

The Lavidge and Steiner model, although not proven in actual practice, has great intuitive and commonsense appeal. It's how "we think consumers purchase." We strongly recommend the use of the L&S model as a measure for the basic Colley approach.

---

7. Robert J. Lavidge and Gary Steiner, "A Model for Predictive Measurements of Advertising Effectiveness," *Journal of Marketing*, 24 (October 1961): 59–62.

Figure 7-3. Effect of Advertising on Consumers: Movement from Awareness to Action

Related behavioral dimensions	Movement toward purchase	Example of types of promotion or advertising relevant to various steps
Conative: The realm of motives. Ads stimulate or direct desires.	Purchase ↑	Point-of-purchase Retail store ads Deals "Last chance" offers Price appeals Testimonials
	Conviction ↑	
Affective: The realm of emotions. Ads change attitudes and feelings.	Preference ↑	Competitive ads Argumentative copy "Image" copy Status, glamour appeals
	Liking ↑	
Cognitive: The realm of thoughts. Ads provide information and facts.	Knowledge ↑	Announcements Descriptive copy Classified ads Slogans Jingles Skywriting
	Awareness	Teaser campaigns

SOURCE: Robert J. Lavidge and Gary A. Steiner, *Journal of Marketing*, 1961.

One thing should be mentioned, however. Since the introduction of the Lavidge and Steiner model, several researchers have pointed out some defects. Although it does not destroy the model itself, the advertising campaign planner should be aware of some of the later questions that have been raised.

1. For some products, consumers might not go through the sequence as it is set out; i.e., they may start and stop, or they may make mistakes and start over, etc.
2. Feedback at various stages might allow later events to have an influence on earlier activities.
3. Some consumers might collapse the entire process into a split second particularly for low-risk, low-cost products.

Figure 7-4.   Altered Hierarchy Model

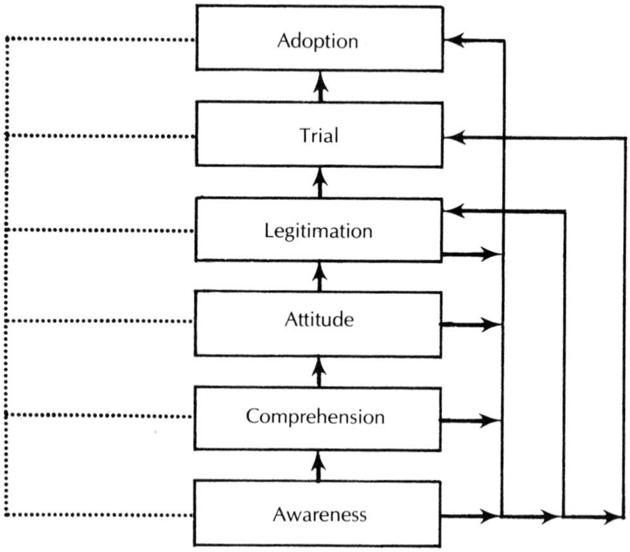

SOURCE: Vaughn, "How Advertising Works," p. 29.

4. Some consumers might not follow the process at all. They might make purchasing decisions under some other system.

Robertson, in 1971, presented the adoption process model illustrated in Figure 7-4. As Richard Vaughn described it:

> This modified "hierarchy" model proposes that some consumers, under some conditions, for some products, might follow a sequential path. The dotted lines [in Figure 7-4] are feedbacks which can alter outcomes. Other decision patterns on the right track consumers as they violate the formal sequence of the hierarchy. Thus, consumers can learn from previous experience and swerve from the awareness-to-purchase pattern.[8]

8. Richard Vaughn, "How Advertising Works: A Planning Model," *Journal of Advertising Research* 20, 5 (October 1980): 28–29. © Copyright Foote, Cone, & Belding Communications, Inc. 1979. Reprinted by permission.

In spite of these irregularities, the Lavidge and Steiner model still provides the best method of establishing firm, measurable advertising objectives for the campaign planner.

In summary, whatever measurement is used and however the measurement is conducted, the important point is that the advertising campaign planner must establish clear, concise, measurable advertising objectives at the initiation of the advertising campaign. The example that Colley offers provides a guideline for all advertising objectives:

> To increase among 30 million homemakers who own automatic washers the number who identify brand X as a low-sudsing detergent and who are persuaded that it gets clothes cleaner—from 10 percent to 40 percent in one year.[9]

If advertising objectives are stated in this way, they can be measured and the results can be evaluated. It's as simple as that.

Some Practical Examples

Several alternative ways in which advertising objectives may be stated have been shown. The best illustrations, however, are practical examples. The statement of advertising objectives in Figure 7-5 is taken from a student

---

Figure 7-5.   Advertising Objectives—A Student Plan

1. To create awareness of Brand X among 70 percent of our target market (primarily women in the top 100 markets, ages 18 to 49, with one or more children under age 18, and having annual household incomes of approximately $15,000 plus) by the end of Year 1, the introductory year of our national campaign.

2. To have 70 percent aided recall among our target market of our advertising promise as stated in the creative strategy.

3. To have 65 percent of our target market report a preference for Brand X over other competitive brands.

Through a combination of advertising and marketing efforts:

4. To generate a 39 percent trial rate in our target market within the designated distribution areas by the end of the introductory year.

5. To achieve a 65 percent repurchase rate (an average of five purchases per year/six packages per purchase) in our target market by the end of the introductory year.

---

9. Colley, *Defining Advertising Goals,* p. 7.

Figure 7-6.   Advertising Objectives—A National Program

	National overlay (percent)	Heavy-up markets (55) (percent)
Awareness	30	75
Correct image perception	20	60
Liking	15	50

(In addition to these three objectives, which can be linked directly to advertising, three behavior-related objectives of the total advertising, marketing, and promotion program were stated:)

Ultimate objectives of advertising, marketing, and promotion

	National overlay (percent)	Heavy-up markets (55) (percent)
Trial	10	40
Repurchase rate	50	50
Franchise	5	20

The national objectives are explained as follows:

1. Awareness. When asked to name all brands that come to mind, 30 percent of the target market will name Brand X.

2. Correct image perception. 20 percent of the target market will acquire the correct perception of the product image from Brand X's advertising messages. Image perception is measurable by checklists, semantic differentials, and projective techniques.

3. Liking. 15 percent of the target market will prefer Brand X to other brands in the product category. Liking can be measured by rank order of preference or by rating scales.

4. Trial. 10 percent of the target market will purchase one package of Brand X once during the first year. Trial can be measured by store audits or surveys as well as by coupon redemption.

5. Repurchase rate. 50 percent of those who try the product during the first year will purchase it again. This can be measured by diaries or tracking studies.

6. Franchise. The end results of trial and repurchase rates will constitute our market share or franchise.

advertising plans book for a "real-world" client. Note how specifically the advertising objectives are stated, i.e., to achieve 70 percent awareness of the product in a very specific target market. Notice how the advertising campaign objectives are separate from the marketing objectives in numbers 4 and 5. These final objectives deal specifically with behavior, and since there are intervening variables such as marketing and promotional programs, they are separated from the advertising objectives that deal only with communication effects.

Advertising objectives can also be much more complex than those illustrated in Figure 7-5. For example, the statement of advertising objectives in Figure 7-6 illustrates a different set of objectives for an advertising campaign. This plan involved a national overlay program plus a heavy-up campaign in 55 additional high-potential markets. As is shown, separate advertising objectives were developed for each portion of the campaign based on the differing levels of media weight and market conditions. The awareness goal nationally, for example, was set at 30 percent while, in the heavy-up markets, the objective was 75 percent.

Again, the advertising objectives and marketing objectives have been separated. In these examples, advertising is evaluated in terms of communication effects. Marketing is evaluated according to trial, repurchase rate, and franchise obtained.

Advertising objectives, as illustrated by these examples, can be made measurable. For proper evaluation of the campaign results, they must be measurable. These measurable results greatly simplify the advertising campaign planner's task. If the objectives are clear, complete, and measurable, the advertising plan (which follows in the next chapter) almost writes itself.

Summary   One of the keys to success is knowing what you want the advertising campaign to do. For different organizations this can vary greatly, but it must be stated clearly before the campaign itself is developed. First the planner must understand the corporation's overall objectives, and then its marketing objectives. Then comes a standard for measuring the outcomes. Is the advertising supposed to create greater awareness, greater liking, or is it supposed to increase trial of the product or market share? These are very different objectives and will influence how the campaign is developed. But it is important to establish objectives for writing the plan.

Case for Discussion:
America Helps

America Helps is a national fund-raising organization that was founded in 1971. Designed to provide funds to public service groups in the nation's small towns and rural areas (communities with populations under 10,000), America Helps allocated funds of between $1,000 and $10,000 to over 4,000 groups in nearly 450 communities in 1982. Donations to America Helps totaled $28 million in 1982, a 6 percent increase over 1981 levels.

Areas that receive funds from America Helps are referred to as "America Helps Communities." Contributors can specify that their money go to a particular community or a particular organization; this was the case for roughly 35 percent of all donations each year. America Helps' chief purpose is to ensure that service groups can spend the majority of their time in serving, not raising money. Among those receiving funding from America Helps are 4-H clubs, counseling groups such as Alcoholics Anonymous, and a variety of other organizations. The community groups are required to undergo a rigorous financial and organizational audit to qualify for America Helps funds and are reassessed every nine months.

Juliana Coffman had recently joined the staff of America Helps as Director of National Advertising. This was a new position, since America Helps had traditionally left any advertising to the local groups. Coffman had been brought on in the hope that a national advertising campaign could help redirect the company in several areas.

Long-range corporate plans called for America Helps to be active in 600 communities, spread throughout the 50 states, by January 1985. To meet this goal, a regular increase in yearly donations was essential. Since its inception, donations to America Helps had increased from year to year at a rate of between 4 and 7 percent. Donations came from several sources, and 1982 had been a typical year in terms of breakdown by source.

Seventy-seven percent of the donations received in 1982 had come from individuals. Ninety percent of these were from people who lived in or near an America Helps community. Corporations had donated 11 percent of the 1982 total. This represented several large contributions from firms with plants near America Helps communities. The remaining 12 percent of donations came from miscellaneous sources, such as foundations, estates, and community fund raisers.

In response to difficult economic conditions, the America Helps board of directors wanted to attract a broader donation base, including contributions from persons and businesses that have no direct ties to America Helps communities. The board reasoned that the types of organizations that received America Haelps funds would earn the interest and support of many potential individual and corporate donors. Despite the competition for charitable dollars from larger fund-raising organizations, America Helps felt their grassroots image could make an impact in larger areas. Coffman's job was to tap that potential through advertising.

Since national advertising was a new concept at America Helps, Coffman felt it was vital to establish some clear-cut objectives that would be discussed with the board of directors before any advertising dollars were spent. She reasoned that having preestablished objectives would not only facilitate the development of the advertising campaign, but also provide positive proof of the campaign's success, proof that would be very important when she presented her budget for succeeding years.

After reviewing the history of America Helps (particularly the 1982 results) and the board's stated objectives, Coffman developed the following advertising objectives for her first-year campaign.

1. To create awareness of America Helps among 75 percent of the national population.

2. To lay the groundwork for America Helps' expansion to 50 new communities in 1984.

3. To have 60-percent knowledge among the Fortune 500 companies of America Helps' methods and services.

4. To increase overall giving by 11 percent.

5. To increase corporate giving from 11 percent of total donations to 22 percent.

6. To increase donations from persons outside of America Helps communities from 8.5 percent of the total to 14 percent.

Questions

1. Is each objective measurable? What additional information, if any, might Coffman need to prove the success of her campaign based on these objectives?

2. Is each objective an *advertising* objective, a goal that can be achieved through advertising?

3. Based on the objectives, what type of plan might Coffman develop? Who would be the target audience? What media might she use?

4. Are Coffman's objectives in keeping with corporate strategy?

5. Are Coffman's objectives relevant to the time frame of a first-year advertising campaign?

6. Refer to the section on "Factors Influencing the Establishment of Advertising Objectives" on page 175 of this chapter. Have all six factors discussed been considered in the above objectives?

7. Evaluate Coffman's objectives using the Lavidge and Steiner model.

8 Determining the Advertising Budget

Setting advertising objectives and establishing an advertising budget are directly related. The objectives establish what the planner *wants* to do, and the budget limits what the planner *can* do. The two must be dealt with together rather than separately. We separate them here only for the organization of the text.

While objectives and budgeting are inseparable—each influences the other—this chapter will deal primarily with the hows and whys of budgeting. The primary focus will be on a review and explanation of various methods of determining and establishing a budget for most products or services.

What Advertising Is Supposed to Do

The amount of money an advertiser might logically invest in advertising has a direct relationship to his or her expectations. In other words, what is an advertising expenditure supposed to accomplish? As was discussed in Chapter 2, advertising's primary task is to communicate a sales message to customers and prospects in the marketplace. The goal of these messages is to create a measurable attitudinal and/or behavioral change that should result in the purchase of the advertised brand and, thus, additional sales for the advertiser. While this advertising-to-sales relationship is somewhat tenuous in some situations, that is the basic objective.

The next step involves looking at what specific sales advertising might generate. Kenneth Longman, who several years ago developed an advertising investment model based on marginal analysis, contends that advertising can only be effective between two sales points for any brand. Those sales, Longman says, are between the threshold and the maximum sales level.[1] The concept is illustrated in Figure 8-1.

---

1. From *Advertising* by Kenneth A. Longman, © 1971 by Harcourt Brace Jovanovich. Reproduced by permission of the publisher.

Figure 8-1. Sales Related to the Advertising Expenditure

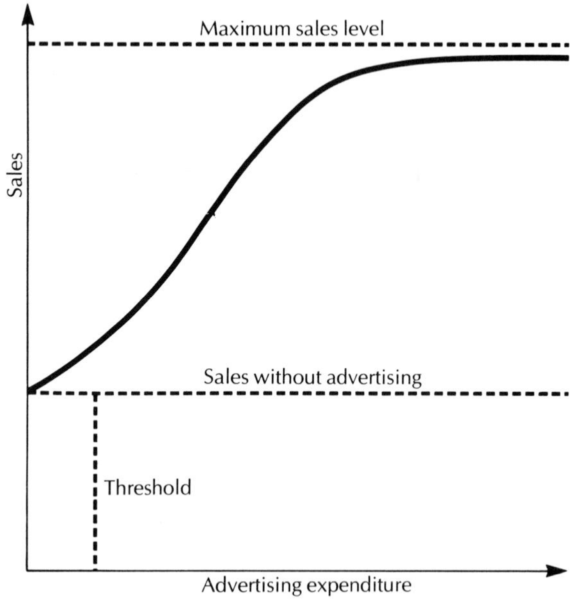

SOURCE: From *Advertising* by Kenneth A. Longman, 1971.

In Longman's model, a certain level of brand sales will be generated without any advertising at all. He calls that the "threshold" level. Further, Longman contends that there is a maximum point above which sales cannot rise. This limit may be due to plant capacity, market saturation, raw ingredient availability, or a variety of other factors. It is between these two points, the threshold and maximum sales level, that advertising actually has some effect on generating sales. In Longman's opinion, the key to successful advertising is to generate the greatest amount of sales dollars between these two points with the minimum advertising investment. Longman suggests this point can be measured through marginal analysis and the point identified where sales reach the maximum and the advertising is most efficient. While the actual calculation of marginal utility is somewhat out of the scope of the average advertising planner, this idea of a maximum and minimum attainable sales level and the understanding of where advertising investments operate is a key concept in developing and determining an advertising budget. The general idea is to spend the least amount of money and achieve the greatest amount of *additional* sales dollars. Sometimes that basic idea gets lost in the advertising planning process when planners start to think about various advertising alternatives and options.

The Budgeting Challenge

Of all the proposals an advertising planner must develop to prepare an advertising campaign plan, the budget often seems to be the most difficult and the least precise. Budgeting is fraught with difficulties ranging from the calculation of such things as returns on investment to overcoming the sometimes staid and traditional thinking of "it's the amount we have always spent" or "that's the way we've always budgeted." If the planner understands the problems inherent in any budgeting situation, solutions and rationales can be developed to deal with and overcome those problems, and the correct budgeting procedure can be developed.

The Budget as a Forecast

A proposed budget is a forecast, an estimate not only of what the planner proposes to do with the advertising expenditures but also of what he or she thinks will occur as a result of those advertising expenditures. Forecasting any marketing operation is difficult, and forecasting advertising results may be the most difficult of all the marketing tasks. Since perfect information about what may happen in many areas doesn't exist, most forecasts are based on inferences, extrapolations, and intuition. As a result, there must always be some margin of error.

Measurement

If it was possible to determine precisely what we achieved with previous advertising expenditures, then it should be possible to get a better fix on what is possible in the future. But it isn't. Thus, the planner is forced to use estimates of results and surrogate measures for the effects of advertising. (See Chapter 6.) That's what makes peering into the future especially difficult.

Present or Future Returns

A basic, still unanswered, question about advertising is, how does one deal with lagged effects? If it was possible to know what advertising impression was made on consumers as a result of previous efforts, planners would have a better chance of estimating what the current effect might be. Since all advertising effects are not instant and there is some building of effects and some carryover, the basic problem for the advertising planner is to estimate what advertising effects have already occurred and to determine how to build on that base. One problem with that approach, as was pointed out in Chapter 1, is that all expenditures will be charged against current year sales and profits. Thus, the planner must allocate funds for advertising for the current period even though he may not see any results until future periods.

In spite of these problems, an advertising budget must be established and justified. The planner often can't solve the problems just mentioned, but by knowing what they are and what causes them, he can attempt to accommodate them in the plan. The next step is to look at some of the factors that directly influence the amount that should be budgeted for a brand.

Factors Influencing the Advertising Budget

Several factors have a direct influence on the size of the advertising budget. Several of them have already been mentioned in Chapter 6. We'll review them here.

Components of the Advertising Budget

First and foremost, the planner must know what expenditures are to be charged against the advertising budget for the brand. While planners like to keep the advertising budget clear and involved strictly with the campaign, that often isn't possible. If by company policy, for example, the annual company picnic is considered an advertising expenditure and is included in the advertising budget, then that will reduce the amount available for the actual campaign.

Generally, the campaign planner has little control over what is charged against the advertising budget. That is commonly decided by management and/or the accounting department. But, no matter who decides what goes in, the planner must keep any noncampaign charges in mind when establishing the overall brand budget. While this may not be as great a problem as it once was, the planner may sometimes find some rather unusual items and expenses charged against advertising simply because the company has always done it that way or has no other place to put the charges. When this is the case, these costs must simply be included in the budget and acknowledged as one of the campaign planning problems. These costs or charges, however, should not be included when an evaluation of the campaign results is made (see Chapter 14).

In 1981, Charles Patti and Vincent Blasko made a survey of the 100 Leading Advertisers to see what costs were commonly charged to the advertising budget. While their goal was to see what changes had occurred

---

Figure 8-2.   Advertising Charges

White List—Charges commonly made against advertising budget by 66 percent or more of respondents

Space time and costs in media
Advertising pretesting services
Institutional advertising
Media costs for consumer contests

Advertising in Yellow Pages
Local cooperative advertising
Storage of advertising materials

Gray List—Charges commonly made against advertising budget by 33–66 percent of respondents

Advertising consultants
Catalogs for consumers
Direct mail to consumers
Space in irregular publications
Advertising aids for sales staff
Financial advertising
Advertising-association dues
Subscriptions to periodicals

Readership or audience research
Advertising-department travel or
    entertainment expense
Cost of contest entry blanks
Cross-advertising enclosures
Premium handling charges
Advertising department salaries

Black List—Charges made against advertising budget by less than 33 percent of respondents

House-to-house sample distribution
Direct mail to dealers
Industry directory listings

Coupon redemption costs
Cost of merchandise for tie-in
    promotion

SOURCE: Patti and Blasko, "Budgeting Practices of Big Advertisers," p. 96.

---

from previous listings, the results (see Figure 8-2) give a good idea what advertisers do and don't charge to the advertising budget.[2]

Obviously, any additional expenses over and above the cost of the actual proposed campaign which are charged to the advertising budget will have a great effect on the amount of money which can be allocated to specific campaign activities.

New or Existing Product

Whether the product is just being introduced or has been on the market for several years usually has a great effect on the budget required. Often, established products require only maintenance advertising schedules.

---

2. Charles H. Patti and Vincent Blasko, "Budgeting Practices of Big Advertisers," *Journal of Advertising Research*, 21, 6 (December 1981): 23–29.

These can be much less expensive than a campaign designed to introduce the brand and initiate first-time trial. The difference between budgeting for an existing and a new product is described in detail elsewhere in this chapter.

Brand Consumer Base or Market Share

The number of customers the brand presently has or the share of market it enjoys has much to do with the advertising appropriation. Generally, it is less expensive to keep a brand with a high market share at that level than it is to build market share by taking business from competitors. The size of market share also indicates the number of current users for the product. There are definite economies of scale in media. Thus, if the user base is large, it is generally less expensive to deliver the campaign message on a cost-per-impression basis than if the user base is very small and select. Thus, market share and size of customer base usually have a great influence on the budget.

Competition and Clutter

The strength and number of competitors have much to do with the amount of advertising money needed to achieve some advertising objectives. For example, if there are a large number of competitors and they are all advertising extensively, then simply having a brand message heard may require heavier than normal advertising investment. A very competitive marketplace is usually a costly advertising arena.

Because there are limited media advertising opportunities for all advertisers, there is much "clutter" in the media. Clutter simply means there are many advertising messages directed to an audience. While all of these messages may not be directly competitive to the brand, they are certainly competitive in terms of attention.

Competition and clutter will not subside. They will likely only become more of a problem for the advertising planner in the future. If the brand competes in the very cluttered atmosphere of television, a larger budget is often required than if the major media choice for the brand is trade and industrial magazines.

The Effects of Advertising Frequency

The effects of advertising frequency—the repetition of the message for the brand in the media—also has much to do with the size of the advertising budget. While little is actually known about the effects of frequency on purchasing decisions, a certain minimum number of repetitions is usually necessary to register the brand and the advertising message in the mind of the consumer. There is also some evidence that these effects vary by medium used, message, product, and even advertising execution.

Generally, three exposures of a message are considered necessary to generate recall among most consumers. This varies widely however. More will be said about the effects of frequency in Chapter 12, Media Planning.

Meanwhile, the planner must recognize that frequency of the message often has much to do with the success of the campaign. Additionally, since advertising (in the media) is sold based on frequency, volume and discounts sometimes influence the amount of money to be allocated to the advertising campaign.

Product Position in the Life Cycle

The position of the brand in its life cycle has much to do with the advertising developed for it and with the level of expenditure necessary to make it successful. For example, a brand in the introductory stage of its life cycle will likely require more space or time for the explanation of its merits than a product in the maturity stage which is well known and understood.

Product Risk and Substitutability

Finally, the risk of the product to the consumer often has much to do with the type and style of advertising that should be used, and that has an effect on the budget required to properly advertise the brand. Consumer risk in a brand can be judged in two ways: (1) monetary risk in terms of actual cost of the product, and (2) risk that the product will fill the need or solve the problem of the consumer who purchases it. In most cases, advertised brands in the U.S. tend to be low risk, both in terms of money and consumer satisfaction. Therefore, brands are often considered quite substitutable for each other.

Often the only differentiating feature between brands in a category is the advertising. When this is the case, advertising is a much more important marketing ingredient than when the brand has a unique physical benefit or feature. When advertising is the major difference between the brands and the risk to consumers is low, advertising expenditures generally must be quite high. Advertising is needed to continually remind the consumer of the brand. When this is necessary, it has a direct effect on the allocated budget.

Steps in Planning and Implementing a Budget

While in any given brand situation, other factors may have an influence on the budget, these are the major ones for consumer package goods. For

Figure 8-3.   A Process for Planning and Evaluating the Advertising Budget

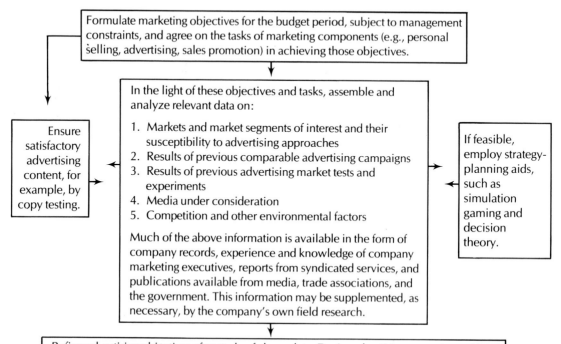

Formulate marketing objectives for the budget period, subject to management constraints, and agree on the tasks of marketing components (e.g., personal selling, advertising, sales promotion) in achieving those objectives.

In the light of these objectives and tasks, assemble and analyze relevant data on:

1. Markets and market segments of interest and their susceptibility to advertising approaches
2. Results of previous comparable advertising campaigns
3. Results of previous advertising market tests and experiments
4. Media under consideration
5. Competition and other environmental factors

Much of the above information is available in the form of company records, experience and knowledge of company marketing executives, reports from syndicated services, and publications available from media, trade associations, and the government. This information may be supplemented, as necessary, by the company's own field research.

Ensure satisfactory advertising content, for example, by copy testing.

If feasible, employ strategy-planning aids, such as simulation gaming and decision theory.

Refine advertising objectives after study of above data. Devise advertising campaign, with supporting detailed budget, to cover:

1. The campaign proper
2. If appropriate, one or more experimental campaigns (i.e., campaigns in markets or regions to receive advertising treatment different from that used in the campaign proper)
3. Contingency reserve if desired
4. Tracking of results

Submit proposals to top management for review. Revise objectives, campaign, and budget as required by any additional constraints.

1. Conduct the campaign proper and any experimental campaigns
2. Use contingency reserve to capitalize on unforeseen opportunities and cope with unexpected difficulties
3. Track results of items 1 and 2

Repeat cycle

SOURCE: . Hurwood and Brown, *Some Guidelines for Advertising Budgeting,* 1972, pp. 22–23.

other products, such as durables, industrial goods, and business products, other factors are very important, such as dealers and distributors, the sales force, the type of response desired, and the number of people involved in the purchase decision. When developing the budget, the campaign planner must have a clear, concise view of what the objectives of the campaign are and what the campaign is expected to achieve—in other words, the advertising objectives. They have a major influence on the budgeting procedure.

While there are as many ways to plan an advertising budget as there are planners, a well-conceived, step-by-step process is usually the best. Often the budgeting procedure for each brand is time and situation specific. However, the planning sequence developed by David L. Hurwood and James K. Brown works for most products or services in most situations.[3] It should work as well for you whether you're an experienced planner or a novice. (See Figure 8-3.)

Methods of Budgeting

With the preceding background on the nature of advertising budgets and the planning sequence, the next step is to review the major methods by which advertising planners establish budgets. There are six major approaches. Each is discussed below.

Guidelines

Guidelines are methods that use historical data or a judgmental approach to determine the advertising budget. With the use of guidelines, the advertising planner makes the assumption there is some relationship between what has happened in the past and what will happen in the future. Three basic types of guidelines used for establishing the advertising budget are discussed.

Ratios. These are usually stated as percentages based on some measurable fact or amount. Typical bases for ratios are percentage of sales (either past or future), percentage of gross margin (again either past or expected in the future), and percentage of net income. Percentage of sales and percentage of gross margin are both explained below since they are so widely used by all types of businesses.

1. Percentage of sales. This is the most widely used method of guideline budgeting and may be based on past or expected future sales. The ratio

---

3. David L. Hurwood and James K. Brown, *Some Guidelines for Advertising Budgeting* (New York: The Conference Board, 1972), pp. 22–23.

Figure 8-4.   100 Leaders Advertising as Percent of Sales

	RANK	COMPANY	ADVERTISING	SALES	ADV. AS % OF SALES
Airlines	57	Trans World Corp.	$95,235,900	$5,265,500,000	1.8
	75	UAL Inc.	70,585,100	5,141,174,000	1.4
	87	Eastern Air Lines, Inc.	54,100,000	3,727,093,000	1.5
	89	American Airlines, Inc.	51,496,900	4,108,699,000	1.2
	91	Delta Air Lines Inc.	44,500,000	3,533,326,000	1.3
Appliances, TV, Radio	17	RCA Corp.	208,798,300	8,004,800,000	2.6
	35	General Electric Co.	164,696,300	27,240,000,000	0.6
	65	North American Philips Corp.	83,881,400	3,030,044,000	2.8
Automobiles	5	General Motors Corp.	401,000,000	62,698,500,000	0.6
	11	Ford Motor Co.	286,686,600	38,247,100,000	0.7
	24	Chrysler Corp.	193,000,000	10,821,600,000	1.8
	51	Toyota Motor Sales, U.S.A., Inc.	106,186,700	17,014,984,000	6.2
	62	Nissan Motor Corp., U.S.A.	87,884,100	15,680,000,000	5.6
	67	Volkswagen of America, Inc.	81,000,000	16,118,505,500	0.5
	76	American Motors Corp.	70,000,000	2,588,923,000	2.7
	78	American Honda Motor Co.	68,346,800	7,945,401,000	0.9
Chemicals	44	American Cyanamid Co.	138,000,000	3,649,073,000	3.8
	53	E.I. du Pont de Nemours & Co.......	105,000,000	22,810,000,000	0.5
	58	Union Carbide Corp.	90,000,000	10,168,000,000	0.9
Communications, Entertainment	37	Warner Communications Inc.	159,000,000	3,237,153,000	4.9
	43	Time Inc.	141,144,000	3,296,382,000	4.3
	46	CBS Inc.	134,010,000	4,125,954,000	3.0
	80	MCA Inc	63,600,000	1,328,988,000	4.8
	90	Columbia Pictures Industries, Inc.	47,500,000	686,600,000	6.9
	99	American Broadcasting Cos.........	40,000,000	2,443,713,000	1.6
Drugs	40	Richardson-Vicks, Inc.	149,000,000	1,088,100,000	13.7
	48	Schering-Plough Corp.	119,768,600	1,808,000,000	6.6
	59	Sterling Drug Inc.	89,700,000	1,792,925,000	5.0
	60	SmithKline Corp.	89,265,000	1,985,341,000	4.5
	73	Miles Laboratories, Inc.	72,084,700	767,606,000	9.4
	83	Pfizer Inc.........................	59,000,000	3,249,700,000	1.8
Food	3	General Foods Corp.	456,800,000	8,351,100,000	5.5
	7	Nabisco Brands, Inc.	340,983,000	5,819,200,000	5.9
	15	McDonald's Corp.	230,248,200	7,129,000,000	3.2
	19	General Mills Corp.	207,306,100	5,312,100,000	3.9
	25	Ralston Purina Co.	192,984,000	5,224,700,000	3.7
	30	Dart & Kraft, Inc.	177,042,100	10,211,000,000	1.7
	31	Esmark, Inc.	175,065,000	3,132,349,000	5.6
	33	Beatrice Foods Co.	170,000,000	9,023,520,000	1.9
	34	Consolidated Foods Corp.	166,399,700	5,800,000,000	2.9
	36	H.J. Heinz Co......................	160,175,000	3,688,500,000	4.3
	39	Norton Simon Inc.	149,875,600	3,191,898,000	4.7
	47	Pillsbury Co.	131,015,100	3,385,100,000	3.9
	54	Kellogg Co.	102,111,300	2,321,300,000	4.4
	56	Quaker Oats Co.	95,597,100	2,599,500,000	3.7
	61	Nestle Enterprises	88,000,000	2,387,000,000	3.7
	63	CPC International Inc...............	87,000,000	4,343,100,000	2.0
	74	Campbell Soup Co.	70,757,000	2,950,000,000	2.4
	92	Borden, Inc.	44,019,000	4,415,174,000	1.0
	94	Morton-Norwich Products, Inc.	42,483,800	957,584,000	4.4

RANK	COMPANY	ADVERTISING	SALES	ADV. AS % OF SALES	
69	Mars, Inc.	$78,400,000	$1,350,000,000	5.8	**Gum, Candy**
81	Wm. Wrigley Jr. Co.	63,526,300	607,834,000	10.5	
86	Hershey Foods Corp.	56,516,000	1,451,000,000	3.9	
55	Eastman Kodak Co.	101,000,000	10,337,500,000	1.0	**Photographic Equipment**
88	Polaroid Corp.	51,750,000	1,419,600,000	3.6	
100	Canon U.S.A.	36,525,800	705,000,000	5.2	
2	Sears, Roebuck & Co.	544,104,500	27,360,000,000	2.0	**Retail Chains**
6	K mart Corp.	349,611,000	16,527,012,000	2.1	
18	J.C. Penney Co., Inc.	208,600,000	11,860,000,000	1.8	
1	Procter & Gamble Co.	671,757,400	11,944,000,000	5.6	**Soaps, Cleaners (and Allied)**
13	Colgate-Palmolive Co.	260,000,000	5,261,364,000	4.9	
27	Unilever U.S.	188,878,800	2,840,170,000	6.7	
68	Clorox Co.	80,761,000	714,023,000	11.3	
79	S.C. Johnson & Son, Inc.	66,560,000	2,000,000,000	3.3	
14	PepsiCo, Inc.	260,000,000	7,027,443,000	3.7	**Soft Drinks**
22	Coca-Cola Co.	197,831,700	5,889,035,000	3.4	
9	American Telephone & Telegraph Co.	297,000,000	58,214,000,000	0.5	**Telephone Service, Equipment**
38	International Telephone & Telegraph Co.	153,000,000	17,306,189,000	0.9	
4	Philip Morris Inc.	432,971,400	10,885,900,000	4.0	**Tobacco**
8	R.J. Reynolds Industries, Inc.	321,279,600	11,691,800,000	2.7	
21	B.A.T. Industries PLC	199,301,800	4,592,259,000	4.3	
66	American Brands Inc.	82,218,900	6,538,161,000	1.3	
93	Liggett Group Inc.	43,500,000	1,192,481,000	3.6	
12	Warner-Lambert Co.	270,400,000	3,379,092,000	8.0	**Toiletries, Cosmetics**
16	American Home Products Corp.	209,000,000	4,131,237,000	5.1	
20	Bristol-Myers Co.	200,000,000	3,496,700,000	5.7	
23	Johnson & Johnson	195,000,000	3,025,900,000	6.4	
32	Gillette Co.	171,900,000	2,335,000,000	7.4	
42	Loews Corp.	141,384,400	4,776,000,000	3.0	
45	Chesebrough-Pond's Inc.	136,241,000	1,529,674,000	8.9	
50	Revlon, Inc.	106,638,750	2,365,938,000	4.5	
77	Beecham Group Ltd.	69,123,200	2,947,930,000	2.3	
96	Noxell Corp.	41,082,100	233,112,000	17.6	
97	Jeffrey Martin, Inc.	41,000,000	75,000,000	54.7	
28	Anheuser-Busch Cos.	187,228,500	4,409,600,000	4.2	**Wine, Beer, Liquor**
29	Heublein, Inc.	187,000,000	2,050,121,000	9.1	
41	Seagram Co. Ltd.	145,000,000	2,772,733,000	5.2	
70	Brown-Forman Distillers Corp.	78,000,000	860,556,000	9.1	
85	Jos. E. Schlitz Brewing Co.	56,763,500	881,674,000	6.4	
95	Hiram Walker Resources Ltd.	42,283,000	2,945,300,000	1.4	
10	Mobil Corp.	293,103,200	68,587,000,000	4.3	**Miscellaneous**
26	U.S. Government	189,026,000	—	—	
49	Mattel Inc.	110,600,000	1,134,252,000	9.8	
52	Gulf & Western Industries, Inc.	106,140,900	7,409,000,000	1.4	
64	Xerox Corp.	84,150,000	8,691,000,000	1.0	
71	American Express Co.	76,036,000	7,211,000,000	1.1	
72	Greyhound Corp.	75,592,100	5,164,000,000	1.5	
82	Kimberly-Clark Corp.	62,440,000	2,900,000,000	2.2	
84	Exxon Corp.	58,062,000	115,148,321,000	0.1	
98	International Business Machines Corp.	40,700,000	29,070,000,000	0.1	

SOURCE: *Advertising Age,* Sept. 9, 1982, p. 8.

used is often determined by past experience or industry or category guidelines.

The computation is fairly simple. A given percentage of the previous year's sales or the forecasted sales for the coming year for the brand determines the allocation. For example, if sales totaled $100,000 last year, and 2 percent was the arbitrary figure selected as appropriate for advertising, the budget for the coming year would be $2,000 ($100,000 × .02 = $2,000). A percentage of forecasted sales can also be used; the calculation is done in the same way.

While the percentage-of-sales method is quick, easy, and accepted by many firms, it has an inherent weakness. When sales are good, the advertising budget increases. When sales are bad, advertising is reduced. The basic principle at work is that advertising becomes a *result* of sales, which is contrary to a basic belief that advertising should generate sales, not the other way around.

An additional problem in the percentage-of-sales budgeting approach is the lag effect in planning. For example, a 1987 marketing plan would be developed in 1986. The advertising budget would be based on the last full year's sales; in this case, that would be 1985. As a result, the advertising budget for 1987 would actually be based on sales figures that would be two years old by the time the budget was implemented.

Figure 8-4 illustrates examples of the budgeting approach using advertising as a percentage of past sales for the top national U.S. advertisers in 1982. As you can see, the percentages used in various industry categories vary widely as does the percentage of sales allocated by individual companies.

2. Percentage of gross margin. Another popular method of advertising budgeting is a percentage of the gross margin (net sales less cost of goods) of the company or brand. The calculation of the budget is determined simply as a percentage of past or anticipated gross margin. For example, if a company has a gross profit margin on a brand of $1,000,000 and invests 5 percent in advertising, the A/M (advertising as a percentage of gross profit) ratio would provide a budget of $50,000. Figure 8-5 shows advertising as a percentage of net sales (A/S) and the A/M by industry for the year 1981.

Allocation per unit, unit of sales, or retail outlet. In this method, a certain dollar amount is allocated on the basis of the number of units produced, the number of units sold, for each retail location or the like. These approaches are widely used in durable goods or where the retail outlet is the key sales factor such as convenience stores or fast food outlets. For example:

1. Unit of sales. This is similar to but not quite the same as the percentage-of-sales method. Here a dollar amount per unit sold or produced is allocated to advertising. This amount may be based on any factor such as cents per case or dollars per unit. For example, an affordable advertising cost per unit is determined by the advertiser. By estimating the number of units that will be sold, the advertiser determines the advertising budget.

   The automobile industry often uses this type of budgeting. If an advertising investment, for example, of $25 per automobile is believed to be sufficient, and 50,000 units are forecast to be sold, the advertising budget would be $1,250,000 (50,000 units × $25 = $1,250,000). This method has the advantage of tying the advertising appropriation directly to the unit of sale, but it begs the same question of whether advertising creates sales or is the result of sales. In some cases, the advertising budget is not actually generated until the unit is sold, which can create additional problems.

2. Per outlet. Many durable goods manufacturers or service firms that rely heavily on the retailer for a personal selling effort set advertising budgets according to the number of outlets through which the product will be sold. For example, a consumer loan organization may determine the company can invest $100 in advertising per loan office per year to generate personal loan applications. If there are 5,000 loan offices across the country, the advertising budget would be $500,000 (5,000 loan offices × $100 = $500,000).

   The per-outlet approach has simplicity and is easily calculated. It does, however, ignore the fact that all loan offices are not alike. Some offices may need considerably more than $100 per year in advertising support, and others less. In effect, the approach suggests that the cost of supporting an office in New York City is the same as that in Seminole, Oklahoma. A major difference, if only in media costs, makes this approach somewhat questionable for many types of products.

Arbitrary Appropriations

While certainly not a scientific method, a number of organizations allocate their advertising budget arbitrarily. Little regard is given in this method to the objectives to be achieved or the results to be obtained from the advertising. Instead, the arbitrary appropriation is usually established by top management or the financial department through some form of executive judgment. The most common of these approaches follow.

Management decision. The budget is established by top management and is simply allocated as the amount available to be spent. It may or may not

Figure 8-5. Estimates of Average Advertising Sales and Advertising to Gross Profit Margin by Industry

INDUSTRY	SIC	A&P AS % Sales 1978	A&P AS % Margin 1978	INDUSTRY	SIC	A&P AS % Sales 1978	A&P AS % Margin 1978
Agriculture production-crops	100	4.2	8.2	Rubber & misc. plastics prods	3000	1.3	4.9
Agriculture production-livestock	200	1.0	4.9	Fabricated rubber prods NEC	3060	1.9	7.0
Metal mining	1000	0.1	0.2	Misc. plastic products	3070	0.9	3.3
Copper ores.	1020	0.2	0.9	Footwear except rubber.	3140	2.3	7.1
Lead & zinc ores	1030	0.0	0.1	Leather goods NEC	3190	1.6	3.9
Gold ores.	1040	0.0	0.0	Flat glass.	3210	0.8	2.4
Bituminous Coal & Lignite Min.	1210	0.0	0.0	Glass containers	3220	5.9	16.1
Crude petroleum & natural gas.	1310	0.1	0.3	Cement hydraulic	3240	0.1	0.2
Drilling oil & gas wells.	1380	0.1	0.3	Structural clay products	3250	1.1	10.0
Misc. nonmetallic minerals.	1490	−0.0	−0.0	Pottery products NEC	3260	2.5	6.8
General building contractors	1520	0.8	5.5	Concrete gypsum & plaster	3270	0.4	1.6
Operative builders	1530	1.0	4.2	Abrasive asbestos & misc. min.	3290	0.5	2.1
Construction-not bldg. constr.	1600	0.3	1.2	Blast furnaces & steel works	3310	0.2	1.1
Construction-spl contractors	1700	0.5	1.9	Iron & steel foundries	3320	−0.0	−0.0
Food & kindred products	2000	3.3	9.8	Prim smelt-refin nonfer. mtl.	3330	0.5	2.1
Meat products	2010	1.2	7.7	Second smelt-refin. nonfer. mtl.	3340	0.2	0.9
Dairy products	2020	1.7	11.6	Rolling & draw nonfer. metal	3350	0.5	2.3
Canned-preserved fruits-vegs	2030	2.3	10.2	Misc. primary metal products	3390	0.6	1.9
Flour & other grain mill prods	2040	1.9	10.8	Metal cans & shipping cont.	3410	1.9	8.8
Bakery products	2050	1.6	3.8	Hardware NEC	3420	1.7	5.0
Cane sugar refining	2060	2.4	6.4	Heating equip. & plumbing fix.	3430	1.3	4.7
Fats & oils	2070	2.5	20.1	Misc. metal work	3440	0.9	3.2
Beer, alcoh bev & soft drink	2080	5.1	14.8	Bolts-nuts-screws-riv-washrs	3450	0.5	1.6
Food preparations NEC.	2090	1.2	3.1	Ordnance & accessories	3480	2.9	29.6
Cigarets.	2110	6.2	14.7	Valves-pipe fittings ex brass	3490	1.2	3.7
Cigars	2120	2.3	8.2	Engines & turbines.	3510	1.0	2.8
Textile mill products	2200	0.8	3.7	Farm & garden machinery & eqp.	3520	1.1	4.3
Floor covering mills	2270	1.3	4.5	Construction machinery & eqp.	3530	0.8	3.0
Apparel & other finished prods	2300	1.7	6.0	Metalworking machinery & eqp.	3540	0.8	2.7
Lumber & wood products	2400	0.7	3.2	Special industry machinery	3550	1.3	3.4
Wood buildings-mobile homes.	2450	0.9	5.2	General industrial mach. & eqp.	3560	1.1	3.4
Household furniture	2510	1.7	7.2	Office computing & acctg. mch.	3570	1.3	2.8
Office furniture	2520	0.9	3.0	Refrig & service ind. machine.	3580	1.8	6.9
Paper & allied products	2600	0.9	3.0	Elec. & electr. mach. eq. & supp.	3600	1.4	4.8
Convert paper-paperbd pd NEC	2640	1.7	4.1	Elec. transmission & distr. eqp.	3610	1.1	3.3
Paperboard containers-boxes	2650	−0.0	−0.0	Industrial controls	3620	0.7	2.1
Printing publishing & allied	2700	4.4	11.5	Household appliances	3630	3.9	12.9
Newspapers: publishing-print	2710	2.8	13.7	Electric lighting-wiring eqp.	3640	1.9	4.8
Periodicals: publishing-print	2720	3.9	14.4	Radio-tv receiving sets	3650	3.8	11.8
Books: publishing & printing.	2730	4.2	7.6	Tele & telegraph apparatus	3660	1.6	6.2
Commercial printing	2750	0.9	2.7	Electronic components & acces.	3670	1.1	3.2
Manifold business forms	2760	0.6	1.5	Electrical machy-equip NEC	3690	1.7	4.6
Greeting card publishing	2770	2.3	4.0	Motor vehicles & car bodies	3710	1.6	8.0
Service indus for print trade	2790	0.7	1.3	Aircraft & parts.	3720	0.8	4.0
Chemicals & allied prods	2800	1.9	5.0	Ship-boat building-repairing	3730	2.1	9.6
Indl. inorganic chemicals	2810	1.9	4.3	Railroad equipment	3740	0.1	0.7
Plastic matr-synthetic resin	2820	5.6	8.8	Motorcycles bicycles & parts	3750	−0.0	−0.0

INDUSTRY	SIC	A&P AS % Sales 1978	A&P AS % Margin 1978	INDUSTRY	SIC	A&P AS % Sales 1978	A&P AS % Margin 1978
Drugs	2830	6.4	12.5	Guided missiles & space vehc.	3760	0.3	1.7
Soap, detergents & cosmetics	2840	10.4	19.1	Travel trailers & campers	3790	0.9	6.9
Paints-varnishes-lacquers.	2850	1.8	5.9	Engr. lab & research equip.	3810	1.4	3.3
Industrial organic chemicals	2860	−0.0	−0.0	Measuring & controlling inst.	3820	1.5	3.7
Agriculture chemicals	2870	1.4	3.0	Optical instruments & lenses	3830	1.7	4.3
Misc. chemical products	2890	2.2	5.1	Surg. & med. instruments & app.	3840	1.5	3.7
Petroleum refining	2910	0.6	3.0	Photographic equip. & suppl.	3860	1.9	4.6
Paving & roofing materials	2950	1.0	3.3	Watches clocks & parts	3870	1.7	6.9
Jewelry-precious metals	3910	5.6	12.4	Retail-jewelry stores	5940	3.0	8.6
Musical instruments.	3930	2.1	5.9	Retail-mail order houses	5960	13.4	27.9
Toys & amusement sport goods	3940	5.2	16.3	Retail-stores NEC	5990	3.0	10.0
Pens-pencil & other office mat.	3950	3.8	10.1	Savings & loan associations	6120	0.9	2.0
Misc. manufacturing	3990	1.1	4.2	Personal credit institutions.	6140	1.7	4.0
Railroads-line haul operating	4010	1.3	5.9	Business credit institutions	6150	1.2	2.1
Trucking-local-long distance	4210	0.4	2.0	Finance-services.	6190	1.7	7.8
Water transportation	4400	0.1	0.2	Security & commodity brokers	6200	1.9	9.4
Air transportation-certified	4510	1.5	5.9	Insurance agents & brokers	6400	1.0	11.0
Pipe lines ex natural gas	4610	0.0	0.0	Real estate	6500	1.9	7.0
Transportation services	4700	0.9	6.8	Subdiv. develop. ex cemetery	6550	2.0	7.7
Telephone communication	4810	0.5	1.3	Miscellaneous investing	6790	2.6	14.3
Radio-tv broadcasters	4830	2.6	4.8	Hotel-motels	7010	2.5	11.2
CATV	4890	1.6	6.0	Serv-personal	7200	3.0	10.5
Natural gas transmission	4920	0.1	0.2	Serv-linen supply	7210	0.4	1.4
Sanitary services	4950	0.2	0.5	Serv-advertising agencies	7310	1.6	5.1
Whsl-autos & parts	5010	1.3	7.1	Serv-clean & maint to bldg NEC	7340	0.2	1.2
Whsl-lumber & constr. matl.	5030	0.8	5.0	Serv-computer & data process	7370	0.9	4.1
Whsl-sporting & recrea goods	5040	4.3	13.6	Serv-R&D labs & profess serv	7390	2.7	10.7
Whsl-metals & minerals	5050	0.2	1.2	Serv-automotive repair & serv.	7500	1.2	5.1
Whsl-elec. apparatus & equip.	5060	3.8	12.2	Serv-motion picture production	7810	7.6	32.3
Whsl-hardwr. plum. heat. equip.	5070	0.3	1.5	Serv-motion picture theatres	7830	3.7	30.5
Whsl-machinery & equipment	5080	1.0	3.4	Serv-racing incl. track oper.	7940	3.1	19.0
Whsl-scrap & waste materials	5090	5.7	13.7	Serv-misc amusement & recreat.	7990	3.5	11.4
Whsl-drugs & proprietary	5120	1.9	4.1	Serv-nursing & personal care.	8050	2.2	4.2
Whsl-groceries & related prods	5140	0.6	2.9	Serv-hospitals	8060	0.6	1.7
Whsl-nondurable goods NEC	5190	0.7	2.8	Serv-educational.	8200	6.3	18.5
Retail-lumber-other bldg. mat.	5210	3.2	9.3	Serv-engineering & architect	8910	0.4	1.8
Retail-mobile home dealers	5270	0.8	4.9	Conglomerates	9990	1.2	4.4
Retail-department stores	5310	2.9	9.9				
Retail-variety stores.	5330	2.3	8.9				
Retail-grocery stores	5410	1.3	5.8				
Retail-auto dealers gas stat.	5500	2.1	8.9				
Retail-apparel & access. store	5600	2.6	7.2				
Retail-women's ready to wear	5620	2.0	12.1				
Retail-shoe stores	5660	2.1	5.0				
Retail-furniture stores	5710	5.8	17.6				
Retail-hshold. appliance stores	5720	3.5	15.3				
Retail-eating places	5810	2.9	15.4				
Retail-drug-propriet. stores	5910	1.8	8.3				

Legend:

A&P	=	Advertising & promotion.
−0.0	=	No data available for this value.
NEC	=	Not Elsewhere Classified
SIC	=	Standard Industrial Classification
A&P % SALES	=	A&P EXPENDITURES/NET SALES
A&P % MARGIN	=	A&P EXPENDITURES/(NET SALES—COST OF GOODS SOLD)

SOURCE: Schonfeld & Associates Inc.
120 South LaSalle Street
Chicago, Illinois 60603 (312) 236-5846

SOURCE: Adapted from *Advertising Age*, July 23, 1979.

be tied to the needs of the brand or the company. When this is the case, the campaign planner really is concerned only with the allocation and control of the advertising, not in budget determination.

What can be afforded. Top management allocates the advertising budget on the basis of what is believed to be affordable either by the brand or the company. The overriding factor in this management decision is usually the total profit desired on the brand as a return on investment. Here, too, the advertising planner is involved only in allocation and control of the budget, not in determination.

Go for broke. In rare instances, management may make a decision that advertising can be used either to capture a market or to attempt to save a dying brand. Advertising funds are then allocated with no relationship to sales, profits, or even return on investment. The basic plan simply is to attempt to overwhelm consumers or competition in the marketplace with advertising. Although rare, this type of budgeting approach is sometimes successful. Top management is usually responsible for the budget allocation, since the plan has a direct bearing on the overall financial stability of the company.

Minimum campaign. Although not exactly an arbitrary decision, it is described here because the determination of what is a minimum campaign falls into that category. Some advertisers believe there is a certain minimum amount of advertising, particularly in television, that must be placed against the consumer to rise above the noise or clutter in the medium. Simon Broadbent has called it the "minimum campaign"[4] while Dorothy Cohen refers to it as meeting the level of "advertising noise."[5] Regardless of the label, the idea is that, below a certain level of investment, the advertising may not be heard in the marketplace. It is simply covered up with other advertisers' messages.

There is some value to this concept, but the problem is in determining what the minimum campaign level for the brand should be. That minimum level is largely a matter of judgment. There appear to be no hard-and-fast rules for determining what minimum level is required or even if it exists. Thus, this approach is purely judgmental.

Inflation. In the general economy inflation has ebbed and flowed for a

---

4. Simon Broadbent, *Spending Advertising Money* (London: Business Books Limited, 1975), p. 165.
5. Dorothy Cohen, *Advertising* (New York: John Wiley & Sons, 1972), pp. 272–73.

number of years. But for advertisers the path has been virtually straight up-hill. A number of advertisers now use a basic figure plus an inflation term to determine their budgets. This inflation percentage increase can be tied to any number of factors, but the most common is an estimate of the increase in media costs for the budget period.

No doubt, rapid rises in media costs have seriously eroded the buying power of all types of advertising budgets over the past few years. Media rate increases of 15 to 20 percent per year are not uncommon. Advertisers using a fixed percentage of their sales are probably actually losing message penetration as compared with a few years ago: i.e., unless brand sales are increasing at the same rate as media inflation, the advertisers' real-dollar investments must be declining. While inflation may be a way of trying to keep message levels the same, advertisers who attempt to use this method may find the required allocation beyond their means. Thus, they may be spending more and still getting less.

Unfortunately, although guidelines and arbitrary appropriations are by far the most widely used advertising budgeting methods in the U.S., they are also the most unscientific and commonly the most unreliable. None is directly related to a campaign's advertising objectives. Thus, generally, these approaches are not desirable. Other methods seem to provide a better approach to properly establishing an advertising budget.

Theoretical and Empirical Methods

Although these budgeting methods are extremely complex and require rather sophisticated use of the computer, previous sales data, and models, they are likely the path of the future. Unfortunately, most of them are still proprietary, and details are not widely available outside the organization that has developed the model or computer system. The basic methods used will be covered rather briefly here since most are extremely complex. Some additional information can be found in market or media research texts or scholarly journals.

Theoretical methods. Theoretical approaches to advertising budgeting are usually based on some form of mathematical model using historical data as input. In spite of many advancements, most models are proprietary or require information that is not obtainable at a reasonable cost. In many cases, these approaches are not practical for any except large companies with extensive available funds.

James F. Engel, Hugh G. Wales, and Martin R. Warshaw identify the primary quantitative methods as follows:

1. Sales model. Advertising is regarded as the only variable affecting sales. Thus, an optimization approach is used to determine the ideal advertising budget.

2. Dynamic models. These models attempt to account for the effects of advertising on sales over time. A typical approach is to incorporate the carry-over effects of present advertising into the future through modeling.

3. Competitive models. Another approach is to create a model of the activities of one's competition. Most such models are based on some form of game theory, in which it is assumed that all players are inter-dependent and that uncertainty results from not knowing what the others will do. A strategy is then developed for reducing and controlling this uncertainty through the model.

4. Stochastic models. Two major approaches using the laws of prob-ability have been developed. One is based on Markov Chains; the other on the Stochastic Learning Model.

5. Simulation. Several computer models have been developed that simu-late consumer behavior from stored data. Through experimental ap-proaches, various levels of budget allocations are tested to determine the most effective return based on investment. While some success has been achieved, much work remains before this becomes a practical budgeting option.[6]

One of the most successful commercial theoretical techniques is the Hendry model, which has been used by many companies, apparently with great success. The details of the model, unfortunately, are secret, but it is believed to be based on a mathematical model containing the "fundamental laws of consumer behavior which have been deductively derived." Developed in 1962, the Hendry model correlates the rela-tionship between varying levels of the advertising expenditure and the resulting share of market and contribution to profit. Because inputs (the direct manufacturing margin, the advertising expenditure level, and share of market) are easily obtained, the system has a number of followers who believe strongly in it.[7]

Empirical approaches. The empirical method is different since it is built on experimental feedback rather than historical data. It is sensitive to specific

6. James F. Engel, Hugh G. Wales and Martin R. Warshaw, *Promotional Strategy,* rev. ed. (Homewood, IL: Richard D. Irwin, 1971), pp. 213–23.

7. M. A. McNiven, Ed. *How Much to Spend for Advertising* (New York: Association of National Advertisers, 1969), pp. 5, 67–71.

characteristics of a given product class and to the marketing factors acting on the product at the time the concept is set.

Because experimentation requires trial and evaluation over time, it can be used only for specific brands and cannot be projected to other product classes or even to other brands in the same category. Most empirical approaches to budgeting are highly proprietary, and little is known of them.

A typical example of an experimentation approach might be the use of a series of test markets. For example, assume the product for which the budget is being developed is a brand of frozen orange juice. Initially, in several test markets of equal population, frozen orange juice usage and brand share were selected and matched as closely as possible. Varying budget expenditure levels were set for the markets. For example, Market A might have been budgeted at the current national program level for that particular brand. Market B might have been set at 50 percent of that amount and Market C at 150 percent. Advertising results in terms of both brand and total frozen orange juice category sales would have been measured. In addition, communications effects would have been tracked. Through a comparison of the results obtained over time, estimates could then be made of how the varying budget levels might perform on a broad-scale basis. As a result of these experiments, budget levels for the frozen orange juice brand could be established with more precision than with other less-sophisticated approaches.

While both theoretical and empirical budgeting approaches will doubtless bring greater precision to the budgeting process, they are limited at this time to only the more sophisticated organizations that can develop or furnish the necessary background and information to make the systems practical and effective. For the general advertising campaign planner, the following three budgeting approaches seem more appropriate at this point.

Competitive Approach

An approach that relates the proposed expenditure for the brand to the expenditures of competitors has gained considerable support from package-goods marketers. Often called the "share of voice" budgeting technique because the basic idea is to relate the amount invested in advertising to the share of market held in sales and the share of all advertising investments being made in the product category, it works on the hypothesis that advertising in a particular product category is mutually exclusive to other advertising in general. In other words, advertising for a brand of dog food competes for the consumer's attention primarily with the advertising of other brands of dog food. It does not, for example, compete with advertising for automobiles, calculators, beer, or fast food restaurants. Therefore, the share of advertising done by an advertiser can be related to the share of attention the brand will receive, which relates to the share of market that can be obtained. The idea boils down to a rather simple equation:

$$\frac{\text{Share of}}{\text{Media Voice}} = \frac{\text{Share of}}{\text{Consumer Mind}} = \frac{\text{Share of}}{\text{Market in Sales}}$$

In other words, the share of media advertising voice or share of total advertising expenditures in the category can be equated to the amount of attention, interest, or preference in the mind of the consumer. That, in turn, can be related to the share of market or share of sales the brand will receive.

How it works. The budgeting procedure is quite simple, which is one of the reasons the approach is so appealing. All the planner needs is the share of market that the brand presently has in the particular product category and the total amount of advertising invested by all advertisers in the category for the past year or the expected amount for the coming year. These figures can usually be estimated or obtained from various research sources.

Once the share of market and the total amount of advertising (voice) are known, the calculation is quite simple because it is assumed that for an existing product, there is a one-to-one relationship. To hold share, the advertiser spends at a ratio of market share to advertising share. To gain share, the ratio is increased. For example, assume a budget for Ralph's Dog Food is being developed. We know that our brand, Ralph's, holds a 15 percent share of the market in terms of sales. Through research, we determine all dog food advertisers invested $50,000,000 in media this past year. A 10 percent media increase is expected for the coming year, which would mean a total of $55,000,000 in dog food advertising. Thus, to hold our present share, our budget for Ralph's Dog Food for the coming year should be $8,250,000 [$50,000,000 in dog food advertising category plus 10 percent increase for the coming year = $55,000,000 × .15 (our share of market) = $8,250,000 budget for the coming year]. If we hoped to gain share, we would budget over $8,250,000. More on this in the next section.

Advantages and disadvantages. The obvious advantage of the share of voice system is that it is easy to calculate and maintains competitive parity with other advertisers in the category. The major disadvantage is that the budget is not directly related to the advertising objectives that may have been set.

While several other arguments may be brought against the competitive system, there is increasing evidence that the parity approach works. Also, there appears to be a fairly strong relationship between advertising expenditures, consumer awareness, and share of market.

J. O. Peckham, formerly of A. C. Nielsen Company, has charted the correlation between share of advertising voice and share of sales for a number of products over a number of years. While much of Peckham's data deals with new products and the resulting market share they achieve over time compared to their advertising share of voice, the same ratio seems to hold true even after introduction. Generally, he has found a one-to-one relationship between share of voice and share of market for existing or established products and a 1.5–2.0 to 1.0 relationship for new products.

Figure 8-6 illustrates the actual experience of a new product in the

Figure 8-6. Ratio of Share of Advertising to Share of Market

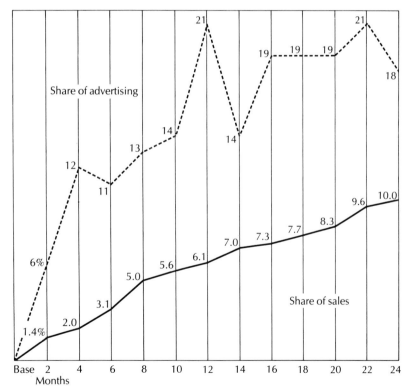

SOURCE: J. O. Peckham, *The Wheel of Marketing* (Scarsdale, NY: Privately printed, 1975), pp. 73–76.

food category over an initial two-year introductory period as charted by Peckham. The ratio of share of advertising to share of market was 1.6.[8]

DAGMAR: Objective and Task

This approach was suggested and formalized by Russell H. Colley in his study for the Association of National Advertisers, *Defining Advertising Goals for Measured Advertising Results* (DAGMAR).[9] While it is by far the most logical of all advertising budgeting approaches, it still does not appear to be widely used. In spite of this, we strongly endorse its use.

How it works. In the DAGMAR approach, specific advertising campaign objectives are set in advance. Based on those objectives, whether they are awareness, brand trial, or other results, the amount of advertising necessary to accomplish those goals can then be determined. The advertising budget is built from the ground up to achieve the predetermined goals rather than past or future results. The DAGMAR, or objective-and-task, approach provides an opportunity to measure the results of the campaign and whether or not the goals set for the advertising campaign are achieved.

Advantages and disadvantages. The major difficulty in using the objective-and-task budgeting method is that although advertising goals and objectives are set in advance, it is sometimes difficult to determine just how much money is needed to achieve those goals. For example, the objective of chieving 20 percent awareness of the advertising campaing theme is easily set by the planner. It is quite another task, however, to determine how much media reach and frequency will be needed to achieve that 20 percent awareness goal among consumers. While the objective-and-task method of advertising budgeting is more scientific and solidly based than other methods, the chief advantage may be in the ability to determine whether the money was well spent after the fact, rather than in setting the original budget.

The Capital Investment Approach

A budgeting approach that has gained considerable attention, particularly in these somewhat troubled economic times, considers advertising and the

---

8. J. O. Peckham, *The Wheel of Marketing* (Scarsdale, NY: Privately printed, 1975), pp. 73–76.

9. Russell H. Colley, *Defining Advertising Goals for Measured Advertising Results* (New York: Association of National Advertisers, 1961).

advertising expenditure as a capital investment. The prime evaluation of the budget is on the basis of return on investment (ROI) or some form of return on the capital spent on advertising. While the approach has great appeal to financial people, it lacks the direct relationship to the advertising campaign's objectives or the goals found in the DAGMAR method. Capital investment looks at advertising as an expenditure and gives a measure of the return on that investment. Nothing more. Nevertheless, the capital investment approach has its adherents.

How it works. The first step is to measure the cost of capital or funds for the particular advertising project. That, of course, requires an investigation not only of the cost of the funds but their availability as well. The next step is to calculate the time-discounted rate of return expected from the advertising investment. This is done by estimating the return on the investment in each future period and discounting that by a time factor until those funds are received. These estimated returns, or cash flows, at the discounted rate then show the value of the investment over time. The formula to make the calculation is:

$$PV = \frac{1}{(1 + r)^n}$$

where

$$PV = \text{present value of a dollar}$$
$$n = \text{periods in the future}$$
$$r = \text{effective rate of interest (or cost of capital)}$$

The obvious effect of having to wait a long time for a dollar to return is to reduce the present value of this future payment. Similarly, the present value of a future payment is therefore reduced as the cost of capital is increased.

Advantages and disadvantages. The most apparent advantage of this approach is to give management a view of the return on the advertising investment when compared to other capital expenditures. The disadvantages are the lack of relationship of the budget to the advertising objectives and the inability of management in many instances to accurately determine the value of the advertising over a period of time or even to determine the length of time over which the advertising should be valued.[10]

---

10. Adapted from Anthony F. McGann and J. Thomas Russell, *Advertising Media: A Managerial Approach* (Homewood, IL: Richard D. Irwin, 1981), pp. 64–67.

All of the advertising budgeting methods outlined above have their supporters and their detractors. In actual fact, the advertising planner's budgeting decision may well be determined by previous methods used by the organization. When this is the case, the best advice is to compare the method used previously with one of the methods listed above to determine if they provide the same general budget amount. If there is a great discrepancy, perhaps it is time to investigate or suggest another method to management.

While all these budgeting methods can and have been used by many organizations for all types of products, there are major differences between budgeting for an existing product and for a new product. In the next section, there are recommended approaches for both.

Budgeting for Existing Products or Services

One of the major problems many advertising planners face is developing an advertising budget for existing or established products. The planner may find that previous budgets have been woefully inadequate and sufficient advertising funds have not been invested in the brand. In those instances, the planner then develops a new plan and a bigger budget needed to achieve the goals that have been established for the brand. This type of situation often occurs when a new advertising agency starts to work on a brand. The first goal of the new agency always seems to be to increase the advertising budget and advertising expenditure. While these increases may be justified, often the feeling of the planner seems to be that any brand's sales, marketing, and advertising problems can be solved with increased spending. While that sometimes may be the case, it often isn't.

Novice campaign planners often face this increased budget problem in a different way. They have a lack of realism as to just exactly what a particular brand can actually afford in terms of an advertising investment. Often, this is caused by a lack of understanding of just how a brand generates advertising dollars and how many dollars that particular brand actually has available for advertising at any given time. A review of where marketing and advertising dollars really come from would seem to be in order, for that will lead directly into a recommended method of budgeting for existing or established brands.

Where Marketing and Advertising Dollars Come From

Figure 8-7 is a hypothetical combined operating statement for a typical consumer product. The letters at the left of each of the entries are used for descriptive purposes.

**Figure 8-7.   Hypothetical Operating Statement for a
Nondurable Consumer Product**

(A)	Retail price 69¢ per can/12 per case		$8.28
(B)	Retailer's margin @ 20%		1.66
(C)	Gross price to retailer		6.62
(D)	Less trade promotions/deals @ 2%		.13
(E)	Net price to retailer		6.49
(F)	Wholesale/broker commission @ 7%		.45
(G)	Net sales price		6.04 (100%)
(H)	Cost of goods		3.32 (55%)
(J)	Fixed costs, 20%	$ .66	
(K)	Variable costs, 80%	2.66	
(L)	Gross margin		2.72 (45%)
(M)	Distribution expense		.12 (2%)
(N)	Contribution margin		2.60 (43%)
(P)	Direct expenses		
(Q)	Advertising	.36	(6%)
(R)	Consumer merchandising	.24	(4%)
(S)	Management and sales expense	.92	(15%)
(T)	Research and development	.06	(1%)
(U)	Total direct expenses		1.58 (26%)
(V)	Product margin		1.02 (17%)

Assume you are the brand manager for Ferd's Food Company. Your primary brand responsibility is canned marinated eggrolls. The eggrolls are packaged in 14-oz. cans containing approximately 17 eggrolls and are shipped 12 cans to the case. The normal retail price (out-of-store) is 69¢ per can.

Line A illustrates the retail price of a case of 12 cans of eggrolls at 69¢ each. From the retail price of 69¢, the retailer usually obtains a gross margin of 20 percent. Thus, on a per-case basis, the retailer's gross profit is $1.66 (Line B). Ferd's Food's gross price to the retailer on a case of eggrolls is $6.62 (Line C).

From the gross trade price, a deduction for trade promotions or deals must be made (Line D). In this case, Ferd's Food plans to offer trade promotions amounting to 2 percent of gross sales to the retailer. The discount is offered on all purchases made during the year if the retailer will run a reduced-price feature on eggrolls during the Chinese New Year's promotion. The cost of the trade promotions is deducted from the gross price to retailer to give a net price to retailer (Line E). Thus, the net price (per case) to the retailer is $6.49.

Ferd's eggrolls are not sold directly to the retailer but through a broker or wholesaler system. The broker's commission, therefore, must be deducted. The average commission to a broker (or the margin required by a wholesaler) is 7 percent of the gross price (Line F), in this case, 45¢. This amount is deducted from the net price to retailer, leaving a net sales price for the eggrolls of $6.04 per case (Line G). This is what Ferd's Food Company will receive for the sale of each case of marinated eggrolls.

The cost of manufacturing and packaging the eggrolls must be deducted from the net sales price. The total cost-of-goods, as determined by the production and accounting departments, amounts to $3.32 per case, or 55 percent of the net sales price. The fixed costs (Line J), your share of the company's general overhead, is calculated at 20 percent of the cost-of-goods, or 66¢ per case. The variable costs (Line K) are calculated at 80 percent of the cost-of-goods of the product, or $2.66 per case. The variable costs include such items as raw materials, manufacturing cost, filling and packaging the eggrolls, and storage and handling until the products are put into the distribution stream. Thus, deducting cost-of-goods (Line H) from the net sales price yields the gross margin on the product (Line L). The gross margin is the amount available for transportation and marketing expenses plus any profit to Ferd's Food Company on the sale of each case of eggrolls.

From the gross margin available (Line L) of $2.72 per case, deduct distribution expense (Line M). This is the actual cost of physically moving the product from the manufacturing plant to the wholesale warehouse or retail store. Here, the distribution expense is estimated to be 2 percent of net sales, or 12¢ per case. Subtracting the distribution expense from the gross margin leaves a contribution margin of $2.60 per case (Line N). If there were no selling or other expenses, this contribution margin would be the amount each case of eggrolls could contribute to the profit of the company. Realistically, however, there are promotional expenses, which are referred to as direct expenses (Lines P and U).

Direct expenses include all promotional costs such as advertising (Line Q), consumer merchandising (Line R), management and sales expense (Line S), and an allocation for research and development of new or improved eggrolls (Line T). These costs are combined as total direct expenses (Line U).

While the final profit on each case of eggrolls is shown as product margin (Line V) and appears to be what is left after all costs and expenses have been deducted, the format is somewhat misleading. Usually, management of Ferd's Food Company, after reviewing sales and expense forecasts for all company products and brands for the coming year, assigns a profit margin percentage (or a total dollar figure) to the eggroll brand manager as a goal for the coming year. This goal is determined on the basis of projecting an adequate return on the company's investment in the eggroll brand and as a proper contribution to the overall financial income and profit of the company. Thus, in actuality, using the profit goals established by management for the brand, the funds available for marketing—including advertising, promotion, sales, and R&D—is the difference between the contribution margin (Line N) and the product margin (Line V) or, in this case, $1.02 per case of eggrolls sold. It is from this total direct expense amount (Line U) that the brand manager must make the allocation for an advertising campaign.

There are, of course, circumstances that might help to increase or decrease the funds available for total direct expense (Line U). As manufacturing economies of scale are realized, such factors as increased sales might reduce the variable cost of the product (Line K). The possibility exists of reducing or completely deleting all trade promotions/deals (Line D). If sales could be concentrated closer to the manufacturing plant, distribution expenses (Line M) might be lowered. A change in any of these costs will directly affect the number of dollars available to the product manager for total direct expenses (Line U). For purposes of this illustration, however, the assumption is made that the sales forecast is fairly firm, that the trade promotions and deals are already established, and that distribution expenses will not vary. It is within this framework that the brand manager and the advertising agency must determine how best to allocate the available marketing funds, which include the cost of the advertising campaign.

In most instances, management and sales expense (Line S) and research and development costs (Line T) are most difficult to manipulate. For example, management and sales expenses (Line S) consist of the salaries and expenses of the sales force calling on the trade. In a multiproduct company, this expense is usually allocated to individual brands on the basis of total sales volume, or brand managers determine how much of the sales force's time they would like to be devoted to the brand. The cost to the brand is then determined as a percentage of overall sales costs. In addition, the salaries of the product manager, any assistants, and the clerical staff are included in this figure. As a result, reduction of management and sales expense is a difficult task, although some options are available.

The same is true of research and development costs (Line T). In this instance, because Ferd's Food Company manufactures many products, a general research and development program for the entire company is operated under an R&D unit. Because this group works on behalf of all brands, costs of their efforts are allocated on an equalized basis. The eggroll brand pays a pro-rated share of all costs of research and development with the understanding that the group is working on behalf of the eggroll brand a proportionate share of the time. R&D expenses charged to the eggroll brand often are allocated by top management and are difficult to reduce.

From this example, it quickly becomes evident that the actual funds available for an advertising campaign are greatly constrained. The funds available are the result of sales and expense forecasts made by brand or top management. Any increases in funds available for advertising must be a direct result of increased sales or reduced costs. That's a key point when budgeting for any brand.

The Profit Planning Approach to Advertising Budgeting

For existing products, under the brand management system, it should be clear that advertising budgeting is often less a case of budgeting and more a case of allocating available funds. In practice there is a basic approach to budgeting and allocation that takes into account the situation described above and gives the advertising planner a sound, proven method of budgeting. It's called the profit planning approach. It consists of four basic steps:

1. Develop an accurate forecast of predicted sales for the coming budget period. This assumes the planner has a reasonably firm estimate of fixed and variable product manufacturing costs.
2. Convert the sales forecast into a contribution margin for the product or brand (see Figure 8-7).
3. The planner must have an understanding of the desired profit margin for the product, company, or brand either in total dollars or as a percentage of net sales price or gross margin.
4. The planner then allocates the available direct expense funds for marketing into advertising, promotion, selling expense, and research and development budgets.

This method permits the planner to approach advertising budgeting from a managerial standpoint. The emphasis is on achieving the desired profit margin for the firm by adjusting sales forecasts or direct expenses as necessary to achieve those goals. Each step of the profit planning advertising budgeting approach is outlined below.

Step 1: Forecast accurately. Profit planning budgeting places primary emphasis on the ability of the planner to know three basic things: what the fixed and variable manufacturing costs for the product are at all levels of sales; the specific percentage or dollar amount desired as a profit margin for the company, product, or brand; and a clear picture of the competitive market situation and consumers so an accurate sales forecast can be made.

Figure 8-7 shows that, with a top line established by the sales forecast and a bottom line dictated by the desired profit margin, the product manager can manipulate only a few variables in developing an advertising budget. Once the desired profit margin has been established, assuming a competitive pricing situation, the only true variables are the number of units forecast to be sold, the variable product cost, and the direct expenses to be allocated. Thus, primary emphasis in the profit planning approach to budgeting is on developing the sales forecast.

Initially, the sales forecast should be made in units rather than dollars. The unit forecast can then be converted into dollars based on the selling price less the necessary discounts, which leads to the second step.

Step 2: Estimate the contribution margin. Once the net sales price of the product has been determined, the cost-of-goods on the forecasted sales is deducted. This gives the gross margin. Distribution expense is then deducted, leaving the contribution margin. (See Figure 8-7.) This contribution margin truly defines the funds available for all marketing expenditures, including advertising.

Step 3: Deduct the desired product margin. Once the product margin has been established, either as a lump sum or as a percentage of net sales price, it is deducted from the contribution margin of the product. The result is the total amount available for marketing (direct expenses).

Step 4: Allocate the marketing funds. The total available marketing funds (direct expenses in Figure 8-7) are now established. Based on that amount, the planner can then allocate the available funds among sales expense, advertising and promotion investments, and research and development to achieve the best return. This is the point at which the planner knows the true alternatives available. It is also the point where the effects of various expenditures for personal sales vs. advertising, or advertising vs. sales promotion, can be estimated with some accuracy.

The major differences between the profit planning method and more traditional budgeting approaches involve viewing the advertising budget within the framework of the entire product operating sheet rather than as a separate entity. Advertising is a function directly related to the profit margin and is a part of the total mix of product income and expense. Advertising is not theoretical: It is a practical device that can be used by the campaign planner.

In the profit planning approach—because advertising is directly related to the sales forecast—effective advertising results in increased advertising dollars. Advertising and sales are inextricably intertwined. Also, the advertising budget is in the hands of the person responsible for the sale and profit of the product. By developing the sales forecast, estimating sales and costs, and knowing other expenses charged against the product, that person can justify the advertising investment to management.

The profit planning approach may not be feasible for some advertising budgeters because of lack of information on such factors as costs and profit margins desired. However, it is a sound, real-world approach to establishing an advertising budget.

Budget Constraints and Considerations for Established Products

While the profit planning system is a highly desirable approach, some additional factors usually have a direct bearing on what the budget should be and how those funds should be allocated. Some of them were discussed previously, but they will be highlighted here.

1. Long-term vs. short-term goals for the brand. Is this budget designed to provide immediate results, or is the brand being built for the future?
2. Competitive spending. Often, investment spending by competition forces investment spending by the brand to maintain share. How close to the proper ratio of share of voice to share of market is the planned spending for the brand?
3. Type of product. Sometimes the type of product and the expected life cycle determine changes that should be made in the budget. How close is the proposed budget to the norm for the product category?
4. Existing markets/target markets. The geographic market location and target market selected for sales efforts have much to do with the advertising budget. Some markets and some target groups are much more expensive to reach with media than are others.
5. Distribution. How widely is the product available or what is the distribution pattern? Is the goal of the plan to build sales in the distribution system or with consumers? That decision has much to do with the budget allocated.
6. Noise levels in media. How much noise or clutter exists in the area or the media that is planned for use? Often, that suggests increasing or decreasing the budget.

With these factors in mind, the planner should be able to develop a sound, defensible budget for the brand that will achieve the previously established advertising objectives.

Advertising Budgeting for New Products

Budgeting advertising for a new product or brand requires a different approach from those discussed previously. The most common technique is based on a payout plan. The rationale is based on the belief that a new brand or product requires a heavier investment in advertising and promotion to get started than is needed by established brands. Because the new brand has no sales income to pay for the advertising, the company must forego profits on the brand until it can pay its own way. Therefore, the parent company should invest funds in advertising and sales promotion for the new brand until it is established. As the new brand achieves sales and profits in the market, the investment money and previously lost profits can be repaid to the parent company. Because this payback procedure usually cannot be accomplished in one budgeting period (ordinarily one year), a payout plan is developed in which the advertising planner for the new brand budgets the payoff of the parent's investment over a period of several budgeting periods, usually one to two years for a consumer product. This rationale parallels the philosophy of the product life cycle concept.

The procedure for developing a payout plan consists of four steps which are discussed below and illustrated in Figure 8-8.

Estimate the Share Goal

The total market must be determined for the product category the new brand is entering. This estimate is usually based on research. Using the

Figure 8-8.   Three-Year Payout Plan: Hypothetical Consumer Product

		Theoretical marketing years		
		Year 1	Year 2	Year 3
(A)	Total market in units	20,000	22,000	23,000
(B)	Average percent of market share goals	8	10	11
(C)	Market sales in units	1,600	2,200	2,530
(D)	Pipeline in units	288	50	28
(E)	Factory shipments in units	1,888	2,250	2,558
(F)	Net trade sales @ $6 per unit	$11,328	$13,500	$15,348
(G)	Less fixed and variable cost of goods			
(H)	@ 3.50 per unit	$ 6,608	$ 7,875	$ 8,953
(J)	Gross margin	$ 4,720	$ 5,625	$ 6,395
(K)	Less distribution expense @ 10¢ per unit	$ 189	$ 225	$ 256
(L)	Contribution margin	$ 4,531	$ 5,400	$ 6,139
(M)	Advertising	$ 3,000	$ 2,500	$ 2,000
(N)	Promotion	$ 5,000	$ 1,000	$ 1,000
(O)	Product margin (or loss)	$ (3,469)	$ 1,900	$ 3,139*
(P)	Product margin as a percent of sales	—	14.1	20.4
(Q)	Cumulative product margin	$ (3,469)	$ (1,569)	$ 1,570

*Product pays out at Month 30

total estimated market, a growth projection based on the budget period is then prepared. This usually covers three to five years.

As illustrated in Figure 8-8, the total market for the hypothetical product illustrated is estimated at 20,000 units in Year 1. The market is expected to grow by 10 percent to 22,000 units in Year 2 and by 4.5 percent or to 23,000 units in Year 3 (Line A).

The new brand's estimated share of the total market must then be determined. Because a new brand's sales typically start slowly and increase until reaching a certain level, an average share for the year is often used. For example, the average market share goal for Year 1 is 8 percent (Line B). For the company to achieve that goal, brand share would probably have to be above 8 percent at the end of Year 1 to average out to that level. Most new brands reach their peak sales share between three and nine months after introduction. After that time, they may slowly decline to a stable position as new triers either become loyal users or switch again to another brand.

Determine the Trade Inventories (Pipeline)

In addition to consumer sales, an estimate must be made of the sales that will be made to the trade to stock the warehouses and shelves at retail. This is called the "pipeline." Typically, pipeline sales occur only at introduction. However, as a brand's distribution increases or more product is stocked on retail shelves, additional sales may be made into the pipeline. All pipeline sales are one time only and usually decline dramatically after Year 1 (see Line D).

When introducing a new product, several methods of estimating the amount of product going into the pipeline may be used. One is a straight-line projection based on the percentage of estimated sales of the product for the year. This figure varies widely depending on the speed with which the product sells and how large a display is normally found in the store.

A more widely used method is to estimate the number of units of the product that would be on display plus the amount stocked as backup (that found in the storeroom of the retail outlet). This sum is then multiplied by the number of stores in which distribution is expected to be achieved. For example, assume a planner is introducing a new line of packaged dry soup mixes packed 24 packages to the case per flavor for three flavors. Normal retail display is one case of 24 packages per flavor per store. Because the sales volume of dry soup mix is fairly high, the retail store usually maintains one additional case per flavor per store in the back room for restocking the shelves. In other words, the planner estimates that, for all the stores in which distribution is obtained, there will be two cases per flavor in the pipeline. If the estimated distribution volume of 10,000 stores is achieved nationwide, there would be 60,000 cases of the product in the pipeline (2 cases per flavor $\times$ 3 flavors = 6 cases per store $\times$ 10,000 stores = 60,000 cases of the product). There are alternative methods of determining the pipeline, but this is a common approach.

Determine the Advertising/Promotion Expense

No hard-and-fast rules exist for budgeting advertising and sales promotional expenditures for a new product. There are, however, some rules of thumb that have proven successful for a number of marketers.

As shown in the hypothetical example (Figure 8-8), advertising and promotion expenditures are normally heavier in the introductory year than in the following years (see Lines M and N). This is logical since the product is unknown to the consumer and the trade. It simply costs more to get consumer interest and trial in a new product than to maintain an existing known product.

Three basic methods of budget allocation are used.

Buy-your-way-in. This allocation entails budgeting enough money in dealer incentives and activities, such as promotional discounts or price allowances, to achieve the needed retail distribution. At the same time, heavy advertising and consumer sales promotion are used so that, once the product is on the dealers' shelves, consumers are encouraged to try it. The budget is set simply by estimating the cost of the required trade and consumer advertising and sales promotion and then allocating that amount. In effect, this budget plan is a form of the go-for-broke approach previously described. While the method is expensive and not always successful, in some instances it is the only approach that will generate distribution and consumer sales.

Competitive expenditure approach. The competitive expenditure approach to budgeting is widely used. The rule of thumb says the advertiser must spend at a rate of one and one-half to two times the annual advertising rate per share point of competitors to reach a share objective. For example, assume Brand V has an 8 percent market share goal for the first year (Figure 8-8). Studies are made of competitive market shares to learn which brand has approximately that share of the total we seek. Assume Brand Z has an 8 percent market share. Based on that, an estimate is then made of the annual advertising expenditure for Brand Z. If it is $1,500,000, the company should invest between $2,250,000 and $3,000,000 for Brand V, approximately one and one-half to two times the annual rate for competitive Brand Z and its 8 percent share.

As was discussed previously, over several years, J. O. Peckham has gathered evidence of a strong correlation between what is invested in advertising as a share of the category total and the share of market achieved. Peckham illustrates this concept with examples of several brands in the food and household-products categories. (See Figure 8-9.) The first set of bars illustrates the share of sales attained by each brand over a two-year introductory period. The second set of bars illustrates the share of advertising for each brand over the same two-year period. The ratio is obtained by dividing share of advertising by share of sales. For the food product category, the average ratio of share of advertising to share of sales is 1.7 and the median 1.5. In the toiletry product category, the average ratio of share of advertising to share of sales is 1.5 and the median 1.5.

While the cases illustrated here are only examples, Peckham has more than 40 years' experience with Nielsen figures to substantiate the general rule of thumb of a ratio of approximately 1.5 to 2.0 share of advertising to share of sales needed for the successful launching of a new brand in the marketplace. The approach is often called "Peckham's Law."[11]

The profit planning approach. While buy-your-way-in and competitive-expenditure methods have been successful, they ignore the basic reason for the payout planning program, namely, the payout. In most consumer, nondurable product companies, there is an acceptable payback period for new products, usually between 12 and 30 months. With this guideline, the same budgeting approach as was recommended for existing products, profit planning can be used to determine the introductory budget.

Using the profit planning approach, the length of the payout period is determined. Based on that, the advertising budget for the new product introduction can be calculated. For example, in Figure 8-8, the hypothetical product illustrated has a payout or break-even point at approximately Month 30. (Sufficient profit will accrue in the sixth month of Year 3 to erase the carry-over deficit from Years 1 and 2, as illustrated by Lines P and R.) Had there been a management decision that the new product had to pay out in 24 months, the only options would have been to raise the market share goal (Line B) or reduce the advertising or promotion expenditures during the introductory periods (Lines M and N). Either step would have allowed an earlier payout as required by management.

Although the profit planning approach is a more complex new product budgeting procedure than the alternatives previously discussed, it adopts a management viewpoint that is guided by the needs of the brand and the entire company. Other allocation methods lack this profit-oriented view, particularly the buy-your-way-in approach, which conceivably could end up as a major expense, rather than a payout, to the company.

---

11. Peckham, *Wheel of Marketing,* pp. 73–76.

Figure 8-9A.   Two-Year Summary. Share of Advertising—Share of Sales Relationships for New Brands of Food Products

	Attained share of sales	Average share of advertising	Ratio of share of advertising to share of sales
Brand 101	12.6%	34%	2.7
102	10.0	16	1.6
103	7.6	8	1.1
104	2.6	4	1.5
105	2.1	3	1.4

Figure 8-9B.   Two-Year Summary. Share of Advertising—Share of Sales Relationships for New Brands of Toiletry Products

	Attained share of sales	Average share of advertising	Ratio of share of advertising to share of sales
Brand 401	19.5%	30%	1.5
402	16.5	25	1.5
403	16.2	20	1.2
404	9.4	12	1.3
405	8.7	16	1.8
406	7.3	19	2.6
407	7.2	14	1.9
408	6.0	10	1.7
409	6.0	7	1.2
410	5.9	6	1.0
411	5.9	10	1.7
412	5.2	6	1.2

SOURCE: Peckham, *The Wheel of Marketing*, 1975.

Determine the payout period. The final step in the development of a payout plan in the profit planning approach is the determination of the length of the payout. The actual calculation is a straightforward one. The cumulative product margin (Line R) is carried from period to period until the product margin (Line P) exceeds the amount previously invested. At the point where the product margin gains exceed the cumulative product margin losses, the brand has returned all the initial seed money to the company and is now on a profit-making basis.

In the competitive expenditure and buy-your-way-in methods, the calculation of the payout period is a result of the calculations, not a preplanned length of time. In the profit planning approach, however, it is an integral part of the development of the advertising and sales promotion budget, since the payout time is the basis on which the available funds are determined. This is another reason the profit planning approach is suggested for a new product.

While the profit planning payout plan does require some assumptions and estimates of what can or might occur in the future, it is the soundest method of determining and allocating an advertising budget for a new product. Although the method is subject to variations in estimates, management is given a clear picture of exactly what is proposed, the amount of money involved, and the length of time deemed necessary to recoup the investment.

Management decisions on new product introductions are usually based on (a) the amount of money risked the first year should the goals not be achieved and an absolute disaster occur and (b) the sales and brand share the first year after the payout is achieved. This is usually indicative of the return that can be expected from the new brand on an ongoing basis. Using these two figures, management can then determine the ratio of the risk to the return when the plan is compared to alternative uses of the funds.

Determination of an advertising budget for a new product is probably the least precise of any budget that might be developed for a company. There is no past experience on which to base one's plans, and there is no successful way of knowing the future. The only option is to approach the problem in the most logical and systematic manner possible. That approach appears to be the profit planning payout plan.

How Do Most Advertisers Set Advertising Budgets?

With the rather extensive descriptions of how advertising budgets should be determined and the rationale for each approach which has preceded, the natural question arises, What is the most widely used method or which ones are in most common use by major advertisers? Based on a study done by Patti and Blasko in 1981, the answer is objective and task, closely

Figure 8-10.   Comparison of Methods Used to Set Advertising Budgets

| | Percent of respondents using each method | | | | | |
Method	San Augustine and Foley	"100 leading advertisers"	Percent difference	Z*	P	Sig. level
Quantitative methods	4	51	+47	−6.38	.0000	.05
Objective and task	12	63	+51	−7.78	.0000	.05
Percent anticipated sales	52	53	+1	.11	.4562	N.S.
Unit anticipated sales	12	22	+10	−1.63	.0516	N.S.
Percent past year's sales	16	20	+4	−.60	.2725	N.S.
Unit past year's sales	12	N/A**	N/A	N/A	N/A	N/A
Affordable	28	20	−8	1.25	.1056	N.S.
Arbitrary	16	4	−12	2.58	.0049	.05
Match competitors	N/A	24	N/A	N/A	N/A	N/A
Others	20	N/A	N/A	N/A	N/A	N/A

SOURCE: Charles H. Patti and Vincent Blasko, "Budgeting Practices of Big Advertisers," *Journal of Advertising Research,* 21, 6 (December 1981): 25.

*Z ± 1.96 = sig.
**This method was not included in this study.

followed by percentage of anticipated sales, and a rapidly increasing use of various forms of quantitative methods. (See Figure 8-10.) The companies surveyed were those listed as the 100 Leading Advertisers in 1980 as reported in *Advertising Age.* Their budgets accounted for 54.3 percent of the total advertising spending in the country for that year.[12]

When comparing Patti and Blasko's results to previous studies, the most common result is that advertisers are placing more and more emphasis on the proper planning and budgeting of advertising and less emphasis on arbitrary judgment. Of course, the results are shown for large, usually sophisticated advertisers with massive resources. It does indicate, however, that advertising budgeting is an increasingly important area for these companies that will likely filter down to the smaller organizations in the next few years.

Allocating Funds Between Advertising and Sales Promotion

While somewhat related to the advertising budget, the question of allocation of the budget between advertising and sales promotion naturally arises after the basic budget has been determined. The rule of thumb for most package goods advertisers seems to be a 50-50 split, but that, of course,

12. Charles H. Patti and Vincent Blasko, "Budgeting Practices of Big Advertisers," *Journal of Advertising Research,* 21, 6 (December 1981): 23–29.

depends greatly on the advertising objectives, the situation of the brand, competition, and other considerations. We'll deal more specifically with how the budget can and should be allocated between advertising and sales promotion in Chapter 13. The key element to remember is the allocation should be based primarily on which approach is most likely to achieve the advertising objectives. That should be the overriding goal.

Summary   After objectives have been set, it is necessary to determine how much will be needed to accomplish those objectives. Planners normally forecast budgets in terms of a desired advertising to sales, but the problem is in the nature of forecasting. This chapter discussed the factors that influence the advertising budget, including the costs of media, testing, and other costs of the corporation. Other factors such as present share of market, projected share for the brand, and the brand's stage in the product life cycle are a few things that will influence the budget. The major steps from establishing objectives through evaluating the campaign were discussed. The profit planning approach has proven itself to be the most reliable method for most companies.

Case for Discussion: Cristel Products

In January of 1982, Charles Dobbs was faced with his biggest challenge since joining Cristel Products in 1979. During his time with Cristel, a major food marketer, Dobbs had worked as an assistant brand manager on several products. He had recently been appointed brand manager for a new product, frozen french fries. Dobbs had worked with a top-level committee to develop objectives for the product, which would be Cristel's first new product introduction in several years and its first national frozen food entry.

Frozen potato products, primarily french fries, were purchased by 46.1 percent of all U.S. homemakers (34,581,000). The market was dominated by one brand, which had accounted for 55 percent of all sales last year. The rest of the market was divided among 6 small brands and various regional distributors and store brands.

Cristel had decided to enter the market for several reasons:

1. they had a ready source of potatoes;
2. french fries could be packaged and processed using present equipment, although additional workers would have to be hired;
3. the company was eager to expand into the frozen food area;
4. despite the market's dominance by one company, Cristel felt their established name and reputation of quality would give them an excellent entry into the market.

A Year 1 share goal of 6 percent had been established for the french fries, increasing to 12 percent in Year 3. Cristel anticipated no problems in gaining distribution equivalent to 83 percent of All Commodity Volume, as they had long-standing relationships with many retailers.

In line with the market share goal, the following objectives had been established for the advertising campaign:

1. achieve 80 percent awareness among french fry purchasers
2. among those aware, achieve 70 percent knowledge of Cristel's product as a quality french fry
3. among those with knowledge, achieve 60 percent preference
4. among those with preference, achieve 45 percent conviction to purchase Cristel french fries

5. among those with conviction, achieve 40 percent actual purchase of Cristel.

Dobbs was working to prepare the 3-year budget/payout plan for the product. He had before him figures on various cost elements, but had yet to determine the advertising and promotion budget:

	Year 1	Year 2	Year 3
Market sales in units (case of 30 2-lb. bags)	46,108,000	47,952,320	49,390,889
Market share goal	6%	10%	12%
Market sales in units	2,766,480	4,795,232	5,926,907
Pipeline	15,000	8,000	4,000
Factory shipments	2,781,480	4,803,232	5,930,907
Sales @ $45.36/unit ($1.19 retail price)	$126,167,933	$217,874,604	$269,025,942
Fixed & variable costs @ $32.50/yr. 1	90,390,100		
$29.50/yr. 2+		141,685,344	174,961,757
Gross margin	35,769,833	76,189,260	94,064,185
Distribution @ $11.75/unit .	32,682,390	56,437,976	69,688,157
Contribution margin	$ 3,087,443	$ 19,751,284	$ 24,376,028

In addition to the established objectives, there were several other points Dobbs needed to take into account in setting a recommended advertising and promotion budget:

1. The market leader had spent an estimated $20,000,000 on advertising during the past year and was expected to continue spending at that level.

2. Cristel sales reps had suggested an additional $3.00/case allowance in Year 1 to ensure that retailers would give the new product freezer space.

3. The category was characterized by heavy use of couponing.

4. Cristel traditionally maintained an advertising to sales ratio of 2.5 percent.

5. Management, while eager for the product to succeed, was not eager to spend a tremendous amount on advertising.

Questions

1. Using the Share of Voice = Share of Market technique, what would the Cristel advertising budget be for Years 1–3?

2. What would the Year 1 advertising budget be under Cristel's traditional 2.5 advertising to sales ratio?

3. In addition to the suggested $3/case allowance to retailers, what other types of costs might be included in the sales promotion budget?

4. How might Dobbs take advantage of Cristel's strong reputation in determining his advertising budget?

5. Can you see any problems with using the Share of Voice approach in this situation?

6. What information would Dobbs need to use the DAGMAR approach in his budgeting?

9 Developing the Creative Strategy

Thus far in the advertising campaign planning cycle, the primary concern has been with rather hard, cold, measurable information and facts, i.e., the gathering of information on the marketplace, product pricing and distribution, learning a bit about where the product is sold and who buys it, setting some objectives to be achieved with the advertising and evaluating, and determining the amount of money that can be invested in the campaign. With all the previous planning steps taken, it would seem that the next step, determining or formulating the sales message to be delivered to customers and prospects for the product or service, should be quite simple. Unfortunately, just the opposite is true. This is the most difficult step by far unless you are blessed with a unique product or service. Yet this is where the practical success or failure of the campaign actually occurs. Quite simply, if the sales message is not clear, does not provide a benefit, or does not solve a problem for prospective purchasers, then the advertising campaign is bound to fail. It really matters little how brilliant the media plan, how substantial the investment, or how attractively or excitingly the message is packaged. If the sales message is poor, weak, or ill-conceived, the campaign will fail or certainly not come close to reaching its potential. That idea is often difficult for the campaign planner to accept, but it's true.

The campaign planner may not be specifically required to personally develop the final advertisements or commercials. But it is nearly always the responsibility of the planner to either direct the development of the message or give the final approval of the message to be used. Therefore, the development of the advertising sales message is still the most important step in the campaign.

If the advertising sales message is truly the heart of the campaign, one would think there must be a sure-fire method of developing or assuring the development of an effective sales message for every campaign. Unfortunately no such magic formula exists, although the search has been going on for generations. The development of the sales message falls into that vague, mystical area called "creative." And since people have a great deal of difficulty just identifying that elusive thing called "creativity," much less harnessing it, most advertising practitioners agree that developing the creative portion of the campaign is by far the most difficult part of the campaign process. However, there are some sound, systematic methods of developing effective sales messages. The chief method and the one discussed in this chapter is the use of an advertising strategy. But first some preliminary steps must be taken.

Preparation for Developing the Sales Message

Writing an ad sounds easy, doesn't it? Most people have seen literally thousands of advertisements, ranging from messages on the backs of cereal boxes at breakfast to full-scale, production-number television commercials. And most people consider themselves experts when it comes to advertising. Even five- and six-year-old children can make suggestions and recommendations on how to write advertisements for products they know.

Why, then, do we see so much advertising that is dumb or boring or even insulting to us as consumers and certainly disturbing to us as professionals? The reason is that many writers of advertising have forgotten some of the very basic elements of developing advertising messages. They have forgotten or overlooked the purpose of advertising. They have forgotten why it is used, why it works and doesn't work. In many cases these basics determine the success or failure of the campaign. Because they are so important, they will be reviewed first before starting to develop advertising sales messages for the campaign.

Preparing to Sell

To develop an effective advertising message, it is necessary to go through all those steps covered thus far in this text. That is, the planner must have an understanding of basic marketing, must know how and why consumers act and react as they do to advertising messages, and must have a basic understanding of communication principles. If a planner can't communicate, the advertising can't possibly succeed. Obviously, the planner must know and understand the product or service (if you haven't tried the product you're trying to sell, how can you possibly influence others to try or use it?) and must have some idea of what customers or prospects should do as a result of seeing the advertising. That is, should they order directly from the advertisement, rush to their nearest dealer or distributor, or simply change their idea or opinion about the product or service? And, finally, based on the amount of money to be invested in the campaign, what limitations and restrictions may this impose on what can be done? For example, it does little good to develop a sales message that requires a 60-second television commercial when enough money is available for only a few black-and-white ads in the local newspaper. In short, you must master all the things that have been covered so far in this text before you're ready or able to develop or to approve the advertising sales message for the campaign. That's the starting point and that's where too many advertising campaigns fail. They fail because their planners and developers haven't or didn't master or remember the basics.

Advertising Is Always a Sales Message

Anybody in advertising who doesn't say his purpose is to sell is either ignorant or a phony.

The above quote has been attributed to one of the greatest creative people of modern advertising, William Bernbach of Doyle Dane Bernbach. Unfortunately, it appears his message hasn't received widespread enough distribution, for there are apparently many in the advertising business who believe their job is simply to entertain or amaze or even to confuse, all at the expense of the sales message for the product or service being featured.

The campaign planner should always remember: The primary and often the sole purpose of an advertising campaign is to either generate a direct sale of the product or service or to influence customers and prospects for the advertised product in such a way that they consider it for a future purchase. Consumer reaction to an advertising message may not always result in an immediate purchase, but the ultimate goal is to get someone to buy something. Therefore, if the advertising campaign doesn't deliver a *sales* message, it is not successful.

Obviously, sales messages can come in many forms. A sales message doesn't have to be "hard sell" or "schlock" or "hit 'em over the head" advertising to be successful. It simply means the advertising must provide a sound, legitimate benefit or tell why the advertised brand should be either preferred, purchased, or repurchased over competition.

The Consumer Buying Equation

To create effective sales messages, you obviously have to know why people buy. The entire theory of buying and selling can be summed up in the equation in Figure 9-1. Benefit divided by price equals value. When the benefit is greater than the price, value will equal more than one, and the person will probably buy. When the price is greater than the benefit, value will equal less than one, and the person probably will *not* buy. While this equation is simple, it's the foundation of the entire advertising and selling business. In fact, it's the foundation of any business.

Figure 9-1.   Theory of Buying and Selling

$$\frac{B}{P} = V$$

B = Benefit   P = Price   V = Value

What really happens in a buying situation is quite simple to explain but quite complex in reality. Every time a consumer is confronted with a buying decision, he or she subconsciously and subjectively assigns a worth to the benefit that is perceived in having the product or service. At the same time, he or she assigns a worth to the price that must be paid. If the benefits outweigh the price, he or she will buy. If through this mental calculation process the price outweighs the benefits, the person will likely not buy. This simple equation works for all types of products in all types of purchasing situations. If there is a "law" of consumer behavior, this is it.

This simple but very demanding equation is very important. A discussion of each element follows.

Price can be defined as anything of value the purchaser has to give up to get the benefit promised by the product or service. Obviously, one of the most important in our economy is money. A dollar amount is asked for the product or service. And to purchase a certain product or service, the purchaser may not be able to make another purchase—if I buy the shoes, I can't buy the purse. Or the purchaser may have to give up time or energy to learn or use the product or service. Or the consumer may be asked to give up the assurance of what they are doing now for the risk of a new idea or a new method of doing something. And the new product may not always work as well or as easily in the beginning. Therefore, price can be anything the purchaser has to give up to obtain the benefit that the product or service being advertised provides.

Value is the easiest of the three concepts to understand, although, again, it is a bit difficult to explain. The value of a product or service lies in the consumer's comparison and evaluation of the price benefit ratio compared to other available alternatives. Thus, every person brings a different value ratio into a buying-selling situation. What is of great value to one person may be of little or no value to another. The value of the advertised product or service is usually determined by the strength or importance to the individual of the benefit being provided: "cheap" and "expensive" are relative terms that depend on the importance of the product to the individual.

The third concept, benefit, is the most difficult and yet the easiest of the three elements to explain because the benefit a product or service provides the purchaser is totally subjective. And, unfortunately, too often this point is totally confused by advertising campaign planners because a benefit is something that personally affects the consumer or purchaser of a product or service. It always exists independently of and apart from the merchandise or service being provided.

Figure 9-2 may help with this very important concept. Pictured is a stereo FM radio. It has two three-way speakers. That's not a benefit. It's a selling point or a product feature or attribute. A selling point, or product feature, is something inherent in the merchandise or service that makes possible and supports the benefit. The fact that the stereo radio has two three-way speakers is merely a selling point. It is part of the merchandise or service. By itself, it means little or nothing to the customer. Its function is to make the benefit both possible and believable.

The fact that you can enjoy lifelike, three-dimensional sound from the radio is the benefit. It is this enjoyment that affects the buyer personally. A buyer doesn't need this radio to have the benefit of lifelike, three-dimensional sound. He or she can go to a concert and get that benefit. This benefit is made possible, and believable, by the fact that the radio has two three-way speakers.

Another example: a consumer couldn't care less about the triple-widget ratchet. If, however, because of the triple-widget ratchet, the job for which the consumer is considering the product can be done in half the time or with half the effort of a regular screwdriver, he or she is likely to care and maybe care enough to buy.

Remember, it is the *benefit* that affects the customer personally. This is

Figure 9-2.   Product Feature or Benefit

what he or she really wants. It is the *selling point or feature* that makes the benefit possible and believable.[1]

The Consumer's View

Closely related to the points above is the selection of the benefit to be featured in the advertising. Oftentimes, advertising campaign planners fall into a trap that can destroy the campaign before it even gets started. It's the difference between taking the consumer's view of a benefit or the manufacturer's view. In too many cases, the manufacturer tries to feature what she thinks is important or considers to be the real value of the product rather than trying to get on the consumer's side of the buying equation and to determine what prospects really want.

In the previous example of the triple-widget ratchet, it is easy for the advertising campaign planner to believe "Hey, look! We're the only ratchet with a triple-widget. That's our benefit." From the manufacturer's view that might be important, since all the competition may have only "double-widgets." To develop a successful sales message for the campaign, however, the planner must take the consumer's view of the benefit or benefits the "triple-widget" provides. Many times advertising campaigns talk to the prospect about benefits that are of little or no importance. When that happens, it's usually because the advertiser is talking about what is important to him or her, not prospective purchasers. To be successful, the campaign planner must start from the purchaser's view of the product or service, not the manufacturer's.

One of the key ingredients of successful advertising is to start where the consumer is. Not where you are.

Some Definitions

Too many times the words "objective" and "strategy" and "execution" are used in widely varying ways by people in advertising. These terms should be defined clearly before proceeding.

- Advertising objective. The clearly stated, measurable end result of an advertising message, messages, campaign, or program. Usually the advertising objective is measured in terms of a change in awareness, preference, conviction, or other communication effect.
- Advertising strategy. The benefit, problem solution, or other product

---

1. "Advertising Is Always a Sales Message" and "The Consumer Buying Equation" above were adapted from a speech by Don Kanter, Stone & Adler Advertising, Chicago, to students at the Medill School of Journalism Graduate Program in Advertising, 1982. Used with permission of Mr. Kanter.

advantage, either physical or psychological, that is the benefit or general idea of the advertising or the promise made to the purchaser through the advertising message.[2]

- Advertising execution. The physical form in which the advertising appears. This includes such items as the art, illustration, copy, music, or other physical or emotional characteristic through which the advertising strategy is translated and presented to the target market to achieve the advertising objective.

The actual development of the creative message starts with the selection of or development of the advertising strategy.

Understanding the Advertising Strategy

With these guidelines and definitions in mind, the planner begins the actual development of "what" he or she plans to say about the product or service in the advertising campaign. This "what to say" goes under many different names in the advertising world. They range from "copy platform" to "copy policy" to "advertising or creative strategy" or even "end user benefit statement." No matter what terminology is used—"advertising strategy" will be used here—the object is always the same: to identify the best target market and to develop and articulate the most important consumer benefit that the product or service can offer.

What Is an Advertising Strategy?

A visit to any supermarket or grocery store will show a wide variety of detergent products. Some if not all of the brands listed below are on display. Each is attempting to appeal to a separate segment of the detergent-buying population, and usually this segmentation is accomplished through the advertising strategy. The following detergents have the following sales messages:

Oxydol—Bleaches as it washes
Dreft—The detergent for baby's laundry
Ivory Snow—Softens as it cleans
Gain—A clean you see—a fresh you smell
Cheer—All-temperature Cheer
Bold 3—Detergent plus fabric softener
Tide—America's favorite
Dash—Low-suds concentrate

---

2. Often this is referred to as a creative strategy. The terms are not used interchangeably here.

Some consumers might ask, "Why do American consumers need all these different detergents?" After all, they're all designed to do pretty much the same thing, to remove the dirt and odor from clothing and other washables when used in an automatic washing machine. So, why are there so many brands? Why so many claims?

The answer is simple. Over the years detergent manufacturers have successfully segmented the laundry washing market by offering products with different features or ingredients. In every case each brand was developed to fill an individual consumer need or want. Some consumers wanted the advantage of a bleach in their detergent. Others wanted low suds. Still others wanted a product that can be used in all water temperatures.

To communicate the various benefits of each brand, the manufacturer first developed the product to fill the need and then translated that benefit into an advertising strategy that summed up in a phrase or a few words what the product would do or the benefit it offered the purchaser. While all the detergents generally will accomplish the same task of cleaning items in the laundry, the thing that sets them apart from each other in the consumer's mind is the benefit they provide or the problem the product will solve. That is expressed in the advertising strategy. All these products also have something else in common. They are all manufactured by the same company, Procter & Gamble.

Over the years, P&G has almost perfected market positioning, segmentation, and advertising strategy development. All these laundry products compete in the same detergent category and, to a certain extent, among themselves. Their primary job, however, is to compete against non–P&G brands. To do so, the advertising strategies, as they are here, must be very clear, very complete, and very concise. Since advertising is the primary way in which consumers learn about detergent products, if the strategy were not as on-target as are those listed above, consumers could not or would not be able to differentiate the various brands. Each would lose its clear, concise market positioning and ultimately sales in the marketplace.[3]

The Importance of a Sound Advertising Strategy

Several years ago, to determine the differences in the effect of advertising headlines, Dr. Alfred Politz, famed marketing and advertising researcher, conducted a split-run print study. Using a home study course in the

---

3. Adapted in part from Don E. Schultz, *Essentials of Advertising Strategy* (Chicago: Crain Books, 1981), p. 32.

operation of television equipment as the advertised product, Dr. Politz developed two identical advertisements in terms of size, offer, and details. The only difference in the two was the headline—the "what" being said about the product. In one advertisement the headline used was:

"New Jobs Offered in TV Station"

In the second advertisement, the headline was:

"Television Course for $11.97 per Week"

While Dr. Politz was testing the individual effects of the headlines, he was also testing the strategy. The first advertisement was based on a strategy of offering job opportunities, while the second was built around a strategy of economy or low price for the course. Then Dr. Politz placed these two advertisements in a split-run edition of a magazine that would reach persons who might logically be interested in such a home study course. Again, the advertisements were identical with the exception of the headline and the response key that identified the advertisement to which consumers were responding.

Can you guess which ad pulled the best response? It was the first. It got over five times more inquiries than the "Economy" strategy and headline. The "what you say" about your product or service *is* vital to success.[4]

| **Formalizing the Advertising Strategy: A Recommended Form** | Over the years most major advertisers and advertising agencies have developed some formal method of developing an advertising strategy. Some use a form, others a step-by-step development process, others simply list the basics of the product and the promise to be made to the consumer. Why do they formalize the advertising strategy? Why go to the trouble of developing a strategy when everyone knows what needs to be done? In those two questions likely lies the answer to why most advertisers and agencies formalize the advertising strategy with some form or standardized approach. |

1. A standard form or approach assures that everyone involved in the development of the creative product is in agreement as to who the target market is, what the message is to achieve, what benefit of the product is to be featured, and so on.

---

4. Adapted in part from Alfred Politz, "The Decline of Creative Advertising," *Journal of Marketing,* 25 (October 1960): 1–6.

2. The development of an advertising strategy makes sure the emphasis of the creative work is on the message and not the execution in the media.

3. The development of an advertising strategy helps assure that the advertising message is developed from the point of view of the consumer and not the advertiser.

While most agencies and most advertisers agree that formalized advertising strategy is needed in the development of an advertising campaign, they don't all agree on exactly how one should go about developing that strategy. Thus, there are as many approaches to advertising strategy development as there are agencies and advertisers. The following general advertising strategy development form consists of five basic steps and some substeps in developing the target market.

A. Key fact
B. Primary marketing problem
C. Communication objective
D. Message strategy
    1. The target market
        a. Geographics
        b. Demographics
        c. Psychographics
        d. Media patterns
        e. Buying/use patterns
    2. Primary competition
    3. Promise
    4. Reason why
E. Corporate/divisional requirements[5]

Going through the form step-by-step will illustrate just what is required to develop an effective advertising strategy. This strategy form is basically a chain of logic that forces the planner to think about all phases and areas of the advertising problem. That is the basic benefit of using this form.

Key Fact

This should be a single-minded statement that sorts out all the information about the product, the market, competition, usage, etc., from the con-

---

5. This form is adapted in part from material obtained from Young & Rubicam U.S.A. and Phil Peppis, "Can Creativity, Efficiency Have Shotgun Wedding and Live Happily Ever After?" *Advertising Age*, April 3, 1978, pp. 44+.

sumer's view. In other words, what single thing is causing consumers either to not purchase the product or service or not give the brand proper consideration. The single element or single problem which advertising can overcome to move consumers toward purchase or consideration of the product or service must be identified.

Note here: the problem must be one advertising can solve, and it must be stated from the consumer's view, not the advertiser's.

Primary Marketing Problem

This grows out of the key fact and is directly related, but it states the problem from the marketer's view. The marketing problem may be a product perception problem, a market problem, a competitive problem, or even an image problem, but it must be something on which advertising can have an effect. For example, if the product has recently been improved and the company failed to communicate that to the consumer, that's a problem advertising can solve. If, however, the product is inferior, it is a marketing problem that advertising cannot solve or on which it can have only limited effect. It is important to remember what advertising can and can't do.

Communication Objective

This should be a clear, concise statement of the effect the advertising should have on the target market. For example, what message is to be conveyed to the prospect for the advertising? How should the prospect react after seeing or hearing the message? Often an active verb such as "convince" or "persuade" is used to identify the effect the message is to have. The more specifically the message's purpose is defined, the stronger the advertising strategy.

The next section of the advertising strategy form deals with the specifics of how the plan will achieve the communication objective that will solve the key fact and will cause the primary marketing problem to disappear. This is really the "heart" of the advertising strategy.

Creative Strategy

Target market. The planner draws the most complete, concise picture possible of the prime prospects for the product or service to be advertised. At this stage, thinking of one person who is representative of the group to be reached makes it much easier to identify and empathize with the market. For example, a person selling pots and pans door-to-door, wouldn't find women 18 to 49, in middle-income with 2.6 children, when a door was opened. Instead, that person might find a single individual with a set income, a certain number of children, a specific lifestyle, and so on. Therefore, it is important to think about the target market as people, ideally as a single person, not as statistics when developing this portion of the strategy form.

For as clear a picture as possible of the typical prospect, the following should be included:

1. Geographics. For most products or services, it's important to identify the general geographic area of the country in which the representative consumer is located. That means not only where in the country in terms of region but the more specific details such as urban, suburban, inner-city, small town, rural, and so on. The more specific this is, the better.

2. Demographics. These are the hard, cold, measurable facts about prospects. These should include age, income, sex, marital status, education, and number of children, at a minimum. All those important things about a person that can be easily measured.

3. Psychographics. A "lifestyle" profile should also be developed, including life and leisure patterns, attitudes toward the use of various products and the brand in particular, how the product might fit into or conflict with the way the person lives, and so on. The fuller the lifestyle picture of the typical prospect, the better the chance of finding an advertising message that is important to him or her.

4. Media patterns. The media to which the target consumer is exposed should be listed. This is not the media plan to be used but the media the consumer uses. Often, they're not the same. If possible, the amount of time spent with each medium also should be listed. If there are programming or content differences, they should be noted, i.e., daytime, early or late fringe, prime time, and so on, for TV or programming format of radio stations and the like.

5. Buying and use patterns. Whether or not the target market uses the brand should be noted. If so, with what frequency. If not, why not. In other words, is the prime prospect a non-user; a light user in which case the advertiser wants to increase usage frequency? Or is the prospect a present user the advertiser is trying to hold? Further, if possible, how the product is purchased, how often, at what type of store, and so on should be described. If the prospect is a non-user of the brand but a user in the category, how does he or she purchase the brand presently used, and why? All this information can help in drawing a clear, complete picture of the person to whom the advertising message is to be directed. Obviously, information of this sort will have a direct effect on the actual message that is developed.

Primary competition. This is not a listing of every product or brand in the category. It is identification of the segment or area in which the brand competes. For example, is it the high-priced oleomargarine market? Diet cola soft drink market? The luxury family automobile market, or what?

This step is vital, for the planner must know and identify what prime competitors are promising to the target market to be able to clearly state how and why the brand is different, or better, or provides a greater benefit, and so on. If the product is new on the market, this might, instead of listing competitors, simply be a statement of the reason for being for the product.

Promise. This is the basic benefit or problem solution that the product or service should provide. It should say to the prospect, "If you buy this product, you will get this benefit or you will solve this problem." The promise should be phrased as a consumer benefit or the solution to a consumer problem. The promise must be strong enough to motivate consumers to act. Featuring a nonimportant benefit such as "Now, our product comes in three colors instead of two" or not being able to separate product attributes from consumer benefits creates the biggest problem in developing a campaign promise for most advertising planners. A sound advertising promise has three vital ingredients. They are:

1. The promise must offer a consumer benefit or solve a consumer problem.
2. The benefit offered or the problem solved by the promise must be important and wanted or needed by the prospect.
3. The brand must be totally integrated into the benefit offered or the problem solved.

Finally, the advertising promise must be made as competitive as possible. If a planner is trying to take business from a specific competitor, it must be clear to that competitor's users that the promise is directed to them.

Reason why. The reason or reasons why are the supporting facts that allow the planner to make the product's claim. The key checkpoint is, "Does the reason why support the promise?" If it doesn't, it should be replaced by the reason that will support the claim.

Ideally, the reason why is a single fact or a single statement. Sometimes it isn't, although the shorter, more concise it is, the better.

In some cases, it is not possible to physically prove or support the promise being made. In those cases, the use of an authority figure may be used to support the claim. For example, gourmet taste claims are often supported by testimonials from famous chefs, cookbook authors, or the like. In other situations, where no authorities are available, manner and

Figure 9-3.   The Reason-Why Statement

BOY: Hey Patty, what's it take
to be a Pepper?
PATTY: It's easy.

PATTY (Singing): To be a
Pepper, original like a Pepper,
all you gotta do is taste.

SINGERS: Be a Pepper

To know the pleasure of a
flavor you will treasure

All you gotta do is taste.
Be a Pepper.

The flavor's got a feeling,
original and appealing, and
all you gotta do is taste.

To be a Pepper, open up a
Dr Pepper, and all you gotta
do is taste.

The more you pour it
The more you will adore it
All you gotta do is taste.

To be a Pepper
Open up a Dr Pepper
All you gotta do is taste.

Be a Pepper, drink Dr Pepper.
Be a Pepper, drink Dr Pepper, yeah.

SOURCE: Courtesy of Dr. Pepper Co.

mood can be used to support the claim. A prime example is the "Be a Pepper" theme that pushed Dr Pepper to the third position in soft drinks. The entire idea is summed up in the mood and manner of the television commercials, which translate the idea being presented to the target market.

Whatever reason why is used, it must be legally supportable and, at the same time, believable.

Corporate/Divisional Requirements

Here is where any mandatory requirements that must be included in the development of advertising should be listed. For example, there are a myriad of details, specific forms, and methods that must be used in automobile mileage comparisons. Or, it is this place in the form where the need for a corporate slogan or signature in the advertising may be noted. In short, all those details and notes on what is required to appear in the advertising but which might be overlooked if not specifically itemized should be included.

If the campaign planner can't complete the form in detail, there is evidence that the prior steps in the advertising campaign development haven't been properly completed. The planner should review what is needed before proceeding.

An Example of a Completed Advertising Strategy Form

Probably the best method of illustrating the advertising strategy form and its use is through an example. The following strategy form was developed by a student group using information in an Intercollegiate Case Clearing House case. Although this example does not include the product, market, or even consumer background available, it does demonstrate how the advertising strategy form actually contains almost all the information which creative people might need to develop sound advertising executions.

Recommended Listerine Lozenges Advertising Strategy

A. Key fact

A recent consumer research study has indicated that consumers do not believe Listerine Lozenges are effective in relieving temporary sore throats.

B. Primary marketing problem

Brand sales in the category and brand awareness have slipped in the past year. As brand leader, Listerine Lozenges must improve efficacy position of the brand to increase share of existing market and initiate brand demand.

C. Communication objective

To convince temporary sore throat sufferers that Listerine Lozenges are the most effective product available for the relief of temporary sore throats.

D. Creative strategy
1. Prospect definition
    a. Geographics
        Alice lives in Grand Island, Nebraska. C county. Non-SMSA.
    b. Demographics
        Woman. White. Age 23. Works. Not a homemaker. Rents. Single. High school grad. Some college. HH income $12,500.
    c. Psychographics
        Not a career girl. Independent. Brand name buyer. Health-conscious. Self-medication. Always on the go.
    d. Media patterns
        Heavy TV/heavy magazines. Mostly prime-time movies. Heavy late-night/Carson. Cosmo and McFadden group. Progressive rock radio. Few newspapers.
    e. Buying/use patterns
        Buys lozenges at food or drug store. Buys as needed. Heaviest usage in October-April period. Does not stock up. Single unit purchase. Fairly brand loyal. Expects relief.
2. Principal competition
    Position Listerine as brand leader in a category and against other premium, medicated lozenges, such as Sucrets and Cepacol, not against throat candies.
3. Promise
    Listerine Lozenges provide effective relief for temporary sore throats.
4. Reason why
    Listerine Lozenges have been specifically formulated to relieve temporary sore throats two ways: (1) to provide anesthetic relief by soothing infected throat tissue; (2) to attack the cause of temporary soreness with germ-killing antiseptic action.

E. Divisional/corporate requirements

Any and all health or health-related claims must be supported with laboratory evidence.[6]

---

6. Listerine Lozenges, Case #9-574-062, Copyright 1974 by the President and Fellows of Harvard College. While the original case dealt with the Listerine situation in Canada, information was transferred to the U.S. for this particular example.

Although background of the actual problem is incomplete, this outline gives a clear, concise picture of the market situation, the target market, the competition, and the "what to say" about the product based on the strategy form. From this, the creative people should be able to develop several ways to present this sales message in the media.

The Built-In Advantage and a Few Cautions About Using the Advertising Strategy Form

The Advantages

One of the advantages of the previous example that the use of this advertising strategy form provides is the built-in system of checkpoints that can be used to determine if a sound, effective strategy has been developed. Here are just a few examples.

1. Does the *reason why* support the *promise?* If not, why not? It must. And, ideally, it should be a single idea.

2. Is the promise easily overcome or discounted by primary competition? Test the promise against what competition is offering. If it's too close to what primary competition is already saying in their advertising, the planner risks offering only a "me-too" benefit.

3. Would the promise logically influence the prospect to purchase or to consider the purchase of the product or service? Is the promise strong enough or important enough to generate some form of action? If it's not, it should be replaced.

4. Does the promise fulfill the communications objective? In other words, will the promise "convince" or "persuade" or "get consumers to consider." If the promise won't fulfill the communications objective, the strategy is sure to fail.

5. If the communications objective is achieved, the key fact should be solved or disappear. In other words, if the planner achieves the communications objective, the consumer should no longer have the problem that is preventing him or her from purchasing or considering or feeling positive about or whatever that is preventing them from purchasing at this time. Here's a quick check. The key fact should no longer exist after the communications objective has been achieved.

6. When the key fact no longer exists, the primary marketing problem for the company or organization should disappear. Thus, if the communications objective disposes of the key fact, it should also dispose of the primary marketing problem. If the key fact and primary marketing problem aren't both solved by the communications objective, then there is a problem either in the key fact or the primary marketing problem. They must be interrelated.

From these few questions, the basic advantages of using this particular advertising strategy development form should be clear. The interrelated nature of the form and its resulting problem-solution format forces the planner to develop sound, effective, clear-cut advertising messages that must be of interest to the target market.

Two Cautions about Strategy Development

While the advertising strategy form recommended above can help the planner organize his or her thoughts and lead to an orderly and organized solution to the defined problem, there are a couple of pitfalls that often cause inexperienced advertising planners some problems. They are:

1. Simply trying to cram too many ideas into a strategy. This usually occurs when the strategy is not totally clear in the planner's mind or when too many people have been involved in the strategy development. The best advertising strategy usually consists of one clear, concise benefit or problem solution directed to a single target market. The planner should avoid a laundry list of benefits. If there are benefits for more than one target market, a separate strategy for these markets and a separate advertising execution should be developed. In the case of advertising strategies, more is usually not better. It's simply confusing.

2. Trying to talk to too many people. Closely allied to trying to cram too many ideas into the strategy is the hazard of trying to reach or talk to too many people with the strategy. Trying to stretch a benefit to a wider market in hopes of attracting a few more people is almost always a mistake. It is much better to take a rifle shot approach at the best prospect than to use a shotgun approach in the hope of hitting a few of the entire market. The planner must know who the target market is and talk directly to them.

The Creative Complaint

In some instances, creative people complain that the advertising strategy form is a straightjacket. They feel it stifles their creativity. They often say: "It's too structured." "It's too orderly to permit the development of really 'creative' approaches." Nothing could be further from the truth. The advertising strategy form really is the most basic aid creative people can have, for it outlines all the information and material known about the advertising problem to be solved. Thus, if the advertising strategy is seen and approved not only by the advertising agency and the client but also by all those who will have ultimate responsibility for approval of the campaign, many missed steps, calls for revisions, and last-minute concerns about whether or not the advertising campaign is a sound one are avoided.

Therefore, the final step in the use of the advertising strategy form is to have everyone who has approval or rejection power over the campaign to see and approve the final strategy before any creative work starts on executions. This point will be discussed more in the following chapter.

How to Develop an Advertising Strategy

To this point, most of the emphasis in this chapter has been on the use of the advertising strategy form. The following shows some ways of identifying or selecting the strongest possible advertising message that can be used in the promise and supported by the reason why.

A brief review of some of the best-known and most widely accepted methods of developing advertising messages will help.

Rosser Reeves's "Unique Selling Proposition"

In his immensely successful and influential book, *Reality in Advertising,* Rosser Reeves, then at Ted Bates & Company, outlined that agency's concept of developing advertising messages. He called it the "Unique Selling Proposition." Reeves described the USP as having three parts:

1. Each advertisement must make a proposition to the consumer. Not just words, not just product puffery, not just show-window advertising. Each advertisement must say to each reader: "Buy this product and you will get this specific benefit. . . . "
2. The proposition must be one that the competition either cannot or does not offer. It must be unique either in the brand or in the claim. . . .
3. The proposition must be strong enough to move the mass millions, i.e., pull over new customers to your brand. . . .[7]

Because of technological developments and the increased complexity of the marketplace, many advertising practitioners have considered the USP passé for today's campaign development needs. There's no question USPs for products or services certainly aren't as easy to develop as they were in the early 1960s, but they are still possible, and they certainly provide very sound selling messages for many advertisers. For example, in one of the most successful new pet food introductions in years, Kibbles and

---

7. Rosser Reeves, *Reality in Advertising* (New York: Alfred A. Knopf, Inc., 1961).

Figure 9-4.　Unique Selling Proposition: Kibbles and Bits

1. DOG: Kibbles 'n Bits,...

2. ...Kibbles 'n Bits, I'm gonna get me some...

3. ...Kibbles...

4. ...'n Bits.

5. Kibbles 'n Bits, (PANT)...

6. ...Kibbles 'n Bits, I'm gonna get me some...

7. ...Kibbles...

8. ...'n Bits.

9. VOA: Kibbles 'n Bits from Ken-L Ration. It's different.

10. Look. It's two great dog foods in one.

11. Kibbles--a crunchy meaty-tasting dry, and Bits--a chewy burger-style food.

12. He'll crunch it, chomp it...absolutely devour it.

13. Kibbles 'n Bits.

14. Two great dog foods in one.

15. DOG: Kibbles 'n Bits, Kibbles 'n Bits, I'm gonna get me more Kibbles 'n Bits. (LIP SMACK)

SOURCE:　Courtesy of Quaker Oats Company.

Bits promised owners their dogs would love the taste of the new dog food because it offered the unique two-part form—kibbles and bits. That uniqueness is inherent in the product itself. (See Figure 9-4.)

Another example of a unique selling proposition is illustrated by the Land O'Lakes "4-Quart Cheeses" in Figure 9-5. While the selling proposition, four quarts of fresh milk in every pound, could most likely be duplicated by competition, Land O'Lakes has succeeded in offering a unique consumer benefit, extra taste, through their advertising strategy.

Figure 9-5.   Unique Selling Proposition: 4-Quart Cheese

SOURCE: Courtesy of Land O'Lakes, Inc.

Figure 9-6.   The Marlboro Image

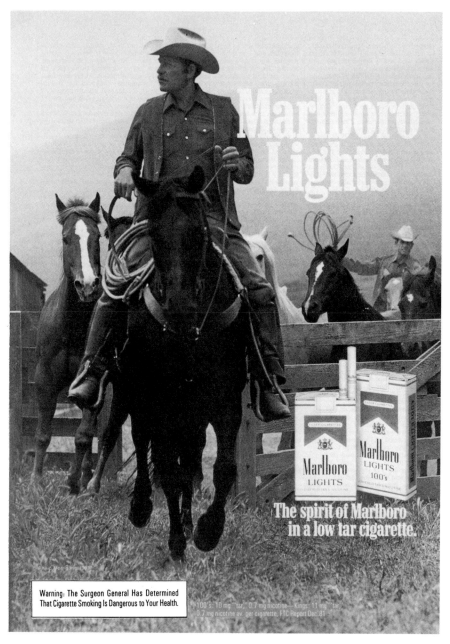

SOURCE: Courtesy of Philip Morris, Inc.

Figure 9-7. The Chanel No. 5 Image

(MUSIC THROUGHOUT)

WOMAN: (VO) I am made

...of blue sky

...and golden light

...and I will feel this way

...forever.

MALE: (VO) Share the Fantasy.

CHANEL N°5

SOURCE: Courtesy of Chanel, Inc.

David Ogilvy's "Brand Image"

In the mid-1960s, David Ogilvy popularized the idea of "Brand Image" through his book, *Confessions of an Advertising Man.* The concept, as Ogilvy expressed it, was that every advertisement should be considered a long-term investment in the overall makeup of the brand. Thus, each brand and each product develops or projects an image which is generally conveyed to customers and prospects through the various promotional techniques, but particularly through the advertising. Based on this image of the product or brand, the consumer doesn't buy just the product; he or she buys the physical and psychological benefits which the product or brand promises to deliver. Thus, what is said about the product in advertising is often more important in the purchase decision than the actual physical attributes which the product possesses.[8]

Over the years many products have developed very clear-cut brand images. One of the best known is that of Marlboro cigarettes. The Marlboro "cowboy" has been riding through the media in "Marlboro Country," inviting smokers to "come to where the flavor is" since the mid-1950s. The image Marlboro and Leo Burnett U.S.A., its agency, have created have stood them in good stead: Marlboro is the largest selling cigarette in the world.

Imagery can be created in many different ways. For example, Chanel No. 5 has created an image of their product through the use of fantasy in television commercials, such as the one in Figure 9-7. These commercials totally involve the viewer with the messages and let the viewer, in effect, create his or her own image of the Chanel No. 5 user.

Jack Trout and Al Reis: "Positioning"

In the early 1970s, Jack Trout and Al Reis introduced the concept of "positioning" in a series of articles that appeared in *Industrial Marketing* and later *Advertising Age.* (See April 24, May 1, and August 8, 1972, issues of *Advertising Age.*) The concept has since been expanded, revised, and adapted so that it is now considered one of the most basic methods of advertising strategy development.

The general idea of positioning is that advertising is used to locate a "position" for the product in the mind of the consumer. Once that position is established, the consumer should consider that product or brand every time the need for the solution to that particular problem arises. Thus, rather than advertising specific product advantages, "positioning" advertising

---

8. David Ogilvy, *Confessions of an Advertising Man* (New York: Atheneum Publishers, 1963).

Figure 9-8.   The Puritan Oil Positioning Statement

Puritan
vs.
Cholesterol

In a University Study, 43 families on low saturated fat, low cholesterol eating plans reduced serum cholesterol an average of 9.6% in three weeks. For cooking and salad dressings they used Puritan Oil, because it's low in saturated fats, with no cholesterol.

Q. Who were these people? Experts on nutrition?

A. No. They were ordinary people, a group of families who lived near the University.

Q. Did the University serve them their meals?

A. No. They were given eating plans and nutritional guidance, but they cooked their own meals in their own homes. Nobody snooped.

Q. How did they get the kids to follow the eating plans?

A. We're not sure! We think it was because the eating plans weren't drastically different from their previous diets. The foods on the eating plans tasted good. And there was no skimping on desserts.

Q. How did these eating plans differ from the average American's diet?

A. The families consumed less cholesterol and saturated fats. They ate more fish, more chicken, more fruits and vegetables. And when they ate meat, they chose veal or lean cuts of beef.

Q. How does Puritan Oil fit into the picture?

A. The families were supplied with Puritan Oil for salads and cooking because Puritan is low in saturated fats and contains no cholesterol.

Q. Would this way of eating work for my family?

A. That was the whole purpose of this University study: to see if average families, eating their meals at home, could lower cholesterol levels. The study seems to say: it *can* be done.

Puritan knows you're fighting serum cholesterol.
Puritan wants you to win.

SOURCE: Courtesy of The Proctor & Gamble Company.

Figure 9-9.　The Kool-Aid Positioning Statement

SOURCE:　Courtesy of The Proctor & Gamble Company.

seeks to make a brand fill all the consumer needs or desires in that specific product category.

While Trout and Reis do not specifically discuss it in their descriptions of positioning, this approach is basically one of offering or providing an "alternative." The advertiser, using a positioning approach, essentially says, "You know what product X is. Here's why or how my product Y is different or better or more effective or whatever from what you know." Therefore, in many advertising campaigns the brand is being "positioned as," "positioned against," "positioned in place of," and so on. For example, Puritan vegetable oil positions itself clearly against cholesterol in the advertisement shown in Figure 9-8. Thus, Puritan hopes that whenever consumers become concerned about the saturated fats in the cooking oil they are using, they will consider switching to their product.

A more specific example of positioning is the Kool-Aid ad shown in Figure 9-9. Kool-Aid is directly positioning itself against carbonated soft drinks and pointing out the differences and advantages between the two products. While many people might not consider Kool-Aid a substitute for a carbonated beverage since it lacks the "fizz" and bottle, it is widely used by children who are the prime market for Kool-Aid. This type of advertising attempts to make that positioning and the interchangeability of the products more evident.

Summary: On to the Creative Execution

With a soundly developed advertising strategy and a clear-cut advertising promise supported by a sound reason why, many advertising campaign planners believe they have devised an advertising campaign that is sure to succeed. While we, too, believe that "what you say" is of much greater importance than "how you say it," the advertising strategy is a critical element of success. While a sound strategy will usually succeed at some level, a truly outstanding advertising execution can increase the response to the campaign by a thousand-fold. The difference between a "good" and a "great" campaign is often the result of the advertising execution. That's the next step in advertising campaign development.

Case for Discussion:
T. White and Associates

T. White and Associates, a Stamford, Connecticut-based rehabilitation consulting firm, recently opened a branch office in Richmond, Virginia. Other branches are located in Baltimore, Maryland, and Youngstown, Ohio. Each office is staffed with a branch manager, 4–15 counselors, and supporting clerical staff.

T. White was formed in 1968 under the auspices of the Phoenix Mutual Casualty Insurance Company. T. White and similar companies were organized in response to the desire on the part of both insurance carriers and attorneys specializing in workers' compensation claims for an outside agent to supervise rehabilitation efforts. Through the counselor approach, claimants are provided with a trained, concerned intermediary who is presumably less likely to be biased in favor of economic concerns over time and quality elements of the rehabilitative effort. Carriers benefit because an outside consultant relieves some of the workload formerly carried by claims representatives. Also, the counselor's specialized training often leads to quicker rehabilitative results. While not all major insurance carriers utilize counseling firms, acceptance is currently estimated at 55 percent.

Persons filing job-related injury claims are assigned a counselor who oversees any medical care needed and supervises physical and vocational rehabilitative efforts. This may include working with an employer to modify the physical requirements of a job if the claimant is to return to his pre-injury employment. If the nature of the injury is such that the claimant can no longer perform the same type of work, the counselor works with the claimant and attorney to identify areas of vocational interest suitable to the claimant's physical capabilities. The counselor then ensures that necessary training is provided and aids the claimant in obtaining a job in the field. Supervision is maintained for up to one year to ensure a proper "fit" between the claimant and the job.

Some counseling supervision is strictly medical, while other cases entail psychological counseling and a high degree of vocational support. A relationship of mutual trust between claimant and counselor is vital for successful rehabilitation. Counselors usually have either medical (RN) or psychological training. T. White requires that all counselors undergo a six-week on-the-job training period that includes specialized classes in vocational and medical guidance. Counselors are also expected to attend seminars on work-related topics, and tuition fees for applicable courses are paid by the company. A typical counselor caseload is 10 to 15 persons in varying stages of rehabilitation.

Although originally established by the Phoenix Company, T. White now works with a number of carriers. Case references are also obtained through physicians and corporations familiar with past cases, as well as attorneys specializing in workers' compensation cases. All fees are handled through the involved insurance company, and bills are submitted monthly. Carrier approval must be obtained for any rehabilitative efforts such as physical therapy and vocational training. The claimant's attorney is also consulted on all major decisions.

The Richmond office was opened to service the claims resulting from the involvement of a regular T. White client, Timber Mutual, with a large tobacco-processing plant located in Richmond. After six months of operation, Larry Wenska, the branch manager, filed a report with the home office. He noted that the number of cases from Timber Mutual was currently 37, a workload that the four Richmond counselors were easily able to handle. Wenska predicted that this figure would remain fairly constant, taking into account the flow of completed cases and new claims. Although income from this business source was more than sufficient to justify the office's existence, Wenska was eager to solicit other clients. He felt that the Richmond market was very attractive for several reasons:

- many large corporations were located in or near the city
- many of the major insurance carriers had established regional offices in the area
- the number of personal injury claims had increased slightly from the past year, in comparison with a decline in the national trend.

On the negative side, Wenska noted that there were four other rehabilitation consulting firms of varying size operating in the city. Each counted one or more of the large insurance carriers among its major clients. The environment for new referrals was somewhat competitive.

After reviewing Wenska's report, the home office informed him that they had decided to make Richmond a testing ground. The field of rehabilitation consulting had been reluctant to use advertising as a marketing tool in the past, being content to rely upon counselors' personal contacts with insurance carriers. T. White management felt that, if properly done, advertising could prove effective for tapping new sources of business, as well as reinforcing old contacts. Therefore, Wenska was to develop an advertising campaign for the Richmond office. Management placed the following stipulations on the campaign:

1. Its fundamental strategy was to be readily transferrable to other offices.

2. It must result in a 75 percent increase in case referrals within nine months of inception. (Approval was given for the hiring of additional counselors, as needed.)

3. It was to be accomplished within a budget of $500,000.

Although the main office's enthusiasm was greater than he had anticipated, Wenska realized that he now had an opportunity to put some of his marketing ideas to work. All he needed to do was review the media vehicles available to him and start spending money.

Richmond is served by two daily newspapers and several community weeklies. Four television stations are based in town, and viewers can also pick up several Washington, D.C. stations. There are 26 radio stations, encompassing a variety of formats.

Feeling that rehabilitation consulting was still relatively unknown and that broad public awareness was the key, Wenska bought a full page in each of the daily papers and ran an advertisement which outlined T. White's services. He also taped a 30-second radio spot to be broadcast on an all-news station exhorting listeners to "check today's paper for important news regarding your health and future." Two weeks later, only one referral had come in attributable to the "campaign." Realizing that perhaps there was more to successful advertising than he had thought, Wenska asked a friend in marketing for advice. After listening to a description of the company's services (he hadn't read the ad) and reading Wenska's original report, the friend suggested that Wenska answer the following questions before spending any more money:

- Who was the primary audience? insurance companies? corporations/unions? doctors? lawyers? potential claimants?
- Having identified the audience, what type of message would best attract them? Would they need basic information as to what the company is and offers, or would they be more interested in how it differs from similar companies?
- What media vehicles would be most likely to get the message to the right audience?

Questions

1. Develop advertising strategies for at least two of the potential audiences. Include a justification for addressing that particular audience.

2. Which potential strategy would be most effective? Why?

3. If T. White were to stress new business solicitation through carrier contacts as a primary aspect of counselors' responsibilities, would the advertising strategy change? Why?

10 The Advertising Execution: From Strategy to Effective Sales Messages in the Media

While there's little question the "what you say" is the most important decision in an advertising campaign and all other decisions simply reinforce or help magnify that decision, the advertising execution or the "how the advertising strategy is communicated to the prospect" does have a very strong effect on the overall campaign. Generally, a sound strategy will succeed regardless of the execution. If "what you say" is of benefit to the prospect or solves a prospect's problems, some response will usually occur. However, if the strategy is presented in an interesting, exciting, and memorable way, larger numbers of prospects will likely respond to the message or respond more quickly. Thus, to qualify this position a bit, while the "what you say" is vital, the "how you say it" can really prove to be the difference between a successful campaign and an outstanding one.

An example will illustrate the point. Quaker Oats Company's LIFE cereal was first introduced to the national market in 1961. After several moderately successful attempts to sell this new nutritional, ready-to-eat cereal to different target markets, Quaker Oats and the advertising agency at that time, LaRoche, McCaffrey & McCall, developed the basic strategy of promoting LIFE as "the nutritional cereal which tastes good." After several years and several different advertising executions, this new "what to say" strategy about the product had started to generate interest among consumers. Sales were growing, but the product was not an overwhelming success.

In 1968, sales of the cereal really started to grow. And that movement can be directly traced to an executional form of the basic strategy which was new and exciting. Specifically, it was a television commercial that has come to be known simply as "Mikey." The strategy did not change. The execution did. The "Mikey" commercial immediately got the attention of ready-to-eat cereal buyers and users, and LIFE began its sales climb. The decision to feature "taste" in the advertising as the "what to say" started

Figure 10-1.   LIFE Cereal's "Mikey": Execution Improves Success

1ST BOY: What's this stuff?
2ND BOY: Some cereal. Supposed to be good
for you.

1ST BOY: D'you try it?
2ND BOY: I'm not gonna' try it, you try it.

1ST BOY: I'm not gonna' try it.

2ND BOY: Let's get Mikey!
1ST BOY: Yeah!

2ND BOY: He won't eat it. He hates everything.

2ND BOY: He likes it!

Hey Mikey!
ANNCR: (VO) When you bring Life home,
don't tell the kids it's one of those

nutritional cereals you've been trying to get
them to eat. You're the only one who has to
know.

SOURCE: Courtesy of Quaker Oats Company.

the cereal on the road to success. The translation of that strategy through the "Mikey" commercial really provided the impetus to make it a winner. Now, 15 years after the "Mikey" commercial first appeared, it is still winning new customers for LIFE cereal, and there is little evidence that it will not continue to do so.

Similarly, Miller Brewing Company's campaign for their Lite Beer has been greatly enhanced by some brilliant executions of a basic creative strategy of "tastes great, less filling" that was developed and refined over the past several years. While any reduced calorie beer could likely make this claim, the manner in which Miller presented the strategy with past sport hero figures arguing whether the major advantage of Lite Beer from Miller was "great taste" or "less filling" helped immediately establish the product as the category leader. Since the campaign started, more than 25 commercials on this same theme have been developed and aired. Some of the commercials have been good. Some have been excellent. One, however, is always well received. That is where all the sports heroes who make up the series gather for a special event. One storyboard is reproduced in Figure 10-2.

In this instance, a brilliant execution of an extremely sound strategy has resulted in one of the most effective and memorable television commercials in recent years. These are only two examples of how a "big idea" can extend and expand sales for a product for a number of years.

Executions can make a difference in an advertising campaign. They can bring the strategy to life and expand the impact of the campaign immeasurably.

The "Big Idea"

Great advertising campaigns, particularly those which are brought about by great advertising executions, are usually the result of what is termed in the business a "big idea." As with the "Mikey" and Miller Lite examples above, the "big idea" is usually very simple, but it brings a realism, an understanding of the marketplace and an empathy with the target market that literally makes the advertisement jump off the page or off the television screen and into the life of the reader or viewer.

A Few Examples

In actual fact, in terms of what they do and how they operate, stock brokerage houses are pretty much alike. They work under certain restrictions imposed by the Securities & Exchange Commission. Their primary income-producing activities are commissions earned on the purchase and sale of stocks and bonds for their clients. Therefore, when it comes to

Figure 10-2.   Lite Beer from Miller: "Bowling Tournament"

JONES: Deacon's my name, and bowling's my game.

MADDEN: Gutter Ball! Gutter Ball!

BUTKUS: (VO) How you going to score that?
MARTIN: Come on, three strikes and you're out.

HEINSOHN: We just won another round of Lite Beer from Miller.

RED AUERBACH: Well, Lite sure tastes great!

CROWD: LESS FILLING!!! TASTES GREAT!!!

POWELL: Hold it! Hold, it, Jim.

You're going the wrong way. There it is down there.

MIZERAK: Eight ball in the pocket.

BUTKUS: Hey Bubba, this ball doesn't have any holes in it.

SMITH: Now it does.

MEREDITH: The score is all even.
NITSCHKE: Last frame. Who's up?

CARTER: Rodney...

CROWD: RODNEY???
BUTKUS: Got to be a mistake.

DANGERFIELD: Hey you kidding. It's a piece of cake.

DAVIDSON: All we need is one pin Rodney.

ANNCR: (VO) Lite Beer from Miller. Everything you always wanted in a beer. And less.

MADDEN: I didn't get my turn yet. I'm gonna break this tie.

SOURCE: Courtesy of Miller Brewing Company.

Figure 10-3.   E. F. Hutton

1.   TEACHER: Alright children. Who's going to be the first one to recite the alphabet?

2.   How about you Ann?

3.   ANN: A, B, C, D, E, F...

4.   E. F., EF Hutton.

5.   (SFX AND PAUSE)

6.   ANN: When EF Hutton talks people listen.

7.   (SILENT)

SOURCE: Courtesy of E. F. Hutton & Co.

differentiating among stock brokerage houses, advertising people find it a rather difficult task since the physical activities and operations are pretty much the same. The real or perceived difference is usually in the experience, background, or ability of the people in the brokerage house and the guidance they can give their clients. As a result, the formal advertising strategy that E. F. Hutton Company uses is not all that unusual or unique. In fact, a number of other brokerage houses could have used it or developed it, for, in essence, the Hutton strategy is simply that the background and experience in the stock, bond, and market exchange that Hutton personnel bring to their clients is very sound and dependable. That strategy is summarized in the phrase "When E. F. Hutton talks, people listen." This idea runs consistently throughout their advertising.

While the strategy is sound—after all, that is what investors come to a brokerage house for—it is the execution of that basic strategy and promise that really helps E. F. Hutton get their message across. That is done with the now familiar period of silence in the television commercials when everyone stops to hear what E. F. Hutton has to say. A storyboard of one of the recent commercials is illustrated in Figure 10-3.

That's the beauty of a really "big idea." It brings the message home in

Figure 10-4.   Country Time Lemonade Drink Mix

(MUSIC UNDER)
GRANDSON 1: I think you pour water in the hole,

then you put the tree in. . .

GRANDSON 2: I dunno. . .

Grandpa!

GRANDPA: We-I-II. . .I can show you the old-fashioned way!

MOTHER: Old-fashioned? You mean. . .

like the taste of good old-fashioned lemonade?

AVO: Country Time Lemonade Flavor Drink. . .

Not too tart. . .not too sweet.
GRANDPA: (OC) Tastes like good old-fashioned lemonade!

GRANDSON 1: Hey, Grandpa. . .have you ever planted a tree before?

SONG: Country Time. . .Country Time. . .

. . .tastes like good old-fashioned lemonade!

SOURCE: Courtesy of General Foods Corporation.

in a way that customers and prospects enjoy and believe in but, most of all, react to.

Another example of a big idea is the campaign developed by Ogilvy & Mather for General Food's Country Time Lemonade. The concept is quite simple but the promise is extremely strong: "Country Time Lemonade, although it is a mix, tastes as good as homemade lemonade." Again, the theme line is summed up in one simple phrase "Tastes Like Good Old-Fashioned Lemonade," a promise that has great appeal to the target market.

It was and is, however, the creative execution of the advertising which really sets Country Time apart from the competition. Since 1976 Harry Holcombe has portrayed the "Grandpa" in the Country Time television commercials. Because of the situations in which he has been placed and the general tone of the commercials developed by Ogilvy & Mather, Inc., Mr. Holcombe has brought the big idea to life for the product. Country Time has become an extremely successful product in a very competitive product category as a result of outstanding commercials such as the one illustrated in Figure 10-4.

There's really nothing that unusual about the concept, the situation, or even the promise being made to consumers, but when these three things are blended together into a brilliant execution, the advertising can literally work miracles for the brand.

A final example of a big idea in advertising is the "Talking Tub" approach developed by Needham, Harper & Steers advertising agency for their client, Kraft Food's Parkay margarine. Again, the strategy developed for Parkay is quite simple: among the premium-priced margarine brands against which Parkay competes, Parkay tastes more like butter. The strategy is summed up in just two words: "Parkay . . . Butter." While all margarine brands claim to taste more like butter than their competitors, through the execution developed by NH&S, Parkay margarine really pre-empts that idea and that position in the mind of the consumer. It's all done with a very simple but very effective device, the Parkay tub "talks." And when the Parkay tub talks, it says only one thing—"Butter." Thus, while the talking tub gains the attention of the viewer, the actor in the commercial delivers all the selling messages for the brand. One of the commercials is illustrated in Figure 10-5.

Those are just three examples of a really big idea in an advertising execution. For the most part, they are simple and direct, they translate the advertising strategy clearly and completely, they clearly state the sales message being delivered; but, most of all, they empathize with the audience—the customers and prospects for the brand. It is this understanding of the people to whom the advertising is directed that usually separates a big idea from the run-of-the-mill variety. And a big idea can really make a difference. For example, Country Time Lemonade moved from new prod-

Figure 10-5.   Parkay Margarine Talking Tub

SOURCE: Courtesy of Kraft, Inc.

uct introduction to the number one brand in the category using the "Tastes Like Good Old-Fashioned Lemonade" big idea. Parkay moved from the number three brand to number one brand with the help of the Talking Tub. And E. F. Hutton continues to be one of the largest and most successful brokerage houses by using the "When E. F. Hutton Talks, People Listen" idea, in spite of increased competition at all levels. Big ideas can result not only in big advertising successes in the marketplace but in big sales successes as well.

How to Develop a Big Idea

A big idea is often quite simple. There's no great complexity to a "Talking Parkay Tub" or a grandfather figure talking about how Country Time "Tastes Like Good Old-Fashioned Lemonade." Yet they are still considered quite "creative." But in these cases they are controlled creativity— ideas that work and sell.

The big question now, though, is, how does one come up with really great ideas that will turn a sound strategy into a winning advertising campaign—a "Mikey"? That usually is the result of ideation or the development of ideas. But how? Can a person learn to generate ideas, to come up with new and exciting concepts and approaches that will grab the attention of the audience and literally drive the sales message home in an interesting and effective way?

The answer is yes. While there are some people who seem to have an innate gift for generating ideas, most anyone can be taught to develop sound advertising executions. Generally, a big idea is more the result of perspiration than inspiration. That simply means that if a person uses a sound, logical, proven approach as preparation for having ideas, they will usually come. Not all will be a talking tub, but they will be sound, exciting advertising ideas and not simply rehashes of all the dull, boring advertisements that currently flood the marketplace.

The basic psychological literature on creativity comes from several theories that attempt to explain creativity and how it occurs. These range from the psychoanalytic theories of Freud, Kris, and Kubie, to the Gestalt theories of Wertheimer; to the association theories of Mednick; to the composite theories of Koestler, Gruber, and Hadamand. All have contributed something to the understanding of how the mind works and how people generate new approaches, new concepts, and new solutions to old problems.[1] While a thorough study and explanation of these theories of creativity is beyond the scope of this book, three particular concepts and techniques have proven helpful to students in understanding how ideas come about or in actually helping generate effective ideas for advertising practitioners.

The James Webb Young "Technique for Producing Ideas"

By far the most widely known, and perhaps the most widely accepted method of developing advertising ideas is that proposed by James Webb Young, a creative executive with J. Walter Thompson advertising agency. Young developed his concept of idea generation in 1940, and it has been widely quoted and discussed since that time. In summary, Young has suggested that a "new idea is nothing more or less than a *new combination* of old elements." The primary question that Young addresses in his book, *A Technique for Producing Ideas,* however, is how to bring about these new combinations of old elements. He suggests there are five specific steps in developing ideas:

> First, the gathering of raw materials—both the materials of your immediate problem and the materials which come from a constant enrichment of your store of general knowledge.

---

1. Thomas V. Busse and Richard S. Mansfield, "Theories of the Creative Process," *The Journal of Creative Behavior,* 14, 2 (1980): 91–103.

Second, the working over of these materials in your mind.

Third, the incubation state, where you let something besides the conscious mind do the work of synthesis.

Fourth, the actual birth of the idea—the "Eureka! I have it!" stage.

And fifth, the final shaping and development of the idea to practical usefulness.[2]

Since Young's formula sounds so simple, perhaps a few words of explanation will illustrate the process better.

Gathering raw materials. Young suggests there are two types of materials to be gathered: the specific and the general. Specific refers to those elements and information directly related to the product or service to be advertised. The general materials are all those things about life and events that a person gathers in living and being interested in the things around him or her. Since Young says all ideas are simply new combinations of old elements, obviously the more elements available for this combining procedure, the greater the possibility of developing a combination that can be truly exciting and effective.

Working over the materials in the mind. In this step Young likens the ideation process to eating food; you masticate the materials for digestion. So he says, you turn all the materials over in your mind. As Young states, "[You] take the different bits of material which you have gathered and feel them all over, as it were, with the tentacles of the mind." Here he also suggests "that facts sometimes yield up their meaning quicker when you do not scan them too directly, too literally." In other words, look for the meaning, not the absolute facts in the combinations.

The incubation stage. Again, according to Young, "In this third stage you make absolutely no effort of a direct nature. You drop the whole subject and put the problem out of your mind as completely as you can." In other words, you turn the problem over to your unconscious mind and let it do the work. It is here that new combinations, new processes, and new meanings really occur.

The birth of the idea. According to Young, "Now, if you have really done your part in these three stages of the process, you will almost surely experience the fourth.

2. James Webb Young, *A Technique for Producing Ideas* (Chicago: Crain Books, 1975), pp. 53–54.

Out of nowhere the idea will appear.

It will come to you when you are least expecting it. . . .''

In other words, there is no explanation of how the new combination of old elements comes about; it simply occurs as a result of the first three steps. That's the mysterious but always exciting part of the process. But, there is one final stage in the process.

The final shaping and development of the idea. Once more, quoting Young, ''[this is] the stage which might be called the cold, grey dawn of the morning after.'' Here, Young suggests that not every idea is totally complete. Often the idea requires work and/or adaptation to make it exactly fit the situation. It is here at this stage that Young suggests many good ideas are lost. They are lost simply because the idea generator wasn't patient enough to go through this final adaptation process, this final shaping of the raw idea into a really big idea.[3]

Will Young's method work for you? It could. It has worked for many successful advertising people. But, Young's approach is not the only way to develop a big idea. Some others follow.

Arthur Koestler's ''The Act of Creation''

While not specifically related to the development of advertising, Arthur Koestler's concepts of how ideas are developed and created has had much influence on how people believe the mind works. Generally, Koestler's concept is built around the idea of ''bisociation.'' That simply means a new idea often occurs when two thoughts collide and combine. He describes it more fully as occurring when two frames of reference (''matrices'') coincide. The coincidence or collision of these matrices results in a combination that previously had not been considered or had not been thought of. In other words, two rather common concepts or thoughts or situations or even events, when brought together through ''bisociation,'' result in a new and original idea. In fact, he describes it as being ''an act of liberation—the defeat of habit by originality.''[4]

One need only look at various advertising executions to see how Koestler's bisociation concept works. It's in the ''Mikey'' commercial: ''a nutritional cereal that tastes good.'' It's in the Parkay ''Talking Tub: a margarine that says Butter,'' and so on.

David Bernstein, in his book, *Creative Advertising,* provides an excellent example of Koestler's concept of bisociation. Although not directly

---

3. Young, *Technique for Producing Ideas,* pp. 30–54.
4. Arthur Koestler, *The Act of Creation* (New York: The Macmillan Co., 1964), p. 96.

written to this point, the following example illustrates how ideas come into conflict and create a new idea.

PROPOSITION
    Lowenbrau is very expensive but it is the best quality beer you can buy.
    (Note, however, that I have both here and subsequently cut the strategy down to the barest detail. Also I am in most cases post-rationalizing the proposition wherever I was not involved in the account. The strategy for Lowenbrau would almost certainly have defined the consumer and his motivation. Nevertheless, for the sake of brevity in this chapter of practical exercises, I state merely the essential fact about the product.)
    The Lowenbrau proposition gives you little to work on. If there were a "product plus"—an ingredient, strength or price advantage—an idea would be easier to arrive at. . . . If you were launching the first ever German beer on the domestic U.S. market, you could simply state that fact. . . . But if you accept that premise in this case you end up with a headline such as:

"Lowenbrau—supreme quality"

or

"Lowenbrau—when only the best will do"

or

"The mark of excellence"

And so on. Ad nauseum (which is a good name for this sort of advertisement). Brian Palmer has a favorite all-purpose headline for this proposition. "Preferred by those who like it best." It has the merit of sounding impressive and being totally acceptable to Weights and Measures Inspectors.
    But to return to the Lowenbrau proposition . . . and the idea.

IDEA
    "When they run out of Lowenbrau order champagne."

OBSERVATIONS
1. The idea re-presents the proposition. It says that Lowenbrau is a top quality beer without saying "Lowenbrau is a top quality beer."
2. The idea is a relationship. The product has been associated with another, more accepted, symbol of quality. The association, more-over, justifies the price.

3. The idea is a reversal of normal thought processes. Instead of the beer being an acceptable alternative to champagne, it suggests the reverse.[5]

(Note: The above campaign was used successfully in Europe.)

As Bernstein shows, two ideas that were normally thought not to be even related and even in conflict have collided and produced another, even more compelling idea. That's how bisociation works. And it can work for any advertiser. Bisociation uses thoughts, concepts, and relationships, in new and different combinations. That's how ideas are born.

Edward deBono's "Lateral Thinking"

Again, although this approach was not specifically designed to assist in the generation of advertising ideas, it is a method that the planner can use to help generate new approaches, new concepts, and new ideas for advertising campaigns. Edward deBono, in his book, *Lateral Thinking for Management,* defines "lateral thinking":

> Vertical thinking is traditional logical thinking. It is called vertical thinking because you proceed directly from one state of information to another state. It is like building a tower by placing one stone firmly on top of the preceding stone; or like digging a hole by making deeper the hole you already have.[6]

He contrasts vertical thinking with what he calls lateral thinking. Lateral thinking generally can be considered to be "discontinuity" or "change for the sake of change" thinking. Perhaps the best way to explain lateral thinking is to contrast it with the more traditional or vertical thinking which most of us practice. DeBono gives several examples.

a. Vertical thinking is selective, lateral thinking is generative.
b. Vertical thinking moves only if there is a direction in which to move, lateral thinking moves in order to generate a direction.
c. Vertical thinking is analytical, lateral thinking is provocative.
d. Vertical thinking is sequential, lateral thinking can make jumps.
e. With vertical thinking one has to be correct at every step, with lateral thinking one does not have to be.
f. With vertical thinking one uses the negative in order to block off certain pathways. With lateral thinking there is no negative.

5. David Bernstein, *Creative Advertising, For This You Went to Oxford?* (London: Longman Group Ltd., 1974), pp. 86–88.

6. Reprinted by permission of the publisher from *Lateral Thinking for Management* by Edward deBono, p. 4. © 1971 by American Management Association. All rights reserved.

g. With vertical thinking one concentrates and excludes what is irrelevant, with lateral thinking one welcomes chance intrusions.
h. With vertical thinking categories, classifications, and labels are fixed, with lateral thinking they are not.
i. Vertical thinking follows the most likely paths, lateral thinking explores the least likely.
j. Vertical thinking is a finite process, lateral thinking is a probabilistic one.[7]

In short, lateral thinking seeks to explore new relationships among elements or situations or events or even activities to generate new and unique ideas. These new relationships are necessarily simple because we tend to think in patterns or in some sort of self-organizing system. While this is highly advantageous to deal with the myriad of rather mundane but necessary activities required to survive in our environment, they tend to inhibit any new approaches or new concepts from being developed. Lateral thinking attempts to break out of these patterns and to look at new and previously unexplored relationships or areas of possibility. In summary, deBono describes lateral thinking as follows:

The purpose of lateral thinking is the generation of new ideas and escape from the old ones. The need for lateral thinking arises from the patterning behavior of the mind which is not good at restructuring ideas to bring them up to date and allow full use of available information. The traditional habits of thinking are very effective at developing ideas but not very good at restructuring them. Lateral thinking is designed to supplement traditional thinking and especially to introduce discontinuity that is necessary for restructuring ideas. The basic process of lateral thinking is the escape from old ideas and the provocation of new ones. The ideas generated by lateral thinking are selected and developed by traditional thinking methods. . . .
        The principles of lateral thinking could be summarized as follows:

1. Recognition of dominant or polarizing ideas.
2. The search for different ways of looking at things.
3. The relaxation of the rigid control of vertical thinking.
4. The use of chance and provocative methods in order to introduce discontinuity. . . . [8]

7. Edward deBono, *Lateral Thinking: Creativity Step by Step* (New York: Harper & Row, 1970), pp. 39–46. Copyright © 1970 by Edward deBono. By permission of Harper & Row Publishers, Inc.
8. DeBono, *Lateral Thinking for Management,* pp. 50–51.

DeBono lists several methods that can be used to stimulate lateral thinking and to break the vertical thinking pattern. Among those are such things as (a) generate alternatives to present situations; (b) challenge present assumptions; (c) innovate; (d) suspend judgment for a period of time; (e) reverse a common approach; (f) develop analogies for the situation; (g) brainstorming and so on.[9] The primary idea is to look at things differently, in nontraditional, lateral thinking patterns. In other words, turn the idea upside-down and look at it a different way.

While there is not sufficient space to enumerate all of deBono's suggestions on how to induce lateral thinking, it should be clear that rather than "thinking through" as in traditional vertical thinking, the concept of lateral thinking is to "think out" into new and previously unconsidered approaches and ways in which a problem might be solved.

The person who is responsible for the actual translation of the advertising strategy into the advertising execution should examine these three basic approaches to developing a big idea for the campaign.

From Idea to Execution

Actually, the most difficult part of translating the advertising strategy into a sound, effective advertisement or commercial is getting started. Sometimes the greatest concepts, the really big ideas, can get lost when the writer or art director sits down to put the idea on paper.

Over the years, Don Kanter, Stone & Adler, Inc., Chicago, has developed a list of guidelines for copywriters. While Kanter and Stone & Adler specialize in direct response advertising, the guidelines Kanter has developed will work just as well for any type of advertising translation or execution.

Guideline One: Know the Product

The first guideline, of course, is that you do not write a word until you have studied your product or service and dug out every possible benefit you can . . . along with the selling points. While, in a classroom exercise you can do it on your own, in real life you should not try to do it that way. Talk to people. Talk to the buyer, the product manager, the account executive . . . whoever. Look at ads and mailings for competitive products or services. If it's possible, try the product or service yourself.

Then build your copy skeleton. List the benefits and selling points. Rank them. Outline them.

---

9. De Bono, *Lateral Thinking for Management,* pp. 50–51.

This is the tough part of copywriting. In some classroom exercises you'll have only 15 minutes to do it, but in real life it can take more time than actually writing the copy. And it is particularly hard for writers who think they are quote—writers—unquote and want to get to the typewriter and start writing. Yet it is the most vital and important part of copywriting because it undergirds every word you write. I repeat: if you realize that your job is to sell, you will realize that you cannot sell until you know as much as possible about what you are selling.

Guideline Two: Know Your Market

Now that you know your product, learn your market. To whom is this product or service going to be sold? What is he or she (or they) like? What are their demographics, their lifestyles? Where do they live?

Again, don't try to reason this out for yourself. Talk to people to find out.

Then visualize your prospect and talk directly to him or her, as if you were selling in person. Keep in mind that you are selling, and that you are substituting the written word for the spoken word.

One obvious caution here: I am not telling you to write precisely as you would speak—far from it. As anybody who's read the Nixon tapes knows, literal spoken dialogue does not make very good written copy. I am telling you to write directly to your prime prospect.

This market knowledge is another part of the writing process that lies underneath that part of the iceberg which is visible: your copy. But like product knowledge, market knowledge undergirds what you write.

With the product and market knowledge, and with the outline done, we are now ready—honest—to start writing copy. And I have more guidelines which I hope you will find helpful.

Remember, I said guidelines, not rules. And remember that there are exceptions to everything. I've found these guidelines to be valid and helpful, but I'll occasionally go against them—*if* there is a good and valid reason to do so.

Guideline Three: Talk to Your Prospect

Talk to your prospect—not to everybody. You know, this is where the copywriter has an advantage over the face-to-face salesperson. A salesperson will generally sell one product or line of products—to one audience. As writers, we get the chance to sell many different kinds of products and services to many different audiences. It's almost like being an actor: talking with kings and princes . . . and with peasants and paupers . . . and talking to each group so that they understand you—and more important, believe you.

Guideline Four: Make a Promise

Make a promise to your prospect—and then prove that you can deliver what you promise.

That's really putting the benefit/selling point theory into practice: the benefit is the promise you make, and the selling points are the way you prove that you will deliver on the promise. It's an obvious point, but worth repeating: unless there is something of value in it for the prospect, he is not interested.

Guideline Five: Get to the Point

Make that promise right away. In other words, get to the point.

This is probably a pet gripe of mine, but it's amazing how much copy I see that wanders around, tries to tease or tell stories . . . and takes forever to get to the point—by which time you've probably lost the prospect.

How many times have you heard a writer say: "We'll I've got this tremendous teaser line, and everybody who sees it will be beside himself with curiosity."

You know, all of us are human beings. We have problems: the kids are sick, we've got to pay the bills somehow, Dick Tracy is in bad trouble this week, the Cubs (or the Cards or Mets) blew last week's game—you know, important things to think about.

But somehow we assume that everybody in America is vitally interested in our copy—that they dash home, throw off their coats and grab the magazine or the newspaper or that day's mail so that they can ponder every word of what we wrote. Baloney; they have lots of things to worry about more important than our copy. We're lucky if we can get their attention, much less sell them anything—and we will get their attention only if we tell them quickly what's in it for them . . . if we make that promise and make it fast.

Get to the point.

Guideline Six: Be Germane

Be germane and specific to your selling proposition.

There's a fairly simple test for this. Look at your major headline, or headline and subhead combination. If you could use that for anything other than the specific product or service you are selling, something's wrong. Fix it.

Guideline Seven: Be Concise

There's a relatively simple test for this one, too: take what you write—then cut it by 20 percent. Almost without exception, you will find that not only hasn't it hurt your copy, it has really improved it by making it sharper and more to the point.

When you write space or broadcast, the disciplines of the space or time available will help you write lean, working copy. When you're writing direct mail, there's often a problem of overwriting. If it were up to me, I would make every copywriter go through two years in the catalog copy department of Sears or Wards. When you're given six lines of 32 characters—including the article number, shipping weight, and price—you learn how to sell with a minimum of words.

Guideline Eight: Be Logical

Once you've hooked your reader with your promise, lead him or her through your selling proposition logically, smoothly. Don't jump to one subject, then to another, then back to the first one again.

Guideline Nine: Be Enthusiastic

If you don't believe in what you're selling, how do you expect your prospect to believe in it?

Caution: enthusiasm doesn't mean adding an exclamation point to every other sentence. That doesn't make your copy enthusiastic. 'Enthusiasm' is when you believe that what you are selling is good, and a good value . . . and this comes through in your copy.

Guideline Ten: Be Complete

Good advice for any copywriter . . . but absolutely essential for a direct response copywriter. You are the only salesperson there is, and if you leave something out, there's nobody the prospect can ask. You may well do a brilliant job of organizing, researching, outlining and writing . . . only to lose the sale because you forgot to include the size . . . or some other obvious point.

Guideline Eleven: Don't Try to Dazzle

Don't try to dazzle your audience with the brilliance of your craft. If anybody says, ''Gee, that's a great ad (or a great mailing piece or a great commercial," you've gotten the wrong reaction. The reaction you want is "Gee, that's a great product (or service)—I've got to have that." Save your brilliant word-smithing for the Great American Novel I'm sure you've already started.

Guideline Twelve: Respect the English Language

This is the tool with which you earn your living, and every good craftsman treats his tools with respect and care. I'm sorry, I am not one of those persons who agrees that the English language is whatever popular usage says it is. I think that makes for sloppy, uncommunicative language. The English language is a beautiful thing. It has its rules, and I believe they should be observed. I still cringe when I hear phrases like "will everybody take their seats" . . . or when somebody doesn't know whether or not to include an apostrophe in the word "i-t-s" . . . or when I see Oldsmobile's line: "Can we build one for you?" (Yes, Oldsmobile, you *may* if you *can*.) Respect the language.[10]

In addition to Kanter's twelve guidelines, four others might be added that both students and professionals seem to have difficulty with in strategy translation. Again, as Kanter says, these are merely guidelines. They are not straight-jackets. They are suggestions that will help keep the idea development on track and make sure that the big idea comes through clearly, quickly, and completely.

Guideline Thirteen: Empathize

Be able to empathize with customers and prospects. Most great advertising comes about because the writer is able to put himself or herself in the place of the person to whom they are writing or speaking. To use the old Chinese phrase, they are "able to walk in the other person's shoes." That simply means being able to understand what it is like to have the problem the product or service will solve. What it is like to be the person to whom the advertising is being directed.

A couple of examples might help. What would it be like to be a mother with a sick child? What would it be like to be 65 years old and on the last day at your job? What would it be like to be a farmer who is trying to decide whether or not to buy a new tractor for the farm or to send one of his children to college? Or what would it be like to live in a small town in Georgia? If the writer can imagine what it would be like to be in those

---

10. From a presentation by Don Kanter to students at Medill School of Journalism, Northwestern University, Evanston, IL, 1982. Used with permission of Mr. Kanter.

situations, he or she is likely well on the way to being able to translate sound advertising strategies into outstanding advertisements.

Developing empathy for customers and prospects often isn't easy. But it's vital for the strategy to really hit home through advertising translation.

Guideline Fourteen: Have a Specific Response in Mind

Often, one of the biggest problems advertising writers have is "they are simply writing advertising." They really don't have a purpose in mind, other than to get the ad done and into the newspaper, or on the radio, or on TV. And the advertising shows it. The problem is that the copywriter really doesn't have a clear idea of how the prospect is to respond or what the prospect should do as a result of seeing the advertisement. In short, what is supposed to happen? Is the reader/listener/viewer supposed to change his or her opinion or image of the product? Should they put the brand on a shopping list? Should they mentally jot the product down as a "possibility" on the next shopping trip? Or should they leap from their chair, rush to their nearest dealer, and make a purchase as quickly as possible?

The answers to these questions can make a big difference in the way the advertising is approached, the actual content used, and the tone employed. If the writer wants people to rush out of their homes to buy, he had better tell them where the product is available. If he wants them to write for more information or send for a brochure, the advertisement should lead up to that point. If the writer can't identify what prospects should do after seeing the advertisement, he needs a different advertisement.

Guideline Fifteen: Offer Benefits, Not Gimmicks

A major problem in advertising today is the reliance of advertising writers on gimmicks rather than promises and benefits for consumers. Too often, advertisements tend to rely on new technology such as computer animation, new lighting, overprinting, or visual effects to take the place of sound, logical, usable consumer benefits that will be received as a result of using the product. Thus there are advertisements in which the actual value of the product or service is totally lost in the final presentation or execution simply because customers and prospects wouldn't, couldn't, or didn't dig through all the gimmicks to find the offer or the promise or the benefit that was available to them. An example should help.

A few years ago, an automobile marketer put one of its cars on top of a mesa in the desert Southwest. Pictures were taken with a model standing beside the car, the wind blowing through her hair, a beautiful sunset, the light just right. The picture was brilliant, and it appeared in numerous advertisements in national magazines and might have even been on television. Most people recall the picture. It was great. But few can remember the brand of automobile or why it was on top of the mesa. Remember Don Kanter's admonition: Don't try to dazzle your audience. That ad did.

Just a few years later, a pet food company developed a television commercial that used a similar mesa. The name of the product was "Come and Get It," a dog food manufactured by Carnation Company. The television storyboard is reproduced as Figure 10-6.

The "Come and Get It" commercial is more memorable than the name of the automobile—even to non-dog owners—because the situation on the mesa is an integral part of the "Come and Get It" commercial. There was a real reason to use a mesa location and a situation like that to get across the idea that dogs will come from everywhere to get the great taste of "Come and Get It." There is no apparent reason for the auto to be on the mesa—or the reason is totally obscured. And that is the point. The elements of the advertising execution should be meaningful, and the benefits should be relevant and clear. That's what makes advertising memorable. Not gimmicks. Not tricks. Not the latest fad. Good, solid, honest benefits for the consumer dressed up in an interesting and informative way.

Guideline Sixteen: Ask for the Order

One of the things that happens all too often in advertising translations is simply that the writer or art director or others involved in the ad forget they are in the selling business. They forget that the idea of advertising is to make a sale, at least a mental, if not a physical, one. Yet, too many times, advertisements simply present the product benefits or the solution to the consumer's problem and then stop. The message simply sits there. No one asks the customer to buy, or to make a mental pledge to try, or to consider the product or service being advertised. In short, the advertising writer almost seems embarrassed that the advertising is supposed to sell things or to help people buy things. And that is a big mistake.

Every successful door-to-door salesperson knows about the importance of closing the sale. She knocks on the door. The prospect answers. She launches into her sales message. It is loaded with benefits. It solves problems. It may even be the "miracle of the age." And, having delivered the message, she simply turns around and leaves. After all, she has given her sales message. Does the prospect who opened the door run after her, screaming, "I want to buy. I want to buy. Let me have one now, please." Not likely. The next logical step is to ask for the order.

It's the same with advertising. The ad shouldn't simply turn on its "heel" and "walk" away. The ad must ask the reader or listener or viewer to buy. It must try to "close the sale." If not, nothing will happen.

Figure 10-6. "Come and Get It": Making the Situation Integral

We went out of our way to make a dry dog food thats all together different.

It's new Come 'N Get It variety dinner for dogs.

The taste dogs really go for.

Come 'N Get It has four different flavors. Beef (echo) . . .

cheese (echo) . . .

liver (echo) . . .

chicken (echo) . . .

in four unique shapes. Four flavors. Four shapes. Great new taste.

We put 'em all together . . . in one bag.

New Come 'N Get It! (Echo) (Bark)

The taste that calls dogs to dinner.

SOURCE: Courtesy of Carnation Company

"Closing the sale" doesn't mean that every advertisement must end with a "Buy now!" tag line. It can be any form of action, either physical or mental, but the ad should ask the prospect to do something or think about something or make a mental commitment to the product. Simply making the presentation and walking away won't sell many products door-to-door, and it won't sell many products through advertising, either. Every ad or commercial must ask for the order.

How to Judge Advertising Executions

Sometimes, as it has been assumed up to now, the campaign planner and the advertising copywriter are the same person. In many instances that's the case. In others, however, it isn't. For example, a brand manager or advertising manager for a manufacturer or marketer may be directly involved in the development of the advertising strategy but dependent on the advertising agency creative personnel or perhaps creative people in her own organization to provide the actual physical translations. Similarly, an agency account executive or other manager may have a major hand in developing the strategy but again rely on the creative department to translate that strategy into the actual advertisements or commercials. If either of these is the case, the question then becomes how does the planner evaluate the executions—determine whether advertising translations will be effective? How can the planner recognize a "big idea"? Is there a way to assure that what is presented will work in the marketplace?

Several advertising agencies and advertisers have developed a series of steps or guidelines that assist them in evaluating advertising executions. Below is a list of eight of these guidelines or checkpoints that have proven effective over the years. Again, remember, these are simply guidelines or checkpoints, not rules. Sometimes there is a good reason for breaking the "rules." It's knowing when and why to break them that separates the good advertising campaign planner from the average. Use these checkpoints to make sure that the advertising really is and does what it is supposed to do in the campaign.

Is the Advertisement on Strategy?

Sounds simple but often it's the biggest problem with a campaign. The strategy is planned to say one thing and the advertising ends up saying another. That usually comes about when "creativity" gets in the way of the selling message. So, first look at the strategy statement. Then look at the advertising execution. If the execution doesn't translate the strategy, toss the execution out and start over. Start over no matter how cute, how clever, how exciting the actual advertisement or commercial or poster or whatever seems to be. The first and guiding rule: the advertising must say what it set out to say in the strategy. That means the execution must follow the strategy. No exceptions. (This is the only guideline that should never be broken.)

Will the Execution Appeal to the Right Audience?

A great deal of time has been spent defining and locating the target market for the advertising message. The question now, assuming the ad is on strategy, is, will this execution appeal to that group of people? If not, toss it out and start over.

There are some obvious clues here. If the target market is people over 60, current fads, rock 'n' roll, and the latest "in" graphics are usually totally wasted. You wouldn't try to sell cleric robes to ministers with rap talk. The point here is, if you really know your target market, you should have a strong idea of whether or not a specific execution or interpretation of the strategy will appeal to them, and that means in terms of layout, style, grammar, music, tone, and the rest. The execution should fit the audience.

Would You Say This to Your Prospect in Person?

If you were calling on your prospect in person, would this be what you would say to convince him to buy? Strangely enough, advertisers often hide behind their advertisements when it comes to trying to sell someone something. The anonymity of the printed page or the radio commercial or even the sales brochure seems to open up the doors to all sorts of inane ideas. We put "bells and whistles" on advertisements and commercials that do nothing more than make the message more difficult to read, see, hear, or understand.

One good way to test an advertisement for effectiveness is to mentally imagine yourself selling your product or service door-to-door. When a person answers the door, would you go into a tap dance? Would you tell a joke? Would you show a puppy dog? Not likely. To make the sale, you'd get directly to the point. And you'd fill your sales talk with benefits and features that the prospect would want and could use in making a buying decision in favor of your product. It's the same with advertising. The advertising should not drift off into unrelated sales messages, cute sayings, puns, gimmicks, and the like. Use the same sort of sales approach you would if you were calling on the prospect in person.

From the Marketer's or Consumer's View?

Is the advertisement written from the marketer's or the prospect's view-point? One good check of an advertising execution is simply to ask, "Does this ad help my prospect buy or simply try to help me make a sale?'' And there's a big difference in that view. Boastful, breast-beating advertising that tells how great the advertiser is or how wonderful the product is or how proud the company is to bring the product to the market usually provides no benefit whatsoever to the prospect. Remember the difference between benefits and product features from Chapter 9. An old advertising adage illustrates the point. People buy one-half-inch holes, not one-half-inch drills. In other words, no one really wants a drill. They really want the holes the drill makes. So, in a sense, the question to ask is, ''Are we selling the drill or the holes?''

Is the Execution Clear, Concise, Complete, and Convincing?

A big problem with many advertisements is that the writer often assumes the prospect knows as much about the product as the writer does and is as interested in it as the writer is. When this happens, the reader or listener or person on the other end of the advertisement is often left far behind. So, first, the advertisement must be clear. Is it easy to follow? Are all the benefits listed and supported? Is the advertisement complete? Is there anything important left out—anything the target market might need to know or to have to make a decision in favor of the product or service advertised?

Perhaps it is a good time to reiterate that each advertisement should be single-minded. That simply means there should be a clear benefit, backed up by a strong reason or reasons why that benefit is available or possible. Often, one of the biggest problems advertisers have is trying to cram too much into an advertisement—too many sales points, too many ideas, too many messages. When that happens, instead of talking to everyone, the advertisement usually talks to no one. The execution should be single-minded. That means cutting out all the extraneous ideas, words, and even benefits so that the primary sales message comes through loud and clear. People won't work to read or understand an ad. In fact, it's hard enough to get them to stop to see the really good ones, much less the average.

Finally, the advertisement must be complete. A good check of this is to ask, ''If the prospect never saw another advertisement or commercial for this product or service, would he or she know enough about how to buy and where to buy so that a sale could occur?'' If the answer is no, this is the time to make the necessary changes.

Does the Execution Overwhelm the Message?

A common failing of many advertisements, particularly those on television, is that they succeed in getting themselves, but not the product or the product benefit, remembered. When that happens, it usually is the result of the advertising execution simply overwhelming the advertising message. The layout or color or animation or whatever is so outstanding that it totally overshadows the message the advertiser is trying to get across. We've all experienced that kind of advertising. Someone walks up to us and says, ''I just saw a great ad. There was this man walking a tightrope between the World Trade Towers with a 70 mph wind blowing and it was really exciting.'' Upon questioning, however, it becomes clear that the person who saw this ''great ad'' can't remember who placed it, what the product was, or even how the man on the tightrope related to the situation. The execution simply overwhelmed the message. Beware the lure of the gimmick. Remember, the advertising is there to sell or influence the purchase of a product or service. If it can entertain or amuse or thrill or even bring a tear, wonderful. But the primary job is to sell a product, a service, or an idea. Don't let the execution get in the way.

Is There a Call to Action?

Surprisingly, a great deal of advertising does not ask for any commitment from the viewer, reader, or listener. That is much like a door-to-door salesperson knocking on the door, having it answered, presenting the sales message, and just when the customer starts to respond, simply turning and walking away. No effort to make the sale. No attempt to get some action or commitment from the prospect. The purpose of advertising is to get someone to do something he or she isn't doing now. That something can be a change of opinion, the trial of the product, a mental pledge to consider the product at the next buying opportunity. Or whatever. But advertising should be designed to get some sort of response. And, if the advertisement doesn't ask directly for the desired response, that response probably won't come.

Therefore, every advertisement must have some sort of call to action, something that the reader or viewer or listener is supposed to do as a result of seeing, reading, or hearing that particular advertisement. And it's much easier to get that response if the ad asks for it than if the prospect is left to figure out for himself or herself what he or she is supposed to do. Every execution must ask for some sort of action.

Are You Proud Enough of the Advertisement to Show It to Someone Close to You?

In other words, is this piece of advertising something you are proud of, something you would want your name on if ads were signed? If not, start over. Advertisements of which you wouldn't be proud rarely gain response from others, particularly those you're trying to sell. People hardly ever buy from rude or crude or pushy salespeople. The same thing is true of advertisements. If you want your advertising to succeed, it must make friends with your prospects and customers. Does the execution you're judging accurately reflect you and your product? If not, change it now.

Here, however, pride in authorship is a two-edged sword, because in evaluating an advertising execution, you must be able to separate your personal prejudices from your job as a salesperson. Even if you'd never wear black shoes with a brown suit, millions of people do. And they see nothing wrong with it. So, when judging an ad in terms of whether or not it shows your best work or presents the product in the best light, try to separate personal prejudices from the selling job at hand. You might be very proud of an advertisement that featured a painting by Picasso because you thought it was esthetically pleasing. If, however, your target market thought it was nothing more than a bunch of squiggly lines, go with the view of your audience. The balance is between what you think is important and what your prospects think is important. Be proud of your work but try to keep your personal prejudices out of the evaluation.

Those are basic questions a planner can and should ask about the translation of every advertising strategy. These questions won't make someone an expert on creative executions, but if the answer to each of the eight questions above is yes, the advertising execution has a big lead on advertising that doesn't qualify on all these points. No one can predict the success of an advertising execution, not even the testing services, but these simple questions can assure that almost everything possible has been done to insure success.[11]

A Few Thoughts about Media Translation

While this is certainly not intended to be a text or even a chapter on copywriting or art direction or even esthetics in the media, there are a few things the campaign planner should keep in mind when translating or evaluating the translation of advertising strategies into executions in the various media. All ideas are not equal. And all media are not equal. Each medium has unique strengths and weaknesses just as do the various campaign strategies. It is the ability to capitalize on the strengths of the individual medium and minimize its weaknesses that really makes the advertising campaign planner effective. Again, although the planner may not be charged with the actual translation of the strategy into the media and may have only final approval or control over how the advertising is to

---

11. Adapted in part from John M. Keil, "Can You Become a Creative Judge?, *Journal of Advertising*, 4, 1 (1975): 29–31.

appear, there are a few guidelines that can be helpful in evaluating advertising executions. Again, these guidelines are just that, guidelines, not rules, but they have been proven over time and generally are accepted by advertising professionals everywhere.

Guidelines for Print

1. Is the message clear at a glance? Can you quickly tell what the advertisement is all about? Today, most readers are simply scanners of the print media. To be successful, the print ad must tell the scanner quickly and clearly the message and benefit of the advertisement. It must generate additional attention to get the copy read. Is this advertisement a clear message?

2. Is the benefit in the headline? With scanners, those who only see the headline and the illustration, it's vital for the headline to quickly and clearly tell the prospect the value or benefit or problem-solution being offered. Involved, complicated, difficult-to-understand headlines don't work in today's fast-paced information situations. Is the headline a benefit-oriented message?

3. Does the illustration support the headline? The headline and the illustration must work in concert. Does the illustration lend support to or explain the headline? It should. It should demonstrate why the advertiser can make the claim made in the headline. Support the promise. Does the illustration support and tie into the headline?

4. Does the first line of the copy support or explain the headline and the illustration? Print ads must present a united idea. Immediately supporting the benefit in the headline with a statement of why that benefit is available or why the claim can be made assures that casual scanners get the total message in just a few seconds. If there is interest, they will read on. First, however, make sure the support for the claim is stated immediately. Does the first line of copy support the headline and illustration?

5. Is the ad easy to read and easy to follow? With the average reader spending only fractions of a second deciding whether or not to stop or to move on, the print advertisement must be or appear to be easy to read and easy to follow. That includes both the layout and composition. Does the ad invite readership?

6. Is the type large and legible? In the last few years a mass of "creative" or "artistic" type faces have been developed. While they have their place, usually advertising isn't one of them. Clear, sharp, easy-to-read, and most of all, legible type is a must in print advertising. People simply won't work to learn what you have to say. Is the type in your ad easy to read?

7. Is the sponsor clearly identified? Again, is it clear who is making the offer in the ad? Too many advertisers seem almost embarrassed to present themselves as the seller or the purveyor of the ideas or products or services offered. People want to know who they are dealing with and how to contact them. They want to buy from people they know. Is the advertiser clearly identified in the ad?

8. Are there any excess words, phrases, or even ideas that could be deleted? People are busy. They don't want and won't take time to read extra words and extra phrases that have little or nothing to do with the benefits they seek or the problem they want to solve. If the information is important and helpful, they'll read literally volumes, but if it's simply "fluff," they'll drop it in a second. Are there any words here that could come out? Cut the copy to the bone, but make it complete.

9. If there is a coupon or a clip-out, is it easy to remove or easy to get? In some art director's zeal to make the advertisement a work of beauty, key elements such as coupons, maps, directions, etc., get lost in a wash of creative genius. If the object of the advertisement is to get a person to clip a coupon, make it easy to do. Put it in the corner. Make it big enough to read. If the name is to be added, make sure there is enough room. In short, do everything possible to help the reader, even if it means giving up an art direction award. Are the elements of the ad easy to understand?

Guidelines for Radio

Radio and television have been separated because today they are such totally different media. Below are just a few suggestions on how to evaluate radio commercials.

1. Does the commercial intrude? Today, radio is primarily a background medium. People are doing something else while they are listening. Therefore, you must intrude to get attention. That doesn't mean irritating, but it does mean that it is necessary to break out of the drone and either offer a benefit or gain attention so that prospects will hear the message. Does the commercial intrude enough to get attention?

2. Is the commercial written for the ear and the mind? As members of the first video generation, many young advertising people assume there is a picture available to support their words, whether there is or not. Radio must play on the mind through the ears. That means it must involve the imagination. That's done with sound effects, words, pauses, and so on. Effective radio allows the listener to add content and contrast to the commercial to further support the idea being heard. Take advantage of this unique aspect of radio. Does this commercial involve the imagination?

3. Does the commercial involve the listener? Closely allied with point two above is involvement. One of the major problems with much radio today is that, not knowing how to use it, some advertisers simply have announcers read print advertisements over the air. That is a massive waste of the medium. Radio has the unique ability to involve listeners, to get them to add to and supplement what is actually being said or heard. Does the radio commercial involve the listener or simply present a mass of facts and data? It makes a big difference.

4. Is there only one sales message? Because radio is so easy to produce and so easy to change, many advertisers make the mistake of thinking that they can use radio as one would a laundry bag . . . simply stuff ideas into the time frame until it is full. Nothing could be further from the truth. Good radio commercials have only one major selling point, and it is repeated and embellished during the commercial. Good radio is not what can be crammed into sixty seconds. It's how well the time can be used to build a story for the listener and discuss the benefits of the product or service. Does the commercial have only one main idea?

5. Is the brand clearly identified? Because radio is fleeting and a background medium, too often the brand name or the sponsor is lost. Radio, unlike print, can't be referred back to or reviewed. Once the commercial is broadcast, it is gone forever. Therefore, it is impossible to repeat the brand name or the product benefit too often in radio. Remember when you've tried to recall an address or a telephone number from a radio commercial. It's very difficult to do. The radio commercial should have enough brand and benefit identification so the message gets across.

6. Does the commercial sound the way the target market speaks? The spoken word and the written word are totally different. Radio commercials, written as literary gems, usually fail because thoughts, ideas, and concepts usually are compressed when spoken. People don't speak in complete sentences or even complete phrases. Radio should be written to communicate—to get ideas and information and benefits across to the audience. That means writing for the ear rather than for the eye in the way most people talk. The best thing: read the commercial aloud. Is that how you would tell your benefit in person? If not, loosen up and write as you speak.

A caution here. Writing as you speak doesn't mean using poor grammar or incorrect sentence construction. It simply means use the written word the way you use it in conversation, not as you use it in print. Is your commercial in written or spoken language?

Guidelines for Television

Because of its great range, television is a medium unto itself. To execute successful television commercials, keep these thoughts in mind when evaluating or developing commercials for the campaign.

1. Does the commercial interrupt? Although politeness is generally considered a virtue, it really has no place in a television commercial. People go to television to be entertained, not to see commercials. Therefore, the commercial must break through their relaxation and get their attention. If radio must intrude, television commercials must interrupt. They must break through the wall of interest in the program content and literally call attention to the product and message. This does not mean that a television commercial should be rude or vulgar or irritating, but it does mean that it must interrupt the programming and get attention for the message being presented. So, first check to see if the commercial interrupts and gets attention.

2. Is the commercial a visual idea? Many television commercials are simply stand-up announcers pitching the product to the audience. This is probably the worst possible way to use television. Television is visual. It is movement. It is action. Without those three things, you might as well use print or radio. You can test that by asking yourself: "Is my sales message a visual idea?" If it isn't, you're not taking full advantage of the medium.

3. Does the commercial demonstrate the benefits of the product or service? This follows very closely with the previous point of television being visual. The major feature television offers is the opportunity to actually demonstrate the benefit being offered or the problem being solved by the product or service. Unfortunately, some creative people believe demonstrating the benefit of problem-solution simply means the traditional "slice-of-life" commercial or a hard-hitting, beat-them-over-the-head with a buy-now theme. That's not true. Almost every product or service can be demonstrated, if not the actual thing that the product does then the benefit the user receives or the psychological satisfaction of using the product or service. Does your television commercial demonstrate the benefit you offer?

4. Is there very clear brand identification? One of the major problems in television is misidentification; that is, viewers seeing commercials for one brand and attributing it to or remembering it as another. Some studies have shown that this misidentification runs as high as 50 percent for brands in some categories. A few years ago, B. F. Goodrich was receiving so much misidentification of its advertising (many viewers thought Goodrich commercials were for Goodyear, the market leader) that the company launched a separate advertising campaign to differentiate itself from the competition.

A key point in developing sound television executions is to avoid what are called generic claims; in other words, benefits and problem solutions that are common to the category and cannot be tied directly to the brand. For over 100 years, Ivory soap has used the line "99 and 44/100% pure, it floats." That's a clear brand identification and a clear product benefit. The benefit being offered must be inexorably connected to the brand. Is it?

5. Is there only one clear sales message? Perhaps because of the wide and varied opportunity to insert additional claims either in the audio or video portion of the commercial, too many advertisers try to insert "just one more idea to reach another group of people who may be watching." This is a mistake. Commercials that try to reach everyone with something usually end up reaching no one with anything. Have one clear sales message and one clear idea directed to one clear target market. If the product has other benefits and strategies for them, write additional commercials. Don't confuse your audience. Is your commercial single-minded?

6. Does the commercial properly represent the product? Finally, does the general tone of the commercial properly represent the product? That is, if the product is high-priced, prestigious, does the commercial portray that image? Take a close look at the product and the people who might buy it. Would the commercial appeal to them? If not, change it now before it gets on the air.

In line with this, beware of "Vampire Video," where the execution totally overwhelms the sales message. This is probably a bigger problem in television than in any other medium. The opportunity to have dramatic pictures, exciting music, thrilling movement, and dulcet announcer tones all at the same time often results in a commercial that is well remembered as a commercial but whose sales message is forgotten. Make sure your message doesn't get lost in the translation.

Summary The heart of the advertising execution is the sales message that reflects the strategy. That creative strategy identifies the particular benefit that the product will give the consumer. While that particular benefit has been called the unique selling proposition, the inherent drama, and other names, the strategy and its execution must "position" the product in the consumers' minds. It must state the promise that the product makes and show how it will deliver the benefit promised. The execution should meet the needs and play to the strengths of the medium being used. A sample form for planning and executing creative strategy was shown. While people use different ones, all the good ones follow a basic format: the key fact, the audience, the product promise or benefit, and the media used.

Case for Discussion: Potato Flips

Perfectly Potato Products had been marketing a line of potato chips called "Potato Flips" for 10 months. The product had not been a major success story, having gained only 2 percent national market share, far short of the 20 percent share that had been predicted.

Flips differed from other potato chips in that they were made with one-third less oil. They had been taste tested extensively and had outscored all the national brands. Test participants described them as "light," "fluffy but crunchy," and "very potatoey-tasting."

Although preliminary market and consumer research had suggested that PPP might be able to segment the potato chip market successfully by positioning Flips as a lower-calorie chip to appeal to diet-conscious consumers, top management had vetoed the idea. Corporate pride insisted that a big splash be made in a big market. Consequently, an advertising campaign was developed that focused on the "fun" aspects of the product. Television commercials showed a variety of celebrity look-alikes "flipping" over Flips. The print ads were similar, showing a person "flipping" over Flips. Copy points included the product's great potato taste and briefly mentioned the one-third less oil feature.

Nine months after the national introduction of Flips, PPP was purchased by a large national food marketer. Soon after the merger was completed, Greg Jeffries, the brand manager for Flips, was summoned to give an accounting for his product. Jeffries correctly assumed that Flips' future was in jeopardy and decided to go on the offensive with his presentation.

"Gentlemen," he began, "right now, Flips is a perfect example of a good product being hurt by poor management. There's no doubt that the product *is* good—taste test results and extremely high repurchase rates prove that it's a good product. People who try Flips love them. The problem is, not many people are trying them. Why? Because they like the chip they're used to buying, and we haven't given them a really good reason to buy ours instead. The "Flipping over Flips" campaign has been great for getting recognition—just about everybody's heard of Flips. But they aren't rushing out to buy them."

Jeffries then distributed copies of the research study that had suggested segmenting the market. "I believe that the positioning described in this study is the right answer for Flips. Right now, there are basically two types of potato chips—regular and chips for dips. So why not a brand of chips for slim hips? Seriously, consumer studies show that there are a lot of nutrition-conscious and calorie-conscious people for whom potato chips are almost taboo. With a lower-calorie positioning based on the one-third less oil aspect, we'd not only attract buyers of other chips, but also people who haven't bought a bag of potato chips in months. I think there's a lot of potential here.''

After several minutes of conferring with his colleagues, the marketing vp spoke. ''OK, Jeffries, you may be right. Get together with the agency. We want to see an ad campaign based on the lower-calorie positioning two weeks from today. We'll decide then on the future of Flips.''

Jeffries called the Flips account executive immediately. He outlined the situation, emphasizing that this was do or die. ''Can you put your creative people to work on this? I'd like four separate approaches within the week. You and I can pick which is best and get a big presentation together on it in time for the meeting.''

The AE promised to do his best. He called in four of the agency's resident creative geniuses and put the problem to them. ''I know this is a rush job, but this Flips account could be the intro to big billings with the new parent company. So, I've got copies of the segmentation study, taste test results, and product samples for each of you. Give it your best shot.''

Five days later, Jeffries was looking at storyboards illustrating these four alternatives:

1. UFO: Scene is a military air traffic control room. A large group of people is gathered around a radar screen. Audio: ''F-17, this is Control. Do you have visual?'' ''Negative, Control. Repeat coordinates.'' ''We have you on screen, F-17. Object should be at two o'clock.'' ''Wait, Control. We have visual. It's . . . it's . . . it's a bag of potato chips.'' Close-up on amazed faces. Then cut to bag of Flips floating alongside airplane. Audio: ''Correction, Control. Not potato chips, Potato Flips.'' ''They must have gotten out of a shopping bag. Come back in, F-17. Oh, bring the Flips with you. We're hungry.'' Voiceover while bag continues to float: ''Potato Flips. One-third less oil than regular potato chips makes them *very* light.''

2. The Exploding Potato: Close-up on a potato. As rumbling noises start underneath, the potato begins to rock back and forth. The noise builds and the potato rocks faster. Potato explodes with a boom and Potato Flips flutter down into a Flips bag. Voiceover: ''Potato Flips—one-third less oil and terrific potato taste.''

3. Falling Flips: No sound. Snow, as seen from a distance, fills screen. As camera closes in, crunching sounds begin. Sounds get louder, and snow is seen to be Potato Flips. Voiceover: ''Potato Flips are extra light and crunchy, because they're made with one-third less oil than other potato chips.'' Cut to bag of Flips. Voiceover: ''And less oil here may mean. . . . .'' Split screen; Flips and bathroom scale. Voiceover: ''Less here.''

4. Potato Diet: Woman sitting on a park bench, drinking a diet beverage and eating Flips. She's joined by another woman, who has another diet drink and a container of yogurt. Woman #2: "What happened to your diet?" Woman #1: "Nothing! I'm still eating light." #2: "Come on! Potato chips are hardly diet food." #1: "These are *not* potato chips. They're Potato *Flips*." (Close-up on Flips bag.) #2: "Well, excuse me. But chips or Flips, I still . . . " #1 (interrupting): "Flips are made with a third less oil than potato chips. So, they're still crunchy and potatoey, but not nearly as fattening." #2: "Can I try a Flip?" #1: "OK, but just one. This *is* my lunch." Close-up on Flips bag. Voiceover (#2): "Just one more, please?"

Questions

1. Which execution(s) do you feel is most "on strategy"?
2. Which execution would be most effective in attracting the target market?
3. Which execution is most convincing?
4. Imagine each execution on television. Would they interrupt?
5. Are the executions visual ideas?
6. Do the executions demonstrate the benefit?
7. Assume each execution must be translated into an accompanying print ad. What are some potential headlines?
8. If you were Jeffries, which execution would you select to present to the board as the "salvation" for Flips?

11 Pretesting the Advertising Campaign

Once the advertising strategy has been developed and executed, the next logical question to answer is whether or not the advertising will achieve the objectives set for the campaign. To determine whether or not the advertising communicates the sales message and will be effective in the marketplace, many major advertising elements and most proposed advertising campaigns are pretested in some way. In spite of the inherent value of some form of pretesting, unfortunately how this testing should be done has developed into quite an area of discussion among advertising practitioners. Some are firmly in favor of pretesting and others violently opposed. Even such major industry organizations as the Advertising Research Foundation have wrestled with the copy testing problem for years without a totally satisfactory solution. Much of the disagreement among practitioners about copy pretesting revolves around what the pretesting is supposed to accomplish and the methods to be used.

This discussion of pretesting can be put in proper perspective by reviewing what Russell Colley wrote in *Defining Advertising Goals for Measured Advertising Results* in 1961. That should help clarify the basic purpose for advertising pretesting.

> The purpose of an advertisement is not just to get itself seen. It is not just to get itself heard or read. The purpose of an advertisement is to convey information, an attitude about a product (service, company, cause) in such a way that the consumer will be more favorably disposed toward its purchase. The purpose of an advertisement is to bring about changes in knowledge, attitudes and *behavior* of people with respect to the purchase of the product.[1]

---

1. Russell H. Colley, *Defining Advertising Goals for Measured Advertising Results* (New York: Association of National Advertisers, 1961), p. 35.

With this basic purpose of advertising in mind, perhaps the reason for and methods of pretesting can be better understood.

To Test or Not to Test

The discussion of whether or not any advertising should even be pretested is becoming increasingly heated. Generally, most creative people are opposed to pretesting. They argue that a number can't be put on or a rank given to a creative idea. For example, they question whether or not anyone is capable of evaluating and ranking the Mona Lisa against the statue of David as works of art. Or whether or not it's possible to measure and put a number on how any creative form affects an individual. Furthermore, since advertising is considered a form of creativity, they believe advertising pretesting stifles that creativity. On the other hand, clients and advertising executives are hesitant to invest literally millions of dollars in an advertising campaign with only their own intuitive guidance as to how effective the campaign might be. While the controversy is likely to continue for some time and may never be resolved totally, there are five very good reasons to pretest or evaluate advertising prior to its use in the media or as a part of the final campaign.

To Prevent Disaster

Generally, advertising pretesting gives only a limited amount of information, but that information can be very important. The primary objective is to determine whether or not the advertising campaign is an absolute disaster. That is, will the proposed advertising actually drive people away from the brand? For that purpose, advertising pretesting is usually quite reliable.

To Test New Approaches to Old Problems

Generally, most advertising campaigns submitted for pretesting are for existing or established products. In those cases, the advertiser usually knows how the previous advertising has performed or at least has some idea of what effects it had on consumers. The new advertising can be measured against what has been used before to determine if it is more effective, delivers the sales message more clearly or more efficiently, is better understood, is more important, than what has been done in the past. If, for example, it was found the new advertising was actually less effective than what had been used, the advertiser would want to make changes prior to any major investment in the campaign or perhaps simply revitalize the present campaign.

To Evaluate Alternative Methods of Communicating the Brand's Sales Message

Just as in any sales situation, several things can be said in several ways to communicate the benefits of the brand or to provide the brand's solution to the consumer's problem. Some ways will be better or more effective than others. Usually, however, it is impossible to tell which is best without actually trying the alternatives out with consumers. Therefore, the success of a new campaign isn't simply a judgment that can be made by the advertising's creators. The advertiser really needs to try the proposed alternative creative approaches with consumers to get their reactions. That really is the only way to see which alternative works best. Pretesting, no matter how effective, can't identify what the single best approach may be, but it can identify the best of the alternatives being tested.

To Determine How Well the Advertising Achieves Its Objectives

The pretest gives the planner an opportunity to see how well the proposed new advertising campaign performs in terms of achieving the objectives that have been set. If for example, the major objective of the campaign is to generate brand name awareness, then that can be measured in the pretest. If it doesn't perform well, changes can then be made. In a pretest, many objectives can be measured, such as information communicated, knowledge gained by consumers, changes in conviction, and the like. Thus pretesting advertising gives a preliminary measure of how well the advertising might perform in the marketplace in achieving the objectives that have been set for the campaign.

To Improve the Proposed Advertising Prior to Its Use

Obviously, the planner wants to use the strongest, most effective advertising possible in the campaign. The pretest provides an opportunity to identify any unforeseen weaknesses and correct them prior to the actual campaign. Thus, not only can the advertising be improved, but major savings in production costs may result as well.

In summary, perhaps the best view of why advertising pretesting should be used and what it is all about is provided by Alan Hedges, a market researcher in England:

> We too often speak of testing advertising (a term which should be struck from all our vocabularies) as if we were submitting the piece of film or print to a testing machine (which happens to be made up of consumers) which will accept or reject it; just like the quality control

process at the end of a production line which rejects items which are over or under weight, or whatever it may be.

This is a very misleading way of looking at creative research, and one which I believe is responsible for a good deal of the misdirected activity which we find in this field. We are not *testing* the advertising since we do not have, and cannot have, any such machine. We are *studying consumers* in order to gain some better understanding of the way they are likely to react to stimuli of different kinds, the stimuli being advertisements or advertising ideas. Since both the stimuli and the repertoire of possible responses are highly complex (and since the research situation is a very unusual one), we know that we cannot make any precise and simple formulation of what a given advertisement will achieve—but we *can* improve our understanding to the point where we are better able both to produce relevant and effective ideas and to judge when we have a campaign which is adequate for our purposes.

Therefore advertising research should seek to enrich our *understanding* of the way a particular advertisement is likely to affect people.[2]

What to Pretest   Generally, while pretesting is conducted with advertising that has been developed and is believed ready to be put before the consumer, the best time to test any advertising is at the earliest stage possible. That usually means at the advertising strategy or development stage or at the time when the central sales theme to be communicated to the consumer is being developed. Unfortunately, however, much advertising pretesting occurs much farther down the line when copy has been approved, television commercials bid and sometimes even produced, and the battle lines have been drawn between those who believe the advertising sound and good and those who think it might be improved. Advertising can generally be pretested at four basic stages that will be discussed here.

At the Concept Stage

The most basic measure of the value of a product or brand is often at the concept stage. While concept testing is not an actual advertising testing technique, it is widely used with new product ideas or suggestions and with new approaches for existing products. Thus, it is often the first step in the development of an advertising campaign.

---

2. Alan Hedges, *Testing to Destruction* (London: Institute of Practitioners in Advertising, 1974), pp. 36–37.

The concept statement is a few sentences that outline the attributes, uses, and advantages of a product or a brand to the consumer. Eugene Cafarelli suggests a concept statement should consist of three main points:

1. A statement of the problem that the product is meant to solve.
2. A definition of the type of solution that your product provides.
3. The necessary supporting attributes (both physical and communications) that lend credibility to the product's ability to solve the problem.[3]

Frequently, the concept statement is accompanied by an illustration or picture of what the product looks like or would look like when produced or the solution it might provide. This illustration and the supporting words are called a concept board. It is used to help the consumer visualize what the product might be or might do. Cafarelli offers these rules of thumb about preparing concept boards and statements:

1. Use normal language. Often the concept board will be used when no one is around to explain what a word or term means. Also, make sure the sentences are short. You're not writing a traditional English composition. You are writing more in the style of advertising without attempting to interject creative twists (there are no slogans, etc.).

2. The verbal section of the concept board should have a number of paragraphs. Avoid long, involved paragraphs, particularly when you are referring to several kinds of supporting attributes. It is better to break them into paragraphs that contain one, or at most, a few kinds of supporting attributes.

3. It is best to avoid catchy names in concept statements, unless the name is an integral part of the product concept or aids in the communication of the concept. It is best if the name indicates the function of the product. For example: "A SAFE TRICYCLE" will be better than "HEAVY WHEELS" if you are talking to mothers who are prospective purchasers of a tricycle type toy that will not tip over. Ultimately, you might want to call it something like "HEAVY WHEELS." But that would be a result of what you learned in your positioning research. It almost never is a good idea to use names in concept statements. I must say, though, that like most statements, this may be tempered. In the area of cosmetics, the name often becomes a part of the total package. Therefore, in areas like cosmetics and toiletries sometimes a name has to be part of the concept statement. It is an area in which you need to use good judgment.

---

3. Eugene J. Cafarelli, *Developing New Products and Repositioning Mature Brands* (New York: John Wiley & Sons, 1980), pp. 110–11.

4. Finally, the concept should have a one- or two-sentence summary that puts the concept in perspective.[4]

The Creative Strategy or Promise Statement Stage

The basic sales message or the idea of the advertising is the creative strategy (or advertising strategy) or promise statement. This really is a summation of what benefit or problem solution the advertising is supposed to communicate to the consumer. It is the real "heart" of the advertising campaign. Therefore, it is vital that this statement is sound, believable, important, and persuasive to the consumer; otherwise, the advertising is certain to fail no matter what else is done.

As was discussed previously, the strategy or promise statement must offer a consumer a benefit or provide the solution to a consumer problem. Often the strategy is pretested in the form of a promise statement. An example might be:

> The Grumman American airplane gives you superior fuel and speed efficiency compared to similar models from Piper, Cessna, and Beechcraft.

For pretesting purposes, the statement may be written in a form that provides a summary of the offer by saying, "If you buy this brand, you will get this benefit or it will solve this problem." Often the statement is accompanied by an illustration of the product or the benefit it offers to help the consumer visualize the offer.

The goal of most creative strategy pretesting is to determine which is the strongest of several alternative sales messages that might be used with the brand. Therefore, the strategy testing should take place at a very early stage in the development of the campaign. This truly is the basic reason for pretesting. If the promise made the consumer isn't effective, believable, or persuasive, no advertising, no matter how creative, can make the campaign successful.

The Rough Stage

The most common form in which advertising is pretested is in a rough form or one stage prior to final production. The newspaper or magazine advertisement is done with rough art and the copy may or may not be set in type. The visuals need only illustrate generally the action, event, or situation taking place and can even be stick figures.

---

4. Cafarelli, *Developing New Products,* pp. 110–11.

For broadcast, a radio "scratch track" is often used. This scratch track simply is a recorded rough approximation of what the finished commercial would be. For example, a piano might be used to carry the basic tune although a full orchestra might be planned for in the finished version. Television is usually tested in the form of a storyboard that may be shown to the respondents in its rough art form or photographed in some way to illustrate what is going to take place in the commercial. Many commercials are put into rough storyboard form and then transferred to sound on a film called an "animatic." The sound and the storyboard illustrations can be synchronized so they represent a very rough version of the final commercial. These animatics may be either very rough or almost in finished commercial form depending on the method of testing to be done.

Generally, roughs are used when testing alternative ideas such as promise statements or strategies. They may also be used to test various executions of the same strategy to see which one best communicates the sales message.

Finished Advertising Form

The pretesting of finished advertising is done primarily by large advertisers for major campaigns, and it is a fairly common practice for them. The form used is the finished print ad or commercial in almost exactly the same form that the consumer would actually see it should the campaign be approved for release. The most common reason for pretesting finished advertising is that many sales messages and advertising executions, particularly those that make use of image or mood, cannot be totally or accurately rendered except in the final form. Thus, the argument is made that only a finished ad or a finished commercial can truly represent what the actual response to the advertising might be by the consumer.

Most of the syndicated services that pretest advertising use a finished commercial or a finished print ad for testing. While testing finished advertising is much more expensive than testing at the earlier stages outlined, it is often required with certain types of campaigns.

While the preceding discussion might have made it seem that advertising pretesting in various forms is an either/or situation, it is not. In fact, some advertisers pretest their advertising at all the stages mentioned. This is particularly true for advertising being developed for new products or when major changes are planned for existing products. The pretesting scheme should be developed and implemented by the campaign planner just as are the other parts of the campaign. Budgets must also be set for this pretesting and included in the overall plan.

What to Measure   Obviously, what is to be measured in the pretest is often determined by the form or the stage at which the advertising will be tested. For example, with product concepts it is difficult to test much more than varying levels of appeal. With finished television commercials, however, it is possible to test several things, including understanding, recall, and information communicated. Thus the planner should determine in advance what is to be pretested, when, and in what form.

Measure against Objectives

The first rule of any advertising pretesting is to set objectives for the measurement. In other words, it must clearly be stated what is being measured and what the objectives of the test are. If the importance of varying new product concepts are to be measured, the real objective is to determine if the product as described will actually solve consumer problems or offer strong enough benefits to generate trial. On the other hand, if the objective is to measure the effects of a rough commercial, totally different objectives may be set for the advertising, such as implanting the brand name, getting the sales message across, building knowledge, or the like. Therefore, the advertising pretest should reflect the objectives of the advertising campaign. If the objective is to build awareness of the brand name in the marketplace, then the advertising should be evaluated on the basis of how well it communicates the brand name, not on how well the spokesperson is remembered. A simple rule: the results of the pretest should be measured on the same basis as the objectives that have been set for the campaign.

Results Must Be Measurable

As alluded to above, the results of the pretest must be measurable. Objectives that can't be quantified should not be used. For example, it is most difficult to measure whether or not respondents "liked" an ad or a commercial. Liking has many degrees that are often hard to measure. It is much better to measure quantifiable objectives, such as recall of the sales message, believability of the message, persuasiveness, or a change in attitude.

One must always keep in mind in any pretest situation that the goal of the pretest is not to measure the mere popularity or entertainment value of the advertising. The goal of advertising is to communicate a sales message. That, not how much people liked the advertising, should be the basis of the test.

Effects Measured

Generally, in pretesting, three basic effects can be measured. They are:

Perception. This is the lowest form of communication or understanding of the advertisement. It simply means the person understands that this is an advertisement and that it contains a sales message. Perception is primarily used to determine what the advertising means to the respondent. In other words, the pretest will show how the person perceives what is being said or how he or she interprets the message of the advertisement. It does nothing more.

This measure of perception is important because advertisers often use attention-getting devices or other means of attracting attention or methods of demonstrating the value of the brand outside a straight sales message. It is important that consumers perceive the same message the advertiser is sending.

Comprehension. Do consumers understand what the advertiser is trying to communicate? In other words, do the words and pictures being used properly communicate the sales message? If the goal of the advertising is to demonstrate that the brand is more effective than the competition, it is important to know if consumers take the same message out of the advertising as was intended by the advertiser.

Comprehension is normally measured by asking the consumer to play back or describe the intended message of the advertisement. That can then be checked against the stated objectives of the advertisement.

Reaction. The final measurement in a pretest is normally the reaction of the consumer to the advertisement. In other words, if the consumer perceived the ad and also comprehended it, what is his reaction to that message? The most common measure is an attempt to determine if the message would persuade respondents to change their attitudes or behavior toward the brand after seeing the message. If the goal of the advertising is to stimulate a change in attitude, the pretest can be used to determine whether or not that particular advertisement changed the attitude or simply reinforced what was already there. The reaction of respondents is often the most important measure in a pretest.

By setting measurable objectives for the advertising pretest and then measuring the various levels of perception, comprehension, and reaction, the campaign planner should have a fair idea of whether or not the advertising will be effective when used in the actual advertising campaign.

How to Pretest Advertising

There are two basic methods of pretesting: (1) a custom-developed pretest plan and (2) through the services of a syndicated or formal pretesting organization. In each case, the methods used are determined by the need or level of measurement required, and these dictate the form of the advertising to be pretested. Based on what is to be tested and learned (i.e., is it a concept test, creative strategy, or promise statement, or the advertising in the rough or finished stage?), there are some basic factors that apply to all pretests.

Test with Target Market

No matter how the pretest is being conducted or the form in which the advertising appears, there is one cardinal rule in pretesting: the persons with whom the advertising is being pretested should be members of the proposed target market. While this seems like a very simple idea, it is often overlooked. Usually, because a convenience sample of some sort is used to provide the respondents on which to pretest, the persons actually evaluating the advertising may or may not be logical prospects for the product, service, or brand. In most cases, it is worthless to pretest the advertising on those who are not in the target market for the brand. For example, testing advertising for a teenage product with women in their forties or testing an advertisement for work clothes designed for low income, blue collar workers with white collar workers makes little sense. But while this point sounds obvious, the pretest audience is so often not the target market that much advertising pretesting is of little value to the advertiser. Pretest your advertising with your target market to get accurate results.

Testing Concept Statements, Creative Strategies, and Promise Statements

There are two basic methods of pretesting concepts, strategies, and promise statements: through personal interviews or in focus group situations.

Personal interviews. Conducting personal interviews is the traditional way to pretest concept statements, strategies, and promise statements. The procedure may take many forms. The most common sites for interviews are in the home, at shopping malls, in or near retail outlets, or even at major airports. The primary objective is to find persons fitting the target market description and then conduct the interviews. A prescreening of respondents is often used to make sure the respondent is in the target market. For example, interviews for a new food product concept might be conducted in the food store with persons waiting in the check-out line. The prospects usually have time to answer questions; they are in a shopping situation and have their minds on food and food products.

A typical concept test method is to have the various ideas written on cards that are handed to the respondents. After reading the cards, respondents are asked to summarize the concept in their own words. This confirms that the statement is interpreted as intended.

After reading the concepts, the respondent is then asked to rank-order the concepts based on their appeal. Frequently, questions are asked, such as why the particular selection was made. Demographic data also are gathered to ensure that the respondent is a member of the selected target market (if this has not already been determined in a prescreening). A sample of 50 to 100 respondents is usually sufficient to identify the most salient concept or strategy among those offered. With this number of respondents, responses tend to stabilize and little beyond verification is gained with larger numbers.

Focus groups. An alternative to the personal interview is the "focus group," so called because the attention of the entire group is focused on the product category, concept, or strategy being evaluated.

A group of 8 to 12 respondents from the prospective target market is asked to meet to discuss a particular topic. Led by a trained interviewer, the respondents are shown the material to be tested. The interviewer then guides the group in a discussion. The purpose is to obtain information on the subject, not necessarily direct answers. Discussions are usually tape recorded. After the session, the interviewer or an interpreter analyzes the conversations and develops a summary or consensus of the group. This interpretation gives valuable insight into the deeper feelings of the group members. It also determines how they talk about the product and discloses the language they use.

As in the personal interview technique, small samples such as two or three focus groups from the target market are usually sufficient to give an indication of the value of various concepts or strategies being tested.

The results of both personal interview and focus group methods usually are directional only. Since the sample is small and subject to error, the result of either type of testing should be regarded as a "prevention of disaster" test, or directional guidance for further research rather than absolute truth.

Testing Rough or Finished Advertisements

There are two basic methods of pretesting rough or finished advertisements.

Internal checklists, rating scales, and readability formulas. One of the easiest and most common methods of advertising pretesting is through an internal evaluation by the advertiser or agency. This is commonly done for many industrial product print advertisements. This evaluation may be done by means of a checklist or rating scale system. Checklists are used to:

1. Ensure that all the various components of the advertisement are included, such as coupons, ordering information, sizes, colors, and delivery time.
2. Ensure that the major selling points of the product, service, or brand are included in the advertisement.

Very elaborate checklists have been developed by some advertisers including such topics as checking for "a benefit-oriented headline," "the use of the word 'you' in the copy," and the inclusion of the brand name a certain number of times in the copy. While checklists seem somewhat mechanical, they can play an important part in ensuring that advertisements are complete and that no obvious errors are present.

Some advertisers have developed rating scales that can be used to evaluate and compare alternative advertisements. This might include such subjective evaluations as "Does the first paragraph follow the headline and lead to the body copy?" or "Is the brand name of the product visible at a glance in the layout?" The usual method is to develop a rating scale based on a five-point measure such as:

Very Good	Good	0	Poor	Very Poor
_____	_____	_____	_____	_____

By rating different advertisements on these scales and then totaling the results for each advertisement tested, one can select a winner. These rating scales are often completed by the management of the company, the sales force, or others in a position to judge the merits of the advertisement.

The final method of internal evaluation is a readership test for print ads. Such tests are designed primarily to determine how easy the advertisement is to read and comprehend. Several formulas are available, the most common of which is the Flesch Formula developed by Rudolph Flesch. The computation of the formula is based on:

1. the average sentence length
2. the average number of syllables
3. the percentage of personal words used
4. the percentage of personal sentences in a 100-word sample of the writing

The formula determines whether the writing can be read and understood by the average person. Phillip Ward Burton has said the Flesch formula shows that the most readable copy contains 14 words per sentence, 140 syllables per 100 words, 10 personal words, and 43 percent personal sentences in total.[5]

Checklists, rating scales, and readability levels of advertising are low in cost, easy to apply, and usually reveal any glaring errors. These types of pretests, however, do little to evaluate the effectiveness of the advertisement with the consumer.

Consumer panels. A consumer panel is simply a group of prospective consumers for the product or service who are exposed to and evaluate the proposed advertising in either rough or finished form. Consumer panels may take many forms from prerecruited ongoing groups to persons contacted for a simple interview in the local supermarket or bus station. Regardless of the type of panel used, the primary objective is to get the considered opinion of prospective customers for the product and combine the responses to form a single opinion. A few of the more common evaluation methods using consumer panels are:

1. Order-of-merit test. The order of merit is a simple ranking test of a group of advertisements by respondents. For example, respondents are asked to look at several alternative advertisements and then to rank them in some way. Rankings may be made on almost any basis, but one of the more common ones is the persuasive ability of the advertisement. Questions such as, "Which of these ads would you be most likely to read?", "Which headline makes you want to read further?", "Which of these ads convinces you most of the quality of the product?" and "Which would be most effective in convincing you to buy?" are commonly used in an order-of-merit test.[6]

   In addition to ranking, respondents may be asked to describe why they selected certain advertisements or why they consider one to be better than others. This helps give the researcher or planner a better understanding of the decisions and why they were made.

2. Portfolio. In the portfolio test, unidentified test advertisements are placed in a folder or portfolio with a number of other advertisements that are not being tested. Sometimes the portfolio is made up to simulate a normal magazine or newspaper and may even include editorial

---

5. Phillip Ward Burton, *Advertising Copywriting,* 3rd ed. (Columbus, OH: Grid, Inc., 1974), pp. 366–75.

6. James F. Engel, Hugh G. Wales, and Martin R. Warshaw, *Promotional Strategy,* rev. ed. (Homewood, IL: Richard D. Irwin, 1971), p. 370.

content. Respondents are then shown the portfolio and allowed to look at it as much or as little as they like. After viewing the portfolio, they are asked to recall which ads they saw, what they remembered about each ad, which ad they liked best and why, and so forth. This helps determine how the advertisement should score when placed in a normal environment. In the portfolio test, advertisements must be complete, or else the balance of the materials must be reduced to the completeness of the test ad to permit a fair evaluation to be made. From 5 to 10 ads can be evaluated by the portfolio method at one time. Portfolio tests are probably a stronger method of pretesting than order-of-merit tests or rankings.

3. Rating scales. Rating scales are often used for evaluation of appeals or parts of individual advertisements. They provide an opportunity to isolate dimensions of opinion and can be repeated with other groups for comparisons.

    A method called the semantic differential is often used for this type of pretest. Adjectives that are opposite in meaning are used to either describe the advertisement or to identify claims made in the advertisement. For example, in the illustration in Figure 11-1, a series of bipolar adjectives describing the content of an advertisement has been developed. They describe how the brand works based on the advertisement that has been prepared. Respondents, after reading the advertisement, check the various scales to indicate what information they received from the advertisement or how the brand was described. By evaluating these responses, the planner can determine whether or not the advertisement is achieving the objectives that have been set.

Figure 11-1.   Semantic Differential

After reading this advertisement, would you say that Brand X is

	Very −3	Quite −2	Slight −1	0 0	Slight +1	Quite +2	Very +3	
Hard to use	___	___	___	___	___	___	___	Easy to use
Low quality	___	___	___	___	___	___	___	High quality
Unpleasant	___	___	___	___	___	___	___	Pleasant

The terms used can be applied to the product, the brand, or the advertisement. Rating individual advertisements and their communicative powers makes possible an identification of the best of the group of advertisements being tested.[7]

---

7. Engel, Wales, and Warshaw, *Promotional Strategy*, pp. 371–91.

Other rating scales, such as a scale of the important values the advertisement should contain or of how the brand and its claims compare to competition, can also be used. The inherent problem in scales of this sort is the subjective development of the factors to be evaluated.

4. Paired comparisons. In this methodology, several advertisements are given to panel members. Respondents are then asked to rate each ad individually against the others. For example, if there are three ads to be tested, A would be rated against B, A against C, and B against C. Each ad is thus rated in comparison with each of the others. With this technique, the best ad may be selected through comparison, not simply by ranking. This technique is usually limited to approximately 8 ads which require a total of 28 comparisons. Respondent fatigue often develops beyond that number.

5. Mock magazines. In this method special magazines are printed or regular editions of known magazines are obtained prior to distribution. Sample advertisements are printed and inserted in place of or in addition to those regularly appearing. These specially constructed magazines are then distributed to subscribers or readers. After a suitable time, the respondents who received the magazines are contacted and are asked questions about the magazine and the advertising.

This pretesting technique uses recall as the measure of success. The main advantage is that the advertisement is tested in an actual reading situation rather than in a "forced viewing." Only finished advertisements, however, can be tested, and the investment in production must be made before testing and may be wasted on those ads that are rejected.

6. Projective techniques. While these are not widely used, various forms of projective techniques such as the puzzle game, word association, sentence completion, and role playing are used for pretesting. A good example is the puzzle game. Respondents are given a partially completed advertisement; e.g., the ad might be complete except for the headline or the illustration. Several alternative headlines and/or illustrations are given to respondents, and they are asked to complete the advertisement using the parts furnished. The respondent selects the headline and illustration that he or she thinks would be most suitable. The assumption is that the headline and illustration most often selected would be the most effective. In other forms of projective techniques, respondents are asked to fill in blanks or draw pictures that indicate what would most appeal to them.

7. Storyboard tests. Television storyboards are often tested with consumer juries using roughly the same techniques as those outlined above. Respondents, however, are usually shown more than just layouts. The

television commercial may be shown in slide form with a prerecorded audiotape. Respondents are usually able to make the transition from rather rough art and single-voice recordings to a finished commercial. Also, if needed, particular scenes can be isolated for discussion and evaluation. The major advantage, of course, is the low cost, since expensive television production is not required. Artists' drawings of the various frames to be used appear to be quite satisfactory for testing purposes. As with other forms of testing, a rather small number of respondents is needed since basic reaction comes rather quickly and additional respondents only quantify the results. Normally, 30 to 50 responses are sufficient for general direction.

8. Mail tests. While not widely used, the mail test is still effective. Alternative copy appeals are printed on postcards that are then sent to prospective customers. Offers are made on the cards using various copy approaches. The appeal that draws the most returns is judged to be best. Because this technique requires an offer and a rather long period of time for reply, it is normally used only to test direct mail or direct response advertising prior to major mailings.

9. Focus groups. While not technically a consumer panel, focus groups are often used to pretest advertising, particularly television. They seem to work quite well with children or younger people who often have trouble expressing themselves individually to adults but do quite well in a group setting.

This certainly does not cover the entire list of consumer jury techniques that may be used to pretest advertising. Others are measures of predisposition to buy, forced switching tests, first- and second-brand choices, and even projective buying games. All are designed to achieve the same goal, i.e., to obtain a preliminary evaluation of various alternatives by the prospective target market.

The major advantage of these types of pretests is that consumers generally can separate the good advertisements from the bad. Since the advertisements are tested against consumers rather than advertising experts or other groups, a rather basic understanding of how they would work in the marketplace can be gained. They are fast and easy to use and usually low in cost since samples are limited in size.

Doing one's own pretesting does have some limitations, such as obtaining a representative sample for the test and the artificial nature of the testing situation. In addition, all of these situations are "forced viewing"; that is, people are required to read the advertising. They might not even notice it in real-world situations. Thus, while the pretesting of advertising with forms the planner can do himself are better than no pretesting at all, the campaign planner must keep in mind that most results are only directional in nature and are guides to better advertising, not to assuring that the best advertising available or possible has been done.

Pretesting Hazards

While the preceding pages have given a rather descriptive view of the various techniques and approaches used in advertising pretesting, some basic rules of thumb on the hazards of any form of pretesting should be pointed out.

Pretesting judges only the best of the lot tested. Any pretesting procedure gives one the opportunity to find the best of those advertisements being tested, not the best of all possible approaches. If all the advertisements being tested are in truth quite poor, only the best of the worst will be selected, not the best possible approach.

Pretests should be realistic and practical. While it is always tempting to ask consumers to make many evaluations in a pretest, keep in mind what consumers can and can't judge from the advertising being shown them. They can't, for example, tell whether or not an advertisement will turn the brand's sales around or whether or not it will generate the level of awareness or comprehension the planner is seeking. Respondents can tell you only what the advertising does to them and how they react.

Try to prevent respondent prejudice. One of the most difficult tasks in advertising pretesting is preventing sample respondents from becoming "advertising experts." This simply means that rather than evaluating the advertising as consumers, respondents begin to suggest improvements. When this occurs, the opinions given are often worthless. While "advertising expertise" is a difficult problem to overcome, efforts should be made to confine respondent opinions and comments to their proper role as consumers of advertising, not as advertising directors. Some suggestions are given in the next section on how to avoid this respondent prejudice.

Campaigns can't be tested. All advertising pretesting is for individual advertisements in a given situation. Consumers can't tell you what the effect would be of multiple exposures over time or how differing executions for the same strategy might affect them when coupled with other marketplace activities. Remember, individual advertisements are being tested, not a campaign.

Recognize the inherent problems in pretesting. Some common situations usually occur in any advertising pretesting situation. For example:

1. Negative advertising appeals traditionally score poorly in pretests, yet they are sometimes successful in the marketplace.

2. Advertising that is entertaining, humorous, or light usually scores best in advertising pretests. The entertainment value of the advertisements is usually much more appreciated in a pretest than in the normal media channels.

3. "Hard sell" facts about the product or service usually score the lowest of all on pretests. Yet, there is ample evidence that "hard sell" advertisements and commercials may be most effective in communicating with the intended audience.[8]

Ways to Avoid Respondent Prejudice

As mentioned above, one of the biggest problems in advertising pretesting is simply that all consumers or respondents usually consider themselves to be experts in advertising. Thus, they often try to go far beyond what they are capable of doing in terms of judging or evaluating advertisements. In addition, if they know the advertising is being pretested, they seem to assume there is something wrong with it. Thus, they are anxious to help spot errors or make changes. Advertising is a very personal thing with most people, and as a result, all of us often are tempted to give opinions or suggestions on how advertising should be improved when it is nothing more than our own personal opinion. For these reasons, there are always respondent prejudices involved in any pretesting situation. However, there are some things that can be done to help overcome this prejudice. They are:

1. The respondent should not be preconditioned. The respondent should not be influenced into going in a direction wanted or to support a preconceived notion. Since most consumers quickly learn that the test is for advertising, the researcher try not to influence the test in one way or another. Don't lead or guide the respondent in any of the answers he or she may give.

2. Direct questions, not opinions, should be asked. As an example, the question, "How do you like this ad?" usually leads to opinion answers. The more direct question, "Would this type of advertisement make you want to purchase the product?" is more specific and helps avoid opinions. Short, direct, to-the-point questions should be asked in an advertising pretest.

3. Questions that can be logically answered by the respondent should be asked. Sometimes the respondent is assumed to have knowledge he or

---

8. Engel, Wales, and Warshaw, *Promotional Strategy*, p. 391.

she may not have. Thus, if a person is asked, "What do you think are the advantages of alternating current in an electric razor?" it is likely the answers would vary widely. Most people don't know the answer. When faced with this type of problem, they often make up an answer or guess rather than appear ignorant.

4. Respondents should not be asked to project their answers to others. Even the most informed parent really can't answer how his children would feel or react to a product or an advertisement. Therefore, putting respondents in the position of guessing how others might feel or react only asks for trouble. Respondents know only about their own feelings. When they are asked to project to others, they are being asked to guess. When that situation occurs, respondents often believe it is acceptable to guess in other areas, too.

5. Questions should probe. The first answer may represent the true feelings of the respondent, but often, it is just that—an answer. Follow up by asking such questions as "Why do you say that?" and "What do you mean by that?" Try to get the truth, not merely a superficial answer. When respondents know a probe will follow, they will often dig a bit deeper to give true facts and not just "top-of-mind" replies.

These certainly are not all the available methods of preventing respondents from becoming "advertising experts," or having respondent prejudice. They may, however, help overcome a very common problem in pretesting.

How to Pretest Advertising— Services Available

Over the years, a number of advertising pretesting organizations and testing systems have been developed. Several have been in operation for a number of years and are widely used. On the other hand, new methods and new companies are constantly springing up with new techniques that may seem to offer exciting new opportunities. Because many facilities and techniques are similar, with only minor methodological differences, only the major services and those that have proven themselves over time are discussed here. More specific information can be obtained on each type of pretesting system or approach from any market research text or from the organizations themselves.

Generally, separate research organizations have developed for pretesting print and broadcast. Certainly, broadcast pretesting services are more widespread than print simply because the demand for these services from large advertisers is greater. In addition, most advertising practitioners feel themselves capable of evaluating print advertising better than for radio or television. Over the years, four basic types of formal advertising pretesting methodologies have developed. Each is discussed briefly below.

Objective Mechanical Methods

These techniques are called objective because they rely on mechanical means for measurement rather than opinions or replies from respondents. Tests are usually conducted with individuals in a laboratory setting. These pretesting approaches generally have not gained widespread use, and many are still regarded as experimental rather than conclusive.

Engel, Wales, and Warshaw divide the various techniques into those that measure attention attraction and those that measure response.

Attention attraction.   There are four basic techniques:

1. The HRB-Singer test measures visual efficiency. Recognition is measured under varying conditions such as light and length of exposure and in competition with other advertisements.
2. The eye camera is used primarily to determine the effectiveness of the layout. A machine measures the movement of the eyes and the amount of time devoted to each element in an advertisement.
3. The third technique is the tachistoscope, which is used to measure the perception of the ad through speed, exposure, and illumination.
4. Binocular rivalry is used to determine the effect of different elements on each eye.[9]

Because these techniques are used primarily to measure stationary objects and the perception or movement of the eye against those objects, they are usually limited to evaluation of print advertisements.

Response.   Mechanical devices are also used to measure a respondent's response to advertising exposure. Most techniques measure involuntary physical response because they are believed to offer a clue to the interest or response to the advertising. The basic approaches are:

1. The psychogalvanometer, which is similar to the lie detector in that it measures sweat gland activity and other involuntary actions of the respondent.
2. The pupil dilation device measures the dilation of the respondent's eyes. A wider dilation is believed to indicate a lower interest in the material under test.

---

9. Engel, Wales, and Warshaw, *Promotional Strategy,* p. 392.

3. A salivation test is sometimes used to measure the response to advertisements for food or food products.[10]

4. An analysis of the voice is a new measure currently enjoying some success. Based on the tone and inflection of the voice, researchers believe they can discover underlying feelings toward a brand or claim.

While the above tests have the advantage of being objective, some concern has been expressed about their interpretation and the understanding of exactly what the results mean.

Print Services

Two organizations, Daniel Starch and Staff and Gallup & Robinson, Inc., offer widely used print pretesting services in which preprinted advertisements are tipped into test magazines. These magazines are then circulated to respondent groups. Following an opportunity to read the magazine, respondents are contacted and interviews are conducted concerning the magazine and the advertisements being pretested. The tests are primarily of recognition and recall and provide an effective evaluation technique prior to full-scale schedules in media.

Broadcast Services

The largest number of pretesting services have been developed for broadcast advertising, particularly television. The major difference between the techniques is the situation in which the test commercials are viewed by respondents. Four basic broadcast pretest methodologies are available:

In-home. A small-screen, self-contained projector is taken into the homes of potential target market viewers. Respondents are asked a series of questions, are shown the commercials to be tested, and then are asked another series of questions. This technique has the advantage of gaining the complete attention of the respondent. But the advantage is offset by the unnatural situation in which the viewing takes place. The technique is extremely expensive and thus not as widely used as it once was.

Trailer tests. For the purpose of getting closer to the actual point of decision by the respondents, pretesting is sometimes conducted in a natural-setting/forced-viewing situation. One method is to set up a trailer in a shopping center. Shoppers are invited to enter and are offered prizes for cooperation. First, respondents are asked a series of questions about the

---

10. Engel, Wales, and Warshaw, *Promotional Strategy*, p. 392.

products to be tested and are given an opportunity to select a series of brands in a simulated shopping situation using cents-off coupons or similar incentives. The respondents then view the test commercials along with other material. After seeing the commercials, respondents are given another set of coupons to be used in the stores in the shopping center. Later, coupons given the respondents are retrieved from the stores where they were used. By correlating the choices made prior to viewing the commercials with the coupons used in the actual shopping situation, inferences are drawn about the strength of the commercials in affecting purchasing behavior.

Theater tests. A widely used technique for pretesting is forced viewing in a theater setting. Audience Studies, Inc. (ASI) and AC-T (Advertising Control for Television) and ARS (Advertising Research Service) ask respondents to come to a theater supposedly to view a potential new television series. At the beginning of the show, respondents select brands of products from among the categories to be tested. (They are told that the selections are door prizes.)

The actual test consists of showing a nontelevised pilot or other entertainment piece followed by a series of commercials and more entertainment. After the showing, respondents are again asked to make brand selections from various categories. Differences between the brand choices prior to viewing the commercials and those after the viewing are assumed to indicate the potential power of the commercials. Other evaluations are made in this type of setting through questionnaires and mechanical devices to measure such factors as attention value, effect of "clutter," persuasiveness of the commercial, and recalled sales points.

Theater testing is fast, and fairly inexpensive, and can be replicated if necessary. Another advantage is that research organizations have tested many commercials in most consumer categories. Test commercials may be compared with previously tested commercials or the "norms" that have been established. This comparison gives an indication of the relative strength of the test commercial compared to others that have been tested. A disadvantage is the forced-viewing situation and the fact that the audience is often in the theater to be entertained. This sometimes leads to false assumptions of how the commercial will do in a real-world situation.

On-air/recruited natural environment. On-air commercial tests have been developed to try to overcome the problems of forced viewing. It is hoped that as natural a setting as possible will improve predictions.

These tests, typified by Burke Market Research, Gallup & Robinson In-View, Mapes & Ross, and Sherman BUY, use an unassigned channel on a cable television system or programming on a regular UHF station as the pretest vehicle. Prospective respondents are either recruited to watch the programming on the channel during the time the test commercials will be shown or selected afterwards based on proven recall of the programming. Since respondents are not told which commercials are being tested, real-world viewing is simulated as closely as possible. After the commercial has appeared, the recruited respondents are called by telephone and asked a series of questions about what they saw and remembered during the time the test commercials were shown. Response to the questions and recall of the test commercials are the normal measures used to rate success.

The major advantage of this technique is the real-world atmosphere in which the commercial appears with all the normal distractions and competition from the programming and other commercials. The major disadvantage is the fairly high cost of the technique and the lack of projective ability in respect to what will happen in repeated viewings.

A variation of these techniques has been developed by AdTel. Test sites are located in several communities in which matched samples of homes have been connected to cable television. Respondents keep diaries of such factors as purchases and television viewing. By controlling the source of the programming through the cable system, the research organization is able to show one commercial in one set of homes while a different commercial is seen by the other sample. Respondents are not aware of what is being tested. Through a comparison of the purchasing behavior of each group of viewers and their exposure to the alternatives, the commercials can be evaluated. While this technique completely simulates the actual conditions under which commercials are seen, it is quite expensive and only a limited number of advertisers can use the system at any one time.

Sales Tests

The sales test attempts to replicate the actual response the advertisement would receive in the real world. Three techniques deserve mention, although they are not as widely used as might be expected. They are inquiries, split runs, and scanner tests.

Inquiries. Inquiry tests are conducted by means of running advertisements in regular media and judging the effectiveness according to the number of inquiries generated. The standard approach is to run different advertisements at different times in the same publication or at the same time in different publications. Based on the number of inquiries received, the advertisement to be used on a broad scale or continuing basis is selected.

Split runs. Split-run testing simply means that different advertisements are run in the same edition of a publication. This can be done by having the publication use different ads in alternating issues or by running one ad in half the press run and a different ad in the other half. Such items as headlines, appeals, and offers can be evaluated according to the response achieved.

The major advantage of these two sales test forms is that the advertising is being evaluated under real-world conditions. The disadvantage is that these approaches can be used only for print advertising and are limited to those publications that have split-run capabilities. Also, split-run testing may not work for all types of products. An appeal for an automobile, for example, would be difficult to test in an inquiry or split-run technique.

Scanner tests. A variation of the AdTel split cable with recruited panels is now being developed by a number of organizations. These involve recruiting panels of people, usually in somewhat isolated markets with cable service and giving them user identification cards. Through the use of scanners in food and drug stores, each person's purchases can be monitored over time through the coded card and scanner. The research company can control the television advertising that goes into the home. Thus, because what advertising was sent into the home is known and then sales are measured through the use of the personalized purchasing card through the scanners in stores, individual purchases can be monitored. With this system, a true advertising-related-to-sales measurement can be made of varying advertising messages and campaigns over time. AdTel and SAMI have developed a system of this sort, as has BehaviorScan. These new types of sales measurements of advertising effects have great promise for advertising pretesting in the future.

What Makes a Good Advertising Pretest?

A number of major factors must be considered in any type of pretest. Some of the more important ones have been identified.

Determine first how the advertising should be judged. Should recall, persuasion, or communication of a specific product benefit be used and at what level? Usually, determining this need clarifies what techniques should be used.

When deciding to pretest, describe the problem to be solved to the research people involved, not the methodology to be used. This is especially important if outside research organizations are to be used.

Whenever and where ever possible, disguise the true purpose of the pretesting, the name of the advertiser, and other campaign themes. Try to have the respondent perceive the advertising as a customer and not as an advertising expert.

Be sure the right sample is selected, i.e., that the respondents logically are in the target market and are prime prospects for the product or service.

If possible, use several markets to avoid geographic bias in the pretest.

Understand the results of the study. The scores on pretests are only approximations. What is the range of the scores? What is the confidence level of the study? Understand the statistical and methodological terminology used in the results.

Test only one thing, not several things, at one time. If several of the test items are too varied, there is no way to know what stimulated the response. Hold everything constant in the pretest except the item to be evaluated.

Use good judgment. Don't rely totally on the results of pretests. If something sounds unusual or the results seem out of the ordinary, go back to the study. Check the verbatim comments. Understand what the respondents were trying to say. Use common sense.[11]

Other rules-of-thumb in advertising pretesting can be cited, but those described here seem to cover the major points. Advertising pretesting should be used primarily to guard against disasters. Guaranteed techniques and completely foolproof tests simply do not exist.

**Revising—
Or Will You
Accept the Truth?**

One of the most difficult things to accept in advertising pretesting is the result. Much work has gone into the development and formulation of the campaign, much research has been done, long hours have gone into developing appeals and yet, a group of 50 consumers in a period of only a few minutes can totally reject the entire premise of a campaign. One's natural reaction is to seek another jury, find another group who truly understands the campaign. Test and retest.

Unfortunately, although results of pretesting are only directional, they may uncover major flaws in the thinking and planning of a campaign. If that is the case, accept the truth. Determine, if possible, exactly what went wrong. Learn why the theme or appeal is weak or has little potential.

Most of all, learn to accept the fact that not every campaign will test well, not every campaign idea is a winner. If the pretest should prove that the campaign is a poor one, certainly an attempt should be made to determine why. But, a vendetta against the "dummies in the market" who don't understand the campaign approach is the fault of the planner, not the respondents. Accept the results as a guide for improvement. That is often one of the most difficult parts of advertising campaign development.

---

11. Kenneth Roman and Jane Maas, *How to Advertise* (New York: St. Martin's Press, 1976), pp. 104–5.

Summary The major source of controversy about pretesting really relates to the problem of establishing objectives. Just as a planner must ask what a campaign is supposed to accomplish when setting objectives for a campaign, the planner must ask what is the pretest going to measure? The concept stage, the strategy stage, the promise stage—these are some key times to test an advertising execution. Whether testing is done internally by the organization or is conducted by an outside service, at its best testing can help creative people and can be used to form better advertising.

Case for Discussion: Demeter Teas

Demeter Teas, an Aberdeen, North Carolina-based company, marketed a nationally distributed line of decaffeinated teas. Their 20-item line consisted of a variety of fruit, spice, and herb-based teas packaged in boxes of 40 teabags. Demeter had been operating for five years.

The market for bagged teas in 1977 was as follows:

- Households drinking tea = 39,619,000 (55.6 percent)
- Average number of cups per day = 2.8[1]

Demeter, the only national decaffeinated brand, had sold 20,367,120 units in 1977. This represented 14.1 percent of total U.S. tea sales.

While Pat Curtis, v.p. marketing, felt these results were good, given the company's relative newness, she also believed there was a great deal of room for growth. Decaffeinated drinkers made up 35.8 percent of all coffee drinkers,[2] and she believed that the tea market held similar potential. The key to tapping that potential was in product presentation through advertising.

Demeter's present advertising campaign, which had been used since 1975, consisted of monthly half-page, four-color advertisements in six national women's magazines. Also, an advertisement with a coupon was run quarterly as a Sunday supplement in newspapers in the top 100 markets. The coupon was usually for 25¢ off on the purchase of one box of tea bags. (Average retail price was $1.79 per box.) The coupon was usually good for any flavor, unless the accompanying advertisement introduced a new flavor.

Although actual copy varied, Demeter's advertisements always focused on the teas' natural goodness, citing the fruit, spice, and herb flavors and tying the product to the mythical Demeter, the Greek goddess of agriculture. Although the product was described as a caffeine-free tea, the no-caffeine feature was not emphasized.

Curtis called a meeting with the three managers in charge of fruit, spice, and herb teas, respectively. After reviewing the current advertising campaign and some recent sales figures (market share holding steady through the past two quarters), she explained why a new emphasis on no-caffeine was desirable. She went on to say, "I'd like some suggestions from you on how we should present the no-caffeine benefit to the consumers. You are all very familiar with the tea market and the tea consumer. We'll meet again next week to discuss your ideas."

---

1. W. R. Simmons & Associates Research, Inc., 1976–77.
2. W. R. Simmons & Associates Research, Inc., 1976–77.

When the group reconvened the following week, Curtis called on Susan Allison, the fruit teas manager.

"It seems to me," Allison began, "that we should define Demeter as the *only* caffeine-free tea available to consumers. I think that most people are aware of caffeine's effects. Pointing out that we're the only tea without caffeine should attract health-conscious drinkers."

Alan Henry, the spice teas manager, spoke next. "I disagree, Susan. I don't think people associate caffeine with tea the way they do with coffee. A lot of people who drink tea assume it doesn't have caffeine to begin with. Yes, we need to say that we're caffeine-free, but first we've got to point out that tea does have caffeine."

"I think you're both a bit off track," said herb tea manager Flip James. "I agree that people know about caffeine's effects, and I think they associate caffeine with tea. But, I think most tea drinkers, especially the cup-a-day group, think that tea's weaker than coffee, so it's got less caffeine. They figure it'll take longer for the caffeine in tea to affect them. You know, two cups of coffee equals four cups of tea, that kind of reasoning. I think we should show that a cup of tea and a cup of coffee both have about the same amount of caffeine and then say that we take care of the problem because we don't have any caffeine."

"Let me see if I understand each of you," said Curtis. "Susan, you say people know about caffeine, so all we need to say is 'We're caffeine free' and they'll know why that's good. Alan says most people don't think tea has any caffeine, so we should tell them 'Did you know all tea has caffeine—except Demeter?' Flip says people know tea's got caffeine, but they think it's negligible and we need to tell them 'Your cup of tea has as much caffeine as a cup of coffee—unless it's Demeter.' "

"It seems to me that you're all saying the same thing, just in a different way. Frankly, I don't know which is best. No matter what we go with, we'll be reinforcing our current 'natural' image, so I don't think we're likely to lose any customers. But, I'm not sure which appeal is likely to bring in the most new Demeter drinkers. I'd like to think on what you've said for a few days."

Questions

1. Would an advertising pretest be helpful in this situation? Explain your answer.

2. How would you test this case: as a concept, a promise statement, a rough, or in finished form?

3. Assume you are each of the three managers. What would you expect your alternative to accomplish in terms of comprehension?

4. Can you establish one comprehension-related objective against which all three alternatives could be measured?

5. Who would the target market be for this advertising pretest?

6. Would you recommend that the alternatives be tested through personal interviews or focus groups?

7. Can you see any obvious hazards in this pretest situation?

12 Media Planning: Optimizing Message Delivery

The "big idea" of the advertising campaign rarely originates with the media planner, but the financial consequences of media strategy are widespread. Media is usually the largest item in the advertising budget and in some instances, particulary for consumer products, is the largest portion of the entire marketing effort. For many products and services, millions are invested in advertising annually. The pressures to optimize budgets are enormous. Even with so much riding on the development of effective media strategy, it is important to keep in mind that the best media plan cannot rescue a poor creative execution. Sound execution, on the other hand, is wasted if inefficiently delivered or improperly directed to the wrong prospects. Effective advertising requires both first-rate copy and proper message delivery.

Prior to the emergence of television in the 1950s, media selection was relatively simple. Newspapers, several large magazines, and radio were the choices. Television did more than add another vehicle. It altered people's lives by becoming the primary entertainment force and the major news source for most people and started a technological evolution that is still exerting substantial influence on the advertising industry.

The Changing Media World

Today's media world is vast and complex. The TV industry is composed of over 750 commercial and 200 public TV stations. Dozens of cable TV networks provide programming to 5,000 cable systems. Nearly 8,000 radio stations, over 1,700 daily newspapers, and hundreds of consumer magazines exist. Countless additional media vehicles are available to reach general audiences and specialized groups.

Obviously, the enormity of this array of media makes the planning process complicated and perhaps awesome. Yet the sheer magnitude of choice creates opportunities for advertisers and allows many who cannot afford $500,000 Super Bowl half-minute commercials to effectively promote their products and services in less expensive but effective ways. The complexity of the media world can be viewed as a blessing also.

Advertisers are always seeking better ways to sell ideas, services, and products. Advertising media likewise are extremely dynamic. Television, the advertising darling of package goods manufacturers, produced stable, growing audiences from the late Fifties to the late Seventies. Agencies, advertisers, and TV executives could count on these viewers—always present in larger numbers habitually watching more TV. Then came cable, video cassette recorders, and subscription TV. The audience research showed strange aberrations. At first, there were merely minor shifts in audience patterns, but recently pronounced declines in traditional viewing are appearing.

The transitory nature of the advertising media world requires innovation and demands originality in approaching the media planning process. Such changes enable opportunity, but creative exploration of media alternatives is increasingly vital.

Media Building Blocks: Basic Media Concepts

Several important terms and concepts have been developed to explain the dynamics of media planning. These are discussed in this section.

Rating

Sometimes referred to as coverage, a rating is the percentage of a specified population exposed to a single issue of a print or broadcast vehicle. The group measured must be defined but can be any target audience (women, men, children, households, etc.). Table 12-1 shows a sample rating group.

TV programs, radio shows, newspaper audiences, outdoor billboard traffic, virtually any medium's audience can be expressed as a rating. Some typical ratings for women are shown in Table 12-2.

Up to this point, national ratings have been discussed. Ratings generally relate to standard geographical areas, metropolitan statistical area, or more commonly an area of dominant influence, the latter an Arbitron research service term for 212 separate TV areas in the U.S.

Table 12-1. Sample Rating Group

	Total women	Women 18–49
U.S. population	90.0 million	55.0 million
Reader's Digest readers .	31.5 million	16.5 million
Reader's Digest ratings . .	35%	30%

Table 12-2. Typical Ratings for Women

	Women	Men	Teens	Children
Prime network TV program	14	12	10	11
Daytime network TV program	5	1	1	1
Early news network TV program . .	9	9	4	4
Late night network TV program . . .	5	4	2	–
Sat. morning network TV program	1	–	4	10
Early morning local radio show . . .	2	3	3	–
Network radio news program	1	1	1	—
Women's service magazine	20	2	4	–
Men's magazine	2	10	2	–
Daily newspaper	30	35	4	1

Table 12-3. Sample Media Schedule

TV	Ratings (women)	Number of announcements or insertions	GRPs
Hill Street Blues	20	2	40
All My Children	7	3	21
Good Morning America .	3	4	12
General Hospital	5	1	5
As the World Turns	4	2	8
Love Boat	9	1	9
Evening News	6	2	12
Magazines			
Better Homes & Gardens	19	2	38
Family Circle	20	1	20
Reader's Digest	35	1	35
Total GRPs			200

Gross Rating Points

The arithmetic sum of all the individual ratings in a media schedule is called *gross rating points*. GRPs is a measure of the total intensity or pressure of a media plan. The period of time represented by the GRP should be specified (week, four weeks, length of the campaign, etc.).

In Table 12-3, television and magazine women's ratings are added to sum 200 total gross rating points for the schedule.

Cumulative Audience

GRPs tell how much weight or total pressure is expected by the number of advertising messages but they do not tell how many different people are exposed to the messages. That is the function of reach, the number or percentage of a given population exposed to at least one of the advertising messages over the course of a schedule. Synonyms are cumulative (cume) audience, net audience, or unduplicated audience.

Reach or the dispersion of an advertising schedule is determined by the number of dayparts, programs, stations, media, magazines, etc., employed. For instance, the largest TV audiences and, thus, the largest reach levels are generated at night when most people are home from work, school, or other activities. TV reach is increased by running announcements in the late evening, morning, and afternoon so they will be seen by people who work during the evening and may be available during the afternoon. Since magazines appeal to specific groups of people, the greater the number of different titles used in a campaign, the greater the reach of the schedule. Size of magazine is important also. Large circulation magazines like *TV Guide* and *National Geographic* reach more people than specialized books (*Golf Digest, Soap Opera Digest*).

Reach divided into gross rating points produces average frequency, a measure of a campaign's depth. Frequency is the number of times a person sees the advertising message. In the example of 200 gross rating points, assume 50 percent of all women are exposed to at least one message. The average frequency is four.

$$\frac{\text{Gross Rating Points}}{\text{Reach}} = \text{Average Frequency}$$

$$200/50 = 4$$

The formula is usually expressed in this fashion: $R \times F = GRPs$. To facilitate the use of these concepts, the advertising profession has developed tables of reach and frequency. Computers are often used to generate these numbers.

The above example is typical of a daytime TV schedule composed of serials and game shows. During the prime evening hours, 200 GRPs would generate broader reach—approximately 80 percent of women, resulting in an average frequency of 2.5 times. Thus, varying the mix of dayparts influences reach and frequency of an advertising schedule. The total number of spots aired and the number of different programs employed also affects reach/frequency patterns. In radio, the number of spots, dispersion of spots across the day, and number of stations used influences reach/frequency relationships. As the number of magazines and their editorial differences increases, the greater the reach.

Reach and frequency help in evaluating alternative schedules in planning. If reach is the most important criteria, the schedule that produces the greatest reach would be chosen. If frequency of exposure is more important, then the schedule concentrating the most exposures has the advantage. At a given budget level and similar GRPs, reach and frequency analysis is invaluable in deciding the best alternative to achieve the objectives of the advertising program.

Cost Per Thousand

The universal calculation of media efficiency is cost per thousand (CPM), the cost of delivering one thousand impressions of a specified population.

$$\text{CPM} = \frac{\text{Cost (dollars)}}{\text{Impressions or People (in thousands)}}$$

Table 12-4 shows some typical women 18–49 CPMs.

Table 12-4.   Typical CPMs

	Cost	W 18–49 impressions	Calculation	CPM
Prime network TV (:30) ...	$100,000	12,500,000	$\frac{\$100,000}{12,500}$	= $8.00
Day network TV (:30)	$ 20,000	4,250,000	$\frac{\$20,000}{4,250}$	= $4.70
Reader's Digest	$100,000	25,000,000	$\frac{\$100,000}{25,000}$	= $4.00

CPM cuts through different audience sizes and costs to create one simple expression of efficiency: the cost to reach 1,000 people as specified.

Effective Reach

A refinement of the reach concept used more frequently in media circles is the idea of effective reach, sometimes confusingly referred to as effective frequency. Take your pick, the term *effective reach* seeks to answer the old question: How much advertising is enough? Effective reach is simply how many people receive sufficient frequency of the advertising to become aware of the message and comprehend its content.

The optimum level of frequency for any product depends upon a host of factors, including the product purchase cycle, complexity of the message, competitive position and communications, brand awareness, and

Figure 12-1.   Effective Reach and Frequency

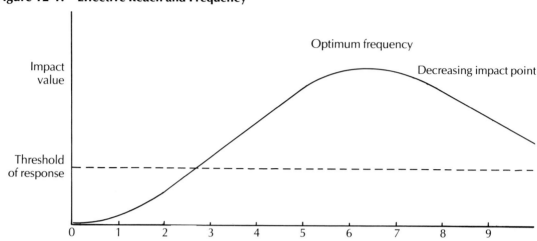

communication properties of media vehicles (which will be discussed more completely later). Numerous studies have been undertaken to determine the optimum level of advertising frequency. The conclusions are the same: it depends. However, for most branded package goods, these observations are generally recognized:

1. One exposure is of little value.
2. A second adds some value.
3. Three exposures a month (or during a purchase cycle) is needed to produce sufficient communication.
4. After a certain level of frequency, succeeding exposures produce increasingly *less* value.
5. At certain frequency levels, the commercial execution becomes ineffective. Negative reactions may result.

In the theoretical model in Figure 12-1, people exposed less than three times are of little value. The optimum level of exposure is six messages. But after eight exposures people grow weary of the message, succeeding impressions are less effective, and negative attitudes may be generated.

Frequency Distribution

Users of reach and frequency sometimes forget that frequency is an average. Some people see more impressions, and an equal number see fewer

Table 12-5. Sample TV Quintile Analysis

	Reach	Frequency	GRPs
Heaviest viewing 20%	12.4	9.2	114
Next heaviest viewing 20%	12.4	6.5	80
Third heaviest viewing 20%	12.4	2.9	36
Fourth heaviest viewing 20%	12.4	1.6	20
Lightest viewing 20%	12.4	0.4	5
Average	62	4.1	255

impressions than the average. To visualize more clearly the flow of impressions, a frequency distribution chart or table similar to the one in Figure 12-1 should be consulted.

Another means of looking at frequency distribution is to divide the population into groups based on exposure behavior. For instance, Table 12-5 shows a typical TV quintile analysis. The total TV audience is divided into five equal parts based upon overall viewing patterns—heaviest to lightest TV viewing.

Note that the two heaviest viewing quintiles (40 percent) account for 76 percent of the total GRPs, a typical TV relationship.

Quintile and frequency distribution charts aid in determining how to schedule advertising in a medium and give some insight into when to add a second or third medium to a campaign. For instance, in the above quintile distribution, 40 percent of the TV viewers account for 76 percent of total exposures of the TV schedule. If a magazine schedule were added to that campaign, more impressions would be delivered to the lighter viewing quintiles. People who are heavy readers of magazines are lighter TV viewers. Subsequently, when print is added to a TV schedule, impressions build against lighter viewing quintiles, evening out or flattening frequency of exposure. Thus, instead of adding more frequency on top of the original frequency, the planner, through the use of quintile analysis, can see when to stop using TV and when to add magazines or radio or some alternative medium. As in the case of reach/frequency analyses, computer programs are now available to assist in constructing quintile distribution charts.

Armed with the basic media concepts, the planner is ready to build the media strategy and plan.

Building Media Strategy

Media planning is dependent upon marketing objectives and strategy, and the media plan becomes an integral part of the overall marketing plan. Media interacts with all elements of marketing strategy. The first step in media planning is a thorough review of all marketing information. The planner must understand the advertising and marketing goals so that the media plan supports those objectives.

Relating Media Planning to Marketing

Marketing objectives. Critical to proper media planning are the marketing objectives that set the overall goals of all promotional, advertising, and merchandising activities. Marketing objectives address sales goals and marketing budget, prime prospects for the product or service, geographical sales and sales potential, sales seasonality, promotions, creative direction, and competitive issues.

Product characteristics and consumption patterns. The nature of the product itself can determine media employed. Certain personal items are inappropriate for early evening TV, for example, while other products may require complex copy. Consumption patterns are critically important in determining where to promote products. Regional peculiarities must be considered as well as what types of people might consume or need the item.

Distribution patterns. The geographical distribution channels and availability of products and services must be evaluated in structuring strategy. Even though products may be consumed nationally, individual brands may not be sold across the country or attain sufficient strength to justify universal advertising support.

Promotion and merchandising strategies. During the 1970s inflation altered America's economic structure and the nature of marketing changed as well. Promotion and merchandising activity increased as consumers became more cost conscious. The relationship between advertising and promotion narrowed and is highly interrelated today. Advertising works hand-in-hand with couponing, point-of-sales promotion, sampling, and merchandising tools.

Competitive activity. Media planning requires thorough knowledge of competitive marketing and advertising efforts. Plans often address threats of new or existing competitors and category spending. Standard industry sources provide the base for competitive expenditure analysis.

Financial constraints. Media budgets sometimes are established by marketing people unfamiliar with the realities of the media world. The planner must have adequate financial footing to achieve advertising's role in the marketing plan. Budget parameters must be established before planning commences.

Creative execution. Creative strategy and particularly the kinds of executions to be utilized are vital to media planning. Unless copy conforms to the media recommended, time is wasted.

Establishing Media Objectives

Media objectives are positive statements of what the media budget will achieve in the promotional plan. Media objectives answer five universal questions plus other considerations unique to the particular marketing situation. Objectives tell *what* will be done, not how it will be accomplished.

Who is to be reached? The target audience for advertising communications is identified as precisely as possible. Prospects are commonly defined in terms of socioeconomic characteristics (age, sex, income, education, race, family size, employment status, etc.). Two other means of defining the target audience are source of business (users/buyers) or psychographical/lifestyle characteristics. If more than one target audience is employed, the relative importance (weighting) of each needs to be established. Indirect secondary groups (sales force, agents, employees, etc.) important to the plan should be noted.

What is to be accomplished? What is the media plan to accomplish against the target audience? Increase awareness of the brand or service? Alter an attitude about the product? Introduce a product? Reinforce promotional activities? Remind customers of the product? Block or meet a new competitive product? Encourage sales force response? Precise identification of the primary tasks of the media process should be outlined.

When does the advertising appear? This goal establishes the proper timetable for spending:

- lead the peak sales season?
- conform to monthly sales?
- support promotions?
- counter competitive threats?
- remind shoppers prior to purchase (time of day)?
- relate to weather, holidays, or quarters?

Where does the advertising occur? Establishing geographical priorities for spending emphasis ties directly back to consumption, distribution, and sales patterns. Some issues to consider:

- national vs. regional vs. local support
- actual brand sales development vs. category sales characteristics
- problem areas due to competitive introductions or testing
- population density (city, suburban, rural promotion).

How much advertising should be scheduled? This objective determines the required advertising pressure necessary to accomplish results. Often, advertising weight goals are defined in terms of reach and frequency during flights or on a monthly basis. If season or geographical emphasis changes, the resulting reach and frequencies are also detailed.

Other considerations: special needs of the situation. Exceptional marketing or advertising goals should be specifically addressed beyond the above five areas. Special trial or inducement marketing activities may need communication support. Flexibility in committing budgets or the need to cancel plans should be detailed. Matching peculiar creative ideas might be required. The need for testing alternative strategies, copy, or marketing approaches for future efforts is critical and is established in the media objectives. Any special company standards (i.e., avoiding certain media vehicles, etc.) as well as significant competitive issues should be addressed.

The media objectives establish goals of the plan. The remainder of the plan goes about the business of accomplishing the tasks and outlining specific media elements to be used during the course of the plan, usually a year.

Strategic Issues

Media strategies are solutions to the media objectives and tell how those goals will be achieved. Addressing these issues is challenging and requires a generous amount of judgment.

Geographical strategic allocations. Products nationally distributed have three basic spending options:

- 100 percent directly into national media.
- A mix of national and local media.
- Employ local media only across the country or a significant portion of the country.

To aid in solving this issue, managers often analyze brand and category sales. An easy method is to index brand sales and category sales to

Table 12-6. Brand Development Profile

	Brand Sales (units)	Brand %	Category Sales (units)	Category %	Brand development index
Eastern region	50	24	150	25	96
Baltimore	10	4	50	8	50
Boston	20	10	60	10	100
New York	20	10	40	7	143
Southern region	70	33	100	17	194
Jackson	20	10	20	3	333
Atlanta	15	7	30	6	117
Dallas	35	16	50	8	200
Central region	30	14	100	17	82
Chicago	5	2	20	3	67
Detroit	10	5	40	7	71
Minneapolis	15	7	40	7	100
Western region	60	29	250	41	71
Los Angeles	20	10	50	8	125
Denver	15	7	100	17	41
Kansas City	15	7	50	8	88
San Francisco ...	10	5	50	8	63
Total U.S.	210	100	600	100	—

construct a BDI or brand development index. In Table 12-6, brand geographical sales are related to overall category sales to show where the brand is strong or weak compared to the entire market. Eastern region sales represent 24 percent of the brand's total sales and 25 percent of the category's total sales. Thus, the BDI is 96 (24/25). Brand sales nearly match category sales in the Eastern region. Not so in Baltimore, however, where brand sales are below category sales (50 index). In New York brand sales are quite strong (143 BDI). An index is merely a percentage relationship between two other percentages. Indices are an easy method to uncover differences among many statistics.

If brand sales closely match category sales, spending may conform to the market. However, if sales deviate substantially from the overall category, strategic decisions have significant impact on possible results. A very successful strategy is to follow the brand's sales pattern. This conservative approach is to identify markets or areas having growth potential and invest (overspend) in these (Western region in the example). Still another

Figure 12-2. **Media Strategies: BDI/CDI System**

	High	Category development Low
Brand development High	• Saturation brand and category sales • Incremental spending unproductive • Defensive spending • Sustained advertising	• Brand strong but consumer spending low • Added spending ineffective • Seek to build category frequency of purchase
Low	• Competition strong; brand relatively weak • Investment spending potentially effective • Build frequency at key periods (peak sales) • Seek intensive or flighted activity	• Limit advertising to peak sales periods • Is advertising necessary? No sales potential; brand weak • Support promotions to avoid distribution losses

approach is to identify weak markets and promote in these (Baltimore for instance).

Another helpful way to focus on product and category strategic issues is to group markets in a matrix (see Figure 12-2).

Target audience analysis. Because several groups may be important to the product or service, weighting of the relative significance of each group should be established. How much advertising weight or emphasis should be given each target is often a marketing decision. Sometimes research must be conducted to decide where to place emphasis.

In this example of a woman's product, the planner determines whether to target media strategy against category or brand users. Category users are younger, but the individual brand's franchise is middle-aged. In selecting media and individual vehicles, it makes significant difference which profile to target advertising to. (See Table 12-7.)

In the next example of an all-family product, advertising might be directed to both women and children. Although all ages consume the

Table 12-7.   Sample Target Audience Analysis for a Woman's Product

Women	% population	% category users	% brand users
18–34	36	45	25
35–54	31	30	50
55+	33	25	25

Table 12-8.   Sample Target Analysis for an All-Family Product

	% population	% consumption
Women	39	32
Men	35	25
Teens	10	12
Children	16	31

Table 12-9.   Sample Strategic Weighting

	% consumption	% of total impressions delivered			
		Day TV	Weekend TV	Sports TV	Combined
Women . . .	32	75	3	18	32
Men	25	10	2	63	25
Teens	12	5	20	11	12
Children . . .	31	10	75	8	31

product, children on a per capita basis consume twice as much as any other group. Women exceed children in total consumption and are the major family food shoppers. These two groups probably exert much more influence over other family members in the purchase decision. (See Table 12-8.)

Should one target advertising to women (buyers), or children (major consumers) or perhaps both? Media reaching women (daytime TV, women's service magazines) and children (Saturday morning TV) or perhaps vehicles that attract both groups such as early evening situation comedy TV shows could be employed.

Strategic weighting, based upon the relative significance of several important consuming groups, is another possible approach. For instance, in the all-family product example, a combination of TV dayparts selected in such a way to deliver advertising impressions in the same proportion (weight) as consumption might be attempted in developing a media strategy. (See Table 12-9.)

Note that the combination of day, weekend children's, and sports programming distributes weight exactly in proportion to consumption. Similar advertising weighting can be accomplished using various media to reach a certain mix of women of different ages—daytime soap operas for younger women and evening news programs to reach older women who might not be busy preparing family meals at that time of day.

Reach and frequency issues. Another major question for which no definitive research is available is how much reach and frequency is enough. Many factors—marketing and media objectives, competitive positioning and pressure, brand's marketing position, and a host of others—can affect this judgment. As a broad gauge, reach or frequency are emphasized in these instances unless other factors preclude the strategies:

Reach situations	Frequency situations
New products	Strong competitors
Expanding category	Complex story
Flanker brand	Frequently purchased
Strong brand franchise	category
Undefined target market	Weak loyalty to brand
Infrequent purchase cycle	Narrow target market
	Consumer resistance to
	brand or category

Scheduling options. The ideal advertising situation is strong, year-around support at high effective reach levels, but of course, that's impractical for virtually all advertisers. Like other strategic issues, scheduling involves the planner's judgment. There are several major methods of scheduling advertising, each with its benefits and trade-offs.

Continuous advertising is weight scheduled throughout the advertising period. Variations in sales plus high media costs generally preclude continuous pressure. Continuous scheduling might be used in these instances:

- Expanding market situations
- Frequently purchased items
- Tightly defined buyer category

Flighted advertising comes in periodic waves separated by periods of no activity (hiatuses). Most brands employ some form of flighting due to media costs.

Situations lending themselves to flighting include:

- Limited funding
- Relatively infrequent purchase cycle
- Seasonal items
- Market share building programs

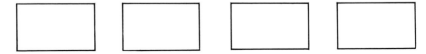

Communication models indicate that forgetting occurs during periods of inactive advertising. Usually the loss is gradual, although numerous factors spread memory delay (competitive clutter, product importance, campaign maturity, seasonality, budget size, copy execution, etc.). Scheduling can dramatically influence campaign results.

In this example, two sixteen-week campaigns are scheduled differently, yet at the end of the sixteen-week period average reach and frequency are equal:

16 weeks
50 GRPs/week

4 weeks	4 weeks	4 weeks	4 weeks
100 GRPs/wk.		100 GRPs/wk.	

	Average 4-week during 16 weeks	
	Continuous	Flighted
GRPs	200	200
Average 4-week reach	75%	75%
Average 4-week frequency	2.7×	2.7×

However, during advertising periods, pressure and reach are surprisingly dissimilar:

	Average 4-week flight	
	Continuous	Flighted
Total GRPs	200	400
4-week reach	75%	89%
4-week frequency	2.7×	4.5×

Compromise scheduling strategies have been developed to draw upon the strengths of continuous (no voids) advertising and flights (increased intensity of exposure). The first, pulsing, is continuous advertising at low weight levels reinforced periodically by waves of heavier activity. If some media vehicles can be identified that efficiently concentrate on a portion of the target audience, continuous support at low weights may be feasible. Then, at strategic points, such as consumer promotions or peak seasonal periods, more intense pressure is activated.

Blinkering, another compromise, is total-in and total-out advertising periods of short duration. Blinkering generates strong pressure while advertising and keeps hiatuses short. The brand may appear as a continuously advertised product without doing so.

Blinkering and pulsing represent economical ways of blending the two original scheduling strategies, but both require extremely careful implementation and can lead to inefficiencies in strong marketplaces.

Media mix. Advertising campaigns in a single medium tend to build impressions against a portion of the population because each medium has a hard core of listeners, viewers, or readers. Using a number of media tends to disperse advertising impressions more effectively than a single medium. Mixing several media tends to balance frequency.

If people are divided into groups based upon patterns of media consumption, we can see how advertising impressions accumulate against these groups. (See Table 12-10.)

Varying message delivery by media generally produces better advertising results than concentration in a single medium or area within a medium (e.g., early morning in the case of TV or a selected group of magazines):

1. As indicated earlier, using several media can level out impressions against target audiences and avoid intense concentration against a single portion of the audience. Caution: sometimes this characteristic is desirable, especially if the medium concentrates impressions against a good cross-section of the desired audience for the campaign.

Table 12-10.   Cumulative Effects of Advertising Impressions

	Adults	Adults 18–49, $20,000+ income, and some college	Index
Heavy TV viewers/light magazine readers .	32%	17%	53
Light TV/heavy magazine	32%	54%	169
Heavy TV/light radio	33%	24%	73
Light TV/heavy radio	33%	43%	130

2. Sometimes a synergistic effect on advertising recall or awareness is generated through a combination of media. TV messages are reinforced and re-created in the mind's eye when a related radio jingle is heard. This "imagery transfer" greatly improves effectiveness.

3. A second medium usually increases frequency against lighter users of the first medium. Thus effective reach can be enhanced.

4. Media mix is only valuable when sufficient resources are available to add a second or third medium. Achieve effective reach levels in the primary medium before dispersing advertising impressions via other media.

Creative values and audience adjustments. Most advertising practitioners believe that media communicate in unique ways. An impression in one medium is not the same as an exposure in another. Media have individual "impact" values. TV commercials produce different results compared to radio commercials or newspaper ads. TV commercials within the TV medium may also produce differing effects. (A commercial for breakfast products may be more meaningful in the morning when people eat breakfast.)

Judgment is needed to determine creative values. Usually a combined agency/client judgmental decision is established based upon campaign objectives. Print may be best for a long, complicated story. Newspapers serve to announce new information forcefully. TV provides visual demonstrations. Radio reinforces many campaigns adding extra intensity near the time of purchase. Each medium has unique communication characteristics.

Closely related to creative values is the concept of audience adjustment. Fortunately, more research is available here, but considerable judgment is needed to properly employ the concept in planning. Most media research measures vehicle audience, not commercial or ad delivery. Audiences should be adjusted downward to reflect the fact that not everyone who watches a program or reads a magazine sees the commer-

---

Table 12-11.   CPM Comparison—Women 25–54

Vehicle	Gross vehicle CPM	Index	"Eyes-on" factor	Creative impact weight	Adjusted W 25–54 CPM	Index
Prime net TV .	$12.00	(100)	68%	1.00	$17.65	(100)
Day net TV . .	4.80	(40)	60%	1.00	8.00	(45)
Magazines . . .	6.60	(55)	85%	.50	15.52	(88)

(Magazines = $6.60 ÷ 85% = $7.76 ÷ 50 = $15.52)

SOURCE: J. Walter Thompson Company

---

cial or the ad. Through various print and broadcast studies, factors have been established to reflect the lower commercial audiences. These adjustments are based upon broad-scale averages, however, and should not be taken as gospel. These "eyes on" and "pages turned" kind of research can be used to refine inter- and intra-media comparisons.

Often agencies will combine creative values and audience adjustments into comparisons. Table 12-11 is an example by J. Walter Thompson Company.

Once creative values and audience adjustment factors are taken into account, effective reach takes on additional meaning, especially when the media planner is attempting to decide upon the relative advertising impact of several potential media strategies.

Product life cycle strategies. Most products, certainly most branded consumer goods, have a life cycle. New products are introduced to the market, grow to maturity, and eventually are forced into decline by competitive or innovative new items. In broad terms, these stages call for significantly varying media strategies, as noted in Table 12-12.

From this point the media planner has established media goals and addressed overall strategic issues. These strategies should relate back to the media goals. The next job is to marry media vehicles with the strategies to produce the optimum message delivery.

Market—Media Research Services

The client marketing research group may provide considerable information to the media planning function concerning target audiences, sales, distribution patterns, and other marketing elements. Sometimes this information is not available internally and must be obtained from other sources. A number of media research firms supply syndicated market and media research data. Mediamark Research, Inc., and Simmons Market Research

Table 12-12.   Product Life Cycle Media Strategies

	New product	Growing product	Mature product	Declining product
Target audience	Widespread (possibly unknown or unclear)	Defined	Users	Users
Advertising reach/ frequency	Reach with effective frequency	Frequency on prospects	Frequency on narrow group of users	Reach among users
Geographical emphasis	National	Natural/basic, additional emphasis on opportunity areas	Best markets	Best areas
Advertising pattern	Strong introduction, continuous follow-ing anticipated sales	Heavy during season	Leading into and during seasonal peaks	Support promotions only

Bureau, Inc., are two of the most widely used services for product usage and media audience data.

The two services are highly competitive, employ different methodologies, and produce a wealth of market information. As an example of the extensiveness of the data provided, SMRB breakouts for several ready-to-eat cereals are shown in Table 12-13. Demographic consumption data can be cross-tabulated with a host of media vehicles. On-line time-sharing enables numerous cross-tabs and manipulation of these extensive data banks across some 750 product/service categories, 3,500 brands, and numerous media audiences (print, broadcast, cable, outdoor, even Yellow Pages).

SMRB reports can be intimidating, but they are not difficult to understand. Breakfast cereals are purchased primarily by female homemakers that are categorized in the left column and cross-referenced to all demographic and other categories reported. Column "A" under the brand tells how many female homemakers are users/purchasers of the brand. (In category sections of SMRB, consumers/purchasers are divided according to purchase/consumption frequency.) The "B" column describes brand purchasers in terms of demographics. Note that the six age breaks add to 100 percent. All purchases are accounted for by homemakers 18 to 65 or older.

The last two columns are quite helpful in marketing and media planning. Column "C" indicates relative consumption by all the categories listed on the left. This column is indexed ("D"). A high index (over 100) means that group (age for instance) purchases more than would be expected based on its proportion of all people. A low index (below 100) means below average consumption.

Table 12-13.   Sample Simmons Market Research Bureau Breakouts

0095
P-20

BREAKFAST CEREALS (COLD): BRANDS
(FEMALE HOMEMAKERS)

0095
P-20

	TOTAL U.S. '000	POST RAISIN BRAN A '000	B % DOWN	C % ACROSS	D INDX	POST SUPER SUGAR CRISP A '000	B % DOWN	C % ACROSS	D INDX	POST TOASTIES A '000	B % DOWN	C % ACROSS	D INDX	POST 40% BRAN FLAKES A '000	B % DOWN	C % ACROSS	D INDX
TOTAL FEMALE HOMEMAKERS	77506	17129	100.0	22.1	100	4740	100.0	6.1	100	4461	100.0	5.8	100	5217	100.0	6.7	100
MKDAY LOCAL EVENING TV NEWS																	
NETWORK AFFILIATES - EARLY	25416	5107	29.8	20.1	91	1247	26.3	4.9	80	1580	35.4	6.2	108	2007	38.5	7.9	117
NETWORK AFFILIATES - LATE	18757	4159	24.3	22.2	100	1205	25.4	6.4	105	1289	28.9	6.9	119	1357	26.0	7.2	107
INDEPENDENTS - LATE	2476	437	2.6	17.6	80	106	2.2	4.3	70	141	3.2	5.7	99	187	3.6	7.6	112
TV EVENING NTWK 6 PM - 2 AM																	
ABC FRIDAY NIGHT MOVIE A	4978	1250	7.3	25.1	114	307	6.5	6.2	101	329	7.4	6.6	115	287	5.5	5.8	86
ABC NEWS: NIGHTLINE A	2266	579	3.4	25.6	116	140	3.0	6.2	101	140	3.1	6.2	107	163	3.1	7.2	107
ABC WORLD NEWS TONIGHT A	5871	1355	7.9	23.1	104	236	5.0	4.0	66	391	8.8	6.7	116	481	9.2	8.2	122
ABC WRLD NEWS TONIGHT-SUN A	2084	502	2.9	24.1	109	**113	2.4	5.4	89	*130	2.9	6.2	108	*132	2.5	6.3	94
ARCHIE BUNKER'S PLACE C	7966	1689	9.9	21.2	96	438	9.2	5.5	90	504	11.3	6.3	110	643	12.3	8.1	120
BARBARA MANDRELL N	5626	1097	6.4	19.5	88	*279	5.9	5.0	81	426	9.5	7.6	132	548	10.5	9.7	145
BARNEY MILLER A	8228	1757	10.3	21.4	97	401	8.5	4.9	80	551	12.4	6.7	116	632	12.1	7.7	114
BENSON A	7000	1425	8.3	20.4	92	333	7.0	4.8	78	451	10.1	6.4	112	517	9.9	7.4	110
BOOK OF LISTS C	5214	1337	7.8	25.6	116	*321	6.8	6.2	101	*242	5.4	4.6	81	*243	4.7	4.7	69
BRET MAVERICK N	5458	1167	6.8	21.4	97	323	6.8	5.9	97	*266	6.0	4.9	85	353	6.8	6.5	96
CBS EVENING NEWS - DEAN C	3645	797	4.7	21.9	99	*149	3.1	4.1	67	*182	4.1	5.0	87	*223	4.3	6.1	91
CBS EVENING NEWS - RATHER C	7761	1625	9.5	20.9	95	451	9.5	5.8	95	509	11.4	6.6	114	599	11.5	7.7	115
CBS SAT. NEWS - SCHIEFFER C	3875	750	4.4	19.4	88	*176	3.7	4.5	74	256	5.7	6.6	115	308	5.9	7.9	118
CBS SAT. NIGHT MOVIE C	5273	1231	7.2	23.3	106	372	7.8	7.1	115	304	6.8	5.8	100	302	5.8	5.7	85
CBS SUNDAY NIGHT - OSGOOD C	2130	385	2.2	18.1	82	**85	1.8	4.0	65	**84	1.9	3.9	69	*132	2.5	6.2	92
CBS WEDNESDAY NIGHT MOVIE C	6817	1398	8.2	20.5	93	465	9.8	6.8	112	506	11.3	7.4	129	477	9.1	7.0	104
CHICAGO STORY N	3093	767	4.5	24.8	112	**152	3.2	4.9	80	*215	4.8	7.0	121	*299	5.7	9.7	144
CHIPS N	7786	1671	9.8	21.5	97	491	10.4	6.3	103	432	9.7	5.5	96	418	8.0	5.4	80
DALLAS C	10915	2268	13.2	20.8	94	717	15.1	6.6	107	654	14.7	6.0	104	779	14.9	7.1	106
DIFF'RENT STROKES N	9535	2171	12.7	22.8	103	844	17.8	8.9	145	537	12.0	5.6	98	546	10.5	5.7	85
DUKES OF HAZZARD C	7935	1723	10.1	21.7	98	616	13.0	7.8	127	485	10.9	6.1	106	521	10.0	6.6	98
FACTS OF LIFE N	8082	1802	10.5	22.3	101	558	11.8	6.9	113	474	10.6	5.9	102	491	9.4	6.1	90
FALL GUY A	8200	1847	10.8	22.5	102	569	12.0	6.9	113	413	9.3	5.0	88	475	9.1	5.8	86
FAME N	6263	1205	7.0	19.2	87	556	11.7	8.9	145	331	7.4	5.3	92	304	5.8	4.9	72
FANTASY ISLAND A	9027	1712	10.0	19.0	86	638	13.5	7.1	116	453	10.2	5.0	87	532	10.2	5.9	88
FATHER MURPHY N	4724	956	5.6	20.2	92	259	5.5	5.5	90	331	7.4	7.0	122	323	6.2	6.8	102
GIMME A BREAK N	8983	1963	11.5	21.9	99	839	17.7	9.3	153	477	10.7	5.3	92	466	8.9	5.2	77
GREATEST AMERICAN HERO A	6628	1513	8.8	22.8	103	510	10.8	7.7	126	436	9.8	6.6	114	368	7.1	5.6	82
HAPPY DAYS A	8265	1681	9.8	20.3	92	697	14.7	8.4	138	499	11.2	6.0	105	470	9.0	5.7	84
HARPER VALLEY N	3816	708	4.1	18.6	84	*226	4.8	5.9	97	263	5.9	6.9	120	390	7.5	10.2	152
HART TO HART A	11762	2677	15.6	22.8	103	735	15.5	6.2	102	630	14.1	5.4	93	858	16.4	7.3	108
HILL STREET BLUES N	9045	1955	11.4	21.6	98	749	15.8	8.3	135	437	9.8	4.8	84	490	9.4	5.4	80
INCREDIBLE HULK C	4712	932	5.4	19.8	89	297	6.3	6.3	103	289	6.5	6.1	107	325	6.2	6.9	102
LAVERNE & SHIRLEY A	8279	1807	10.5	21.8	99	699	14.7	8.4	138	445	10.0	5.4	93	436	8.4	5.3	78
LITTLE HOUSE - PRAIRIE N	10207	1800	10.5	17.6	80	606	12.8	5.9	97	603	13.5	5.9	102	604	11.6	5.9	88
LOU GRANT C	8042	1808	10.6	22.5	102	482	10.2	6.0	98	461	10.3	5.7	100	471	9.0	5.9	87
LOVE BOAT A	11480	2318	13.5	20.2	91	795	16.8	6.9	113	567	12.7	4.9	86	639	12.2	5.6	83
MAGNUM, P.I. C	10658	2162	12.6	20.3	92	570	12.0	5.3	87	499	11.2	4.7	81	553	10.6	5.2	77
M*A*S*H A	9369	2253	13.2	24.0	109	733	15.5	7.8	128	687	15.4	7.3	127	694	13.3	7.4	110
MORK & MINDY A	4737	1229	7.2	25.9	117	289	6.1	6.1	100	307	6.9	6.5	113	352	6.7	7.4	110
NBC MAGAZINE N	4118	873	5.1	21.2	96	*203	4.3	4.9	81	305	6.8	7.4	129	331	6.3	8.0	119
NBC MONDAY NIGHT MOVIES N	7285	1670	9.7	22.9	104	461	9.7	6.3	103	399	8.9	5.5	95	495	9.5	6.8	101
NBC NIGHTLY NEWS N	5866	1122	6.6	19.1	87	254	5.4	4.3	71	314	7.0	5.4	93	422	8.1	7.2	107
NBC NIGHTLY NEWS - SAT. N	2990	482	2.8	16.1	73	**100	2.1	3.3	55	*151	3.4	5.1	88	256	4.9	8.6	127
NBC NIGHTLY NEWS - SUN. N	3166	458	2.7	14.5	65	**87	1.8	2.7	45	*186	4.2	5.9	102	339	6.5	10.7	159
NBC SUNDAY NIGHT MOVIE N	7514	1797	10.5	23.9	108	384	8.1	5.1	84	530	11.9	7.1	123	463	8.9	6.2	92
ONE DAY AT A TIME C	8157	1747	10.2	21.4	97	498	10.5	6.1	100	521	11.7	6.4	111	600	11.5	7.4	109
ONE OF THE BOYS N	3347	625	3.6	18.1	82	*219	4.6	6.4	104	268	6.0	7.8	135	331	6.3	9.6	143
QUINCY, M.E. N	9880	2042	11.9	20.7	94	557	11.8	5.6	92	525	11.8	5.3	92	724	13.9	7.3	109
REAL PEOPLE N	9143	2014	11.8	22.0	100	494	10.4	5.4	88	648	14.5	7.1	123	784	15.0	8.6	127
60 MINUTES C	12666	2826	16.5	22.3	101	582	12.3	4.6	75	874	19.6	6.9	120	1162	22.3	9.2	136
TAXI A	8204	1942	11.3	23.7	107	438	9.2	5.3	87	507	11.4	6.2	107	594	11.4	7.2	108
TEACHERS ONLY N	6998	1774	10.4	25.4	115	515	10.8	7.4	120	522	11.7	7.5	130	515	9.9	7.4	109
THAT'S INCREDIBLE A	7495	1663	9.7	22.2	100	447	9.4	6.0	98	418	9.4	5.6	97	498	9.5	6.6	99
THREE'S COMPANY A	12031	2922	17.1	24.3	110	894	18.9	7.4	122	671	15.0	5.6	97	758	14.5	6.3	94
TONIGHT SHOW N	2727	629	3.7	23.1	104	115	2.4	4.2	69	209	4.7	7.7	133	214	4.1	7.8	117
TOO CLOSE FOR COMFORT C	11418	2719	15.9	23.8	108	864	18.2	7.6	124	716	16.1	6.3	109	756	14.5	6.6	98
TRAPPER JOHN, M.D. C	11694	2763	16.1	23.6	107	897	18.9	7.7	125	734	16.5	6.3	109	759	14.5	6.5	96
20/20 A	9204	2035	11.9	22.1	100	444	9.4	4.8	79	571	12.8	6.2	108	664	12.7	7.2	107
WALT DISNEY C	4583	1011	5.9	22.1	100	277	5.8	6.0	99	*260	5.8	5.7	99	267	5.1	5.8	87
TV VIEWING SPORTS EVENTS																	
BASEBALL	10670	2609	15.2	24.5	111	528	11.1	4.9	81	899	20.2	8.4	146	1076	20.6	10.1	150
BASKETBALL - COLLEGE GAMES	4501	1343	7.8	29.8	135	*448	9.5	10.0	163	*531	11.9	11.8	205	*371	7.1	8.2	122
BASKETBALL - PRO-GAMES	4600	1203	7.0	26.2	118	*332	7.0	7.2	118	*480	10.8	10.4	181	*456	8.7	9.9	147
BOWLING	4732	923	5.4	19.5	88	*375	7.9	7.9	130	*274	6.1	5.8	101	*399	7.6	8.4	125
BOXING	5042	1597	9.3	31.7	143	698	14.7	13.8	226	*360	8.1	7.1	124	*409	7.8	8.1	121
FOOTBALL-COLLEGE GAMES	8758	2764	16.1	31.6	143	725	15.3	8.3	135	771	17.3	8.8	152	851	16.3	9.7	144
FOOTBALL-PROFESSIONAL GAMES	14895	3898	22.8	26.2	118	1312	27.7	8.8	144	1178	26.4	7.9	137	1148	22.0	7.7	115
GOLF	4057	1143	6.7	28.2	127	**249	5.3	6.1	100	*356	8.0	8.8	152	*411	7.9	10.1	151
POST-SEASON COLL. FOOTBALL	6612	1822	10.6	27.6	125	*468	9.9	7.1	116	*591	13.2	8.9	155	579	11.1	8.8	130
POST-SEASON PRO FOOTBALL	9284	2572	15.0	27.7	125	747	15.8	8.0	132	754	16.9	8.1	141	758	14.5	8.2	121
TENNIS	3738	973	5.7	26.0	118	**216	4.6	5.8	94	**229	5.1	6.1	106	**257	4.9	6.9	102

BREAKFAST CEREALS (COLD): BRANDS
(FEMALE HOMEMAKERS)

	TOTAL U.S. '000	QUAKER CAP'N CRUNCH A '000	B % DOWN	C % ACROSS	D INDX	QUAKER LIFE A '000	B % DOWN	C % ACROSS	D INDX	QUAKER PUFFED RICE A '000	B % DOWN	C % ACROSS	D INDX	QUAKER PUFFED WHEAT A '000	B % DOWN	C % ACROSS	D INDX
TOTAL FEMALE HOMEMAKERS	77506	6014	100.0	7.8	100	4209	100.0	5.4	100	4417	100.0	5.7	100	3970	100.0	5.1	100
18 - 24	9335	1118	18.6	12.0	154	652	15.5	7.0	129	•460	10.4	4.9	86	••289	7.3	3.1	60
25 - 34	18029	1820	30.3	10.1	130	1485	35.3	8.2	152	975	22.1	5.4	95	849	21.4	4.7	92
35 - 44	13417	1443	24.0	10.8	139	944	22.4	7.0	130	713	16.1	5.3	93	642	16.2	4.8	93
45 - 54	11632	998	16.6	8.6	111	•535	12.7	4.6	85	773	17.5	6.6	117	779	19.6	6.7	131
55 - 64	11283	••269	4.5	2.4	31	•375	8.9	3.3	61	634	14.4	5.6	99	660	16.6	5.8	114
65 OR OLDER	13811	•366	6.1	2.7	34	•217	5.2	1.6	29	862	19.5	6.2	110	751	18.9	5.4	106
18 - 34	27364	2938	48.9	10.7	138	2137	50.8	7.8	144	1434	32.5	5.2	92	1138	28.7	4.2	81
18 - 49	46197	4987	82.9	10.8	139	3346	79.5	7.2	133	2547	57.7	5.5	97	2150	54.2	4.7	91
25 - 54	43078	4261	70.9	9.9	127	2965	70.4	6.9	127	2461	55.7	5.7	100	2270	57.2	5.3	103
35 - 49	18833	2049	34.1	10.9	140	1209	28.7	6.4	118	1113	25.2	5.9	104	1012	25.5	5.4	105
50 OR OLDER	31310	1027	17.1	3.3	42	863	20.5	2.8	51	1870	42.3	6.0	105	1820	45.8	5.8	113
GRADUATED COLLEGE	9890	•422	7.0	4.3	55	715	17.0	7.2	133	503	11.4	5.1	89	441	11.1	4.5	87
ATTENDED COLLEGE	12236	948	15.8	7.7	100	861	20.5	7.0	130	720	16.3	5.9	103	742	18.7	6.1	118
GRADUATED HIGH SCHOOL	32853	3093	51.4	9.4	121	1843	43.8	5.6	103	1979	44.8	6.0	106	1665	41.9	5.1	99
DID NOT GRADUATE HIGH SCHOOL	22527	1552	25.8	6.9	89	789	18.7	3.5	64	1215	27.5	5.4	95	1122	28.3	5.0	97
EMPLOYED	37446	3008	50.0	8.0	104	2302	54.7	6.1	113	2029	45.9	5.4	95	1886	47.5	5.0	98
EMPLOYED FULL-TIME	29717	2270	37.7	7.6	98	1484	35.3	5.0	92	1495	33.8	5.0	88	1379	34.7	4.6	91
EMPLOYED PART-TIME	7729	738	12.3	9.5	123	818	19.4	10.6	195	•533	12.1	6.9	121	•507	12.8	6.6	128
NOT EMPLOYED	40060	3006	50.0	7.5	97	1907	45.3	4.8	88	2388	54.1	6.0	105	2084	52.5	5.2	102
PROFESSIONAL/MANAGER	10614	•640	10.6	6.0	78	562	13.4	5.3	98	501	11.3	4.7	83	•462	11.6	4.4	85
CLERICAL/SALES	14780	1227	20.4	8.3	107	1038	24.7	7.0	129	922	20.9	6.2	109	850	21.4	5.8	112
CRAFTSMEN/FOREMEN	824	••108	1.8	13.1	169	••85	2.0	10.3	190	••61	1.4	7.4	130	••53	1.3	6.4	126
OTHER EMPLOYED	11229	1032	17.2	9.2	118	617	14.7	5.5	101	545	12.3	4.9	85	•521	13.1	4.6	91
SINGLE	8267	626	10.4	7.6	98	522	12.4	6.3	116	423	9.6	5.1	90	•313	7.9	3.8	74
MARRIED	50768	4088	68.0	8.1	104	3138	74.6	6.2	114	2961	67.0	5.8	102	2649	66.7	5.2	102
DIVORCED/SEPARATED/WIDOWED	18471	1299	21.6	7.0	91	549	13.0	3.0	55	1033	23.4	5.6	98	1008	25.4	5.5	107
PARENTS	31500	4286	71.3	13.6	175	2630	62.5	8.3	154	1956	44.3	6.2	109	1588	40.0	5.0	98
WHITE	67876	5244	87.2	7.7	100	3925	93.3	5.8	106	4071	92.2	6.0	105	3684	92.8	5.4	106
BLACK	8235	700	11.6	8.5	110	•185	4.4	2.2	41	•296	6.7	3.6	63	•250	6.3	3.0	59
OTHER	1395	••70	1.2	5.0	65	••99	2.4	7.1	131	••50	1.1	3.6	63	••37	0.9	2.7	52
NORTHEAST-CENSUS	16922	1342	22.3	7.9	102	1130	26.8	6.7	123	1493	33.8	8.8	155	950	23.9	5.6	110
NORTH CENTRAL	20200	2051	34.1	10.2	131	1227	29.2	6.1	112	1393	31.5	6.9	121	1533	38.6	7.6	148
SOUTH	26132	1805	30.0	6.9	89	1124	26.7	4.3	79	763	17.3	2.9	51	696	17.5	2.7	52
WEST	14252	816	13.6	5.7	74	729	17.3	5.1	94	768	17.4	5.4	95	792	19.9	5.6	108
NORTHEAST-MKTG.	17524	1440	23.9	8.2	106	1192	28.3	6.8	125	1454	32.9	8.3	146	879	22.1	5.0	98
EAST CENTRAL	11814	1204	20.0	10.2	131	710	16.9	6.0	111	913	20.7	7.7	136	972	24.5	8.2	161
WEST CENTRAL	13479	1236	20.6	9.2	118	932	22.1	6.9	127	912	20.6	6.8	119	1031	26.0	7.6	149
SOUTH	22875	1542	25.6	6.7	87	899	21.4	3.9	72	551	12.5	2.4	42	•567	14.3	2.5	48
PACIFIC	11814	593	9.9	5.0	65	•477	11.3	4.0	74	586	13.3	5.0	87	•521	13.1	4.4	86
COUNTY SIZE A	31229	2468	41.0	7.9	102	1729	41.1	5.5	102	1917	43.4	6.1	108	1417	35.7	4.5	89
COUNTY SIZE B	23352	1792	29.8	7.7	99	1497	35.6	6.4	118	1213	27.5	5.2	91	1141	28.7	4.9	95
COUNTY SIZE C	12137	1026	17.1	8.5	109	•715	17.0	5.9	108	782	17.7	6.4	113	815	20.5	6.7	131
COUNTY SIZE D	10789	728	12.1	6.7	87	•268	6.4	2.5	46	505	11.4	4.7	82	597	15.0	5.5	108
METRO CENTRAL CITY	23359	1737	28.9	7.4	96	1220	29.0	5.2	96	1040	23.5	4.5	78	863	21.7	3.7	72
METRO SUBURBAN	34657	2799	46.5	8.1	104	2132	50.7	6.2	113	2296	52.0	6.6	116	2083	52.5	6.0	117
NON METRO	19491	1478	24.6	7.6	98	857	20.4	4.4	81	1080	24.5	5.5	97	1024	25.8	5.3	103
TOP 5 ADI'S	17725	1293	21.5	7.3	94	1055	25.1	6.0	110	1183	26.8	6.7	117	696	17.5	3.9	77
TOP 10 ADI'S	25079	2096	34.9	8.4	108	1556	37.0	6.2	114	1608	36.4	6.4	113	1114	28.1	4.4	87
TOP 20 ADI'S	35085	2839	47.2	8.1	104	1941	46.1	5.5	102	2143	48.5	6.1	107	1549	39.0	4.4	86
HSHLD INC. $40,000 OR MORE	8818	•646	10.7	7.3	94	627	14.9	7.1	131	•505	11.4	5.7	100	•459	11.6	5.2	102
$30,000 OR MORE	18653	1521	25.3	8.2	105	1153	27.4	6.2	114	1122	25.4	6.0	106	1050	26.4	5.6	110
$25,000 OR MORE	25911	2178	36.2	8.4	108	1537	36.5	5.9	109	1514	34.3	5.8	103	1366	34.4	5.3	103
$20,000 - $24,999	9349	787	13.1	8.4	108	848	20.1	9.1	167	•528	12.0	5.6	99	•508	12.8	5.4	106
$15,000 - $19,999	8862	869	14.4	9.8	126	620	14.7	7.0	129	•397	9.0	4.5	79	•515	13.0	5.8	113
$10,000 - $14,999	13844	1138	18.9	8.2	106	545	12.9	3.9	72	836	18.9	6.0	106	600	15.1	4.3	85
UNDER $10,000	19541	1041	17.3	5.3	69	659	15.7	3.4	62	1141	25.8	5.8	102	981	24.7	5.0	98
HOUSEHOLD OF 1 PERSON	11894	•178	3.0	1.5	19	375	8.9	3.2	58	604	13.7	5.1	89	510	12.8	4.3	84
2 PEOPLE	25454	949	15.8	3.7	48	791	18.8	3.1	57	1355	30.7	5.3	93	1211	30.5	4.8	93
3 OR 4 PEOPLE	28521	2756	45.8	9.7	125	1964	46.7	6.9	127	1521	34.4	5.3	94	1656	41.7	5.8	113
5 OR MORE PEOPLE	11637	2132	35.5	18.3	236	1080	25.7	9.3	171	937	21.2	8.1	141	•594	15.0	5.1	100
NO CHILD IN HSHLD	43986	1396	23.2	3.2	41	1425	33.9	3.2	60	2353	53.3	5.3	94	2314	58.3	5.3	103
CHILD(REN) UNDER 2 YRS	5651	691	11.5	12.2	158	•583	13.9	10.3	190	•418	9.5	7.4	130	••295	7.4	5.2	102
2 - 5 YEARS	12521	1691	28.1	13.5	174	1133	26.9	9.0	167	893	20.2	7.1	125	725	18.3	5.8	113
6 - 11 YEARS	15766	2572	42.8	16.3	210	1436	34.1	9.1	168	962	21.8	6.1	107	757	19.1	4.8	94
12 - 17 YEARS	16144	2376	39.5	14.7	190	1252	29.7	7.8	143	910	20.6	5.6	99	798	20.1	4.9	97
RESIDENCE OWNED	55460	4079	67.8	7.4	95	3048	72.4	5.5	101	3282	74.3	5.9	104	3251	81.9	5.9	114
VALUE: $50,000 OR MORE	28563	2154	35.8	7.5	97	1768	42.0	6.2	114	1574	35.6	5.5	97	1511	38.1	5.3	103
VALUE: UNDER $50,000	26897	1924	32.0	7.2	92	1281	30.4	4.8	88	1708	38.7	6.4	111	1740	43.8	6.5	126

Table 12-13.　(continued)

BREAKFAST CEREALS (COLD): BRANDS
(FEMALE HOMEMAKERS)

	TOTAL U.S. '000	QUAKER CAP'N CRUNCH A '000	B % DOWN	C % ACROSS	D INDX	QUAKER LIFE A '000	B % DOWN	C % ACROSS	D INDX	QUAKER PUFFED RICE A '000	B % DOWN	C % ACROSS	D INDX	QUAKER PUFFED WHEAT A '000	B % DOWN	C % ACROSS	D INDX
TOTAL FEMALE HOMEMAKERS	77506	6014	100.0	7.8	100	4209	100.0	5.4	100	4417	100.0	5.7	100	3970	100.0	5.1	100
MAGAZINES																	
QUINTILE 1	14450	1048	17.4	7.3	93	938	22.3	6.5	120	1063	24.1	7.4	129	796	20.1	5.5	108
QUINTILE 2	17861	1486	24.7	8.3	107	792	18.8	4.4	82	1261	28.5	7.1	124	974	24.5	5.5	106
QUINTILE 3	15911	1459	24.3	9.2	118	952	22.6	6.0	110	815	18.5	5.1	90	744	18.7	4.7	91
QUINTILE 4	17318	1311	21.8	7.6	98	1034	24.6	6.0	110	799	18.1	4.6	81	958	24.1	5.5	108
QUINTILE 5	11967	710	11.8	5.9	76	*494	11.7	4.1	76	479	10.8	4.0	70	499	12.6	4.2	81
NEWSPAPERS																	
QUINTILE 1	12468	1020	17.0	8.2	105	823	19.6	6.6	122	984	22.3	7.9	138	699	17.6	5.6	109
QUINTILE 2	23121	1983	33.0	8.6	111	1214	28.8	5.3	97	1514	34.3	6.5	115	1292	32.5	5.6	109
QUINTILE 3	11493	797	13.3	6.9	89	670	15.9	5.8	107	*516	11.7	4.5	79	533	13.4	4.6	91
QUINTILE 4	13169	813	13.5	6.2	80	613	14.6	4.7	86	642	14.5	4.9	86	678	17.1	5.1	101
QUINTILE 5	17255	1401	23.3	8.1	105	889	21.1	5.2	95	762	17.3	4.4	77	768	19.3	4.5	87
OUTDOOR																	
QUINTILE 1	14564	1447	24.1	9.9	128	955	22.7	6.6	121	914	20.7	6.3	110	852	21.5	5.9	114
QUINTILE 2	15716	1312	21.8	8.3	108	1071	25.4	6.8	125	1051	23.8	6.7	117	828	20.9	5.3	103
QUINTILE 3	17253	1317	21.9	7.6	98	887	21.1	5.1	95	945	21.4	5.5	96	1057	26.6	6.1	120
QUINTILE 4	17084	1279	21.3	7.5	96	829	19.7	4.9	89	843	19.1	4.9	87	684	17.2	4.0	78
QUINTILE 5	12888	660	11.0	5.1	66	*468	11.1	3.6	67	664	15.0	5.2	90	549	13.8	4.3	83
RADIO-DRIVE TIME																	
QUINTILE 1	14947	1215	20.2	8.1	105	821	19.5	5.5	101	813	18.4	5.4	95	688	17.3	4.6	90
QUINTILE 2	16214	1403	23.3	8.7	112	946	22.5	5.8	107	981	22.2	6.1	106	747	18.8	4.6	90
QUINTILE 3	13989	984	16.4	7.0	91	871	20.7	6.2	115	789	17.9	5.6	99	748	18.8	5.3	104
QUINTILE 4	16905	1330	22.1	7.9	101	898	21.3	5.3	98	928	21.0	5.5	96	873	22.0	5.2	101
QUINTILE 5	15452	1082	18.0	7.0	90	673	16.0	4.4	80	906	20.5	5.9	103	914	23.0	5.9	115
RADIO-MID-DAY																	
TERCILE 1	20499	1775	29.5	8.7	112	1279	30.4	6.2	115	1245	28.2	6.1	107	1128	28.4	5.5	107
TERCILE 2	20662	1794	29.8	8.7	112	1240	29.5	6.0	111	1084	24.5	5.2	92	929	23.4	4.5	88
TERCILE 3	36346	2445	40.7	6.7	87	1690	40.2	4.6	86	2088	47.3	5.7	101	1913	48.2	5.3	103
RADIO-TOTAL																	
QUINTILE 1	14968	1390	23.1	9.3	120	865	20.6	5.8	106	801	18.1	5.4	94	769	19.4	5.1	100
QUINTILE 2	15619	1147	19.1	7.3	95	1019	24.2	6.5	120	928	21.0	5.9	104	658	16.6	4.2	82
QUINTILE 3	15270	1146	19.1	7.5	97	839	19.9	5.5	101	982	22.2	6.4	113	885	22.3	5.8	113
QUINTILE 4	16444	1353	22.5	8.2	106	873	20.7	5.3	98	835	18.9	5.1	89	833	21.0	5.1	99
QUINTILE 5	15205	978	16.3	6.4	83	613	14.6	4.0	74	871	19.7	5.7	101	826	20.8	5.4	106
TV-PRIME TIME																	
QUINTILE 1	15300	1006	16.7	6.6	85	599	14.2	3.9	72	940	21.3	6.1	108	725	18.3	4.7	93
QUINTILE 2	15998	1381	23.0	8.6	111	969	23.0	6.1	112	932	21.1	5.8	102	861	21.7	5.4	105
QUINTILE 3	15302	1198	19.9	7.8	101	861	20.5	5.6	104	894	20.2	5.8	103	748	18.8	4.9	95
QUINTILE 4	15556	1124	18.7	7.2	93	941	22.4	6.0	111	998	22.6	6.4	113	826	20.8	5.3	104
QUINTILE 5	15350	1306	21.7	8.5	110	838	19.9	5.5	101	652	14.8	4.2	75	810	20.4	5.3	103
TV-DAYTIME																	
TERCILE 1	25639	1957	32.5	7.6	98	1287	30.6	5.0	92	1715	38.8	6.7	117	1497	37.7	5.8	114
TERCILE 2	25556	2088	34.7	8.2	105	1664	39.5	6.5	120	1132	25.6	4.4	78	1083	27.3	4.2	83
TERCILE 3	26311	1969	32.7	7.5	96	1259	29.9	4.8	88	1570	35.5	6.0	105	1391	35.0	5.3	103
TV-TOTAL																	
QUINTILE 1	15533	1216	20.2	7.8	101	674	16.0	4.3	80	943	21.3	6.1	107	707	17.8	4.6	89
QUINTILE 2	15660	1053	17.5	6.7	87	753	17.9	4.8	89	904	20.5	5.8	101	792	19.9	5.1	99
QUINTILE 3	15513	1098	18.3	7.1	91	933	22.2	6.0	111	958	21.7	6.2	108	944	23.8	6.1	119
QUINTILE 4	15787	1194	19.9	7.6	97	1003	23.8	6.4	117	888	20.1	5.6	99	826	20.8	5.2	102
QUINTILE 5	15014	1453	24.2	9.7	125	845	20.1	5.6	104	723	16.4	4.8	84	701	17.7	4.7	91
MAGAZINES-NEWSPAPERS: DUAL	20558	1579	26.3	7.7	99	1096	26.0	5.3	98	1551	35.1	7.5	132	1056	26.6	5.1	100
MAGAZINE IMPERATIVE	20063	1580	26.3	7.9	101	1057	25.1	5.3	97	1065	24.1	5.3	93	966	24.3	4.8	94
NEWSPAPER IMPERATIVE	21681	1812	30.1	8.4	108	1391	33.0	6.4	118	1263	28.6	5.8	102	1228	30.9	5.7	111
MAGAZINES-OUTDOOR: DUAL	17015	1507	25.1	8.9	114	1004	23.9	5.9	109	1241	28.1	7.3	128	890	22.4	5.2	102
MAGAZINE IMPERATIVE	25016	1828	30.4	7.3	94	1195	28.4	4.8	88	1569	35.5	6.3	110	1294	32.6	5.2	101
OUTDOOR IMPERATIVE	23031	1977	32.9	8.6	111	1508	35.8	6.5	121	1134	25.7	4.9	86	1340	33.8	5.8	114
MAGAZINES-RADIO: DUAL	16347	1349	22.4	8.3	106	901	21.4	5.5	101	919	20.8	5.6	99	794	20.0	4.9	95
MAGAZINE IMPERATIVE	25186	2008	33.4	8.0	103	1271	30.2	5.0	93	1812	41.0	7.2	126	1357	34.2	5.4	105
RADIO IMPERATIVE	22493	1770	29.4	7.9	101	1422	33.8	6.3	116	1201	27.2	5.3	94	1056	26.6	4.7	92
MAGAZINES-TELEVISION: DUAL	15880	1153	19.2	7.3	94	876	20.8	5.5	102	1058	24.0	6.7	117	823	20.7	5.2	101
MAGAZINE IMPERATIVE	26737	2325	38.7	8.7	112	1553	36.9	5.8	107	1823	41.3	6.8	120	1415	35.6	5.3	103
TELEVISION IMPERATIVE	24463	1711	28.5	7.0	90	1187	28.2	4.9	89	1174	26.6	4.8	84	1228	30.9	5.0	98
NEWSPAPERS-OUTDOOR: DUAL	16208	1477	24.6	9.1	117	957	22.7	5.9	109	1142	25.9	7.0	124	929	23.4	5.7	112
NEWSPAPER IMPERATIVE	26117	1870	31.1	7.2	92	1383	32.9	5.3	98	1621	36.7	6.2	109	1331	33.5	5.1	99
OUTDOOR IMPERATIVE	23098	1871	31.1	8.1	104	1452	34.5	6.3	116	1173	26.6	5.1	89	1293	32.6	5.6	109
NEWSPAPERS-RADIO: DUAL	16533	1406	23.4	8.5	110	1240	29.5	7.5	138	1048	23.7	6.3	111	820	20.7	5.0	97
NEWSPAPER IMPERATIVE	26132	2061	34.3	7.9	102	1275	30.3	4.9	90	1729	39.1	6.6	116	1506	37.9	5.8	113
RADIO IMPERATIVE	22172	1747	29.0	7.9	102	1159	27.5	5.2	96	1138	25.8	5.1	90	1104	27.8	5.0	97
NEWSPAPERS-TELEVISION: DUAL	16544	1384	23.0	8.4	108	949	22.5	5.7	106	1054	23.9	6.4	112	867	21.8	5.2	102
NEWSPAPER IMPERATIVE	25715	2186	36.3	8.5	109	1517	36.0	5.9	109	1713	38.8	6.7	117	1391	35.0	5.4	106
TELEVISION IMPERATIVE	22566	1416	23.5	6.3	81	922	21.9	4.1	75	1137	25.7	5.0	88	1107	27.9	4.9	96
OUTDOOR-RADIO: DUAL	15950	1398	23.2	8.8	113	1163	27.6	7.3	134	1028	23.3	6.4	113	896	22.6	5.6	110
OUTDOOR IMPERATIVE	24960	2082	34.6	8.3	107	1423	33.8	5.7	105	1500	34.0	6.0	117	1497	37.7	6.0	117
RADIO IMPERATIVE	24159	1840	30.6	7.6	98	1210	28.7	5.0	92	1289	29.2	5.3	94	1093	27.5	4.5	88
OUTDOOR-TELEVISION: DUAL	14262	1240	20.6	8.7	112	846	20.1	5.9	109	834	18.9	5.8	103	831	20.9	5.8	114
OUTDOOR IMPERATIVE	26094	2316	38.5	8.9	114	1767	42.0	6.8	125	1685	38.1	6.5	113	1536	38.7	5.9	115
TELEVISION IMPERATIVE	26419	1658	27.6	6.3	81	1180	28.0	4.5	82	1491	33.8	5.6	99	1286	32.4	4.9	95
RADIO-TELEVISION: DUAL	14718	1095	18.2	7.4	96	766	18.2	5.2	96	793	18.0	5.4	95	566	14.3	3.8	75
RADIO IMPERATIVE	25164	2150	35.7	8.5	110	1636	38.9	6.5	120	1510	34.2	6.0	105	1403	35.3	5.6	109
TELEVISION IMPERATIVE	25828	1708	28.4	6.6	85	1094	26.0	4.2	78	1582	35.8	6.1	107	1449	36.5	5.6	110

0098
P-20

BREAKFAST CEREALS (COLD): BRANDS
(FEMALE HOMEMAKERS)

0098
P-20

	TOTAL U.S. '000	QUAKER CAP'N CRUNCH A '000	B DOWN	C ACROSS %	D INDX	QUAKER LIFE A '000	B DOWN	C ACROSS %	D INDX	QUAKER PUFFED RICE A '000	B DOWN	C ACROSS %	D INDX	QUAKER PUFFED WHEAT A '000	B DOWN	C ACROSS %	D INDX
TOTAL FEMALE HOMEMAKERS	77506	6014	100.0	7.8	100	4209	100.0	5.4	100	4417	100.0	5.7	100	3970	100.0	5.1	100
BARRON'S	•186	••33	0.5	17.7	229	••31	0.7	16.7	307	••1	0.0	0.5	9	••18	0.5	9.7	189
BETTER HOMES & GARDENS	14982	1240	20.6	8.3	107	866	20.6	5.8	106	1092	24.7	7.3	128	864	21.8	5.8	113
BON APPETIT	2027	••116	1.9	5.7	74	•218	5.2	10.8	198	•133	3.0	6.6	115	•128	3.2	6.3	123
BUSINESS WEEK	882	••39	0.6	4.4	57	••89	2.1	10.1	186	••47	1.1	5.3	94	••14	0.4	1.6	31
CAR AND DRIVER	•287	••71	1.2	24.7	319	••30	0.7	10.5	192	••13	0.3	4.5	79	••13	0.3	4.5	88
CBS MAGAZINE NETWORK (GROSS)	1005	••48	0.8	4.8	62	••52	1.2	5.2	95	••120	2.7	11.9	210	••89	2.2	8.9	173
CHANGING TIMES	1078	••54	0.9	5.0	65	••105	2.5	9.7	179	••74	1.7	6.9	120	••66	1.7	6.1	120
CONDE NAST MAG. PKG. (GROSS)	11194	870	11.1	6.0	77	634	15.1	5.7	104	579	13.1	5.2	91	553	13.9	4.9	96
COSMOPOLITAN	6485	579	9.6	8.9	115	325	7.7	5.0	92	366	8.3	5.6	99	234	5.9	3.6	70
COUNTRY LIVING	1190	••89	1.5	7.5	96	••65	1.5	5.5	101	••73	1.7	6.1	108	••71	1.8	6.0	116
CUISINE	1112	••83	1.4	7.5	96	••50	1.2	4.5	83	••59	1.3	5.3	93	••63	1.6	5.7	111
CYCLE WORLD	•260	••14	0.2	5.4	69	••0	0.0	0.0	0	••26	0.6	10.0	175	••3	0.1	1.2	23
DECORATING & CRAFT IDEAS	2036	•172	2.9	8.4	109	•171	4.1	8.4	155	•280	6.3	13.8	241	•246	6.2	12.1	236
DEC CRFT ID/SOUTH LIV(GROSS)	5461	321	5.3	5.9	76	373	8.9	6.8	126	348	7.9	6.4	112	342	8.6	6.3	122
DISCOVER	505	••18	0.3	3.6	46	••10	0.2	2.0	36	••32	0.7	6.3	111	••8	0.2	1.6	31
EBONY	3092	322	5.4	10.4	134	••97	2.3	3.1	58	•154	3.5	5.0	87	••114	2.9	3.7	72
ESQUIRE	663	••29	0.5	4.4	56	••82	1.9	12.4	228	••38	0.9	5.7	101	••41	1.0	6.2	121
ESSENCE	1399	••95	1.6	6.8	88	••45	1.1	3.2	59	••57	1.3	4.1	71	••38	1.0	2.7	53
FAMILY CIRCLE	14658	1189	19.8	8.1	105	827	19.6	5.6	104	1089	24.7	7.4	130	877	22.1	6.0	117
THE FAMILY HANDYMAN	918	••103	1.7	11.2	145	••140	3.3	15.3	281	••81	1.8	8.8	155	••51	1.3	5.6	108
FAMILY WEEKLY	12554	1087	18.1	8.7	112	754	17.9	6.0	111	767	17.4	6.1	107	670	16.9	5.3	104
FIELD & STREAM	1562	••109	1.8	7.0	90	••115	2.7	7.4	136	••162	3.7	10.4	182	••145	3.7	9.3	181
FORBES	489	••40	0.7	8.2	105	••20	0.5	4.1	75	••22	0.5	4.5	79	••14	0.4	2.9	56
FORTUNE	625	••0	0.0	0.0	0	••19	0.5	3.0	56	••19	0.4	3.0	53	••8	0.2	1.3	25
GENTLEMEN'S QUARTERLY	421	••34	0.6	8.1	104	••7	0.2	1.7	31	••7	0.2	1.7	29	••7	0.2	1.7	32
GLAMOUR	4136	231	3.8	5.6	72	•236	5.6	5.7	105	•219	5.0	5.3	93	•226	5.7	5.5	107
GOLF DIGEST	627	••21	0.3	3.3	43	••68	1.6	10.8	200	••43	1.0	6.9	120	••36	0.9	5.7	112
GOLF DIGEST/TENNIS (GROSS)	1023	••35	0.6	3.4	44	••131	3.1	12.8	236	••54	1.2	5.3	93	••47	1.2	4.6	90
GOLF MAGAZINE	368	••23	0.4	6.3	81	••14	0.3	3.8	70	••26	0.6	7.1	124	••21	0.5	5.7	111
GOLF MAGAZINE/SKI (GROSS)	701	••35	0.6	5.0	64	••19	0.5	2.7	50	••56	1.3	8.0	140	••35	0.9	5.0	97
GOOD HOUSEKEEPING	14160	1123	18.7	7.9	102	731	17.4	5.2	95	926	21.0	6.5	115	770	19.4	5.4	106
HARPER'S BAZAAR	2244	••83	1.4	3.7	48	••114	2.7	5.1	94	•163	3.7	7.3	127	••72	1.8	3.2	63
HEALTH	1499	••91	1.5	6.1	78	••67	1.6	4.5	82	••94	2.1	6.3	110	••58	1.5	3.9	76
HEARST MAG CORP. BUY (GROSS)	36944	2818	46.9	7.6	98	1971	46.8	5.3	98	2347	53.1	6.4	111	1768	44.5	4.8	93
HEARST MEN'S PACKAGE (GROSS)	1771	••107	1.8	6.0	78	••77	1.8	4.3	80	•155	3.5	8.8	154	••98	2.5	5.5	108
HOUSE BEAUTIFUL	3321	•184	3.1	5.5	71	•246	5.8	7.4	136	•189	4.3	5.7	100	•155	3.9	4.7	91
INDUSTRY WEEK	••65	••0	0.0	0.0	0	••0	0.0	0.0	0	••14	0.3	21.5	378	••6	0.2	9.2	180
INSIDE SPORTS	•213	••23	0.4	10.8	139	••23	0.5	10.8	199	••4	0.1	1.9	33	••3	0.1	1.4	27
JET	2540	229	3.8	9.0	116	••61	1.4	2.4	44	•112	2.5	4.4	77	••96	2.4	3.8	74
LADIES' HOME JOURNAL	11577	822	13.7	7.1	92	513	12.2	4.4	82	762	17.3	6.6	115	613	15.4	5.3	103
LHJ FAMILY GRP COMBO (GROSS)	15051	1190	19.8	7.9	102	774	18.4	5.1	95	912	20.6	6.1	106	728	18.3	4.8	94
LIFE	3934	271	4.5	6.9	89	•247	5.9	6.3	116	•234	5.3	5.9	104	•191	4.8	4.9	95
L.A. TIMES HOME MAGAZINE	1253	••35	0.6	2.8	36	••72	1.7	5.7	106	••71	1.6	5.7	99	••78	2.0	6.2	122
MADEMOISELLE	2385	•190	3.2	8.0	103	•125	3.0	5.2	97	•117	2.6	4.9	86	••100	2.5	4.2	82
MC CALL'S	12042	947	15.7	7.9	101	693	16.5	5.8	106	873	19.8	7.2	127	659	16.6	5.5	107
MECHANIX ILLUSTRATED	697	••98	1.6	14.1	181	••39	0.9	5.6	103	••51	1.2	7.3	128	••31	0.8	4.4	87
METROPOLITAN HOME	642	••32	0.5	5.0	64	••85	2.0	13.2	244	••27	0.6	4.2	74	••14	0.4	2.2	43
MONEY	1369	••91	1.5	6.6	86	••82	1.9	6.0	110	••80	1.8	5.8	103	••57	1.4	4.2	81
MONTHLY MAG OF FOOD & WINE	310	••10	0.2	3.2	42	••5	0.1	1.6	30	••14	0.3	4.5	79	••8	0.2	2.6	50
MS.	999	••68	1.1	6.8	88	••47	1.1	4.7	87	••49	1.1	4.9	86	••45	1.1	4.5	88
NATIONAL ENQUIRER	8699	907	15.1	10.4	134	486	11.5	5.6	103	767	17.4	8.8	155	599	15.1	6.9	134
NATIONAL GEOGRAPHIC	8895	537	8.9	6.0	78	538	12.8	6.0	111	637	14.4	7.2	126	530	13.4	6.0	116
NATIONAL SUPPLEMENT PACKAGE	46099	3650	60.7	7.9	102	2756	65.5	6.0	110	2912	65.9	6.3	111	2582	65.0	5.6	109
NATURAL HISTORY	557	••64	1.1	11.5	148	••11	0.3	2.0	36	••22	0.5	3.9	69	••27	0.7	4.8	95
NEWSWEEK	5803	439	7.3	7.6	97	385	9.1	6.6	122	400	9.1	6.9	121	310	7.8	5.3	104
NEW YORK INCLUDING CUE	517	••47	0.8	9.1	117	••12	0.3	2.3	43	••57	1.3	11.0	193	••45	1.1	8.7	170
THE N.Y. TIMES DAILY EDITION	1226	••82	1.4	6.7	86	••34	0.8	2.8	51	••96	2.2	7.8	137	••52	1.3	4.2	83
THE N.Y. TIMES MAGAZINE	1725	••116	1.9	6.7	87	••78	1.9	4.5	83	•135	3.1	7.8	137	••80	2.0	4.6	91
THE NEW YORKER	997	••46	0.8	4.6	59	••30	0.7	3.0	55	••81	1.8	8.1	143	••48	1.2	4.8	94
OMNI	945	••44	0.7	4.7	60	••38	0.9	4.0	74	••56	1.3	5.9	104	••32	0.8	3.4	66
1001 HOME IDEAS	1975	•277	4.6	14.0	181	•194	4.6	9.8	181	••56	1.3	2.8	50	••57	1.4	2.9	56
ORGANIC GARDENING	1561	•141	2.3	9.0	116	••64	1.5	4.1	75	••70	1.6	4.5	79	••94	2.3	6.0	116
OUI	•193	••24	0.4	12.4	160	••8	0.2	4.1	76	••16	0.4	8.3	145	••10	0.3	5.2	101
OUTDOOR LIFE	1013	••39	0.6	3.8	50	••32	0.8	3.2	58	••68	1.5	6.7	118	••64	1.6	6.3	123
PARADE	20439	1536	25.5	7.5	97	1236	29.4	6.0	111	1417	32.1	6.9	122	1257	31.7	6.2	120

Table 12-13.   (continued)

BREAKFAST CEREALS (COLD): BRANDS
(FEMALE HOMEMAKERS)

	TOTAL U.S. '000	QUAKER CAP'N CRUNCH A '000	B DOWN	C % ACROSS	D INDX	QUAKER LIFE A '000	B DOWN	C % ACROSS	D INDX	QUAKER PUFFED RICE A '000	B DOWN	C % ACROSS	D INDX	QUAKER PUFFED WHEAT A '000	B DOWN	C % ACROSS	D INDX
TOTAL FEMALE HOMEMAKERS	77506	6014	100.0	7.8	100	4209	100.0	5.4	100	4417	100.0	5.7	100	3970	100.0	5.1	100
PARENTS	2831	338	5.6	11.9	154	•264	6.3	9.3	172	•227	5.1	8.0	141	•194	4.9	6.9	134
PENTHOUSE	1031	••87	1.4	8.4	109	••62	1.5	6.0	111	••95	2.2	9.2	162	••58	1.5	5.6	110
PEOPLE	10610	912	15.2	8.6	111	653	15.5	6.2	113	732	16.6	6.9	121	560	14.1	5.3	103
PLAYBOY	1829	••114	1.9	6.2	80	••173	4.1	9.5	174	••188	4.3	10.3	180	••109	2.7	6.0	116
POPULAR HOT RODDING	•176	••11	0.2	6.3	81	••5	0.1	2.8	52	••26	0.6	14.8	259	••0	0.0	0.0	0
POPULAR MECHANICS	876	••80	1.3	9.1	118	••56	1.3	6.4	118	••71	1.6	8.1	142	••52	1.3	5.9	116
POPULAR SCIENCE	627	••85	1.4	13.6	175	••89	2.1	14.2	261	••48	1.1	7.7	134	••28	0.7	4.5	87
PREVENTION	2932	•144	2.4	4.9	63	•121	2.9	4.1	76	•170	3.8	5.8	102	•192	4.8	6.5	128
PSYCHOLOGY TODAY				AUDIENCE DATA NOT SHOWN BECAUSE OF CHANGE IN RATE BASE CIRCULATION													
READER'S DIGEST	20834	1658	27.6	8.0	103	1076	25.6	5.2	95	1279	29.0	6.1	108	1275	32.1	6.1	119
REDBOOK	6928	629	10.5	9.1	117	373	8.9	5.4	99	413	9.4	6.0	105	342	8.6	4.9	96
ROAD & TRACK	•188	••15	0.2	8.0	103	••34	0.8	18.1	333	••32	0.7	17.0	299	••7	0.2	3.7	73
ROLLING STONE	848	••113	1.9	13.3	172	••42	1.0	5.0	91	••86	1.9	10.1	178	••45	1.1	5.3	104
RUNNER'S WORLD	297	••19	0.3	6.4	82	••26	0.6	8.8	161	••0	0.0	0.0	0	••0	0.0	0.0	0
SATURDAY EVENING POST	1248	••97	1.6	7.8	100	••66	1.6	5.3	97	••109	2.5	8.7	153	••74	1.9	5.9	116
SCIENCE DIGEST	426	••27	0.4	6.3	82	••21	0.5	4.9	91	••58	1.3	13.6	239	••26	0.7	6.1	119
SCIENCE 82	521	••51	0.8	9.8	126	••7	0.2	1.3	25	••55	1.2	10.6	185	••65	1.6	12.5	244
SCIENTIFIC AMERICAN	368	••19	0.3	5.2	67	••14	0.3	3.8	70	••12	0.3	3.3	57	••17	0.4	4.6	90
SELF	1435	••67	1.1	4.7	60	••78	1.9	5.4	100	••72	1.6	5.0	88	••79	2.0	5.5	107
SEVENTEEN	1814	••169	2.8	9.3	120	••62	1.5	3.4	63	••44	1.0	2.4	43	••33	0.8	1.8	36
SKI	333	••12	0.2	3.6	46	••5	0.1	1.5	28	••30	0.7	9.0	158	••14	0.4	4.2	82
SMITHSONIAN	2149	•105	1.7	4.9	63	••108	2.6	5.0	93	•149	3.4	6.9	122	••101	2.5	4.7	92
SOAP OPERA DIGEST	2599	•237	3.9	9.1	118	••141	3.3	5.4	100	••176	4.0	6.8	119	••87	2.2	3.3	65
SOUTHERN LIVING	3424	•148	2.5	4.3	56	•202	4.8	5.9	109	••68	1.5	2.0	35	••97	2.4	2.8	55
SPORT	477	••91	1.5	19.1	246	••19	0.5	4.0	73	••44	1.0	9.2	162	••10	0.3	2.1	41
THE SPORTING NEWS	•226	••15	0.2	6.6	86	••4	0.1	1.8	33	••13	0.3	5.8	101	••6	0.2	2.7	52
SPORTS AFIELD	469	••1	0.0	0.2	3	••0	0.0	0.0	0	••25	0.6	5.3	94	••20	0.5	4.3	83
SPORTS ILLUSTRATED	2106	••167	2.8	7.9	102	••159	3.8	7.5	139	••168	3.8	8.0	140	••81	2.0	3.8	75
STAR	5900	536	8.9	9.1	117	269	6.4	4.6	84	635	14.4	10.8	189	468	11.8	7.9	155
SUNDAY	21600	1871	31.1	8.7	112	1312	31.2	6.1	112	1585	35.9	7.3	129	1331	33.5	6.2	120
SUNSET	2137	••95	1.6	4.4	57	••89	2.1	4.2	77	•181	4.1	8.5	149	••127	3.2	5.9	116
TENNIS	396	••14	0.2	3.5	46	••63	1.5	15.9	293	••11	0.2	2.8	49	••11	0.3	2.8	54
TIME	8036	588	9.8	7.3	94	563	13.4	7.0	129	627	14.2	7.8	137	437	11.0	5.4	106
TOWN & COUNTRY	766	••16	0.3	2.1	27	••38	0.9	5.0	91	••41	0.9	5.4	94	••22	0.6	2.9	56
TRAVEL & LEISURE	872	••42	0.7	4.8	62	••31	0.7	3.6	65	••33	0.7	3.8	66	••45	1.1	5.2	101
TRUE STORY	2894	•233	3.9	8.1	104	••72	1.7	2.5	46	••152	3.4	5.3	92	••91	2.3	3.1	61
TV GUIDE	17478	1512	25.1	8.7	111	1009	24.0	5.8	106	1170	26.5	6.7	117	782	19.7	4.5	87
US	1865	••122	2.0	6.5	84	••194	4.6	10.4	192	••160	3.6	8.6	151	••132	3.3	7.1	138
U.S. NEWS & WORLD REPORT	3094	•214	3.6	6.9	89	•200	4.8	6.5	119	•199	4.5	6.4	113	•148	3.7	4.8	93
VOGUE	3238	•181	3.0	5.6	72	•194	4.6	6.0	110	•172	3.9	5.3	93	•148	3.7	4.6	89
WALL STREET JOURNAL	1916	••86	1.4	4.5	58	••79	1.9	4.1	76	•150	3.4	7.8	137	•107	2.7	5.6	109
WOMAN'S DAY	13991	1198	19.9	8.6	110	809	19.2	5.8	106	982	22.2	7.0	123	916	23.1	6.5	128
WORKING MOTHER	733	••107	1.8	14.6	188	••82	1.9	11.2	206	••30	0.7	4.1	72	••8	0.2	1.1	21
WORKING WOMAN	941	••40	0.7	4.3	55	••50	1.2	5.3	98	••53	1.2	5.6	99	••21	0.5	2.2	44
WORLD TENNIS	209	••3	0.0	1.4	18	••0	0.0	0.0	0	••25	0.6	12.0	210	••33	0.8	15.8	308
ZIFF-DAVIS MAG NETWK (GROSS)	2155	•207	3.4	9.6	124	••125	3.0	5.8	107	••146	3.3	6.8	119	••76	1.9	3.5	69
DAILY NEWSPAPERS																	
READ ANY	51006	3980	66.2	7.8	101	2778	66.0	5.4	100	3220	72.9	6.3	111	2723	68.6	5.3	104
READ ONE	42326	3340	55.5	7.9	102	2249	53.4	5.3	98	2537	57.4	6.0	105	2235	56.3	5.3	103
READ TWO OR MORE	8679	640	10.6	7.4	95	529	12.6	6.1	112	683	15.5	7.9	138	487	12.3	5.6	110
WEEKEND/SUNDAY NEWSPAPERS																	
READ ANY	51231	4044	67.2	7.9	102	2942	69.9	5.7	106	3198	72.4	6.2	110	2785	70.2	5.4	106
READ ONE	45002	3535	58.8	7.9	101	2565	60.9	5.7	105	2659	60.2	5.9	104	2474	62.3	5.5	107
READ TWO OR MORE	6229	509	8.5	8.2	105	376	8.9	6.0	111	540	12.2	8.7	152	311	7.8	5.0	97
OUTDOOR																	
100 SHOWING - 1 DAY GROSS	42314	3892	64.7	9.2	119	2518	59.8	6.0	110	2585	58.5	6.1	107	2504	63.1	5.9	116
30 DAY NET	64618	5354	89.0	8.3	107	3741	88.9	5.8	107	3753	85.0	5.8	102	3421	86.2	5.3	103
50 SHOWING - 1 DAY GROSS	21207	1950	32.4	9.2	119	1264	30.0	6.0	110	1299	29.4	6.1	107	1267	31.9	6.0	117
30 DAY NET	59637	5079	84.5	8.5	110	3553	84.4	6.0	110	3558	80.6	6.0	105	3265	82.2	5.5	107
25 SHOWING - 1 DAY GROSS	10594	977	16.2	9.2	119	629	14.9	5.9	109	648	14.7	6.1	107	630	15.9	5.9	116
30 DAY NET	53098	4541	75.5	8.6	110	3177	75.5	6.0	110	3236	73.3	6.1	107	3032	76.4	5.7	111
CABLE TV: HOME WIRED	21929	1915	31.8	8.7	113	1522	36.2	6.9	128	1453	32.9	6.6	116	1239	31.2	5.7	110
HOME NOT WIRED	55577	4099	68.2	7.4	95	2687	63.8	4.8	89	2964	67.1	5.3	94	2731	68.8	4.9	96
HAVE PAY CABLE	11408	1238	20.6	10.9	140	915	21.7	8.0	148	733	16.6	6.4	113	•497	12.5	4.4	85

0100
P-20

BREAKFAST CEREALS (COLD): BRANDS
(FEMALE HOMEMAKERS)

0100
P-20

	TOTAL U.S.	QUAKER CAP'N CRUNCH				QUAKER LIFE				QUAKER PUFFED RICE				QUAKER PUFFED WHEAT			
	'000	A '000	B % DOWN	C % ACROSS	D INDX	A '000	B % DOWN	C % ACROSS	D INDX	A '000	B % DOWN	C % ACROSS	D INDX	A '000	B % DOWN	C % ACROSS	D INDX
TOTAL FEMALE HOMEMAKERS	77506	6014	100.0	7.8	100	4209	100.0	5.4	100	4417	100.0	5.7	100	3970	100.0	5.1	100
RADIO AVG. DAILY (M-F) CUME																	
6:00 AM - 10:00 AM	42199	3433	57.1	8.1	105	2328	55.3	5.5	102	2391	54.1	5.7	99	2081	52.4	4.9	96
10:00 AM - 3:00 PM	29804	2588	43.0	8.7	112	1840	43.7	6.2	114	1724	39.0	5.8	102	1560	39.3	5.2	102
3:00 PM - 7:00 PM	31338	2623	43.6	8.4	108	1970	46.8	6.3	116	1765	40.0	5.6	99	1583	39.9	5.1	99
7:00 PM - MIDNIGHT	16050	1483	24.7	9.2	119	1071	25.4	6.7	123	963	21.8	6.0	105	983	24.8	6.1	120
MIDNIGHT - 6:00 AM	9729	748	12.4	7.7	99	512	12.2	5.3	97	559	12.7	5.7	101	508	12.8	5.2	102
6:00 AM - MIDNIGHT	56771	4734	78.7	8.3	107	3355	79.7	5.9	109	3253	73.6	5.7	101	2926	73.7	5.2	101
ENTIRE DAY	57438	4766	79.2	8.3	107	3361	79.9	5.9	108	3278	74.2	5.7	100	2957	74.5	5.1	101
AVG DAILY M-F CUME: 6AM-MDNT																	
FORMATS: ADULT CONTEMPORARY	16644	1356	22.5	8.1	105	986	23.4	5.9	109	906	20.5	5.4	96	833	21.0	5.0	98
ALL NEWS	2143	••119	2.0	5.6	72	••115	2.7	5.4	99	•133	3.0	6.2	109	••37	0.9	1.7	34
AOR/PROGRESSIVE	3061	320	5.3	10.5	135	•282	6.7	9.2	170	•200	4.5	6.5	115	••143	3.6	4.7	91
BEAUTIFUL MUSIC	6442	568	9.4	8.8	114	453	10.8	7.0	129	425	9.6	6.6	116	334	8.4	5.2	101
BLACK	3168	267	4.4	8.4	109	•117	2.8	3.7	68	•201	4.6	6.3	111	••143	3.6	4.5	88
CLASSICAL	1353	••153	2.5	11.3	146	••70	1.7	5.2	95	••70	1.6	5.2	91	••61	1.5	4.5	88
CONTEMPORARY	4721	481	8.0	10.2	131	267	6.3	5.7	104	•196	4.4	4.2	73	•296	7.5	6.3	122
COUNTRY	11091	855	14.2	7.7	99	649	15.4	5.9	108	469	10.6	4.2	74	555	14.0	5.0	98
GOLDEN OLDIES	1572	••110	1.8	7.0	90	••78	1.9	5.0	91	••110	2.5	7.0	123	••72	1.8	4.6	89
MIDDLE OF THE ROAD	4977	444	7.4	8.9	115	309	7.3	6.2	114	316	7.2	6.3	111	332	8.4	6.7	130
NEWS/TALK	4382	•222	3.7	5.1	65	•205	4.9	4.7	86	220	5.0	5.0	88	•203	5.1	4.6	90
RELIGIOUS	2210	•258	4.3	11.7	150	•245	5.8	11.1	204	••104	2.4	4.7	83	•137	3.5	6.2	121
SOFT ROCK	1028	••63	1.0	6.1	79	••49	1.2	4.8	88	••59	1.3	5.7	101	••19	0.5	1.8	36
WIRED NETWORKS:																	
ABC CONTEMPORARY	4303	441	7.3	10.2	132	•337	8.0	7.8	144	•341	7.7	7.9	139	•249	6.3	5.8	113
ABC ENTERTAINMENT	4546	374	6.2	8.2	106	•248	5.9	5.5	100	202	4.6	4.4	78	168	4.2	3.7	72
ABC FM	1536	•139	2.3	9.0	117	••101	2.4	6.6	121	••140	3.2	9.1	160	••99	2.5	6.4	126
ABC INFORMATION	5203	386	6.4	7.4	96	258	6.1	5.0	91	298	6.7	5.7	101	337	8.5	6.5	126
CBS	5342	254	4.2	4.8	61	243	5.8	4.5	84	261	5.9	4.9	86	321	8.1	6.0	117
NBC	5044	320	5.3	6.3	82	349	8.3	6.9	127	319	7.2	6.3	111	261	6.6	5.2	101
RKO ONE	3194	328	5.5	10.3	132	•178	4.2	5.6	103	•160	3.6	5.0	88	•162	4.1	5.1	99
THE SOURCE	2366	•257	4.3	10.9	140	•215	5.1	9.1	167	••117	2.6	4.9	87	••99	2.5	4.2	82
NON-WIRED NETWORK:																	
TORBET	6816	607	10.1	8.9	115	559	13.3	8.2	151	546	12.4	8.0	141	420	10.6	6.2	120
TELEVISION AVG. HALF HOUR																	
WKDAY 7:00 AM - 9:00 AM	7578	567	9.4	7.5	96	357	8.5	4.7	87	456	10.3	6.0	106	304	7.7	4.0	78
WKDAY 9:00 AM - 1:00 PM	11656	897	14.9	7.7	99	552	13.1	4.7	87	729	16.5	6.3	110	574	14.5	4.9	96
WKDAY 1:00 PM - 4:30 PM	15625	1303	21.7	8.3	107	744	17.7	4.8	88	917	20.8	5.9	103	769	19.4	4.9	96
WKDAY 4:30 PM - 7:30 PM	20457	1352	22.5	6.6	85	903	21.5	4.4	81	1200	27.2	5.9	103	999	25.2	4.9	95
WKDAY 7:30 PM - 8:00 PM	27889	1912	31.8	6.9	88	1247	29.6	4.5	82	1625	36.8	5.8	102	1370	34.5	4.9	96
WKDAY 11:00 PM - 11:30 PM	24724	1811	30.1	7.3	94	1352	32.1	5.5	101	1479	33.5	6.0	105	1188	29.9	4.8	94
WKDAY 11:30 PM - 1:00 AM	8170	590	9.8	7.2	93	502	11.9	6.1	113	508	11.5	6.2	109	381	9.6	4.7	91
M-SAT 8-11 PM+SUN 7-11 PM	29906	2255	37.5	7.5	97	1535	36.5	5.1	95	1794	40.6	6.0	105	1507	38.0	5.0	98
WKDY DAYTIME NTWK 7AM-4:30PM																	
ALICE M-F C	2093	244	4.1	11.7	150	78	1.9	3.7	69	94	2.1	4.5	79	•93	2.3	4.4	87
ALL MY CHILDREN C	6821	669	11.1	9.8	126	418	9.9	6.1	113	431	9.8	6.3	111	353	8.9	5.2	101
ANOTHER WORLD N	3408	310	5.2	9.1	117	162	3.8	4.8	88	150	3.4	4.4	77	••110	2.8	3.2	63
AS THE WORLD TURNS C	5446	274	4.6	5.0	65	169	4.0	3.1	57	297	6.7	5.5	96	244	6.1	4.5	87
CAPITOL C	2817	197	3.3	7.0	90	•90	2.1	3.2	59	159	3.6	5.6	99	101	2.5	3.6	70
DAYS OF OUR LIVES N	5496	470	7.8	8.6	110	312	7.4	5.7	105	317	7.2	5.8	101	193	4.9	3.5	69
EDGE OF NIGHT A	2294	223	3.7	9.7	125	•99	2.4	4.3	79	•131	3.0	5.7	100	•96	2.4	4.2	82
FAMILY FEUD A	2796	230	3.8	8.2	106	110	2.6	3.9	72	185	4.2	6.6	116	114	2.9	4.1	80
GENERAL HOSPITAL A	6569	615	10.2	9.4	121	371	8.8	5.6	104	519	11.8	7.9	139	395	9.9	6.0	117
GOOD MORNING, AMERICA-730 A	3283	231	3.8	7.0	91	115	2.7	3.5	65	227	5.1	6.9	121	•106	2.7	3.2	63
GOOD MORNING, AMERICA-830 A	3337	203	3.4	6.1	78	148	3.5	4.4	82	188	4.3	5.6	99	•134	3.4	4.0	78
GUIDING LIGHT C	5920	408	6.8	6.9	89	187	4.4	3.2	58	336	7.6	5.7	100	321	8.1	5.4	106
LOVE BOAT DAYTIME A	2754	279	4.6	10.1	131	142	3.4	5.2	95	173	3.9	6.3	110	166	4.2	6.0	118
ONE LIFE TO LIVE A	5712	534	8.9	9.3	120	303	7.2	5.3	98	409	9.3	7.2	126	361	9.1	6.3	123
PRICE IS RIGHT 1 C	4160	290	4.8	7.0	90	113	2.7	2.7	50	242	5.5	5.8	102	223	5.6	5.4	105
PRICE IS RIGHT 2 C	4267	316	5.3	7.4	95	119	2.8	2.8	51	264	6.0	6.2	109	238	6.0	5.6	109
RYAN'S HOPE A	3330	360	6.0	10.8	139	161	3.8	4.8	89	231	5.2	6.9	122	•103	2.6	3.1	60
TEXAS	2414	242	4.0	10.0	129	•109	2.6	4.5	83	143	3.2	5.9	104	•62	1.6	2.6	50
TODAY SHOW - 7.30AM N	2313	148	2.5	6.4	82	•121	2.9	5.2	96	••129	2.9	5.6	98	•132	3.3	5.7	111
TODAY SHOW - 8.30AM N	2173	•99	1.6	4.6	59	169	4.0	7.8	143	183	4.1	8.4	148	•174	4.4	8.0	156
WHEEL OF FORTUNE N	2126	153	2.5	7.2	93	•73	1.7	3.4	63	194	4.4	9.1	160	130	3.3	6.1	119
YOUNG AND THE RESTLESS C	5706	540	9.0	9.5	122	204	4.8	3.6	66	256	5.8	4.5	79	251	6.3	4.4	86
WEEKEND DAYTIME NTWK PRE 6PM																	
ABC WIDE WORLD-SPORTS SAT A	2332	•131	2.2	5.6	72	•95	2.3	4.1	75	•100	2.3	4.3	75	•85	2.1	3.6	71
ABC WIDE WORLD-SPORTS SUN A	1752	•175	2.9	10.0	129	••109	2.6	6.2	115	•119	2.7	6.8	119	•110	2.8	6.3	123
CBS SPORTS SATURDAY C	1151	••93	1.5	8.1	104	••24	0.6	2.1	38	••68	1.5	5.9	104	••49	1.2	4.3	83
MEET THE PRESS N	1486	••60	1.0	4.0	52	••32	0.8	2.2	40	••87	2.0	5.9	103	••26	0.7	1.7	34
NBC MAJOR LEAGUE BASEBALL N	1449	••63	1.0	4.3	56	••40	1.0	2.8	51	•92	2.1	6.3	111	••60	1.5	4.1	81
NBC MAJOR LEAGUE PRE GAME N	1387	••67	1.1	4.8	62	••48	1.1	3.5	64	••76	1.7	5.5	96	••24	0.6	1.7	34
PRO BOWLERS - SPRING ED. A	1606	••94	1.6	5.9	75	••88	2.1	5.5	101	••103	2.3	6.4	113	••100	2.5	6.2	122
SPORTSWORLD N	1331	•97	1.6	7.3	94	••87	2.1	6.5	120	•87	2.0	6.5	115	••71	1.8	5.3	104
SUNDAY MORNING C	1866	•104	1.7	5.6	72	••30	0.7	1.6	30	•146	3.3	7.8	137	••110	2.8	5.9	115

Table 12-13. (continued)

BREAKFAST CEREALS (COLD): BRANDS
(FEMALE HOMEMAKERS)

	TOTAL U.S. '000	QUAKER CAP'N CRUNCH A '000	B % DOWN	C % ACROSS	D INDX	QUAKER LIFE A '000	B % DOWN	C % ACROSS	D INDX	QUAKER PUFFED RICE A '000	B % DOWN	C % ACROSS	D INDX	QUAKER PUFFED WHEAT A '000	B % DOWN	C % ACROSS	D INDX
TOTAL FEMALE HOMEMAKERS	77506	6014	100.0	7.8	100	4209	100.0	5.4	100	4417	100.0	5.7	100	3970	100.0	5.1	100
WKDAY LOCAL EVENING TV NEWS																	
NETWORK AFFILIATES - EARLY	25416	1465	24.4	5.8	74	1008	23.9	4.0	73	1465	33.2	5.8	101	1219	30.7	4.8	94
NETWORK AFFILIATES - LATE	18757	1436	23.9	7.7	99	1107	26.3	5.9	109	1210	27.4	6.5	113	915	23.0	4.9	95
INDEPENDENTS - LATE	2476	116	1.9	4.7	60	127	3.0	5.1	94	111	2.5	4.5	79	153	3.9	6.2	121
TV EVENING NTWK 6 PM - 2 AM																	
ABC FRIDAY NIGHT MOVIE A	4978	355	5.9	7.1	92	307	7.3	6.2	114	351	7.9	7.1	124	266	6.7	5.3	104
ABC NEWS: NIGHTLINE A	2266	154	2.6	6.8	88	115	2.7	5.1	93	175	4.0	7.7	136	126	3.2	5.6	109
ABC WORLD NEWS TONIGHT A	5871	377	6.3	6.4	83	274	6.5	4.7	86	371	8.4	6.3	111	318	8.0	5.4	106
ABC WRLD NEWS TONIGHT-SUN A	2084	••117	1.9	5.6	72	••92	2.2	4.4	81	••102	2.3	4.9	86	••87	2.2	4.2	82
ARCHIE BUNKER'S PLACE C	7966	449	7.5	5.6	73	324	7.7	4.1	75	445	10.1	5.6	98	334	8.4	4.2	82
BARBARA MANDRELL N	5626	452	7.5	8.0	104	•219	5.2	3.9	72	282	6.4	5.0	88	312	7.9	5.5	108
BARNEY MILLER A	8228	688	11.4	8.4	108	555	13.2	6.7	124	530	12.0	6.4	113	510	12.8	6.2	121
BENSON A	7000	438	7.3	6.3	81	289	6.9	4.1	76	517	11.7	7.4	130	459	11.6	6.6	128
BOOK OF LISTS C	5214	318	5.3	6.1	79	•217	5.2	4.2	77	•204	4.6	3.9	69	•218	5.5	4.2	82
BRET MAVERICK	5458	316	5.3	5.8	75	•206	4.9	3.8	70	387	8.8	7.1	124	•247	6.2	4.5	88
CBS EVENING NEWS - DEAN C	3645	•213	3.5	5.8	75	••104	2.5	2.9	53	•233	5.3	6.4	112	•158	4.0	4.3	85
CBS EVENING NEWS - RATHER C	7761	455	7.6	5.9	76	258	6.1	3.3	61	439	9.9	5.7	99	460	11.6	5.9	116
CBS SAT. NEWS - SCHIEFFER C	3875	•188	3.1	4.9	63	••107	2.5	2.8	51	•222	5.0	5.7	101	•230	5.8	5.9	116
CBS SAT. NIGHT MOVIE C	5273	419	7.0	7.9	102	341	8.1	6.5	119	302	6.8	5.7	100	266	6.7	5.0	98
CBS SUNDAY NEWS - OSGOOD C	2130	••111	1.8	5.2	67	••54	1.3	2.5	47	•149	3.4	7.0	123	•101	2.5	4.7	93
CBS WEDNESDAY NIGHT MOVIE C	6817	524	8.7	7.7	99	412	9.8	6.0	111	320	7.2	4.7	82	318	8.0	4.7	91
CHICAGO STORY N	3093	•300	5.0	9.7	125	••144	3.4	4.7	86	•210	4.8	6.8	119	••254	6.4	8.2	160
CHIPS N	7786	769	12.8	9.9	127	405	9.6	5.2	96	487	11.0	6.3	110	462	11.6	5.9	116
DALLAS C	10915	858	14.3	7.9	101	445	10.6	4.1	75	675	15.3	6.2	109	499	12.6	4.6	89
DIFF'RENT STROKES N	9535	803	13.4	8.4	109	462	11.0	4.8	89	525	11.9	5.5	97	412	10.4	4.3	84
DUKES OF HAZZARD C	7935	780	13.0	9.8	127	322	7.7	4.1	75	408	9.2	5.1	90	281	7.1	3.5	69
FACTS OF LIFE N	8082	665	11.1	8.2	106	423	10.0	5.2	96	606	13.7	7.5	132	414	10.4	5.1	100
FALL GUY A	8200	767	12.8	9.4	121	355	8.4	4.3	80	395	8.9	4.8	85	345	8.7	4.2	82
FAME N	6263	461	7.7	7.4	95	395	9.4	6.3	116	390	8.8	6.2	109	326	8.2	5.2	102
FANTASY ISLAND A	9027	805	13.4	8.9	115	450	10.7	5.0	92	505	11.4	5.6	98	387	9.7	4.3	84
FATHER MURPHY N	4724	477	7.9	10.1	130	•212	5.0	4.5	83	213	4.8	4.5	79	•216	5.4	4.6	89
GIMME A BREAK N	8983	696	11.6	7.7	100	451	10.7	5.0	92	507	11.5	5.6	99	369	9.3	4.1	80
GREATEST AMERICAN HERO A	6628	596	9.9	9.0	116	330	7.8	5.0	92	318	7.2	4.8	84	292	7.4	4.4	86
HAPPY DAYS A	8265	888	14.8	10.7	138	539	12.8	6.5	120	445	10.1	5.4	94	430	10.8	5.2	102
HARPER VALLEY N	3816	•243	4.0	6.4	82	•174	4.1	4.6	84	226	5.1	5.9	104	•234	5.9	6.1	120
HART TO HART A	11762	1070	17.8	9.1	117	738	17.5	6.3	116	845	19.1	7.2	126	829	20.9	7.0	138
HILL STREET BLUES N	9045	831	13.8	9.2	118	593	14.1	6.6	121	540	12.2	6.0	105	498	12.5	5.5	107
INCREDIBLE HULK C	4712	365	6.1	7.7	100	207	4.9	4.4	81	276	6.2	5.9	103	232	5.8	4.9	96
LAVERNE & SHIRLEY A	8279	912	15.2	11.0	142	522	12.4	6.3	118	427	9.7	5.2	91	409	10.3	4.9	96
LITTLE HOUSE - PRAIRIE N	10207	688	11.4	6.7	87	•344	8.2	3.4	62	667	15.1	6.5	115	445	11.2	4.4	85
LOU GRANT C	8042	594	9.9	7.4	95	541	12.9	6.7	124	450	10.2	5.6	98	561	14.1	7.0	136
LOVE BOAT A	11480	965	16.0	8.4	108	551	13.1	4.8	88	673	15.2	5.9	103	495	12.5	4.3	84
MAGNUM, P.I. C	10658	635	10.6	6.0	77	392	9.3	3.7	68	532	12.0	5.0	88	434	10.9	4.1	79
M*A*S*H C	9369	844	14.0	9.0	116	622	14.8	6.6	122	606	13.7	6.5	113	558	14.1	6.0	116
MORK & MINDY A	4737	571	9.5	12.1	155	292	6.9	6.2	114	264	6.0	5.6	98	•198	5.0	4.2	82
NBC MAGAZINE N	4118	•192	3.2	4.7	60	•154	3.7	3.7	69	293	6.6	7.1	125	221	5.6	5.4	105
NBC MONDAY NIGHT MOVIES N	7285	539	9.0	7.4	95	384	9.1	5.3	97	548	12.4	7.5	132	438	11.0	6.0	117
NBC NIGHTLY NEWS N	5866	298	5.0	5.1	65	263	6.2	4.5	83	365	8.3	6.2	109	286	7.2	4.9	95
NBC NIGHTLY NEWS - SAT. N	2990	••148	2.5	4.9	64	•97	2.3	3.2	60	•210	4.8	7.0	123	•138	3.5	4.6	90
NBC NIGHTLY NEWS - SUN. N	3166	•244	4.1	7.7	99	•153	3.6	4.8	89	•152	3.4	4.8	84	•193	4.9	6.1	119
NBC SUNDAY NIGHT MOVIE N	7514	605	10.1	8.1	104	419	10.0	5.6	103	424	9.6	5.6	99	305	7.7	4.1	79
ONE DAY AT A TIME C	8157	505	8.4	6.2	80	342	8.1	4.2	77	425	9.6	5.2	91	320	8.1	3.9	77
ONE OF THE BOYS N	3447	•194	3.2	5.6	73	•181	4.3	5.3	97	205	4.6	5.9	104	•212	5.3	6.2	120
QUINCY, M.E. N	9880	864	14.4	8.7	113	548	13.0	5.5	102	601	13.6	6.1	107	612	15.4	6.2	121
REAL PEOPLE N	9143	642	10.7	7.0	90	508	12.1	5.6	102	549	12.4	6.0	105	536	13.5	5.9	114
60 MINUTES C	12666	682	11.3	5.4	69	579	13.8	4.6	84	719	16.3	5.7	100	691	17.4	5.5	107
TAXI A	8204	769	12.8	9.4	121	618	14.7	7.5	139	511	11.6	6.2	109	463	11.7	5.6	110
TEACHERS ONLY N	6998	575	9.6	8.2	106	403	9.6	5.8	106	530	12.0	7.6	133	401	10.1	5.7	112
THAT'S INCREDIBLE A	7495	614	10.2	8.2	106	400	9.5	5.3	98	437	9.9	5.8	102	313	7.9	4.2	82
THREE'S COMPANY A	12031	1236	20.6	10.3	132	773	18.4	6.4	118	781	17.7	6.5	114	699	17.6	5.8	113
TONIGHT SHOW N	2727	156	2.6	5.7	74	228	5.4	8.4	154	191	4.3	7.0	123	181	4.6	6.6	130
TOO CLOSE FOR COMFORT A	11418	1331	22.1	11.7	150	861	20.5	7.5	139	760	17.2	6.7	117	745	18.8	6.5	127
TRAPPER JOHN. M.D. C	11694	882	14.7	7.5	97	504	12.0	¯4.3	79	638	14.4	5.5	96	672	16.9	5.7	112
20/20 A	9204	617	10.3	6.7	86	474	11.3	5.1	95	538	12.2	5.8	103	492	12.4	5.3	104
WALT DISNEY C	4583	360	6.0	7.9	101	•217	5.2	4.7	87	252	5.7	5.5	96	•218	5.5	4.8	93
TV VIEWING SPORTS EVENTS																	
BASEBALL	10670	809	13.5	7.6	98	687	16.3	6.4	119	739	16.7	6.9	122	764	19.2	7.2	140
BASKETBALL - COLLEGE GAMES	4501	•388	6.5	8.6	111	••304	7.2	6.8	124	••155	3.5	3.4	60	••175	4.4	3.9	76
BASKETBALL - PRO-GAMES	4600	•441	7.3	9.6	124	•251	6.0	5.5	100	•348	7.9	7.6	133	•272	6.9	5.9	115
BOWLING	4732	•315	5.2	6.7	86	••248	5.9	5.2	97	500	11.3	10.6	185	•421	10.6	8.9	174
BOXING	5042	•486	8.1	9.6	124	•326	7.7	6.5	119	•217	4.9	4.3	76	•256	6.4	5.1	99
FOOTBALL-COLLEGE GAMES	8758	989	16.4	11.3	146	••673	16.0	7.7	142	514	11.6	5.9	103	•401	10.1	4.6	89
FOOTBALL-PROFESSIONAL GAMES	14895	1587	26.4	10.7	137	836	19.9	5.6	103	907	20.5	6.1	107	837	21.1	5.6	110
GOLF	4057	••235	3.9	5.8	75	••138	3.3	3.4	63	•286	6.5	7.0	124	•387	9.7	9.5	186
POST-SEASON COLL. FOOTBALL	6612	•547	9.1	8.3	107	•388	9.2	5.9	108	•344	7.8	5.2	91	•361	9.1	5.5	107
POST-SEASON PRO FOOTBALL	9284	922	15.3	9.9	128	•517	12.3	5.6	103	•444	10.1	4.8	84	511	12.9	5.5	107
TENNIS	3738	•404	6.7	10.8	139	••190	4.5	5.1	94•	••113	2.6	3.0	53	••122	3.1	3.3	64

0102
P-20

BREAKFAST CEREALS (COLD): BRANDS
(FEMALE HOMEMAKERS)

0102
P-20

	TOTAL U.S. '000	QUAKER 100% NATURAL A '000	B % DOWN	C % ACROSS	D % INDX	TOTAL A '000	B % DOWN	C % ACROSS	D % INDX	TRIX A '000	B % DOWN	C % ACROSS	D % INDX	WHEATIES A '000	B % DOWN	C % ACROSS	D % INDX
TOTAL FEMALE HOMEMAKERS	77506	3004	100.0	3.9	100	5417	100.0	7.0	100	5140	100.0	6.6	100	9408	100.0	12.1	100
18 - 24	9335	••348	11.6	3.7	96	•576	10.6	6.2	88	842	16.4	9.0	136	936	9.9	10.0	83
25 - 34	18029	780	26.0	4.3	112	1273	23.5	7.1	101	1903	37.0	10.6	159	1911	20.3	10.6	87
35 - 44	13417	630	21.0	4.7	121	884	16.3	6.6	94	1465	28.5	10.9	165	2352	25.0	17.5	144
45 - 54	11632	•582	19.4	5.0	129	835	15.4	7.2	103	•586	11.4	5.0	76	1680	17.9	14.4	119
55 - 64	11283	•339	11.3	3.0	78	888	16.4	7.9	113	••129	2.5	1.1	17	1207	12.8	10.7	88
65 OR OLDER	13811	•326	10.9	2.4	61	962	17.8	7.0	100	••215	4.2	1.6	23	1322	14.1	9.6	79
18 - 34	27364	1128	37.5	4.1	106	1849	34.1	6.8	97	2745	53.4	10.0	151	2847	30.3	10.4	86
18 - 49	46197	2106	70.1	4.6	118	3122	57.6	6.8	97	4567	88.9	9.9	149	5949	63.2	12.9	106
25 - 54	43078	1991	66.3	4.6	119	2992	55.2	6.9	99	3955	76.9	9.2	138	5943	63.2	13.8	114
35 - 49	18833	978	32.6	5.2	134	1273	23.5	6.8	97	1821	35.4	9.7	146	3102	33.0	16.5	136
50 OR OLDER	31310	898	29.9	2.9	74	2295	42.4	7.3	105	•574	11.2	1.8	28	3459	36.8	11.0	91
GRADUATED COLLEGE	9890	571	19.0	5.8	149	882	16.3	8.9	128	•407	7.9	4.1	62	1266	13.5	12.8	105
ATTENDED COLLEGE	12236	601	20.0	4.9	127	938	17.3	7.7	110	744	14.5	6.1	92	1778	18.9	14.5	120
GRADUATED HIGH SCHOOL	32853	1320	43.9	4.0	104	2040	37.7	6.2	89	2553	49.7	7.8	117	4146	44.1	12.6	104
DID NOT GRADUATE HIGH SCHOOL	22527	•513	17.1	2.3	59	1558	28.8	6.9	99	1435	27.9	6.4	96	2218	23.6	9.8	81
EMPLOYED	37446	1800	59.9	4.8	124	2215	40.9	5.9	85	2715	52.8	7.3	109	4959	52.7	13.2	109
EMPLOYED FULL-TIME	29717	1317	43.8	4.4	114	1644	30.3	5.5	79	2082	40.5	7.0	106	3647	38.8	12.3	101
EMPLOYED PART-TIME	7729	•484	16.1	6.3	162	571	10.5	7.4	106	633	12.3	8.2	123	1311	13.9	17.0	140
NOT EMPLOYED	40060	1204	40.1	3.0	78	3203	59.1	8.0	114	2425	47.2	6.1	91	4449	47.3	11.1	91
PROFESSIONAL/MANAGER	10614	731	24.3	6.9	178	803	14.8	7.6	108	•634	12.3	6.0	90	1401	14.9	13.2	109
CLERICAL/SALES	14780	666	22.2	4.5	116	872	16.1	5.9	84	991	19.3	6.7	101	2132	22.7	14.4	119
CRAFTSMEN/FOREMEN	824	••20	0.7	2.4	63	••20	0.4	2.4	35	••60	1.2	7.3	110	••138	1.5	16.7	138
OTHER EMPLOYED	11229	•383	12.7	3.4	88	519	9.6	4.6	66	1030	20.0	9.2	138	1288	13.7	11.5	94
SINGLE	8267	•234	7.8	2.8	73	549	10.1	6.6	95	478	9.3	5.8	87	828	8.8	10.0	83
MARRIED	50768	2208	73.5	4.3	112	3736	69.0	7.4	105	3720	72.4	7.3	110	6854	72.9	13.5	111
DIVORCED/SEPARATED/WIDOWED	18471	562	18.7	3.0	79	1132	20.9	6.1	88	942	18.3	5.1	77	1727	18.4	9.3	77
PARENTS	31500	1496	49.8	4.7	123	2557	47.2	8.1	116	4038	78.6	12.8	193	4637	49.3	14.7	121
WHITE	67876	2779	92.5	4.1	106	5016	92.6	7.4	106	4413	85.9	6.5	98	8744	92.9	12.9	106
BLACK	8235	•190	6.3	2.3	60	380	7.0	4.6	66	613	11.9	7.4	112	553	5.9	6.7	55
OTHER	1395	••35	1.2	2.5	65	••22	0.4	1.6	23	••114	2.2	8.2	123	••111	1.2	8.0	66
NORTHEAST-CENSUS	16922	•861	28.7	5.1	131	1682	31.1	9.9	142	1027	20.0	6.1	92	2260	24.0	13.4	110
NORTH CENTRAL	20200	734	24.4	3.6	94	1389	25.6	6.9	98	1819	35.4	9.0	136	4016	42.7	19.9	164
SOUTH	26132	726	24.2	2.8	72	1373	25.3	5.3	75	1297	25.2	5.0	75	1481	15.7	5.7	47
WEST	14252	•682	22.7	4.8	123	974	18.0	6.8	98	998	19.4	7.0	106	1651	17.5	11.6	95
NORTHEAST-MKTG.	17524	963	32.1	5.5	142	1614	29.8	9.2	132	1015	19.7	5.8	87	2055	21.8	11.7	97
EAST CENTRAL	11814	•406	13.5	3.4	89	818	15.1	6.9	99	1092	21.2	9.2	139	2339	24.9	19.8	163
WEST CENTRAL	13479	611	20.3	4.5	117	962	17.8	7.1	102	1034	20.1	7.7	116	2511	26.7	18.6	153
SOUTH	22875	•533	17.7	2.3	60	1279	23.6	5.6	80	1153	22.4	5.0	76	1129	12.0	4.9	41
PACIFIC	11814	•491	16.3	4.2	107	745	13.8	6.3	90	847	16.5	7.2	108	1375	14.6	11.6	96
COUNTY SIZE A	31229	1373	45.7	4.4	113	2277	42.0	7.3	104	2279	44.3	7.3	110	3811	40.5	12.2	101
COUNTY SIZE B	23352	995	33.1	4.3	110	1783	32.9	7.6	109	1648	32.1	7.1	106	2368	25.2	10.1	84
COUNTY SIZE C	12137	•404	13.4	3.3	86	•809	14.9	6.7	95	•632	12.3	5.2	79	1607	17.1	13.2	109
COUNTY SIZE D	10789	•233	7.8	2.2	56	548	10.1	5.1	73	•581	11.3	5.4	81	1622	17.2	15.0	124
METRO CENTRAL CITY	23359	875	29.1	3.7	97	1528	28.2	6.5	94	1685	32.8	7.2	109	2335	24.8	10.0	82
METRO SUBURBAN	34657	1712	57.0	4.9	127	2850	52.6	8.2	118	2466	48.0	7.1	107	4258	45.3	12.3	101
NON METRO	19491	•417	13.9	2.1	55	1040	19.2	5.3	76	989	19.2	5.1	77	2814	29.9	14.4	119
TOP 5 ADI'S	17725	868	28.9	4.9	126	1362	25.1	7.7	110	1289	25.1	7.3	110	1962	20.9	11.1	91
TOP 10 ADI'S	25079	1198	39.9	4.8	123	1826	33.7	7.3	104	1792	34.9	7.1	108	2933	31.2	11.7	96
TOP 20 ADI'S	35085	1509	50.2	4.3	111	2555	47.2	7.3	104	2317	45.1	6.6	100	4046	43.0	11.5	95
HSHLD INC. $40,000 OR MORE	8818	•658	21.9	7.5	193	644	11.9	7.3	104	•543	10.6	6.2	93	1283	13.6	14.5	120
$30,000 OR MORE	18653	1249	41.6	6.7	173	1379	25.5	7.4	106	1134	22.1	6.1	92	2828	30.1	15.2	125
$25,000 OR MORE	25911	1501	50.0	5.8	149	1997	36.9	7.7	110	1659	32.3	6.4	97	3834	40.8	14.8	122
$20,000 - $24,999	9349	••359	12.0	3.8	99	715	13.2	7.6	109	•587	11.4	6.3	95	1129	12.0	12.1	99
$15,000 - $19,999	8862	•256	8.5	2.9	75	664	12.3	7.5	107	751	14.6	8.5	128	1189	12.6	13.4	111
$10,000 - $14,999	13844	421	14.0	3.0	78	717	13.2	5.2	74	1099	21.4	7.9	120	1622	17.2	11.7	97
UNDER $10,000	19541	467	15.5	2.4	62	1324	24.4	6.8	97	1043	20.3	5.3	80	1633	17.4	8.4	69
HOUSEHOLD OF 1 PERSON	11894	299	10.0	2.5	65	783	14.5	6.6	94	••143	2.8	1.2	18	801	8.5	6.7	55
2 PEOPLE	25454	865	28.8	3.4	88	1771	32.7	7.0	100	807	15.7	3.2	48	2475	26.3	9.7	80
3 OR 4 PEOPLE	28521	1305	43.4	4.6	118	1688	31.2	5.9	85	2406	46.8	8.4	127	4073	43.3	14.3	118
5 OR MORE PEOPLE	11637	•535	17.8	4.6	119	1176	21.7	10.1	145	1785	34.7	15.3	231	2059	21.9	17.7	146
NO CHILD IN HSHLD	43986	1475	49.1	3.4	87	2793	51.6	6.3	91	888	17.3	2.0	30	4470	47.5	10.2	84
CHILD(REN) UNDER 2 YRS	5651	•355	11.8	6.3	162	•585	10.8	10.4	148	799	15.5	14.1	213	685	7.3	12.1	100
2 - 5 YEARS	12521	•561	18.7	4.5	116	1137	21.0	9.1	130	1697	33.0	13.6	204	1487	15.8	11.9	98
6 - 11 YEARS	15766	513	17.1	3.3	84	1131	20.9	7.2	103	2318	45.1	14.7	222	2605	27.7	16.5	136
12 - 17 YEARS	16144	743	24.7	4.6	119	1406	26.0	8.7	125	2013	39.2	12.5	188	2790	29.7	17.3	142
RESIDENCE OWNED	55460	2148	71.5	3.9	100	4001	73.9	7.2	103	3531	68.7	6.4	96	7124	75.7	12.8	106
VALUE: $50,000 OR MORE	28563	1455	48.4	5.1	131	2290	42.3	8.0	115	1746	34.0	6.1	92	3878	41.2	13.6	112
VALUE: UNDER $50,000	26897	•694	23.1	2.6	67	1712	31.6	6.4	91	1785	34.7	6.6	100	3246	34.5	12.1	99

SOURCE: 1982 Study of Media and Markets, Simmons Market Research Bureau, Inc., 1982, Vol. P-20, pp. 96-101.

Close inspection of the indices can provide considerable insights into category and brand target consumers and the media that reach them. Note that SMRB data covers most major media types, specific vehicles, and various quintile categories.

Another interesting market media research organization is Claritas Corp's PRIZM. PRIZM is based upon groupings of neighborhood areas into 40 homogeneous clusters based upon census blocks and zip codes. Claritas profiles a business against the 40 socioeconomic zip clusters using company-generated and syndicated data. The profile provides a means for targeting advertising and media investments. Clarita's zip-clusters are labeled with clever names such as "Money and Brains," swank townhouses, and mid-rise apartments on tree-lined urban streets. "Furs and Station-wagons" are young, well-educated professionals living in new suburban neighborhoods. "Bunker's Neighbors" is a take-off from the TV show.

Other marketing media research firms provide surveys on special areas, such as upper income groups, business professionals, and product categories. Some media audience research companies exist to supply tailor-made audience profiles for TV, radio, magazine, newspaper, and outdoor media and their respective trade organizations.

Selecting and Buying Media Finding and selecting the optimum combination of media vehicles is dependent upon the objectives of the plan, the resulting strategic decisions, plus a background knowledge of the various media and how people relate to these media. The media planner systematically searches through available media types evaluating each against the criteria established by the objectives and strategies. A host of factors are considered:

- Target audience
- Geographical pattern
- Seasonality
- Competitive activity
- Budget flexibility
- Budget size
- Promotions
- Timing of audience response
- Creative

Of course, before selecting the media, the planner must understand the media and what each can do in the advertising program.

Broadcast Television

Television is available in nearly all American homes. Color penetration exceeds 88 percent, more than half of American homes have two or more TV sets, and over 35 percent are able to receive cable programming.

Table 12-14.   Percent Composition of Viewing Audiences

	Women	Men	Teens	Children
Total U.S.	38%	35%	11%	16%
Daytime	61	19	9	11
Early evening . .	40	27	13	20
Prime	43	34	11	12
Late evening . .	49	40	8	3

Table 12-15.   Audiences by Type of Program

Daytime	Women	Men	Teens	Children
Serials	69%	16%	8%	7%
Games	57	24	7	12
Prime				
Drama	48%	32%	9%	11%
Movies	44	38	10	8
Sit coms	43	31	11	15

Table 12-16.   The Elements of the Typical TV Day

	Time period	Source of program	Program types
Early morning	Mon.–Fri./7AM–9AM	Network	News, talk
Morning	Mon.–Fri./9AM–10AM	Local	Talk, reruns, movies
Daytime	Mon.–Fri./10AM–4:30PM	Network	Quiz shows, specials, sit coms
Early evening	Mon.–Fri./4:30–7PM	Local	Talk, reruns, movies, local news
Early news	Mon.–Fri./7–7:30PM	Network	News
Access	Mon.–Fri./7:30–8PM	Local	Game shows, international, animal shows
Prime	Mon.–Sun./8–11PM	Network	Various
Late news	Mon.–Sun./11–11:30PM	Local	News
Late evening	Mon.–Sun./11:30PM–1AM	Network	Talk, news, movies, drama, reruns

Table 12-17.   Hours:Minutes of Women Viewing Weekly

	November	February	March	July
Daytime	6:16	6:55	5:59	5:54
Early evening	5:01	5:27	4:08	3:45
Prime	10:51	11:37	9:54	8:17
Late evening	3:01	3:10	3:05	3:01
Other times	8:22	9:09	7:02	6:23
Total	33:31	36:18	30:08	27:20

Table 12-18.   Cumulative Weekly Reach

	Women	Women 18–54	Working women
Daytime	63%	63%	45%
Early evening	79	76	75
Prime	89	88	88
Late evening	47	49	46

Table 12-19.   Typical Television Costs

		Cost (:30)	Household Rating	CPM
Daytime	Network	$15,000	6.0	$3.00
Prime	Network	85,000	17.5	6.00
Evening news	Network	45,000	12.5	4.50
Tonight Show	Network	35,000	7.0	5.50
Early and late fringe	Spot	Varies	7.0	5.00

Advertising is purchased nationally through the three networks (each with approximately 200 affiliates), in the 212 local markets (called TV areas of dominant influence or ADIs) or nationally through syndicators who build à la carte networks market by market. Table 12-14 illustrates the composition of audiences by the typical TV time periods, source of origination, and types of programs offered.

Total audiences vary during the day and by programming type. (See Tables 12-15 and 12-16.) Audiences are highly seasonal, peaking in the winter months and turning lowest in the summer. (See Table 12-17.) Men, teens, and children follow seasonal viewing patterns. Television reaches large numbers of people as typified by the medium's penetration among men, younger women, and working women. (See Table 12-18.) Note that nearly half of all working women watch some daytime TV (10AM–4:30PM) during the week.

Although television cost efficiencies vary seasonally and by programming type, in general, relative costs are lowest during the daytime hours and highest in the evening when more people view TV. (See Table 12-19.)

Network television is employed to efficiently reach broad national audiences. The medium is highly intrusive, for commercials are wedged into programs in fairly short commercial "pods." The level of commercialization is relatively low, ranging from 10 minutes per hour on network affiliates in prime time to 16 minutes during nonprime hours. Various programming options provide some degree of selectivity (daytime for women, men in sports, children on Saturday morning). The vast majority of Americans can be reached in prime time.

To properly employ network, however, large budgets are required and the medium is not considered flexible in terms of budgeting options. Commitments are made months prior to air dates, especially in long-term, up-front negotiations. But the primary drawback is uneven delivery by market. This lack of geographical precision can be overcome by "filling in" with local spot.

Spot, like network, is a highly impactful medium that permits excellent flexibility geographically for both advertising weight and copy. Shorter lead times are needed than with network buys. However, spot is less efficient than network with significant variations in costs by market. Some markets are expensive while others are priced attractively. While network commercials are embedded in programs, many spot availabilities are between shows and viewed less intently.

Because television programming is subject to quick changes and TV audiences shift with alterations in shows, weather conditions, and other factors, buyers must provide a stewardship or post-analysis reports. These

Table 12-20.   Network Radio

Network	Formats	Affiliates	Audience skew
NBC	Adult contemporary, MOR*	355	25+
CBS	News, MOR, adult contemporary	428	25+
Mutual	News, MOR, country	850	25–54
ABC-Contemporary	Adult contemporary	364	12–49
ABC-Entertainment	Adult contemporary, MOR, contemporary	478	25–54
ABC-FM	Adult contemporary	140	12–34
ABC-Informational	News, MOR, country	577	25+
National Black	Black urban contemporary	91	Black
Sheridan	Black urban contemporary	116	Black
The Source	Album-oriented rock	180	12–34
RKO I	Adult contemporary	220	12–34
WSJ Report	News, talk, MOR	65	25+
Country Coast to Coast	Country	50	25–49
RKO II	Talk, MOR	155	25–54
Star Station	Adult contemporary	35	18–49
ABC-Direction	News, MOR	122	25–49
ABC-Rock	Album-oriented rock	54	12–34
RadioRadio (CBS)	Adult contemporary, rock	85	18–34
CNN Radio	News	25	35+
RKO III	Adult contemporary, MOR	Varies	Varies
Stardust	MOR ('40s–'60s)	N.A.	35+
Transtar	Adult contemporary	75	25–34
Talkradio	Talk	25	25–34

SOURCE: BBDO   *MOR = Middle of the Road

reports recap budget and audience goals and then provide actual final schedule costs and audience deliveries. The post-analysis tells if the TV schedule performed as anticipated and planned.

Radio

Radio is the most ubiquitous medium because radios are mobile and are found everywhere—in the home, in the car, and recently on the street via headphone sets. The typical household has six radios. As a commercial medium, radio is extremely local because most station signals are limited and people listen to hometown stations. However, numerous wired and nonwired radio networks exist. (See Table 12-20.)

Network programming is confined to short-form news and informational shows throughout the day and occasional hour-long special concerts and entertainment programs. Local programming consists of talk, news, or music. The variety of choice is almost unlimited ranging from album rock, progressive rock, standard rock, to beautiful music or symphonic music, or country music, and so on.

The radio day is divided into segments based upon available audiences:

Mon.–Fri.	6AM–10AM	Morning
Mon.–Fri.	10AM–3PM	Housewife time
Mon.–Fri.	3PM–7PM	Afternoon drive
Mon.–Sun.	7PM–12M	Evening
Sat.–Sun.	6AM–7PM	Weekend

Radio prime time is morning drive. (See Table 12-21). Radio is bought much differently than TV. Many stations compete for available audiences, and people tend to be "loyal" to a limited number of stations. For these reasons, radio is purchased on a "cume" basis. Packages of announcements (12, 18, 24, etc.) are spread throughout the day and week on numerous stations in order to build reach. Because of stable, loyal audiences, frequency is generated easily. Reach is more difficult to achieve.

Spot radio is usually employed along with network radio. Network radio has exceptionally wide variations in market-to-market deliveries, and local stations are normally added to compensate in poorly covered

Table 12-21. Percent Listening to Radio during Average Quarter Hour

Monday–Friday	Men	Women	Teens (12–17)
6–10AM	22%	27%	14%
10AM–3PM	18	21	8
3PM–7PM	17	17	16
7PM–12AM	8	8	13

areas. Radio is most efficient on a CPM basis, especially network, but on a national basis, the medium can absorb large out-of-pocket budgets if significant reach is desired. Many spots are needed and the cumulative cost builds quickly. For this reason, radio has become primarily a local advertising medium.

While network radio is efficient compared to TV and builds frequency, the medium is less instrusive than TV. Radio is a background medium and requires large budgets to achieve high reach. Local radio enables the advertiser to quickly move into a market, change copy easily, tie-in to local events with hometown personalities and to selectively support areas of importance. Radio complements TV in a media mix.

Consumer Magazines

Magazines are employed to reach large general audiences (*TV Guide, Time, Reader's Digest*) or a multiplicity of special interests. In recent years, the trend is toward specialized publications carefully edited to appeal to designated audiences. This editorial direction has meant increasing ability to target advertising toward very narrow groups:

- Geographically by regions, markets, zip codes
- Demographically by income, occupation, behavior
- Space unit by size (pages, partial pages, etc.) and coloration

Standard Rate & Data lists over 50 types of magazines that cover just about every interest.

Magazine advertising costs vary widely, but generally there is a relationship based on size of circulation and narrowness of the editorial appeal. (See Table 12-22.)

Another important factor in magazine selections and cost relationships is the proportion of a magazine's audience that reads the issue in the household that pays for it (primary audience) and the percentage that receives the book from someone else (pass-along readers). Primary reader-

Table 12-22.   Representative Magazine Costs

	Cost page 4/C ad	Circulation (000)	CPM
TV Guide	$80,000	17,500	$ 4.57
Woman's Day	60,000	7,000	8.57
People	35,000	2,500	14.00
House & Garden	27,000	1,200	22.50
Golf Digest	28,000	1,000	28.00

Table 12-23.   Magazines: Primary and Pass-Along Readership

	% primary	% pass-along
Sunday supplements (Parade, Family Weekly)	95%	5%
Reader's Digest	80	20
Newsweeklies (Time, Newsweek)	45	55
Women's service (McCall's, Redbook)	40	60
Fashion/glamour (Vogue)	20	80

ship is considered advantageous; those who pay are more intent readers. (See Table 12-23.)

Magazines offer numerous advertising advantages:

1. Demographic, geographic selectivity
2. Long life of message
3. Excellent color reproduction
4. Numerous size and coloration options
5. Long message potential
6. Couponing availability
7. Reasonable efficiencies
8. Compatible editorial positioning possibilities.

But magazines require fairly long lead times (about three months for monthlies), slow accumulation of readership, premium prices for geographical editions, and uneven market-to-market circulation like most national media.

Newspapers

Because almost all newspapers are published and printed locally, the medium is evaluated as a local medium. A few papers are national in scope *(Wall Street Journal, USA Today, National Enquirer)* but have limited penetration in any specific local area. Newspapers are available daily or weekly and on Sundays.

Newspapers are accepted and read by a broad cross-section of people but tend to skew somewhat toward people 35 and older, higher incomes ($25,000+) with some degree of advanced education. Generally speaking, however, newspapers penetrate deeply among all adults in a market.

General newspapers tend to be relatively expensive compared to other consumer media because farily large space sizes are employed, and papers have such deep penetration reaching 50 percent or more of households. Newspapers immediately penetrate a local market (one day), enable excellent geographical flexibility (county, metropolitan area, suburban, city editions), are highly promotable to the trade distributors, permit numerous ad size possibilities, and can be used in a matter of days.

Running a schedule of several ads requires a large budget because of the depth of newspaper exposure. Additionally, newspapers, with the exception of high-cost preprinted sections and weekend magazines, do not enable good color reproduction. Although much progress has been achieved recently in standardizing newspaper ad sizes and costs, local publishing requirements and varying cost efficiencies have hampered newspapers as a national medium.

Space does not allow a complete discussion of all the various advertising media available today. The basic four—TV, radio, magazines, and newspapers—are the primary vehicles employed to promote and advertise consumer products. Many other media can be brought into a campaign to reach specialized audiences or enable unique creative approaches. The planner has to evaluate other media as occasions arise.

Media Models

The advertising profession has invested considerable amounts attempting to duplicate the advertising process, especially media dynamics, in computer-based models. Today these simulations are employed as tools to aid in sifting through the many media vehicles and to simplify the planning process. Thanks to syndicated media planning systems, both large and small advertising agencies have access to computer models that rapidly and inexpensively perform some analysis functions:

1. Help in assessing alternative media plans by tabulating reach, frequency, CPMs, and other descriptive summaries of plans for evaluation.
2. Analyze media and marketing data bases to organize information in establishing media objectives and strategies. Computers may analyze market segments to determine best prospects, cross-tabulate two groups (say, age and sex) to determine the interaction of demographic characteristics on consumption.

   Independent media computer firms like Telemar and IMS (Interactive Market Systems) provide these general data analyses.
3. Other more specialized functions are found among a few marketing research firms or large advertising agencies. Simulations of test market strategies, sales prediction systems, market share forecasting, and consumer behavior prediction models are not universally available or recognized.

At one time, perhaps 15 to 20 years ago, computers and models were expected to totally perform the media planning process. Time and experience have shown that the planning function is too complex to be handled solely by linear programming or heuristic methods. Models and computer simulators have been a tremendous asset to the advertising profession in simplifying media analysis and assuming complex computational chores. However, human judgments and creative evaluations are vital to advertising media planning.

New Media Developments

During the 1980s several video communication media are expected to grow into significant entertainment forms and alter the impact of other consumer media. For some advertisers, these newer technologies will be an asset permitting more effective creative approaches and allowing greater demographic selectivity. On the other hand, these media may erode the value of existing media for those advertisers seeking broad-scale audiences. The new media, thus, may be both an opportunity and a spoiler.

Scope of New Media

Cable TV is the forerunner of the new video forms. Cable is as old as TV. It originally was employed to improve picture quality in areas with poor reception. Advanced technology now permits transmission of up to 120 channels over wires that handled 12 channels previously. As older systems are upgraded and additional towns are wired for cable, people will have more channels to choose from and smaller audiences will result. For those seeking narrowly defined audiences, cable may simplify their task and improve relative efficiencies. For those wishing broad audiences, costs will rise as more channels are needed to obtain acceptable reach levels.

In addition to cable, other home-video forms will emerge:

- Interactive (two-way) communication permits viewers to respond to video signals and perform certain jobs at home (banking, merchandise ordering, etc.) through the TV or telephone. Warner Amex's QUBE is an example.
- Teletext writes on to the home TV screen lines of information contained in portions of conventional broadcast signals. Viewers control the data displayed by means of a handheld decoder box similar to remote-control TV devices.
- Viewdata systems link home TV sets to computers. Subscribers access the systems via a keyboard. Viewdata is similar to teletext in that large amounts of alphanumeric information can be obtained but different in that teletext is one-way and viewdata is interactive.

- Subscription TV (STV) uses conventional TV broadcast stations to transmit coded programming. Viewers need a decoder box to unscramble the picture.
- Multipoint distribution service is similar to STV except microwave signals are employed. MDS is found primarily in large cities that are not wired for cable.
- Direct broadcast satellites is similar to STV except the signal is transmitted from earth-orbiting satellites to roof-top dish antennas.
- Video cassette recorders and video disc players allow people to view information and programming completely at will.

The growth of these new media is not easily projected, for much depends upon government regulations and economic conditions. Batten, Barton, Durstine & Osborn's forecasts indicate rapid growth for cable and VCRs during the 1980s. (See Table 12-24.)

The influence of cable has only begun to be felt in recent years. Audience surveys are beginning to reflect the shift of viewing from network affiliates to independent TV stations, cable advertiser-supported networks, and pay cable channels. Nielsen's spring 1982 *Cable TV—A Status Report* shows significant cable viewing. (See Table 12-25.)

Table 12-24.   Percent U.S. Penetration

	1982	1985	1990
Basic cable	34	40	65
Pay cable	19	26	50
STV	2	6	12
VCR	3	8	22
Video text	–	6	12

Table 12-25.   Average Hours Viewed per Week, May 1982

	Non-cable homes		Cable homes		Pay cable homes	
	Prime	Day	Prime	Day	Prime	Day
Network affiliates	45.9	17.8	40.0	16.0	38.5	15.1
Other over-the-air stations .	9.5	4.0	12.1	5.7	13.6	7.0
Cable originated TV	–	–	2.9	1.3	4.3	2.3
Pay cable	–	–	–	–	14.5	4.0
Total	55.4	21.8	55.0	23.0	70.9	28.4

SOURCE: A. C. Nielsen, *Cable TV—A Status Report,* May 1982.

Pay cable homes watch more TV but spend less time viewing network affiliated stations. As cable penetration expands, schedules will be affected and different media strategies will evolve. In the next few years, advertisers will experiment with cable and some other new technologies, but eventually, permanent strategy changes will be needed as the impact of the emerging video forms are felt.

Numerous cable networks have developed in recent years and more are planned. Table 12-26 is a partial listing. Most are advertiser-supported and unlike the broadcast networks, concentrate on a specific type of programming—news, weather, sports, religion, children, etc. The pay channels typically provide movies and some general entertainment specials or major sports events.

At the current time, cable rates are low, reflecting small audience delivery, and reliable research is not available. Even so, cable offers several values:

1. Low unit prices
2. Inexpensive testing facility
3. Ability to build frequency
4. Highly selective audiences
5. Flexibility in copy lengths
6. Inexpensive sponsorship opportunities
7. Compatible programming adjacencies
8. Commercial tag opportunities
9. Franchise positioning

Cable offers the low cost and frequency of radio, video of TV, selectivity of magazines, and local interest of newspapers (cable franchises are awarded by municipalities). Although infants today, the new video media promise to alter American lifestyles and advertising approaches. The process will be gradual, but it is beginning.

The Media Plan   Media Plan Document

1. Executive summary. One- or two-page review of basic strategy and plan elements for senior client executives not intimately involved in product marketing operations.
2. Background commentary and situational analysis. Briefly describes the market situation for the product or service, recaps marketing and advertising goals, and indicates creative direction.
3. Media objectives. Specific, actionable statements of what the media plan will accomplish.

Table 12-26.   Average Hours Viewed Per Week, May 1982

Basic services		Subscribers (millions)
Alpha Repertory Television Service	Cultural	8.0
Appalachian Community Service Network	Educational	2.0
Black Entertainment Network	Black entertainment	10.0
Cable News Network	News	15.0
CNN Headline News	News headlines	2.0
C-SPAN	Informational	12.0
Cable Network	Various	17.0
Daytime	Women's service	6.0
Dow Jones Cable News	News service	0.6
ESPN	Sports	18.0
Eternal Word	Religion	0.5
Financial News Network	Business	0.5
Modern Satellite Network	Home shopping	5.0
Music TV	Music	5.0
National Christian Network	Religion	0.8
National Jewish Network	Religion	2.5
Nickelodeon	Children's	9.0
People That Love	Religion	6.0
Satellite News Chennels	News headlines	3.0
Satellite Program Network	Various	5.0
Spanish International Network	Spanish-language	NA
Trinity	Religion	3.0
USA	Women's, children's, sports	13.0
The Weather Channel	Weather	5.0
WGN	TV station—Chicago	9.0
WOR	TV station—New York City	5.0
WTBS (Superstation)	TV station—Atlanta	22.0

Pay services		
Cinemax	Movies, specials	2.0
Playboy	Movies, specials	0.4
Galavision	Spanish films	0.2
Home Box Office	Movies, sports, specials	10.0
Home Theater Network-Plus	Family movies	1.0
The Movie Channel	Movies	2.5
Showtime	Movies, specials	4.0
Spotlight	Movies	NA

SOURCE: *Cablevision Magazine.*

4. Media strategies. Planned options to achieve media objectives; strategies outline how media objectives will be achieved.

5. Plan description. Executional elements of the media plan, alternative strategies considered, justification for recommendations. All tactical components are included in this section.

A sample media plan follows in the next section.

Evaluating the Media Plan

Evaluations of media plans involve reviewing alternatives presented and considering the effectiveness of the options. The first step is to ask if objectives support overall marketing goals. Assuming basic direction is on-target, the next step is to determine which recommended strategies are the most efficient, effective combinations of media to fulfill the objectives. The properly written media plan will expedite evaluations by outlining alternative possibilities and rationalizing the recommended course of action.

Several other elements make for good planning. Are the planning group's assumptions and judgments clearly outlined? Were innovative ideas considered even if not recommended? Were any tests proposed to learn for future planning? Are cost elements specifically and accurately outlined? Does the plan leave room for adjustments should marketing conditions change? Is substantiation thorough and clear? In the end, judgments will play a major role in evaluating media plans, but the plan must and should relate directly to marketing goals and other advertising plans.

Sample Media Plan—Goody Cereal

The following ready-to-eat cereal product media plan illustrates organization and style of media plans. Some of the tactical detail is removed, primarily supporting exhibits, but the essence of the strategic issues remains. Goody Cereal is a competitively priced, all-family, ready-to-eat (RTE). The product's main attributes are its good taste and appeal to adults and children alike. Introduced seven years previously, Goody Cereal enjoyed continuous growth until the last year when shipments plateaued. In the year ahead, additional budget is authorized in an effort to re-establish the brand's historical growth pattern.

Goody Cereal Media Plan

Executive Summary

- Planned spending will be up 23 percent over last year:

This year's plan	$7,000M
Last year's plan	5,710M
Percent change	+19%

  Real dollars, which take into consideration media inflation, reflect a 10 percent increase in expenditures.

- An all-television media plan will be continued in light of:
  — Its effectiveness in relaying the copy message
  — The competitive influence on TV.

  Heavier national levels will be implemented this year to support a revitalized creative campaign.

- A print-TV option will be tested at 30 percent incremental spending.

Objectives/Strategies

1. Direct advertising support toward the Goody Cereal target audience defined as:
   - Women 25–54 primarily
   - Teens and kids secondarily
   - $25,000 household income

2. Geographically, direct support in line with the product's sales.

3. Advertising will be flat throughout the year reflecting the lack of seasonal sales skews.

4. Plan Summary:

Vehicle	W 25–54 weekly GRPs	Number of weeks	$(000)	%
Prime network	29	26	$3,600.0	49
Day network	39	26	2,200.0	30
Total network	68		$5,800.0	79
Spot TV (45% U.S.)	32	26	$1,200.0	16
Total media			$7,000.0	95
Production			$ 350.0	5
Total advertising			$7,350.0	100

Background

Goody Cereal has enjoyed excellent growth since its introduction seven years ago. Last year, sales followed the industry pattern and were flat for the first time. The corporation wishes to renew Goody's growth trend. To return Goody to upward sales momentum, advertising budgets will be increased and creative will be freshened.

Independent promotions will run in the first quarter to build volume. By this time, the cumulative effects of new creative will be felt and brand awareness will begin building. Goody is expected to grow 10 percent next year and achieve a 3 percent year-end share.

The challenge facing Goody's franchise is to renew growth despite stagnation in the ready-to-eat category. Growth must derive from increased penetration that is below industry norms. Achieving this penetration through sales promotion initially and improved awareness from advertising later is the focus of next year's marketing plan.

Marketing budgets have been established at levels higher than inflation in order to achieve the company's growth target.

Media Objectives

1. Within the $7 million media budget, increase Goody Cereal awareness and reestablish growth, especially in areas where the brand has shown above-average sales development.

2. Direct advertising to the primary purchasing agent in households with $25,000+ income, women 25–54. Secondarily, target advertising to children 6–11 and teens 12–17 who consume 40 percent of the product.

3. Achieve minimum four-week reach of 75 percent and 3.5× average frequency against the primary target. Expand reach/average frequency to 85 percent/4.5× in high potential areas.

4. Provide strong national support complemented by additional emphasis in high volume/BDI markets where growth has exceeded national rates.

5. Maintain year-around advertising support because of flat sales.

6. Recognize that the brand has been successfully built with an established TV campaign that is revitalized for the upcoming year.

7. Test a 30% increase in budget to determine if adding women's service magazines can significantly improve awareness. Funding will be incremental. Test area to be determined and schedule prepared during first quarter of the year.

Media Strategy

A medium that can effectively reach both adult women family food shoppers and children/teens is vital to the Goody advertising strategy:

Age of user	% Goody volume	Index to RTE volume
–6	5	87
6–8	13	122
9–12	12	130
13–18	15	132
19–34	19	101
35–54	23	136
55+	8	36

Television remains Goody Cereal's advertising medium because of the:

- Proven effectiveness in providing broad reach efficiently against the primary and secondary targets.
- Audio/video capabilities.
- Strong competitive presence in this medium; ready-to-eat cereals concentrate their efforts in TV.

Prime network. Prime network will be utilized to generate broad reach and rapid awareness. A base of prime is recommended to reach approximately 65 percent of women 25–54 an average of once every two weeks while advertising. The program environment and higher viewer attentiveness of the daypart will provide an impactful presentation of the Goody message.

Element	Attentiveness levels as a % of prime
Prime	100
Day	92
Late night	97
Early news	95

The chart below details the weekly reach potential among the primary and secondary audiences.

Element	Weekly reach potential by daypart		
	Women 25–54	Teens 12–17	Kids 6–11
Prime (M–Su/8–11P)	92%	86%	94%
Day (M–F/10–4:30P)	63	60	66
Late night (M–F/11:30P–1A) ..	50	35	19
Early fringe (M–F/4:30–7:30P)	80	76	91

In addition, prime network will generate visibility for Goody Cereal because it has the least commercial clutter of all TV dayparts:

Element	Commercial minutes allowed per hour
Prime	10.0
Day	16.0
Late night	16.0
Early fringe	16.0

Day network. Day network represents the most efficient media vehicle to reach women 25–54, even when adjusted by relative media values:

Element	Unadjusted W25–54 CPM	Index	Impact values	Adjusted CPM	Index
Day	$ 5.56	100	70	$ 7.94	100
Prime	12.25	220	100	12.25	154
Late night	9.56	172	85	11.25	142
Early news	12.17	219	75	16.23	204
Early morning ..	5.93	107	60	9.88	124
Early fringe spot	8.25	148	75	11.00	139
Magazines	5.66	102	70	8.09	102

Day network is utilized to provide additional reach as well as frequency of exposures against the prime prospect:

W25–54, average 4-week R/F	Prime only	Prime and day	Index
Reach	65	76	117
Frequency	1.8	3.6	200

Spot TV. The addition of spot television to the network base plan insures adequate spending behind the high BDI/high volume markets. Goody cereal will cover 45 percent of the U.S. in spot. These areas account for 55.2 percent of total volume (average BDI 123). Without spot television, the high BDI/high volume areas would be underdelivered based on sales contribution:

	Spending vs. Ideal				
	% U.S. pop.	% volume	BDI	Ideal dollars*	Dollars allocated
Spot areas	45	55.2	123	$3,864.0	$3,800.0
Remainder U.S. .	55	44.8	81	3,136.0	3,200.0
Total	100	100.0	100	$7,000.0	$7,000.0

*Ideal dollars = % volume × $7,000,000 budget

Scheduling. Due to the continuous purchasing pattern of ready-to-eat cereals, TV activity will be scheduled year-around. Network will run for 26 weeks in 4- to 5-week flights. Local TV is broken out into three priority groups:

	% U.S.	Number of weeks of spot TV
Group I	36	26
Group II	6	25
Group III	3	22

RTE and Goody Cereal sales are relatively flat throughout the year:

Quarter	Total RTE index*
JFM	98
AMJ	102
JAS	104
OND	96

*5 years of SAMI data

Plan Description   Flow Chart

Impression Analysis

Comparison with Previous Year

Alternative Plans

Spot TV Allocation

Goody Cereal Flow Chart

(W25-54 GRP's)

MONTH STD BRDCST CALENDAR	JAN	FEB	MAR	APR	MAY	JUN	JUL	AUG	SEP	OCT	NOV	DEC
Prime Network $3,600.0	:29:/464.0		:29:/511.2		:29:/800.2		:29:/650.3		:29:/594.1		:29:/594.2	
Day Network $2,200.0	:39:/291.7		:39:/309.5		:39:/453.3		:39:/425.1		:39:/362.2		:39:/362.2	
Total Network W25-54 4-Wk. R&F $5,800.0	76%/3.6x											
SPOT TV $2,200.0	180.0		178.1		239.4		218.1		189.0		195.4	
Group I												
Group II												
Group III												

W25-54 4-Wk. R&F	45%/2.8	
Combined R&F	87%/4.6	
$7,000.0		
Spending By Quarter	23%	25%	27%	25%

Impression Analysis (Thousands)

Element	Women 25–54	Teens 12–17	Kids 6–11
Prime network	315,398	130,187	124,051
Day network	424,156	59,176	46,519
Total network	739,554	189,363	170,570
Spot TV (45% U.S.)	155,671	77,171	89,854
Total	895,225	266,534	260,424
% by target	63%	19%	18%

Goody Cereal Recommended Plan vs. Previous Year

	Previous actual	Recommended	Index
Number of weeks	24	26	108
Total budget	$5,710.3	$7,000.0	123
W25–54 avg. 4-wk. R/F			
Spot universe:			
R	85	87	102
F	4.3	4.6	107
Remainder U.S.:			
R	72	76	106
F	3.0	3.6	120
Impressions (MM)	706.5	895.2	127
CPM	$8.08	$7.82	97
Adj. impressions (MM) . .	575.2	729.1	127
Adj. CPM	$9.93	$9.60	97

Alternative Plans   The following alternatives have been examined:

- Alternative I   Prime and day network
- Alternative II   Prime/day network and magazines
- Alternative III   Prime/day network, spot TV, and magazines

Alternative I

Description:

- All network plan.
- Utilize the same network elements—prime and day.
- Weekly network GRPs higher.

Reasons for rejection:

- Provides comparable reach/frequency levels against national schedule.
- Underdelivers against the spot areas, which accounts for 55.2 percent of volume in 45 percent of U.S.

W25–54 spot universe	Recommended	Alternative I	Index
R	87	80	92
F	4.6	4.0	87
3+	58	47	81
Total unadj. imp. (MM) . .	488.5	395.3	81
Total adj. imp. (MM)	392.3	327.5	83
Remainder U.S.			
R	76	80	105
F	3.6	4.0	111
3+	42	47	112
Total unadj. imp. (MM) . .	406.7	483.1	119
Total adj. imp. (MM)	336.8	400.3	119

Alternative II

Description:

- Total national plan/no spot.
- Utilize prime/day network and magazines
- Weekly network GRPs are identical to recommended plan.
- Magazines are substituted for spot TV.

Reasons for rejection:

- Underdelivers against the spot areas, which accounts for 55.2 percent of volume in 45 percent of U.S.

W25–54 spot universe	Recommended	Alternative II	Index
R	87	89	102
F	4.6	4.3	93
3+	58	60	103
Total unadj. imp. (MM) . .	488.5	425.3	87
Total adj. imp. (MM)	392.3	340.3	87
Remainder U.S.			
R	76	76	100
F	3.6	3.6	100
3+	42	42	100
Total unadj. imp. (MM) . .	406.7	519.8	128
Total adj. imp. (MM)	336.8	415.9	124

Alternative III

Description:

- National and spot plan.
- Utilize prime/day network, spot TV and magazines.
- 8 weeks of prime are eliminated in the most expensive quarters to afford a magazine schedule.

Reasons for rejection:

- Deletion of 8 weeks of a historically proven and impactful prime day-part. As a base media type, 18 weeks of prime time are unacceptable.

W25–54 spot universe	Recommended	Alternative III	Index
R	87	89	102
F	4.6	4.8	104
3+	58	60	103
Total unadj. imp. (MM) . .	488.5	541.2	111
Total adj. imp. (MM)	392.3	416.1	106
Remainder U.S.			
R	76	80	105
F	3.6	3.8	106
3+	42	47	112
Total unadj. imp. (MM) . .	406.7	469.9	116
Total adj. imp. (MM)	336.8	365.0	108

Spot TV
Allocation

1. Selected markets with significant BDIs/volume contribution. A market list was compiled by the brand group indicating markets with:

- BDIs over 100 and
- Goody Cereal volume contribution above .65%

Within the list, markets were prioritized into three groups.

2. Equal weight methodology. Based on marketing input, each of the selected markets was to receive equal weekly weight. A goal of 95 W25–54 GRPs (network and spot) was set for each market.

Network delivery in the individual markets was first taken into consideration. Spot GRPs were then derived by subtracting the network GRPs from the total weekly goal of 95.

3. Market prioritization. Markets were prioritized into three groups based on volume contribution, BDI and volume/share trends. The number of weeks scheduled for each priority group follows:

Group	% U.S.	Number of weeks	Total cost
I	36	26	$ 950.0
II	6	25	150.0
III	2	22	100.0
Total	45		$1,200.0

Goody Cereal Spot TV Allocation (95 GRP goal/35 markets)

	Markets	Percent U.S.	Average weekly W25–54 GRPs Network	Spot	Number of weeks in spot
Group I:	Albany	.55	63	32	26
	Baltimore	1.14	60	35	
	Boston	2.42	54	41	
	Buffalo	.79	61	34	
	Chicago	2.95	54	41	
	Cleveland	1.87	65	30	
	Denver	1.03	63	32	
	Des Moines	.42	69	26	
	Detroit	2.30	71	24	
	Flint	.57	80	15	
	Indianapolis ...	1.01	67	28	

	Markets	Percent U.S.	Average weekly W25–54 GRPs		Number of weeks in spot
			Network	Spot	
Group I (cont.)	Los Angeles	5.17	61	34	(26)
	Milwaukee	.89	63	32	
	Philadelphia . . .	3.32	67	28	
	Pittsburgh	1.54	82	13	
	Providence	.67	73	22	
	Sacramento	.91	67	28	
	San Diego	.79	60	35	
	San Francisco . .	2.42	58	37	
	Seattle-Tacoma .	1.16	58	37	
	Syracuse	.43	63	32	
	Tampa	.84	65	30	
	Washington	2.01	51	44	
	Subtotal	36.20			
Group II:	Columbus	.71	73	22	25
	Grand Rapids . .	.69	71	24	
	Harrisburg	.60	71	24	
	Minneapolis . . .	1.32	54	41	
	Omaha	.43	77	18	
	Phoenix	.74	71	24	
	Rochester	.42	63	32	
	Salt Lake City . . .	.59	62	33	
	Wilkes-Barre . . .	.55	84	11	
	Subtotal	6.05			
Group III:	Cincinnati	.87	63	32	22
	Hartford	1.04	55	40	
	Portland	.84	65	30	
	Subtotal	2.77			
	Grand total	45.02	63	32	

Case for Discussion:
G & T Associates

Brian Harper, an account executive with G & T Associates, a Washington, D.C. advertising agency, was faced with a difficult situation in the spring of 1983. His chief client, a major savings and loan institution, was reducing its advertising budget by 55 percent in response to corporate losses and the economic situation. In the past, the company had handled its own media buying, relying on the agency only for creative. However, as part of the streamlining, the corporate media buyer position had been eliminated and placement responsibility had also been turned over to the agency.

Harper met with Linda Britten of the agency's media department to discuss strategy. His review of the situation included these facts:

> The area's three leading savings and loans had a combined net income of −$49,575,000 for 1980. Our client had the lowest loss, and currently has a market share of 23.6 percent, the number 1 position. The market is highly competitive and has become more so with recent changes in banking regulations. Area savings and loans have introduced an average of five new accounts this year, each with heavy advertising support. In response to consumer confusion, most of this advertising has been very informational in nature (i.e., long copy print ads).
>
> In terms of year-round corporate advertising, savings and loan services in the Washington area are advertised through daily and weekly newspapers (46.6 percent), consumer magazines (3.3 percent), outdoor, spot radio (16 percent), spot TV (6.7 percent), exhibits, the Yellow Pages, and point-of-purchase items such as brochures.
>
> Our client has been the leading spender ($1,867,000 last year). Here's how we compare to the competition:

	Advertising expenditure	Share of voice	Share of market
Our client .	$1,867,000	41.3%	23.6%
S&L B	934,000	20.6	23.1
S&L C	594,000	13.1	22.6

Harper went on to observe:

> Based on the share of voice = share of market theory, spending hasn't been very efficient, since market share should be much higher. I believe there are two primary reasons for the problem. First, in the past

the advertising strategy was very general. Basically, we just said "We're the biggest," suggesting that being the biggest was the same as being the best. We've refined that; now we're stressing that we're a "strong, well-managed" savings and loan so that people will feel confident about letting us handle their money. We think this is a key concern, especially since two area S&Ls closed down last year and three others were forced to merge to survive. Second, our media strategy (and the competition's) has been to spend continuously and spread the message broadly. There has not been any attempt to target consumers through strategic media placement. It seems to me that careful targeting and scheduling can help overcome the negative effects of the budget cutback. With the 55 percent reduction, the 1983 budget will be $840,150. That's still more than the number 3 S&L spent last year. Both our chief competitors lost money too, so I doubt their spending will increase much, if at all.

Britten asked, "How locked in are these people? What I mean is, would they be responsive to some major changes in their media strategy? If so, I think there are several things we can do that might prove very effective."

"I don't think they'd be averse to something different," Harper said. "I'm not going to tell them their past strategy was lousy, but I think they know the results weren't what they might have been. As long as you've got good support for your recommendations, I think there's an excellent chance they'll support a change. Some things to keep in mind, though: there'll probably be at least two more new account introductions next year. Plus, a new securities investment service will be opening in several of the branches. Those will have to be planned for. Can you come up with the basics by next week?"

Britten agreed to present her recommendation to the S&L's marketing vp the next week.

Questions/Guidelines

Recommend media vehicles (and scheduling guidelines, i.e., flighting, continuous, etc.) that might prove effective for the S&L. Justify each. Be creative! The following information on the Washington metro area is provided to help you in your recommendations.

	Population (000)				
	18–24	25–34	35–49	50–64	Total
Women	199	273	320	247	1,175
Men	206	251	307	225	1,078

Children   2–11:   432,000
            12–17:   312,000

Households: 1,157,480

Consumer spendable income 1/80–1/82: $38,604,498

Spendable income per household: $33,352

Retail sales per household: $15,446

Media

30+ radio stations, variety of formats. Costs for 60-second spot range from $7 to $300, 30 seconds from $5 to $248.

3 network affiliated TV stations
3 independent stations
2 public stations
1 subscription TV service
5 communities with cable service (20 percent of area population)

2 area-wide daily newspapers:
Washington Post: circ. 549,244 (47 percent of HHs)
    $10.50/line in weekly business magazine section
    $ 8.60/line daily edition
    $10.50/line Sunday edition

Washington Times: circ. 104,000
    $1.00/line

9+ daily community papers, $1.89–$2.53/line

Washington circulation of selected consumer magazines

Magazine	# circulation	% circulation penetration
Family Circle	125,733	11
National Geographic .	172,070	15
Reader's Digest	229,838	20
TV Guide	175,702	15
Better Homes	115,452	10
Parade	682,634	59
Time	124,970	11
Woman's Day	120,984	10
Smithsonian	139,066	12
Money	29,429	3
Business Week	20,795	2
Forbes	16,025	1
Fortune	16,255	1

National savings data

Percentage of population having:

Checking account at an S&L .. 19.3

Savings account at an S&L 29.8

IRA/Keogh account 5.5

Certificates of deposit 12.4

S&L loan 3.2

S&L mortgage 10.9

SOURCES:

Population and spending data and radio cost figures: Standard Rate and Data Service, *Spot Radio,* 65, 3 (March 1, 1983).

Newspaper costs and circulation and magazine circulation: SRDS, *Newspapers,* 65, 3 (March 12, 1983).

Financial data: Simmons Market Research Bureau, 1980, Vol. P-5.

13 Sales Promotion: The Extra Ingredient in the Advertising Campaign

While sales promotion is really a separate topic and is often handled by a group of experts either in the advertising or sales promotion agency or the marketing organization, it is included in the development of the advertising campaign because it is often such a vital element in the overall promotional plan for the brand. In addition, the success of the advertising campaign is usually the result of the combination of advertising and sales promotion techniques rather than either alone. Thus, sales promotion must be integrated into the advertising program.

Unfortunately, in too many cases the sales promotion plan is simply an "add-on," tacked on at the last minute to "flesh-out" the campaign. But increasingly advertising campaign planners are finding that sales promotion and sales promotional activities are just as important to the success of the campaign as are the more traditional media programs. In fact, marketers now invest more in sales promotion than in advertising. And the percentage of the total promotion mix allocated to sales promotion is growing at a faster rate than that for advertising.[1] (See Figure 13-1.)

Despite the fact that sales promotion is a key promotional element, it is often misunderstood and misused by advertising campaign planners. Part of the reason for this confusion may be that sales promotion often makes use of many of the same tools and techniques as are used in the advertising campaign. Therefore, campaign planners may view sales promotion as just another form of advertising and treat it in the same way. But sales promotion is a separate field and while related to advertising, there are some major differences.

---

1. Russell D. Bowman, "Fourth Annual Report: Advertising and Promotion Expenditures," *Marketing Communications,* (August 1983), pp. 5–8.

Figure 13-1.   Year-to-Year Growth of Advertising and Sales Promotion

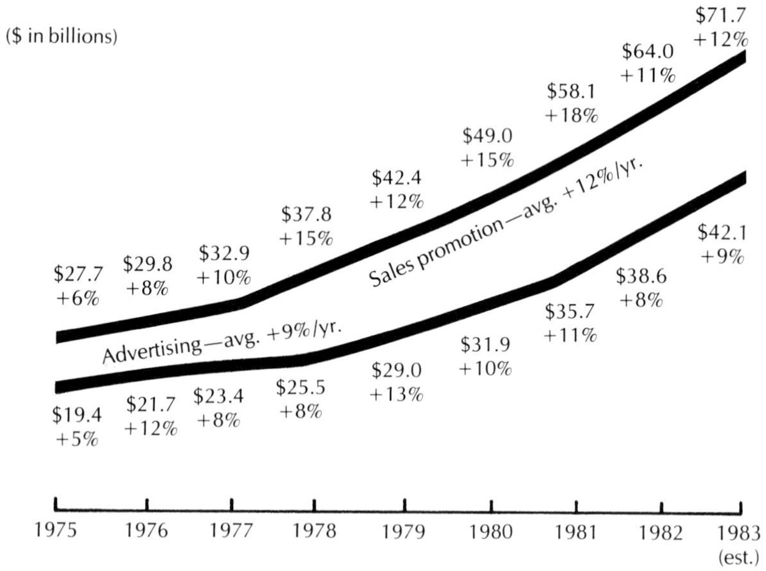

Source: Bowman, "Fourth Annual Advertising and Sales Promotion Report," *Marketing Communications* (August 1983), p. 6.

Defining Sales Promotion

William A. Robinson, *Advertising Age* columnist and sales promotion agency president, has defined sales promotion as "an activity in which a short-term incentive is offered to the trade or consumer to induce the purchase of a particular product."[2] The difference, of course, is the incentive, and the incentive is usually the key element in the sales promotion plan. Advertising and sales promotion can be differentiated in the following way: advertising offers the consumer a product with a *reason* to buy while sales promotion offers the product with an *incentive* to buy. Usually that incentive is either money, merchandise, or an additional service that ordinarily does not come with the product.

Since sales promotion comes in so many various forms, that often adds to the confusion. Indeed, not all people agree on even what constitutes sales promotion. Figure 13-2 illustrates the major areas of sales promotion and the percentage each accounted for in the total 1982 investment. The eight major areas of sales promotion investment are meetings and conventions; couponing; printing, audiovisual and miscellane-

---

2. Russell D. Bowman, "Third Annual Report: Advertising and Promotion Expenditures," *Marketing Communications* (September 1982), pp. 49–51.

Figure 13-2.   Major Areas of Sales Promotion Spending

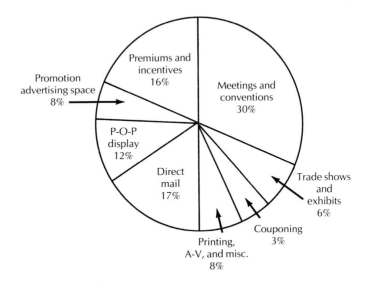

Source: Bowman, "Fourth Annual Advertising and Sales Promotion Report," *Marketing Communications* (August 1983), p. 6.

ous; promotion advertising space; direct mail; point-of-purchase display; trade shows and exhibits; and premiums and incentives.[3] Obviously, not all these areas of sales promotion will be important to the advertising campaign planner. Therefore, in this chapter, we'll concentrate on those segments and those sales promotion techniques which might be most helpful in the development of an advertising campaign.

With this brief description of what constitutes sales promotion, perhaps a look at the differences between advertising and sales promotion will help clarify how and why sales promotion is so important in the development of an advertising campaign.

Differences Between Advertising and Sales Promotion

While there are many obvious differences in the techniques used in advertising and sales promotion, there are five differences in objectives between the two.

1. As mentioned above, advertising attempts to communicate a sales message. Sales promotion offers an incentive to purchase at that particular time.

---

3. Bowman, "Fourth Annual Advertising and Sales Promotion Report, p. 6.

Figure 13-3. Seasonal Sales Levels as a Function of Base Business and Marketing Variables

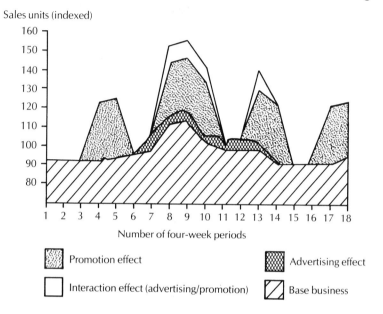

Source: Don Sunoo and Lynn Y. S. Lin, "Sales Effects of Promotion and Advertising," *Journal of Advertising Research,* 18, 5 (October 1978): 37.

2. Advertising is usually considered to be long term. That is, advertising may not seek an immediate consumer response. Sales promotion, however, is designed for immèdiate response and usually for a limited period of time.

3. Advertising is often used to create an image for the product or to give it a mood or feeling or identify those who use the brand. Sales promotion, however, is action oriented. The goal is an immediate sale.

4. Advertising may be used to help relate the product to competition through some comparison. Sales promotion attempts to differentiate the brand at a given place and time from all other brands in the field.

5. Advertising usually adds some perceptual value to the brand. Sales promotion, however, adds actual value in the attempt to create a sale.

Further, there are specific actions each of the two generate for the brand. For example, advertising is generally better at building brand awareness and at positioning the brand among the competition. It's also much better at building an image for the brand. Sales promotion, however, is much stronger in stimulating trial of a product by consumers. And, sales promotion is much more effective in improving distribution for a brand and in helping to get consumers to stock up on a brand. While there are major differences between advertising and sales promotion, these will likely become obvious as the various techniques and approaches used with sales promotion are explained.

The Synergism of Advertising and Sales Promotion

One of the most important things the advertising campaign planner must understand is that while advertising and sales promotion are indeed different and perform different functions in the promotion mix, when properly planned and executed they truly work together to assure a successful campaign. Together, they can generate response to the campaign far beyond that of either being used alone. A certain synergism in the use of advertising and sales promotion results when the combination is correctly developed. This synergism is illustrated in Figure 13-3, which shows the results of an 18-month test conducted for a major package goods advertiser using a cable television test system. The researchers, using several methodologies, were able to manipulate the advertising and sales promotion activities and then measure the effect of each. In addition, they could also measure the results when the two were used together. From the base business that the brand had, advertising was able to increase the sales a certain amount, sales promotion contributed another amount, and then, particularly in the peak periods, the combination of the two generated additional sales. This is the sort of effect the campaign planner hopes to achieve when developing a plan for the brand.[4]

Purposes of Sales Promotion

When people consider sales promotion and its purposes, generally various sales promotion techniques, such as coupons or sampling or contests or sweepstakes events, come to mind. In truth, there are several ways to look at sales promotion. The primary one to consider is the market to whom sales promotion is directed and the purpose for which sales promotion is used. There are three basic markets for sales promotion: (1) the consumer, (2) the trade or the people in the retail or distribution network, and (3) the sales force for the brand.

In general, sales promotion activities directed to the consumer have the basic purpose of inducing purchase of the brand. The typical goals are

4. Don Sunoo and Lyn Y. S. Lin, "Sales Effects of Promotion and Advertising," *Journal of Advertising Research* 18, 5 (October 1978): 37–40.

to either increase use among present users, to get prospects to switch from another brand, or simply to get people to start using a brand in the product category. Sales promotion activities directed to the trade or members of the retail distribution system are generally designed to either gain or increase distribution of the brand or to encourage the retailer to conduct some sort of special merchandising activity at the store level, such as reducing the price, building a display, or advertising the brand in the local market. The goal of sales promotion directed to the sales force usually is to encourage the sales force to make an extra effort in selling the brand, getting displays in retail stores, or simply to talk about the brand with their customers. Generally, these are the major uses of sales promotion in the advertising campaign.

Like advertising, sales promotion works best in certain marketing situations. For example, sales promotion works best in introducing new brands or in announcing significant improvements in existing brands. It seems to work well in supporting existing or established products with the retailer. Often, existing brands get lost in the maze of new products and sales promotion is used to remind the reseller and the consumer about the brand. Finally, sales promotion and various forms of merchandising are most effective when used to supplement ongoing media advertising campaigns. Sales promotion is the extra step. It can contribute to the success of the media campaign by providing the immediate stimulus to act.

Sales Promotion: Uses and Limitations

A brief review of what sales promotion can and can't do will be helpful.

What Sales Promotion Can Do

Generally, sales promotion can be used to accomplish five basic tasks for the brand.

Obtain trial of a product. Because sales promotion techniques are designed to provide short-term incentives to the consumer or reseller, trial of a new product, a reformulation of an existing product, or trial of a new category often can be achieved. While trial may be obtained, usually it is only initial trial. The product must provide the benefits promised to the consumer for long-term sales to be established.

Establish a purchasing pattern by persuading initial triers to repurchase. If the product delivers the benefit promised, sales promotion can aid in obtaining repeat purchases. This may establish purchase patterns. For example, a continuing sales promotion program requiring consumers to save for a premium may encourage repeat purchases enough so that a habit is formed. Thus, the sales promotion program solidifies the response by providing the repurchase incentive to obtain the promotional item.

Increase consumption of a product.   By identifying new or additional uses for an established product through sales promotion, consumption can often be increased. For example, a common sales promotion technique is the development and promotion of new recipes using the product as an ingredient. Sometimes these new recipes are compiled into a cookbook that is then used as a sales promotion feature. Similarly, a promotion that combines two products may help increase the consumption of both. An excellent example is the promotion developed by the Puerto Rican rum industry and Coca-Cola, which combined to promote the two products as a refreshing drink.

Neutralize competitive promotions.   Sales promotion is often used to help offset activities by competitors, particularly those that employ an especially effective competitive media campaign. By the same token, if competition has developed an effective sales promotion program, an offsetting advertising and sales promotion plan may be developed with the objective of holding present customers. Advertisers of leading brands, who seek to hold their share of market against invasion, often use sales promotion in this way.

Affect the sales of companion products.   Interestingly, sales promotion can not only increase the sale of the brand, but it can also have an influence on the sale of companion products as well. For example, A. C. Nielsen Company found that sales promotion activities supporting a brand of table syrup had an effect on the entire pancake mix category. (See Figure 13-4.)

What Sales Promotion Can't Do

Even the most brilliant sales promotional program cannot achieve some objectives.

Sales promotion can't build loyalty.   Sales promotion can achieve trial of a product or service, but it is always a short-term incentive. Only satisfaction with the product or service can build brand loyalty. Promotional methods may keep customers buying in the short run, but once the promotion stops, customers may switch to another brand unless the product fills a real need. Business bought with promotion can often be lost to promotion.

Sales promotion can't reverse a declining sales trend.   If the product has been in a lengthy sales decline or is in the latter stages of the product life

---

Figure 13-4.   The Side Effects of Sales Promotion

Both product categories are indexed at 100 in week 1, and over the course of the eight-week analysis you'll note a similarity in the direction of the trend lines. During the time interval there were no major promotions in the pancake mix product class; however, sales ranged as high as 67 percent greater in week 5 versus the base week. All of this sales movement appeared to trace to major promotions in the table syrup category during weeks 3 through 8. It is interesting to note the promoted brand in weeks 3 through 7 was the same (note the diminished effect upon product class sales), while in week 8 another brand was promoted for the first time and caused both product classes to respond.

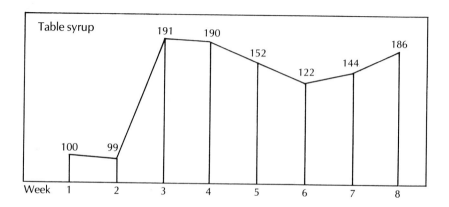

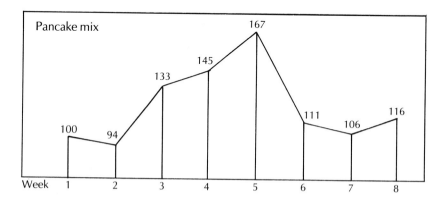

Source: A. C. Nielsen Company, *Nielsen National ScanTrack Service: Applications,* Sept. 1980, p. 11.

cycle, sales promotion can provide only momentary sales gains to stave off the eventual demise. It cannot save a dying brand or product. An outstanding sales promotion program, for example, could not have saved the buggy whip industry any more than it could have rescued the slide rule when hand-held calculators were introduced. While sales promotion is effective in many instances, it is not the panacea for all the ills of a product line or category.

Sale promotion cannot change the "nonacceptance" of a product. Quite the contrary, if a product is of little value or does not provide a consumer benefit, sales promotion, rather than increasing sales, may well hasten the decline. For example, assume a manufacturer of premixed soups develops a new flavor that does not match the quality of the rest of his line. In an effort to beat competition to the market, he does no consumer testing. A promotion program is designed to obtain trial for the newly developed flavor. Customers who try the new soup flavor reject it. Not only do they reject the new flavor, they assume the same poor flavor is in the rest of the product line. Thus, the more trial the promotion achieves, the fewer prospects the manufacturer has. Under normal circumstances, without sales promotion, trial of the new flavor might not have been so great. Product quality might have been improved before it was too late. Thus, while sales promotion obtained trial of the product, the long-term success of the promotion was actually negative.

Consumer Sales Promotion

Consumer sales promotion programs used in the advertising campaign are most often developed by the campaign planner, the advertising department, the advertising or sales promotion agency, or staff sales promotion experts. These plans are then usually executed by sales promotion specialists either inside or outside the organization. On the other hand, sales promotion efforts directed toward the trade and the sales force are usually planned and executed by the sales department or sales staff. The advertising campaign planner usually has some input and often is responsible for the general approach. The reason for the different task assignment is that the sales department is usually more closely involved with the wholesalers and retailers and is thus more attuned to what might be most effective to accomplish the objectives that have been set.

The discussion of sales promotion activities and techniques that follows will be based on the assumption that the advertising campaign planner is responsible for the actual events. In many cases today, however, the campaign planner consults with or develops the sales promotion program in cooperation with internal or external sales promotion experts or with a sales promotion agency.

Objectives of Consumer Sales Promotion Programs

Sales promotion plans can be designed to influence almost any target market the advertising campaign planner may define. Further, because of the wide variety of sales promotion techniques available and the combinations that can be developed, an effective plan can be structured to meet almost any objective the campaign planner may set from getting present customers to use more of the product to encouraging nonusers of the product category to try the product or service. The real strengths of sales promotion are its wide variety and appeal.

The standard approach to integrating sales promotion into the overall advertising campaign is, first, to use the target market description developed in the creative strategy. (See Chapter 9.) Next, determine exactly what the sales promotion program is supposed to accomplish and set some definite measurable objectives for the plan. While objectives will vary from campaign to campaign, any sales promotion plan usually has one or more of the following six basic objectives.

To attract customers not presently using. The objective of many sales promotion programs is to attract new triers. This usually means giving some incentive to users of competitive products to encourage them to try the brand. An alternative approach is to attract persons not using any brand in the particular product category. This is usually a more difficult task than a simple brand switch, although many successes have been reported.

To hold present customers. Most products rely on a stable base of users for much of their business. Therefore, it is usually as important to hold present customers as to attract new ones. Thus, while competitors attempt to take customers away with sales promotions designed to attract new triers, marketers develop programs they hope will hold their present customers.

To load current users. One way to hold current customers is to "load them with the product" or "take them out of the market" for a period of time. This plan encourages present customers to purchase a large enough supply of the product so they will not be purchasing again in the near future. This serves two purposes. First, it ensures that customers will continue using the advertiser's product since it is on hand. Second, with a sufficient supply of the product available, there is little likelihood that present customers will respond to a competitor's promotional offer.

To increase product usage. As was previously discussed, one of the major objectives of many sales promotion plans is to increase product usage. With a slowly growing consumer population, new or other uses must be found for many products to increase consumption. Continually attempting to take business from the competition is a very expensive proposition and, in the long run, usually results in constant consumer brand switching that results in negligible increases for any brand. A better long-term strategy may be to increase the user base for the product or service.

One of the most common methods of increasing product usage is through suggesting additional uses. A common method used by food advertisers is to develop new recipes or new uses for the product or brand.

To trade consumers up to a higher quality or higher price level. An objective for many brands is to get consumers to "trade up" or buy a more expensive brand or model than that which they would normally use. This is often done through a reduced price offer of some sort. Many automobile manufacturers, for example, often promote specially equipped models with stereo radio, air conditioning, bucket seats, and other options with a reduced or combination price. The objective is to get customers accustomed to these conveniences so their next purchase may be made at the regular price. Similarly, a bar soap manufacturer might attempt to move its present customers up to a higher price or level of quality through promotional activity such as multipacks, a new size, or the inclusion of free face cloths.

To reinforce brand advertising. Last, but certainly not least, is the objective of increasing awareness of or simply reinforcing the current brand advertising. A common example is a consumer premium tied to the advertising campaign such as the inflatable Dole banana, the Jolly Green Giant kite, or cowboy accessories sold through the "Marlboro Country Store," all designed to support the advertising campaign. In some instances, the advertising itself becomes an effective sales promotion tool, as in the use of advertising jingles that are turned into popular songs and sold as records.

Consumer Sales Promotion Techniques

Just as various advertising appeals can be developed to impart specific sales messages to consumers, various sales promotion techniques can be used to achieve specific sales promotion objectives such as trial for a brand or increased usage or repeat purchase. While it might seem unlikely to the novice planner, all consumer sales promotion activities can be traced back to ten basic sales promotion techniques.[5] It is the combination and variation of these techniques however that enables the campaign planner to

---

5. Don E. Schultz and William A. Robinson, *Sales Promotion Essentials* (Chicago: Crain Books, 1982).

develop a novel and unique approach for the sales promotion plan. When the creative approaches that can be used with each of the ten techniques or combination of techniques available are included, an almost limitless supply of sales promotion ideas, strategies, and executions can be developed for most any brand. That's the beauty of sales promotion. The real key to successful use of sales promotion in the advertising campaign is to know and understand the various available techniques. It is the job of the campaign planner to maximize these strengths and minimize those weaknesses that really determines how successful the sales promotion segment of the campaign will be.

Figure 13-5.   Coupon

Ragu foods introduced its new Homestyle Spaghetti Sauce with large value coupons such as this in newspapers across the country.

Source: Courtesy of Ragu Foods, Inc.

Coupons. Coupons are one of the oldest yet still one of the most effective sales promotion tools available to the campaign planner.

There are two types of coupons: manufacturer-distributed coupons and store coupons. Manufacturer-distributed coupons make an offer on a particular brand by the manufacturer of the product. These coupons may be redeemed at any retail store that carries the product. For example, a coupon good for 40¢ off the purchase price on Ragu Homestyle Spaghetti Sauce could be redeemed at any retail outlet that stocked the product. (See Figure 13-5.) Store coupons, on the other hand, are redeemable only at the store that offers the coupon. For example, if A&P placed a coupon in its newspaper advertisement offering 10¢ off on the purchase of Ragu Home-style Spaghetti Sauce, that coupon would be good only at the A&P store, not at Safeway or Kroger. Stores develop their own coupons to generate promotional activity or, in some cases, to tie in with manufacturer promotions.

The basic advantage of the coupon is that it allows the advertiser to reduce the price of his or her product at retail by a specific amount without relying on cooperation from the retailer. Coupons are used to induce trial of a new product or to gain trial of a new or improved product. They may also be used as distribution-forcing devices, as competitive weapons against promotional activities by competitors, and as control techniques to limit the number of redemptions of certain types of promotions. While the primary purpose of coupons is to induce trial, they are also used to encourage repeat purchase of the product. For example, often a manufacturer will attach a coupon to the product good for a certain amount off on the purchase of the product the next time. This is a form of reward to the customer for use and encourages a repeat purchase.

Couponing can take many forms. The most traditional is a cents-off coupon distributed through media channels. Figure 13-6 illustrates the distribution of coupons by medium for a three-year period as measured by Nielsen Clearing House. Coupons may be distributed by attaching them to or including them in the package. Another approach is the "cross-ruff." This is a coupon for one product that is either packaged with or printed on the package of another, often complementary, product but not necessarily from the same manufacturer. Another popular method of coupon distribution is through cooperative mailings to selected homes. In these co-op mailings, an independent organization gathers the coupons of several marketers and mails or delivers them in a single envelope to consumer homes. The distribution cost is thus split among the participants.

The value of coupons varies as widely as the products on which they are used. The range for package goods coupons is usually from 10¢ to 50¢, although there are no prescribed norms. The most popular coupon value is now 15¢, although this tends to increase according to the retail price of the

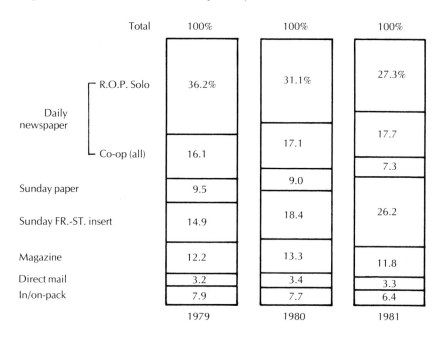

Figure 13-6.　Distribution of Coupons by Media

	Total	100%	100%	100%
Daily newspaper { R.O.P. Solo		36.2%	31.1%	27.3%
				17.7
Co-op (all)		16.1	17.1	7.3
Sunday paper		9.5	9.0	
Sunday FR.-ST. insert		14.9	18.4	26.2
Magazine		12.2	13.3	11.8
Direct mail		3.2	3.4	3.3
In/on-pack		7.9	7.7	6.4
		1979	1980	1981

Source: A. C. Nielsen Company, *NCH Reporter*, No. 1, 1982, p. 1.

product. The "buy one—get one free" coupon is increasingly popular. It is commonly used with existing products when the advertiser is attempting to take the consumer out of the marketplace for a period of time. A relatively recent innovation is the "self-destruct" coupon. Two coupons are printed together in an overlapping fashion. One coupon is for a lesser amount on the small size or purchase of one item, while the overlapping coupon has a greater value on a large size or multiple purchase. When one coupon is used, the second is destroyed. Another type, the so-called "instant reward" coupon, is attached to the package. The consumer rips off the coupon and redeems it at the checkout—thus the "instant reward" name.

Advertisers are constantly devising new couponing techniques. For example, some retail outlets use a specially printed roll of cash register tape. On the back of the tape are printed coupons good for reduced prices at the store itself or at other retail outlets located nearby. For example, a food store might carry a coupon for a movie theater on the back of its cash register tapes.

Coupons are an increasingly popular method of consumer promotion, as is shown in Figures 13-6 and 13-7, from information developed by the A. C. Nielsen Company. Figure 13-7 shows the increasing use of coupons by manufacturers from 1977 to 1981. The 65 percent usage increase reflects not only an increasing number of coupons by manufacturers but also an increasing number of companies using coupons as a promotion tool.

One of the major difficulties in a couponing program is determining the estimated level of redemption the coupon may achieve. Few, if any, coupons are ever redeemed at 100 percent rate. In addition, the method of distribution of the coupon has a direct effect on the redemption. Figure 13-8 shows the average redemption rate for the various types of grocery product class coupons in 1979 through 1981, as measured by Nielsen Clearing House. As can be seen, although newspapers still account for the largest number of coupons, they have a low redemption rate, trailing only magazines.

Coupon promotion costs are not limited to the value of the coupon. Several other factors must be included as well. Traditionally, coupons redeemed through retail stores allow an amount for retailer handling. Currently, retailers receive 7¢ per retail coupon for handling regardless of coupon value. This amount is subject to change by agreement with the retailers or their trade organizations. In addition, a charge is made by the clearing house or other organization that gathers the coupons, reimburses the retailer, and bills the manufacturer. While costs vary tremendously according to type of coupon, distribution, and other factors, the rule of thumb is to include about 4¢ per coupon for this service. Thus, a 15¢ coupon actually will cost the manufacturer about 26¢ for each redemption made (15¢ coupon value + 7¢ retailer handling + 4¢ clearing house = 26¢ total).

Another consideration in couponing is the length of time during which coupons may be redeemed. In most instances, an expiration date is included on the coupon. A cents-off coupon is usually valid from six months to one year after distribution. While the majority of redemptions will occur in the first three months, redemptions may continue for the length of the coupon offer and sometimes after if retailers fail to honor the expiration date and continue to redeem the coupons at retail. Sufficient funds must be set aside by the campaign planner for estimated coupon redemption when this type of promotion is being planned.

Misredemption is a major factor to be considered in any coupon redemption costs; i.e., incorrectly or fraudulently redeemed coupons. Misredemption can occur anywhere along the distribution channel from the consumer to the retailer to the wholesaler. For example, the consumer may ask that the coupon be allowed on the purchase of a competitive product or simply that the money be refunded. The retailer may accept

Figure 13-7.   Trend in Coupon Distribution

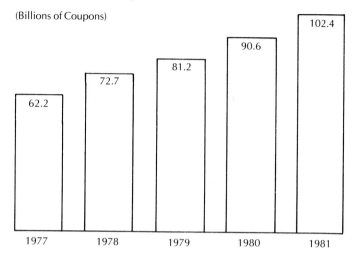

(Billions of Coupons)

Source: A. C. Nielsen Company, *NCH Reporter,* No. 1, 1982.

Figure 13-8.   Coupon Redemption Rates by Media

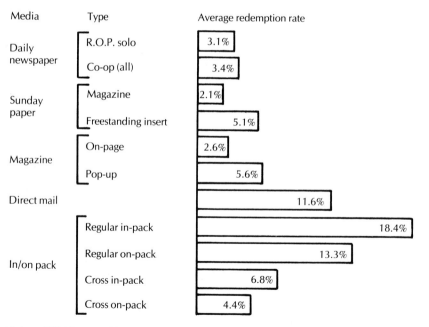

Source: A. C. Nielsen, *NCH Reporter,* No. 1, 1982.

out-of-date coupons or buy up large quantities of newspapers, cut the coupons, and redeem them without selling the product. Sometimes, criminals actually print up numbers of valuable coupons and sell them to unscrupulous merchants who in turn redeem them from the manufacturer. Misredemption requires constant policing. The major problem, however, is that misredemption is usually discovered only after it has occurred and there is little recourse for the advertiser. Most advertisers allocate a certain percentage for misredemption into their estimates since they have little control over this problem.

A factor that affects the number of redemptions of coupons is the value of the coupon itself. For example, a coupon good for $1.00 off has much more appeal than one for 10¢. Other factors are the product category, whether the product is purchased regularly or occasionally, the amount of discount off the regular retail price, and the percentage discount off the purchase price that the coupon allows, to mention just a few. Most clearing houses have developed estimates of redemption based on their experience with various types of coupons. These may be used to help determine the amount that should be set aside to help cover the cost of a couponing program.

Sampling. With most new products, particularly package goods, one of the primary marketing objectives is to obtain trial usage. Because most prospective customers already use an established brand, simply getting a presently satisfied user of a competitive product to switch to a new brand may be a herculean task. One method that has proved successful over the years is sampling. It also appears to work successfully for product reformulations and the reinforcing of current brand usage for existing products.

Sampling can take many shapes and forms. (See Figure 13-9.) For low-priced products, the least expensive sampling unit is often the regular product. For more expensive products or those in which several uses or servings are purchased at one time, a sample package may be developed. The purpose of a sample is to provide a sufficient supply of the product so the consumer can judge its merits.

While samples are normally distributed to prospects at no charge, another technique that is gaining importance is the sale of a trial package at retail. This is usually a special size of the product for which the advertiser charges a price to offset some of his or her costs. The trial-size offer has appeal to the retailer who receives a profit on the sales of sample goods rather than seeing them given away. The sale of the trial sample appears to be particularly appealing to advertisers whose products have a relatively high unit price such as cosmetics, drugs, and health and beauty aids.

The chief problem inherent in any sampling program is finding an effective yet cost-efficient method of distribution. Many methods are used, but four basic approaches are most common: through-the-mail, hand delivered to the prospects' door, as an on-pack with an existing product, and in-store sampling by demonstrators.

The through-the-mail method offers the advertiser the obvious advantage of being able to control fairly closely where and when the product is distributed. This permits demographic or geographic targeting. Cost and postal limitations on some products are usually the primary problems with through-the-mail.

The problem of cost is the major disadvantage of delivery to the prospect's door. The opportunity to control where and when the samples are distributed and the fact that almost any product can be distributed are almost overwhelmed by the sheer cost of personal delivery. Cooperative ventures, where several products are distributed at once often helps reduce the cost problem of door-to-door delivery.

Personal Products Company developed the sample package of their Sure & Natural Maxishields to distribute to prospective users. The sample packet illustrated in Figure 13-9 was sent to females through the mail and delivered directly to the home. It contained five units, enough for the woman to accurately determine the value of the product. While this particular sample was distributed free, some samples are sold through retailers at a low price to encourage trial. Many of the samples sold in stores are miniatures of the actual product package. That way, the consumer who has used the sample knows what to look for when shopping for a full-size package of the product.

Figure 13-9.   Product Sample through the Mail

Source: Courtesy of Personal Product Co. Sure & Natural is the trademark of Personal Products Company, Milltown, NJ 08850.

The on-pack sample has the major advantage of low cost. The disadvantage, however, is that it is distributed only to those persons who purchase the product with which it is packaged. Thus, packing a sample of a new soy sauce with a brand of chow mein limits the product trial to purchasers of the specific brand of chow mein selected and not the entire market.

In-store sampling is becoming increasingly important in many areas, particularly for food products. In these cases, persons, usually called "demonstrators," set up a table or booth, prepare the product, and offer samples to shoppers. This approach is particularly effective for food products because the consumer has an opportunity to taste the product prior to purchase. In addition, the "demonstrator" can often deliver a sales message during the sampling. The major disadvantages are the extremely high cost and limited number of stores in which the promotion can be conducted. It requires space, product, personnel, and a great deal of planning. It can, however, be one of the most effective of all sampling methods.

New and unique methods of sampling through the media are being developed. Samples of the product often can be bound into a magazine or

Figure 13-10.   Media Sampling for a Product

Source: Courtesy of General Foods Corporation. BRIM is a registered trademark of General Foods Corp.

included with the local newspaper. (See Figure 13-10.) An interesting way to sample a product is through the media-delivered sample used by Brim Decaffeinated Coffee. A packet of the coffee was attached to a page in a preprinted Sunday newspaper insert and distributed to all newspaper purchasers on that specific day. Brim was able to reach newspaper readers at a fraction of the cost of other forms of sample distribution. This, of course, applies only to a limited number of small, inexpensive, nonbreakable products.

Sampling is a big business and brings dramatic results. Advertisers are willing to invest large sums of money to achieve trial. For example, a few years ago, Procter & Gamble, to introduce a new brand, distributed over a million one-pound samples of coffee in one geographic area of the country.

The campaign planner has several cost factors to consider in a sampling program. First is the cost of the sample itself. Next is the cost of distribution. Often special packages or promotional literature to accompany the sample must be printed. When a coupon is included to encourage trial, its cost must also be included. Sampling is expensive but can be worth it. Because sampling is such a complex operation, the campaign planner usually relies on advice from one of the many specialized sampling organizations when planning this type of promotion.

In short, sampling works and works well. The key to successful sampling is to obtain cost efficiency while still distributing the product to the proper target market.

Contests and sweepstakes. Contests and sweepstakes generate a great deal of interest among consumers, especially if the prize structure is appealing. The major question, however, is whether running the contest or sweepstakes will contribute to product sales. Most of the promotion supporting a sweepstakes or contest is directed only to the contest, not the brand. Unless the campaign is carefully planned, the brand's sales message may easily get lost in the excitement of the promotion. The contest or sweepstakes may be a success, but the advertiser may fail to achieve the desired sales goals.

Figure 13-11 illustrates a contest and a sweepstakes for the same brand. The sales promotion event on the left is a contest for Chef Boyardee pizza mix and Ekco's Baker's Secret Bakeware. Entrants are required to develop a pizza recipe, which requires a form of skill or ability. Prizes will be awarded on the basis of the recipe received. On the right is a sweepstakes event developed for the Chef Boyardee line. All contestants had to do was send in the entry blank. Prizes were then awarded on the basis of a drawing among all entries received. Each of the events was designed to achieve specific sales promotion objectives but each is dramatically different.

Figure 13-11.   Contests and Sweepstakes

Source: Courtesy of American Home Products.

While contests and sweepstakes are often lumped together in the same promotional category, a major difference exists between them. Contests are promotions in which participants compete for a prize or prizes based on some sort of skill or ability. Usually this consists of answering questions, completing sentences, or writing phrases or paragraphs about the product or its advantages, all of which require some form of talent. Sweepstakes, on the other hand, require only that the entrant submit his or her name to be included in a drawing or other form of awarding prizes. Because of the additional effort required of contest entrants, sweepstakes promotions usually draw about ten times more entries than contests.

Contests and sweepstakes appear to work best in generating interest in a parity product or one that has no particular promotional advantage. They may also be used to help renew enthusiasm for the product at the retail level or to help in revitalizing an existing advertising campaign theme.

In addition, sweepstakes and contests do increase the readership of the advertising in which they are promoted. Consumers who have an interest in the promotion usually read the advertising more thoroughly than they do normal product advertising. Another advantage of a contest or sweepstakes is the opportunity to tie the promotion directly to the creative approach being used in regular advertising. For example, if a pineapple processor's advertising campaign is built around the sunny climate of Hawaii, a sweepstakes or contest built around trips to the islands will help reinforce the brand's sales message.

Finally, advertisers can often develop a large sweepstakes or contest prize list for a relatively small amount of money. Many manufacturers are willing to sell their products at less than retail cost to sweepstakes or contest promoters simply to obtain the additional advertising exposure their products will receive.

A major consideration in a contest or sweepstakes is preventing the event from becoming a lottery, which is illegal under federal laws. Lotteries have three basic elements: luck or chance, prizes or awards, and consideration on the part of the contestant. The consideration portion of a lottery is where problems usually occur. Any campaign planner contemplating a contest or sweepstakes should consult qualified promotion and legal experts to ensure compliance with all federal, state, and local regulations.

Although contest and sweepstakes promotions seem to rise and fall in popularity with advertisers, some factors remain fairly constant; e.g., sweepstakes are usually more popular with entrants than contests, and cash and merchandise seem to generate the most enthusiasm as prizes. Oddly enough, offering too many prizes can create problems. Many contest developers suggest no more than a total of 100 prizes. Finally, the value of the contest or sweepstakes must be carefully weighed. With many states now conducting monthly legal lotteries with prizes up to and including $1,000,000 in cash, the prize structure of a contest or sweepstakes must be carefully planned.

Recent federal regulations require that all prizes offered in a contest or sweepstakes be awarded or that notification be made if all prizes are not to be awarded. Prior to this ruling, advertisers offered large prize structures and gambled that only part of the prizes would be collected. Now, however, the total prize package is a known cost, plus the advertising support required to promote it properly.

Refund offers. Refunds are offers to return all or part of the product purchase price when a certain requirement is met such as supplying proofs of purchase. (See Figure 13-12.) Many advertisers believe this type of promotion builds brand loyalty. They reason that if the consumer uses the product a number of times to obtain necessary proofs of purchase for the refund, a purchase habit or brand loyalty will result. Also, when consumers

Figure 13-12.   Refund Offer

Source: Courtesy of the Green Giant Company, a subsidiary of the Pillsbury Company.

take advantage of refund offers, the advertiser obtains their names and addresses. This helps pinpoint the user market and also offers followup sales opportunities.

Refunds are growing rapidly in popularity with sales promotion planners, and consumers are responding to refund offers. Manufacturer's Marketing Services found the percentage of homes responding to refund offers increased from 34 percent in 1978 to 59 percent in 1979.[6] Doubtless that number will grow in the future.

While refund offers can be designed to have many purposes, the basic objectives usually set for this technique are to (a) obtain product trial, (b) reward customers, and (c) provide some form of continuity purchase program for the brand. Refund offers designed to generate trial typically appear in media advertising. Those offers that seek to reward present users appear in or on the package.

One of the newest forms of refunds is to offer varying refunds based on

---

6.   Louis J. Haugh, "Cash Refunds Multiply," *Advertising Age*, May 5, 1980, p. 48.

the number of labels returned or the number of units of the brand purchased. (See Figure 13-12.) In addition, refund offers may be made for the value of the product purchased, a set amount or a varying amount based on other factors. The refund is limited only by the imagination of the planner.

Refunds are particularly attractive to many advertisers because of their relatively low cost. In many refund offers, consumers will start to save for the refund and never get around to collecting enough proofs of purchase or simply forget to send them in. This is called "slippage" and occurs with almost all refund offers. Typically, the refund offer will not redeem more than 1 to 2 percent of the media circulation in which the offer is made. Thus, the advertiser gets the benefit of the promotion, but the actual cost may be relatively low.

The Green Giant offer in Figure 13-12 illustrates a basic refund offer in which money is returned for purchasing the product. In addition, to make the incentive greater and to encourage multiple purchases, Green Giant offers multiple refunds for multiple purchases. For example "collect 4 symbols, receive $1; collect 8 symbols, receive $2; or collect 12 symbols, receive $3." In addition, note how the proof-of-purchase requirement is identified to make it easy for the consumer to know what to do.

The primary disadvantage of the refund offer is that it actually amounts to a discount on the product. While the offer must be large enough to gain attention, making it too great may result in the majority of refunds going to present users so that no additional sales result. In addition, many refund offers hold low interest for consumers. For example, brand-loyal customers don't respond to refund offers for competing products, so there is little trial among this important group. Finally, most refund offers don't generate immediate sales increases. Since it takes time for consumers to purchase and use the product, sales results often aren't noticeable for several weeks.

Several cost factors must be considered in a refund offer. First is the value of the refund. Also, most offers are handled through clearing house organizations such as Nielsen, which charge for handling the redemption plus the return postage. With a charge of approximately 11.5¢ for each redemption handled plus the return postage, 31.5¢ must be added to the value of the refund offer to determine redemption costs to the advertiser.

One reason many advertisers like to use refunds is that the response can be varied simply by manipulating three factors: (a) by varying the value of the refund; (b) by raising or lowering the number of proofs-of-purchase required for the refund; and (c) varying the ways in which the offer is advertised. Refunds can provide major incentives to the advertiser, and the alert campaign planner will usually consider some form of refund offer in the overall advertising plan.

Price-offs.   A promotional tool often used in connection with an advertising campaign is the price-off or price pack. This promotion may take many forms. The two most common are a cents-off label or a two-for-the-price-of-one offer. (See Figure 13-13.)

Since the FTC investigations of the early 1960s into the misuse of these promotions, stringent rules have been developed on the use of cents-off labels and price packs. For example, the FTC has developed a series of "guides," which are used as aids in developing advertising and merchandising materials. The "Guide Against Deceptive Pricing" covers such areas as former price comparisons, retail price comparisons, comparable value comparisons, advertising retail prices that have been established or suggested by manufacturers or other nonretail distributors, and bargain offers based on the purchase of other merchandise. These guides outline suggested methods of presenting offers fairly to the consuming public.

Generally, the guides require that price comparisons be legitimate and bona fide, based on former pricing of the products. Thus, if a two-for-the-price-of-one offer is made, the suggested price for both products must equal the former price for only one. The same is true for other types of promotional activities that involve previous, prior, or combination pricing.

The price-off technique offers the advertising campaign planner broad promotional opportunities. For example, with the cents-off label, a significant price reduction can be promoted to the consumer with the assurance the savings will actually be passed along and not absorbed in the retail channels. The price pack offers the same advantages as the retail coupon but has none of the accompanying redemption costs for retailers or clearing houses. Additionally, accurate estimates of the promotion costs can be determined in advance. Finally, the use of special product labels can actually turn the package into a sales promotion tool at the retail level. This is increasingly important as self-service increases in retail outlets.

Procter & Gamble reduced the price of the 20-sheet Bounce Fabric Softener package by 15¢ as illustrated in Figure 13-13. Note that the offer.

Figure 13-13.   Price-Off Promotion

Source: Courtesy of Procter & Gamble.

a 15¢ reduction from the regular price. Price-off promotions can be used with almost any type of product that has a label or package simply by printing the spot or burst and explaining the offer.

The major disadvantage of the price pack is that, to be most effective, the offer must be advertised to the consumer. Without advertising, the reduced price may go unnoticed unless the consumer is shopping for the specific item. Therefore, cents-off or price packs usually work best for established products, since consumers have a base against which to judge the price reduction on an established brand. In spite of this, promoters of new brands often make use of the price pack or cents-off label promotion.

Bonus packs. Another method marketers use to assure that their sales promotion offers reach the consumer is through the bonus pack. This is usually a larger size of the standard package or a standard pack with additional merchandise offered at the current price. It is widely used in the food and health and beauty aids categories. An example might be an offer from a marketer of vitamin pills to include 25 extra pills in a bottle of 100. The unit is priced the same as a 100-pill pack, and the 25 are thus a "bonus" to the consumer. (See Figure 13-14.)

Bonus packs are widely used by marketers who are planning on introducing a new, larger size of their product. For example, a ketchup marketer might plan on replacing the 26 oz. size bottle with a 30 oz. bottle over the course of several months. While the changeover is taking place, a label might be placed on the 30 oz. bottle identifying it as a "bonus pack," with a line that might say: "4 ounces of ketchup free in this bottle." Once

Figure 13-14.   Bonus Pack

Source: Courtesy of Consumer Products Division, Abbott Laboratories.

the old containers have been sold out of the market, then the price of the 30 oz. size can then be increased and the bonus pack offer ended simply by changing the label.

Bonus packs, like price-offs, appeal primarily to present users. They are used to encourage more or additional use of the brand by those who already buy since the offer acts as a reward for purchase. They can also be used to "load" customers with the product, i.e., give them additional product they might not have had. The bonus pack is also used to try and hold present users in the face of some competitive sales promotion or advertising activity.

Selsun Blue made use of the bonus pack when they included 35 percent more shampoo in the package illustrated in Figure 13-14. The consumer received 9.5 oz. of the product at the price of 7 oz., or a 35 percent increase at the same price. This bonus pack should give the consumer quite an incentive to purchase at this time. And, by doing so, Selsun Blue would take them out of the market for any competitive promotions.

Generally, bonus packs do little to induce trial or help to build the brand image of the product. They also can be quite expensive since they often require special packaging and additional handling in the plant and in the retail store. The bonus pack offers the campaign planner an effective tool when the objective of the campaign is to either build total volume for the brand or to reward present users.

In-pack, on-pack, near-pack premiums and reusable containers. While these promotional vehicles are related, they have distinct characteristics and will be discussed separately. The mention of in-pack or on-pack premiums immediately brings to mind ready-to-eat cereals. Yet, in-packs and on-packs also are strong incentives for many other product categories. The only difference between the in-pack and on-pack premiums is the manner in which it is included in the package. (See Figure 13-15.) The major advantage of these offers is that the product must be purchased for the consumer to obtain the premium. If a very desirable premium is available and promoted, substantial sales may be achieved that would not otherwise occur. Because all in-pack and on-pack premiums will eventually be distributed, premiums are usually low cost or are built into the retail price of the product.

A different form of in-pack premium is the continuity program, in which a series of premiums is collected by consumers over a period of time. For example, some detergent manufacturers have in-pack continuity programs that encourage the consumer to continue to purchase the brand time after time to obtain the full set of dishes, towels, or kitchen gadgets.

For campaign planners, the advantages of the in-pack or on-pack premium are the known cost of the promotion and the opportunity to promote the premium. Each package is known to contain the premium and

Figure 13-15.   In-Pack and On-Pack Premiums

Sources: Post and Honeycomb are registered trademarks of General Foods Corporation, White Plains, NY. Edge lathering gel courtesy of Personal Care Division, S. C. Johnson & Son, Inc.

ensures that promotional expenditures will not be wasted by the lack of premium availability at the retail level.

In Figure 13-15 (left) the Honeycomb ready-to-eat cereal package illustrates how an in-pack premium is featured on the box. A free pack of Trident sugarless gum was packed in each Honeycomb cereal box as a special incentive to buy. A second promotion, "Post Fun 'n Fitness," which was described elsewhere on the box, was an additional reason to buy. On the right, a free Schick Super II razor was attached as an on-pack premium to each package of Edge lathering gel for a limited period of time. The promotion was also featured on the can itself to call attention to the offer.

Recent events have discouraged some marketers from using in-pack and on-pack premiums as heavily as in the past. First, of course, is cost. Finding a desirable premium at a reasonable cost becomes more and more difficult as prices continue to increase. Recent Federal Trade Commission and National Association of Broadcasters codes have placed stringent requirements on television advertising of premiums, particularly to children. The U.S. Food and Drug Administration also has quite stringent regulations about premiums packed with food products based on such factors as size, shape, and packaging of the premium. Thus, before deciding that an in-pack premium is an attractive promotional tool, the advertising campaign planner should seek the advice of an expert in the field.

Near-pack premiums are offered by the manufacturer but are not attached in any way to the package. The near-pack premium offer is usually made by offering the premium with the purchase of the product. For example, a Chinese food manufacturer may offer a Chinese kite with the purchase of chow mein noodles. Since the premium cannot be attached, it is stocked nearby (near pack), and the offer is made on the package or through promotional signs that a kite may be taken if the noodles are purchased. The near-pack is simply a method of offering a large or bulky premium with the purchase of the product.

The reusable container is exactly that—the product is packed in a container that can be used for other things around the home after the product has been used up. Coffee and drink mix manufacturers have made wide use of reusable containers as a method of differentiating their product from competition.

Free-in-the-mail premiums. The name describes the technique. An offer of a free premium or gift, which is sent through the mail, is made to the consumer. Typically, this offer is made on the basis of sending in proof-of-purchase symbols or other signs that the product has been purchased. Normally, more than one proof-of-purchase is required to obtain the premium. (See Figure 13-16.)

Trix and Lucky Charms combined two sales promotion techniques in this advertisement. They offer coupons good for cents-off on the products plus a free-in-the-mail premium. The premium is imprinted with either the Trix rabbit or the Lucky Charms leprechaun and the brand slogan. It is available free for proof-of-purchase of five packages of either of the products.

Free-in-the-mail premiums, unlike other premiums, do not immediately reward the purchaser, since typically there is a delay in receiving the premium and an even greater delay when multiple proofs-of-purchase are required. In spite of this, this technique seems to work very well in competitive situations in which there is little or no product difference. In many cases, the premium offered can be personalized or made more attractive in some way since it must be ordered and then shipped. To be effective, most free-in-the-mail premiums must be promoted through

Figure 13-16.   Free-in-the-Mail Premiums

Source: Courtesy of General Mills, Inc.

media advertising to call attention to the offer. Thus, there is additional expense involved with this type of technique.

The primary goal of most free-in-the-mail promotions is to reward present customers and to keep them buying. It also works in creating a trial or brand switch if the premium is attractive enough. In most instances, free premiums tend to have utilitarian value and are closely allied to the product being promoted. It is assumed that the premium will continue to remain with the consumer and serve as a reminder of the brand. Thus, many free-in-the-mail premiums are imprinted with the name of the manufacturer, a brand, or logotype.

Because of the wide variety of free premiums, it is impossible to give rule-of-thumb estimates of costs. The campaign planner should consult a premium-manufacturing firm or sales promotion organization.

Self-liquidating premiums. Self-liquidating premiums are items offered, usually with proof of purchase of the product, at a price that covers the out-of-pocket cost of the item. For example, a soup manufacturer may offer a set of specially designed soup mugs for proof of purchase of the product

Figure 13-17.   Self-Liquidating Premium

Source: Courtesy of The Pillsbury Company.

and a certain amount of money. The price paid by the consumer covers the actual premium cost plus postage and handling. Because self-liquidating premiums are purchased in large quantities by the advertiser, the price is usually much lower than if the same item were purchased at retail. Thus, there is a savings to the consumer. (See Figure 13-17.)

The Pillsbury Company offered a "Pillsbury's BEST Heritage Can-nister" for $2.50 plus two proofs of purchase from a 5-pound bag or larger of Pillsbury's BEST flour. The illustration on the cannister was a reproduction of the original poster artwork commemorating Pillsbury's "A" Mill, where Pillsbury's BEST flour began in 1879. Thus, consumers are reminded of the Pillsbury heritage every time they take flour from the cannister in the home. In addition to the self-liquidating premium, Pillsbury backed up the promotion with a 15¢-off coupon on the purchase of the product.

Self-liquidators offer the advertiser several advantages. First, the cost of the premium is borne by the consumer. Second, the premium is often tied directly to the advertising campaign or theme, and thus the advertising message is extended at no cost. An excellent example is the wide use

Budweiser and Coca-Cola have made of premiums using their brands and logotypes on all types of clothing, glassware, and other items. Third, by purchasing in large quantities, the manufacturer can offer excellent values on products used as premiums and thus generate interest in the brand.

The major disadvantage of the self-liquidating approach is the usual requirement by the premium supplier that the sales of a certain number of the premiums be guaranteed. If the premium is a success, there is no problem. However, if the premium redemption does not achieve the guaranteed number, the advertiser may find him- or herself holding a large supply of premiums that have little appeal to the consumer or that are tied to last year's advertising.

A major change in self-liquidating premiums has occurred in the past few years. Some advertisers are now promoting premiums that have no brand identification. Others have selected premiums with rather high prices. Usually self-liquidating premiums have been in the under-$20 category, but some advertisers have had success with more expensive premiums such as the KOOL cigarette sailboat at well over $500. The real success of a self-liquidating premium is usually the premium itself and the amount of promotion put behind the offer.

An alternative way to judge the value of a self-liquidating premium, other than counting the number of premiums redeemed, is the number of in-store or retailer displays that are gained through the use of the premium. Often, in fact, the goal of the self-liquidating premium is to gain retail displays with the actual distribution of the premiums a secondary consideration. The display of a self-liquidating premium with the product in a retail store can often move much merchandise on an impulse basis when combined with a well-planned advertising campaign.

Stamp and continuity plans. Stamp and continuity plans are simply promotional programs in which the consumer either collects stamps, coupons, or receipts and redeems them for free or reduced prices on gifts or prizes. By collecting the required proofs of purchase the consumer is encouraged to either purchase a brand on a regular basis or to shop at a particular retail store to fulfill the particular game plan. Continuity programs are particularly widespread among supermarket chains, some of which seem to have an endless parade of continuity plans, such as a set of dishes, pots and pans, jewelry, lawn furniture and the like. (See Figure 13-18.)

Stamps and continuity plans seem to rise and fall in popularity with the public and with marketers. A few years ago, nearly every supermarket and gasoline service station had some type of trading stamp. Today, hardly any feature this type of sales promotion program.

A prime example of the stamp-type plan among consumer brands is

Figure 13-18. Retail Continuity Plan

Source: Courtesy of Dominick's Finer Foods, Inc.

the General Mills program featuring Betty Crocker coupons. On General Mills consumer food products ranging from ready-to-eat cereals to cake mixes, the consumer can find Betty Crocker coupons either in or on the packages. By saving those coupons, the consumer may order flatware, kitchen utensils, and the like from a catalog at greatly reduced prices. The plan has been in existence since 1930. (See Figure 13-19.)

Figure 13-19. Stamp or Coupon Continuity Plan

Source: Courtesy of Betty Crocker Division, General Mills, Inc.

The obvious objective of the stamp or continuity plan is to encourage present users to continue to purchase the brand or shop the retail store. These types of programs are usually most effective with present users and they do give a method of differentiating among parity brands. In addition, they are usually fairly low in cost since many people start to save but never redeem the coupons for the gifts or prizes. (This is the slippage that also characterizes refund offers.)

The major disadvantage of a program such as this is the length of time over which the program must be conducted. There is a commitment on the part of the advertiser to keep the program going and that may preclude other more attractive programs later on. In addition, in this age of instant reward, continuity and stamp plans don't seem to appeal to many people. They prefer to have an immediate reward for purchasing or for continuing to buy.

While stamp and continuity plans do represent some opportunities for the advertising campaign planner, they are very complex and require the talents of a specialist.

Allocating the Budget Between Advertising and Sales Promotion

As has been stated previously, the key to successful sales promotion is to integrate it with the advertising. The question naturally arises, "How much of the budget should be allocated to advertising and how much to sales promotion?" Unfortunately, there isn't any pat answer to the question. It simply depends on the objectives of the marketer, the goals of the campaign, and the situation in the marketplace. Generally, the budget is split 50/50 between advertising and sales promotion for most consumer package goods products. This ratio, however, may vary according to the brand and the market situation.

Although there are no hard and fast rules about advertising and sales promotion allocation, one method of determining how much should go to each has been developed by Robert M. Prentice. It is based on what he calls "consumer franchise building" or simply CFB. Since CFB does give a broad basis for advertising and sales promotion allocation and seems to have some logical value, it is reviewed below.

In several studies on consumer product brands, Prentice found that when funds were invested in specific advertising and sales promotion techniques, they achieved better long-term sales and profits than did brands in which other combinations were used. Based on these evaluations, Prentice developed a rationale for his consumer franchise building approach.

1. To generate profit over an extended period, a brand must build a strong consumer franchise. It must establish a significant, lasting value in the minds of an important segment of consumers.

2. But value isn't enough. Consumers must believe that the brand's value is worth the price. If they don't, the marketer will have to reduce the price or increase the value to the point where they are willing to buy it—to the point where consumers believe that value and price are in balance. But the marketer must realize that if he hasn't established a high value in the consumer's mind, a price reduction will generally cut into his profit.

3. A brand's share of market at any given time reflects how consumers perceive the brand's price/value relationship in comparison with other brands.

4. How does the consumer arrive at his or her perception of brand value? Obviously, a lot depends on experience with the product and on its unique performance and the satisfaction it provides. But, a lot also depends on the ideas the consumer gets about the brand which make it uniquely different—in important respects—from competitive brands. These ideas arise from the brand's name, its positioning, the package, and the various marketing activities that implant unique and important ideas about the brand in the mind.

5. What kinds of marketing activities do this? I call them Consumer Franchise Building (or CFB) activities. They include:

   Advertising. Perhaps the most common way to register such ideas (although some advertising, we have to admit, does a fairly poor job in this respect).

   Certain types of promotion. If they register unique and important selling ideas about the brand such as:

   > *Sampling*—because the package highlights the product's advantages, because the proof of the pudding is in the eating and because a descriptive folder with a strong selling message usually accompanies the sample—an ad, if you will.
   > *Cents-off coupons*—distributed by the manufacturer by mail, or in print ads, or in or on a package. These coupons can also register unique and important ideas about the brand—provided that an effective selling message accompanies the coupon or appears on it. This distinction is important, for it excludes most coupons that appear in retailers' own ads, which usually say "Brand X, 10¢ off with this coupon. Good only in this store for this week only." There is no selling message with these trade coupons, nothing about the brand's unique attributes or advantages—they are simply a means of cutting the price. Therefore, trade in-ad coupons are not considered a CFB activity.

Demonstrations—either in-store or before home economic or other groups of consumers, are CFB activities. Service, material, recipes, etc. which enhance the image of a brand and register ideas of its unique superiority and value are also CFB activities.

All these CFB activites perform two functions: (1) they build long-term brand preference and (2) they generate immediate sales (often more effectively than many people realize).

6. All other activities I classify as non-CFB activities. Their job is to accelerate the buying decision to generate immediate sales, but they generally do not implant unique and important ideas about the brand in the consumer's mind. Instead, they simply reduce the price or add temporary, extraneous value (as in the case of most premiums and contests) or help obtain retail distribution or co-operation. These are important and necessary functions—but they do not register important and unique ideas about a brand in the mind.[8]

While all sales promotion executives do not agree with Prentice's approach to allocation of the advertising and sales promotion budget, he found that among the brands he studied, those that invested less than 50 to 55 percent of their combined advertising/sales promotion budget in CFB activities did not do as well in sales and profits as those who did. That makes a strong argument for the Prentice approach.

Measuring Sales Promotion Activities

It is no longer acceptable in most organizations to simply say, "We'll run a few coupons," or "How about including a contest?" There must be clearly defined measurable goals for sales promotion activities. Unless sales promotion programs have clearly defined objectives that can be achieved, they should not be included in the plan. A poorly planned or poorly executed sales promotion program may often be a detriment to the campaign rather than a help. Whether the CFB approach is used for selecting techniques and allocating funds to sales promotion activities or another method is chosen to support the advertising campaign, one thing is a must: the objectives set for the sales promotion program must be measurable or quantifiable.

Rules for measurement are quite simple. Objectives must be set based on some measurable activity. For example, the objective of a sampling program might be to place the product in the hands of 45 percent of the

8. Robert M. Prentice, "How to Split Your Marketing Funds Between Advertising and Promotion," *Advertising Age,* January 10, 1977, p. 49.

prospective customers in a given area. By carefully developing a mailing list and through selection and distribution methods, this goal could be achieved. Another objective might be to move 90 percent of the old packages off the shelves of retail stores within the next two months, prior to the new package introduction. For this objective, a "two-for-one" promotion might be initiated to speed up the process. Through a store audit, it could quickly be determined whether the promotion was achieving its goal. The key point is that promotional objectives should be set in advance and should be measurable. The quantification may take many forms, but often a before-and-after measure of distribution or shelf space, the number of coupons redeemed, number of retail displays built, and the like are quantifiable objectives for a sales promotion program. Less worthwhile are such things as contest entries or number of premiums redeemed unless specific sales can be traced to the event.

Sales Promotion to the Trade

In spite of Prentice's convincing arguments for CFB, a well-planned and effective sales promotion program to the trade is a basic requirement for most brands under current marketing conditions. Unless there is distribution of the product in retail stores, the most persuasive advertising and sales promotion program cannot be effective with the consumer. If consumers can't find the product, they can't buy it. Thus, while marketers often dislike having to develop price reductions or concessions to achieve trade or retail distribution, they know it is necessary for the survival of the brand.

What Is Trade Promotion?

The most common use of sales promotion to the trade is to obtain, hold, or increase shelf space for the brand in the retail store. That usually consists of some form of price reduction, margin increase, or other activity that will encourage the retailer to cooperate in the distribution and local promotional process for the brand. Generally, trade promotions are developed to either (1) pay the trade for some service they perform for the brand in the local market or in the retail store or (2) as an allowance for quantity, specific product, or volume purchases. Unfortunately, many marketers misinterpret the real success of a trade promotion. Often the belief of the marketer is that if the promotion moves the product from the plant to the wholesaler or to the retail store, then the promotion should be considered a success. In truth, a trade promotion is successful only if (1) more of the product is sold to the trade *and then* to the ultimate consumer or (2) if the promotion increases distribution or shelf space for the brand. The ultimate measure of any trade sales promotion program is to generate final sales. If that doesn't occur, the sales promotion isn't truly successful.

Who Sets Up the Trade Sales Promotion Program?

Generally, the marketing manager or sales department of the marketing organization is responsible for the development of the various trade sales promotion activities. While the advertising campaign planner usually works with these people, it is most often not within the responsibility of the planner to make discount or pricing decisions since they have such a direct effect on the bottom-line profit of the organization. In some situations, the trade sales promotion program may be included as part of the cost of the overall marketing activities. In others, it may even be included as a part of the advertising budget. Generally, however, these trade offers are considered a discount or sales rebate and are thus taken from or charged to a separate budget outside the advertising area. No matter where the budget is located or how involved the planner is in determining the trade promotions, they are a vital ingredient in the success of the campaign.

Trade Promotion Objectives

Most trade promotions have one or more of the following objectives:

1. To obtain trade support for advertising and merchandising activities
2. To gain new distribution
3. To build trade inventories
4. To improve trade relations.

Obtaining trade support. When one thinks of the various types of consumer promotions available to the campaign planner, it becomes clear that the success of many of them depends greatly on retail support. An advertiser, for example, may offer a special price pack and promote it heavily through the media. Unless the retailer stocks the price pack and makes it prominently available, however, the program will fail. The same is true for most other consumer sales promotions. To gain support, advertisers may provide many forms of retail materials to back up their promotions such as trade deals, point-of-purchase materials, cooperative advertising funds, contests, and even push money.

Gaining new distribution. Many trade promotions are designed simply to obtain new or additional distribution. This is particularly important for a new product. Additional distribution is often the goal of existing products, too, as advertisers seek to maximize their media advertising investment by having the product available in as many locations as possible.

Retailers have limited space and usually want products that offer the greatest margin and the fastest turnover. Trade deals, consumer promotion packs, featured items, and other approaches are all appealing since they can be converted into retail promotions. Because many products are at parity, retailers usually feature brands that offer them the greatest potential.

Building trade inventories. Advertisers constantly seek ways to increase the inventory of products stocked by the retailer. Full display shelves in retail stores usually mean greater sales. As the old saying goes, "If the product is not available, it is not sold." Advertisers use promotion, therefore, to encourage retailers to keep larger stocks of the product on hand so that it will be available and will also be promoted.

Improving trade relations. Manufacturers continually seek to improve relations with the trade. With the goodwill of the retailer, it is much easier to introduce new products, obtain promotional activity for existing products, and ensure continued distribution patterns. Most middlemen and retailers have a wide choice of products to stock and sell. The retailer usually favors the advertiser with whom he or she has a good rapport. Advertisers also recognize the importance of middlemen over whom they have little actual control. They try, therefore, to influence middlemen and to gain their support by offering substantial trade discounts, promotional materials, and other sales aids.

Types of Trade Sales Promotion Techniques

It would be almost impossible to list all the various types of sales promotion programs that may be directed to the trade. They are limited only by the imagination of the sales promotion planner. The following, however, are the major types. Others that may be found are often variations on these themes.

Trade deals. Trade deals are usually special price concessions, over and above the normal purchasing discounts, granted to the trade for a limited period of time. They may or may not be tied to a specific performance by the retailer or middleman, such as larger-than-normal purchases, stocking of several sizes, flavors, or colors of the product. Often they are offered as incentives to lower the retail shelf price of the brand to the consumer for a given period. Most trade deals are an incentive to the retailer to cooperate with the advertiser in some out-of-the-ordinary promotional way.

Trade deals are especially important in developing support for a new product, a new advertising campaign or other promotional program. The size and type of the trade deal offered often has a significant impact on the success of the distribution at retail and thus the results of the advertising campaign.

The main advantage of a trade deal to the advertiser is the opportunity to gain retail support for the advertising campaign with special pricing. Another is the control the advertiser can exercise over the amount of "deal" merchandise available. By controlling the size of the deal to the trade, the advertiser has some control over the amount of money allowed as a discount. Finally, with a trade deal, the advertiser can promote when and how he or she chooses. The advertiser can make the deal available when promotion is needed and hold off when it is not required.

The primary disadvantage in trade deals is that, once "dealing" starts, retailers come to expect it in the future. Thus, when an advertiser wishes to develop a promotion without some kind of deal, he or she may find retailers unwilling to cooperate. In addition, trade deals have a tendency to become habit-forming, not just for the retailer but for the advertiser as well. Trade deals may be given when they are not really required to achieve promotional goals. They then develop by force of habit, and retailers and customers alike wait for the "deal" rather than purchase at normal prices.

Deals also are expensive. They have a direct effect on the profit-and-loss sheet. The discount comes directly from the price of the product and is a direct reduction to the retailer. Advertising campaign planners often complain that trade deals absorb dollars that otherwise could have been used for consumer advertising. Because sales promotion provides a short-term incentive to purchase, trade deals cannot and will not build retailer or consumer loyalty. Finally, one of the major disadvantages of trade deals is that they may be absorbed in the retail channel. In other words, the retailer may simply absorb the trade deal discount and not pass the savings along to the consumer. Because the advertiser has no control over the retailer in these types of promotions, trade deals, especially if they are designed to offer a reduced price to the consumer, may often never achieve their goal.

Based on federal regulations, all trade deals must be offered to all retailers on a proportionally equal basis. That is, if a trade deal is made to one retailer or middleman, it must be offered on an equal basis to all retailers to whom the advertiser sells in that market. Offers may be made in various areas of the country or to noncompeting retailers on a selective basis. This practice is designed to prevent unfair trade discounting or pricing under the Robinson-Patman Act.

There are three primary types of trade deals:

1. Price-offs. Often these are called off-invoice or off-list. These are straight discounts off the list price of the product usually for a certain period of time. Often, these discounts take the form of an allowance or discount for purchasing a certain minimum quantity, purchasing a certain number of flavors or sizes, or purchasing during a certain period of time. For example, a soft drink mix manufacturer may offer a $1 per case trade deal featuring an off-invoice allowance from February 1 to

March 15 to encourage retailers to stock the product for the upcoming heavy selling season.

2. Allowances. The allowance is a form of discount that gives the retailer a certain amount off, usually per case, as an allowance for some promotional activity he might conduct on the local level. Most common allowances are for advertising or display.

    a. An advertising allowance is a sum paid to the middleman or retailer for advertising the manufacturer's product in local media. In the soft drink mix example, the advertiser might offer an advertising allowance of 50¢ per case on each case purchased from March 15 to May 1. The retailer, through purchases during that time, would then have a credit with the advertiser or earn a discount that could be used to purchase local advertising. Usually, retailers support their claim for the advertising allowance by furnishing proof-of-performance, such as tear sheets of the ads or affidavits of performance that the advertising actually appeared. Many types and variations of the basic advertising allowance are used, but all are tied to local advertising by the retailer in some way to support the sale of the advertised product. Advertising allowances are usually paid by check direct to the retailer or may be taken off the invoice.

    b. Display allowances are just that. Retailers are given a predetermined allowance for developing a retail display of the advertised product. Guidelines for the display are set; e.g., the display must be of a certain size or contain a minimum number of cases of the product or amount of floor space to qualify. A photograph is used to certify to the manufacturer that the display was actually built.

3. A somewhat different form of trade allowance is the free-goods offer. The soft drink mix advertiser mentioned above, instead of offering a buying allowance, might use a free-goods offer such as one case free with the purchase of ten during the February 1 to March 15 period. In this situation, the free goods are a discount to encourage the retailer or middleman to stock up prior to the selling season and to ensure the availability of a complete line of flavors.

    Many manufacturers prefer the free-goods offer over case allowance for one simple reason: it costs less than the case allowance to the manufacturer. Free goods are priced at wholesale to the retailer, but the manufacturer is really only allowing the actual cost of manufacturing. With case allowances, the percentage deducted from the invoice includes the manufacturer's margin and thus actually amounts to more money.

    In some instances, free goods are offered as an incentive on slow-moving products. Again, taking the example of the soft drink mix advertiser, to ensure the retail display of the full line, an offer of one case of fruit punch (a slow seller) might be offered with each ten cases of the more popular grape or cherry flavors.

Cooperative advertising. While often maligned as being unmanageable and a form of discount and source of dispute between retailer and manufacturer, cooperative advertising is still an excellent way to bring the national campaign to the local level. In many cooperative advertising agreements, the advertiser agrees to pay 50 percent of the cost of the advertising placed locally by the retailer in support of the advertised brand. While many cooperative agreements are set up on a 50-50 basis, they vary widely according to the product category, the amount of advertising done by the manufacturer, the value of local retail advertising to the sale of the product, and other factors. The usual agreement is for newspaper space. Increasing numbers of advertisers, however, are including radio and television in their co-op programs, and some even split the cost of circulars and flyers.

The major advantage most advertisers find in cooperative advertising is local media support for a national or regional campaign. Also, since retail advertising is price-specific, the advertiser gains the benefit of a local price feature by the retailer. In most instances, this price feature is impossible in national campaigns.

The chief disadvantage of cooperative advertising is a limitation on the degree of control that the advertiser can exert over retailers or middlemen who develop the retail advertising. In some cases, less-than-professional-looking advertisements are run under the cooperative program, or the advertisements appear in undesirable media. Usually, unless there is full understanding, the advertiser must share the cost even if it appears that full value was not received.

Another problem is the national-local rate. Often co-op agreements are set up on a shared-cost based on the national rate in the media. If the retailer receives the lower local or retail rate, the advertiser may find he or she is paying 75 percent or even more of the actual cost of the advertising. Also, cooperative advertising is sometimes agreed to by the advertiser to offset competition. Often, the same money might be better spent in some other way. Finally, according to federal law, once a cooperative advertising program is initiated by an advertiser, it must be made available to all retailers under similar conditions. Thus, once a cooperative advertising program is started, it is usually most difficult to stop.

Trade coupons. An increasingly important method of generating local retail activity for a brand is through trade coupons. Simply put, the trade coupon is a cooperative venture between the manufacturer and the

Figure 13-20.   Trade Coupons Offered by a Retailer

Source: Courtesy of Dominick's Finer Foods, Inc.

retailer to offer a reduced price or other inducement at the retail level through a cents-off coupon or other offer. Typically, the trade coupon consists of a coupon in a flyer, in the retailer's newspaper advertisement, on the shelf, or in the store that allows a certain reduction on the price of the brand in that particular store for a limited period of time. It carries the same offer as a manufacturer's coupon with the major difference being that the offer is redeemable only at the particular retail location. Examples of trade coupons can be seen in the in-store coupon sheet in Figure 13-20.

The flyer in Figure 13-20 was distributed by a Chicago-area super-market chain in their stores. A number of trade coupons appear ranging from produce to canned hams to paper products. Each of the coupons offers a discount on the purchase of that particular product in that chain during a limited period of time.

The trade particularly likes these types of coupons since it gives them an edge on competition. Marketers like them because they assure the proper offer by the retailer and get additional exposure either through the newspaper advertising, in the flyer, or on the in-store coupon page.

With a trade coupon, the manufacturer usually agrees in advance with the retailer on how many coupons will be redeemed or the total amount of dollar value in coupons that will be accepted. This is to assure that misredemption is held to a minimum. In some cases, the retailer will add an additional value to the coupon over and above that offered by the manufacturer. For example, if the manufacturer agrees to a 15¢ reduction on the product, the retailer may add an additional discount of 10¢ from his own margin to make the value of the coupon a total of 25¢ and make the offer that much more attractive to the consumers.

An added advantage of the trade coupon to the manufacturer is that the retailer handling and clearing house charges can often be avoided when the coupon is handled directly between the marketer and the re-tailer. Often the retailer will forego the handling charge, and the coupons may well be counted in each store. This provides a savings to both parties that can then be passed along to the consumer in the form of a lower price on the brand.

Point-of-purchase materials. Advertiser-developed point-of-purchase material for use in retail stores is a major sales promotion category. Point-of-purchase materials may range from a simple shelf-talker in a food or drugstore to an elaborate, long-term, moving display for a liquor retailer. Point-of-purchase pieces, originally offered to retailers for displays, often become permanent store fixtures, such as clocks, wall ornaments, product dividers or headers, and other items.

Most point-of-purchase materials are offered or shipped to retailers with little or no restrictions. Because of this, it is estimated approximately half of all POP materials are never used. There are simply too many advertisers sending too much material to a limited number of retailers. In spite of the problems of getting point-of-purchase materials used, their value cannot be doubted. The advent of self-service shopping in all types of retail operations points up the increasingly important role this type of material plays in supporting advertising campaigns at the retail level.

A strong advertising campaign can often be increased manyfold through the use of effective point-of-purchase advertising materials. It is especially effective when the media advertising campaign theme is carried through to retail POP materials.

Dealer loaders. A dealer loader is designed to do exactly what the name implies—load the dealer with a product. One type of dealer loader is packing the product in a display such as a wheelbarrow, wagon, or other valuable premium. The premium and product are used as a display unit. When the product has been sold, the retailer keeps the premium. In addition, self-liquidating premiums (previously discussed) that are used as retail displays are also used as dealer loaders. In this case, after the promotion is over, the dealer keeps the premium included in the display.

Dealer loaders may take almost any form from a small, impersonal gift to sporting goods, clothing, or even expensive foreign trips for the retailer and his family. Dealer loaders are often tied to a specific-size purchase, with the value of the loader being proportionate to the value of the offer. This type of promotion is frequently used to support a new advertising campaign with the loader tied to the theme of the campaign. As with other types of retail deals, if a dealer loader is offered, it must, under federal regulation, be made available to all retailers on a proportionate basis.

Contests. Dealer contests have grown in size and importance over the years. Today it is not unusual for retailers to have opportunities to win very expensive prizes in contests sponsored by advertisers. Contests are usually tied to specific achievements by the retailer such as purchases, total sales, sales based on quotas, sales increases over previous periods, or sales of a new or existing product line. As a general rule, for a contest to be effective, the retailer must be given a reasonable opportunity to win.

Contests often work better with independent retailers than with chain stores. Many chain-store operations have very strict rules about contests, premiums, and gifts that may be given or awarded to their store managers. In these instances, clearance is required from the chain's headquarters office before any type of contest can be conducted with employees.

Contests generate great dealer interest and support while they are going on, but often don't have long-lasting effects. Once the contest is over, the retailers tend to return to their regular promotional activities. It is likely, though, that trade relations are improved through a contest. With the growth of contests and expanding prize structures, many retailers enter only those they have a good chance of winning or which offer a particularly lucrative prize.

Push money. Often called "spiffs" or "PM," push money is money paid by the advertiser directly to sales people to promote specific items in the product line. A refrigerator manufacturer, for example, might offer "PM" or "spiff" on a certain model. During the time the promotion is in effect, the retail sales people are encouraged to personally promote that particular model since they will be rewarded with an additional cash prize. Usually, spiffs or PM works only for those products in which the retail sales person is a key selling factor. The device is not effective for products sold in self-service situations or those with a low selling price.

In nearly every case, the use of PMs requires the cooperation and approval of the store manager or the headquarters office of the retail store. Because offering money to employees is regarded as an inducement, retail management must be consulted prior to the offering of such a program to their employees.

While push money is still used, the legality of the practice has been questioned, and many advertisers are reviewing their use of this promotional tool.

Sales meetings. A final, widely used trade promotional tool is the sales meeting, which is conducted for retailers by the advertiser's sales representative or the broker sales force. Theoretically, all retail store personnel should attend these meetings. In many larger chains, however, those persons aren't available. Thus, sales meetings are often conducted for retail headquarters personnel or merchandising managers who, in turn, hold sales meetings for the retail people on the floor. Obviously, with this approach, something may be lost in the translation of the message. Nevertheless, sales meetings are an important way to merchandise and promote to the trade, especially when a new product, a new promotion, or a new advertising campaign is being introduced.

Sales meetings take many forms, from a simple meeting in a hotel room with a small group to a formal, traveling, professional show. The determining factor is the importance of the announcement to the advertiser and the middleman. The advertising campaign is usually a key feature of a sales-meeting program. Special emphasis is often given to the geographic areas represented by the retailers present. Thus, part of the development of many consumer-product advertising campaigns is a brief outline of how the material will be presented to the retailers and the sales force.

Measuring Trade Promotion Results

Just as with advertising and consumer sales promotion objectives, sales promotion programs directed to the trade must be stated in measurable terms and thus be quantifiable. For example, the objectives of a trade promotion program cannot be stated simply as "to get distribution." Rather, the goal should be stated as "to achieve distribution in retail outlets that account for a minimum of 65 percent of all-commodity volume (ACV)." Quantifiable results should also be projected for other types of trade promotion activities such as "achieving at least three facings in retail stores doing a minimum of $10,000 per week in volume in the top 50 markets." When the promotional goals are stated in such measurable terms, the success of the promotional program can be easily evaluated.

Promoting to the Sales Force

The final but certainly not the least important part of advertising campaign promotion is obtaining the support of the sales force, whether advertiser, employee, broker sales person, or independent sales representative. Enthusiastic support of the campaign by the sales force can often make a major difference in overall results.

Measuring Results

As in consumer or trade promotions, results from sales force promotion must be measurable. This is usually a simple matter of developing objectives for the sales force, then measuring against those objectives. With the introduction of a new advertising or promotion program, for example, each member of the sales force is given a sales quota. Quotas may be based on the territory, increases over existing business, new distribution, or other objectives. Sales quotas are often tied to personal incentives in the form of either money or prizes.

While the advertising campaign planner usually is not involved in the development of sales quotas, he or she should be aware that they are used and that supporting materials may be needed.

Objectives of the Promotion

Most sales force promotions are designed to build sales force enthusiasm for the campaign. This is often difficult because sales forces vary so widely. One advertiser may have a sales force composed entirely of company employees. Another may use broker representatives exclusively. Still another may have commission representatives who also represent 15 to 20 noncompetitive advertisers. And others may have a combination of all of the above. Just getting all these sales people enthusiastic about the advertising campaign so they will stress it to retailers may be a most difficult task.

Sales people who truly believe their company is supporting their sales efforts with advertising and promotion usually work harder to make the program successful. In fact, in some instances, advertising campaigns are developed as much for the benefit of the sales force as they are for the trade and consumer.

Sales force objectives of trade level support take many forms. Objectives may be set, for example, to obtain a certain number of tie-in advertisements from retailers. Others may be designed to obtain a certain number of displays in stores. Often, gaining new distribution in the sales area is one of the primary objectives. Although the objectives vary depending on advertiser needs, the sales force usually has three tasks:

1. To obtain additional sales to the trade.
2. To obtain additional distribution among either present or new retailers.
3. To gain retail support for the campaign in the form of tie-in advertising or merchandising features.

While the campaign planner is usually not responsible for the development of sales force promotional objectives, sometimes such a program is requested.

Types of Promotion to the Sales Force

Sales promotion directed to the sales force takes many forms. The choice usually depends on the type of sales force, the methods of communication, and the closeness with which the advertiser works with his or her sales people. Some fairly standard techniques are used, and they are briefly reviewed here. The campaign planner is sometimes expected to develop sales force promotional materials, particularly for the smaller advertiser. This seems like a natural extension, since elements of the basic advertising campaign are often used as a basis for the promotional program.

Sales meetings. Like trade sales meetings, these can range from brief one- or two-hour meetings to full-scale production numbers at a distant resort. Much depends on the size of the manufacturer, the type of product, and the importance of the campaign. Generally, one of the key ingredients of these sales meetings is the presentation of the advertising campaign. Thus, the advertising campaign planner is often included in the program for such sales meetings.

Sales manuals. The sales manual is a descriptive booklet designed to help sales people do a better job of selling. It is usually designed for internal use. The manual may contain product information, background materials, price lists, models, and other information that will assist in presenting the product line to prospects. The advertising campaign, advertising materials, and promotional program are usually integral parts of a sales manual.

Sales portfolios. Sales portfolios are usually developed as an external selling tool for the sales force. The portfolio may take any form, from looseleaf binders to booklets to brochures to flyers. They are often designed to be left with the prospect. The portfolio contains information on the product being promoted, price lists, the advertising campaign, order forms, and other selling materials. The importance of the campaign, the type of market, and the needs of the sales force dictate the type of sales portfolio to be created. Often, the campaign planner is called on to help develop the sales portfolio because of knowledge of the market, the advertising campaign, and the advertising plan.

Sales letters. Sales letters, expressing the theme of the campaign, are used to announce sales meetings and to keep personnel enthusiastic during the course of a promotion. These sales letters often contain information that can be used in followup calls on prospects by the sales force.

With this look at how sales promotion can and should be used to support the advertising campaign, we move to the final stage of the advertising plan: how to evaluate the success of the campaign. That's handled in Chapter 14.

Summary Sales promotion can be a very important part of an advertising campaign. It can be used to gain trial for the product and reinforce use by current purchasers. It also can be used to get strong support from the trade. These are the reasons why it has become the fastest growing sector of promotion. The planner who properly integrates sales promotion into a campaign will have an important support for other advertising efforts.

Case for Discussion: RealCream

Bossy Products' powdered dairy creamer, RealCream, had been in national distribution for two months when Bob Cubbin, the brand manager, met with top management to review the situation.

RealCream was currently stocked in stores representing 40 percent of national all-commodity volume. The goal for the end of Year 1 had been set at achieving distribution representing 65 percent of ACV. Cubbin felt this objective was still feasible, noting that Bossy's overall distribution represented 75 percent ACV. RealCream was being sold in every major market, but only by small chains and independents. In the large chains, the sales force had not yet been able to gain shelf space. The reason was twofold: the creamer section traditionally generated only average profit for the supermarkets. Consequently, grocers were unwilling to expand the shelf space allotted to the category, and established brands were firmly entrenched. Second, since RealCream was a new product and still an unknown, buyers for major chains had adopted a "wait and see" attitude.

RealCream had been introduced to the trade under Bossy's traditional terms: 1 case free with the purchase of 12. However, the nondairy creamer manufacturers offered a 1 free with 10 allowance. RealCream was also higher priced than nondairy creamers.

Consumer acceptance of RealCream, while good, had not been as strong as expected. In its two months on the market, the product had accounted for 3 percent of the creamer category sales. Year 1 goal had been set at 15 percent. (Bossy's other products, powdered milk and canned condensed milk, had respective market shares of 30 percent and 25 percent.)

According to preliminary trade figures, RealCream's sales had not come at the expense of any one nondairy creamer. The major competitors had experienced slight losses, but overall creamer sales had increased, suggesting that RealCream was bringing new users to the category. Cubbin pointed out that while some category growth had been expected, new users were only a secondary target and the main thrust of the promotional campaign had been to attract competitive users. He reviewed the campaign:

Full-page, four-color advertisements had been placed in seven major women's magazines, *Reader's Digest,* and *TV Guide.* The ad pictured the RealCream jar sitting beside a coffee cup and a woman's hand stirring the coffee. The headline read: "RealCream: It's the Cream in My Coffee." Copy was as follows: "It seems we use so many substitutes these days. Some, like salt substitutes, were developed for health reasons. Those are good substitutes. But others, like nondairy creamers, are used because they're more convenient, not better. I don't use a nondairy creamer anymore, because now there's Real-Cream. Same convenient powder form, but it's a real dairy food, made with real cream. Mmm, RealCream, I'd be lost without you."

Cubbin had asked Bossy's consumer researchers to conduct two focus groups, one with people who had tried RealCream and one with those who had not. Those people who had tried the product had very positive comments. They liked the taste and the idea that it was a real dairy product. Most reported that they had seen the ad. Several had bought RealCream because of the Bossy name (featured prominently on the package). All intended to buy the product again. They agreed it was expensive in comparison to nondairy creamers, but they felt the expense was justified because of the "natural" aspect.

Non-users were somewhat skeptical of RealCream's real dairy claim. "Who ever heard of powdered cream?" asked one panel member. Most participants felt that the product was too expensive in comparison with other creamers. The Bossy name suggested quality, but it was not strong enough to overcome questions about the price-benefit relationship.

In summary, Cubbin stated that he believed RealCream could still achieve the established goals. He reported that 30 percent of the promotional budget had been spent on introductory phase advertising. He wanted permission to allocate at least half of the remaining funds to a sales promotion effort in an attempt to attract competitive users to RealCream.

Bossy had always been reluctant to use major sales promotion plans for their products. Past efforts had been limited to cross-ruff coupons on company products. For example, powdered milk might carry a coupon for Bossy condensed milk. However, the management committee gave Cubbin their approval of his request.

Questions

1. Obviously, one way to increase distribution would be to offer a more competitive free-goods allowance. However, this is not possible because of corporate profit requirements. What other trade measures might you recommend?

2. Do you agree that sales promotion (consumer and/or trade) would be effective for RealCream?

3. Which of the 10 basic consumer sales promotion techniques might Cubbin consider? (Assume that cost is not a factor.)

4. Outline a sales promotion campaign for RealCream that ties into the advertising campaign. Remember that users of competitive products are the primary target.

14 Evaluating the Advertising Campaign

Throughout this text, there has been a recurring theme: set measurable objectives for the various stages and elements in the advertising campaign. Objective setting was stressed when the overall objectives of the campaign were determined, when the budget was established, when the creative strategy was finalized, when the media plan was prepared, even when the extra step of sales promotion was added to the campaign. The time has now come to take those measurements, in other words, to evaluate the advertising campaign. The planner needs to know whether the advertising campaign achieved the goals that were set.

In some companies, this advertising evaluation process is called accountability. Management wants the advertising planners and managers to identify exactly what results were obtained for the advertising investment and to provide evidence of the return on investment. And this is reasonable and logical. After all, advertising uses the scarce resources of the firm, resources that could be invested in a number of ways. Therefore, the real question management poses is, "Is advertising the best way to use those funds?" And it is the job of the advertising campaign planner to be able to answer that question, and to do that usually requires some form of advertising evaluation.

While advertising campaign evaluation is a form of research, it is often quite different from other forms of advertising research. Most advertising research is used to pretest or predict what might occur in the real world marketplace. Evaluation research, on the other hand, is used to determine exactly what did happen. While this information might be used as a basis for what to do in the future, the basic purpose is to measure what occurred as a result of the advertising campaign and therefore what return was received on the investment made.

In summary, the three primary reasons to evaluate the advertising campaign are:

1. To determine if the overall objectives set for the advertising campaign were met. If those overall objectives were not met, determine which of the individual objectives for the various elements of the campaign were met. Based on these evaluations, it can be determined where the failure may have occurred.

2. To quantify and justify the return on the campaign investment. By knowing what was achieved, management can relate that to other potential uses for the funds and determine cost effectiveness of the advertising campaign.

3. To use the measurement information to make changes, additions, or corrections for future campaigns. No advertising campaign is ever totally successful in and of itself. It can always be improved. Evaluations of previous campaigns are a great help in improving and refining the elements and makeup of future campaigns.

In most organizations today, the question is not whether to measure the results of the campaign, it is how to do so. That will be the thrust of the following sections.

What to Measure and Why

If the campaign planner has built measurable objectives into the campaign plan, the evaluation is greatly simplified. There are, however, some rather traditional steps in campaign evaluation and some problems, too. Each is discussed in turn.

Evaluating the Results against the Objectives

In spite of some management's pleas that advertising must always produce sales, the advertising campaign must be evaluated against the objectives of the advertising plan. Thus, if the objective of the campaign was to generate direct sales, then the measurement of success of the campaign must be sales. If the goals were established as obtaining qualified leads for the sales force, then leads obtained as a direct result of the campaign would be the measuring stick. And so on. It is all too easy for the advertising campaign planner to fall into the trap of attempting to measure the total marketing efforts of the organization and relate them to the advertising campaign, rather than to measure the actual effects of the advertising that appeared. The rule is simple: measure and evaluate the advertising campaign on the basis of the objectives contained in the advertising plan. Nothing more, nothing less. The importance of setting specific, measurable advertising objectives for the advertising campaign is critical.

Some Problems in Campaign Measurement

No matter what objectives were set for the campaign, whether sales, market share, communication effects, or something else, some problems are inherent in the measurement process. The campaign planner should be aware of them and try to minimize them when developing the plan.

Most advertising results must have soft objectives. Unlike the hard, physical measurement that can be made of the number of cans of peas processed on a packing line, the objectives of most advertising campaigns are much softer and subject to interpretation. That's an inherent problem when any measurement is being made on people, particularly when the objectives are communication effects such as awareness, knowledge, liking, or even past purchase recall. While measurements can't be as precise as some physical measurements, objectives can be set and effects measured.

Measurement over time. Since most advertising campaigns run over several months or even a year, it is often difficult to pinpoint the exact results of the campaign. In many instances, the campaign effects may build over time. In addition, there is the lagged effect of advertising.

Multiple advertising and marketing variables. Even when measuring the communications effects of the advertising campaign, there is a problem in differentiating between what is advertising and what is not. For example, if the advertising sales message is carried on the product package and the consumer sees the package and remembers it but not the actual media advertising itself, should that then be credited to the advertising campaign? Questions such as this make the identification of actual advertising effects very difficult. Often they really can't be separated from the other marketing efforts on behalf of the brand.

The problems of human memory. Humans simply don't remember everything. And they certainly don't remember all the advertising they have seen or to which they have been exposed. While more and more is being learned about how the human mind works, it still is almost impossible to say whether advertising goes into short-term memory, long-term memory, is dismissed, is stored, or exactly what happens to advertising impressions. Until there is a better understanding of how human memory and information storage works, it is difficult to say exactly what should be measured and even if the use of recall and memory is the best way to evaluate advertising impressions.

In spite of these problems, the results of the advertising campaign must be measured. The measurement of sales messages and communication effects is one sound and accepted way.

Measuring Communication Effects

Because communication of a sales message is the usual goal of advertising, the measurement of some form of communication effect is quite natural. This too seems satisfactory since the goal of most consumer package goods advertising is either to keep present customers purchasing the particular brand or to influence other purchasers who have the brand in their evoked set to give the brand greater preference in future buying decisions. Thus, while it is difficult indeed to measure the absolute effects of advertising in terms of sales, these surrogate measures such as brand awareness, sales messages delivered, and information about the brand transferred can be used as a method of evaluating the effects of the campaign.

What to Measure and Why

The first step in measuring communication effects is to determine what those effects are and what evaluation tool will be used. Earlier the use of the Lavidge and Steiner "Hierarchy of Effects Model" was suggested as a sound, consistent method. Lavidge and Steiner see the movement from "unawareness" to "purchase" of a product as a series of six distinct steps. The first step is "awareness" and the second "knowledge," both of which relate directly to information or ideas about the product or service. The third step, "liking," and the fourth step, "preference," are the "feeling" steps that deal with attitudes about the product. The fifth step, "conviction," and the sixth step, "purchase," are "action" or behavioral steps that result in the actual purchase of the product.

While Lavidge and Steiner have six specific steps in their model, from "awareness" to "purchase," these are usually collapsed into the four used in the evaluation model for advertising campaigns: (1) awareness/knowledge (recall), (2) liking (attitude change), (3) preference, (4) conviction/brand to be purchased or brand bought last.

Translating this concept into the more traditional form of a model, advertising really is intended to move people along a continuum from no information or sales messages to the final purchase behavior. And, adver-

---

Figure 14-1. From Awareness to Purchase

Lack of information or awareness	——————— Communication effects ———————	Behavior
	Awareness/knowledge ♦ Liking ♦ Preference ♦ Conviction	Purchase

---

tising constantly is having some effect on purchasers in either moving them forward or backward toward purchase or helping them to remain where they are.

Awareness and knowledge. The lowest level of communication effect of advertising or the first objective of a sales message is awareness or knowledge of either the brand being advertised or the advertising message itself. When the product is new or unknown, the objective of the campaign may be simply to make the consumer aware that the brand exists. Awareness of either the brand or the sales message is the simplest measure and, therefore, is the most widely used.

For an existing or known brand, the advertising task usually is to develop awareness or knowledge within the target market about a specific benefit the brand provides or the consumer problem it may solve. These measures do not necessarily attempt to determine whether the message has a communication effect. The assumption is made that if the consumer is aware of the message or has gained knowledge about the brand, the advertising has achieved its basic objective.

Under the assumption that the advertising message for the brand was unknown prior to the start of the campaign, the awareness measure can be made at any time after the campaign starts. The usual quantification is determining how many persons are aware of or recognize the product, the campaign theme, the benefit of the promises made, or other identification of the sales message.

Recall. The second level of advertising effectiveness is recall. Persons exposed to the advertising campaign can repeat or play back certain portions or ideas they may have seen or heard. They "recall" the advertising message. Again, no measure is made of the value of the advertising message or the impact it might have on the target market.

Two types of recall are used in advertising evaluation, unaided and aided.

1. In unaided recall, respondents are asked if they remember having seen or heard advertising recently for any brand in a certain product category. No further clues are given to help identify the sponsor, the brand, or the message.

2. In aided recall, certain clues are given to help the respondent remember the advertising. For example, rather than asking only if advertising for a certain product category has been seen or heard, the question might be phrased to see if the respondent could recall which brand or what advertiser used a certain graphic device or made a certain claim in his or her advertising. Thus, the hints or suggestions "aid" in recalling the advertising.

Both aided and unaided recall are used in evaluating an advertising campaign. Unaided recall is believed to be the stronger, however, because the respondent is asked only about the product category and to spontaneously recall or remember the advertising. The assumption is that a longer-lasting impression has been made.

The strongest effect of the campaign at this level is specific information about the brand. If consumers learn from advertising that only one brand of cough drop has the advantage of dual action—e.g., it's both antiseptic and anesthetic—and that the product with these properties is Brand Z, then the assumption is made that knowledge has been communicated. It is assumed this sales message will have some effect on the future purchase behavior of the consumer, although that relationship is somewhat tenuous. Awareness, recall, and knowledge of the brand, the message, or the benefits probably make up the bulk of the content of all campaign evaluation.

Liking and attitude change. The third level of advertising effect is liking the brand. Liking assumes the consumer is aware and has some knowledge either from the advertising or from actual use. Often, it is difficult to separate advertising knowledge from experience, which makes the measure more difficult.

In the liking measure, it is assumed the advertising has had an effect on the consumer's mental condition or that some sort of attitude change has occurred. The consumer has moved beyond the awareness or knowledge stage and has formed a positive opinion about the product. Liking does not mean that the consumer will purchase the product. It simply means that positive feelings or impressions exist.

An example of the "liking" measure is to have a consumer name several acceptable brands of products in a category. The assumption is made that if the products are acceptable, they are liked (the "evoked set"). While liking is an important step in evaluating the results of an advertising campaign, this measure still does not assume a purchase action. A consumer may like many products but purchase only a few.

Preference. The final communications effect to be considered is preference. This means that, among a certain number of brands within a category, one is preferred over the others. In terms of campaign evaluation, an assumption is made that the advertising message has created a level of acceptance for a specific brand, so that among available alternatives the advertised brand is preferred and would likely be purchased.

Because preference indicates that, all things being equal, certain brands will probably be purchased, preference is one of the stronger measures of the effect of advertising. If advertising is the major decision factor in creating product preference, the campaign is usually considered successful whether or not any actual sales result.

Preference is the final communication stage where the actual effects of the advertising campaign can be measured. Once preference has been developed, there is little more that the advertising or the sales messages can do to trigger the purchase decision. From here, the consumer may or may not purchase the product based on many market factors such as price, availability, sales promotion, and the like.

Purchasing behavior. If the advertising message that has been communicated is successful and market conditions and other marketing variables are favorable, the final step in the purchasing process is behavior or actual purchase of the brand. Lavidge and Steiner believe that conviction and purchase are behavioral. There is some question as to whether the concept of conviction is or is not a behavioral variable.

Conviction and behavior are the most difficult concepts to measure because of the many variables involved. There are some instances, though, in which purchase behavior can be traced directly to the advertising message such as in direct response.

In the conviction measure, as in all others, it is assumed that members of the target market have seen and reacted to the advertising message. The consumer has become aware of the brand advertised, has developed a liking, has moved up through the preference stage and is now prepared to take or has taken the final step of conviction to purchase or has actually purchased the brand.

In the Lavidge and Steiner model, conviction and purchase behavior are in the connative or motivational area of behavior. Because a person often cannot accurately describe a conviction, some of the measures in this evaluation require questions of purchase intention or past purchase behavior. Thus, attempts are made to identify advertising as the force that created a switch of brands or stimulated the purchase of a brand in the past or what might occur in the future. Intent to purchase is assumed to be a strong indicator of advertising success.

Most evaluation questions in the area of conviction deal with what was purchased. A given purchase is compared with past or usual behavior to determine if a change occurred. If change, such as a brand switch, did occur or if there was an indication that a brand switch might occur on the next purchase, an attempt is made to link that behavioral change to the advertising. While the link is often questionable, it is used as a form of evaluation, especially if the reason given for the brand switch is implicit in the advertising message.

Many behavioral or psychological models can be used to evaluate advertising. The Lavidge and Steiner hierarchy of effects model or parts of it have gained widespread industry acceptance. The model provides a practical and useful, if somewhat arbitrary, method of advertising campaign evaluation.

Measuring the Advertising Campaign

With this review of the measurement of communication effects of the advertising campaign, the actual methods used to evaluate an advertising campaign can be examined. There are two basic approaches: (1) concurrent (while the campaign is in progress) or (2) the more traditional method of evaluating the campaign after its completion.

Concurrent Evaluation

Today, because of high media costs, varying marketing conditions and the need to react to competition, more and more advertisers are measuring, evaluating, and adjusting their campaigns while they are in progress. This form of evaluation is not a form of pretesting as was discussed in Chapter 11. It is simply a matter of measuring the campaign as it unfolds in the marketplace and then making adjustments and fine tuning it to maximize the results. There are two methods of measuring the communication effects of the campaign while it is in progress.

Coincidental studies. These studies attempt to measure and evaluate consumer exposure and reaction to the advertising while it is appearing. It is particularly effective with broadcast.

The most common type of coincidental study is the telephone interview. For example, an advertiser may want to determine if the advertising message is reaching the correct target market and to learn how and what information is being conveyed. Telephone calls are therefore made to members of the target market while the advertising is being broadcast on either radio or television. By learning what stations or shows are being seen or heard, the advertiser then knows whether or not the target audience is hearing the message and, if so, what information or meaning is being received. Because coincidental surveys are designed to furnish only very basic data, little information about the campaign can be obtained other than a quick reading of message distribution and general information content.

Tracking studies. Studies of this type usually consist of a series of consumer interviews during the course of the campaign. The purpose is to determine the levels of exposure and effect that are being achieved by the advertising campaign. Since it is commonly agreed that advertising effects build over time, tracking studies are usually conducted in "waves" on a predetermined schedule. An example may help.

Assume that on March 1 a new advertising campaign for Millie's Peanuts is started which is to run through November 1. Tracking studies using a telephone survey format are planned for April 1 and June 1.

On April 1, a series of random telephone calls are made to consumers. The sample size is sufficiently large so that reasonable assumptions may be made about the results. The questions asked are such things as:

Question 1: Have you seen or heard any advertising for the peanut category?

If the consumer has seen or heard any advertising for peanuts, the next question is:

Question 2: What brand was it for?

This is followed by such additional questions as:

Question 3: In what medium was the advertising seen or heard?
Question 4: What did the advertising say?
Question 5: What brand do you normally buy?

This first study establishes a benchmark for the campaign. In addition, it spotlights such items as lack of exposure with prospects, misunderstanding of the message, and misidentification of the sponsor that might be occurring. Based on this first "wave," the advertiser can then make any necessary adjustments.

Again, on June 1, another series of random telephone calls is made asking the same questions. Under the assumption that the samples are comparable, comparisons can be made between the first and second "waves" or studies to determine any changes that might have occurred. In addition, it can be learned if the changes made after the first study have corrected any of the problems previously found.

Tracking studies of this kind can be conducted at any time during the campaign at normal intervals of about 60 days. For some product categories, a shorter or longer time period may be required.

Telephone studies are the most common form of tracking, although they may be done through personal interview or diaries or by other means.

The major advantage of concurrent testing is the rapid accumulation of information. Based on this information, any problems can be spotted, and corrections can be made quickly and efficiently. The major disadvantage is the limited amount of information that can be obtained. In addition, since concurrent testing takes place during the campaign, a quick reading may often not accurately reflect what the final results might be.

The coincidental and tracking studies work very well as long as the objectives of the advertising campaign are communication effects. In some cases, however, the goal of the campaign may be to generate actual sales, such as through direct response, or to persuade present users to purchase more of the brand or to use it in additional ways or simply to attempt to develop a brand switch. When one of these is the objective, a different type of concurrent study is undertaken. There are two basic types: (1) the consumer diary and (2) the consumer pantry check.

1. Consumer diaries. These are used by some advertisers to record the behavior of persons in their target market during the campaign. For example, customers or prospects may keep diaries of such activities as brands purchased, brands used for various activities, brand switches, media usage, exposure to competitive promotions, use of coupons, and the like. By reviewing the diaries, an advertiser may determine if the advertising message is being exposed to the target market and what effect this exposure is having. If the respondents are exposed to the advertising message and no attitude or behavioral changes occur, the advertiser may determine the message is not effective. There are obvious limitations on the amount of information that can be obtained through a consumer diary, but the methodology often serves as an early warning system for spotting potential strengths or weaknesses in an advertising campaign and allows the planner to make changes while there is still time.

2. Pantry checks. The alternative to the diary is the pantry check, whereby a research person physically goes to target market homes and asks consumers what brands of products have been purchased or used recently. In some cases, a physical count of products or brands in the home is taken and recorded. This may be done on several occasions over time and changes in purchasing habits noted. A variation used is called the "dust bin" approach, whereby consumers are asked to save empty packages of products they have used. These are then picked up, counted, and evaluated by the research team. In either case, the attempt is to determine what if any changes in purchasing habits may have occurred while the advertising campaign was in progress.

The Post-Test

The traditional campaign evaluation methodology is the post-test, which is conducted at the conclusion of the campaign. While data gathering through panels, diaries, personal interviews, telephone surveys, or other means is common to both the concurrent and the post-test, the primary purpose of this measure is to evaluate the final results of the campaign against predetermined advertising goals or objectives.

In a standard post-test, consumers in the target market or area in which the campaign was conducted are questioned about the advertising and the effects of the message on their opinions, attitudes, and behavior. These results are then weighed against the objectives and goals of the advertising campaign to determine if satisfactory results were achieved for the advertising investment.

The major problem in a simple post-test is lack of information on changes that may have been caused by the advertising campaign. Unless concurrent testing has been done, little may be known about consumer attitudes toward and opinions about the brand prior to the time the advertising messages were placed in the media. It is difficult to determine, therefore, if the advertising had the desired effect or if the attitude and opinions found in the post-test were already present or were caused by other factors. A better approach using a pre-post test can solve this problem.

In the pre-post-testing technique, advertisers conduct a pretest in the market before launching the advertising campaign. This provides a benchmark for later evaluation. By knowing what attitudes and opinions were held by consumers prior to the start of the campaign, a comparison can be made with the findings after the campaign has run.

For example, assume the advertising objective for a specific campaign was to raise the awareness level about a particular product benefit within the target market population by 25 percent. Without a pretest, it would be difficult to determine if the objective had been achieved at the end of the campaign or if that level was already present. If, however, a pre-test were used it might have been found that an awareness level of 16 percent already existed among the target group. Thus, to achieve the goal of a 25 percent increase, awareness of the product benefit at the end of the campaign would have to measure at least 20 percent (a 25 percent increase over the 16 percent base). If, after the campaign had been run, it was found that the awareness level of the specific product benefit was 32 percent among the target population, the campaign could be judged very successful; the advertising goal was only a 25 percent increase in awareness and a 50 percent increase was achieved.

The post-test and pre-post technique can be used to evaluate almost any campaign objective. The chief distinction of the methodology is that the study is conducted after the campaign has been run and there is no opportunity for change or revision. This inability to change or revise is also the chief disadvantage.

Research Methods for Evaluating the Advertising Campaign

While it is usually not the task of the planner to physically conduct the evaluation of the campaign (that usually falls to the research department or an outside research organization), the planner often may be required to specify the particular way in which the campaign should be evaluated. Therefore, whether the evaluation is the task of the planner or a research person, the planner should have an understanding of the various research tools available. That also helps build an evaluation system into the plan. A brief review of the various tools and techniques used to evaluate the campaign follows.

Individual Methods of Measuring the Results of the Campaign

Generally, the evaluation of the campaign is conducted with consumers in the marketplace. Of course, some campaigns are directed to dealers, distributors, or others, but for the most part in package goods advertising, the concern is with how the campaign performed with the ultimate consumer. The most common method of gathering that information is through some form of survey research. While actual structure and development of an evaluation survey is beyond the scope of this text, some general suggestions may be helpful in developing or evaluating a questionnaire to be used in this type of study.

Measuring awareness. Awareness is generally regarded as a measure of knowledge without reference to source. Although the primary interest in campaign evaluation is knowing if there is a relationship between the advertising and consumer awareness, this is usually not possible. There are four primary methods of measuring awareness:

1. Yes-or-no questions. Example: "Have you ever heard of Fred's Flour?" Yes ___ No ___. While the yes-no questions are simple to administer and tabulate, no information is gained beyond the direct answer.

2. Open-end questions. Example: "What companies can you name that package flour?" Here, more information is obtained than that in a yes-no situation, but no relationship to the advertising campaign can be developed.

3. Checklist questions. Example: "Which of the following products does Fred's Company manufacture?" Flour ___ Rolling pins ___ Automobiles ___ Electronic computers ___. Here the answers are easily obtained, although the range of answers is restricted. As in the open-end and yes-no questions, no connection with the advertising campaign can be developed.

4. Rating scales. Examples: "How would you rate Fred's Flour in comparison with other brands of flour you have used?" Better ___ About the same as ___ Not as good as ___. With this approach, a measure of familiarity is achieved, but differences among the persons doing the rating make it difficult to combine answers or interpret the exact results. Additional scales or other approaches are sometimes used to make this form of measurement more reliable.

Measurement of awareness through the above techniques is quick and fairly low in cost since it can be done through the mail or by telephone interview. The results are easy to tabulate and generally straightforward. These advantages are balanced by the lack of knowledge of a significant change in awareness; e.g., awareness may have been higher before the campaign than after. This change is not measurable with a straight awareness approach. In addition, it is difficult to determine the source of the awareness. Awareness may or may not have come from the advertising campaign. While awareness is important to the evaluation of the campaign, it is the simplest of all measures and does not, in most cases, provide a direct relationship.

Measuring recall. In campaign evaluation, measuring recall can be determined by the amount of knowledge among consumers that can be directly related to the advertising and by identifying the campaign as the source of that knowledge. Recall is normally used to determine the extent to which advertising messages have been retained by consumers. Although tenuous, the assumption is made that recall of an advertising message and purchase behavior are related. Thus, recall is believed to be an important measure for the advertising campaign.

As outlined in the previous section, two types of recall can be measured, aided and unaided.

1. Unaided recall. Example: "Can you recall any brands of flour being advertised in the last few weeks?" The respondent is given no clues as to what brand is being investigated or what additional questions might be asked. He or she must recall any or all advertising messages seen in the past and relate them to the question. The assumption is made that advertising remembered without any clues from the interviewer is stronger than that in which some direction is given.

2. Aided recall. Example: "Do you remember seeing or hearing any advertising for Fred's Flour recently?" The respondent's reply is aided by the brand name. Rather than trying to remember all flour advertising, the respondent can concentrate on the particular brand. Care must be

taken that not too much aid is given or the respondent may resort to guessing rather than recalling.

The major advantage of measuring recall is that it allows measurement of at least one aspect of the advertising campaign. If the respondent remembers the campaign message or portions of the actual advertising, a direct correlation can be made. The main problem is that recall and purchase behavior may not be directly connected. In other words, the person may recall the message, but that message may have no effect when the purchase decision is made. In addition, since many campaigns are quite similar over the years, the respondent may actually recall a previous advertising message and put it into the context of the present campaign. It is often difficult to identify or isolate specific campaign features.

Measuring attitudes.   Recall and attitude tests are often combined in an attempt to determine if there are major differences between consumers who remember the advertising message and those who don't. Attitude tests are also used to measure changes in consumer perception of a brand or the degree of acceptance of various claims made in the advertising when used over time.

Five basic techniques are used to measure attitudes:

1. Direct questions. Example: "How would you describe the use of Fred's Flour for baking?" Only a favorable or unfavorable attitude toward the product is measured. The level or degree of feeling is not possible. As a result, this approach may be combined with a rating scale.

2. Rating scales. Example: "How would you describe the self-measuring spout on Fred's Flour packages?" Very easy to use ___ Easy to use ___ Neither easy nor hard to use ___ Hard to use ___ Very hard to use ___. While scales are easy to apply and tabulate, the main problem is the view of the respondent. A "Very easy to use" answer by one person may be the same as an "Easy to use" response from another. In other words, a scale does not discriminate sufficiently to permit a precise line to be drawn between the various attitudes.

3. Checklists. Example: "Which of the following are most important to you when you purchase flour?" Price ___ Package ___ Pre-sifted ___ Reputation of manufacturer ___. The attributes can be easily ranked by the respondents and easily tabulated by the advertiser. The primary problem, however, is there is no assurance that the most important factors have been isolated and listed on the questionnaire. In addition, the meaning of each question is not always totally clear. For example, does "Reputation of manufacturer" mean the same thing to all respondents?

4. Semantic differential tests. Example: "Would you say the user of Fred's Flour is":

A good cook   ___   ___   ___   ___   ___   A poor cook

Extravagant   ___   ___   ___   ___   ___   Price-conscious

Paired opposite descriptive words or phrases are separated on a scale. The respondent is allowed to check the place on the scale where the product would be rated. Thus, the respondent's attitude toward the product can be determined. The scale is easy to use and the results are simple to tabulate. The major problem with this type of measure is that the scale may not be interpreted by all respondents in the same manner.

5. Partially structured interviews. Example: "I'd like you to tell me some of your feelings about baking and the ingredients you use such as flour, butter, and milk." In this approach, an attempt is made to allow the respondent to discuss the general topic area and reveal attitudes about the brand without using a specific set of questions. While the interviewer knows the general areas about which information and attitudes will be sought, the use of the unstructured interview allows the respondent an opportunity to indicate areas of interest that might not have been previously considered.

Attitudinal tests are regarded as quite important in advertising campaign evaluation. A favorable attitude is considered to be an indication that the person is more likely to purchase a brand than if he or she has an unfavorable attitude. As a result, changes in attitudes are regarded as more important in campaign evaluation than awareness or recall. Unfortunately, there is little evidence that a favorable attitude will always result in behavioral change, such as purchase of a brand. The use of attitude measurements is also open to question because it is most difficult to obtain an accurate measure of people's attitudes about any subject.

Measuring brand usage.   Brand usage is the ultimate measure of the effectiveness of an advertising campaign. While it has been stressed that advertising usually should be considered only on the basis of communication effects, in some instances, advertisers want to trace sales results. This is done by measuring such things as movement of goods through store audits, pantry audits, and consumer panels. When consumer interviews are used, they consist primarily of a series of questions about past, present, and future brand usage, such as:

1. "What brand of flour do you normally purchase?" Fred's ___ Harry's ___ Aunt Ethel's ___ Brand X ___

2. "What brand of flour did you buy last?" Fred's ___ Harry's ___ Aunt Ethel's ___ Brand X ___

3. "What brand of flour do you think you will buy next?" Fred's ___ Harry's ___ Aunt Ethel's ___ Brand X ___

By using this type of consumer questionnaire, primarily on a pre-test/post-test basis, changes in purchasing habits can be measured. When these usage changes are combined with tests of awareness, recall, and attitudes, determination of the effects of an advertising campaign is sometimes possible. While the relationship is somewhat tenuous, the attempt to relate advertising to sales is sometimes fruitful when all variables can be controlled.

Syndicated and Custom Research Techniques

A number of syndicated research services specialize in the evaluation of individual advertisements and sometimes advertising campaigns. Because these services vary so greatly in methodology, only the major organizations are covered. Those who wish to investigate specific techniques should consult the individual organization offering the services.

Syndicated print techniques. The most common technique for evaluating print advertisements or campaigns is that employed by Daniel Starch and Staff. Although Starch studies are designed primarily to evaluate individual advertisements in magazines, the technique can be adapted to other forms of print.

The Starch technique consists of a recognition-and-recall test. First, a list of magazines that respondents believe they have seen before is developed. Based on their acknowledged exposure to the publication, respondents are taken through the magazine page by page and are asked questions about each advertisement recognized. Every advertisement in the issue is scored. Advertisers may then compare the score of their advertisement to the scores of others in the same product category or to all advertisements in the magazine.

Other organizations, such as Gallup & Robinson, offer evaluations of print advertisements, and nearly all follow some form of the recognition-and-recall technique. Most industrial publications conduct some form of readership study whereby individual readership scores are computed for each advertisement appearing in the issue.

Starch and Gallup & Robinson syndicated services are widely used by many advertisers. Some advertisers and agencies, however, have reservations about this form of measurement. They cite the fact that these techniques measure only the recall of the advertisement by the reader and notthe selling effectiveness or the persuasive ability of the ad as a whole. In some cases, the argument goes, the very devices used to gain memorability and recall in a Starch or Gallup & Robinson study may work against developing a strong sales message. That is, an advertisement, by its unusual nature, may be remembered for itself, but the brand or sales message forgotten. At best, Starch and Gallup & Robinson scores measure only one aspect of a print advertisement—the ability to be recalled.

Broadcast evaluation techniques. Specifically, there are few if any individual commercial or campaign evaluation techniques used to rate broadcast commercials. Having used a pretest on the commercials, most advertisers are content to use one of the other forms of campaign evaluation to determine the success or failure of the commercials used.

One additional evaluative measure commonly taken by many advertising agencies is the "post-buy media analysis." Since all time purchases on radio and television are based on estimates of the audience that might be exposed to the individual commercial, the real question is how many people were actually in the audience. Therefore, the media department, commonly using Nielsen or Arbitron figures, takes the audience that was estimated and compares it with the measured audience that was actually achieved for each of the commercials on the schedule. Those figures are then compared against the media campaign objectives and estimates. This evaluation tells whether or not the commercials received the expected exposures and how well the media buy was made. Some service organizations provide this type of service to the advertisers and the agency. While these are not technically syndicated services, they do offer another form of campaign evaluation, particularly in the media buy.

Sales results. While our primary emphasis has been on the communication effects of the campaign, advertisers often also use sales or marketing information for evaluation. The chief sources are internal sales data and syndicated or custom research.

Internal sales data are used to learn if product sales are responses to the advertising campaign. This effect can be measured either through comparisons to previous periods or against sales goals that have been set for the brand. A widely used source of information comes from broker or sales force reports.

Syndicated or custom research usually consists of subscription to one of the auditing services as the Nielsen Retail Index or SAMI (Selling Areas

Markets, Inc.). Nielsen makes bimonthly studies of retail food and drug-stores to obtain information on distribution levels, penetration of the product into different types of stores, share of national case volume, share of in-store distribution, product movement, and activities of competitors. SAMI offers a service that measures warehouse withdrawals by food and drugstores, thus indicating the popularity of the product at the retail level.

While many marketing variables are involved in the sale of the product, if sales measurement techniques such as the Nielsen Retail Index are used, one can sometimes determine if the failure or success of the product can be related to the advertising campaign.

Other methods of advertising campaign evaluation, such as personal observation and expert opinion, are sometimes used. The methods listed above, however, make up the bulk of the data gathering and evaluation techniques.

Custom research techniques.   While many forms of data gathering may be used, the four that follow are most commonly used in campaign evaluation.

1. Personal interviews. These are usually considered the most accurate of all advertising campaign evaluation techniques. Whether the evalua-tion centers on past purchase behavior, understanding of present campaign messages, or questions about competitive activity, the per-sonal interview is usually able to elicit the information from the respondent.

    Personal interviews may take many forms, from traditional door-to-door to mall intercepts. The major advantage is the opportunity for face-to-face discussion and clarification of answers to the questions asked. The major disadvantages are the extremely high cost of personal data gathering and the inability of interviewers to make contact with people not at home or to contact responents in certain urban areas.

2. Consumer panels. These are widely used to gather all types of adver-tising information. Panels consist of respondents who agree either to keep records or to answer inquiries on an ongoing basis. Questions asked the panel may take almost any form. The major advantage of the panel is the high rate of return from the respondents, since they are usually committed to the techniques. The major disadvantage is the lack of selectivity among the respondents. In addition, the panel response technique consists of polling those who have agreed to par-ticipate. This group may or may not be representative of the whole population.

3. Mailed questionnaires. Sending questionnaires by mail is a relatively

low-cost method of obtaining an evaluation of an advertising campaign. The mail questionnaire offers many advantages, from selection of the sample to wide geographic distribution for response. Usually, more detailed questions can be asked in a mail survey than any other form. The major disadvantage is the length of time needed to carry out the study and the often low return response rate. Mail surveys are widely used to evaluate industrial advertising studies.

4. Telephone interviewing. This is an increasingly popular form of data gathering for campaign evaluation. The telephone call has many of the advantages of the personal interview, yet it is much less expensive. It can be used in areas where personal interviews cannot be made, and often respondents will answer questions by telephone they will not answer any other way. The obvious disadvantages of telephoning are inability to show advertising materials and asking very complex questions. The innovation of WATS (Wide Area Telephone Service) has enabled advertisers and researchers to poll people on advertising campaigns all over the country from one central location.

Some research organizations offer a syndicated form of custom research for campaign evaluation. Usually, this methodology requires the advertisers to submit one, two, or more questions about the campaign to the research organization. The organization gathers several noncompetitive advertisers who have done the same. The questions are then combined into a usable format, and a certain number of consumers are contacted and asked the questions. Because several advertisers have participated, the price is usually much lower than that for an individual study. Another form of evaluation study is for a research organization to investigate several product categories through consumer studies, compile the data, and then offer this information on a syndicated basis to various companies at a flat rate.

The methodology used for campaign evaluation varies according to factors such as available funds, type of campaign to be evaluated, geographic area, type of product, and advertising media used. Thus, there is no one best way or predetermined methodology that should be used for any given campaign or any type of advertiser. The evaluation should be developed to fit the needs of the advertiser and the marketplace.

The major point in the choice of a technique or methodology to evaluate the campaign is to be sure the technique measures the objectives stated in the campaign strategy. If the intent is to measure advertising awareness, the methodology used should be keyed to fit that goal. If, on the other hand, the goal of the campaign is to increase product preference, the evaluation methodology may be vastly different. Like the development of an advertising campaign, there is no hard-and-fast rule for evaluation. It all depends on the campaign.

Evaluating the Evaluation

For purposes of evaluating the evaluation, certain questions should be asked about the research itself. While numerous considerations can be cited for any research study, Simon Broadbent has suggested four.

Is the Sample Representative?

Obviously, the respondents in the evaluation sample should be members of the target market to whom the advertising campaign is directed. The advertising may do an excellent job of communicating the sales message to women 35 to 49 years of age. But that's of little value if the target group for whom the advertising is intended is young men 18 to 24. The groups simply aren't that much alike.

Does the Respondent Understand the Questions Being Asked?

Too many times, in followup interviews, it has been found that respondents didn't actually understand the questions they were asked. As a result of this misunderstanding, garbled—or even worse—misleading or incorrect information was obtained. To be able to reply with the information sought, the respondent must understand the question being asked.

Are the Conclusions Drawn from the Advertising Campaign Evaluation Substantiated?

Leaping to conclusions is prevalent in campaign evaluation. Because so much time and effort have gone into the campaign, the creators are sometimes inclined to explain away problems or assume as accepted things that may not be true. The research conclusions reached in the campaign must be based solely on the information gathered and reported with a minimum of explanation required.

Was the Sample Large Enough?

A frequent problem in campaign evaluation is finding enough respondents who have seen or are familiar with the advertising to make an adequate evaluation of it. The problem becomes crucial for products that have a small market share, are purchased infrequently, or have a limited media schedule. Yet, for meaningful conclusions to be drawn, the sample base must be of a sufficient size to be statistically accurate.[1]

---

1. Simon Broadbent, *Spending Advertising Money* (London: Business Books, 1975), pp. 210–43.

Test Marketing   Most of the concern in the preceding sections has been with measuring the effects of advertising for existing or established products. While these types of evaluations are satisfactory, they assume that the campaign is being used in a widespread area. In some instances, for both established and new products, test markets are used to evaluate advertising campaigns before large sums of money are invested in national media or national markets.

Why Use Test Markets?

While many reasons exist for using a test market, three are major.

A trial of the campaign. With marketers attempting to take more and more of the risk out of advertising, the test market offers an excellent opportunity to try out the campaign. By testing the campaign in a smaller market or on a reduced scale, the advertiser has the opportunity of seeing how it might work and of making any needed adjustments before moving the campaign into the larger, more expensive broad-scale market.

An opportunity to try variations. Where alternative campaigns have been developed, test markets allow an advertiser to try the variations in an actual market setting to determine the best choice. For example, two or more campaign themes may have been developed, each of which has performed about the same in a pretest format. The test market allows the measurement to be made in a "real world" setting and the results to be evaluated.

A way to reduce the financial risk. With the increasing cost of media and the need to stretch advertising investments as much as possible, the test market gives the advertiser an opportunity to try a campaign in a controlled-risk situation. A failure in a test market is not nearly as costly as one on a national scale.

Types of Test Markets

While test markets may be developed for many reasons, three essential purposes predominate.

Product test. The product test is an opportunity to learn how the product or service is accepted by consumers prior to a national or broad-scale introduction. While preliminary laboratory tests may have proved successful, the acid test for a new product is the response or results in the actual marketplace.

Advertising test. Like the product test, the advertising test is an opportunity to try the advertising campaign on a reduced scale prior to a rollout. As mentioned previously, the advertising program may be fine tuned as a result of test market results or alternatives evaluated on their success or failure in the test market.

Media weight tests/spending level tests. Advertisers often use test markets to evaluate various levels of media weight or various levels of advertising spending. The use of these tests gives the advertiser the opportunity to determine the most effective and efficient spending level for achieving the advertising goals.

How to Develop a Test Market

Two basic steps are required in developing a test market plan. First, the broad-scale or national plan must be developed. This is the advertising campaign that will be used, provided the test market is successful. In other words, all parts of the major program must first be developed in detail. The second step is to reproduce this broad-scale program in miniature. That is, the major plan is then scaled down to fit the test market or markets selected. This is usually done through a translation of the broad-scale program in the form of a percentage of expenditure or investment. For example, if the proposed national advertising investment for the campaign is planned at $5 million, the test market expenditure would be determined based on the test-market size as a percentage of the national program. In this case, if Fort Wayne, Indiana, was selected as the test market and the population of Fort Wayne was determined to be 1 percent of the planned size of the national campaign, then the investment in Fort Wayne would be $50,000 ($5,000,000 × .01 = $50,000). Other relationships may be used, but population, size of the test market as part of the broad-scale plan, and percentage of media costs are the most common methods of determining the amount to be invested in the test market. In addition to the estimated advertising campaign costs, other investments such as sales promotion programs and consumer incentives, are scaled to fit the test market. In short, the entire broad-scale plan is miniaturized to fit the test market.

Developing a Test Market Plan

Several major factors should be considered in developing a test market plan.

Test market size and location. The proposed test market must be large enough to be reasonably representative of the broad-scale market. While test markets should be small enough to control and evaluate, they must be large enough and have enough of the pertinent market variables for the campaign to get a fair test. The test market should be of sufficient size so that the national competitive climate is represented. The same competitors should be present in the test market with approximately the same competitive weight as that found in the national market.

While the test market must be large enough to give the campaign a fair test, it must be small enough to reduce the financial risk to worthwhile proportions. For example, New York City might represent the national program exactly, but it would make a poor test market simply because of the amount of investment required to conduct the program.

Test market media. The test market must also be capable of satisfactorily reproducing the national media plan. For example, if the national plan calls for the use of newspaper supplements, the test market must provide newspaper supplements for an adequate test. Attempting to test a media plan on a reduced scale with other media forms can often be misleading with respect to what national results might be.

Duration of the test. The length of a test market is another major factor in planning. This decision is usually based on the minimum amount of time required to accurately measure the results. Thus, there is no hard-and-fast rule on how long a test market should run. Two major factors are usually considered:

1. The test should run long enough to permit checking the initial levels of product distribution, trade stocking, and displays. With some products, this could be a matter of days, and with others weeks or even months may be required to take the product through the distribution channels.

2. There should be sufficient time to allow for the formation of a clear assessment of the level of consumer trial and the proportion of repeat purchases achieved. In other words, a short test might be misleading as consumers try the product initially but fail to make repeat purchases. Advertisers frequently have read the results of a test market incorrectly because their interpretation was based on initial purchases. The lack of repeat purchases after the first trial was not evaluated and, as a result, what appeared to be a successful product was, in reality, a failure. The same is true of the advertising campaign. Initial awareness might be very high, but knowledge and preference might not develop. Unless sufficient time is allowed for the test market to show the full results of the campaign, the results could be misleading.

Measurement and control of results. The final factor in the determination of the relative success of a test market is the ability to measure the results. Closely allied with that is the control the advertiser has over obtaining or gathering the results of the test market. It does little good to develop a test market and then not be able to obtain the necessary test results or not be able to control some of the factors in the market that would prevent an accurate appraisal. For example, attempting to use a test market in which obtaining sales figures for the product is very difficult only compounds the problem. If a test market is to be used, the measurement and control of the results of that test are vital.

Test Market Problems

While test marketing is widely used by advertisers in many categories, two major problems exist.

Competition reading the test. In most good test markets, it is as easy for the competition as it is for the advertiser to obtain information about the test market. Because all marketers use many of the same techniques and often the same syndicated information sources, it is a simple matter for a competitor to watch a test market while it is in progress. When this occurs, the competitor often knows the success or failure of the campaign as quickly as the advertiser. With this knowledge, a competitor may be able to react and generate a campaign that will offset even an advertiser's success. It is almost impossible to hide the results of a test market from competition.

Competition destroys the test market. Competitors may also take market actions that will give a false reading to the test market. For example, if a campaign is developed with a strong competitive price story, a competitor might lower his price in the test market to make the results inconclusive. A competitor often prefers to destroy the test market with competitive activities rather than risk facing the results of the successful test.

In spite of the cost of development and the risks involved, test markets are an excellent way to learn how an advertising campaign would perform in a real-world setting at a reasonable cost.

Test Areas and Control Groups

A useful way to evaluate a specific advertising campaign on a limited basis is through test areas and control groups. This technique is widely used to evaluate the advertising campaign for new products. It is usually conducted prior to a widespread use of the campaign or a national rollout.

Cities or areas are selected for the test and matched as closely as possible. For example, three different areas might be selected to test an advertising campaign. A similar group of three areas matching as nearly as possible the geographic, demographic, and product-usage patterns of the test cities would then be identified. The advertising campaign being evaluated would be conducted in the three test areas. The three matching markets would receive no advertising and would serve as controls. At the end of the test campaign, studies and comparisons of advertising effects would be made between the test and control markets to determine differences. Because the areas were matched as closely as possible, it could be assumed that the advertising campaign in the advertised markets was the reason for any differences found.

The major advantage of the test-and-control approach is the comparatively low cost of placing and evaluating the campaign in a few limited areas as opposed to widespread use without testing. In addition, if necessary, changes can be made in the materials after the test results are obtained. The major disadvantage of this evaluation method is the difficulty of matching the control and test areas and the possibility that competition may "read" the test and learn what is planned for the future.

Evaluating a Test Market

In the preceding sections, it was assumed that in most cases the test market is simply a test of a new advertising program for an existing product. Indeed, that is often the case. Measuring the results of that type of test market is often quite different from a test for a new product or a new brand. A brief review of test market evaluation for a new product or brand follows.

Awareness. Advertising awareness of the brand or the product is often the major measurement in a test market. Because the product is new, and in some cases may be the first of its kind in the market, just making consumers aware of the product and the brand may be the key ingredient for success. In a test market, advertising often has the double task of making consumers aware not only of the new product type but also of the brand. Evaluating the advertising against these two objectives is often sufficient.

Obtaining distribution. Distribution of the brand may also be an advertising goal in a test market. Because new products have no track record, retailers are sometimes hesitant to stock them until they are in demand. Thus, the use of consumer advertising to "pull" the product through distribution channels is often stated as an advertising objective.

When advertising is powerful enough to have customers ask for the product, particularly to the extent that retailers feel it necessary to stock it, the campaign is usually considered effective. Similarly, if advertising in a test market fails to sufficiently convince customers so they go to the store

and purchase the product after distribution has been achieved, then retailers may discontinue the product. While distribution was obtained, the
advertising was not powerful enough to generate a consumer behavioral
change.

Sales. Sales may be a logical evaluative basis for an advertising campaign
in a test market, all other factors being equal. Many test products are
unknown and rely almost entirely on advertising for achieving awareness
and, ultimately, sales. In these cases, traditional market variables that
impinge on an existing product may not be present for a test product. Thus,
it may be possible to gauge the strength of the advertising campaign on the
basis of sales in a test situation. This seems to be particularly true for a
product that is the first entry in a new category or is the newest brand in an
existing product category.

Summary   One of the most important elements of good advertising and marketing is
the ability to measure results. And that comes from measuring the results
produced by the campaign. As with pretesting, the first issue is, "What will
be measured?" That, of course, involves objectives. Many of the same
problems confront the planner when evaluating the results of a campaign
as with pretests—multiple marketing effects, communications effects,
sales, and so on.

Case for Discussion: Fleur de Lis Cognac

In August of 1983, final plans were being made for the national introduction of Fleur de Lis Importers' new cognac. This would be Fleur de Lis' first nationally marketed product. Due to some processing innovations, Fleur de Lis would be able to sell its premium French cognac at a price well below that of most imports on the market.

During a corporate planning session, Jordan Uland, brand manager for the cognac, reviewed the promotional plan for the national introduction: "As you'll recall, we've established the following objectives for the Fleur de Lis Cognac campaign:

- achieve 90 percent awareness of Fleur de Lis Cognac among brandy and cognac drinkers (22,891,000 adults in the U.S.)
- among those aware, achieve 70 percent knowledge of Fleur de Lis as a low-price, premium cognac
- among those with knowledge, achieve 60 percent preference for Fleur de Lis over other cognacs
- achieve 20 percent purchase among those preferring Fleur de Lis.

This should result in Year 1 market share of approximately 7.6 percent. Approximate market shares for the top five competitors are:

Christian Brothers	24.4%
Courvoisier	15.5
Hennessey	11.6
Remy Martin	6.6
Paul Masson	5.8

We have defined the primary target market as:

Young adults, aged 25–34, both single and recently married (1–2 person households). They work full time in professional or managerial positions and have an annual income above $25,000.

This definition is based on data that indicates that, while the average brandy drinker tends to be older (35–54) and more settled, imported brandies and cognacs appeal to a younger consumer.[1]

---

1. Simmons Market Research Bureau, 1980 data.

Several renowned experts have pronounced Fleur de Lis equal to or better than other cognacs, including other imports. Their endorsement will be a chief component in the advertising campaign. Our theme is that "Fleur de Lis is premium cognac at a pleasing price."

We will advertise in two national weekly news magazines, three monthly business publications, one business weekly, and three monthly food-related magazines. The planned schedule for the first two months is as follows:

Time	1 page, four color, 8 insertions
Newsweek	1 page, four color, 8 insertions
Business Week	1 page, four color, 6 insertions (3-3-)
Fortune	1 page, four color, 2 insertions
Forbes	1 page, four color, 2 insertions
Barron's	1 page, four color, 2 insertions
Gourmet	1 page, four color, 2 insertions
Cuisine	1 page, four color, 2 insertions
Bon Appétit	1 page, four color, 2 insertions

This will give us national reach of approximately 40 percent (95 percent among our target market).

In addition, we will run a full page, four-color advertisement in the following publications to provide localized heavy-up in major markets:

Chicago	*Los Angeles*
Washingtonian	*Boston*
New York	*Philadelphia*
Mpls.-St. Paul	*San Francisco*
San Diego	*Atlanta*
Denver	*D* (Dallas)
Houston City	*Cleveland*
Pittsburgh	

We have two alternative advertising executions. Both have scored well in localized pre-testing. One places primary emphasis on premium quality, one on low price. The first is headlined "A truly excellent cognac" and pictures a gentleman holding a snifter of Fleur de Lis. He is identified as a cognac expert in a caption. Body copy points include the product's premium quality, French origin, and low price. A tag line, positioned beside a photograph of the Fleur de Lis bottle, reads, "Premium cognac at a pleasing price." We have three separate executions in this campaign, each featuring a different expert.

The alternative campaign depicts a young couple relaxing at home, enjoying Fleur de Lis cognac. The headline reads "Fleur de Lis: Premium Cognac at a Pleasing Price." The copy reads "Fleur de Lis is a premium French import. And with a price that's well within our budget, we can afford to indulge ourselves regularly."

Fleur de Lis cognac will be distributed through an established wholesaler we've dealt with in the past. Response from retailers has been very favorable and we are projecting a national distribution level of nearly 75 percent.

We will limit our consumer sales promotion efforts to shelf talkers labeling Fleur de Lis Cognac as a newcomer.

Before we launch the full-scale campaign, and prior to implementing a final import schedule, we'd like to try the product in a test market situation. We will be able to approximate the national media level through use of regional editions of the publications we've identified. In addition, we will use daily newspaper ads during the first two weeks of the test. This test will give us a chance to calculate import quantities based on demand and to test the two advertising campaigns to see which is more effective in an actual market situation.

We have selected two pairs of markets: Boston-Dallas and Philadelphia-San Diego. We will run the "expert" campaign in the first pair of markets and the "couple" campaign in the second pair. Test duration will be six weeks. Assuming all is well, the national introduction should begin on November 1.

Questions

1. Do you agree that Fleur de Lis is a good candidate for a test market?

2. Do you foresee any problems with the test market developed by Uland?

3. At the end of the staff meeting, Uland was told to develop an evaluation plan that would measure the effectiveness of the national campaign.
   a. Would you advocate a concurrent evaluation, or post-test?
   b. Should a pre-post test be used?
   c. Uland decides that telephone surveys might be helpful in the evaluation. Develop some questions that would test achievement of the knowledge objective.
   d. Uland is contacted by a syndicated research service that uses an established base sample in their studies. Before contracting with this service, what questions should be answered?

15 How to Make Winning Presentations

Ron Hoff, creative director for Foote, Cone & Belding, interviewed several senior agency persons in New York and Chicago to find out exactly what annoyed them about presenters. The following "dirty laundry list" tells what is wrong with most presentations. After citing the problems, the rest of this chapter gives specific proven solutions.

David Ogilvy:

"Most presenters are incoherent."

"I don't know what they're talking about."

"Why doesn't anybody start with a short summary of the problem, the research, the strategy, the promise, the media . . . *three minutes worth*."

" . . . listen before you talk."

"I don't know whether to read what he's *showing* or listen to what he's *saying*."

". . . no evidence that the presenter has taken great pains with his presentation."

Arthur Schultz:

"They just don't sell; lack of support for what you're recommending."

"We often repeat what somebody else just said. 'What I think David was trying to say. . . .' "

"Jargon. It's embarrassing."

"Don't paraphrase slides. Read them word for word."

This chapter was condensed from the writings of three senior advertising executives. Drawing from years of experience in internationally famous agencies, they have agreed to share the secrets of their success (and failure) in making client presentations. The late Andrew Kershaw was chairman, Ogilvy and Mather, when he wrote *How to Make Agency Presentations*. Ronald Hoff, executive creative director, Foote, Cone & Belding/New York, is author of a national workshop course, *Agency Presentations*. Paul Repetto, who spent 20 years in the advertising business with N. W. Ayer and Foote, Cone & Belding/Los Angeles, is author of an *Advertising Age* workshop lecture on *Agency Presentations*. Credit to these authors is given in context throughout the chapter.

David Ofner:

"No explanation at the start of *why we are gathered here*. No clear agenda."

"No sense of direction. Imprecise."

"Our presenters lack presence, authority."

"We don't know how to win. . . ."

John O'Toole:

"The purpose of personal presentations is to leave the prospect with the feeling that each of the presenters, with whom he will probably be spending more time than his wife, is the brightest, most professional, most capable person available in the agency business. Precious few of our presenters leave that impression."

Harvey Clements:

"We don't pay attention to lighting. Should be carefully set up and tested."

"We don't plan for involvement by the audience."

"Too many extraneous slides."

"Don't tell the audience how wonderful you think the recommendations are. If the stuff is good, they'll know it."

David Berger:

"The general failing is treating the presentation as yours, instead of the audience's. Presenting what *you* did rather than what *they* need."

"In terms of research this means emphasizing the study rather than the problem and the solution. In terms of media it means counting gross rating points instead of conveying a sense of *how much* advertising people will encounter."

"In terms of account management this means conveying the fact that you did your homework rather than what the listener needs to know."

"In terms of creative it means presenting how hard you worked rather than how the selling problem is being attacked."

Bryan Putnam:

"Too many presenters—amount of detail."

"Presentations in an informal way."

Chuck Winston:

"Too much time on everything."

"We answer the same question over and over. We seem to think that *one* answer for one question is somehow painfully inadequate."

After the critics had spoken, Ron Hoff boiled their grievances down into three cardinal sins.

- Imprecise
- Unorganized
- Deadly dull

Checklist for Preparation

It's easy to avoid these sins if you *prepare*. Look over the following list and spend your time working on areas in which you need to improve.

- Allow enough time for preparation or suffer doom.
- Focus on the lion.
- Treat the client as a person, not an advertising pro.
- Focus attention on the subject.
- Dos and don'ts on opening and closing.
- Approach the client's problem from his point of view—sales.
- Select your presenters carefully.
- The production—pay attention to details.
- How to show off your work.
- Visual aids—getting past the optic nerve.
- Questions—the sudden-death round.
- You can't over-rehearse.
- A checklist of 119 questions and tips.

The suggestions that follow are written from the viewpoint of an agency presenting to a client. However, the ideas are equally applicable to any situation where the planner is presenting advertising to management.

Preparation Time

The marketing, media, and creative are dynamite. Now it's time to present this delicate newborn child to the management. Will the management agree with you? Will he or she see the brilliance? Will he or she embrace it and love it? Only if you put the same loving care into *presenting* the work as you did in creating it. You can't rush it. Remember, the presentation is a finished commercial for your work. The presentation *is* you. To wing it without solid preparation is a waste of everyone's time.

In too many cases, the presentation is treated like a bastard child. It gets whatever scraps of time are left over once everything else is done. Perhaps in one day or a night a hundred slides are shot, developed, and then thrown into a carousel. We rationalize that the stuff is so great, it won't matter how we present it, the audience will rave over it. Foolish thinking. Most clients expect to see evidence of great care and concern on their behalf. Magnificent work can easily be ignored if it is presented in beggar's clothing.

Focus on the Lion   Invariably there is one key person whose blessing is crucial to your success. One in the group you present to will be the *lion,* the others the lambs. Seek out the lion and be sure to give him or her plenty of eye contact during the presentation. Also, tailor your presentation especially for the lion.

Andrew Kershaw tells how:

> In one case, not so long ago, our intelligence came from a former Ogilvy and Mather employee—now working in a division of the prospect company. He characterized the prospect as a martinet, with a great attachment to rigid methods and rules. Another source said that our prospect had been heard to praise our house advertisements, to which he referred as "The Tablets."
>
> Putting this to good use, we built our presentation on the theme of "discipline in advertising." We got the business.

Kershaw emphasizes that intelligence should be verified by two or more reliable sources. You take a very big chance tailoring your whole presentation based on one person's judgment. Especially if you do not know that person very well.

The Client as Person, Not Advertising Pro (According to Paul Repetto)   It's simply more realistic to admit that advertisers are less interested in advertising per se than we are. Their minds are cluttered with a host of other marketing problems besides advertising. Advertising is not their daily bread, it's *our* daily bread.

Paul Repetto points out two very important problems that result. First, management has other things on his or her mind. Plus, management feels uneasy "sitting on the bench" as the supreme judge of advertising. Top managers know deep inside that he or she is not really the expert; you are. So, he or she feels threatened. That person is sitting in front of peers—wide open and vulnerable. A person's natural strategy in this situation is to shield him- or herself, *to take a defensive posture.* Repetto gives the following admonition:

> Failure to recognize the fact that you are in an adversary role with the key person kills more presentations than any other single factor.

Reduce the Tension—Use a Warm-Up

Andrew Kershaw recalls the time when he was the client prospect and Ogilvy and Mather was the presenting agency. "We had the *warm-up* in

David Ogilvy's office and then he led me into the conference room. . . . ''
Ogilvy clearly understood this potential adversary relationship. One
reason for his great success is his understanding of human relations. He has
a natural talent for putting people at ease. And that's the first step in
overcoming this adversary relationship.

**Focus Attention
on the Subject**

Paul Repetto suggests that a good way to start the presentation is with an
agenda. Not a handout, that's distracting. Have the agenda on a poster
board and say, "Here's what we're going to cover this morning." Now,
you've done two important things. The audience knows business has
clearly started. The agenda rivets his or her attention to both you and the
business. Equally important, the agenda helps reduce tension. Because
now the audience gets a clear picture of what's going to happen. No
shocking surprises. He or she knows you aren't trying to be manipulative
and feels you trust him or her and respect his or her intelligence.

Restate the Assignment

Another simple way to reassure the key person is to restate the
assignment, *using exactly the same words he used when he gave it to
you.* First, this reestablishes his authority and helps him feel secure in
that role. Second, it tells him that you've heard him. And third, it
establishes the planner as the problem-solving partner of management, rather than the adversary. —Paul Repetto

---

**Dos and Don'ts on
Opening and Closing**

Andrew Kershaw offers some tips:

- Don't start with a funny story. That's amateurish.
- Don't start until after the beginning. (The actual beginning is not the real
  start.) How much warm-up time is needed is a very subjective thing. You
  have to feel your way along.
- Don't offer profuse thanks and claim what a privilege it is. It is undig-
  nified. But be polite and pleasant.
- A good way to start is with a businesslike agenda.
- Find charming, gentle, and warm ways to introduce your team by name,
  rank, and function.
- When the ''beginning'' is over, *start with something memorable.* Your
  initial impression is critical. If it is dull, you will probably never win the
  audience over.

On Closing

- Do not let the meeting end with a whimper or peter out with a recital of trivia.
- Make the closing memorable. The final impression must *move* the key person closer to agreeing with you.
- Put your strongest presenter at the end.
- Do not end with a peroration. A flowery rhetorical plea for approval of the plan sounds like a desperate prayer. Close confidently; boldly.
- A reprise is acceptable. Restate the original assignment and reinforce how you fulfilled it.
- Make your closing dramatic.
- The leave-behind or plans book must be well typed and contain all the important matters discussed during the presentation. Include a synopsis on each person who will be working on the campaign. Give full details on their experience, skills, and special strengths.
- For agencies, the leave-behind should contain a list of names of present clients with addresses and phone numbers. Suggest that the prospect phone them for more information.

Approach the Client's Problem from His Point of View

Ron Hoff believes that many advertising people have not learned to speak the client's language.

> Your priorities are mixed up when you insist on cramming 107 of your objectives down the client's throat when his greatest interest is *his objectives*.
>
> What kind of objective are we talking about? Marketing objective? Advertising objective? I submit that the *best* presentation technique is to state the *one* objective that is foremost in the client's mind. Advertising is generally judged in terms of sales—in terms of brand share. That's what this business is all about. When sales fall off, advertising agencies get fired. Don't present a whole slew of objectives. Present one . . . and write it from the client's point of view. Get to the heart of it. Don't mince words.
>
> I recall going to a lot of agency Plans Board meetings. Invariably, by the end of the meeting, the walls would be loaded with objectives. Marketing objectives, advertising objectives, research objectives, creative objectives, media objectives—pretty soon it all turned into mulligan stew and you couldn't tell the potatoes from the tomatoes.
>
> I submit to you that this does nothing but confuse everybody. When all the excess verbiage is ruthlessly boiled out of everything, your primary mission usually boils down to one basic objective. Be sure you give that objective center stage with bright flood lights on it.

Keep Your Language Simple

Paul Repetto is fond of a little thing Arthur Kudner wrote to his son. It's all that needs to be said about communicating something important.

> Never fear big, long words. Big long words name little things. All big things have little names. Such as life and death, peace and war, dawn, day, night, hope, love, home. Learn to use little words in a big way. It is hard to do, but they say what you mean. When you don't know what you mean, use big words. They often fool little people.

Select Your Presenters Carefully

Certain members of the planning team may be exceptional in his or her field. Even brilliant. However, he or she may be a lousy speaker; nervous in front of people. Don't force that person on stage just because he or she masterminded the creative strategy. Ideally, the client would like to see the people who will be conducting the campaign. But exceptions can and should be made for people who do not feel comfortable presenting and who do not want to learn how to present.

Andrew Kershaw recommends that you not select the presenters until you know who will be in the audience and how many. Many managers feel uncomfortable if they are outnumbered by the presenting group.

> All the agency people chosen to be present should have some functional role to play in the presentation. It is awful to watch someone sit silently during a presentation, a stuffed dummy, an obvious makeweight.

The Production— Pay Attention to Details

The first thing you must memorize about production is the *Presentation Law of Physics:*

> Audiovisual equipment always breaks down *during* the client presentation. It is programmed that way by mad engineers at the factory.

There are thousands of stories about equipment failures killing presentations. And losing business. And they're all true. The tragic part is how wasteful and stupid we are by not having oil in our lamps so we are ready for any surprise. We deserve to lose the approval when the client looks back and sees the projectionist with his pants down and no spare suspenders.

Kershaw admonished his people to "beware goofing on the staging." You can do everything right. Spend 100 work-hours getting the advertising ready. But one slip and "the audience will *forget the content* and remember only that the slide was upside down."

Here's a checklist based on Andrew Kershaw's experience in stage management. Don't start the presentation without it.

- Study the presentation room well in advance.
- Know where electrical outlets are.
- See if the room can be darkened.
- Is there a screen available?
- Can the lights be dimmed? Who will operate the light switches? Make sure the lighting has been tried and rehearsed.
- Avoid presenting in total darkness. If you can't see the whites of their eyes, and if they can't see yours, you are asking for trouble—or snores.
- If the room lights cannot be dimmed, get some appropriate table lamps or floor lamps with low wattage bulbs.
- Do you need an easel to display your ads? Most ledges in board rooms are too narrow to hold ads.
- Your projectionist must always have spare bulbs and batteries. Make sure he or she has them. It's even a good idea to have a spare projector at the ready in case a slide jams and you can't fix it.
- You will need a pointer. Make sure everyone knows how to use it.
- Carefully arrange tables and chairs in advance. Avoid lining up management and planners as opposing armies, glaring at each other across the table.
- Decide if a mike is necessary. Pray that it is not. But if the room is too large, make sure you test the sound system and have an engineer on hand in case of failure.
- Check out the lectern if you use one. Test the lights, test the lip that holds your papers, test the width for turning your pages. Test its height; you do not want to look diminutive behind it, nor should you loom like the Green Giant.
- Provide your audience with note pads, pencils, and clean ash trays.

Ogilvy and Mather's Presenter's Survival Kit

1. Long extension cords with multiple plug-in capacity
2. Projection bulbs for carousel and movie projectors
3. An exciter lamp for movie projector
4. Push pins
5. A gum eraser
6. Black and colored felt pens (for fixing typos in charts)
7. An emergency splicer
8. Rolls of masking tape, Scotch tape, and duct tape

How to Show Off Your Work

Ron Hoff believes in creating excitement from the moment the client walks in the door. A good way to do that, according to Hoff, is "to show where the campaign will go without doing the whole campaign. Do a batch of headlines, blow them up, mount them, and place them around the room. It will look like you've done a ton of work—and the client will get the feeling the campaign could go on forever."

You can do the same thing with television. Display one board (or a reasonable facsimile thereof) and write brief synopses of follow-up commercials. Blow them up (include a visual of the key frame for each commercial) and display them about the room.

Andrew Kershaw was a believer in creating excitement, too. "If permitted, decorate the walls with ads. Show annual reports, merchandising, posters, booklets, brochures. Make it look exciting."

"Once we made a presentation thousands of miles from home," continued Kershaw. "We erected a temporary wall to display our work in the boardroom. We were successful with the wall but not the account. This proves you can try too hard."

Visual Aids— Getting Past the Optic Nerve

The quickest way to the human brain is through the eye. It's a person's most efficient learning tool. However, the eye is a very impatient organ. Like any of the other physical senses, it needs stimulation to remain alert and fixed in one spot for very long. One study reported that the average adult eye must be stimulated every nine seconds or it will lose interest. That's a pretty big challenge, especially when you consider your prospects are probably thinking about other serious marketing problems, personal problems, dental appointments, a daughter's injury, a son's overnight engagement. As Tom Murray of Murray-Chaney Advertising once said, "The world is not about advertising. It's about people." And that applies to clients as well as consumers. You've got to be compelling if you expect to get past the optic nerve and into the grey matter.

Ron Hoff has written a tablet of valuable "scripture" on making and using slides. If you follow these laws, you'll not only keep the client awake, but he or she will be absorbing your precious information and moving closer to conversion.

The Ten Commandments of Making and Using Slides

1. Limit words per slide: 15 to 20, best. Think of the slide as a *billboard*.
2. Use several *simple* slides in place of one complicated slide.
3. Use *titles* with caution. Good, brief slides don't need them.

4. Dark backgrounds are best. Blue. Black. Red. White on dark blue for *ease* of reading, recall. Sans serif best.
5. Nobody ever complained about words on slides being *too large*. Design slides for "back row viewing."
6. Use color functionally, sparingly. Emphasis, not ornamentation.
7. Don't leave slide on screen *after* you've discussed it. If a lengthy bit of information follows after the slide, go to black.
8. Operate slides *yourself*. White tape on forward button.
9. Always check to make sure slides are right side up, not upside down and backwards. Check it yourself immediately before the presentation starts.
10. Rehearse with everything *exactly* as it will be.

Andrew Kershaw gives the following advice on the use of slides and charts: Study it before and after the visual aids are done.

1. Read everything on the slide exactly as written the instant the slide appears. Having done so, you can give any additional information. Don't show a slide and discuss something else. What the eye sees, and what you say, must march together.
2. Never turn your back on the audience to read a slide or chart. Have note cards or a transcript so you don't have to read from the screen.
3. Visual aids are supposed to help you. When charts fall all over or slides jam or get shown upside down, they are not aids at all—they destroy communication: These things can be prevented by adequate rehearsal.
4. Learn to use a pointer. It is a marvelous instrument. When it is used properly, the audience is riveted to it. And it enables you to maintain a respectable distance from the screen or chart, and you will not be in the line of vision of the audience.
5. White lettering on blue or red or green background is usually most legible. (That is because the room is at least partially darkened: it is not inconsistent with the rules about illegibility of reversed type.)
6. Never show a storyboard in a presentation. Put the frames on separate slides with accompanying words on a tape recorder.
7. If, in the course of your talk, you refer to a booklet, merchandising piece, package, or direct mail piece, always show it to the audience. Then, if possible, hand it to the audience to look at more closely.
8. When you show ads, always read the headline. And read the subhead, too, especially if it is a good one. But never read all the copy—it takes too long.
9. If you play a radio commercial, an ingenious idea is to accompany the commercial with silent-film footage (or a series of slides) of a highway,

taken from the driver's seat, to simulate the effect of a car radio. People will know where to look—and it adds a touch of showmanship.

10. A presenter makes his life a lot easier if he sticks to just one kind of visual aid—to switch from slides to charts to film is asking for trouble.

11. Proofread your material several times. It is an invariable law of presentations that charts and slides always contain a typo or two, misspellings, a wrong figure. (A good trick for spotting errors is to read the words on each slide from back to front.) If an error should slip through undetected and cannot be corrected before the presentation, always point it out. Don't let the audience spot it.

12. Set *early* deadlines or suffer. Waiting until the last minute to make your visual aids is a 90-proof formula for failure. Allow plenty of time to make changes, fix typos, and rehearse.

Questions—
The Sudden-Death
Round

When major agencies compete for accounts, this is where many *eliminations* occur. For example, if six agencies are invited to present, odds are that, based on the presentation alone, two or three will be dead before the questions and answers begin. Assuming that your presentation is right on target, you've still got the highest hurdle left.

An astute client will perform exploratory surgery during the Q&A. The client will make careful incisions into the following areas, and then observe how the agency body responds:

Personnel. Are they bright people? Do they have character? Do they articulate well without a script? Do they answer directly? Are they honest? Are they dignified? Do they like each other? Do they accept their leader? Will they respect our authority? Can we get along with them? Like them?

Substance. Are we hiring professionals? Are they *experts* in their particular fields? Do they know more about advertising than we do? Can they give solid, logical support for the advertising budget they want from us? Do they really understand our product from our point of view (profit and consumer satisfaction)? From the consumer's point of view (problem solving)? Do they show sparks of genius and originality in media and marketing decision making as well as creative strategy?

Aggressiveness. Are they confident in themselves? Do they believe they can deliver the objectives they have set? Do they demonstrate the kind of aggressiveness that is needed to battle for brand shares in our highly competitive market? Are their goals high enough, yet realistic? Will they work toward *our* profit as well as their own?

Sound frightening? Most surgery is. But there are some excellent ways you can prepare for a client's delicate scalpel. Your confidence will increase tenfold if you will give heed to the following advice from Ron

Hoff. It's based on years of winning experience, and just enough losing to know how to avoid it.

How to Cope with Questions

Most politicians have a system you might want to consider. They have their staffs write down every question that might be asked during a press conference—and they make sure they have the answers. The day before your presentation, spend an hour *anticipating* the questions you may get. Write them down.

- "Who is the biggest competitor? What's our share of market?"
- "Will legal let you say that? Have you asked?"
- "Why a :60? Would it be better as a :30?"
- "Does it have enough brand identification?"
- "How much will that commercial cost? Have you thought about shooting in Europe?"
- "Where's the big idea?"
- "Does your theme line clearly position the product?"
- "Have you tested the theme line? What do people think it means?"
- "How did you determine your budget?"
- "Do you think 75 GRPs will deliver enough prospects?"

If you can honestly say, "We looked into that very question—and here's what we found . . . ," you're not going to get much argument from your audience.

If somebody asks a question that you *should* know the answer to but don't—say, "I should know the answer to that but I don't." *Write the question down* so that everybody can see you have every intention of looking into it.

Another tip. Find out about the people you'll be presenting to. Do a little digging. What kinds of questions are they likely to ask? Do they have any pet peeves? Ask around. The more you know about your audience, the better able you'll be to control the situation.

Appoint a Leader for the Q&A Session

There's always the one question everybody is dying to answer. And they all jump in together. So the whole agency dies right there on the spot. Grim, yet so common. Be sure someone is responsible for fielding the questions. This person can easily establish authority at the outset of the Q&A by asking for questions. Then, as questions come, he or she can nod or gesture to the best agency authority on that subject. It maintains order and keeps the impulsive jaws from flapping.

Don't Hitchhike on Each Other's Answers

A sure sign of agency weakness is for Sue to "clarify" what Rick was saying. It may be acceptable to add something to a response now and then, but never say, "What Rick was trying to say is. . . . " That's inviting sudden death.

You Can't Over-Rehearse

How to Defeat Nervousness

There are two important secrets. First, be in complete command of your material. Know exactly what's coming up—what you want to say—how you want to say it—the points you want to register. Rehearse until you're sick of it. The better you know your material—the more you've rehearsed —the less likely you are to be nervous.

Incidentally, if it's possible to rehearse in the same room where you'll be performing, so much the better. The more uncertainties you can remove from your presentations, the fewer butterflies you'll have.

The second secret is one that requires lots of persuasion. Before you get up to talk, tell yourself you know your subject better than anybody in your audience (and you had better). Convince yourself that you're better at what you do than anybody in the place—and that you're going to outshine everybody on the program. Pump yourself up—get your adrenalin going. Tell yourself you're going *to be the best and you will be.*

And, of course, *you've* got to be sold on the material you're presenting, or your audience won't be. This is particularly important if you're presenting work that you didn't create yourself.

Criticism

How do you handle it? The best attitude for a presenter is one of good-natured confidence. Don't be overbearing. Don't be a clown. If you're good-natured, your audience probably will be, too. If you're confident, it gives your audience confidence in you.

But don't be so confident that you're intractable. Don't give the impression that the words are embedded in stone and the pictures are sacrosanct. David Ogilvy has a good point. He says, "Most clients like to have the feeling that they contribute something to the advertising." If the suggestion sounds feasible, say you'll try it. Don't fall in love with your own words—there are 600,000 words in the English language and the possible combinations are endless. Don't act as if you've been mortally wounded if somebody questions your work. Listen before you leap. The true professional gives reasoned responses rather than rash rebuttals.

A Checklist of 119 Questions and Tips (by Andrew Kershaw)

First things:

1. Did you get briefed?
2. Have you gathered intelligence?
3. Have you studied the people attending?
4. Do you know your competition?
5. Have you learned the prospect's needs?
6. Are you sticking to the ground rules?
7. Do you plan to include a little surprise?
8. Will you finish on time?

Matching audience and performers:

9. Will the performers outnumber the audience?
10. Have you matched the prospect by rank?
11. Did you find a part for all in attendance?
12. Have you given your best presenters a dramatic role?

Stage management:

13. Have you tried to present in *your* offices?
14. Away from home, have you checked out, *in advance:* Electrical outlets? Sound system? Projection equipment and method? Lighting? Darkening of room?
15. Have you arranged for these props: Easels? Space for display of ads, etc.? Lectern? Pointer? Pins, tape, and spare bulbs? Note pads? Pencils?
16. Refreshments: How and when?
17. Have you thought about seating?
18. Did you avoid exotic staging?
19. Have you rehearsed slides and film on equipment in presentation room?

Constructing the presentation:

20. Did you combine showmanship with business?
21. Have you remembered that informal is more difficult than formal?
22. Are you appealing to self-interest?
23. Are you flattering prospects by treating their problems as unique?
24. Are you giving evidence of special efforts?
25. If you are in a speculative presentation, are you doing it properly?
26. Is the creative work the high point?
27. Is the boss introducing the team?
28. Have you found an unusual way to recite the facts about the agency?
29. Were you going to show an organization chart? Don't.

30. Are you relating your strong points to the prospects' needs?
31. Are you showing relevant experience?
32. Or how you make up for its absence?

How to use case histories:
33. Are they brief?
34. Are the cases relevant?
35. Don't use involved case histories.
36. Visual illustrations are vital.
37. Have you selected up-to-date cases?

How to select creative material:
38. Did you pick relevant advertising?
39. Did you include humor and emotion?
40. Are you showing categories that appeal to your audience, e.g., cars to males?
41. Show some famous old campaigns
42. Please be careful with long copy.
43. Use foreign examples with discretion.
44. Don't show a standard reel: make one up for each prospect.
45. Did you find dramatic ways of showing material?
46. Do not give elaborate explanations for each commercial.
47. Do you plan to play games to get them involved?

How to use visual aids:
48. Remember to read the slide.
49. Don't turn your back to the audience.
50. Do you have the text of the slides and charts in your script?
51. Have you rehearsed the handling of visual aids?
52. Are you comfortable with the visual aids?
53. Use the pointer.
54. Have you checked the size of the type: is it legible?
55. Flip-charts are good only for small audiences.
56. Don't present storyboards.
57. Read headlines, not body copy.
58. Radio needs special care.
59. Watch the lighting.
60. Use only one kind of visual aid for each presenter.
61. Did you check the slides and charts for typos?

Show that your agency is different:
62. Talk about discipline.
63. Magic lanterns.

64. Stability of staff and clients.
65. Describe growth with clients.
66. Show dedication to creative excellence.
67. Talk about Creative Council.*
68. Explain One Agency Indivisible.*
69. Draw attention to International Management Supervisors.*
70. Say you believe in first-class business.
71. Talk about your agency chief.
*Items unique to Ogilvy and Mather.

How to start and how to close:
72. Be prepared to warm up, but no funny story.
73. Make the start memorable.
74. Are you opening with a film or a reel?
75. Tell them "Why you should pick us."
76. Is the ending memorable?
77. Ask for the order.
78. Are you ending with a film or reel?
79. Have you organized the leave-behind?

Question time:
80. Encourage questions.
81. Be truthful, simple, to the point.
82. Listen to the question.
83. Don't hedge or waffle.
84. Don't minimize problems: acknowledge them.
85. Make them laugh.
86. Don't knock the competition.
87. Don't criticize current advertising.
88. Watch for signs of boredom.
89. Make sure you don't all reply at the same time.
90. Don't make promises you can't deliver.
91. Be ready to offer a list of names of clients.
92. Be ready to deal with the usual objections.

The rehearsal:
93. Rehearse.
94. Rehearse again.
95. You cannot have too many rehearsals.
96. Did you use rehearsals to change the format?
97. Have you cut scripts?
98. Did you consider changing the order?
99. Remember that informality is achieved through rehearsals.

100. Rehearse your ad libs.
101. Watch the timing.
102. Make everyone rehearse.

How to become a better speaker:
103. Encourage courses in public speaking.
104. Listen to yourself on a tape recorder.
105. Watch yourself on video tape.
106. Edit your script.
107. Use quotes or memorable expressions.
108. Do memorable things.
109. Be careful with humor.
110. Stand up.
111. Have you devised a good introduction?
112. Are you disarming and reassuring?
113. Watch your dress, your mannerisms, and your hands.
114. Don't smoke or chew.
115. Gesticulate.
116. Remember to watch for changing moods of the audience.
117. Be ready to improvise.
118. Learn to use your voice.
119. Don't expect applause.

Appendix:
Coors Original Draft

PREFACE

This plans book is the result of an in-depth analysis of the college beer market. Original Draft has examined the multifaceted lifestyle of the college market and has developed a strategy which will promote Coors beer as the natural beer for the student lifestyle.

This strategy is based upon an in-depth survey of 514 beer-drinking college students, 895 smaller intercept, and 32 focus group interviews involving 230 students. We also interviewed 21 bar store managers and 16 distributors and drivers. Our total research effort consists of 1,676 respondents.

Original Draft believes that our primary research, combined with an extensive secondary research effort, provides a solid foundation for our proposed campaign.

SITUATION ANALYSIS

Current status. One of the major reasons brewers compete for the college market is that the sheer *size* of the market makes it attractive. There are over 11 million college students in the United States, with over $10 billion in disposable income. In Coors' 17-state marketing region alone, 3,960,156 students attend 897 colleges or universities. Their disposable income exceeds $3.6 billion yearly. (Figures provided by CASS—Communications & Advertising Services to Students.)

Profile of the college student. College students today are tremendously peer-oriented. Students are very concerned with their ability to relate to others, and they believe that college helps them develop this skill. This trait is important in beer marketing because students use beer as a "social lubricant," using it both as an excuse to gather with friends and to ease tensions when they do get together. Studies show that students who are less adept at relating to others and who are socially concerned, drink slightly more beer than others (Mullins, 1980).

Conservatism and traditionalism also typify this generation of college students. The students tend to be more materialistic, ambitious, and goal sighted than their 1970s counterpart. Majors in liberal arts are becoming less popular as business and professional

---

This advertising plan was developed by students at Michigan State University and entered in the American Advertising Federation student competition in 1981. The student team consisted of Denise Astro, Suzanne Blas, Roger Boettcher, Lisa Cleland, Lyn Fall, Pete Hagan, John Haley, John Hrcka, Rob Jacobs, Brian Juergens, Harry Los, Jeanne Lytle, Marybeth Polzin, Vicky Schonschek, Laurie Selik, Steve Swartz, and Jim Winnale. Their advisor was Professor Sandra Ernst Moriarty. The plans book duplicated here and the student presentation that accompanied it resulted in a first-place award for the group.

While the plans book is written to a very strict format, as required by the student competition, it presents, in our opinion, an excellent example of the thinking, planning, and development required in solving advertising problems. It is presented here as a guide for persons who may be developing their first plans book. Follow this example and you will assure that your campaign plan is in a form your readers can understand and evaluate.

This plans book is used with the permission of the Adolph Coors Company, Golden, Colorado.

studies grow in student popularity. A return to tradition can be seen in the fashion-oriented dressing and make-up that have returned to campus. Greek life is rising in popularity as students regain interest in extracurricular activities.

A study of college student purchase behavior reveals that quality is a major purchase determinant, and the students justify their indulgence by looking at purchases as investments.

College student attitudes toward advertising show that they like ads that reflect their conservatism. Heavily sexist advertising repels a significant portion of students while humor tends to appeal to them most.

Trends. While the college market is considered to be substantial in size, the United States Department of Health, Education, and Welfare has projected a lengthy decline in college student enrollment. This decline will begin with a drop of .2 percent in 1981 and will exceed 5 percent by 1988.

In summary, declining enrollment projections suggest a relatively static market, now and in the future. Existing competitive pressures will only intensify as market share battles within this attractive market become imminent.

The College Beer Market

Current status. Since the minimum legal drinking age varies among 18, 19, and 21 among the 17 states, the total number of college students who can legally drink in Coors' market area is 2,219,719. This college *beer* market represents 56 percent of the total number of college students, a market that continues to be substantial in size.

Profile of the college beer drinker. Original Draft feels that the college beer market is a blue chip investment for future market share battles. Research has shown that many brand loyalties are formed in college. This implies that if a brewer convinces students to drink this beer while they are still in college, there is a strong possibility that this loyalty will continue, thus bolstering future market shares. Making students even more attractive targets is their natural tendency to become affluent professionals. This upscale segment is the most sought-after market in the beer industry today. If a

brewer establishes himself as the students' choice in college, he gets a big jump on the upscale market for the future.

This is where Coors has a definite advantage over its competitors. Original Draft has found that Coors drinkers have an unusually high level of brand loyalty. According to Simmons Market Research Bureau, 1980, over 19 percent, or nearly one in five Coors drinkers, drink only Coors. A comparable figure for the industry is 12.5 percent. This high brand loyalty rate might be associated with the somewhat unique taste of Coors beer, described by students as pure, clear, and full-flavored but light. It is possible that devotees of this taste simply have fewer alternative sources for it among other brews.

Preceding the establishment of brand loyalty, the college beer drinker goes through what is called a formative period. The early stages happen to coincide with the time the student is in college and involve the formation of drinking behaviors. For example, the student who is in the beginning stages of wine drinking behavior will orient himself by selecting light-tasting, often pop wines. As tastes develop and the student grows older, heavier, distinct wines may be selected. The same process holds true for beer. Students often begin with the lighter-tasting beers and as preferences permit, move on to heavier tastes later in life. However, the most important aspect of the students' formative period is the tendency to prefer a light taste in beer as a general starting point. Coors has a definite advantage as it is regarded as having a full-flavored but light taste. Not only is Coors' position advantageous, but a good acceptance record and a high level of brand loyalty indicate that it has superior potential in the college market. The preferred characteristics of Coors will enable the brand to occupy an important niche in the minds of college students.

Demographics and usage rates. Approximately 70 percent of all college students are between the ages of 18 and 24. The largest single age group is the 18-year-old segment.

Due to the differences in minimum legal drinking ages, each state has been analyzed separately according to the number of students who meet the state's legal age requirements. In a state where 19 is the legal drinking age, 84 percent of the market can legally drink. In states with a legal drinking age of 21, 59 percent of the market can legally drink.

Sixty-eight percent of college students drink beer, while fewer students prefer hard liquor or wine. The students who drink beer, drink an average of seven 12-ounce cans or glasses of beer a week. This average usage rate is considered to be a heavy usage rate by Simmons Market Research Bureau.

Males represent 60 percent of the total college beer market, making up a large proportion of medium and heavy users. Cross-tabulations between usage rate and sex allowed us to define the college beer market in the following way:

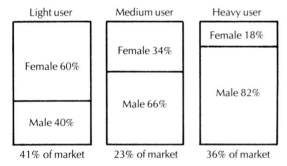

Light user	Medium user	Heavy user
Female 60%	Female 34%	Female 18%
Male 40%	Male 66%	Male 82%
41% of market	23% of market	36% of market

The heavy user drinks seven or more 12-ounce cans or glasses of beer a week, while the medium user drinks between four and six cans or glasses of beer a week, and the light user drinks three or less cans or glasses of beer a week.

Males account for 82 percent of the heavy users, 66 percent of the medium users, and 40 percent of the light users. A high concentration of males in the medium and heavy user segments justifies the conclusion that males are the largest purchasers of beer in the college beer market.

Usage rates varied slightly among the various age groups. Original Draft found that the 18–20 age segment tended to have a heavier usage rate than older age segments.

College students reported that the most important factors in their beer selection are taste, price, and brand name, as revealed by our primary research study. These purchase decision factors are consistent with our focus group findings which indicate that price and brand availability (or brand name) are primary determinants in brand loyalty.

Psychographics. Several other cross-tabulation procedures involving our primary research study allowed us to further define the college beer market. The most favored drinking activity, according to the students surveyed, is partying. However, favorite leisure activities vary by usage rates. Heavy users prefer partying, medium users prefer team sports, and light users prefer rapping.

Among extracurricular activities, both the medium and light users are involved in sports and professional clubs while heavy users are mostly involved in sports and fraternities or sororities. Consistent with the heavy users' Greek life affiliation, we found that 43 percent of all college students surveyed, who live in fraternities or sororities, are heavy drinkers.

College differences. We investigated differences that may exist by type of institution (university, college, urban college, and community college). No significant differences were found among these institutional types for the students' favorite leisure activity, partying. Extracurricular involvement did vary at community colleges though. Instead of fraternity/sorority involvement, the community college student is characterized by more professional club involvement. This is consistent with the finding that the CC student is older than most students (the average age tends to be 25) and therefore more career oriented. Usage rates were found to remain consistent throughout all types of institutions surveyed.

Seasonality. Original Draft found that the majority of college students consume beer during fall and spring sessions. This consumption pattern correlates to the pleasant climate during these periods. Also, a large number of students reported drinking on an equal basis across all seasons.

In summary, Coors appears well suited for the college beer market. A high rate of brand loyalty combined with a well-accepted light taste will become valuable assets for Coors as it establishes a stable position in student formative drinking patterns.

Coors Premium Beer

Product. As mentioned earlier, Coors is currently perceived as a light-tasting beer among college students.

However, this perception appears a bit fuzzy. Results of our primary research study indicate that Coors holds a close position to Miller Lite in the minds of college students:

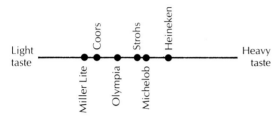

Apparently, the fuzzy brand image is based on the students' confusion over whether Coors is light in taste or light in caloric content. Past advertising which positioned Coors as "America's Fine Light Beer" seems to have clouded this image to some extent.

From a more positive perspective, Coors' position concerning taste and quality showed an extremely favorable image. Coors is even seen as being in a class of its own, exceeding two major competitors—Miller Lite and Olympia.

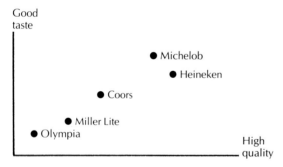

Although most attitudes appear quite favorable, a slightly negative attitude may still exist concerning past problems Coors has had with union members and its image as anti-minority. However, Original Draft believes that the best way to deal with these potential attitudes is to smooth them over with a new positive image.

Other important factors related to the product are the characteristics unique to Coors consumers. These characteristics highlight Coors' potential in the college market. First of all, Coors drinkers are, in general, younger than the average beer market. Coors' largest user segment is between 18 and 24 years old (30.9 percent). This is particularly unusual because 8 out of 17 states have drinking age limits of 21 years old. Target Group Index data indicates that Coors has the largest 18–24-year-old segment of any competing beer.

Coors users are also more educated than the general beer market with over 47 percent of Coors users reporting to have attended college. Coors drinkers are disproportionately professional, managers, in general upscale.

A final important factor in relation to the product is Coors' share of the 17-state college market.

Coors' national college market share (based on "drank most often" percentages from CASS) is 6.64 percent, putting the beer in fifth place to Miller, Budweiser, Miller Lite, and Michelob. However, since Coors is distributed only on a regional basis, its national college share is not an accurate measure of the beer's actual college share.

To overcome this problem, Original Draft set up a ratio of Coors' *national college* share to the beer's *national overall* market share:

$$\frac{\text{Coors' 1980 National College Share}}{\text{Coors' 1980 National Market Share}} = \frac{6.64\%}{7.60\%} = .874$$

The relationship between the two national shares can be seen in the resulting multiplier (.874).

Assuming the same relationship exists at the regional level, Original Draft estimated Coors' *regional college* share by applying the multiplier to Coors' average *regional overall* market share:

Coors' 1980 Average Regional Share (26.0%)

× .874

Coors' 1980 Regional College Share (22.7%)

Thus, Coors' regional college market share for 1980 is 22.7 percent.

Assuming per capita consumption among college students is 1.1 barrels or 34.1 gallons yearly (AAF Casebook), then the legal drinking-age student market represents 2,441,691 in barrel volume. Original Draft projects that Coors' share of this market is 554,264 barrels.

Promotion. In order to develop effective advertising messages geared to the student, we felt it necessary to analyze Coors' past advertising efforts.

Focus-group attitudes towards Coors' 1980 advertising campaign "What If" were consistent with the company's conclusion that the college campaign was ineffective (AAF Casebook). Our focus groups described the "What If" ads this way: "Well, they never really say much about the beer," and "It never tells me anything about how beer tastes." Other reactions cited the extensive copy and the effort required to finally reach the point of the ads.

Coors' national ad campaign "Taste the High Country" was also not well accepted by college students. The ad theme was classed by focus groups as nondistinct and not significantly different from the images presented by other brands of beer and even of some cigarettes. Students characterized the beer as "macho" and "cowboy" and reported, at best, a lack of identification with this theme and, at worst, an absolutely negative reaction.

Coors' ongoing programs, the Intramural Sports Festival and the College Representative Program, are considered to be very effective.

Competition. As competition in the beer industry increases, college advertising budgets are sure to go up. Also, since most students are only lightly exposed to the various media, brewers have been forced to pursue new methods to reach this market. Sales promotion budgets in the college market are growing even more rapidly than the general beer market. Besides the standard frisbee and t-shirt offers, some brewers are expanding into such unusual promotions as national "superstar" sports competitions (Budweiser), vacation package tie-ins (Schlitz), and outright scholarship raffles (Pabst).

Price. Coors was found to be competitively priced with Miller, Budweiser, and Miller Lite. Michelob was priced slightly higher.

Distribution. Distributors are independent businessmen and many of them handle more than one brewer's products. But, exclusive or not, the key to their cooperation is profit. Our task is to convince them that following through with the 1981 campaign will result in increased profits.

Personal interviews with 21 local grocery and party store managers were conducted. The survey findings indicate that the majority of stores based their purchasing and shelf-space decisions for beer on either profits or promotion. The consensus was that the managers like point-of-purchase displays and felt they helped the sale of beer.

Additional published and primary research has told us that distributors want three things from their manufacturers. First, distributors want to be sure that the company is doing all it can to sell the product, and to beer wholesalers this means advertising. Our survey of 16 distributors and drivers found that image advertising was the biggest influence on sales. And if advertising support isn't there, distributors said they can be very uncooperative.

Second, distributors want to feel involved in the total marketing effort. They want both prior information about company plans and a chance to make suggestions. Distributors want the company to be responsive to their needs.

Published research suggests that 59 percent of liquor store owners interviewed feel they are not advised about promotions before the advertisements appear. More dealers in the west and north central regions appeared to be uninformed about scheduled advertising. Perhaps more significantly, the larger volume retailers were apparently less well informed about magazine advertising programs than were smaller retailers. Most dealers (72 percent) further reported that they were not usually provided with materials which would enable them to tie in to magazine advertising campaigns with local promotions and displays. Those who did receive tie-in materials stated that the materials were used.

The third and perhaps most important aspect in distributor relations is that wholesalers want no interference from the company in their local businesses. Distributors surveyed were quick to take offense at any suggestion that the company would go over their heads to reach either drivers or retailers, unless they are given prior notice. Thus, it is crucial that any contact made with these groups be made through distributors.

The actual sales contacts are made most often through the distributors' drivers. Our interviews found that these are usually blue-collar Teamsters, and they work for the distributors, not Coors. Although these drivers are usually very close to retailers and provide fine personal contact, many drivers consider themselves more truck driver than salesman and are less than adept at the latest merchandising methods. They are, however, more than willing to learn any method likely to improve their sales and their commissions.

Problems and Opportunities

Problems. First, in addition to the traditionally heavy competition from Anheuser-Busch, Coors can expect very heavy competition in the 1980s from the Miller Brewing Company. Miller has targeted the Mountain and Pacific regions for special attention.

Second, Coors faces an acute brand switching problem among college students, which will be further aggravated by the Miller competition.

The last problem is Coors' apparent nondistinct image. As mentioned earlier, students described Coors' "Taste the High Country" theme as similar to other brands of beer or even some cigarettes. Focus groups comprised of students from Coors' region seemed eager for a new image. While they greatly enjoyed the beer's taste, the image presented a mental conflict. Confusion over whether the beer is light in taste or light in caloric content is another factor in the beer's nondistinct image.

Opportunities. Coors has the opportunity to develop strong brand loyalties in the college market. The beer's tradition of high brand loyalty, set in a situation where brand loyalties are often formed, could give Coors an edge in establishing a large percentage of students as permanent Coors drinkers, thus bolstering hopes of increasing general market share as the students age.

Finally, Coors has the opportunity to take advantage of its position as the ideal beer for the college market. This market is young, price conscious, and well educated. Original Draft's research shows that Coors appeals to this type of drinker. Hence, Coors fits right into the market. Also, the brand's lighter taste appeals to those in early formative drinking periods.

STRATEGY

Market Objectives

Short-term objectives (1 year)
1. To increase Coors' college market share 3.3 percentage points, from the present 22.7 percent to 26 percent in 1981–82. This translates into a barrel volume increase of 79,000 barrels and a sales increase of $4.5 million.

	1980–81	1981–82	Increase
Market share	22.7%	26.0%	3.3%
Barrel volume	546,000	625,000	79,000
Sales	$31.1 Mil	$35.6 Mil	$4.5 Mil

2. To establish a positive and distinct image for Coors among college students.
3. To attract new college beer drinkers as they reach legal drinking age.
4. To increase Coors' already strong brand loyalty by increasing preference among its occasional users, as well as attracting new ones.

Long-term objectives (3 years)
1. Continue to increase Coors' college and general market share.
2. Continue to develop a positive and distinct image for Coors among college students.
3. Maintain and increase brand loyalty for Coors so that students will continue to be loyal after graduation from college.
4. Establish Coors as the college beer.

Market Strategy

1. Position Coors against competitive brands in the minds of college students and protect Coors' share of market from competitive assault by using "Coors is the college beer," as our position statement.
2. Implement a push/pull promotion strategy in order to involve and strengthen the distribution channel. Efforts aimed at the college student will increase demand for Coors, while increased attention toward the distribution channel will help to insure the brand's availability.
3. Time our marketing program so that the majority of our efforts take place during peak periods in cam-

pus population and college drinking—namely fall and spring.

4. In order to utilize the most efficient mix of promotional activities, special emphasis will be put on ten key states (Levels 1–3), indicated below, which represent a large concentration of target audience members and a large percentage of Coors' total sales. These key states will receive a *combination* of advertising and sales promotion efforts while the seven non-key states (Level 4) will receive *only* sales promotion efforts.

State	10 Key States (Levels 1–3) % Target audience	% Coors sales
Level 1:		
Texas	28.7	24.7
California	28.0	31.6
Level 2:		
Colorado	6.8	5.2
Arizona	6.2	6.5
Kansas	5.6	5.9
Oklahoma	2.4	7.1
Level 3:		
Iowa	4.3	1.4
Washington ..	4.2	1.6
Missouri	3.5	3.3
Nebraska	2.7	.9
Total	92.4	88.2

State	7 Non-Key States (Level 4) % Target audience	% Coors sales
Level 4:		
Utah	1.4	1.5
Idaho	1.3	1.5
Arkansas	1.1	1.4
Montana	1.0	.7
New Mexico ..	.8	3.0
Wyoming	.6	1.0
Nevada	.5	1.9
Total	6.7	11.0

Each level will be budgeted according to its contribution in sales and target audience. For example, Texas and California combined account for over half of target audience and total sales. Therefore, approximately half of our total budget will be spent in these states.

5. Added promotional weight will be given to Iowa, Washington, Missouri, and Nebraska (Level 3). Original Draft sees substantial growth potential for Coors in these states, as indicated by the high category development indices and low brand development indices highlighted in Exhibit 1 on the next page.

6. Creative executions will vary according to differences in the four types of institutions (universities, four-year colleges, community colleges, and urban colleges) which all differ in lifestyle patterns.

Target Market Definition

Primary target market. Our primary audience is the 2.2 million legal-drinking-age students in the 17-state area. However, our creative and sales promotional strategies will specifically focus on the male heavy user segment. Original Draft has determined that this segment represents the best potential to increase Coors' sales. The male heavy user consumes the largest volume of beer, and is the segment most likely to prefer regular premium beer. Also, the male heavy user represents the highest potential for brand loyalty, which will insure a stable share of the college market in the long run.

Target Market Definition

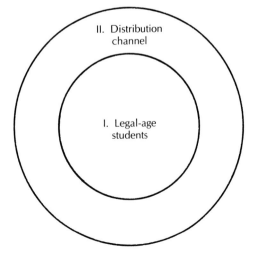

Exhibit 1

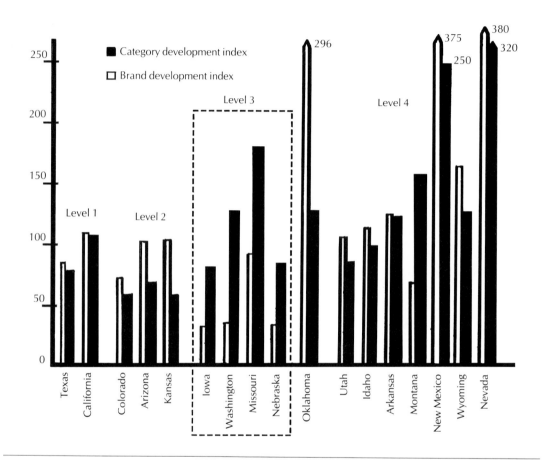

Primary research compiled by Original Draft has shown that our target audience (legal age students) has a strong sense of group affiliation. They are looking for fun. Favorite leisure activities center around partying and other group activities. These students also tend to be price conscious.

Secondary target market. With the need for increased attention on the distribution channel, we have selected this segment for secondary emphasis. Improving trade relations by answering demands of the distribution channel will prove profitable by increasing brand availability. The distribution channel includes dis-

tributors, drivers, sales representatives, retailers, and bar and restaurant owners.

CREATIVE

Creative Recommendations

Advertising objectives. Our overall communication objectives are: (1) to increase preference among those who already consider Coors·as an alternative, and (2) to introduce roughly 10 percent of the market as new users to Coors. Specifically, we will move 4 percent of the market from liking to preferring Coors Premium

Beer and .3 percent from preferring to using Coors solely.

Advertising strategy. Our strategy is: (1) to establish a personality for Coors Premium Beer as the college beer, (2) to appeal directly to the college market by creating interest and involvement, and (3) to develop an image for Coors as the fun, popular beer.

Our copy platform promises that Coors Premium Beer is the popular favorite for the college lifestyle.

Our target audience for the creative message is Joe College, a heavy to moderate drinker from legal drinking age to 24. His main interests are socializing with friends, becoming involved in fraternities and clubs, and having fun in general. Joe is moderately loyal to the beer he drinks and feels the image of a beer is important in brand selection.

The basic execution strategy will depict the image of Coors as the taste of college life. Ads will focus on involvement and fun, keying on unusual activities popular at campuses in the region.

Development of Creative Concept

A total of 32 focus groups involving 230 college students were held to obtain insight from respondents as to their personal preferences for beer, perceptions of brands, media consumption, recall of past advertisements, and advertising creative strategies.

To determine the communication effectiveness of our proposed campaign theme, Original Draft conducted 40 intercept interviews measuring the responses to concepts for a college-market campaign. Respondents were given a questionnaire and asked to rank nine concepts based on their overall appeal. Included with the three Original Draft concepts were four current competitors' ads, the previous Coors' college-market campaign "What If," and Coors' national "Taste the High Country" theme. The four competitors' ads tested were: Busch's "mountaineering" theme, Stroh's college cartoons, Lowenbrau's "good friends" theme, and Budweiser's ads featuring a can breaking through a photograph.

The three concepts developed by Original Draft were:

Games theme: Associated beer with indoor,

everyday games such as darts, pinball, and backgammon which are popular among the college crowd.

Sports theme: Depicted active sports scenes associating the moment of excellence in sports achievement with the "Coors Cup" and beer drinking.

Craze theme: Featured fun, spontaneous moments at college, and emphasized crazes and fads specific to the college lifestyle.

Focus group results. The concepts preferred by the majority of respondents emphasized college lifestyles, fun, and humor. Ranking highest was the "college craze" approach followed closely by the "games" and "good friends" concepts. Respondents felt these approaches appealed directly to the college market in an interesting, original manner. Concepts featuring outdoors, adventure, sports, and solitary activities generally were rated low, as "Taste the High Country," "Mountaineering," and the "Coors Cup" concepts ranked 6, 7, and 8 respectively. Several individual comments to these concepts were: "It sounds like a lot of other beer ads—they all sound the same," and "I don't think of drinking beer when I'm out doing something athletic."

Theme. After the results were calculated, the "college craze" approach was selected as the most effective way to reach our advertising objectives. The games concept is to be included in this approach because it is also a popular craze on campuses today. This will not only offer more variations to expand upon, but will also enable Coors to target directly to the differing lifestyles among the various institutions.

This "college life" theme fits our copy platform by associating Coors Premium Beer directly with everyday college life. Coors achieves a favorable personality as a fun popular beer; it's not only for weekends or special reward situations.

Coors will be differentiated from competition. The campaign will eliminate any confusion or worn-out images of adventure similar to campaigns currently used by other beer companies. Most important, the "college craze" approach is fascinating and involving, and our respondents actually wanted to know more. Depicting specific crazes at different universities creates curiosity as well as memorability.

Execution. The following pages feature print and broadcast advertisements proposed for the 1981–82 campaign. The print executions will run in college newspapers. Advertisements for outdoor and transit, while containing no body copy, will follow a similar visual approach to the newspaper executions. Theater ads will follow a script similar to the radio ads but the video will be in a style reminiscent of 1930s newsreels.

Initial executions include the six featured in the print ads on the following pages. Other proposed variations for both print and broadcast are stated below:

- Express yourself with Coors (visuals depict rubber-like facial expressions called "living droodles")
- Make your night with Coors (nightly "tuck-in" service and serenade)
- Line up a winning shot with Coors (pool table in bar with a lot of people gathered)
- Serve your best with Coors (beach-volleyball)
- Have a blast with Coors (students playing electronic games)
- Step in the right direction with Coors (dance marathon)
- Hit the spot with Coors (dart league in a bar)
- Break the ice with Coors (winter ice festivals)

SALES PROMOTION

Objectives

1. To establish Coors in the students' evoked set of brands and to increase preference among those who already consider Coors as an alternative.
2. To associate Coors with college life by promoting college activities that students can relate to and participate in.
3. To keep the Coors name and our theme in places where the students will encounter them repeatedly.
4. To gain support and active participation from all parts of the distribution chain in presenting Coors' new image and pushing the product through at the retail level.
5. To stimulate impulse purchases by offering small incentives which differentiate Coors from the realm of parity products.
6. To increase reach of the campaign by including students at schools other than those scheduled for media attention.

A. Theater Tie-in Promotion

In September, a tie-in promotion with local movie theaters and entertainment spots will begin. Theaters at 66 colleges in the 10-state market area showing major motion picture releases will be chosen to run Coors theater commercials, a 60-second ad following our "Taste of College Life" theme. The ads will run for the first two weeks of the movie at each theater.

Participating bars will accept movie ticket stubs from the theaters involved for free admission to the bar. The bars will be able to offer special prices on Coors by taking advantage of volume discounts. These discounts will be available to all retailers but only those included in this promotion will have definite reason to use it.

This plan provides increases in both sales and visibility for Coors and offers increased attendance and sales as incentives to both bars and theaters, who will also have a strong incentive to share advertising costs. In addition to increased sales and visibility for the brand, it will increase the percentage of legal drinking-age students present in the audience for our theater ad. This promotion also increases advertising support for the brand by encouraging participants to run joint advertisements promoting our "College Life" theme (although not our brand name) concurrent with our regular newspaper ads. A final advantage of this promotion is its cost—none. Beyond the normal costs of theater advertising, which will be incurred without this promotion, Coors is not liable for any costs involved. In fact, Coors is prohibited by law from sharing any advertising costs with the retailers. Note that there is no such prohibition on bars or theaters sharing advertising costs.

B. Coors' Extramural Festival

To widely promote Coors' new image and strengthen students' involvement with the brand, Original Draft has designed the Extramural Festival. This promotion is designed in many ways to complement, rather than duplicate, the Intramural Festival Coors already sponsors. While the Intramural Festival involves only one team from each school, and limits spectators to only those at the host schools, the Extramural Festival provides four separate opportunities for large numbers of participants and spectators to become involved in the games at 81 different major universities throughout the 17-state region. Also, while the Intramural Festival features somewhat traditional athletic events (softball, soccer), the Extramural Festival features more frivolous, unusual activities, characterizable as "the kind of thing you'd only do in college."

Four events have been chosen as group oriented, likely to attract crowds of both participants and spectators and representative of the fun spirit of the College Life campaign. The four are a jalapeno pepper eating contest; pieing, a team duel using whipped cream pies; earth ball, a team sport using a 6-foot diameter ball; and tip frisbee, a team sport vaguely resembling "Guts." Original Draft feels that by extending Coors' activities to this type of events and broadening the opportunities for direct involvement by students, we can best promote top-of-the-mind awareness and increase consideration of the brand as an alternative, as

HEAD: Hit the hot spot

SUB: with Coors

COPY: Jalapeno pepper eating contests have become one of the hottest crazes at several college campuses. Crowds watch as contestants gulp down the fiery pickled peppers. One heroic participant at the University of X swallowed 17 peppers in less than 10 minutes. Coors put out the fire.

Get together with good friends, have some crazy fun, and enjoy the quality taste of Coors Premium Beer.

Hit the hot spot with Coors.

TAG LINE: Coors, the taste of college life.

HEAD: Top your night

SUB: with Coors

COPY: Cowboy hats, winged hats, and baseball caps are all part of a popular craze at campuses everywhere. "Hat nights" featured by area bars have crowds of students lining up for special deals when wearing their favorite hat. At X State, ten seniors topped off their night by wearing *one* six-foot Stetson.

Get together with good friends, have some crazy fun and enjoy the quality taste of Coors Premium Beer.

Cap off your night with Coors.

TAG LINE: Coors, the taste of college life.

well as increase preference among occasional users. Also, this promotion can capitalize on prior publicity for the Intramural Festival without cannibalizing its results.

The first 50 entrants in each competition, except earth ball, will receive Coors College Life t-shirts. The first 15 earth ball teams will each receive one decorative Coors keg tap. Events will be spread out over the year with earth ball in the fall, jalapeno pepper eating contests in the winter, and pieing and tip frisbee in the spring. Various prizes will be awarded to the top teams in the different events, and posters and newspaper ads will promote the events.

Allocated promotional budget

3 sports × 50 t-shirts × 81 schools × $2.80/t-shirt	= $34,020.00
1 sport × 15 keg taps × 81 schools × $7.00/keg tap	= 8,505.00
70 posters × 4 sports × 81 schools × $.12/poster	= 2,721.60
2 ads × $66/ad (average cost) × 4 sports × 81 schools	= 42,768.00
	$88,014.60

HEAD: Call it a week

SUB: with Coors

COPY: They call it TG-ing at U of X and FAC-ing at X College, but no matter how you spell it, Friday afternoon is a great time to kick off the weekend.

Get together with good friends, have some crazy fun, and enjoy the quality taste of Coors Premium Beer.

Thank goodness for Friday afternoons and Coors.

TAG LINE: Coors, the taste of college life.

HEAD: Break away

SUB: with Coors

COPY: Every year spring break hits campuses across the country like an epidemic. Whether it's spring fever, cabin fever, or winter chills, students flock to sunny beaches and powdered slopes to leave books and classes behind.

It's time to break away with good friends, have some crazy fun, and enjoy the quality taste of Coors Premium Beer.

This spring, break away with Coors.

TAG LINE: Coors, the taste of college life.

C. California Volleyball

Coors will sponsor the first two-on-two volleyball tournament of the year in California. Two-on-two beach volleyball has a large following in California and since most of California's colleges are not residential, we felt a special promotional effort is needed to reach this market.

Coors will hold this opening tournament in the Los Angeles area so that the majority of students who live and commute in this area can attend and participate. The promotion for this four-day event will consist of posters and advertisements placed in the newspapers of 15 local colleges. Coordination for the event will be handled by the Coors student representative. Publicity releases will be supplied to L.A. area radio and TV stations along with local newspapers. Prizes will be presented to winning teams. All entrants and many spectators will receive free t-shirts. In addition, free cooler cups will be distributed on the beach. Once again, this special event will help maintain strong top-of-the-mind recall as well as promoting involvement as discussed in the Extramural Festival section.

HEAD: Make cramming fun

SUB: with Coors

COPY: Universities across the country report that more and more students are cramming and actually enjoying it. Twenty-three students from U of X decided that cramming in a phone booth was more fun than cramming for exams.

Get together with good friends, have some crazy fun, and enjoy the quality taste of Coors Premium Beer.

Let Coors get you out of tight situations.

TAG LINE: Coors, the taste of college life.

HEAD: Get your kicks

SUB: with Coors

COPY: At college it's fun to kick around new ideas. Students at several universities play hacky-sack as a favorite pastime activity. Champions at U of X managed to keep the leather footbag off the ground for 21 minutes.

Get together with good friends, have some crazy fun, and enjoy the quality taste of Coors Premium Beer.

Get your kicks with Coors.

TAG LINE: Coors, the taste of college life.

Allocated promotional budget
70 posters × 15 schools × $.12/poster . = $ 126.00
4⅛-page ads × $66/ad × 15 schools .. = 3,960.00
Write-up and mailing of publicity
   material . . . . =   200.00
500 t-shirts × $2.80/t-shirt . . . . = 1,400.00
1,000 cooler cups/day × 4 days
   × $.125 . . . . =   500.00
                                $6,186.00

D. "Thirst Aid Kits"

Original Draft has developed the "Thirst Aid Kit" as a means of reaching the California commuter student and to heavy up promotion in four key states, Iowa, Washington, Missouri, and Nebraska, which have especially high potential. We found that most of the colleges in California are commuter schools and are located in large metropolitan areas with expensive and wasteful media. Therefore, we need a unique means, like a "Thirst Aid Kit" to reach them. In the four key states, the kits will supplement our advertising efforts. These kits contain four items:

1. ID holder. A plastic ID holder with the Coors logo is an excellent way to build both reach and frequency among our target market. It is very practical and functional and therefore something that everyone can use. Also, students must show their IDs when purchasing beer so the brand name is exposed right at the moment of purchase.

2. T-shirt transfer. This attractive transfer, which will read, "Coors . . . The Taste of College Life" will offer students something they will want to use. The back of the transfer will be printed with an ad for self-liquidating items such as the keg taps and the cooler cups.

Radio Spot (60 seconds): Coors College Update

SFX: NEWSROOM SOUNDS, UP, 4 SEC., TYPEWRITER FOLLOWED BY RIP OF PAPER, DOWN, FADE INTO BACKGROUND.

ANNCR: GRAVEL VOICED, FAST TALKING.
         And hot off the press is today's Coors College Update. Jalapeno pepper eating contests have become one of the hottest crazes at college campuses. Crowds watch as contestants gulp down the fiery pickled peppers. One heroic participant at the U of X swallowed 17 peppers in less than 10 minutes.
             Coors put out the fire. PAUSE
             Universities across the country report that more and more students are cramming and actually enjoying it. Twenty-three crazy students from X College decided cramming into phone booths was more fun than cramming for exams. A cold Coors got them out of this very tight spot.

SFX: RATTLING OF PAPER AS ANNOUNCER TURNS PAGE IN NOTES.

ANNCR: Several western universities are kicking around a new idea. Hacky-sack has become a favorite pastime among the college crowd. Students at U of X managed to keep the leather footbag off the ground for 21 minutes. Afterward, they got their kicks with Coors.

SFX: SHUFFLING PAPERS

ANNCR: That concludes today's Coors College Update. If your craze can top these, we'll feature your school on Coors College Update. Get instructions for the college craze competition when you're buying Coors at your favorite store.

VO: MALE, NORMAL VOICE.
         Coors . . . the taste of college life.

Coors "College Update" Theater Advertisement :60 seconds

LS TO CU: OLD NEWSREEL STYLE. NEWSPAPER SPINS FAST FROM BACKGROUND TO FOREGROUND. HALTS WITH CU ON HEADLINE.

SFX: FAST, EXCITING, BRASSY MUSIC CLIMAXING AT CU, FADE TO BACKGROUND.

ANNCR: And hot off the press is today's Coors College Update.

CUT TO MS OF STUDENTS AROUND TABLE AT PEPPER EATING CONTEST

ANNCR: Jalepeno pepper eating contests have become one of the hottest crazes on campus. Crowds watch as contestants gulp down the fiery pickled peppers. One heroic participant at the U of X swallowed 17 peppers in less than 10 minutes.

    Coors put out that fire.

CUT TO MS OF STUDENTS CRAMMING INTO PHONE BOOTH

ANNCR: Universities across the country report that more and more students are cramming and enjoying it.

    Twenty-three crazy students at College X decided cramming into phone booths was more fun than cramming for exams. A cold Coors got them out of this very tight spot.

CUT TO MS OF STUDENTS KICKING A HACKY-SACK FOOTBAG

ANNCR: Several universities are kicking around a new idea. Hacky-sack is a favorite pastime among the college crowd. Students at U of X kept the leather footbag off the ground for 21 minutes. Afterwards they got their kicks with Coors.

CU TO LS: REVERSE OF OPENING: NEWSPAPER SPINS TO BACKGROUND AND FADES.

ANNCR: That concludes today's Coors College Update. If your craze can top these, we'll feature your school on the Update. Get instructions for the college craze competition when you buy Coors at your favorite store.

FADE-IN OF COORS BOTTLE NEXT TO GLASS. SUPER SLOGAN.

ANNCR: This College Update was brought to you by Coors . . . the taste of college life.

3. Game rule book. This will be a handy rule book for bar games such as darts, backgammon, cardinal, and euchre to promote the image of social activities associated with the campaign theme.
4. Calendar. The calendar is a small but important item in a college student's life. Imprinted with the Coors logo, the calendar will be helpful in building frequency as it is often used for reference. Certain days will be noted as "Time for Coors."

All four will be packaged in a plastic bag that can be used as an in-car litter bag. They will be distributed at fall registration at each school.

By using the "Thirst Aid Kits," we can effectively reach our commuter audience. We are giving the students items they will use or see daily. This will reinforce Coors brand name. The self-liquidating items offered will provide an opportunity for action on the part of the student that Coors will be able to measure in sales. And, of course, the buying of these items will entail an amount of involvement with the brand and so promote use.

Allocated promotional budget.
397,733 = (200,000 California commuters + 197,733 students in colleges in the four key states).

397,733 × $.12/ID holder . . . . = $ 47,727.96
397,733 × $.0625/t-shirt transfer . . . =   24,858.31
397,733 × $.04/rule book . . . . =   15,909.32
397,733 × $.10/calendar . . . . =   39,733.30
397,733 × $.049/plastic bag 19,488.91
$147,757.80

E. "Can You Top This?"

Original Draft has designed two promotions developed to increase both brand visibility and target market involvement with Coors. The "Can You Top This?" promotion is a contest which any group can enter by contacting their college rep and telling him/her about a college event or craze which they feel is fun and representative of the "Taste of College Life" theme. The rep will pass these on to Coors and those events chosen will become the basis for future ads. Also, the "best" event for the duration of the contest (February, March, April) will win a video game for its originators. The contest will be advertised on point-of-purchase

displays which will also serve other functions detailed later.

F. Group Events Incentive

Another related promotion invites groups to contact their college representative. In this case the company will provide $200 worth of prizes for the events the groups organize. Each rep in the 66 schools will be allowed a total of 3 events throughout the duration of the promotion (March, April, May). In return for the prizes, Coors' logo and slogan will appear on all advertising for the events.

This promotion will again create involvement and will saturate the campuses with the Coors' theme as the events occur in the same period as Coors' own scheduled events. This promotion will be announced on in•store displays and in newspaper ads.

Allocated promotional budget
66 reps × 3 events × $200/event . . . . = $39,600

POP cooler cup display. Distributors in college towns in the 17-state region will supply their retailers with a free-standing display containing a supply of Coors cooler cups. These will be sold at cost, two for $.25, only with a Coors purchase. The cups are very useful and a fine value at this price. By offering this incentive for purchasing Coors, we hope to separate Coors from the great mass of brands, which are often seen as parity products. This differentiation will promote impulse purchases and, of course, trial use.

Also, the display will hold a sign with a picture of one of Coors' ad events with students using the cooler cups. Accompanying the picture will be an advertisement of the two promotions, "Can You Top This" and "Group Events Incentive," discussed earlier. Detailed instructions for the promotions will be printed on tear-off pads which may be mounted on the display.

Allocated promotional budget
180 distributors × 80 retailers
× $4.50/display . . . . = $64,800
(Cooler cups are self-liquidating and so present no additional cost.)

Table-top tents. Bars near all 81 schools will be provided with table-top tents. One side will promote the Coors "Taste of College Life" theme while the other side will feature instructions for popular bar games. These will help to associate Coors with fun group activities right at the point of purchase.

Allocated promotional budget
81 schools × 6 bars/school × 50 tents
   × $.08/tent . . . . = $1,944.00
5 printing plates (for 5 different designs)
   × $400/plate . . . . =   2,000.00
                                                        $3,944.00

G. Floor Traffic Display

A stand-up paper triangle surrounded with Coors 12-packs will be used as a floor display. The triangle will feature illustrations taken from ads and the retailer's price. In addition, the beer will be rotated by the drivers to insure freshness. These floor displays are widely recognized as keys to increasing impulse purchases and are currently used by Coors. They will be used intermittently throughout the year.

Allocated promotional budget
3 pieces/triangle × 2 per retailer
   × 14,400 retailers × $.30 . . . . = $25,920.00

H. Keg Taps

Plastic keg taps will be offered for sale at cost, $7.00, to purchasers of Coors kegs. As with the sale of the cooler cups, these taps will help to differentiate Coors from the majority of beers and so will promote a Coors purchase in those that are undecided. Countertop signs will be placed in retail stores to promote the availability of the Coors tap. The decorative tap will be a status symbol as well as a convenience to the owner.

Allocated promotional budget
14,400 retailers × 2 countertop signs
   × $.15/sign . . . . = $4,320

(Keg taps are self-liquidating and present no additional cost.)

I. Sales Incentive Program

To motivate drivers to get behind the new advertising and promotion campaign, there will be a sales incentive program for drivers from September through December. The top salesman, driver, in each of our 17 states will receive a weekend trip to Las Vegas valued at $1,500 (where legal).

Allocated promotional budget
17 trips × $1,500 . . . . = $25,500

J. Driver Merchandising Packets

Coors will distribute to its distributors, who will then give their drivers, a packet containing the latest information on successful beer merchandising. This driver packet will be sent out in late August along with the driver incentive program announcement. The combination of the two will give the drivers an incentive to use the methods described in the driver packet and will make them aware of the upcoming advertising campaign.

Allocated promotional budget
180 distributors × 9 drivers each × 1 packet
   × $7.00/4-color folder (8½″ × 11″)
   packet . . . . = $11,340

K. Direct Mail

To reach our estimated 14,400 retailers in all 17 states, we will send out a letter from Joseph Coors directly to them. The letter will inform them of the start of our new campaign and the impact it will have on their stores and businesses. The letter will be sent out in late summer just before the school year begins. As with all promotions reaching the distribution chain, distributors will have advance notice of these letters. This will avoid any feelings that Coors is interfering.

Allocated promotional budget
14,400 retailers × $.208/letter . . . . = $3,000

Additional Recommendations

Original Draft would like to make two other sales promotion recommendations. First, that those distributors with colleges in their areas receive a special version of the company newsletter specifically detailing college market activities. Second, that Coors establish a vacation tie-in with hotels at major spring vacation destinations (e.g., Padre Island, Texas; Vail, Colorado). The tie-in would involve Coors-sponsored parties, dances, and interschool competitions at each destination for those students who sign up for various special tour priced trips. These trips and events would provide fine publicity and create a sense of involvement with the brand among those on the trips and those at the events. Coors could use the events as opportunities to distribute promotional materials. Also, distributors could be encouraged to offer volume discounts to local retailers, who could take advantage of the brand's popularity during the promotion.

Legal Considerations

All recommended promotional activities are legal as researched in the Michigan Liquor Control Act, Vernon's Texas Annotated Code, and West's Annotated California Code. Naturally, in any areas where a promotion is found to be illegal, the promotion will not be run.

Budget Summary

To recap, Original Draft's total sales promotion budget looks like this:

Extramural festival	$ 88,014.60	20.9%
California volleyball	6,186.00	1.5
"Thirst aid kits"	147,757.80	35.1
Group events incentive	39,600.00	9.4
POP display/cooler cup bins	64,800.00	15.4
Table-top tents	3,944.00	.9
Floor traffic display	25,920.00	6.2
Keg taps	4,320.00	1.0
Sales incentive program	25,500.00	6.1
Driver merchandising packets	11,340.00	2.7
Direct mail	3,000.00	.7
	$420.382.40	

Sales Promotion Payout

Our sales promotion plans are specifically designed to do two things. First, provide involvement with the brand by the target market, and second, stimulate impulse purchases. Both effects flow directly from our communication objectives which, as stated earlier, concentrate mostly on increasing the use of Coors among those who already are occasional Coors users.

To justify our promotion expenditure, Original Draft set as our goal 31.5 percent of the desired sales increase of 79,111 barrels. We used 31.5 percent as a rather arbitrary estimate with this reasoning: sales promotion is more involving and more directly related to sales than is media advertising. Therefore, it must carry double its share of the sales goal. Any more than this would disregard the high influence media has on how the market reacts to sales promotion and the influence of the media advertising itself. Sales promotion's budget is 21 percent of the total. Therefore, 31.5 percent or 24,920 barrels is our sales promotion goal. This equals 8,240,213 bottles.

As noted in the descriptions, each promotional activity provides some combination of impulse purchase stimulation and preference increase through involvement. Estimates presented here are very conservative, they include no residual effects of the promotions after they actually end. Also, numbers presented include only increased sales caused by consumers buying Coors instead of another brand, not extra consumption of beer.

Payout Summary

	Bottles
Extramural festival	2,808,000
California volleyball	150,000
"Thirst aid" kits	795,465
Group events incentive	1,080,000
POP display/cooler cup bins	1,598,197
Table-top tents	1,560,000
College life nights	693,000
"Can you top this?"	86,667
Total paid promotions	9,551,329

9,551,329 bottles = 28,885 barrels

An example of the conservatism of our estimates is the point-of-purchase displays. Our figures represent a sales increase of only 1.5 percent of the market purchasing one additional Coors six-pack every week for only 12 weeks. Retail sources indicate that such displays actually provide much stronger sales increases, often reaching over 400 percent for the duration of their placement. (Figures for other promotions upon request.) Finally, given the number of legal drinkers, each one would only need to drink four bottles of Coors beyond his regular purchase rate of Coors as a result of our promotions to justify our investment. Surely such a yearly figure is very conservative.

MEDIA

Media Plan

Media objectives
1. Reach 35 percent of the total legal-aged college students directly through the media selected.
2. Reach an additional 15 percent of the total legal-aged college students as an overflow from schools not budgeted, but still exposed to our advertising.
3. Reach 5 percent of the total number of legal-aged students through advertising for promotional activities and promotions.
4. Secure a *total reach of 55 percent* for Original Draft's campaign.
5. Secure an *average frequency of 116* for each student reached over the course of our campaign.
6. Use media that selectively delivers students.
7. Use creative media which have the least possible clutter to instill memorability of our creative messages.
8. Use media that can tie into and support our promotional effort.
9. Use media that require low production costs so as to spend as much of the budget as possible on buying space and time.
10. Use media which can deliver the target audience effectively without an excessive total cost and develop tie-in programs where possible and legal.

Media criteria. Several criteria were used to determine each medium's effectiveness in delivering the college student audience. A media matrix which listed each medium and ranked its effectiveness over eight variables was used. (See Appendix.) The variables are:

(1) reach, (2) frequency availability, (3) selectivity, (4) clutter, (5) memorability of message, (6) tie-ins with other media and promotions, (7) production costs, and (8) total costs.

Each variable was then weighted as to its importance to our media objectives.

The unweighted total for each medium represents the medium's rank assuming each variable to be equally important. The weighted total represents each medium's rank based on adjusting the importance of each variable to our media objectives. Results of the media matrix are as follows:

Media Matrix Findings*

Rank	Unweighted total	Weighted total
1. College newspapers	10	8.00
2. Theater advertisements .	11	7.90
3. Transit advertisements ..	8	6.75
4. Outdoor advertisements	8	6.25
5. Radio advertisements** .	7	5.10

*See appendix for complete media matrix.
**Radio will only be used in Iowa, Missouri, Nebraska, and Washington.

Media strategy. Our media strategy is based upon the stated media objectives as well as estimated communication needs to meet those objectives.

1. The Coors "College Life" media campaign will be introduced into 10 carefully selected states in our 17-state marketing region for one full year beginning September 1, 1981. Almost 98.5 percent of our total budget will be spent during the nine-month school year period of September through June.
2. California and Texas will receive a larger portion of our budget because of high consumption patterns existing in those states.
3. Four states (Iowa, Missouri, Nebraska, and Washington) will receive proportionately larger budget shares because of their high potential for brand development.
4. The use of *college newspapers* as the primary medium provides the greatest frequency while reaching 79.0 percent of all college students.
5. *Theater advertisements* have a commanding

presence coupled with selectivity and flexibility. Ads shown on this medium have the highest memorability.

6. *Transit advertising* provides us with selectivity and low cost.
7. *Outdoor advertising* offers geographic flexibility and continuity within the campaign and reaches commuting students.
8. *Radio* offers us a good followup medium for sales promotions in selected areas where university students comprise a large proportion of the audience.
9. Advertising and sales promotion will work hand-in-hand to stimulate top-of-the-mind awareness and consumer demand for Coors Premium Beer.

Media Selection

College newspapers. One advantage of college newspapers is that they allow for relative flexibility within targeted schools. Also, students actively seek editorial and advertising information, and the news content of the newspaper injects the element of immediacy into ads. Disadvantages are that newspapers sometimes have poor reproduction in black and white, and only a few print in color. Also college newspapers have a short life span.

The specific buy is as follows: The CPM is $40.83. Total GRPs for one year of advertising is 3,135, almost half of our campaign's total GRPs. These high GRPs are accomplished with only 33 percent of our total budget. With each run of our selected school newspapers, we'll be reaching 732,000 students in our targeted states. Each school will have the following number of ads: 47 ¼-page ads (33 GRPs each run), 10 ½-page ads (66 GRPs each run) and 7 full-page ads (132 GRPs each run).

Theater advertisements. Advantages of theater advertising include the commanding size of the medium which helps to hold attention. A theater screen is five times the size of an outdoor board. There is little or no clutter associated with this medium; this insures a high rate of memorability and good positioning for the ads. Approximately 83.5 percent of viewers surveyed remember seeing theater advertisements the next day, much higher than comparable figures for other media.

Viewers are in a receptive mood in a relaxed, uninterrupted environment. Theater ads provide the highest degree of localization of any medium. Finally, over 55 percent of college students attend movie theaters at least nine or more times during a school year. The disadvantages are that theater ads are obtrusive since those attending theaters came to watch a movie without interruption. Also, production costs can be high.

The specific buy gives us a CPM of $24. Total GRPs for one year of advertising in theaters is 543. Each commercial and movie is shown approximately 20 times per flight with an average audience of around 500 people per showing. The ratio in each state of the legal-aged drinkers in the audience was used to compute GRPs.

Transit advertising. Advantages of transit include a low cost-per-thousand. Also, for transit serving campuses, exterior advertising has excellent frequency availabilities. The prospect need not buy or tune in to the medium; it is always available. Transit is particularly appropriate for campuses with a large number of commuting students. Disadvantages include the limited availability in our targeted states and the limited time available to view the message.

The specific buy gives us a very low CPM of $.29. The total GRPs for one year is 1,743. There is limited availability for showings in 18 of our targeted college cities.

Outdoor advertising. Outdoor is an efficient way to build high awareness, particularly among commuting students. Outdoor can be effectively localized to obtain specific reach and frequency. It is an excellent impulse trigger, ideal for reminding the prospect at a time when the desire for the product is apt to be high. The disadvantage is that only short messages are possible.

The specific buy will give us a CPM of $13.30. Total GRPs for one year is 585. A 200 showing of the student population is planned for September, April, and June. All other times will have a 100 showing.

Radio advertising. Radio provides local coverage. We found in our research that students listen to a good deal of radio. It also offers a good reminder and tie-in medium for sales promotions. Disadvantages are that a variety of formats may have to be purchased because students listen to a variety of programming. The message is fleeting. There is a tremendous waste in large metropolitan areas. Also, it is difficult to know what time of day our target market is likely to listen to radio.

The specifics of our radio buy will give us a CPM of $7.07. We will only be using radio in university towns where college students make up a large proportion of

the audience in our four targeted key states. Total GRPs for one year is 377. Thirty-two stations will be used with 377 total commercials.

The schedule for the media plan is included in the appendix. The media buy is flighted around major peak selling periods such as fall and spring. A breakdown of our total budget is included in the chart below:

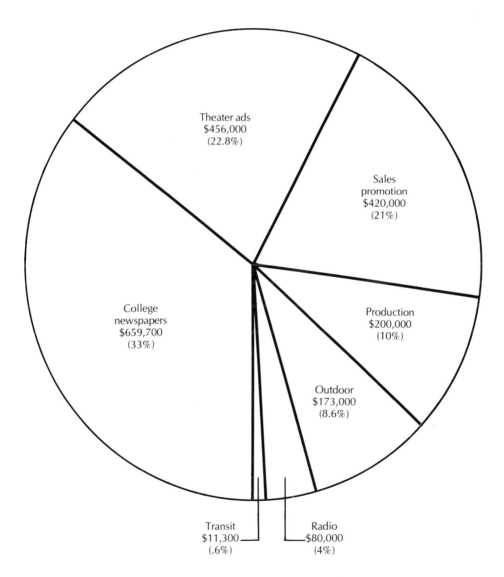

Theater ads
$456,000
(22.8%)

Sales promotion
$420,000
(21%)

College newspapers
$659,700
(33%)

Production
$200,000
(10%)

Outdoor
$173,000
(8.6%)

Transit
$11,300
(.6%)

Radio
$80,000
(4%)

BUDGET JUSTIFICATION

Original Draft has determined that a $2 million budget will result in a $4.5 million increase in college sales. This corresponds to a 3.3 percentage point increase in college market share. The following explains our budget justification process.

1. First, we estimated beer consumption in the 17-state market. Of the beer-drinking students, 2.2 million were found to be of legal age. We multiplied this by the heavy user figure (seven beers a week) and by 52 weeks per year for an estimate of 33.6 million cases. (The heavy user number was used because we determined that beer-drinking college students average a heavy use rate of consumption.) At 14 cases per barrel, this equals roughly 2.4 million barrels.
2. We estimated earlier that Coors' 1980 market share in the 17 states is 22.7 percent. This, multiplied by national barrels, gives us a projection of about 546,000 barrels Coors' college sales in 1980–81.
3. Our research indicates Coors' total sales in 1980 was 13.8 million barrels and Coors' projected total sales in 1981 will be 15.8 million barrels. Therefore, in 1980, 3.9% of the national sales will come from the college market (545,000 ÷ 13.8 Mil.).
4. Using the 3.9 percent ratio, we project 625,000 barrels for the 1981–82 college market (15.8 Mil. × 3.9 percent).
5. This gives us an increase of 79,000 barrels for Coors' college market in 1981–82 (625,000 − 546,000) and an increase in market share of 3.29 percentage points (79,000 ÷ 2.4 Mil.).

Although a 3.29 percentage point increase in market share may seem relatively small for a 53 percent increase in the advertising budget, research has shown that competitors' advertising budgets are increasing at astonishing rates, often more than 50 percent yearly in the college market. This increase in Coors' budget represents only slightly more than a holding action. Also, research shows that the number of students is declining slightly, making the college beer market one of little or no growth. In this case, a large budget increase is absolutely necessary in order to increase only slightly as competition for share becomes more fierce.

EVALUATION OF CAMPAIGN

Communication Objectives

As stated earlier, Original Draft intends to move 10 percent of our target audience from knowledge to liking. In addition, we will move 4 percent from liking to preference and .3 percent from preference to sole use.

Currently our market share is 22.7 percent. This movement will cause a market share increase of 3.3 percentage points, thus creating a new market share of 26 percent.

	Currently
Sole use	4.4% (4.4% market share)
Preference	16.6% (8.3% market share)
Liking	60.0% (10.0% market share)
Knowledge	19.0% (0.0% market share)

	After our campaign
Sole use	4.7% (4.7% market share)
Preference	20.3% (10.15% market share)
Liking	66.0% (11.0% market share)
Knowledge	9.0% (0.0% market share)

These movements are only averages. In reality, categories are not as clear cut as they appear in the chart and so, of course, these are based on average consumption rates (includes heavy, medium, and light beer drinkers).

The "College Life" campaign will create 10 percent more people who drink Coors some of the time in the liking state. More important, it will increase the buying rate of people who are already occasional Coors users.

We've defined each state in relation to where our target audience is. Knowledge is defined as the point where our target audience is just aware of Coors and knows something about the product, with no formation of an attitude. Liking is defined as our target audience considering Coors as one of the brands in their evoked set when they consider purchasing beer. Preference is when our target audience buys Coors most often when they buy beer. Sole use is our brand loyal college students. They drink only Coors when they drink beer.

Suggestions and Proposals

Original Draft suggests that an evaluation of "The Taste of College Life" campaign should be carried out to measure its effectiveness. Certainly, the increase in market share of 3.3 will be evident in barrel volume and sales, but communication objectives can only be tested by primary research. In addition, primary research conducted while our campaign is running gives us the flexibility to key into and update our advertising and promotional efforts. Also, by measuring target market awareness of previous campaigns we have a benchmark with which to compare. These evaluations are only suggested to Coors and are not included in our 2 million dollar budget.

Methodology

We propose a centralized telephone interview to be used in our evaluation plan with a sample size of approximately 250 students from major colleges and universities each time the test is administered. The names of the students to be tested can be obtained from student directories which also list current phone numbers.

Original Draft suggests a pretest in early fall to measure student awareness of Coors' present "Taste the High Country" theme. We feel this pretest is essential to further evaluations as it will measure levels of awareness already existing among our target market and serve as a benchmark for comparison.

We suggest that the second evaluation period take place in October using the same methodology. This second test should measure the impact of the launch of our "Taste of College Life" campaign and allow early fine tuning of the campaign.

The third and final evaluation period is suggested in late May. It is here that we will be spending the largest portion of our advertising budget and the students tested at this time will be fully exposed to our messages. This final test should demonstrate the increased awareness, involvement, and knowledge of the new "college beer" position that our campaign has established in their minds. (Estimated cost for evaluations with computer cross-tabulations: $10,000.00.)

APPENDIX

Media Matrix

	College NP		Theater		Transit		Outdoor		Radio	
	UW	W	UW	W	UW	W	UW	W	UW	W
Reach (weight = 1)	2	2	1	1	1	1	1	1	2	2
Tie-ins (weight = .6)	0	0	2	1.2	1	.6	−1	−.6	1	.6
Total cost (weight = 1)	1	1	2	2	2	2	2	2	−1	−1
Selectivity (weight = .5)	2	1	2	1	2	1	2	1	2	1
Frequency (weight = .75)	2	1.5	1	.75	2	1.5	2	1.5	0	0
Clutter (weight = .35)	0	0	2	.7	−1	−.35	1	.35	0	0
Memorability (weight = 1)	1	1	2	2	0	0	1	1	1	1
Prod. cost (weight = .75)	2	1.5	−1	−.75	1	.75	0	0	2	1.5
Unweighted total	10		11		8		8		7	
Weighted total		8		7.9		6.5		6.25		5.1
Rank		1		2		3		4		5

UW = Unweighted score   W = Weighted score   Score: 2 = very good, 1 = good, 0 = fair, −1 = poor

Media Flow Chart

Media	Sept.	Oct.	Nov.	Dec.	Jan.	Feb.	Mar.	Apr.	May	June	July	Aug.	Cost
Theater commercials	1 flight 2 weeks 90.5 GRPs	1 flight 2 weeks 90.5 GRPs	1 flight 2 weeks 90.5 GRPs	1 flight 2 weeks 90.5 GRPs				1 flight 2 weeks 90.5 GRPs	1 flight 2 weeks 90.5 GRPs				$456,000
Transit	52 weeks 1,743.36 GRPs												$11,300
College newspapers	528 GRPs	66 GRPs	330 GRPs		330 GRPs	66 GRPs		528 GRPs	561 GRPs	726 GRPs			$659,700
Outdoor	#200 showing			#100 showing				#200	#100	#200	#100		$173,000
Radio	82 GRPs	30 GRPs	50 GRPs		30 GRPs	15 GRPs		56 GRPs	56 GRPs	58 GRPs			$80,000
GRPs	923.72	370.75	654.75	184.25	634.75	265.25	184.25	897.72	891.75	1,007.22	184.25	184.25	

Total GRPs: 6381.91

Evaluation Schedule

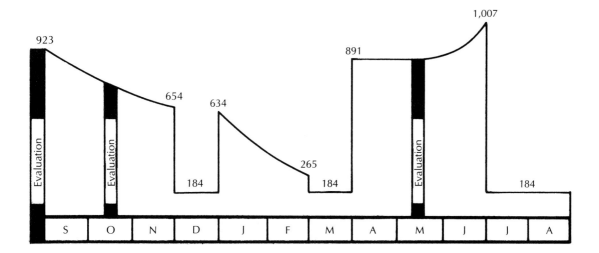

Research

Original Draft has used extensive research in developing Coors "College Life" campaign. The total number of college students used in our research is 1,639.

This figure includes a sample of 514 Michigan students from major universities, four-year colleges, community colleges, and urban universities with personal interviews. In addition, 32 focus groups were used for testing themes/concepts, headlines, copy, layout, tag-lines, visual impact, and product presentation for a total of 230 students. Of that number, 17 percent were from Coors' marketing area states. Also, 13 separate street intercept surveys were conducted to research specific questions regarding strategy with a total of 895 students.

The significant results of the primary research survey are as follows:

Usage patterns
- 62.8 percent drink beer rather than any other beverage in social situations.
- 65.0 percent buy their beer at a party store.
- 78.4 percent drink lights or regular premiums. (Coors is in this category.)

- 65.0 percent purchase a six-pack when buying beer.
- Given seven situations, the majority of students chose beer to drink at a bar, at a party, and at a sporting event.

Purchase decisions
- Price, brand name, and taste are the most important factors considered when purchasing beer.
- 63.2 percent said that they buy most of their beer in fall and spring (excluding summer).
- 74.7 percent of the students have tried Coors.

Media usage
- 73.9 percent read a newspaper every day with school newspaper being second most read, and large metropolitan newspapers being first.
- 57.0 percent of the students read the supplements in their school newspapers.
- 46.7 percent of the students only watch between 3 and 10 hours of television per week.

Advertising recall
- 82.3 percent remembered some advertisement for

beer. The brands remembered were split among four: Stroh's, Miller, Miller Lite, and Budweiser.

Demographics
- 62.6 percent of the students were between 21–24 years old.
- 30.0 percent were between 18–20 years old.
- 41.5 percent were seniors, 26.0 percent were juniors, 16.5 percent were sophomores, 9.8 percent were freshmen, and 6.1 percent were graduate students.
- 59.9 percent of the students live on their own, in an apartment, rented house, duplex, etc.
- 60.9 percent were male, 39.1 percent were female.
- 69.0 percent were from major universities, 10 percent were from urban universities, 10 percent were from 4-year colleges, and 11 percent were from community colleges.

There were 23 states represented in this study; 56.0 percent of the students were from Michigan, 19.0 percent from Coors' marketing area states and the remainder were from other states.

Original Draft also conducted a survey with a sample of 45 students at Michigan State University for further data on advertising to the college-student beer drinker.

The significant results were that 59 percent switched types of beer depending on the situation, while 41 percent drank the same type no matter where they were. In general, the more formal the situation, the more expensive the beer our target audience will drink.

Focus group results
From our focus group results we were able to develop the following psychographic profile of our target audience:

- Students from non-Coors marketing areas have a stronger mountain, macho image of Coors beer.
- Coors marketing area students see Coors as "the cowboy beer" with no distinct or desirable image.
- Coors is perceived as a light-tasting beer which is inexpensively priced.
- Students associate beer with hard work, sports, games, parties, weekends, fun activities, the outdoors, and study breaks.
- College students are not brand loyal because of

differences in price and availability of certain brands. However, they do have a favorite "set" of brands of beer they consider when buying. This favoritism is particularly strong among heavy users.
- Students have a strong, positive reaction toward relating a feature of an everyday slice of college life to drinking Coors beer. They said that it was a good change from the traditional rugged, macho beer ads that don't really relate to college students.
- Many students will buy the beer on special.
- Although students are concerned with the environment and ecology, a theme combining the fact that Coors is all natural and brewed with pure mountain spring water had little impact on them.
- College students are peer oriented and career oriented. There is a trend toward the professional and business career.
- Today's college students are more materialistic and ambitious than their 1970s counterparts.
- Students are getting more involved in political activities and extracurricular activities such as intramural sports.
- There seems to be a trend toward joining fraternities and sororities as indicated by the rising popularity of "Greek life" on college campuses.
- Focus groups indicated their dislike for sexist advertising and indicated preference for down-to-earth, real-life situations in any advertising.
- When Coors marketing area students were asked about the current "Taste the High Country" theme, they indicated that it was not an appealing image for college students. It was more for the "cowboy" beer drinker.
- Coors' copy "This ain't no city dweller's beer, this ain't no flat-land dweller's beer," seemed to eliminate students from the target market and indicated that only cowboys should drink the beer.

We also interviewed members of our secondary target audience, distributors and retailers. We reached 21 retailers from party and grocery stores and found that:

- The majority of stores base their purchasing and shelf-space decisions for beer on either profits or promotion.
- Retailers like point-of-purchase displays and feel that they sell beer.

- Retailers thought that the best selling beers used point-of-purchase displays often, but they were also strongly in favor of off-premise promotions.
- Retailers agreed unanimously that beer is a profitable product.
- Retailers believe that distributors should offer retailers the best possible service.

Original Draft interviewed approximately 11 distributors in the Michigan State University area. Results are as follows:

- Distributors are convinced that image advertising has the biggest influence on beer sales.
- Distributors want to be informed of company changes and plans.
- Distributors indicated that wholesalers want no interference from brewers in their local business. Distributors were offended by any effort of a brewery to go over their heads in an attempt to reach the driver or retailer. Any contact should either be made through the distributor or the distributor should be informed long before any contact is made.
- Distributors and drivers are willing to learn any method that will improve their sales and, therefore, their commissions.

Bibliography

Advertising Age, Dec. 11, 1978; April 9, 1979; May 7, 1979; May 21, 1979; June 11, 1979; July 2, 1979; July 30, 1979; Aug. 6, 1979; Sept. 24, 1979; Oct. 8, 1979; Jan. 19, 1981.

American Advertising Federation, Oct. 3, 1980.

Barron's, May 12, 1980.

"Beer-Wine-Liquor," Time, Inc., 1979.

Beer Paper, Feb. 12, 1980.

Beverage Industry Magazine, Jan. 25, 1980; Feb. 8, 1980; May 9, 1980; May 23, 1980; June 20, 1980.

Beverage World Magazine, Dec. 1978, April 1979, July 1979, Oct. 1979, Nov. 1979, Feb. 1980, Mar. 1980, Apr. 1980, May 1980, June 1980, July 1980, Sept. 1980, Nov. 1980.

Brewers Almanac, 1979.

Communications & Advertising Services to Students, "The College Market/Opportunities of the 1980s."

Communications & Advertising Services to Students,

"1980–81 National Rate Book and College Newspaper Directory."

Domesticated Drug Among Collegians, edited by G. L. Maddox.

Encyclomedia, Decisions Pub., Inc., 1980.

Federal Trade Commission, *The Brewing Industry,* 1978.

Financial World Magazine, Sept. 1, 1979.

Industry Week Magazine, Apr. 2, 1979.

"Liquor, Wine & Beer Sales," Time, Inc.

Modern Brewery Age, Jan. 7, 1980; Jan. 21, 1980; Jan. 28, 1980; Feb. 11, 1980; Apr. 21, 1980; May 12, 1980; June 16, 1980; Aug. 4, 1980; Aug. 18, 1980; Sept. 22, 1980; Oct. 6, 1980; Oct. 13, 1980; Oct. 27, 1980; Nov. 3, 1980.

Montrose Daily Press, Jan. 8, 1981.

New York Times, Apr. 29, 1979; Aug. 9, 1979; Oct. 18, 1979.

"Patterns of Drinking Among College Students," Time, Inc., 1978.

Predicasts Forecasts, Oct. 24, 1980.

Quarterly Media Spending, 1981.

Ryan, Thomas E., Inc., "Produced for Time, Presentation Date for Bureau of Labor Statistics Study of Consumer Expenditures," May, 1979.

Sales and Marketing Management Magazine, Oct. 27, 1980.

Schultz, Don E., and Dennis G. Martin, *Strategic Advertising Campaigns* (Chicago: Crain Books, 1979).

Simmons Market Research Bureau, Inc., 1980.

"Spirits of '79," Time, Inc., 1979.

Standard and Poors, *Industry Surveys,* Mar. 27, 1980.

Standard Directory of Advertisers.

"TAA Rate Directory of Transit Advertising," Nov. 19, 1980.

Target Group Index (TGI) 1977, vol. p-9.

U.S. Bureau of Census.

U.S. Department of Commerce, *Annual Survey of Manufacturers,* 1980.

U.S. Department of Commerce, Industry, and Trade, 1980 U.S. Industrial Outlook.

U.S. National Center for Education Statistics, *Institutions of Higher Education: Number and Enrollment by State,* 1970, 1977.

Wall Street Journal, Mar. 3, 1980; July 31, 1980.

Wall Street Transcript, Mar. 31, 1980.

"1980 Radio Encyclopedia," 1980.

Answers for Cases

1. Taking each factor separately:

   - The social environment has affected the overall market for milk products. Convenience desires of consumers suggest the product would be desirable as a baking aid; the move toward "natural" foods gives strength to the beverage creamer position.
   - The natural environment will impact the company's ability to get raw materials. Since the new product is within the dairy field, the company can rely on its current suppliers.
   - The economic environment is, along with the social environment, the key to the current problem of limited corporate growth.
   - Although not directly mentioned, the company must be operating within the strictures of the governmental environment or it would not be in business after 44 years.
   - The technological environment has made the new product possible.
   - The competitive environment has not been addressed in depth. For a baking aid, competition is seen as non-use because of waste. For a beverage creamer, the competition is defined as nondairy creamers. Other, indirect, competitors might include ready-made foods and mixes. The strength of the competition has not been assessed.
   - In terms of the consumer environment, a consumer panel suggested one use (baking aid) and overall consumer behavior suggests appeal of a *dairy* coffee creamer. Actual consumer desire for such a product (in either use) has not been assessed directly.

2. As a baking aid with a projected 10 percent share of a market with negative growth, the product would be a dog. However, if aggressively marketed so as to promote overall category growth, it could move into the star range as market share increases through the year.

As a beverage creamer with 15 percent of a market whose growth is unknown, star potential is greater. Again, starting as a dog until share picks up throughout the year, if the product can attract competitive users and non-users, there is a chance for category growth.

3. Pricing alternatives would include pricing somewhat higher than non-dairy creamers to emphasize the natural quality image. Pricing the same as nondairy creamers might attract more competitive users, especially on a trial basis. At a lower price, while inferiority might be inferred, it could also suggest that chemicals and preservatives (in nondairy creamers) cost more than the "real thing."

    Placement would either be with other creamers to attract competitive users or in or near the dairy section to appeal to non-users and underline the "natural" claim.

4. Marketing as a baking aid is more in keeping with current corporate know-how. But, since an increased consumer base is a corporate goal and because there is more profit potential, the beverage creamer position is more desirable.

Chapter 2:
The Maverick
Brewing Company

1. The step-flow model of communication can be used to extend the influence of Maverick Brewing Company's new campaign in two different ways. First, opinion leaders can be identified and profiled, and media can be planned to reach this group with the new campaign. Additionally, a creative approach that would select this audience and attract it to the ads for the new super-premium brand can be developed.

    The difficulty with the first approach is in identifying and profiling this group. Who are they? One approach might be to try to identify those most likely to try a new brand of beer in the early stages of its introduction. Perhaps heavy users of beer contain some of these people. A survey might be conducted to identify relevant heavy users. A variation of this first approach could be to consider restaurants, taverns, and retail stores as opinion leaders. Introduction of the new brand to these institutions could help to establish an initial awarenss among their patrons.

    A second approach would be to use recognizable celebrities in the introductory advertising campaign. The goal would be to establish credibility and leverage in the media marketplace against the national competition. In this situation, the celebrity endorsers can be considered opinion leaders.

    Other approaches no doubt can be found for extending the impact of Maverick's campaign. The objective should be to take advantage of opinion leaders' credibility and influence among members of your target audience.

2. The outcome of the case, to a large extent, depends upon Maverick's message leverage against the national competition's money and media weight. Even though Maverick cannot compete with the national brewers on the basis of financial strength alone, it does have the advantage of knowing its audience better. Two things should come to mind immediately. As a local brewer Maverick should be able to take advantage of the common background and experiences it shares with its target audience and communicate them more effectively. Also, the media marketplace is very cluttered. Maverick should have an advantage in breaking through this clutter if it can develop a creative message that effectively communicates its empathy with its customers. This could be its best weapon against the financial clout of the national competition.

3. The complexity of the consumer's decision process regarding the selection of a brand of beer will determine whether a low- or high-involvement learning hierarchy is in operation. There is some support for the notion that heavy users of beer have more simplistic decision rules regarding the selection of a brand of beer than do light users. Assuming that Maverick's target audience is more likely to consist of heavy and medium users, the low-involvement hierarchy is most likely in operation in this case. Therefore, Maverick's goal should be to establish instant recognition for its new super-premium beer among as many members of its target audience as possible. Attitude formation will occur for most consumers after trying Maverick's new beer.

    Brand recognition is a function of both media exposure and the impact of the message. Since Maverick might suffer versus the national competition in establishing high levels of exposure, it will have to compensate by developing ads that strike a responsive chord among members of its target audience.

4. Answers to this question should be based on an extension of the analysis used to answer question 3. The audience members in this case are more likely to be passive catchers than active seekers of Maverick's advertising messages. Therefore, Maverick's advertising should be creatively unique and highly memorable. General consumer media will probably provide the best vehicles for getting across Maverick's message to the target audience.

5. Using Assael's model of how advertising works, Mr. Cummings must take the following steps to be successful in establishing his new super-premium beer in the marketplace.

   a. Mr. Cummings must hope that his selection for the type of product to add to his product line will attract a sufficient number of customers to make its promotion successful. If not, the best advertising possible cannot make the product a success.

   b. Mr. Cummings must select and guide an advertising agency that can develop advertising messages that communicate the right product benefits in a manner that will elicit the desired response from the target audience. This stage requires the correct selection of benefits and manner in which they should be communicated. A mistake in either of these areas can seriously short circuit the effectiveness of the campaign.

   c. Next, Mr. Cummings' agency must plan and select media that can deliver the right audience while providing a good creative environment for the message. These media vehicles must also be able to reach the audience at the most appropriate times, and with sufficient frequency to achieve brand recognition for Maverick's new beer.

   d. Lastly, Mr. Cummings and his agency must monitor the campaign to determine if it is eliciting the correct response from the target audience. If consumer perceptions and interpretations turn out to be incorrect, then adjustments in the campaign should be made.

Chapter 3: Stearns Food Market

1. Social groups—if shopping at Stearns became "trendy" as a result of the specialty store aura, many shoppers might be brought in.

    Family—"low price" appeal would be especially attractive to larger families; specialty stores to those with older or no children; special offerings to teens and men.

    Personal influence—word of mouth could be the key to bringing people in for a trial visit.

2. People who don't consider grocery stores as purchase alternatives for specialty foods would be competitive users. But, people who don't utilize a full-service butcher, or a cheese shop, etc., for reasons such as inconvenience, would be non-users. The goal with these people would be to convince them to utilize *all* of the store's services.

3. Although grocery stores are clearly in the maturity stage, if Stearns can be presented as a new *type* of grocery, rather than just a new store, Louis could capitalize on the excitement and curiosity generated by an introduction.

4. Cost-conscious consumers with the "guaranteed low price" policy and regular special savings. Gourmet shoppers with the specialty shop attraction. Health-conscious consumers with the large produce section, product dating, and on-premises bakery. Convenience-minded shoppers with the deli and large frozen food section.

5. a. Bring emphasis on economy, or health, or convenience in ads: this is important to you, and we've done something about it.
   b. Groceries aren't considered fast shopping places—we've got *2* express lanes. Actually, most of the store's new features were adopted for their saliency.
   c. Meat that's trimmed how you want it, quickly and at no charge, is easier to cook with. Cheese cut while you wait is fresher than prepackaged.
   d. Instead of being second-best, we're best because our store has been remodeled to offer more.
   e. The older type of grocery store is outdated. Ours is the store of the future.

6. Cost-conscious consumers are probably the largest market group. If they are brought in by low prices on traditional grocery offerings, it may be possible to get a portion of them to trade up and try other, specialty items.

Chapter 4:
Sidley's Soft Drinks

1. Plan A: How important are national spending levels to a regional brand? Was a detailed analysis of all new products necessary? Why recommend extending distribution—does this belong in an advertising plan? Is price an important factor in soft drink purchase?

   Plan B: Is enough consideration given to the present situation? Is "home-grown" an important appeal to a significant number of people? What does the target market currently buy? Are they brand loyal? How important to the target audience are the selected media vehicles? What type of evaluation will be used?

   Plan C: How will distributor attitudes be utilized? Focus on region is good—that's the key market area. How cost-effective are local newspapers? How important a force is the target market? Again, how important is a regional appeal in differentiating the product?

2. Plan A: Television and magazines are likely to be effective in reaching the defined target market, and the execution and premiums would seem to have appeal.

Plan B: The target market seems to have been created to match the execution. Since the analysis is scanty, it's hard to tell if this is a logical solution.

Plan C: This follows logically from the analysis. The campaign appears to be designed to appeal specifically to the targeted audience.

Chapter 5: "POPCORN!"

1. See chart below

Question	Primary	Secondary	Best	Why
1. Present subscriber likes and dislikes	Subscriber survey (mail, telephone, door-to-door) Subscriber focus groups Reply card in program guide "Call us" announcement on program	Any letters from subscribers	Focus group	Qualitative input, have names of potential group members 2 wks—telephone 3 months—card in program guide
2. "POPCORN!" pricing	Telephone survey among new and long-time subscribers Reply card in program guide Door-to-door survey Focus group	Any letters from subscribers	Telephone	Gives feedback—can follow up Quick and cheap 2 wks—telephone 3 mos—reply card and telephone follow-up
3. Cable penetration	Random calling in those areas with cable—"Do you have it?"	Cable companies' figures on number of hookups National studies on cable penetration	Company figures	Location specific, accurate, easy to obtain Same for other time frames
4. Viewer extras	Random telephone survey in cable areas	Cable company records National figures	Company records	Fast, accessible 2 wks—same 3 mos—same, but use telephone follow-up for qualitative info
5. Cable pricing	Telephone/door-to-door/mail survey	See if penetration percentage is different in communities where the price differs National studies	Telephone	Qualitative input 2 wks—cable figures 3 mos—telephone

Question	Primary	Secondary	Best	Why
6. People not getting cable	Telephone in cable areas Mail, door-to-door	National studies	Telephone	Qualitative input 2 wks—national studies 3 mos—telephone
7. Ex-subscribers	Telephone/mail/door-to-door to ex-subs	Letters asking to cancel subscription	Telephone	Qualitative—more probing 2 wks, 3 mos—same
8. Cable likes/dislikes	Telephone/mail/door-to-door to cable areas	National studies Cable company studies	Telephone	Qualitative input 2 wks—national studies 3 mos—telephone

In most cases, the secondary information should be used as a starting point, with primary research as a confirmation and localizing factor. Due to time and cost restraints, telephone surveys would be most efficient. Many of the questions can be addressed simultaneously: nos. 1 and 2; 3, 4, 5, 6, 8. The primary advantage or change when using a three-month time phase is that sample sizes can be larger; two weeks forces greater reliance on secondary information, including national trends.

2. Videotapes and videodiscs, which are also in the movie-related home entertainment genre. How many machines are there in the area served by "POPCORN!" and what are purchase projections? How are rental movies priced?

3. No, because of time and cost constraints. Also, the needed information is primarily qualitative, not quantitative.

4. Need to be sure they don't lead people on in pricing questions—there seems to be a tendency to assume that price will be a large factor, i.e., don't ask "Is $20 a month too much to pay?"

5. In other cities, how have STV services responded to increasing cable penetration? Have they been hurt and had to make changes, or has the impact not been large?
   What are "POPCORN!"'s current projections? Are they bringing in new subscribers at a constant rate, or has the influx slowed?

Chapter 6:   1. Yes. The panel is already established, so it's a ready audience. It would
Noile Shampoo   be helpful to see if the product has any appeal for teenagers, especially
                         as the current market tends to be young.

2. The best argument can probably be made for:
    3 & 9 which defines users by age, helping to target the market;
    5 & 7 which would reveal if the perceived benefits vary among heavy
        users and other users;
    1 & 3 which would reveal any pattern between how often people
        shampoo and usage of Noile; 2 & 5 which show if hair condition
        and length vary between heavy users and other users.

3. Harsh-gentle and cleaning-conditioning

4. Yes, the questionnaire suggests there may be a small but well-defined
    market for Noile based on benefits such as oil cutting and long-term
    cleaning.

5. What about the sports-active aspect mentioned in the initial market
    description? Is this a key determinant in usage?

6. How strong are non-users harshness perceptions? Are they aware of
    Noile's conditioners? When do Noile users who don't use the product
    every time they shampoo use it? How important is long-term cleaning?
    To whom?

Chapter 7:   1. Objectives 1 and 3 are measurable, if information is available (or
America Helps   research done) to determine the current level of national awareness and
                         of knowledge among Fortune 500 companies. Objectives 4, 5, and 6
                         are measurable, since data is available on current levels in each cate-
                         gory. Objective 2 is not measurable because it is not clearly defined—
                         what is "the groundwork"?

2. All objectives can be achieved through advertising. Objective 2 is more
    of a general marketing objective, as it almost echoes the corporate goal,
    but advertising can be used to achieve that goal.

3. Coffman would need a two-pronged campaign. One facet, aimed at a
    broad national audience, would be basically informative to carry out
    Objective 1, 75 percent national awareness. Mass media, such as

network television and national magazines, would be most effective. Heavy-up through local media (spot TV, newspapers) could be used in the "50 new communities" of Objective 2.

A second target would be a more detailed message directed to executives in the Fortune 500 companies to fulfill Objective 3. Direct mail and business magazines would be effective here. In both cases, the message would have to include a direct plea for donations in order to help meet Objectives 4, 5, and 6.

4. Yes. Objectives 1 and 3 are designed to broaden the giving base; 4, 5, and 6 to increase donations; and 2 to help branch out into new communities.

5. Probably not. Unless national awareness and corporate knowledge are already high (45–50 percent), or the advertising budget extremely large (doubtful in a charitable organization), this is probably an attempt to do too much too soon. The giving-related objectives, 4–6, are probably more attainable, but they may also be high. If these objectives remain intact, actual performance will likely fall short in Year 1. This could become an issue in future years, since the campaign's achievements may be viewed as "good, but not what we were led to expect."

6. Marketing system—Yes. Giving goals are directly related and easily measured. Communication effects are also very important to America Helps and are accounted for in Objectives 1 and 3.

Type of message—Yes. The basic America Helps message is "please give," so objectives dealing with giving levels are appropriate.

Long- or short-term effects—Both have been considered: Objectives 1–3 are basically long term; 4–6 short term (this year).

Intended audience—Yes. Reaching new targets is desirable, so awareness and knowledge are necessary.

Product familiarity—Yes. Same reasons as above.

Competitive activity—Not clear. There seems to have been little consideration of competition, except in regard to setting reasonable giving increase goals. Might be wise to determine awareness and knowledge levels for other charitable organizations as a guide to what's reasonable/feasible.

7. A key concern is that these objectives seem to assume that awareness and knowledge will generate immediate giving, or "purchase," among a substantial portion of the target audiences. (Objective 1 = Objectives 4, 6); (Objective 3 = Objectives 4, 5.) Whether or not this is true is

largely dependent on outside forces such as competitive appeals and economic conditions.

In the case of Objective 3, is groundwork a "liking" or "preference" for America Helps in 50 communities, or is it "knowledge"? Again, this objective needs to be more clearly defined.

Chapter 8:
Cristel Products

1. Year 1 = $2.2M × 2 = $4.4M
   Year 2 = $3.6M
   Year 3 = $4.4M
   (Assumes competitive expenditure remains constant.)

2. Year 1 = $3.2M

3. Since the category uses couponing extensively, Cristel would probably also want to use this technique. Costs could be kept down by cross-ruffing with other Cristel products, or by including the coupons in advertisements whose costs were included in the advertising budget. Other costs might include any point-of-purchase materials; co-op coupons, if used, etc.

4. Some ads might be run featuring the french fries with another Cristel product, so that costs could be split between the two. This would give the french fries exposure at a lower cost.

5. Dobbs only knows the spending for the number 1 brand. To use SOV effectively, he needs to know spending for other brands whose market shares are closer to Cristel's goals. The actual investment required to achieve a 6 percent market share goal in Year 1 might be more or less than that indicated by comparison with the market leader's spending. Also, it's difficult to judge the impact of a well-recognized company name; Cristel's reputation might mean that a 1.5 factor would be effective in gaining the desired market share, as opposed to a 2.0 factor.

6. Using the established objectives, he would need to determine media requirements to achieve those objectives and calculate the associated costs.

Chapter 9:
T. White and
Associates

1. Major points for each strategy should include:

   Insurance carriers: use a differentiating message, direct mail and/or company newsletters as a vehicle coupled with counselor support with established contacts.

Justification: Control the funds; are familiar with rehab services; have approval; main component of business; can convince T. White is best.

Corporations/unions: basic informational message, direct mail to benefits offices, corporate newsletters, business section of newspapers.
Justification: good public relations for them (employee/member concern); have influence with insurance company to use a rehabilitative service and to make T. White that service.

Lawyers: differentiating message to worker's comp specialists; direct mail and/or local professional newsletters.
Justification: have approval on all activities; extra benefit to their clients; have influence with insurers.

Doctors: basic informational message; direct mail to orthopedic surgeons.
Justification: can recommend use of rehabilitative service when first see patient.

Potential claimants: really too broad, but could use an informational message in corporate newsletters.
Justification: can request use of a rehabilitative service through their benefits office, union representative, or attorney.

2. Insurance carriers are the major force and potentially the most frequent users of the service. Attorneys and corporations are also very strong because of their influencer role. If they are convinced of the benefit of a rehabilitation service and associate those benefits with T. White, T. White is given an edge over other competitors.

3. Wouldn't need to concentrate advertising money on insurance carriers, makes influencers a stronger case.

Chapter 10: Potato Flips

1. Number 1 infers the lower-calorie positioning through its emphasis on lightness, but doesn't directly address it. Number 2 seems to be directed more toward potato taste. Number 3 directly addresses lower calories through the scale motif. Number 4 does the same through a slice-of-life method.

2. Since number 4 depicts two members of the assumed target market, it would probably attract such people. Number 3 would also appeal, in a less blatant fashion.

3. Number 4 clearly outlines the benefit and supporting product attribute and uses a convinced spokesperson.

4. Numbers 1 to 3 are all likely to interrupt, number 1 because of curiosity, number two because of the novelty of the audiovisual combination, and number 3 because of the absence of sound. Number 4 is less likely to interrupt, because of its more familiar, frequently used format.

5. Numbers 2 and 3 are heavily visual; neither would be effective on radio. Number 1 is somewhat visual, but could probably be more so. Number 4 is the least visual; since it relies heavily on dialogue, it could easily be transferred to radio.

6. Number 1 demonstrates lightness through the floating package.
   Number 2 demonstrates flavor through the explosion motif.
   Number 3 demonstrates lightness through the "snow" and lower calories through use of the scale.
   Number 4 demonstrates lower calories through comparison to diet foods.

7. For number 1: "The Light Chip—Potato Flips"
   "The Flip that's Lighter than Air"
   For number 2: "Flips Explode with Potato Taste"
   "Flips Are Bustin' Out All Over"
   For number 3: "Potato Flips—Weigh the Difference"
   "Your Scale Will Tell You—Flips Look Lovely on You"
   For number 4: "My New Diet Food—Potato Flips"
   "Flips Make Counting Calories Taste Great"

8. Although he'd probably want extra time to test numbers 3 and 4 to see which is most effective, number 3 is probably a better bet. It clearly demonstrates the benefit, is much more intrusive, and probably more memorable.

**Chapter 11:
Demeter Teas**

1. Yes. To determine which of the three approaches is most effective in bringing in new customers, they should be tested. Also, this will help show if the idea of concentrating on no-caffeine is generally attractive: do people care that this is a caffeine-free tea?

2. For the basic premise of a caffeine-free tea, a concept test might reveal the saliency of the benefit. However, assuming Demeter is committed to a change, the three alternatives would best be tested in promise statement form. Putting them into rough form or even a finished form using the current Demeter format might help equate the new promise

with the established product, which could aid in estimating appeal to *new* users.

3. Allison—communicate that Demeter is the only caffeine—free tea. Henry—communicate that all tea has caffeine except Demeter. James—communicate that tea has as much caffeine as coffee, except for Demeter.

4. Communicate that Demeter is the only caffeine-free tea.

5. Tea drinkers, but non-users of Demeter. Since the goal is to attract new buyers, non-users would be the primary target.

6. A focus group would be useful in determining the saliency of a no-caffeine appeal. However, personal interviews would probably be best, since comprehension is the key. Using a focus group, the first alternative would probably be chosen, due to varying levels of knowledge. A strong, well-informed leader could overpower other group members, who might be confused on the tea-caffeine issue.

7. It starts by assuming that caffeine is important to tea drinkers. The best message of the three still may not attract new users. Also, "no caffeine" could be perceived as a hard sell fact, with all the inherent disadvantages of that approach in a test situation.

Chapter 12:
G & T Associates

In evaluating media choices, the following should be kept in mind:
1. The creative strategy is addressed at building consumer confidence; media choices should reinforce that goal.
2. Currently, the major advertisers are all using the same media strategy.
3. Most savings and loan advertising is heavily explanatory/informational.

Newspapers. Very good for alerting public to new accounts/services because of immediacy. Also, a flighting schedule would keep name before the public, giving an image of permanency/stability. Probably more cost-effective *not* to advertise in the weekly business magazine section of the *Post* because of price and clutter considerations. Also, probably targeting at a less sophisticated consumer than that likely to read the business magazine section.

Community papers are an ideal forum because of lower cost (especially considering prevalency of copy-heavy ads) and a family/savings oriented suburban audience. Also, the competition probably doesn't use them as heavily, so there would be less clutter.

Radio. Good for name recognition and new offering announcements. Not useful for explaining accounts/services in any detail. Again, can help foster secure image.

Television. Advertising in traditional programming formats can be used for announcements and name recognition. Costs are a key consideration— might not be able to buy enough time to be effective. Again, clutter is a problem. A possible approach would be to buy less expensive cable time, such as long (10- to 15-minute) segments where account features and special services could be explained in detail, perhaps offering interested viewers a chance to telephone in with questions. This would be relatively cost-efficient, very good for image, and extremely useful in building consumer confidence/trust.

Consumer magazines. Probably not cost-effective because of small audiences. Strictly local publications could be used to outline services in some detail.

Miscellaneous. As far as new account types are concerned, direct mail to present customers would be a very useful tool. Information could be sent out with quarterly statements, or as a separate mailing to addresses gleaned from current files. Current customers assumedly have a fairly high level of trust already, and so could be expected to be good prospects for further investment.

Outdoor's value is questionable, given the nature of the business concerned.

Scheduling. The budget does not allow for continuous mass advertising. Flighting using newspaper and radio and/or TV will keep the corporate name in view. A potential problem: a sharp drop in advertising frequency from last year's heavy levels may be perceived by consumers as a sign of instability. The flighting schedule will need to allow for this. A cable TV "segment," such as that described earlier, might provide a bonus in terms of free publicity, which would also counteract any consumer fears.

Chapter 13: RealCream

1. A freestanding dealer loader might be very effective: (1) it would not require shelf space; (2) it would attract attention to the product and to the creamer section; (3) it would offer retailers a chance to evaluate the product's appeal to their customers without forcing a commitment of shelf space. A series of sales meetings would offer chain buyers an opportunity to hear consumer test results and try the product themselves, helping to alleviate any doubts.

2. Since acceptance among users is good, generating trial is needed. This is one of the things for which sales promotion is most effective.

3. Because price seems to be a deterrent to trial, those techniques that decrease the price or offer a chance for trial at a lower price would be most effective: coupons, sampling, refunds, price-offs. In-, on-, or near-pack premiums might be useful if they enhanced the dairy image and had good perceived value.

4. Ideas could include running a coupon with the national ad; coupons on other Bossy products; cross-ruffs with a coffee manufacturer; in-store trial sizes in a display shaped like a coffee cup or cream pitcher; offering a free sample to consumers who send in the label from their nondairy creamer; price-offs; packing in a china creamer; refunds. The plan should be designed to induce trial among competitive users.

Chapter 14: Fleur de Lis Cognac

1. Yes. The test will help minimize financial loss that could come if large quantities are imported and not sold. It will also help indicate which advertising approach will be most effective in attracting the target market.

2. 1—Newspapers aren't being used in the national campaign. Why include them in the test?

   2—The selected market pairs may not be similar enough to yield valid results. What is the target market concentration in each? Are lifestyles similar? Are brandy/cognac consumption levels similar?

   3—Given that the media schedule is spread out over time, is six weeks long enough to judge the effectiveness of either campaign? Note: it may be argued here that use of daily newspapers for two weeks will make judgment easier. But, if it's not to be used in the national campaign, is it valid to use it in the test? After all, the test market may show that greater frequency is needed for the national campaign.

   4—How frequently do people buy cognac; i.e., is it reasonable to expect repurchase within a six-week period? If not, the test will only indicate initial demand, not customer satisfaction and repurchase.

3. a. Because of the long-term nature of the campaign (print ads, weekly frequency), a concurrent campaign probably would not be very helpful. Because specific objectives have been set, a post-test can help determine if they were met. It might be helpful to administer a

mini-test at the conclusion of the two-month introduction, particularly if sales results are not as anticipated.

b. Since this is a new product, awareness, knowledge, preference and purchase are at 0 as the campaign begins. Any gains as indicated by testing at the campaign's conclusion can be attributed to the campaign. A pre-test is unnecessary.

c. "How would you rate Fleur de Lis Cognac with other cognacs in terms of price?" "Do you think Fleur de Lis Cognac is better tasting, not as good, or about the same as other cognacs?"

d. 1—What age groups does the sample include? The target market for Fleur de Lis is clearly defined and those people should make up the sample for any evaluation. Are they covered in this base sample?

2—If the sample base is widespread, can it be segmented so that only the appropriate members are used? There's no sense in paying for testing among a larger group.

3—Does the lifestyle of the sample members match that of the target market for Fleur de Lis?

Index